OXFORD ENGLISH DRAMA

General Editor: MICHAEL CORDNER

Associate General Editors: PETER HOLLAND · MARTIN WIGGINS

THE ALCHEMIST

AND OTHER PLAYS

BEN JONSON, the greatest dramatic satirist of the English Renaissance, was born in London in 1572. As a young man he worked as a bricklayer and served as a soldier in the Netherlands, and in 1594 embarked on a new career as an actor. Three years later he began to write plays, and with the accession of James I in 1603, he also began to compose court masques, often in collaboration with Inigo Jones. He wrote prolifically for both the court and the public theatres, and also established himself as one of the finest poets of the period. His tumultuous private life included several spells in prison, a commuted death sentence for murder, and possible involvement in the Gunpowder Plot. In 1618 he walked to Scotland, where his wittily opinionated views of his contemporaries were recorded by William Drummond. In 1628 Jonson's public life was suddenly terminated by a stroke, and he lay paralysed in bed for the last nine years of his life. He died in 1637, and was buried in Westminster Abbey.

GORDON CAMPBELL is Professor of Renaissance Literature at the University of Leicester. He has published widely on Renaissance literature, especially Milton. His other work for Oxford University Press includes the editorship of the multidisciplinary journal *Renaissance Studies* and the preparation of the second edition of W. R. Parker's *Milton: A Biography*.

MICHAEL CORDNER is Ken Dixon Professor of Drama at the University of York, he has edited George Farquhar's *The Beaux' Stratagem*, the *Complete Plays* of Sir George Etherege, and *Four Comedies* of Sir John Vanbrugh. His editions include *Four Restoration Marriage Comedies* and he is completing a book on *The Comedy of Marriage 1660–1737*.

PETER HOLLAND is McMeel Family Professor in Shakespeare Studies at the University of Notre Dame.

MARTIN WIGGINS is a Fellow of the Shakespeare Institute and Lecturer in English at the University of Birmingham.

OXFORD ENGLISH DRAMA

OXFORD WORLD'S CLASSICS

BEN JONSON

Volpone, or The Fox
Epicene, or The Silent Woman
The Alchemist
Bartholomew Fair

Edited with an Introduction by
GORDON CAMPBELL

OXFORD
UNIVERSITY PRESS

OXFORD

UNIVERSITY PRESS

Great Clarendon Street, Oxford OX2 6DP

Oxford University Press is a department of the University of Oxford.
It furthers the University's objective of excellence in research, scholarship,
and education by publishing worldwide in

Oxford New York

Athens Auckland Bangkok Bogotá Buenos Aires Cape Town
Chennai Dar es Salaam Delhi Florence Hong Kong Istanbul Karachi
Kolkata Kuala Lumpur Madrid Melbourne Mexico City Mumbai Nairobi
Paris São Paulo Shanghai Singapore Taipei Tokyo Toronto Warsaw

with associated companies in Berlin Ibadan

Oxford is a registered trade mark of Oxford University Press
in the UK and in certain other countries

Published in the United States
by Oxford University Press Inc., New York

First published as a World's Classics paperback 1995
Reissued as an Oxford World's Classics paperback 1998
Reissued 2008

British Library Cataloguing in Publication Data

Data available

Library of Congress Cataloging in Publication Data
Jonson, Ben, 1573?–1637.
The alchemist/Ben Jonson; edited with an introduction by Gordon
Campbell.
p. cm.—(Oxford world's classics).
Includes bibliographical references and index.
1. Campbell, Gordon. II. Title. III. Series.
PR2605.A1 1995 822'.3—dc20 94-32779

ISBN 978-0-19-953731-0

5

Printed in Great Britain by
Clays Ltd, St Ives plc

CONTENTS

ACKNOWLEDGEMENTS

Editing is inevitably a collaborative process, because every editor needs to draw on the labours of his predecessors to fill in the gaps in his own knowledge. This practice is not without attendant dangers, in that it can perpetuate errors of annotation and harden dubious hypotheses into facts. I have tried to make my own mistakes rather than replicate those of others, but the extent to which an editor can detach himself from the editorial tradition has its limits, and I am happy to acknowledge my debt to the investigations of earlier editors. Editions such as L. A. Beaurline's *Epicoene* have set formidable textual standards for the editor of Jonson. In common with all other editors, I draw on the unnerving erudition of C. H. Herford and Percy and Evelyn Simpson, and, particularly but not exclusively in the case of *Epicene*, I have benefited from the labours of G. A. Wilkes in the more recent Oxford edition. Of modern editors, the most stimulating have been Martin Butler, John Creaser, and Johanna Procter.

In the course of preparing this edition I have incurred many debts: John Creaser helped me to think afresh about the principles of editing Jonson; Nicholas Davidson and John Law illuminated some of the mysteries of seventeenth-century Venice; Patricia Jones saved me from some foolish errors in my treatment of Jonson's Spanish; Andrew Wear assisted with law and medicine; Roy Flannagan helped to make my notes accessible to American readers; Neil Harris and Anthony Low provided me with scarce modern editions of *Volpone*; Kirsten Campbell assisted with the preparation of the text; and Stella Lanham lavished many hours on the ordering of my chaotic manuscript. My general editor, Michael Cordner, has patiently lived with the consequences of having asked me to prepare this edition, resisting my attempts to modernize beyond the bounds of propriety, offering modestly phrased suggestions that betrayed a daunting command both of Jonson and of the editorial issues peculiar to the editing of dramatic texts, and waiting patiently as I sailed past a succession of deadlines. I should like to dedicate this edition to him and his colleagues at the University of York, to whom 'I owe all that I am in arts.'

Leicester, 1995   *GC*

INTRODUCTION

Life and Writings

Ben Jonson's plays are robust, exuberant, and learned. These traits can also be discerned in the life and personality of their author. Jonson was born in 1572, and so was a younger contemporary of Shakespeare, whose friendship he later enjoyed. Jonson was the posthumous child of an Anglican priest, and shortly after his birth his mother married again. Her new husband was a bricklayer, and in due course Jonson followed his stepfather into the trade. Jonson was not, however, an uneducated bricklayer. As a child he had attended Westminster School and studied under the tutelage of William Camden, 'to whom', as Jonson was later to say in an epigram, 'I owe | All, that I am in arts, all that I know'. In Jonson's case, 'all that I know' consisted of learning so prodigious that in English letters it is equalled only by that of Milton and Coleridge. Many passages in his plays are couched in a demotic English that gives no hint of the passages in the literature of classical antiquity that Jonson is imitating with such consummate skill. These echoes are fainter for a modern audience than they would have been for his contemporaries, partly because our education has lost its classical bias, and partly because Jonson often imitated Renaissance Latin translations of ancient Greek works; such translations would have been familiar to Jonson's audiences, but they have now faded into irredeemable obscurity. There are occasions when his characters speak in Latin: such passages are usually excised in modern performances, and in modern printed texts they are translated in footnotes, so they do not constitute an impediment to modern audiences and readers. Indeed, far from seeming laboriously learned, Jonson's plays have a lightness of touch and quickness of wit that have kept them alive on the English stage.

The extravagant and immoderate characters that people Jonson's plays derive their vitality from a creator whose experience of life ranged beyond that of his contemporaries. He interrupted his labours as a bricklayer with military service in the Netherlands. In an incident which Jonson remembered with satisfaction for the rest of his life, he challenged a Spanish soldier to single combat in the no-man's land between the two armies, killed him, and stripped him of his arms and armour; Jonson's term for this plunder was *opima spolia* (the spoils of honour), a phrase which, in its original context in Livy, refers to arms taken from a vanquished general. Jonson killed his hapless victim in full view of a large audience, and in his appropriation of Livy's phrase exaggerated the dead soldier's importance and rationalized his own looting by reference to a practice characteristic of the battlefields of antiquity. His approach to soldiering was characteristically theatrical.

Jonson returned to England, and in November 1594 he married Anne Lewis. He later described his wife as a shrew, but gratefully acknowledged her chastity, even as he boasted of his own sexual profligacy. Shakespeare led a similar life, but whereas in Shakespeare's comedies there is a strained insistence on the importance of fidelity, Jonson's chaste characters, such as Celia in *Volpone*, are ridiculed for their naïvety. Indeed, the morality of Jonson's plays, about which he is so relentlessly insistent in his prefaces, is not always readily apparent in the plays themselves: Face escapes retribution at the end of *The Alchemist*, and Overdo's generosity at the end of *Bartholomew Fair* is qualified by his curmudgeonly insistence that he be paid compensation.

Jonson's marriage violated the requirement of the Guild of Bricklayers that apprentices remain unmarried for the seven years of their apprenticeship, so it seems likely that by November 1594 he had embarked on a new career as an actor. The playhouses had reopened in June 1594 after a two-year closure occasioned by plague, and Jonson probably entered his new profession at about that time. He acted for several years, touring with the Earl of Pembroke's Men. Jonson's roles included Hieronimo in Kyd's *Spanish Tragedy*, but he seems not to have been regarded as a great actor, and early in 1597 he began to write plays. His earliest known play is *The Case is Altered*, which was performed by the Children of the Chapel Royal in the first half of 1597. That summer Jonson helped to complete a play that Thomas Nashe had abandoned after one act. The play, which is now lost, was called *The Isle of Dogs*; the title suggests its location on the island in the Thames near Greenwich, but gives no hint of its contents. The Privy Council decided that the play was 'lewd' and contained material that was seditious and slanderous. Jonson was imprisoned along with several other members of the company.

He was soon released, and within months *Every Man in His Humour*, which Jonson later saw as his first important play, was performed by the Lord Chamberlain's Men. This promising beginning to a theatrical career almost came to an untimely end in

September 1598, when Jonson fell out with his fellow actor (and former fellow prisoner in Marshalsea) Gabriel Spencer. They met in Hoxton Fields, and Jonson killed Spencer. In later life Jonson described this incident in heroic terms: he had been challenged to a duel and then attacked by Spencer with a sword ten inches longer than his own. The court records present a less heroic version: Jonson was charged with murder, pleaded guilty, was sentenced to be hanged, and evaded the gallows by pleading 'benefit of clergy' (a law that allowed literate criminals a second chance); he was branded on the thumb as a murderer, and his possessions were confiscated. While in prison Jonson had been visited by a recusant priest and had decided to convert to Roman Catholicism. He emerged from Newgate as a branded, dispossessed Roman Catholic. The loss of his goods made it impossible for Jonson to honour his financial commitments, so within two months he was back in prison for having failed to repay a loan of £10.

After his release Jonson collaborated on several plays, and by the end of 1599 he had written another full-length play, *Every Man out of His Humour*. Jonson wrote the play for performances at court and at the Globe, and thereafter prepared a version for publication 'containing more than hath been publicly spoken or acted'. Publication of this play constituted a bid for literary status: Jonson intended it to be read by those who had not seen it performed, just as the plays of Roman and Greek playwrights were read by Jonson's contemporaries.

Every Man out of His Humour was the first salvo in the theatrical dispute, now known as the War of the Theatres, between Jonson and some of his fellow dramatists, notably John Marston and Thomas Dekker. As the protagonists in this quarrel were all playwrights, they attacked each other through their plays. Jonson's next two plays, *Cynthia's Revels* and *Poetaster*, are at one level manifestations of this dispute.

In the small hours of 24 March 1603 Queen Elizabeth died, and the beneficiaries of her patronage scrambled to reposition themselves in order to secure niches in the new order inaugurated by the accession of James VI of Scotland to the throne of England. Jonson was quick off the mark with a pastoral entertainment which was performed before Queen Anne and Prince Henry when they broke their journey from Edinburgh to London at Althorp, home (then as now) of the Spencer family. This launched Jonson as a writer of court masques and entertainments, a career that for the next thirty years ran in tandem with his activities as a playwright. King James was interested in the theatre, and shortly after his coronation had brought the Lord Chamberlain's company under his personal patronage as the King's Majesty's Servants, usually known as the King's Men. Jonson immediately wrote a tragedy for the rechristened company; he had already claimed classic status as a writer of comedy, and with *Sejanus* he could aspire to eminence as a tragedian. He may have completed an earlier tragedy, if a commission in 1602 to write a play about Richard III (*Richard Crouchback*) was fulfilled, but *Sejanus* is Jonson's earliest surviving tragedy. His hopes for *Sejanus* were shaken when the Globe audience hissed it off the stage, and came to grief when he was called to account by the Privy Council to answer accusations that the play was seditious. The outcome of this episode is not known, and it is difficult to judge the extent to which the play could be deemed seditious, because the performance text (which is lost) may have been a collaborative work. When Jonson published the play he explained that in the acted version 'a second pen has had good share', whereas the printed version of the play was entirely his own work. Jonson may have had a collaborator, but it is equally possible that this shadowy figure was invented by Jonson as the author of excised passages that were thought to be seditious.

In 1605 Jonson was in trouble again, and was imprisoned for his part in the writing of *Eastward Ho!*, which was deemed to cast aspersions on the Scottish people and question the integrity of the king. When Jonson was eventually released he celebrated with a party for his friends. In the midst of the festivities Jonson's elderly mother rose to toast her son; she displayed a paper packet, and explained that it contained the poison with which she had planned to kill her son and herself if Jonson had been mutilated as a punishment for his offence. This incident, which constitutes all that is known of Jonson's mother, suggests that his love of theatrical gestures may have been a family trait.

On 9 October 1605 Jonson attended a dinner party at the home of Robert Catesby. Catesby, who was shortly to be exposed as the organizer of the Gunpowder Plot, was a Roman Catholic, as were Jonson and his six fellow guests. Guy Fawkes was not present, but numbered among the guests were several of the chief conspirators in the massacre that was planned for 5 November; Francis Tresham, who inadvertently betrayed the plot, was also present. When Fawkes was captured he insisted that his name was Jonson; his true identity was eventually discovered, and he betrayed the other conspirators under torture. Jonson was not directly implicated, but Fawkes's infelicitous choice of an alias and Jonson's attendance at the dinner party inevitably raised the question of his involvement, and on 7 November he once again appeared before the Privy Council. He somehow persuaded the Council that he was not one of the conspirators, and indeed walked away with a commission to assist with the investigation of the plot.

In the years that followed Jonson pursued his twin careers as a writer of masques and plays, and his four greatest comedies were written and performed: *Volpone* in 1606, *Epicene* in 1609, *The Alchemist* in 1610, and *Bartholomew Fair* in 1614. His private life in this period was a characteristic blend of propriety and profligacy. In 1610 he reconverted to Anglicanism, and in a gesture that reflects both his irrepressible theatricality and his drinking habits, attended holy communion and drank the entire chalice of wine; in the same year, two women, neither of whom was married to Jonson, gave birth within a fortnight of each other, and each recorded the father of her illegitimate child as 'Ben Jonson'. These registrations are the first recorded use of the now familiar shortened form of his Christian name.

By 1611 the fiasco of *Sejanus* had receded, and Jonson, riding on the success of *Epicene* and *The Alchemist*, returned to Roman tragedy with *Catiline*. His attempt to dramatize the conspiracy of Catiline, like those of Crébillon, Voltaire, and Ibsen that were to follow, was a failure: the portion of the audience that had survived the first three acts rebelled against Jonson's 300-line translation of Cicero's speech in Act Four, and the performance was left in ruins. Jonson was never to achieve the supremacy in tragedy that he had secured in comedy. Just as Shakespeare's genius evaporated when he came to write the masques in his late plays, so Jonson's attempts to write tragedy ended in grief.

The disaster of *Catiline* was shortly followed by a collapse in Jonson's career as a court writer; the king was in financial difficulty, and had cut the budget for Jonson's Twelfth Night masque of 1612 to less than a tenth of the usual figure; Prince Henry, who was to have been the chief masquer, declined to participate in this stripped-down spectacle. Jonson decided to accept an invitation to travel to Paris and Brussels as tutor and governor of Walter Ralegh, son of Sir Walter, who was then imprisoned in the Tower of London. Jonson and young Ralegh spent a riotous year abroad, and then Jonson returned to the London stage with *Bartholomew Fair*.

In 1616 Jonson published a sumptuous folio edition of his collected *Works*. The folio assembles his poems (*Epigrams* and *The Forest*), masques, entertainments, and nine of his plays; in the case of *Every Man in His Humour*, the text is a wholesale revision of the earlier quarto text. The poems establish Jonson as one of the greatest poets of the English Renaissance, but it was not these that caused a stir. It was the inclusion of plays in a collection of literary works that irritated Jonson's contemporaries, who were contemptuous of the notion that modern plays should be presented in the literary format traditionally reserved for classical drama. Jonson was by now well positioned to ignore such sniping, because in 1616 he started to receive public recognition beyond the world of the theatres. In February the king granted him a pension, and Jonson thus became the first holder of the honour which was later to be associated with the title of Poet Laureate.

In the autumn of 1618 Jonson set out on a walking tour to Scotland. His motives are unknown, but his atavistic attachment to Scotland (he believed himself descended from a border family), together with a timely curiosity about Scotland engendered by the accession of a Scottish king to the English throne, may have prompted the journey. The decision to walk rather than travel by ship seems an improbable one for a grossly overweight, hard-drinking 45-year-old, but it is consistent with Jonson's lifelong enthusiasm for public acts of heroic individualism. In Scotland he met the poet William Drummond of Hawthornden, who subsequently recorded their conversations; Drummond's notes survive in a transcription by the antiquary Sir Robert Sibbald which was eventually published as *Conversations with William Drummond* (1711, abridged; 1833, unabridged). The only other substantial record of Jonson's opinions and omnivorous reading is his commonplace book, of which Jonson had planned to publish a selection; he did not do so, but the book was posthumously published in the 1640 Folio as *Timber: or Discoveries*. The image of Jonson that emerges from *Conversations* and *Timber* is of an extravagantly learned and wittily opinionated man of letters who was capable of violence (for example, 'he beat Marston, and took his pistol from him', in *Conversations*); this image may have been a conscious creation, but Jonson endeavoured to live up to it.

On returning to England Jonson assumed the role of an important literary figure, accepting an honorary MA from Oxford in 1619 and an appointment as City Chronologer in 1628, and presiding over a literary circle that became known as the 'tribe of Ben'. Late in 1628 his public life was suddenly terminated by a stroke, and he lay paralysed in bed for the last nine years of his life. Jonson never again left his house, but none the less sustained his public presence throughout these years of incapacity with a steady stream of poems and plays. He died on 16 August 1637, and was buried in Westminster Abbey. His achievements were celebrated in a commemorative volume of poetry in English, Greek, and Latin, and in a two-volume folio edition of his *Works*. Three-and-a-half centuries later his poems and masques are still read by students of English Renaissance literature, and his plays are watched by large audiences. The most popular are his four great comedies, *Volpone*, *Epicene*, *The Alchemist*, and *Bartholomew Fair*.

Volpone

In the verse prologue to *Volpone* Jonson claims that 'five weeks fully penned it'. These five weeks fell in February and March 1606, and a few weeks later the play was staged at the Globe by the King's Men. In the summers of 1606 and 1607 the company took the play to Oxford and Cambridge. Jonson may have added learned scenes such as the Pythagorean satire of 1.2 to the Globe version of the play with a view to pleasing academic audiences; their enthusiasm is fulsomely acknowledged in Jonson's Dedication and Epistle.

Volpone retains its power to hold audiences, and is probably performed more often than any of Jonson's other plays. It was successfully revived after the Restoration, and many of its comic stratagems were imitated in the plays of Restoration and eighteenth-century playwrights. Its earthy language gradually alienated it from increasingly prudish audiences, and in the late eighteenth century it was first bowdlerized (1771) and then dropped from the repertoire. It was revived for a popular audience in 1921 (Lyric, Hammersmith) and for an academic audience in 1923 (Cambridge). Since then it has been performed regularly throughout the English-speaking world and occasionally beyond it.

The play is set in a Venice that owes more to Jonson's imagination than to the early seventeenth-century city-state. The presiding spirit of this Venice of the mind is a fox who conspires with a fly to defraud various repugnant birds. The narrative draws in part on the medieval stories of Reynard the Fox, who at various points in the cycle commits rape, deceives a crow and a rook, and stands trial for his crimes. In the bestiaries of the ancient world the fox is characterized as sly and brutal, and in the New Testament Herod is described as a human fox. In production this element of analogy can usefully be accentuated through costumes that emphasize the animalistic characterizations implied by the names of the characters. In an age well before Landseer's sentimental anthropomorphic depictions, a comparison of human beings to animals was intended to emphasize the domination of base appetites over noble spiritual elements. Volpone is not the urban fox eagerly studied by conservationists, but rather the ruthless predator hunted by gamekeepers. In a sermon published in 1612, the eminent principal of St Edmund Hall, Oxford, distinguished between helpful beasts, to which man should be merciful, and foxes, who were 'not helpful, but hurtful', and therefore undeserving of pity.

There is an obvious sense in which Jonson's characters are not naturalistic, but it would be imprudent to assume that they are merely comic stereotypes. It is true that his characters, unlike Shakespeare's, do not constantly articulate their thoughts and motives, but in that respect they are more naturalistic than are Shakespeare's creations. Jonson constructs an element of naturalistic psychological depth for his characters by giving them lines that encourage audiences to infer the motives that lie behind actions. Thus Volpone hints that behind his lust for Celia lies a fear of impotence; similarly, the audience gradually comes to realize that Volpone's insistent celebration of the life of pleasure is in part an attempt to recapture the fading joys of such a life, just as his assumed illnesses furtively acknowledge his actual decay. The characters of *Volpone* are on one level repugnant, but Jonson's characterizations enable the audience to understand the forces that have shaped their despicable actions. Corbaccio's attempt to become Volpone's heir is at one level reprehensible, but recognition of the fact that the ailing Corbaccio has constructed a sustaining illusion to the effect that he will outlive Volpone endows the audience with a degree of sympathy and understanding that would not be possible if Jonson's characters were merely caricatures. This capacity to induce a sympathetic understanding of villainy without sentimentalizing the villains is a mark of Jonson's supreme abilities as a dramatist. The same feat was later accomplished in poetry with Milton's Satan and in prose with George Eliot's Casaubon, but those writers worked in forms that permitted commentary by a narrator; Jonson repeatedly achieved the same effect without a narrator, instead facilitating the requisite disclosures through the prism of phrases and actions that reveal more than is intended.

Jonson's subject in *Volpone* is human greed, but if his play were merely an attack on the wickedness of greed, audiences would suffer such complacent banality in the spirit that one endures a sermon. Jonson's play transcends the limitations of homily because it dramatizes in a spirit of high comedy an enquiry into the corrupting nature of this vice. That is why the play is set in Venice, which was associated in the minds of those who had never been there with untrammelled greed and corruption.

One point which might offend the sensibilities of a modern audience is the comic depiction of Volpone's court, and especially Nano the dwarf. Some directors deal with the problem simply by cutting the part, but of course it must remain in the printed text, where it points to a darker side of Jonson's comedy. King James had an unhealthy predilection for people who had been unkindly treated by nature, and Jonson's figures of a dwarf, a eunuch, and a catamite ('hermaphrodite') must on one level have been designed to please the king's known fancies. On another level these figures associate the court of Volpone with the court of James, and thus hint at the greed and corruption of the latter. From time to time allegedly seditious elements in plays to which he had contributed had landed Jonson in prison, but on this occasion he escaped censure by virtue of the ambiguity of his criticism.

Epicene

On 9 December 1609 the London theatres reopened after an eighteen-month closure occasioned by an epidemic of plague. On 4 January 1610 the children's company for which *Epicene* was written received its patent as the 'Children of Her Majesty's Revels' and officially took possession of its new private playhouse, the Whitefriars. The play was performed either before the official opening (the text dates it '1609'), or, if 1609 reflects the traditional calendar year which ended on 24 March, in January 1610. By February the play had been suppressed, following a complaint by Lady Arabella Stuart, the king's cousin, that the play contained a slighting allusion (at 5.1.20–1) to her alleged engagement to a fraudulent continental prince. The suppression seems to have been quickly forgotten, because the play was printed in 1616 and occasionally revived by adult companies until the theatres were closed in 1642. When the theatres were reopened in June 1660 *Epicene* was the first play to be performed. Pepys recorded in his diary his view that it was 'the best comedy, I think, that ever was wrote'.

After the Restoration women were allowed to act in public theatres, and in 1663 Mrs Knepp became the first actress to play the title role. The procession from a children's company to an adult male company to a mixed company inevitably affects an audience's perceptions of the gender reversal that is unleashed in the final scene, and the casting of Epicene remains a critical decision in modern productions.

In the twentieth century *Epicene* has largely been the preserve of university productions and small theatre companies, partly because, as Dryden remarked, its wit seems to derive from the universities rather than from London society, and partly because the comic power of the closing scenes is vitiated by a popular audience's inability to cope with the substantial amount of Latin. In 1989, however, the Royal Shakespeare Company mounted an exuberant production of the play at the Swan in Stratford. Epicene was played by John Hannah, whose name appeared in the programme as Hannah John; most members of the audience thought that he was a woman, so the revelation of his true sex at the end of the play caught the audience by surprise, as it must have done in the early productions, in which all the actors were male.

The political agenda of many radical academic literary critics includes the redemption of sexual preferences such as homosexuality and paedophilia that have hitherto been regarded as deviant. Viewed through such a prism, *Epicene* becomes a play about transvestism and the crossing of gender boundaries. In the 1989 Stratford production this interest in the androgynous was extended beyond Epicene to several other characters: in the opening scene, for example, Clerimont entered wearing bloomers and was dressed in effeminate clothes by his 'boy', who was played by a young woman; similarly, the conversation of Clerimont and Truewit was punctuated by camp gestures. It is perfectly natural to read the literature of the past in terms of the preoccupations of the present, but sexual orientation is a culturally conditioned phenomenon, and it is not safe to assume that the range of alternative sexualities in Jacobean England was broadly similar to our own. Truewit's witty description of Clerimont's boy as his catamite ('ingle'), for example, must be considered in the complicated context of classical sanction, clerical abomination, and royal practice. The revelation of Epicene's true gender, on the other hand, is probably no more than a dramatic device to humiliate Morose. Similarly, the notion of a silent woman was delicately balanced between a Christian ideal (as articulated by male polemicists) and a comic oxymoron, whereas the male-dominating women such as

Mistress Otter and Centaure would have been seen by members of Jonson's overwhelmingly male audience as monstrous inversions of nature. As for marriage, the ideal, in the words of Shakespeare's Petruccio, was to 'wive it wealthily'. The perversion of Morose's marriage is not that it lacks love, but that it is grounded in a mean desire to disinherit a relative.

Epicene is comedy untainted by overt morality; it contains few concessions to the usual values of comedy: there is no affirmation of the value of friendship or love, no banishing of villains, no triumph of happiness. The opening scene firmly situates the play in the context of the plague that had been devastating London for more than a year. In its affirmation of the consolatory power of laughter at such a time, *Epicene* recalls the ending of *Love's Labour's Lost*, in which Rosaline commands Biron 'to enforce the pained impotent to smile'. Biron's reply, that 'mirth cannot move a soul in agony', is dismissed by Rosaline, who knows that mirth can do precisely that. *Epicene*, like Shakespeare's play, 'move[s] wild laughter in the face of death'. It accomplishes its end by subjecting to comic dissection the quirks, pretensions, and complacent social conventions of its characters.

The Alchemist

The calculations of Ananias in Acts 3 and 5 of *The Alchemist* show that Jonson intended the play to open at the Blackfriars playhouse in the autumn of 1610. This intention was frustrated by an epidemic of plague that kept the theatres closed until the end of November. The restrictions occasioned by the plague in London did not apply in provincial centres, and Jonson was therefore able to mount a performance in Oxford in September 1610. The long record of public and private performances shows that the play sustained its popularity throughout the seventeenth and eighteenth centuries. It was even performed (in a shortened version) in private houses during the Interregnum, when the public theatres were closed. Like Jonson's other plays, *The Alchemist* disappeared from the repertoire during the nineteenth century, but it has been regularly revived throughout the twentieth century.

In the early seventeenth century, chemistry, which was usually known as alchemy (*al* means 'the' in Arabic), was dedicated to the production of pharmaceutical medicines and the scientific study of elements and their compounds. These twin purposes are reflected in the ambiguity in modern British English of the word 'chemist', which can denote both a pharmacist and a specialist in chemistry. The ultimate aim of pharmaceutical chemistry was the production of a panacea that would cure all diseases and prolong life indefinitely. The scientific study of chemicals was often skewed towards the aim of transmuting base metals into silver and gold. The subsequent development of chemistry has demonstrated that both aims were futile, but it cannot be safely assumed that alchemy was a pseudo-science like palmistry or phrenology. Just as the astrologers established a connection between the moon and the tides, so the Renaissance alchemists developed efficacious medicines and laid the foundations of descriptive chemistry. The unachieved and unachievable aims of discovering a panacea and transmuting base metals, however, created openings for charlatans and genuine, but inept, scientists who claimed to have achieved these ends.

Jonson and his audiences would rightly have regarded alchemy as a combination of science and imposture. Some of Jonson's characters and some members of his audiences half believed in the claims of alchemy in much the same way that some members of his modern audiences dismiss astrology as a pseudo-science but none the less furtively read their horoscopes in the newspapers. This vestigial and partial belief creates the ambiguity that Jonson exploits comically in his play. Just as Conrad's *Victory* opens with an affirmation of the 'very close chemical relation between coal and diamonds' and then goes on to explore the chemical relations that link its characters, so Jonson deploys the metaphors of alchemical transformation to delineate the mutability and instability of his characters and their social relationships.

In Marlowe's tragic accounts of human aspiration, characters who seek transformation of their lives are heroic; in Jonson's comic inversions such ambition is ridiculed as folly. The hopes of his gulls, like those who nowadays play the pools in the vain hope of transfiguring their lives, render them vulnerable to exploitation by unscrupulous rogues. In the hierarchy of values in Jonson's comedies, however, stupidity is a moral failing, intelligence a virtue. At the end of *The Alchemist*, when one might expect retribution, Subtle and Doll are allowed to escape, albeit empty-handed, and Face, the clever villain who has outwitted all the other characters, adeptly reassumes his role as Jeremy, the faithful servant of Lovewit. The gulls, on the other hand, are ruthlessly castigated. Dapper aspires to success as a gambler, and loses his money; Sir Epicure Mammon's belief that the philosopher's stone would give him a life of unbridled sensuality is subjected to comic derision; Drugger's naïve aspiration to be a successful business man married to Dame Pliant is exploited without mercy. The most embittered attack is reserved for the theocratic Puritans Ananias and Tribulation Wholesome, whose smarmy and oppressive piety is exposed when their avarice draws them into a scheme to counterfeit Dutch money. The modicum of pity that Jonson allots to his victims does not extend to Puritans: his other gulls are merely foolish, but his Puritans are wicked.

If the foolishness and vanity of human aspiration that occupy the moral centre of the play had been allowed to shape its language and dramatic effects, *The Alchemist* would be lifeless. The unrestrained vitality of the language, be it the invidious cant of Puritanism, Mammon's vision of a voluptuous paradise, or Subtle's exposition of the mysteries of alchemy, transforms bland morality into a rich banquet of verbal delicacies. Similarly, the serial presentation of the dupes occasions a procession of some of the funniest scenes in English drama, ranging from the humiliation of the blindfolded Dapper, who is gagged with gingerbread and locked in the privy, to Doll Common's impersonation of the Queen of Fairy. Jonson effects the alchemical transformation of base morality into the rich ore of dramatic comedy; tragedy, in Aristotle's improbable view, is said to purge the emotions, but the sheer vitality of *The Alchemist* facilitates laughter that is arguably more therapeutic than the solemn experience of tragedy.

Bartholomew Fair

Bartholomew Fair, the last of Jonson's four great comedies, was the inaugural production of the Hope, a theatre and bear-pit in Southwark. The play opened on 31 October 1614, and the following day was performed at Whitehall in the presence of the king. The prospect of a court performance seems to have weighed on Jonson's mind as he wrote the play, for it clearly reflects many of the king's personal concerns: James deplored the eating of pork, and inveighed against the evils of tobacco; his campaign to contain the Puritans, whom he regarded as a menace, had begun in 1604 with the Hampton Court Conference; similarly, James had both learned and practical interests in the reform of the activities of the justices of the peace, whose administration of the countryside and oppositional stances in parliament he deplored: in April 1614 James had summoned parliament (the 'Addled Parliament') and in June had dissolved it in a spirit of rage and frustration.

After the two productions in 1614, *Bartholomew Fair* disappears from the dramatic record for almost fifty years; although it was printed in 1631, this text was not published until 1640, so no printed text was available for reading or production. The play was revived after the Restoration, when its attack on Puritanism rendered it particularly attractive to a society emerging from the reign of the godly. In the course of the next eighty years the play was often revived when Bartholomew Fair was taking place. The play then disappeared from the repertoire for 200 years, but since 1950 has been produced regularly. The play is sometimes set in Victorian England (for example, Nottingham Playhouse, 1976, and the National Theatre, 1988), a transformation that substitutes a sentimental Dickensian fair for Jonson's anarchic and sinister setting and creates an odd context for his satire on Puritanism. The more sympathetic productions, such as Bogdanov's at the Young Vic in 1978, have eschewed an anti-quarian setting and managed to capture Jonson's equivocal oscillation between untrammelled farce and comedy darkened by brutality and the humiliation of its victims.

The structure of *Bartholomew Fair* is episodic, and its cohesion derives from its highly focused setting rather than its sparse and disparate narrative. The virtual absence of a plot can frustrate a reader, whereas a member of a theatre audience retains a strong visual sense of both characters and setting, and can derive enormous pleasure from the deftness and wit with which Jonson embroils the visitors to the fair in its myriad temptations. The fair was part of the experience of living in Jacobean London, and those who attended Jonson's play must have recognized on the stage many of the characters associated with the fair. It should not, however, be assumed that the earthiness of Jonson's characters makes them naturalistic or realistic: Jonson is writing in a tradition of caricature analogous to the visual satires of Bellini and Hogarth, in which the comic urge to create grotesque characters is curbed by the need to ensure that the originals are clearly discernible. Thus Zeal-of-the-Land Busy, for example, is not a Jacobean Puritan, but his exaggerated mannerisms are sufficient-ly reminiscent of the theatre-goers' sense of Puritanism for Jonson to present with dramatic conviction his dubious contention that beneath the rectitudinous godliness of Puritans lay natures that were corrupt and materialistic. Jonson's comic attempt to undermine the moral authority of Puritanism was, of course, related to the perception, shared by the king and eventually vindicated by the Puritan revolution, that Puritanism constituted a political threat to the absolutist authority of the monarchy.

The climactic device of the puppet-show allows Jonson to extend his dramatic presentation of the voracity of human nature by means of puppets whose appetites are utterly unbridled. The ignoble urges of ordinary human beings may be constrained by the niceties of social intercourse, but Littlewit's puppets feel no such inhibitions. Jonson's method, perhaps surprisingly in a play, is predominantly literary rather than dramatic. The puppets dramatize a comically conflated version of the stories of Hero and Leander and Damon and Pithias. In the classical and post-classical accounts both stories are exemplary: Hero and Leander are virtuous lovers, and Damon and Pithias are types of self-sacrificing friendship. In Jonson's puppet-show their true natures are shown to be as unlovely as those of his flesh-and-blood characters. Hero and Leander think of nothing but food, drink, and sex; Hero has slept with both Damon and Pithias, whose legendary friendship quickly turns out to be paper-thin as they loudly denounce each other and quickly turn to violence. In the anarchy of the fairground, love and friendship are exposed as fraudulent.

Comedy normally provides a protagonist through whose actions and perceptions the moral perspective of the play is focused. *Bartholomew Fair* contains no such starring role because, as the title indicates, it is the fair rather than any particular character that is at the centre of the action. In order to bring the play to a coherent conclusion, however, Jonson introduces the slowly emerging figure of Justice Overdo, so that at the end he can preside over the resolution. Overdo comes to the fair with a view to exposing its corruption and, like the Duke in *Measure for Measure*, disguises himself in order to watch unnoticed. Once the dramatic contrivance becomes apparent, the audience, guided by the conventions of comedy, assumes that Overdo will overcome his ineptitude and assert his moral authority at the end of the play. This expectation is fulfilled structurally, in that in the final scene Overdo reveals his true identity and prepares to dispense justice, but Jonson quickly silences him by making his wife vomit, and then allows Quarlous to usurp Overdo's judicial prerogative. In Jonson's world no one has sufficient moral purity to pass judgement on others.

NOTE ON THE TEXT

The task of an editor of Jonson is to mediate between seventeenth-century texts and twentieth-century readers. Neither the readers nor the texts are unproblematical. Readers include students of English literature who need to understand Jonson's language, students of English Renaissance drama who need to understand how the plays were originally performed, and the producers, directors, and actors who mount modern productions, who must understand the dramatic mechanisms of the plays; an editor has to offer assistance to all these groups. The printed texts of Jonson's plays are literary versions of his original acting texts, and literary conventions such as divisions into acts and scenes and the listing of all characters in a scene at its outset have been added, sometimes by Jonson, to his dramatic texts. The retention of acts and scenes is an uncontentious matter, but the modern editor must often judge the point at which characters enter and exit, and that is a matter of editorial discretion. I have, therefore, supplemented the stage directions in the original texts with new stage directions, which I enclose in square brackets.

Jonson is often said to have closely supervised the preparation of his texts for publication; there is indeed some evidence of authorial intervention, but there is also evidence of carelessness in proofreading, especially in words and phrases written in languages other than English. There are also some lapses in punctuation, which suggests that Jonson did not always see the final versions of his carefully punctuated texts. I have retained much of the original punctuation, which is for the most part a very precise guide to phrasing and expression, but have not hesitated to modify or supplement pointing in the interests of rhetorical, syntactical, or theatrical clarity.

I am an unapologetic modernizer of spelling, but in some cases I have had to curb my enthusiasm in order to preserve metre. Editors whose texts are otherwise modernized have often retained the seventeenth-century spellings of proper nouns and of words in languages other than English. Such reticence seems to me pointless. I have modernized the spelling of the names of characters, so that Epicoene appears as Epicene and Kastril as Kestrel; I have, however, resisted the temptation to rechristen Volpone as Volpe, because the older form survives in modern Italian. I have modernized occasional words in

Dutch and German, and lines in Italian and Spanish; in the case of the Spanish in *The Alchemist*, the process of modernization reveals the metrical structure of the lines. I have also 'classicized' the spelling of Latin. In *Epicene* 5.3, for example, Otter says that Morose is utterly useless *ad thorum*; editors have suggested that *thorum* is a comic blunder for *torum* ('wedding bed') and have seen a witty quibble on Greek *thoros* ('semen'). In fact, the intrusive 'h' is a commonplace of Renaissance Latin, and the *th* spelling is preserved in the legal notion of divorce *a mensa et thoro*. I have spelt the word *torum* in the hope of avoiding such confusion. Had my usually accommodating general editors allowed me to do so, I would have translated *exit* and *exeunt*, as the distinction is lost on many students through no fault of their own.

Volpone survives in two texts, the quarto of 1607 and the folio of 1616; most of the differences between the two texts disappear in the process of modernizing, though I have noted a few variations that may be related to censorship. There is only one authoritative text of *Epicene*, the 1616 folio, but in that text the first act and the first two scenes of the second act survive in both an uncorrected and a corrected version; the 1620 quarto has no independent authority. A quarto of *The Alchemist* was published in 1612, and a slightly revised version of this text appeared in the 1616 folio. *Bartholomew Fair* was for some reason excluded from the 1616 folio. An edition was printed in 1631, probably for a projected second folio; this folio was never published, but the printed sheets of *Bartholomew Fair* were eventually used in the 1640 folio. I have sometimes incorporated readings from the second (1640) and third folios (1692) into my text, and have on occasion accepted emendations proposed by subsequent editors, but my texts are essentially modernized versions of the early folio texts, supplemented with stage directions designed to facilitate the imaginative reconstruction of the plays in performance.

SELECT BIBLIOGRAPHY

Biography. The standard scholarly biography is David Riggs's *Ben Jonson: A Life* (1989), which supersedes earlier biographies by Marchette Chute (*Ben Jonson of Westminster*, 1954) and Rosalind Miles (*Ben Jonson: His Life and Work*, 1986). The fundamental recasting of the history of the early seventeenth century in recent years has occasioned new thinking about Jonson's career in works such as Philip Edwards's *Threshold of a Nation* (1979), Jonathan Goldberg's *James I and the Politics of Literature* (1983), and David Norbrook's *Poetry and Politics in the English Renaissance* (1983).

Editions. The standard edition of Jonson is the eleven-volume *Works of Ben Jonson*, ed. C. H. Herford and Percy and Evelyn Simpson (1925–52). A four-volume modernized version of the Herford and Simpson text, with corrections and light annotation, was edited by G. A. Wilkes (1981–2). The best of the modern selected editions is the two-volume *Selected Plays of Ben Jonson* (1989): volume one (ed. Johanna Procter) includes *Volpone* and *Epicene*; volume two (ed. Martin Butler) includes *The Alchemist* and *Bartholomew Fair*. There is a large number of recent editions of single plays. The best *Volpone* is John Creaser's edition in the London Medieval and Renaissance Series (1978); there are also competent editions by Alvin B. Kernan (Yale Ben Jonson, 1962), Philip Brockbank (New Mermaids, 1968), and R. B. Parker (Revels Plays, 1983). The Herford and Simpson text of *Epicene* is flawed, partly because they confused the corrected and uncorrected folio texts, and partly because they unaccountably used as copy text for the last three acts an unreliable edition by Aurelia Henry (1906). These errors contaminated subsequent editions, and the muddle was not fully resolved until L. A. Beaurline published his scrupulous Regents Renaissance Drama edition (1966). Fully annotated editions of *Epicene* have been published by Edward Partridge (Yale Ben Jonson, 1971) and R. V. Holdsworth (New Mermaids, 1979). The most helpful editions of *The Alchemist* are those prepared by F. H. Mares (Revels Plays, 1968) and Alvin B. Kernan (Yale Ben Jonson, 1982); Douglas Brown's New Mermaids edition (1966) is eccentric and uneven. The best edition of *Bartholomew Fair* is G. R. Hibbard's New Mermaids edition (1977), which by virtue of its strong annotation and carefully meditated text supersedes the earlier New Mermaids edition by Maurice Hussey (1964) and the editions of E. A. Horsman (Revels Plays, 1960), Eugene M. Waith (Yale Ben Jonson, 1963), and Edward B. Partridge (Regents Renaissance Drama, 1964).

Criticism. The most authoritative literary study of Jonson's plays is Anne Barton's *Ben Jonson, Dramatist* (1984); the best theatrical study is Richard Cave's *Ben Jonson* (1991). Peter Womack's *Ben Jonson* (1986) is the most fruitful of the recent studies informed by theory, in this case Bakhtinian. Early criticism is collected in *Ben Jonson: The Critical Heritage,* 1599–1798, ed. D. H. Craig (1990). The torrent of critical work on Jonson published in the past fifty years was initiated by L. C. Knights's *Drama and Society in the Age of Jonson* (1937). Edward B. Partridge's *The Broken Compass* (1958) and Jonas Barish's *Ben Jonson and the Language of Prose Comedy* (1960) are valuable for their accounts of Jonson's imagery and language. The best general accounts of Jonson are Alexander Leggatt's *Ben Jonson: His Vision and his Art* (1981), Richard Dutton's *Ben Jonson: To the First Folio* (1984), and Rosalind Miles's *Ben Jonson: His Craft and Art* (1990).

A CHRONOLOGY OF BEN JONSON

1572	(11 June) Ben Jonson born, posthumous son of a minister.
1573(?)	Remarriage of Jonson's mother to a bricklayer.
1579–89(?)	Attends Westminster School.
1589–91(?)	Works as a bricklayer.
1591–2	Military service in the Low Countries.
1594	(14 November) marriage to Anne Lewis.
1597	Employed as an actor; imprisoned for his contribution to *The Isle of Dogs*, a (lost) play regarded as seditious.
1598(?)	*The Case is Altered* performed; *Every Man in His Humour* performed by the Lord Chamberlain's Men at the Curtain Theatre in Shoreditch; (22 September) kills Gabriel Spencer, a fellow actor, in a duel; avoids death sentence by pleading benefit of clergy; converted to Roman Catholicism while in prison.
1599	(January) imprisoned for debt.
1599–1602	'War of the Theatres':
1599	Marston satirizes Jonson in *Histriomastix*; Jonson satirizes Marston's style in *Every Man out of His Humour* (performed by the Chamberlain's Men at the Globe and at court).
1600	Marston satirizes Jonson in *Jack Drum's Entertainment*.
1601	Jonson satirizes Marston and Dekker in *Cynthia's Revels* (acted by the Children of Queen Elizabeth's Chapel); Marston satirizes Jonson in *What You Will*; Jonson satirizes Marston and Dekker in *Poetaster* (performed by the Children of the Chapel at the Blackfriars); Dekker (possibly assisted by Marston) satirizes Jonson in *Satiromastix*.
1601	(25 September) Jonson paid £2 for additions to Kyd's *Spanish Tragedy*.
1602	(22 June) Jonson commissioned to write a play called *Richard Crookback* (i.e. Richard III); the play, which may not have been completed, is lost.
1603	*Sejanus* performed by the King's Men; Jonson arraigned on charges of popery and treason; (25 June) *Entertainment at Althorp* performed.
1604	(15 March) *King's Entertainment* and (1 May) *Entertainment at Highgate* performed.
1605	(6 January) *Masque of Blackness* performed; imprisoned for his contribution to *Eastward Ho!*; (9 October) present at a dinner party attended by several Catholics who were later exposed as Gunpowder Plot conspirators.

1606	(5 and 6 January) *Hymenaei* performed; (April) indicted (with his wife) as a recusant; *Volpone* performed by the King's Men in Oxford, Cambridge, and London.
1608	(10 January) *The Masque of Beauty* performed; (9 February) *The Haddington Masque* performed.
1609	(2 February) *The Masque of Queens* performed.
1609	(or early 1610) *Epicene* performed by the Children of the Queen's Revels at the Whitefriars.
1610	(6 January) *Prince Henry's Barriers* performed; *The Alchemist* performed by the King's Men at the Globe; granted a pension by the king; re-converted to Anglicanism.
1611	(1 January) *Oberon, The Fairy Prince* performed; (3 February) *Love Freed from Ignorance and Folly* performed; *Catiline* performed by the King's Men.
1612	(6 January) *Love Restored* performed.
1612–13	Travels in France as tutor to Walter Ralegh (son of Sir Walter).
1613	(27 December, and 1 January 1614) *A Challenge at Tilt* performed; (29 December, and 3 January 1614) *The Irish Masque* performed.
1614	*Bartholomew Fair* performed by the Lady Elizabeth's Men at the Hope Theatre (31 October) and at court (1 November).
1615	(6 and 8 January) *Mercury Vindicated from the Alchemists* performed.
1616	(1 and 6 January) *The Golden Age Restored* performed; granted royal pension; publication of Folio *Works*; *The Devil is an Ass* performed by the King's Men at the Blackfriars; (December) *Christmas His Masque* performed.
1617	(6 and 19 January) *Vision of Delight* and (22 February) *Lovers Made Men* performed.
1618–19	Visit to Scotland.
1618	(6 January) *Pleasure Reconciled to Virtue* and (17 February) *For the Honour of Wales* performed.
1619	(17 July) awarded honorary MA by Oxford University.
1620	(17 January and 29 February) *News from the New World* and (May) *Entertainment at the Blackfriars* performed and (19 June) *Pan's Anniversary* scheduled for performance (and possibly performed) at Greenwich.
1621	*The Gypsies Metamorphosed* performed at Burley-on-the-Hill (3 August), Belvoir Castle (5 August), and Windsor (September).
1622	(6 January) *The Masque of Augurs* performed.
1623	(19 January) *Time Vindicated* performed.
1623	(or 1624) *Pan's Anniversary* performed.
1624	(6 January) *Neptune's Triumph* scheduled for performance but cancelled and (19 August) *The Masque of Owls* performed.
1625	(9 January) *The Fortunate Isles* performed.

1626   *The Staple of News* performed by the King's Men at the Blackfriars.

1628   Paralysed by a stroke.

1629   (19 January) *The New Inn* performed by the King's Men.

1630   (26 March) royal pension increased by King Charles and supplemented with an annual cask of canary wine.

1631   (9 January) *Love's Triumph through Callipolis* and (22 February) *Chloridia* performed.

1633   *A Tale of a Tub* performed by Queen Henrietta's Men at Cockpit and (January 1634) at Whitehall; (21 May) *King's Entertainment at Welbeck* performed.

1634   (30 July) *Love's Welcome at Bolsover* performed.

1637   (16 August) death of Jonson.

VOLPONE

or

THE FOX

TO THE MOST NOBLE
AND MOST EQUAL
SISTERS
THE TWO FAMOUS UNIVERSITIES,°
FOR THEIR LOVE
AND
ACCEPTANCE
SHOWN TO HIS POEM°
IN THE PRESENTATION:
BEN JONSON
THE GRATEFUL ACKNOWLEDGER
DEDICATES
BOTH IT, AND HIMSELF.

There follows an Epistle, if
you dare venture on
the length.

THE EPISTLE

Never (most equal sisters)° had any man a wit so presently excellent,°
as that it could raise itself, but there must come both matter, occasion,
commenders, and favourers to it. If this be true, and that° the fortune
of all writers doth daily prove it, it behoves the careful to provide well
toward these accidents; and having acquired them, to preserve that   5
part of reputation most tenderly, wherein the benefit of a friend° is
also defended. Hence is it that I now render myself grateful, and am
studious to justify the bounty of your act,° to which, though your
mere° authority were satisfying, yet (it being an age wherein poetry
and the professors of it hear so ill° on all sides) there will a reason be   10
looked for in the subject.° It is certain, nor can it with any forehead
be opposed, that the too much licence of poetasters in this time hath
much deformed their mistress;° that every day their manifold and
manifest ignorance doth stick unnatural reproaches upon her. But° for
their petulancy, it were an act of the greatest injustice either to let the   15
learned suffer, or so divine a skill (which indeed should not be
attempted with unclean hands) to fall under the least contempt. For
if men will impartially, and not asquint, look toward the offices and
function of a poet, they will easily conclude to themselves the
impossibility of any man's being the good poet, without first being a   20
good man.° He that is said to be able to inform young men to all good
disciplines, inflame grown men to all great virtues, keep old men in
their best and supreme state, or as they decline to childhood, recover
them to their first strength; that comes forth the interpreter and
arbiter of nature, a teacher of things divine no less than human, a   25
master in manners; and can alone (or with a few) effect the business
of mankind°—this, I take him,° is no subject for pride and ignorance
to exercise their railing rhetoric upon. But it will here be hastily
answered, that the writers of these days are other things; that not only
their manners but their natures are inverted; and nothing remaining   30
with them of the dignity of poet but the abused name, which every
scribe usurps; that now, especially in dramatic or (as they term it)
stage poetry, nothing but ribaldry, profanation, blasphemy, all licence
of offence to God and man, is practised. I dare not deny a great part
of this (and am sorry I dare not) because in some men's abortive   35
features° (and would they had never boasted the light) it is over-true.

3

But that all are embarked in this bold adventure for hell is a most
uncharitable thought, and, uttered, a more malicious slander. For my
particular,° I can (and from a most clear conscience) affirm that I have
ever trembled to think toward the least profaneness; have loathed the   40
use of such foul and unwashed bawdry as is now made the food of the
scene. And howsoever I cannot escape from some the imputation of
sharpness, but that they will say I have taken a pride or lust to be
bitter, and not my youngest infant° but hath come into the world with
all his teeth, I would ask of these supercilious politics, what nation,   45
society, or general order, or state I have provoked? What public
person? Whether I have not (in all these) preserved their dignity, as
mine own person, safe? My works are read, allowed° (I speak of those
that are entirely mine);° look into them. What broad reproofs have I
used? Where have I been particular? Where personal, except to a   50
mimic,° cheater, bawd, or buffoon—creatures (for their insolencies)
worthy to be taxed? Yet to which of these so pointingly as he might
not either ingenuously have confessed or wisely dissembled his disease?
But it is not rumour can make men guilty, much less entitle me to
other men's crimes. I know that nothing can be so innocently writ or   55
carried,° but may be made obnoxious to construction;° marry, whilst
I bear mine innocence about me, I fear it not. Application° is now
grown a trade with many; and there are that profess to have a key for
the deciphering of everything. But let wise and noble persons take heed
how they be too credulous, or give leave to these invading interpreters,   60
to be over-familiar with their fames, who cunningly and often utter
their own virulent malice under other men's simplest meanings. As for
those that will (by faults which charity hath raked up, or common
honesty concealed) make themselves a name with the multitude, or (to
draw their rude and beastly claps) care not whose living faces they   65
entrench with their petulant styles,° may they do it without a rival, for
me; I choose rather to live graved in obscurity than share with them
in so preposterous a fame. Nor can I blame the wishes of those severe
and wiser patriots who providing° the hurts these licentious spirits may
do in a state, desire rather to see fools and devils° and those antique   70
relics of barbarism retrieved, with all other ridiculous and exploded
follies, than behold the wounds of private men, of princes and nations.
For, as Horace makes Trebatius speak, among these

———*Sibi quisque timet, quamquam est intactus, et odit.*°

And men may justly impute such rages, if continued, to the writer,   75
as his sports.° The increase of which lust in liberty, together with the

4

present trade of the stage, in all their misc'line interludes,° what
learned or liberal soul doth not already abhor? Where nothing but the
filth of the time is uttered, and that with such impropriety of phrase,
such plenty of solecisms, such dearth of sense, so bold prolepses, so   80
racked metaphors, with brothelry able to violate the ear of a pagan,
and blasphemy to turn the blood of a Christian to water. I cannot but
be serious in a cause of this nature, wherein my fame and the
reputations of divers honest and learned are the question; when a
name° so full of authority, antiquity and all great mark, is (through   85
their insolence) become the lowest scorn of the age; and those men
subject to the petulancy of every vernaculous° orator, that were wont
to be the care of kings and happiest monarchs. This it is, that hath
not only rapt me to present indignation, but made me studious
heretofore, and by all my actions to stand off from them: which may   90
most appear in this my latest work (which you, most learned
arbitresses, have seen, judged, and to my crown,° approved) wherein
I have laboured, for their instruction and amendment, to reduce not
only the ancient forms, but manners of the scene—the easiness, the
propriety, the innocence and last the doctrine which is the principal   95
end of poesy: to inform men in the best reason of living. And though
my catastrophe may, in the strict rigour of comic law,° meet with
censure, as turning back to my promise, I desire the learned and
charitable critic to have so much faith in me to think it was done of
industry.° For with what ease I could have varied it nearer his scale   100
(but that I fear to boast my own faculty) I could here insert. But my
special aim being to put the snaffle in their mouths that cry out, we
never punish vice in our interludes etc., I took the more liberty—
though not without some lines of example,° drawn even in the ancients
themselves, the goings-out of whose comedies are not always joyful,   105
but oft-times, the bawds, the servants, the rivals, yea, and the masters
are mulcted; and fitly, it being the office of a comic poet to imitate
justice and instruct to life, as well as purity of language, or stir up
gentle affections. To which I shall take the occasion elsewhere° to
speak. For the present (most reverenced sisters) as I have cared to be   110
thankful for your affections past, and here made the understanding°
acquainted with some ground of your favours, let me not despair their
continuance, to the maturing of some worthier fruits; wherein, if my
muses be true to me, I shall raise the despised head of poetry again,
and stripping her out of those rotten and base rags wherewith the   115
times have adulterated her form, restore her to her primitive habit,°
feature and majesty, and render her worthy to be embraced and kissed

5

of all the great and master-spirits of our world. As for the vile and
slothful, who never affected° an act worthy of celebration, or are so
inward with their own vicious natures as they worthily° fear her, and   120
think it a high point of policy to keep her in contempt with their
declamatory and windy invectives: she shall out of just rage incite her
servants (who are *genus irritabile*)° to spout ink in their faces that shall
eat farther than their marrow, into their fames; and not Cinnamus°
the barber with his art shall be able to take out the brands, but they   125
shall live and be read till the wretches die, as things worst deserving
of themselves in chief, and then of all mankind.

THE PERSONS OF THE PLAY

VOLPONE,° a Magnifico°
MOSCA,° his Parasite°
VOLTORE,° an Advocate
CORBACCIO,° an old gentleman
CORVINO,° a merchant
AVVOCATI,° four Magistrates
NOTARO,° the Register°
NANO,° a dwarf
CASTRONE,° an eunuch
GREGGE°
SIR POLITIC° WOULD-BE, a
knight

PEREGRINE,° a gentleman-traveller
BONARIO,° a young gentleman
[*Corbaccio's son*]
FINE° LADY WOULD-BE, the knight's
wife
CELIA,° the merchant's wife
COMMENDATORI,° Officers
MERCATORI,° three merchants
ANDROGINO,° a hermaphrodite
SERVITORE,° a servant
TWO WOMEN, [*Lady Would-be's
attendants*]

THE SCENE

Venice

V olpone, childless, rich, feigns sick, despairs,
O ffers his state to hopes of several heirs,°
L ies languishing; his parasite receives
P resents of all, assures, deludes; then weaves
O ther cross-plots, which ope themselves, are told.°   5
N ew tricks for safety are sought; they thrive; when, bold,
E ach tempts th'other again, and all are sold.°

Prologue

Now, luck God send us, and a little wit°
    Will serve, to make our play hit;
According to the palates of the season,
    Here is rhyme, not empty of reason:
This we were bid to credit, from our poet,°   5
    Whose true scope, if you would know it,
In all his poems, still, hath been this measure,
    To mix profit with your pleasure;
And not as some (whose throats their envy failing)°
    Cry hoarsely, 'All he writes is railing';   10
And when his plays come forth, think they can flout them,
    With saying, 'He was a year about them'.°
To these there needs no lie, but this his creature,°
    Which was, two months since, no feature;
And though he dares give them five lives to mend it,   15
    'Tis known, five weeks fully penned it—
From his own hand, without a co-adjutor,°
    Novice, journeyman or tutor.
Yet, thus much I can give you, as a token
    Of his play's worth: no eggs are broken   20
Nor quaking custards with fierce teeth affrighted,°
    Wherewith your rout are so delighted;
Nor hales he in a gull, old ends reciting,°
    To stop gaps in his loose writing;
With such a deal of monstrous and forced action   25

As might make Bedlam a faction:°
Nor made he his play, for jests, stolen from each table,
   But makes jests to fit his fable.°
And so presents quick comedy, refined°
   As best critics have designed,   30
The laws of time, place, persons he observeth,°
   From no needful rule he swerveth.
All gall and copperas from his ink he draineth,°
   Only a little salt remaineth°
Wherewith he'll rub your cheeks, till red with laughter,   35
   They shall look fresh a week after.

1.1

[*Enter*] *Volpone* [*and*] *Mosca*

VOLPONE Good morning to the day; and next, my gold!
Open the shrine that I may see my saint.
[*Mosca reveals the treasure*]
Hail the world's soul, and mine. More glad than is°
The teeming earth to see the longed-for sun
Peep through the horns of the celestial ram,°   5
Am I, to view thy splendour, darkening his:
That lying here, amongst my other hoards,
Show'st like a flame by night; or like the day°
Struck out of chaos, when all darkness fled
Unto the centre.
[*Picks up a coin*]
　　　　　　O, thou son of Sol,°   10
(But brighter than thy father) let me kiss,
With adoration, thee, and every relic
Of sacred treasure in this blessed room.
Well did wise poets, by thy glorious name,
Title that age, which they would have the best;°   15
Thou being the best of things—and far transcending
All style of joy, in children, parents, friends,
Or any other waking dream on earth.
Thy looks, when they to Venus did ascribe,°
They should have given her twenty thousand Cupids;   20
Such are thy beauties, and our loves! Dear saint,
Riches, the dumb god, that giv'st all men tongues:°
That canst do naught, and yet mak'st men do all things;
The price of souls; even hell, with thee to boot,°
Is made worth heaven! Thou art virtue, fame,   25
Honour, and all things else! Who can get thee,
He shall be noble, valiant, honest, wise—°
MOSCA And what he will, sir. Riches are in fortune
A greater good than wisdom is in nature.°
VOLPONE True, my beloved Mosca. Yet, I glory   30
More in the cunning purchase of my wealth°
Than in the glad possession; since I gain
No common way: I use no trade, no venture;

I wound no earth with ploughshares; fat no beasts°
To feed the shambles; have no mills for iron,   35
Oil, corn, or men, to grind 'em into powder;°
I blow no subtle glass; expose no ships°
To threat'nings of the furrow-facèd sea;
I turn no moneys in the public bank;°
Nor usure private—

MOSCA   No, sir, nor devour°   40
Soft prodigals. You shall ha' some will swallow°
A melting heir as glibly as your Dutch°
Will pills of butter, and ne'er purge for't;°
Tear forth the fathers of poor families
Out of their beds, and coffin them, alive,   45
In some kind, clasping prison, where their bones
May be forthcoming when the flesh is rotten:
But your sweet nature doth abhor these courses;
You loathe the widow's, or the orphan's tears
Should wash your pavements, or their piteous cries   50
Ring in your roofs, and beat the air, for vengeance—

VOLPONE Right, Mosca, I do loathe it.

MOSCA   And besides, sir,
You are not like the thresher that doth stand
With a huge flail, watching a heap of corn,
And, hungry, dares not taste the smallest grain,   55
But feeds on mallows and such bitter herbs;°
Nor like the merchant, who hath filled his vaults
With Romagna, and rich Candian wines,°
Yet drinks the lees of Lombard's vinegar;°
You will not lie in straw, whilst moths and worms   60
Feed on your sumptuous hangings and soft beds.°
You know the use of riches, and dare give, now,
From that bright heap, to me, your poor observer,°
Or to your dwarf, or your hermaphrodite,
Your eunuch, or what other household trifle   65
Your pleasure allows maintenance—

VOLPONE   Hold thee, Mosca,°
    [*Gives him money*]
Take, of my hand; thou strik'st on truth in all:
And they are envious, term thee parasite.°
Call forth my dwarf, my eunuch and my fool,

And let 'em make me sport.
    [*Exit Mosca*]
                           What should I do   70
But cocker up my genius and live free°
To all delights my fortune calls me to?
I have no wife, no parent, child, ally,
To give my substance to; but whom I make
Must be my heir—and this makes men observe me.°   75
This draws new clients, daily, to my house,°
Women and men of every sex and age,
That bring me presents, send me plate, coin, jewels
With hope, that when I die (which they expect
Each greedy minute) it shall then return,   80
Tenfold upon them; whilst some, covetous
Above the rest, seek to engross me, whole,°
And counterwork the one unto the other,
Contend in gifts, as they would seem in love:
All which I suffer, playing with their hopes,°   85
And am content to coin 'em into profit,
And look upon their kindness, and take more,
And look on that; still bearing them in hand,°
Letting the cherry knock against their lips,°
And draw it by their mouths and back again.   90
How now!

1.2

    [*Enter*] *Mosca* [*with*] *Nano, Androgino,* [*and*] *Castrone* [*presenting
    a dramatic entertainment*° *to Volpone*]
NANO Now, room for fresh gamesters, who do will you to know,°
    They do bring you neither play nor university show;°
And therefore do entreat you that whatsoever they rehearse,°
    May not fare a whit the worse for the false pace of the verse.°
If you wonder at this, you will wonder more ere we pass,   5
    For know, here is enclosed the soul of Pythagoras,°
    [*He points to Androgino*]
That juggler divine, as hereafter shall follow;°
    Which soul (fast and loose, sir) came first from Apollo,°
And was breathed into Aethalides, Mercurius his son,°

Where it had the gift to remember all that ever was done.　　10
From thence it fled forth, and made quick transmigration
　　To goldy-locked Euphorbus, who was killed in good fashion°
At the siege of old Troy, by the cuckold of Sparta.°
　　Hermotimus was next (I find it in my charta)°
To whom it did pass, where no sooner it was missing,　　15
　　But with one Pyrrhus of Delos it learned to go a-fishing,°
And thence did it enter the Sophist of Greece.°
　　From Pythagore, she went into a beautiful piece°
Hight Aspasia, the meretrix; and the next toss of her°
　　Was, again, of a whore—she became a philosopher,°　　20
Crates the Cynic (as itself doth relate it);°
　　Since, kings, knights and beggars, knaves, lords and fools gat it,°
Besides ox and ass, camel, mule, goat and brock,
　　In all which it hath spoke, as in the cobbler's cock.°
But I come not here to discourse of that matter,　　25
　　Or his one, two or three, or his great oath, 'By Quatre!'°
His musics, his trigon, his golden thigh,°
　　Or his telling how elements shift; but I°
Would ask how of late thou hast suffered translation,°
　　And shifted thy coat in these days of reformation?°　　30
ANDROGINO Like one of the reformèd, a fool, as you see,
　　Counting all old doctrine heresy.°
NANO But not on thine own forbid meats hast thou ventured?°
ANDROGINO On fish, when first a Carthusian I entered.°
NANO Why, then thy dogmatical silence hath left thee?°　　35
ANDROGINO Of that an obstreperous lawyer bereft me.
NANO Oh wonderful change! When Sir Lawyer forsook thee,
　　For Pythagore's sake, what body then took thee?
ANDROGINO A good dull mule.
NANO　　　　　　　　　　And how! By that means,
　　Thou wert brought to allow of the eating of beans?°　　40
ANDROGINO Yes.
NANO　　　　　　　But, from the mule, into whom didst thou pass?
ANDROGINO Into a very strange beast, by some writers called an ass;
　　By others, a precise, pure, illuminate brother,°
　　　Of those devour flesh, and sometimes one another;°
And will drop you forth a libel, or a sanctified lie,　　45
　　Betwixt every spoonful of a nativity-pie.°
NANO Now quit thee, for heaven, of that profane nation;°
　　And gently report thy next transmigration.

ANDROGINO To the same that I am.

NANO   A creature of delight?
    And, what is more than a fool, an hermaphrodite?   50
    Now 'pray thee, sweet soul, in all thy variation,
        Which body would'st thou choose to take up thy station?

ANDROGINO Troth, this I am in, even here would I tarry.

NANO 'Cause here the delight of each sex thou canst vary?

ANDROGINO Alas, those pleasures be stale and forsaken;   55
        No, 'tis your fool wherewith I am so taken,
    The only one creature that I can call blessèd:
        For all other forms I have proved most distressèd.

NANO Spoke true, as thou wert in Pythagoras still.
        This learned opinion we celebrate will,   60
    Fellow eunuch, as behoves us, with all our wit and art,
        To dignify that where of ourselves are so great and special a part.°

VOLPONE Now very, very pretty! Mosca, this
    Was thy invention?

MOSCA   If it please my patron,
    Not else.

VOLPONE It doth, good Mosca.

MOSCA   Then it was, sir.   65
            SONG° [*sung by Nano and Castrone*]
            Fools, they are the only nation
            Worth men's envy or admiration;
            Free from care or sorrow-taking,
            Selves and others merry making.°
            All they speak or do is sterling;   70
            Your fool, he is your great man's darling,
            And your ladies' sport and pleasure;°
            Tongue and bauble are his treasure.°
            E'en his face begetteth laughter,
            And he speaks truth, free from slaughter;   75
            He's the grace of every feast,
            And sometimes the chiefest guest;
            Hath his trencher and his stool,
            When wit waits upon the fool.
                Oh, who would not be   80
                He, he, he?°
        [*Someone knocks offstage*]
    VOLPONE Who's that? Away!
        [*Exeunt Nano and Castrone*]

Look, Mosca.

MOSCA [*to Androgino*]   Fool, begone,
     [*Exit Androgino*]
   'Tis Signor Voltore, the advocate;
   I know him by his knock.

VOLPONE   Fetch me my gown,
   My furs and night-caps; say my couch is changing;°   85
   And let him entertain himself awhile
   Without i' the gallery.
     [*Exit Mosca*]
      Now, now, my clients°
   Begin their visitation! Vulture, kite,
   Raven and gor-crow, all my birds of prey   90
   That think me turning carcass, now they come—
   I am not for 'em yet.
     [*Enter Mosca with Volpone's gown, furs, and night-caps*]
                    How now? The news?

MOSCA A piece of plate, sir.

VOLPONE   Of what bigness?

MOSCA   Huge,
   Massy, and antique, with your name inscribed,
   And arms engraven.

VOLPONE   Good! And not a fox   95
   Stretched on the earth, with fine delusive sleights,
   Mocking a gaping crow? Ha, Mosca?

MOSCA   Sharp, sir.° [*laughs*]

VOLPONE Give me my furs. Why dost thou laugh so, man?
     [*Mosca dresses Volpone*]

MOSCA I cannot choose, sir, when I apprehend
   What thoughts he has, without, now, as he walks: 100
   That this might be the last gift he should give;
   That this would fetch you; if you died today
   And gave him all, what he should be tomorrow;
   What large return would come of all his ventures;
   How he should worshipped be, and reverenced;   105
   Ride, with his furs, and foot-cloths; waited on°
   By herds of fools and clients; have clear way
   Made for his mule, as lettered as himself;°
   Be called the great and learnèd advocate:
   And then concludes, there's naught impossible.   110

VOLPONE Yes, to be learnèd, Mosca.

MOSCA   Oh no: rich
Implies it. Hood an ass with reverend purple,°
So you can hide his two ambitious ears,°
And he shall pass for a cathedral doctor.
VOLPONE My caps, my caps; good Mosca, fetch him in.   115
MOSCA Stay, sir, your ointment for your eyes.
          [*Mosca anoints Volpone's eyes*]
VOLPONE That's true;
Dispatch, dispatch—I long to have possession
Of my new present.
MOSCA   That, and thousands more,
I hope to see you lord of.
VOLPONE   Thanks, kind Mosca.   120
MOSCA And that, when I am lost in blended dust,
And hundred such as I am, in succession—
VOLPONE Nay, that were too much, Mosca.
MOSCA   You shall live,
Still, to delude these harpies.
VOLPONE   Loving Mosca,° [*Looks in a mirror*]
'Tis well; my pillow now [*jumps into bed*] and let him enter.   125
          [*Exit Mosca*]
Now, my feigned cough, my phthisic and my gout,°
My apoplexy, palsy and catarrhs,
Help with your forcèd functions this my posture,
Wherein, this three year, I have milked their hopes.°
He comes, I hear him—uh! uh! uh! uh! Oh—°   130

1.3

          [*Enter*] Mosca [*with*] Voltore [*carrying a piece of plate*]
MOSCA [*to Voltore*] You still are what you were, sir. Only you,
Of all the rest, are he, commands his love;
And you do wisely to preserve it thus,
With early visitation, and kind notes°
Of your good meaning to him, which, I know,   5
Cannot but come most grateful. [*To Volpone*] Patron, sir.°
Here's Signor Voltore is come—
VOLPONE   What say you?
MOSCA Sir, Signor Voltore is come this morning,

To visit you.

VOLPONE   I thank him.

MOSCA   And hath brought
A piece of antique plate, bought of St Mark,°   10
With which he here presents you.

VOLPONE   He is welcome.
Pray him to come more often.

MOSCA   Yes.

VOLTORE   What says he?

MOSCA He thanks you, and desires you see him often.

VOLPONE Mosca.

MOSCA   My patron?

VOLPONE   Bring him near, where is he?
I long to feel his hand.

MOSCA   The plate is here, sir.   15

VOLTORE How fare you, sir?

VOLPONE   I thank you, Signor Voltore.
Where is the plate? Mine eyes are bad.

VOLTORE [*gives plate to Volpone*]   I'm sorry,
To see you still thus weak.

MOSCA [*Aside*]   That he is not weaker.

VOLPONE You are too munificent.

VOLTORE   No, sir, would to heaven,
I could as well give health to you as that plate.   20

VOLPONE You give, sir, what you can. I thank you. Your love
Hath taste in this, and shall not be unanswered.°
I pray you see me often.

VOLTORE   Yes, I shall, sir.

VOLPONE Be not far from me.

MOSCA [*aside to Voltore*]   Do you observe that, sir?

VOLPONE Hearken unto me still; it will concern you.   25

MOSCA You are a happy man, sir, know your good.

VOLPONE I cannot now last long—

MOSCA [*aside to Voltore*]   You are his heir, sir.

VOLTORE Am I?

VOLPONE   I feel me going—uh! uh! uh! uh!
I am sailing to my port—uh! uh! uh! uh!
And I am glad I am so near my haven.   30

MOSCA Alas, kind gentleman, well, we must all go—

VOLTORE But, Mosca—

MOSCA   Age will conquer.

VOLTORE   Pray thee hear me.
    Am I inscribed his heir for certain?
MOSCA   Are you?°
    I do beseech you, sir, you will vouchsafe
    To write me i' your family. All my hopes°   35
    Depend upon your worship. I am lost,°
    Except the rising sun do shine on me.
VOLTORE It shall both shine and warm thee, Mosca.
MOSCA   Sir,
    I am a man that have not done your love
    All the worst offices; here I wear your keys,   40
    See all your coffers and your caskets locked,
    Keep the poor inventory of your jewels,
    Your plate and moneys, am your steward, sir,
    Husband your goods here.
VOLTORE   But am I sole heir?
MOSCA Without a partner, sir, confirmed this morning;   45
    The wax is warm yet, and the ink scarce dry
    Upon the parchment.
VOLTORE   Happy, happy, me!
    By what good chance, sweet Mosca?
MOSCA   Your desert, sir;
    I know no second cause.
VOLTORE   Thy modesty
    Is loath to know it; well, we shall requite it.°   50
MOSCA He ever liked your course, sir—that first took him.°
    I oft have heard him say how he admired
    Men of your large profession, that could speak°
    To every cause, and things mere contraries,
    Till they were hoarse again, yet all be law;   55
    That with most quick agility could turn,
    And re-turn; make knots, and undo them;
    Give forkèd counsel; take provoking gold°
    On either hand, and put it up—these men,°
    He knew, would thrive, with their humility.   60
    And, for his part, he thought he should be blessed
    To have his heir of such a suffering spirit,
    So wise, so grave, of so perplexed a tongue,
    And loud withal, that would not wag, nor scarce
    Lie still, without a fee; when every word   65
    Your worship but lets fall, is a sequin!°

Another knocks
Who's that? One knocks, I would not have you seen, sir.
And yet—pretend you came and went in haste;
I'll fashion an excuse. And, gentle sir,
When you do come to swim in golden lard,   70
Up to the arms in honey, that your chin
Is borne up stiff with fatness of the flood,
Think on your vassal; but remember me:°
I ha' not been your worst of clients.
VOLTORE   Mosca—
MOSCA When will you have your inventory brought, sir?   75
Or see a copy of the will? [*More knocking*] Anon!°
[*To Voltore*] I'll bring 'em to you, sir. Away, be gone,
Put business i' your face.
        [*Exit Voltore*]
VOLPONE   Excellent, Mosca!°
Come hither, let me kiss thee.
MOSCA   Keep you still, sir.
Here is Corbaccio.
VOLPONE   Set the plate away,   80
        [*Gives the plate to Mosca*]
The vulture's gone, and the old raven's come.

1.4

MOSCA Betake you to your silence and your sleep.
        [*Adds plate to collection*]
Stand there, and multiply. Now shall we see°
A wretch, who is indeed more impotent,
Than this can feign to be; yet hopes to hop°
Over his grave.
        [*Enter Corbaccio carrying a bag of coins*]
                Signor Corbaccio!   5
You're very welcome, sir.
CORBACCIO   How does your patron?
MOSCA Troth, as he did, sir, no amends.
CORBACCIO   What? Mends he?
MOSCA No, sir—he is rather worse.
CORBACCIO   That's well. Where is he?

MOSCA Upon his couch, sir, newly fallen asleep.

CORBACCIO Does he sleep well?

MOSCA   No wink, sir, all this night,   10
Nor yesterday, but slumbers.

CORBACCIO   Good! He should take°
Some counsel of physicians: I have brought him
An opiate here, from mine own doctor—

MOSCA He will not hear of drugs.

CORBACCIO   Why? I myself
Stood by, while 'twas made; saw all the ingredients: 15
And know it cannot but most gently work.
My life for his, 'tis but to make him sleep.

VOLPONE [aside] Aye, his last sleep, if he would take it.

MOSCA   Sir,
He has no faith in physic.

CORBACCIO   Say you? Say you?

MOSCA He has no faith in physic: he does think   20
Most of your doctors are the greater danger,°
And worse disease t'escape. I often have
Heard him protest that your physician
Should never be his heir.

CORBACCIO   Not I his heir?

MOSCA Not your physician, sir.

CORBACCIO   Oh, no, no, no,   25
I do not mean it.

MOSCA   No sir, nor their fees
He cannot brook: he says, they flay a man,
Before they kill him.

CORBACCIO   Right, I do conceive you.

MOSCA And then, they do it by experiment;
For which the law not only doth absolve 'em,   30
But gives them great reward: and he is loath
To hire his death so.

CORBACCIO   It is true, they kill,
With as much licence as a judge.

MOSCA   Nay, more;
For he but kills, sir, where the law condemns,
And these can kill him too.

CORBACCIO   Aye, or me,°   35
Or any man. How does his apoplex?
Is that strong on him still?

MOSCA   Most violent.
His speech is broken, and his eyes are set,
His face drawn longer than 'twas wont—
CORBACCIO   How? How?
Stronger than he was wont?
MOSCA   No, sir; his face   40
Drawn longer than 'twas wont.
CORBACCIO   Oh, good.
MOSCA   His mouth
Is ever gaping, and his eyelids hang.
CORBACCIO   Good.
MOSCA A freezing numbness stiffens all his joints,
And makes the colour of his flesh like lead.
CORBACCIO   'Tis good.
MOSCA His pulse beats slow and dull.
CORBACCIO   Good symptoms still.   45
MOSCA And from his brain—
CORBACCIO   Ha? How? Not from his brain?°
MOSCA Yes, sir, and from his brain—
CORBACCIO   I conceive you, good.
MOSCA Flows a cold sweat, with a continual rheum,
Forth the resolvèd corners of his eyes.°
CORBACCIO Is't possible? Yet I am better, ha!   50
How does he with the swimming of his head?
MOSCA Oh, sir, 'tis past the scotomy; he now
Hath lost his feeling, and hath left to snort:°
You hardly can perceive him, that he breathes.°
CORBACCIO Excellent, excellent, sure I shall outlast him: 55
This makes me young again, a score of years.
MOSCA I was a-coming for you, sir.
CORBACCIO   Has he made his will?
What has he given me?
MOSCA   No, sir.
CORBACCIO   Nothing? Ha?
MOSCA He has not made his will, sir.
CORBACCIO   Oh, oh, oh.
What then did Voltore the lawyer here?   60
MOSCA He smelt a carcass, sir, when he but heard
My master was about his testament—°
As I did urge him to it, for your good—
CORBACCIO He came unto him, did he? I thought so.

MOSCA Yes, and presented him this piece of plate.   65
CORBACCIO To be his heir?
MOSCA   I do not know, sir.
CORBACCIO   True,
  I know it too.
MOSCA [*aside*] By your own scale, sir.
CORBACCIO   Well,°
  I shall prevent him yet. See, Mosca, look
  Here, I have brought a bag of bright sequins,
  Will quite weigh down his plate.
MOSCA [*taking the bag*]   Yea, marry, sir!°   70
  This is true physic, this your sacred medicine,
  No talk of opiates, to this great elixir.°
CORBACCIO 'Tis *aurum palpabile*, if not *potabile*.°
MOSCA It shall be ministered to him, in his bowl?
CORBACCIO Aye, do, do do.
MOSCA [*pouring coins into the bowl*]
                    Most blessed cordial!   75
  This will recover him.
CORBACCIO   Yes, do, do, do.
MOSCA I think, it were not best, sir.
CORBACCIO   What?
MOSCA   To recover him.
CORBACCIO Oh, no, no, no; by no means.
MOSCA   Why, sir, this
  Will work some strange effect, if he but feel it.
CORBACCIO 'Tis true, therefore forbear; I'll take my venture:°   80
  Give me it again.
MOSCA   At no hand, pardon me;
  You shall not do yourself that wrong, sir. I
  Will so advise you, you shall have it all.
CORBACCIO How?
MOSCA   All, sir, 'tis your right, your own; no man
  Can claim a part: 'tis yours, without a rival,   85
  Decreed by destiny.
CORBACCIO   How? How, good Mosca?
MOSCA I'll tell you, sir. This fit he shall recover—
CORBACCIO I do conceive you.
MOSCA   And on first advantage
  Of his 'gained sense, will I reimportune him
  Unto the making of his testament   90

And show him this. [*Points to the bowl of coins*]
CORBACCIO   Good, good.
MOSCA   'Tis better yet,
    If you will hear, sir.
CORBACCIO   Yes, with all my heart.
MOSCA Now, would I counsel you, make home with speed;
    There frame a will, whereto you shall inscribe
    My master your sole heir.
CORBACCIO   And disinherit   95
    My son?
MOSCA Oh, sir, the better: for that colour°
    Shall make it much more taking.
CORBACCIO   O, but colour?°
MOSCA This will, sir, you shall send it unto me.
    Now, when I come to enforce (as I will do)°
    Your cares, your watchings, and your many prayers,°   100
    Your more than many gifts, your this day's present,
    And, last, produce your will; where (without thought,
    Or least regard, unto your proper issue,°
    A son so brave, and highly meriting)
    The stream of your diverted love hath thrown you   105
    Upon my master, and made him your heir:
    He cannot be so stupid, or stone dead,
    But, out of conscience, and mere gratitude—
CORBACCIO He must pronounce me, his?
MOSCA   'Tis true.
CORBACCIO   This plot
    Did I think on before.
MOSCA   I do believe it.   110
CORBACCIO Do you not believe it?
MOSCA   Yes, sir.
CORBACCIO   Mine own project.
MOSCA Which when he hath done, sir—
CORBACCIO   Published me his heir?
MOSCA And you so certain to survive him—
CORBACCIO   Aye.
MOSCA Being so lusty a man—
CORBACCIO   'Tis true.
MOSCA   Yes, sir—
CORBACCIO I thought on that too. See, how he should be   115
    The very organ to express my thoughts!

MOSCA You have not only done yourself a good—
CORBACCIO But multiplied it on my son?
MOSCA   'Tis right, sir.
CORBACCIO Still, my invention.
MOSCA   'Las sir, heaven knows,
  It hath been all my study, all my care,   120
  (I e'en grow grey withal) how to work things—
CORBACCIO I do conceive, sweet Mosca.
MOSCA   You are he,
  For whom I labour here.
CORBACCIO   Aye, do, do, do:
  I'll straight about it.
MOSCA [aside]   Rook go with you, raven.°
CORBACCIO I know thee honest.
MOSCA [aside]   You do lie, sir.
CORBACCIO   And—   125
MOSCA [aside] Your knowledge is no better than your ears, sir.
CORBACCIO I do not doubt to be a father to thee.
MOSCA [aside] Nor I, to gull my brother of his blessing.°
CORBACCIO I may ha' my youth restored to me, why not?
MOSCA [aside] Your worship is a precious ass—
CORBACCIO   What sayst thou?   130
MOSCA I do desire your worship to make haste, sir.
CORBACCIO 'Tis done, 'tis done, I go.
    [Exit Corbaccio]
VOLPONE [leaping from his bed]   Oh, I shall burst;
  Let out my sides, let out my sides—
MOSCA   Contain°
  Your flux of laughter, sir: you know, this hope°
  Is such a bait, it covers any hook.   135
VOLPONE Oh, but thy working, and thy placing it!
  I cannot hold; good rascal, let me kiss thee:°
  I never knew thee in so rare a humour.
MOSCA Alas, sir, I but do as I am taught;
  Follow your grave instructions; give 'em words;°   140
  Pour oil into their ears, and send them hence.°
VOLPONE 'Tis true, 'tis true. What a rare punishment
  Is avarice to itself.
MOSCA   Aye, with our help, sir.
VOLPONE So many cares, so many maladies,
  So many fears attending on old age,   145

Yea, death so often called on, as no wish
Can be more frequent with 'em; their limbs faint,
Their senses dull, their seeing, hearing, going,
All dead before them; yea, their very teeth,
Their instruments of eating, failing them—   150
Yet this is reckoned life! Nay, here was one,°
Is now gone home, that wishes to live longer!
Feels not his gout nor palsy, feigns himself
Younger by scores of years, flatters his age
With confident belying it, hopes he may   155
With charms, like Aeson, have his youth restored;°
And with these thoughts so battens, as if fate
Would be as easily cheated on as he,
And all turns air!
    Another knocks
                Who's that there now? A third?°
MOSCA Close, to your couch again; I hear his voice.   160
  It is Corvino, our spruce merchant.
VOLPONE [*lying down*]   Dead.
MOSCA Another bout, sir, with your eyes.
    [*Anointing them*]
                     Who's there?

1.5

[*Enter*] *Corvino* [*carrying a pearl and a diamond*]
MOSCA Signor Corvino! Come most wished for! Oh,
  How happy were you, if you knew it, now!
CORVINO Why? What? Wherein?
MOSCA   The tardy hour is come, sir.
CORVINO He is not dead?
MOSCA   Not dead, sir, but as good;
  He knows no man.
CORVINO   How shall I do then?
MOSCA   Why, sir?   5
CORVINO I have brought him, here, a pearl.
MOSCA   Perhaps he has
  So much remembrance left as to know you, sir;
  He still calls on you; nothing but your name

Is in his mouth. Is your pearl orient, sir?°
CORVINO Venice was never owner of the like.   10
VOLPONE [*faintly*] Signor Corvino.
MOSCA   Hark.
VOLPONE   Signor Corvino.
MOSCA He calls you, step and give it him. [*To Volpone*] He's here, sir,
    And he has brought you a rich pearl.
CORVINO [*giving the pearl to Volpone*] How do you, sir?
    [*To Mosca*] Tell him, it doubles the twelfth carat.
MOSCA   Sir,°
    He cannot understand, his hearing's gone;   15
    And yet it comforts him, to see you—
CORVINO   Say
    I have a diamond for him, too.
MOSCA   Best show't, sir,
    Put it into his hand; 'tis only there
    He apprehends—he has his feeling yet.
    See how he grasps it!
CORVINO   'Las, good gentleman!   20
    How pitiful the sight is!
MOSCA   Tut, forget, sir.
    The weeping of an heir should still be laughter
    Under a visor.
CORVINO   Why? Am I his heir?°
MOSCA Sir, I am sworn I may not show the will
    Till he be dead. But here has been Corbaccio,   25
    Here has been Voltore, here were others too,
    I cannot number 'em, they were so many,
    All gaping here for legacies; but I,
    Taking the vantage of his naming you,
    'Signor Corvino', 'Signor Corvino' took   30
    Paper and pen and ink, and there I asked him,
    Whom he would have his heir? 'Corvino.' Who
    Should be executor? 'Corvino.' And,
    To any question he was silent to,
    I still interpreted the nods he made   35
    Through weakness, for consent; and sent home th'others,
    Nothing bequeathed them, but to cry and curse.
CORVINO Oh, my dear Mosca.
        (*They embrace*)
                        Does he not perceive us?

MOSCA No more than a blind harper. He knows no man,°
 No face of friend, nor name of any servant,   40
 Who 'twas that fed him last, or gave him drink;
 Not those he hath begotten or brought up
 Can he remember.
CORVINO   Has he children?
MOSCA   Bastards,
 Some dozen or more, that he begot on beggars,
 Gipsies and Jews and black-moors, when he was drunk. 45
 Knew you not that, sir? 'Tis the common fable.°
 The dwarf, the fool, the eunuch are all his;
 He's the true father of his family,°
 In all save me—but he has given 'em nothing.
CORVINO That's well, that's well. Art sure he does not hear us? 50
MOSCA Sure, sir? Why, look you, credit your own sense.
   [*He shouts into Volpone's ear*]
 The pox approach and add to your diseases,
 If it would send you hence the sooner, sir.
 For your incontinence, it hath deserved it
 Throughly, and throughly, and the plague to boot—   55
 [*To Corvino*] You may come near, sir—would you would once close°
 Those filthy eyes of yours, that flow with slime,
 Like two frog-pits; and those same hanging cheeks,
 Covered with hide instead of skin—[*to Corvino*] nay, help, sir—
 That look like frozen dish-clouts, set on end.   60
CORVINO Or like an old smoked wall, on which the rain
 Ran down in streaks.
MOSCA   Excellent, sir, speak out;
 You may be louder yet: a culverin
 Dischargèd in his ear, would hardly bore it.
CORVINO His nose is like a common sewer, still running. 65
MOSCA 'Tis good! And what his mouth?
CORVINO   A very draught.
MOSCA
  [*picking up a pillow*]
 Oh, stop it up—
CORVINO   By no means.
MOSCA   Pray you let me.
 Faith, I could stifle him rarely with a pillow,
 As well as any woman that should keep him.
CORVINO Do as you will, but I'll be gone.
MOSCA   Be so;   70

It is your presence makes him last so long.

CORVINO I pray you, use no violence.

MOSCA   No, sir? Why?
  Why should you be thus scrupulous, pray you, sir?

CORVINO Nay, at your discretion.

MOSCA   Well, good sir, be gone.

CORVINO I will not trouble him now, to take my pearl?°   75

MOSCA Puh, nor your diamond. What a needless care
  Is this afflicts you! Is not all here yours?
  Am not I here? Whom you have made? Your creature?
  That owe my being to you?

CORVINO   Grateful Mosca!
  Thou art my friend, my fellow, my companion,   80
  My partner, and shalt share in all my fortunes.

MOSCA Excepting one.

CORVINO   What's that?

MOSCA   Your gallant wife, sir.
      [*Exit Corvino*]
  Now, is he gone: we had no other means
  To shoot him hence but this.

VOLPONE   My divine Mosca!
  Thou hast today outgone thyself.
      Another knocks

                        Who's there?   85
  I will be troubled with no more. Prepare
  Me music, dances, banquets, all delights;
  The Turk is not more sensual, in his pleasures,
  Than will Volpone.
      [*Exit Mosca*]
                  Let me see, a pearl?
  A diamond? Plate? Sequins? Good morning's purchase;°   90
  Why, this is better than rob churches yet;
  Or fat, by eating once a month a man.
      [*Enter Mosca*]
  Who is't?

MOSCA The beauteous Lady Would-be, sir,
  Wife to the English knight, Sir Politic Would-be,   95
  (This is the style, sir, is directed me)
  Hath sent to know, how you have slept tonight,
  And if you would be visited.

VOLPONE   Not now.
  Some three hours hence—

MOSCA   I told the squire so much.°

VOLPONE When I am high with mirth and wine; then, then.   100
   'Fore heaven, I wonder at the desperate valour
   Of the bold English, that they dare let loose
   Their wives to all encounters!

MOSCA   Sir, this knight
   Had not his name for nothing; he is politic,
   And knows, how e'er his wife affect strange airs,   105
   She hath not yet the face to be dishonest.
   But had she Signor Corvino's wife's face—

VOLPONE Has she so rare a face?

MOSCA   Oh, sir, the wonder,
   The blazing star of Italy! A wench
   O' the first year! A beauty ripe as harvest!°   110
   Whose skin is whiter than a swan, all over!
   Than silver, snow, or lilies! A soft lip,
   Would tempt you to eternity of kissing!
   And flesh that melteth in the touch to blood!°
   Bright as your gold! And lovely as your gold!   115

VOLPONE Why had not I known this before?

MOSCA   Alas, sir.
   Myself but yesterday discovered it.

VOLPONE How might I see her?

MOSCA   Oh, not possible;
   She's kept as warily as is your gold—
   Never does come abroad, never takes air   120
   But at a window. All her looks are sweet
   As the first grapes or cherries; and are watched
   As near as they are.

VOLPONE   I must see her—

MOSCA   Sir,
   There is a guard of ten spies thick upon her—
   All his whole household—each of which is set   125
   Upon his fellow, and have all their charge,
   When he goes out, when he comes in, examined.°

VOLPONE I will go see her, though but at her window.

MOSCA In some disguise then.

VOLPONE   That is true. I must
   Maintain mine own shape still the same; we'll think.°   130
     [Exeunt]

2.1

[Enter] Sir Politic Would-be [and] Peregrine

SIR POLITIC Sir, to a wise man, all the world's his soil.°
  It is not Italy, nor France, nor Europe,
  That must bound me, if my fates call me forth.
  Yet I protest it is no salt desire
  Of seeing countries, shifting a religion,   5
  Nor any disaffection to the state
  Where I was bred (and unto which I owe
  My dearest plots) hath brought me out; much less
  That idle, antique, stale, grey-headed project
  Of knowing men's minds and manners, with Ulysses:°   10
  But a peculiar humour of my wife's,
  Laid for this height of Venice, to observe,°
  To quote, to learn the language, and so forth—
  I hope you travel, sir, with licence?°
PEREGRINE   Yes.
SIR POLITIC I dare the safelier converse—How long, sir,   15
  Since you left England?
PEREGRINE   Seven weeks.
SIR POLITIC   So lately!
  You ha' not been with my lord ambassador?°
PEREGRINE Not yet, sir.
SIR POLITIC   Pray you, what news, sir, vents our climate?°
  I heard last night a most strange thing reported
  By some of my lord's followers, and I long   20
  To hear how 'twill be seconded!
PEREGRINE   What was't, sir?
SIR POLITIC Marry, sir, of a raven that should build°
  In a ship royal of the King's.
PEREGRINE *[aside]*   This fellow
  Does he gull me, trow? Or is gulled? *[To Sir Politic]* Your name,
    sir?°
SIR POLITIC My name is Politic Would-be.
PEREGRINE *[aside]*   Oh, that speaks him.   25
  [To Sir Politic] A knight, sir?
SIR POLITIC   A poor knight, sir.
PEREGRINE   Your lady

Lies here in Venice for intelligence
Of tires, and fashions, and behaviour,
Among the courtesans? The fine Lady Would-be?°
SIR POLITIC Yes, sir, the spider and the bee oft-times   30
Suck from one flower.
PEREGRINE   Good Sir Politic!°
I cry you mercy; I have heard much of you.
'Tis true, sir, of your raven.
SIR POLITIC   On your knowledge?
PEREGRINE Yes, and your lion's whelping, in the Tower.°
SIR POLITIC Another whelp!
PEREGRINE   Another, sir.
SIR POLITIC   Now, heaven!   35
What prodigies be these? The fires at Berwick!°
And the new star! These things concurring, strange!°
And full of omen! Saw you those meteors?°
PEREGRINE I did, sir.
SIR POLITIC   Fearful! Pray you sir, confirm me,
Were there three porpoises seen above the bridge,°   40
As they give out?
PEREGRINE   Six, and a sturgeon, sir.°
SIR POLITIC I am astonished!
PEREGRINE   Nay, sir, be not so;
I'll tell you a greater prodigy than these—
SIR POLITIC What should these things portend?
PEREGRINE   The very day
(Let me be sure) that I put forth from London,   45
There was a whale discovered in the river,°
As high as Woolwich, that had waited there
(Few know how many months) for the subversion
Of the Stade fleet.
SIR POLITIC   Is't possible? Believe it,°
'Twas either sent from Spain, or the Archdukes!°   50
Spinola's whale, upon my life, my credit!°
Will they not leave these projects? Worthy sir,
Some other news.
PEREGRINE   Faith, Stone the fool is dead;°
And they do lack a tavern fool extremely.
SIR POLITIC Is Mas' Stone dead!
PEREGRINE   He's dead, sir. Why? I hope   55
You thought him not immortal? [Aside] Oh, this knight

(Were he well known) would be a precious thing
To fit our English stage; he that should write
But such a fellow, should be thought to feign
Extremely, if not maliciously.

SIR POLITIC   Stone dead!   60

PEREGRINE Dead. Lord! How deeply, sir, you apprehend it?
He was no kinsman to you?

SIR POLITIC   That I know of.°
Well! That same fellow was an unknown fool.°

PEREGRINE And yet you knew him, it seems?

SIR POLITIC   I did so. Sir,
I knew him one of the most dangerous heads   65
Living within the state, and so I held him.

PEREGRINE Indeed, sir?

SIR POLITIC   While he lived, in action.
He has received weekly intelligence,
Upon my knowledge, out of the Low Countries,°
(For all parts of the world) in cabbages;°   70
And those dispensed again to ambassadors,
In oranges, musk-melons, apricots,
Lemons, pome-citrons and such like—sometimes,
In Colchester oysters, and your Selsey cockles.°

PEREGRINE You make me wonder!

SIR POLITIC   Sir, upon my knowledge.   75
Nay, I have observed him at your public ordinary
Take his advertisement from a traveller
(A concealed statesman) in a trencher of meat;°
And instantly, before the meal was done,
Convey an answer in a toothpick.

PEREGRINE   Strange!°   80
How could this be, sir?

SIR POLITIC   Why, the meat was cut
So like his character, and so laid, as he
Must easily read the cipher.

PEREGRINE   I have heard°
He could not read, sir.

SIR POLITIC   So 'twas given out
In polity by those that did employ him;°   85
But he could read, and had your languages,
And to't, as sound a noddle—

PEREGRINE   I have heard, sir,°

That your baboons were spies; and that they were°
A kind of subtle nation near to China.

SIR POLITIC Aye, aye, your *Mammalucci*. Faith, they had°   90
Their hand in a French plot or two; but they°
Were so extremely given to women, as
They made discovery of all; yet I
Had my advices here (on Wednesday last)
From one of their own coat, they were returned,   95
Made their relations (as the fashion is)
And now stand fair for fresh employment.

PEREGRINE [*aside*]   'Heart!
This Sir Pol will be ignorant of nothing.
[*To Sir Politic*] It seems, sir, you know all?

SIR POLITIC   Not all, sir. But
I have some general notions; I do love   100
To note and to observe; though I live out,
Free from the active torrent, yet I'd mark
The currents and the passages of things,
For mine own private use, and know the ebbs
And flows of state.

PEREGRINE   Believe it, sir, I hold   105
Myself, in no small tie unto my fortunes
For casting me thus luckily upon you;
Whose knowledge, if your bounty equal it,
May do me great assistance, in instruction
For my behaviour and my bearing, which   110
Is yet so rude and raw—

SIR POLITIC   Why, came you forth
Empty of rules for travel?

PEREGRINE   Faith, I had
Some common ones, from out that vulgar grammar,°
Which he that cried Italian to me taught me.

SIR POLITIC Why, this it is that spoils all our brave bloods;   115
Trusting our hopeful gentry unto pedants:
Fellows of outside, and mere bark. You seem
To be a gentleman, of ingenuous race—°
I not profess it, but my fate hath been°
To be where I have been consulted with,   120
In this high kind, touching some great men's sons,°
Persons of blood and honour—

PEREGRINE
      [*seeing two people approach*]
          Who be these, sir?

2.2

      [*Enter*] *Mosca* [*and*] *Nano* [*disguised as a mountebank's attendants
      and carrying materials for a stage*]

MOSCA Under that window, there't must be. The same.
      [*They start to assemble a stage with a banner at the front; a
      crowd gathers as they work*]

SIR POLITIC Fellows, to mount a bank! Did your instructor°
  In the dear tongues never discourse to you
  Of the Italian mountebanks?

PEREGRINE   Yes, sir.

SIR POLITIC   Why,
  Here shall you see one.

PEREGRINE   They are quacksalvers,   5
  Fellows that live by venting oils and drugs?

SIR POLITIC Was that the character he gave you of them?

PEREGRINE As I remember.

SIR POLITIC   Pity his ignorance.
  They are the only knowing men of Europe!
  Great general scholars, excellent physicians,   10
  Most admired statesmen, professed favourites,
  And cabinet counsellors to the greatest princes!°
  The only languaged men of all the world!°

PEREGRINE And I have heard they are most lewd impostors;
  Made all of terms and shreds; no less beliers   15
  Of great men's favours than their own vile medicines;
  Which they will utter upon monstrous oaths—
  Selling that drug for twopence, ere they part,
  Which they have valued at twelve crowns before.

SIR POLITIC Sir, calumnies are answered best with silence.   20
  Yourself shall judge. Who is it mounts, my friends?

MOSCA Scoto of Mantua, sir.

SIR POLITIC   Is't he? Nay, then°
  I'll proudly promise, sir, you shall behold

Another man than has been fant'sied to you.
I wonder, yet, that he should mount his bank   25
Here in this nook, that has been wont to appear
In face of the Piazza! Here, he comes.°
    [*Enter Volpone on to the stage, disguised as a mountebank*]
VOLPONE [*to Nano*] Mount, zany. [*Nano mounts the stage*]
GREGGE   *Follo, follo, follo, follo, follo.*°
SIR POLITIC See how the people follow him! He's a man
    May write ten thousand crowns in bank here. Note,   30
    Mark but his gesture: I do use to observe
    The state he keeps, in getting up!
PEREGRINE   'Tis worth it, sir.
VOLPONE Most noble gentlemen, and my worthy patrons, it may
    seem strange that I, your Scoto Mantuano, who was ever wont to
    fix my bank in face of the public Piazza, near the shelter of the   35
    portico to the Procuratìa,° should now (after eight months' absence
    from this illustrious city of Venice) humbly retire myself into an
    obscure nook of the Piazza.
SIR POLITIC Did not I, now, object the same?
PEREGRINE   Peace, sir.
VOLPONE Let me tell you: I am not (as your Lombard proverb saith)   40
    cold on my feet,° or content to part with my commodities at a
    cheaper rate than I accustomed—look not for it. Nor that the
    calumnious reports of that impudent detractor, and shame to our
    profession—Alessandro Buttone,° I mean—who gave out, in pub-
    lic, I was condemned a 'sforzato to the galleys,° for poisoning the   45
    Cardinal Bembo's°—cook, hath at all attached, much less dejected
    me. No, no, worthy gentlemen, to tell you true, I cannot endure
    to see the rabble of these ground *ciarlatani,*° that spread their
    cloaks on the pavement, as if they meant to do feats of activity,°
    and then come in, lamely, with their mouldy tales out of Boccac-   50
    cio,° like stale Tabarin,° the fabulist: some of them discoursing
    their travels, and of their tedious captivity in the Turks' galleys,
    when indeed (were the truth known) they were the Christians'°
    galleys, where very temperately they ate bread and drunk water, as
    a wholesome penance (enjoined them by their confessors) for base   55
    pilferies.
SIR POLITIC Note but his bearing, and contempt of these.
VOLPONE These turdy-facy-nasty-paty-lousy-fartical° rogues, with
    one poor groats-worth of unprepared antimony, finely wrapped up
    in several *scartoccios,*° are able, very well, to kill their twenty a   60

week, and play; yet these meagre starved spirits, who have
half-stopped the organs of their minds with earthy oppilations,
want not their favourers among your shrivelled, salad-eating°
artisans who are overjoyed that they may have their ha'p'orth of
physic, though it purge 'em into another world, it makes no   65
matter.

SIR POLITIC Excellent! Ha' you heard better language, sir?

VOLPONE Well, let 'em go. And gentlemen, honourable gentlemen,
know that for this time our bank, being thus removed from the
clamours of the *canaglia*, shall be the scene of pleasure and   70
delight—for I have nothing to sell, little or nothing to sell.

SIR POLITIC I told you, sir, his end.

PEREGRINE   You did so, sir.

VOLPONE I protest, I and my six servants are not able to make of
this precious liquor so fast as it is fetched away from my lodging
by gentlemen of your city; strangers of the Terra Firma; worship-   75
ful merchants; aye, and senators too, who ever since my arrival
have detained me to their uses, by their splendidous liberalities.
And worthily. For what avails your rich man to have his magazines
stuffed with *moscatelli*, or of the purest grape, when his physicians
prescribe him—on pain of death—to drink nothing but water,   80
cocted with aniseeds? Oh, health! Health! The blessing of the rich!
The riches of the poor! Who can buy thee at too dear a rate, since
there is no enjoying this world without thee? Be not then so
sparing of your purses, honourable gentlemen, as to abridge the
natural course of life—   85

PEREGRINE You see his end?

SIR POLITIC   Aye, is it not good?

VOLPONE For when a humid flux or catarrh,° by the mutability of
air, falls from your head into an arm or shoulder or any other part,
take you a ducat, or your sequin of gold, and apply to the place
affected: see what good effect it can work. No, no, 'tis this blessed   90
unguento, this rare extraction, that hath only° power to disperse all
malignant humours that proceed either of hot, cold, moist or
windy causes—

PEREGRINE I would he had put in dry° too.

SIR POLITIC   Pray you, observe.

VOLPONE To fortify the most indigest and crude stomach, aye, were   95
it of one that through extreme weakness vomited blood, applying
only a warm napkin to the place, after the unction and fricace; for
the *vertiginè* in the head, putting but a drop into your nostrils,

likewise behind the ears—a most sovereign and approved remedy;
the *mal caduco*, cramps, convulsions, paralyses, epilepsies, *tremor*   100
cordis, retired nerves,° ill vapours of the spleen, stoppings of
the liver, the stone, the strangury, *hernia ventosa*, *iliaca passio*;
stops a *dysenteria* immediately; easeth the torsion of the small
guts;° and cures *melancolia hypocondriaca*,° being taken and applied
according to my printed receipt. (*Pointing to his bill° and his glass*)   105
For this is the physician, this the medicine; this counsels, this
cures; this gives the direction, this works the effect; and, in sum,
both together may be termed an abstract of the theoric and practice
in the Aesculapian art.° 'Twill cost you eight crowns. [*To Nano*]
And, Zan Frittata,° pray thee sing a verse, *extempore*, in honour of   110
it.

SIR POLITIC How do you like him, sir?
PEREGRINE   Most strangely, I!°
SIR POLITIC Is not his language rare?
PEREGRINE   But° alchemy,
  I never heard the like—or Broughton's° books.

    SONG [*Sung by Nano, accompanied by Mosca*]
      Had old Hippocrates, or Galen,°   115
      (That to their books put medicines all in)
      But known this secret, they had never
      (Of which they will be guilty ever)
      Been murderers of so much paper,
      Or wasted many a hurtless taper: 120
      No Indian drug had e'er been famèd,
      Tobacco, sassafras not namèd;°
      Ne yet of guacum one small stick, sir,°
      Nor Raymond Lully's great elixir;°
      Ne had been known the Danish Gonswart,°   125
      Or Paracelsus, with his long-sword.°

PEREGRINE All this, yet, will not do; eight crowns is high.
VOLPONE No more. Gentlemen, if I had but time to discourse to you
  the miraculous effects of this my oil, surnamed *oglio del Scoto*;°
  with the countless catalogue of those I have cured of the aforesaid,   130
  and many more diseases; the patents and privileges of all the
  princes and commonwealths of Christendom; or but the deposi-
  tions of those that appeared on my part, before the Signory of the
  Sanità,° and most learned College of Physicians; where I was
  authorized, upon notice taken of the admirable virtues of my   135
  medicaments, and mine own excellency in matter of rare and

unknown secrets, not only to disperse them publicly in this famous
city, but in all the territories that happily joy under the government of the most pious and magnificent states of Italy. But may
some other gallant fellow say 'O, there be divers that make   140
profession to have as good, and as experimented receipts,° as
yours.' Indeed, very many have assayed, like apes in imitation of
that which is really and essentially in me, to make of this oil;
bestowed great cost in furnaces, stills, alembics, continual fires and
preparation of the ingredients (as indeed there goes to it six   145
hundred several simples, besides some quantity of human fat, for
the conglutination, which we buy of the anatomists); but, when
these practitioners come to the last decoction, blow, blow, puff,
puff, and all flies *in fumo*.° Ha, ha, ha. Poor wretches! I rather pity
their folly and indiscretion than their loss of time and money; for   150
those may be recovered by industry, but to be a fool born is a
disease incurable. For myself, I always from my youth have
endeavoured to get the rarest secrets, and book them; either in
exchange, or for money; I spared nor cost nor labour where
anything was worthy to be learned. And, gentlemen, honourable   155
gentlemen, I will undertake, by virtue of chemical art, out of the
honourable hat that covers your head, to extract the four elements—that is to say, the fire, air, water, and earth—and return
you your felt without burn or stain. For whilst others have been
at the *pallone*,° I have been at my book; and am now past the   160
craggy paths of study, and come to the flowery plains of honour
and reputation.

SIR POLITIC I do assure you, sir, that is his aim.

VOLPONE But, to our price.

PEREGRINE   And that withal, Sir Pol.

VOLPONE You all know, honourable gentlemen, I never valued this   165
ampulla, or vial, at less than eight crowns; but for this time I am
content to be deprived of it for six; six crowns is the price; and
less in courtesy I know you cannot offer me; take it or leave it
howsoever, both it and I am at your service. I ask you not as the
value of the thing, for then I should demand of you a thousand   170
crowns, so the Cardinals Montalto,° Fernese,° the great duke of
Tuscany,° my gossip, with divers other princes have given me; but
I despise money: only to show my affection to you, honourable
gentlemen, and your illustrious state here, I have neglected the
messages of these princes, mine own offices, framed my journey   175
hither, only to present you with the fruits of my travels. [*To Nano*

and Mosca] Tune your voices once more to the touch of your
instruments, and give the honourable assembly some delightful
recreation.

PEREGRINE What monstrous and most painful circumstance   180
   Is here, to get some three or four *gazets*!
   Some threepence i'the whole, for that 'twill come to.
        SONG [*Sung by Nano, accompanied by Mosca*]
            You that would last long, list to my song,
            Make no more coil, but buy of this oil.
            Would you be ever fair? And young?   185
            Stout of teeth? And strong of tongue?
            Tart of palate? Quick of ear?
            Sharp of sight? Of nostril clear?
            Moist of hand? And light of foot?°
            Or I will come nearer to't—   190
            Would you live free from all diseases?
            Do the act your mistress pleases;
            Yet fright all achès from your bones?°
            Here's a medicine for the nones.°
        [*Celia appears at the window*]

VOLPONE Well, I am in a humour at this time to make a present of 195
   the small quantity my coffer contains: to the rich, in courtesy, and
   to the poor, for God's sake. Wherefore, now mark; I asked you six
   crowns; and six crowns, at other times, you have paid me; you shall
   not give me six crowns, nor five, nor four, nor three, nor two, nor
   one; nor half a ducat; no, nor a *mocenigo*: six—pence° it will cost   200
   you, or six hundred pound—expect no lower price, for by the
   banner of my front, I will not bate a *bagattino*, that I will have only
   a pledge of your loves, to carry something from amongst you, to
   show I am not contemned by you. Therefore now toss your
   handkerchiefs,° cheerfully, cheerfully; and be advertised, that the   205
   first heroic spirit that deigns to grace me with a handkerchief, I
   will give it a little remembrance of something beside, shall please
   it better than if I had presented it with a double pistolet.°

PEREGRINE Will you be that heroic spark, Sir Pol?
        Celia at the window throws down her handkerchief
   Oh, see! The window has prevented you.   210

VOLPONE Lady, I kiss your bounty; and for this timely grace you
   have done your poor Scoto of Mantua, I will return you, over and
   above my oil, a secret of that high and inestimable nature, shall
   make you forever enamoured on that minute wherein your eye first

descended on so mean (yet not altogether to be despised) an object.   215
Here is a powder, concealed in this paper, of which, if I should
speak to the worth, nine thousand volumes were but as one page,
that page as a line, that line as a word—so short is this pilgrimage
of man (which some call life) to the expressing of it. Would I
reflect on the price? Why, the whole world were but as an empire,   220
that empire as a province, that province as a bank, that bank as a
private purse, to the purchase of it. I will only tell you: it is the
powder that made Venus a goddess (given her by Apollo), that
kept her perpetually young, cleared her wrinkles, firmed her gums,
filled her skin, coloured her hair; from her, derived to Helen, and   225
at the sack of Troy unfortunately lost; till now, in this our age, it
was as happily recovered by a studious antiquary out of some ruins
of Asia, who sent a moiety of it to the court of France (but much
sophisticated) wherewith the ladies there now colour their hair.
The rest, at this present, remains with me, extracted to a quintes-   230
sence, so that wherever it but touches, in youth it perpetually
preserves, in age restores the complexion; seats your teeth, did
they dance like virginal jacks,° firm as a wall; makes them white as
ivory, that were black as—

2.3

[*Enter*] *Corvino*

CORVINO Blood o' the devil and my shame! [*To Volpone*] Come
down here,°

He beats away the mountebank, etc.

Come down! No house but mine to make your scene?
Signor Flaminio, will you down, sir? Down?
What, is my wife your Franciscina, sir?

[*Exit Celia from the window*]

No windows on the whole Piazza here   5
To make your properties, but mine? But mine?
'Heart! Ere tomorrow I shall be new-christened,
And called the *Pantalone di Besogniosi*
About the town.

[*Exit Corvino; the Crowd disperses*]

PEREGRINE   What should this mean, Sir Pol?°
SIR POLITIC Some trick of state, believe it. I will home.   10

41

PEREGRINE It may be some design on you.
SIR POLITIC   I know not.
  I'll stand upon my guard.
PEREGRINE   It is your best, sir.
SIR POLITIC This three weeks, all my advices, all my letters,
  They have been intercepted.
PEREGRINE   Indeed, sir?
  Best have a care.
SIR POLITIC   Nay, so I will.   15
          [*Exit Sir Politic*]
PEREGRINE   This knight,
  I may not lose him, for my mirth, till night.
          [*Exit*]

2.4

          [*Enter*] Volpone [*and*] Mosca
VOLPONE O, I am wounded!
MOSCA   Where, sir?
VOLPONE   Not without;
  Those blows were nothing—I could bear them ever.
  But angry Cupid, bolting from her eyes,
  Hath shot himself into me like a flame;
  Where now he flings about his burning heat,   5
  As in a furnace an ambitious fire
  Whose vent is stopped. The fight is all within me.
  I cannot live, except thou help me, Mosca;
  My liver melts, and I, without the hope°
  Of some soft air from her refreshing breath,   10
  Am but a heap of cinders.
MOSCA   'Las, good sir!
  Would you had never seen her.
VOLPONE   Nay, would thou
  Hadst never told me of her.
MOSCA   Sir, 'tis true;
  I do confess, I was unfortunate,
  And you unhappy: but I'm bound in conscience,   15
  No less than duty, to effect my best
  To your release of torment, and I will, sir.

VOLPONE Dear Mosca, shall I hope?

MOSCA   Sir, more than dear,
  I will not bid you to despair of aught,
  Within a human compass.

VOLPONE   O, there spoke
  My better angel. Mosca, take my keys,°
  Gold, plate and jewels, all's at thy devotion;
  Employ them how thou wilt; nay, coin me, too.
  So thou in this but crown my longings—Mosca?

MOSCA Use but your patience.

VOLPONE   So I have.

MOSCA   I doubt not
  To bring success to your desires.

VOLPONE   Nay then,
  I not repent me of my late disguise.

MOSCA If you can horn him, sir, you need not.

VOLPONE   True;
  Besides, I never meant him for my heir.
  Is not the colour o' my beard and eyebrows°
  To make me known?

MOSCA   No jot.

VOLPONE   I did it well.

MOSCA So well, would I could follow you in mine
  With half the happiness; and yet I would
  Escape your epilogue.

VOLPONE   But, were they gulled
  With a belief that I was Scoto?

MOSCA   Sir,
  Scoto himself could hardly have distinguished!
  I have not time to flatter you, we'll part;
  And as I prosper, so applaud my art.
    [*Exeunt*]

2.5

    [*Enter*] Corvino [*and*] Celia

CORVINO Death of mine honour, with the city's fool?
  A juggling, tooth-drawing, prating mountebank?
  And at a public window? Where, whilst he,

With his strainèd action, and his dole of faces,
To his drug-lecture draws your itching ears,   5
A crew of old, unmarried, noted lechers
Stood leering up, like satyrs—and you smile,
Most graciously! And fan your favours forth,
To give your hot spectators satisfaction!
What, was your mountebank their call? Their whistle?°   10
Or were you enamoured on his copper rings?°
His saffron jewel, with the toadstone in't?°
Or his embroidered suit, with the cope-stitch,
Made of a hearse-cloth? Or his old tilt-feather?
Or his starched beard? Well, you shall have him, yes.   15
He shall come home, and minister unto you
The fricace for the mother. Or, let me see,°
I think you'd rather mount? Would you not mount?
Why, if you'll mount, you may; yes truly, you may—°
And so you may be seen down to the foot.   20
Get you a cittern, Lady Vanity,°
And be a dealer with the virtuous man;
Make one—I'll but protest myself a cuckold,
And save your dowry. I am a Dutchman, I!°
For if you thought me an Italian,°   25
You would be damned ere you did this, you whore;
Thou'dst tremble, to imagine that the murder
Of father, mother, brother, all thy race,
Should follow as the subject of my justice!
CELIA Good sir, have patience!
CORVINO [*draws his dagger*]   What couldst thou propose   30
  Less to thyself, than, in this heat of wrath,
  And stung with my dishonour, I should strike
  This steel into thee, with as many stabs,
  As thou wert gazed upon with goatish eyes?
CELIA Alas, sir, be appeased! I could not think   35
  My being at the window should more now
  Move your impatience than at other times.
CORVINO No? Not to seek and entertain a parley
  With a known knave? Before a multitude?
  You were an actor, with your handkerchief!   40
  Which he, most sweetly, kissed in the receipt,
  And might no doubt return it, with a letter,
  And point the place where you might meet: your sister's,

Your mother's, or your aunt's might serve the turn.
CELIA Why, dear sir, when do I make these excuses? 45
    Or ever stir abroad, but to the church?
    And that so seldom—
CORVINO   Well, it shall be less;
    And thy restraint before was liberty,
    To what I now decree; and therefore, mark me.
    First, I will have this bawdy light dammed up; 50
    And, till't be done, some two or three yards off
    I'll chalk a line, o'er which if thou but chance
    To set thy desperate foot, more hell, more horror,
    More wild, remorseless rage shall seize on thee
    Than on a conjurer, that had heedless left 55
    His circle's safety, ere his devil was laid.°
    Then, here's a lock, which I will hang upon thee;
        [*Holds up a chastity belt*]
    And, now I think on't, I will keep thee backwards;
    Thy lodging shall be backwards; thy walks backwards;
    Thy prospect—all be backwards; and no pleasure, 60
    That thou shalt know, but backwards. Nay, since you force°
    My honest nature, know it is your own
    Being too open makes me use you thus.
    Since you will not contain your subtle nostrils
    In a sweet room, but they must snuff the air 65
    Of rank and sweaty passengers—(*Knock within*) One knocks.
    Away, and be not seen, pain of thy life;°
    Not look toward the window: if thou dost—
        [*Celia starts to leave*]
    Nay stay, hear this—let me not prosper, whore,
    But I will make thee an anatomy,° 70
    Dissect thee mine own self, and read a lecture
    Upon thee to the city and in public.
    Away!
        [*Exit Celia*]
        Who's there?
        [*Enter Servitore*]
SERVITORE   'Tis Signor Mosca, sir.

2.6

CORVINO Let him come in, his master's dead:
    [*Exit Servitore*]
                                              there's yet
    Some good, to help the bad.
        [*Enter Mosca*]
                            My Mosca, welcome,
    I guess your news.
MOSCA   I fear you cannot, sir.
CORVINO Is't not his death?
MOSCA   Rather the contrary.
CORVINO Not his recovery?
MOSCA   Yes, sir.
CORVINO   I am cursed,   5
    I am bewitched, my crosses meet to vex me.
    How? How? How? How?
MOSCA   Why, sir, with Scoto's oil!
    Corbaccio and Voltore brought of it,
    Whilst I was busy in an inner room—
CORVINO Death! That damned mountebank! But for the law,   10
    Now I could kill the rascal; 't cannot be
    His oil should have that virtue. Ha' not I
    Known him a common rogue, come fiddling in
    To the *osteria*, with a tumbling whore,°
    And, when he has done all his forcèd tricks, been glad°   15
    Of a poor spoonful of dead wine, with flies in 't?
    It cannot be. All his ingredients
    Are a sheep's gall, a roasted bitch's marrow,
    Some few sod earwigs, pounded caterpillars,
    A little capon's grease, and fasting spittle;°   20
    I know 'em, to a dram.
MOSCA   I know not, sir,
    But some on't, there, they poured into his ears,
    Some in his nostrils, and recovered him;
    Applying but the fricace.
CORVINO   Pox o' that fricace.
MOSCA And since, to seem the more officious,   25
    And flattering of his health, there they have had
    At extreme fees the college of physicians

Consulting on him, how they might restore him;
Where one would have a cataplasm of spices,
Another, a flayed ape clapped to his breast,   30
A third would ha' it a dog, a fourth an oil
With wild cats' skins; at last, they all resolved
That to preserve him was no other means
But some young woman must be straight sought out,
Lusty, and full of juice, to sleep by him;°   35
And to this service—most unhappily,
And most unwillingly—am I now employed,
Which here I thought to pre-acquaint you with,
For your advice, since it concerns you most,
Because I would not do that thing might cross   40
Your ends, on whom I have my whole dependence, sir:
Yet, if I do it not, they may delate
My slackness to my patron, work me out
Of his opinion; and there all your hopes,°
Ventures, or whatsoever, are all frustrate.   45
I do but tell you, sir. Besides, they are all
Now striving, who shall first present him. Therefore—°
I could entreat you, briefly, conclude somewhat;°
Prevent 'em if you can.
CORVINO   Death to my hopes!
This is my villainous fortune! Best to hire   50
Some common courtesan?
MOSCA   Aye, I thought on that, sir.
But they are all so subtle, full of art,
And age again doting and flexible,
So as—I cannot tell—we may perchance
Light on a quean, may cheat us all.
CORVINO   'Tis true.   55
MOSCA No, no; it must be one that has no tricks, sir,
Some simple thing, a creature made unto it;
Some wench you may command. Ha' you no kinswoman?
God's so—Think, think, think, think, think, think, think, sir.°
One o' the doctors offered there his daughter.   60
CORVINO How?
MOSCA   Yes, Signor Lupo, the physician.°
CORVINO His daughter?
MOSCA   And a virgin, sir. Why? Alas
He knows the state of 's body, what it is;

That naught can warm his blood, sir, but a fever;
Nor any incantation raise his spirit—°   65
A long forgetfulness hath seized that part.
Besides, sir, who shall know it? Some one or two—
CORVINO I pray thee give me leave. [*He walks aside*] If any man
But I had had this luck—the thing, in 'tself,
I know, is nothing—wherefore should not I   70
As well command my blood and my affections°
As this dull doctor? In the point of honour,
The cases are all one of wife and daughter.
MOSCA [*aside*] I hear him coming.
CORVINO [*aside*]   She shall do't: 'Tis done.°
'Slight, if this doctor, who is not engaged,   75
Unless it be for his counsel (which is nothing),
Offer his daughter, what should I, that am
So deeply in? I will prevent him: wretch!
Covetous wretch! [*To Mosca*] Mosca, I have determined.
MOSCA How, sir?
CORVINO   We'll make all sure. The party you wot of   80
Shall be mine own wife, Mosca.
MOSCA   Sir, the thing
(But that I would not seem to counsel you)
I should have motioned to you at the first;
And, make your count, you have cut all their throats.
Why, 'tis directly taking a possession!°   85
And, in his next fit, we may let him go.
'Tis but to pull the pillow from his head,
And he is throttled; 't had been done before,
But for your scrupulous doubts.
CORVINO   Aye, a plague on't,
My conscience fools my wit. Well, I'll be brief,   90
And so be thou, lest they should be before us;
Go home, prepare him, tell him with what zeal
And willingness I do it; swear it was
On the first hearing—as thou mayest do, truly—
Mine own free motion.
MOSCA   Sir, I warrant you,°   95
I'll so possess him with it that the rest
Of his starved clients shall be banished all,
And only you received. But come not, sir,
Until I send, for I have something else

To ripen for your good; you must not know it.   100
CORVINO But do not you forget to send now.
MOSCA   Fear not.
    [*Exit Mosca*]

2.7

CORVINO Where are you, wife? My Celia? Wife?
    [*Enter Celia, crying*]
                              What, blubbering?
Come, dry those tears. I think thou thought'st me in earnest?
Ha? By this light, I talked so but to try thee.
Methinks the lightness of the occasion°
Should ha' confirmed thee. Come, I am not jealous.   5
CELIA No?
CORVINO Faith, I am not, I, nor never was:
It is a poor, unprofitable humour.
Do not I know, if women have a will,
They'll do 'gainst all the watches o' the world?°   10
And that the fiercest spies are tamed with gold?
Tut, I am confident in thee, thou shalt see 't:
And see, I'll give thee cause too, to believe it.
Come, kiss me. [*Celia kisses him*] Go, and make thee ready straight,
In all thy best attire, thy choicest jewels,   15
Put 'em all on, and with 'em thy best looks:
We are invited to a solemn feast
At old Volpone's, where it shall appear
How far I'm free from jealousy or fear.
    [*Exeunt*]

3.1

[Enter] Mosca

MOSCA I fear I shall begin to grow in love
With my dear self, and my most prosp'rous parts,
They do so spring and burgeon; I can feel
A whimsy i' my blood. I know not how,
Success hath made me wanton. I could skip   5
Out of my skin, now, like a subtle snake,
I am so limber. O! Your parasite
Is a most precious thing, dropped from above,
Not bred 'mongst clods and clot-polls, here on earth.
I muse the mystery was not made a science,   10
It is so liberally professed! Almost°
All the wise world is little else in nature
But parasites or sub-parasites. And yet,
I mean not those that have your bare town-art,°
To know who's fit to feed 'em; have no house,   15
No family, no care, and therefore mould
Tales for men's ears, to bait that sense; or get°
Kitchen-invention, and some stale receipts
To please the belly and the groin; nor those,
With their court-dog-tricks, that can fawn and fleer,   20
Make their revenue out of legs and faces,°
Echo my lord, and lick away a moth:°
But your fine, elegant rascal, that can rise
And stoop (almost together) like an arrow;
Shoot through the air, as nimbly as a star;   25
Turn short, as doth a swallow; and be here,
And there, and here, and yonder, all at once;
Present to any humour, all occasion;°
And change a visor swifter than a thought!°
This is the creature had the art born with him;   30
Toils not to learn it, but doth practise it
Out of most excellent nature; and such sparks
Are the true parasites, others but their zanies.

3.2

[Enter] Bonario

MOSCA Who's this? Bonario? Old Corbaccio's son?
  The person I was bound to seek. Fair sir,
  You are happ'ly met.
BONARIO   That cannot be by thee.
MOSCA Why, sir?
BONARIO   Nay, 'pray thee know thy way, and leave me;
  I would be loath to interchange discourse   5
  With such a mate as thou art.
MOSCA   Courteous sir,
  Scorn not my poverty.
BONARIO   Not I, by heaven—
  But thou shalt give me leave to hate thy baseness.
MOSCA Baseness?
BONARIO   Aye, answer me, is not thy sloth
  Sufficient argument? Thy flattery?   10
  Thy means of feeding?
MOSCA   Heaven, be good to me.
  These imputations are too common, sir,
  And easily stuck on virtue when she's poor;
  You are unequal to me, and howe'er
  Your sentence may be righteous, yet you are not,   15
  That ere you know me, thus proceed in censure;
  St Mark bear witness 'gainst you, 'tis inhuman.°
      [He weeps]
BONARIO *[aside]* What? Does he weep? The sign is soft and good!
  I do repent me that I was so harsh.
MOSCA 'Tis true that, swayed by strong necessity,   20
  I am enforced to eat my careful bread
  With too much obsequy; 'tis true, beside,
  That I am fain to spin mine own poor raiment,°
  Out of my mere observance, being not born
  To a free fortune. But that I have done   25
  Base offices in rending friends asunder,
  Dividing families, betraying counsels,
  Whispering false lies, or mining men with praises,
  Trained their credulity with perjuries,
  Corrupted chastity, or am in love   30

With mine own tender ease, but would not rather
Prove the most rugged and laborious course
That might redeem my present estimation,
Let me here perish in all hope of goodness.
BONARIO [*aside*] This cannot be a personated passion!   35
[*To Mosca*] I was to blame, so to mistake thy nature;
Pray thee forgive me, and speak out thy business.
MOSCA Sir, it concerns you; and though I may seem
At first to make a main offence in manners,°
And in my gratitude unto my master,   40
Yet for the pure love which I bear all right,
And hatred of the wrong, I must reveal it.
This very hour your father is in purpose
To disinherit you—
BONARIO   How!
MOSCA   And thrust you forth
As a mere stranger to his blood; 'tis true, sir,   45
The work no way engageth me, but as
I claim an interest in the general state
Of goodness and true virtue, which I hear
T'abound in you; and for which mere respect,°
Without a second aim, sir, I have done it.   50
BONARIO This tale hath lost thee much of the late trust,
Thou hadst with me; it is impossible—
I know not how to lend it any thought,
My father should be so unnatural.
MOSCA It is a confidence that well becomes   55
Your piety; and formed, no doubt, it is
From your own simple innocence, which makes
Your wrong more monstrous and abhorred. But, sir,
I now will tell you more. This very minute,
It is, or will be doing: and if you   60
Shall be but pleased to go with me, I'll bring you
(I dare not say where you shall see), but where
Your ear shall be a witness of the deed;
Hear yourself written bastard: and professed
The common issue of the earth.
BONARIO   I'm 'mazed!°   65
MOSCA Sir, if I do it not, draw your just sword,
And score your vengeance on my front and face;
Mark me your villain. You have too much wrong,

And I do suffer for you, sir. My heart
Weeps blood, in anguish—
BONARIO   Lead. I follow thee.   70
    [Exeunt]

3.3

    [Enter] Volpone, Nano, Androgino [and]Castrone
VOLPONE Mosca stays long, methinks. Bring forth your sports
    And help to make the wretched time more sweet.
NANO Dwarf, fool, and eunuch, well met here we be.
    A question it were now, whether of us three,
Being, all, the known delicates of a rich man,°   5
    In pleasing him, claim the precedency can?
CASTRONE I claim for myself.
ANDROGINO   And so doth the fool.
NANO 'Tis foolish indeed: let me set you both to school.
    First for your dwarf, he's little and witty,
        And everything, as it is little, is pretty;   10
    Else why do men say to a creature of my shape,
        So soon as they see him, 'It's a pretty little ape'?
    And why a pretty ape? But for pleasing imitation
        Of greater men's action, in a ridiculous fashion.
    Beside, this feat body of mine doth not crave   15
        Half the meat, drink and cloth, one of your bulks will have.
    Admit, your fool's face be the mother of laughter,
        Yet, for his brain, it must always come after;
    And though that do feed him, it's a pitiful case,
        His body is beholding to such a bad face. (*One knocks*)   20
VOLPONE Who's there? My couch, away, look, Nano, see:
    Give me my caps first—go, enquire.
        [Exeunt Nano, Androgino, Castrone]
                          Now, Cupid
    Send it be Mosca, and with fair return.°
        [Enter Nano]
NANO It is the beauteous Madam—
VOLPONE   Would-be—is it?
NANO The same.
VOLPONE   Now, torment on me; squire her in—   25

For she will enter, or dwell here forever.
Nay, quickly, that my fit were past.
    [*Exit Nano*]
        I fear
A second hell too, that my loathing this
Will quite expel my appetite to the other:°   30
Would she were taking now her tedious leave.
Lord, how it threats me, what I am to suffer!

3.4°

[*Enter*] Nano [*and*] Lady Would-be
LADY WOULD-BE [*to Nano*] I thank you, good sir. Pray you signify
    Unto your patron I am here. [*Examining herself in a mirror*]
                        This band
Shows not my neck enough—I trouble you, sir,
Let me request you, bid one of my women
Come hither to me—
    [*Exit Nano*]
                    in good faith, I am dressed   5
Most favourably today, it is no matter,
'Tis well enough.
    [*Enter Nano and First Woman*]
                Look, see, these petulant things!
How they have done this!
VOLPONE [*aside*]   I do feel the fever
Ent'ring in at mine ears; o for a charm
To fright it hence.
LADY WOULD-BE   Come nearer: is this curl   10
In his right place? Or this? Why is this higher
Than all the rest? You ha' not washed your eyes yet?
Or do they not stand even i' your head?
Where's your fellow? Call her.
    [*Exit First Woman*]
NANO [*aside*]   Now, St Mark
Deliver us! Anon she'll beat her women,   15
Because her nose is red.
    [*Enter First and Second Women*]
LADY WOULD-BE   I pray you, view

This tire, forsooth—are all things apt, or no?

SECOND WOMAN One hair a little, here, sticks out, forsooth.

LADY WOULD-BE Does 't so, forsooth? And where was your dear
  sight
  When it did so, forsooth? What now? Bird-eyed?   20
  And you, too? Pray you both approach, and mend it.
  Now, by that light, I muse, you're not ashamed!
  I, that have preached these things so oft unto you,
  Read you the principles, argued all the grounds,
  Disputed every fitness, every grace,   25
  Called you to counsel of so frequent dressings—

NANO [aside] More carefully than of your fame or honour.

LADY WOULD-BE Made you acquainted what an ample dowry
  The knowledge of these things would be unto you,
  Able, alone, to get you noble husbands   30
  At your return; and you thus to neglect it?°
  Besides, you seeing what a curious nation
  Th' Italians are, what will they say of me?
  The English lady cannot dress herself;
  Here's a fine imputation to our country!   35
  Well, go your ways, and stay i' the next room.
  This fucus was too coarse too, it's no matter.
  Good sir, you'll give 'em entertainment?°
     [Exeunt Nano and Women]

VOLPONE [aside] The storm comes toward me.

LADY WOULD-BE   How does my Volp?

VOLPONE Troubled with noise, I cannot sleep; I dreamt   40
  That a strange fury entered now my house,
  And with the dreadful tempest of her breath,
  Did cleave my roof asunder.

LADY WOULD-BE   Believe me, and I
  Had the most fearful dream, could I remember't—

VOLPONE [aside] Out on my fate; I ha' given her the occasion   45
  How to torment me: she will tell me hers.

LADY WOULD-BE Methought the golden mediocrity°
  Polite, and delicate—

VOLPONE   Oh, if you do love me,
  No more; I sweat and suffer at the mention
  Of any dream: feel, how I tremble yet.   50

LADY WOULD-BE Alas, good soul! The passion of the heart.
  Seed-pearl were good now, boiled with syrup of apples,

Tincture of gold, and coral, citron-pills,
Your elecampane root, myrobalanes—
VOLPONE [*aside*] Aye me, I have ta'en a grasshopper by the wing.   55
LADY WOULD-BE Burnt silk, and amber; you have muscatel
Good i' the house—
VOLPONE   You will not drink and part?
LADY WOULD-BE No, fear not that. I doubt we shall not get
Some English saffron (half a dram would serve)
Your sixteen cloves, a little musk, dried mints,   60
Bugloss, and barley-meal—
VOLPONE [*aside*]   She's in again.
Before I feigned diseases; now I have one.
LADY WOULD-BE And these applied with a right scarlet-cloth—
VOLPONE [*aside*] Another flood of words! A very torrent!
LADY WOULD-BE Shall I, sir, make you a poultice?°
VOLPONE   No, no, no;   65
I'm very well: you need prescribe no more.
LADY WOULD-BE I have, a little, studied physic; but now
I'm all for music—save i' the forenoons
An hour or two for painting. I would have
A lady, indeed, t'have all letters and arts,   70
Be able to discourse, to write, to paint,
But principal (as Plato holds) your music—°
And so does wise Pythagoras, I take it—°
Is your true rapture; when there is concent
In face, in voice, and clothes—and is, indeed,   75
Our sex's chiefest ornament.
VOLPONE   The poet°
As old in time as Plato, and as knowing,
Says that your highest female grace is silence.
LADY WOULD-BE Which o' your poets? Petrarch? Or Tasso? Or
Dante?
Guarini? Ariosto? Aretine?   80
Cieco d'Adria? I have read them all.°
VOLPONE [*aside*] Is everything a cause to my destruction?
LADY WOULD-BE I think I ha' two or three of 'em about me.
VOLPONE [*aside*] The sun, the sea will sooner both stand still,
Than her eternal tongue! Nothing can 'scape it.   85
LADY WOULD-BE Here's *Pastor Fido*—
VOLPONE [*aside*]   Profess obstinate silence,°
That's now my safest.

LADY WOULD-BE   All our English writers,
I mean such as are happy in th'Italian,
Will deign to steal out of this author mainly,
Almost as much as from Montagnie:°   90
He has so modern and facile a vein,
Fitting the time, and catching the court-ear.
Your Petrarch is more passionate, yet he,
In days of sonneting, trusted 'em with much.
Dante is hard, and few can understand him;   95
But for a desperate wit, there's Aretine!
Only, his pictures are a little obscene—°
You mark me not?

VOLPONE   Alas, my mind's perturbed.

LADY WOULD-BE Why, in such cases, we must cure ourselves,
Make use of our philosophy—

VOLPONE   *Ohimè.*   100

LADY WOULD-BE And as we find our passions do rebel,
Encounter 'em with reason; or divert 'em,
By giving scope unto some other humour
Of lesser danger—as in politic bodies,°
There's nothing more doth overwhelm the judgement,   105
And clouds the understanding, than too much
Settling and fixing and (as 't were) subsiding
Upon one object. For the incorporating
Of these same outward things into that part
Which we call mental, leaves some certain faeces°   110
That stop the organs, and, as Plato says,
Assassinates our knowledge.

VOLPONE [*aside*]   Now the spirit°
Of patience help me!

LADY WOULD-BE   Come, in faith, I must
Visit you more a-days, and make you well;
Laugh and be lusty.

VOLPONE [*aside*]   My good angel save me!   115

LADY WOULD-BE There was but one sole man in all the world,
With whom I e'er could sympathise; and he
Would lie you often, three, four hours together,°
To hear me speak; and be sometime so rapt,
As he would answer me quite from the purpose,°   120
Like you, and you are like him, just. I'll discourse—
An't be but only, sir, to bring you asleep—

How we did spend our time and loves together,
For some six years.
VOLPONE   O, o, o, o, o, o.
LADY WOULD-BE For we were *coaetanei*, and brought up—   125
VOLPONE [*aside*] Some power, some fate, some fortune rescue me!

3·5

[*Enter*] *Mosca*
MOSCA God save you, madam.
LADY WOULD-BE   Good sir.
VOLPONE   Mosca! Welcome,
Welcome to my redemption.
MOSCA   Why, sir?
VOLPONE   O,
Rid me of this my torture, quickly, there;
My madam, with the everlasting voice;
The bells in time of pestilence ne'er made°   5
Like noise, or were in that perpetual motion;
The cockpit comes not near it. All my house,
But now, steamed like a bath, with her thick breath.
A lawyer could not have been heard; nor scarce
Another woman, such a hail of words   10
She has let fall. For hell's sake, rid her hence.
MOSCA Has she presented?
VOLPONE   O, I do not care,
I'll take her absence upon any price,
With any loss.
MOSCA   Madam—
LADY WOULD-BE   I ha' brought your patron
A toy, a cap here, of mine own work—
MOSCA   'Tis well.   15
I had forgot to tell you, I saw your knight,
Where you'd little think it—
LADY WOULD-BE   Where?
MOSCA   Marry,
Where yet, if you make haste, you may appre'nd him,
Rowing upon the water in a gondola,
With the most cunning courtesan of Venice.   20

LADY WOULD-BE Is't true?

MOSCA   Pursue 'em, and believe your eyes.
    Leave me to make your gift.
        [*Exit Lady Would-be*]
                    I knew 'twould take.
    For lightly, they that use themselves most licence
    Are still most jealous.

VOLPONE   Mosca, hearty thanks
    For thy quick fiction, and delivery of me.
    Now, to my hopes, what sayest thou?   25
        [*Enter Lady Would-be*]

LADY WOULD-BE   But do you hear, sir?—

VOLPONE [*aside*] Again! I fear a paroxysm.

LADY WOULD-BE   Which way
    Rowed they together?

MOSCA   Toward the Rialto.

LADY WOULD-BE I pray you lend me your dwarf.

MOSCA   I pray you, take
    him.
        [*Exit Lady Would-be*]
    Your hopes, sir, are like happy blossoms, fair,   30
    And promise timely fruit, if you will stay
    But the maturing; keep you at your couch—
    Corbaccio will arrive straight, with the will;
    When he is gone, I'll tell you more.
        [*Exit Mosca*]

VOLPONE   My blood,
    My spirits are returned; I am alive;   35
    And like your wanton gamester at primero,
    Whose thought had whispered to him 'not go less',
    Methinks I lie, and draw—for an encounter.°
        [*He hides in his bed*]

3.6

      [*Enter*] *Mosca* [*and*] *Bonario*

MOSCA Sir, here concealed, you may hear all. But 'pray you
    Have patience, sir; (*One knocks*) the same's your father knocks;
    I am compelled to leave you.

BONARIO   Do so. Yet
        [*Exit Mosca*]
    Cannot my thought imagine this a truth.
        [*He hides*]

    3.7

        [*Enter*] *Mosca, Corvino* [*and*] *Celia*
MOSCA Death on me! You are come too soon, what meant you?
    Did not I say I would send?
CORVINO   Yes, but I feared
    You might forget it, and then they prevent us.
MOSCA [*aside*] Prevent? Did e'er man haste so for his horns?°   5
    A courtier would not ply it so, for a place.°
    [*To Corvino*] Well, now there's no helping it, stay here;
    I'll presently return.
        [*Goes to Bonario*]
CORVINO   Where are you, Celia?
    You know not wherefore I have brought you hither?
CELIA Not well, except you told me.
CORVINO   Now I will:°   10
    Hark hither.
        [*They whisper apart*]
MOSCA (*to Bonario*) Sir, your father hath sent word
    It will be half an hour ere he come;
    And therefore, if you please to walk the while
    Into that gallery—at the upper end
    There are some books to entertain the time;   15
    And I'll take care no man shall come unto you, sir.
BONARIO Yes, I will stay there [*Aside*] I do doubt this fellow.
        [*Exit Bonario*]
MOSCA There, he is far enough; he can hear nothing:
    And for his father, I can keep him off.
        [*Goes to Volpone*]
CORVINO Nay, now, there is no starting back; and therefore   20
    Resolve upon it; I have so decreed.
    It must be done. Nor would I move 't afore,
    Because I would avoid all shifts and tricks
    That might deny me.

CELIA   Sir, let me beseech you,
  Affect not these strange trials; if you doubt   25
  My chastity, why, lock me up, for ever:
  Make me the heir of darkness. Let me live
  Where I may please your fears, if not your trust.
CORVINO Believe it, I have no such humour, I.
  All that I speak I mean; yet I am not mad—   30
  Not horn-mad, see you? Go to, show yourself
  Obedient, and a wife.
CELIA   O heaven!
CORVINO   I say it,
  Do so.
CELIA   Was this the train?
CORVINO   I've told you reasons;
  What the physicians have set down; how much
  It may concern me; what my engagements are;   35
  My means; and the necessity of those means
  For my recovery; wherefore, if you be
  Loyal, and mine, be won, respect my venture.
CELIA Before your honour?
CORVINO   Honour? Tut, a breath;
  There's no such thing in nature—a mere term   40
  Invented to awe fools. What, is my gold
  The worse for touching? Clothes, for being looked on?
  Why, this 's no more. An old decrepit wretch
  That has no sense, no sinew; takes his meat
  With others' fingers; only knows to gape,   45
  When you do scald his gums; a voice; a shadow;
  And what can this man hurt you?
CELIA [aside]   Lord! What spirit
  Is this hath entered him?
CORVINO   And for your fame,
  That's such a jig; as if I would go tell it,
  Cry it on the Piazza! Who shall know it   50
  But he that cannot speak it and this fellow,
  Whose lips are i' my pocket: save yourself
  If you'll proclaim 't, you may. I know no other
  Should come to know it.
CELIA   Are heaven and saints then nothing?
  Will they be blind, or stupid?
CORVINO   How?

CELIA   Good sir,   55
  Be jealous still, emulate them; and think
  What hate they burn with, tòward every sin.
CORVINO I grant you; if I thought it were a sin,
  I would not urge you. Should I offer this
  To some young Frenchman, or hot Tuscan blood,   60
  That had read Aretine, conned all his prints,°
  Knew every quirk within lust's labyrinth,
  And were professed critic in lechery,°
  And I would look upon him, and applaud him,°
  This were a sin. But here, 'tis contrary,   65
  A pious work, mere charity, for physic,
  And honest polity to assure mine own.
CELIA O heaven! Canst thou suffer such a change?
VOLPONE [aside to Mosca] Thou art mine honour, Mosca, and my
    pride,
  My joy, my tickling, my delight! Go, bring 'em.   70
MOSCA [to Corvino] Please you draw near, sir.
CORVINO   Come on, what—
  You will not be rebellious? By that light—
MOSCA Sir, Signor Corvino here is come to see you.
VOLPONE O.
MOSCA   And hearing of the consultation had
  So lately for your health, is come to offer,   75
  Or rather, sir, to prostitute—
CORVINO   Thanks, sweet Mosca.°
MOSCA Freely, unasked, or unentreated—
CORVINO   Well.
MOSCA As the true, fervent instance of his love,
  His own most fair and proper wife; the beauty,°
  Only of price in Venice—
CORVINO   'Tis well urged.°   80
MOSCA To be your comfortress, and to preserve you.
VOLPONE Alas, I'm past already! Pray you, thank him
  For his good care and promptness; but for that,
  'Tis a vain labour, e'en to fight 'gainst heaven;
  Applying fire to a stone—uh, uh, uh, uh—   85
  Making a dead leaf grow again. I take
  His wishes gently, though; and you may tell him,
  What I've done for him. Marry, my state is hopeless!
  Will him to pray for me; and t'use his fortune

With reverence, when he comes t'it.

MOSCA   Do you hear, sir?   90
   Go to him with your wife.

CORVINO   Heart of my father!
   Wilt thou persist thus? Come, I pray thee, come.
   Thou seest 'tis nothing, Celia. By this hand
   I shall grow violent. Come, do't, I say.

CELIA   Sir, kill me rather. I will take down poison,   95
   Eat burning coals, do anything—

CORVINO   Be damned.°
   Heart, I will drag thee hence home by the hair;
   Cry thee a strumpet through the streets; rip up
   Thy mouth unto thine ears, and slit thy nose,°
   Like a raw rochet—Do not tempt me, come.   100
   Yield, I am loath—Death! I will buy some slave,
   Whom I will kill, and bind thee to him, alive;°
   And at my window hang you forth—devising
   Some monstrous crime, which I, in capital letters,
   Will eat into thy flesh, with aqua-fortis   105
   And burning corsives, on this stubborn breast.
   Now, by the blood thou hast incensed, I'll do it.

CELIA   Sir, what you please, you may; I am your martyr.

CORVINO   Be not thus obstinate, I ha' not deserved it:
   Think who it is entreats you. Pray thee, sweet;   110
   Good faith, thou shalt have jewels, gowns, attires,
   What thou wilt think, and ask. Do but go kiss him.
   Or touch him, but. For my sake. At my suit.
   This once. No? Not? I shall remember this.
   Will you disgrace me thus? Do you thirst my undoing?   115

MOSCA   Nay, gentle lady, be advised.

CORVINO   No, no.
   She has watched her time. God's precious, this is scurvy;°
   'Tis very scurvy: and you are—

MOSCA   Nay, good sir.

CORVINO   An arrant locust, by heaven, a locust. Whore,
   Crocodile, that hast thy tears prepared,°   120
   Expecting how thou'lt bid 'em flow.

MOSCA   Nay, pray you, sir,°
   She will consider.

CELIA   Would my life would serve
   To satisfy—

CORVINO   'Sdeath, if she would but speak to him,
  And save my reputation, 'twere somewhat;
  But spitefully to effect my utter ruin!   125
MOSCA Aye, now you've put your fortune in her hands.
  Why i' faith, it is her modesty, I must quit her;
  If you were absent, she would be more coming;
  I know it, and dare undertake for her.
  What woman can, before her husband? Pray you,   130
  Let us depart, and leave her here.
CORVINO   Sweet Celia,
  Thou mayst redeem all yet; I'll say no more:
  If not, esteem yourself as lost. Nay, stay there.
    [Exit Corvino with Mosca]
CELIA O God, and his good angels! Whither, whither
  Is shame fled human breasts? That with such ease,   135
  Men dare put off your honours and their own?
  Is that, which ever was a cause of life,
  Now placed beneath the basest circumstance?
  And modesty an exile made, for money?
VOLPONE (*he leaps off from his couch*) Aye, in Corvino, and such
    earth-fed minds,   140
  That never tasted the true heaven of love.
  Assure thee, Celia, he that would sell thee,
  Only for hope of gain, and that uncertain,
  He would have sold his part of paradise
  For ready money, had he met a cope-man.   145
  Why art thou 'mazed, to see me thus revived?
  Rather applaud thy beauty's miracle;
  'Tis thy great work, that hath, not now alone,
  But sundry times raised me in several shapes
  And but this morning like a mountebank,   150
  To see thee at thy window. Aye, before
  I would have left my practice for thy love,
  In varying figures, I would have contended
  With the blue Proteus, or the hornèd flood.°
  Now, art thou welcome.
CELIA   Sir!
VOLPONE   Nay, fly me not.   155
  Nor let thy false imagination
  That I was bed-rid make thee think I am so:
  Thou shalt not find it. I am now as fresh,

As hot, as high, and in as jovial plight,
As when, in that so celebrated scene   160
At recitation of our comedy
For entertainment of the great Valois,°
I acted young Antinous; and attracted°
The eyes and ears of all the ladies present,
To admire each graceful gesture, note, and footing.   165

SONG°

> Come, my Celia, let us prove,
> While we can, the sports of love;
> Time will not be ours forever,
> He, at length, our good will sever;
> Spend not then his gifts in vain.   170
> Suns that set may rise again:
> But if once we lose this light,
> 'Tis with us perpetual night.
> Why should we defer our joys?
> Fame and rumour are but toys.   175
> Cannot we delude the eyes
> Of a few poor household-spies?
> Or his easier ears beguile,
> Thus removèd by our wile?
> 'Tis no sin love's fruits to steal,   180
> But the sweet thefts to reveal;
> To be taken, to be seen,
> These have crimes accounted been.

CELIA Some sèrene blast me, or dire lightning strike
This my offending face.
VOLPONE   Why droops my Celia?   185
Thou hast in place of a base husband found
A worthy lover; use thy fortune well,
With secrecy, and pleasure. See, behold, [*shows the treasure*]
What thou art queen of; not in expectation,
As I feed others: but possessed and crowned.   190
See, here, a rope of pearl; and each more orient
Than that the brave Egyptian queen caroused:°
Dissolve, and drink 'em. See, a carbuncle,
May put out both the eyes of our St Mark;°
A diamond would have bought Lollia Paulina,°   195
When she came in like star-light, hid with jewels
That were the spoils of provinces; take these,

And wear, and lose 'em: yet remains an earring
To purchase them again, and this whole state.
A gem but worth a private patrimony   200
Is nothing—we will eat such at a meal.
The heads of parrots, tongues of nightingales,
The brains of peacocks, and of ostriches
Shall be our food: and could we get the phoenix,
Though nature lost her kind, she were our dish.°   205
CELIA Good sir, these things might move a mind affected
With such delights; but I, whose innocence
Is all I can think wealthy, or worth th'enjoying,
And which once lost, I have naught to lose beyond it,
Cannot be taken with these sensual baits   210
If you have conscience—
VOLPONE   'Tis the beggar's virtue,
If thou hast wisdom, hear me, Celia.
Thy baths shall be the juice of Jùly-flowers,
Spirit of roses, and of violets,
The milk of unicorns, and panther's breath°   215
Gathered in bags, and mixed with Cretan wines.
Our drink shall be preparèd gold and amber;°
Which we will take, until my roof whirl round
With the vertìgo: and my dwarf shall dance,
My eunuch sing, my fool make up the antic.   220
Whilst we, in changèd shapes, act Ovid's tales,°
Thou like Europa now, and I like Jove,°
Then I like Mars, and thou like Erycine,
So of the rest, till we have quìte run through
And wearied all the fables of the gods.   225
Then will I have thee in more modern forms,
Attirèd like some sprightly dame of France,
Brave Tuscan lady, or proud Spanish beauty;
Sometimes unto the Persian Sophy's wife,
Or the Grand Signor's mistress; and, for change,°   230
To one of our most artful courtesans,
Or some quick Negro, or cold Russìan;
And I will meet thee in as many shapes:
Where we may so transfuse our wand'ring souls,°
Out at our lips, and score up sums of pleasures,   235
                That the curious shall not know,
                How to tell them as they flow;°

> *And the envious, when they find*
> *What their number is, be pined.*°

CELIA If you have ears that will be pierced—or eyes°   240
  That can be opened—a heart may be touched—
  Or any part that yet sounds man—about you:°
  If you have touch of holy saints or heaven—
  Do me the grace to let me 'scape.—If not,
  Be bountiful, and kill me.—You do know   245
  I am a creature hither ill-betrayed,
  By one whose shame I would forget it were.—
  If you will deign me neither of these graces,
  Yet feed your wrath, sir, rather than your lust—
  It is a vice, comes nearer manliness—   250
  And punish that unhappy crime of nature,
  Which you miscall my beauty—flay my face,
  Or poison it with ointments for seducing
  Your blood to this rebellion.—Rub these hands
  With what may cause an eating leprosy,   255
  E'en to my bones and marrow—anything,
  That may disfavour me, save in my honour—
  And I will kneel to you, pray for you, pay down
  A thousand hourly vows, sir, for your health—
  Report, and think you virtuous—

VOLPONE   Think me cold,   260
  Frozen, and impotent, and so report me?
  That I had Nestor's hernia, thou wouldst think.°
  I do degenerate and abuse my nation,
  To play with opportunity thus long;
  I should have done the act, and then have parleyed.   265
  Yield, or I'll force thee.

CELIA   O just God!

VOLPONE   In vain—

  He [Bonario] leaps out from where Mosca had placed him.

BONARIO Forbear, foul ravisher, libidinous swine!
  Free the forced lady, or thou diest, impostor.
  But that I am loath to snatch thy punishment
  Out of the hand of justice, thou shouldst yet   270
  Be made the timely sacrifice of vengeance
  Before this altar, and this dross, thy idol.
  Lady, let's quit the place, it is the den
  Of villainy; fear naught, you have a guard:

And he ere long shall meet his just reward.   275
    [Exit Bonario with Celia]
VOLPONE Fall on me, roof, and bury me in ruin,
Become my grave, that wert my shelter. Oh!
I am unmasked, unspirited, undone,
Betrayed to beggary, to infamy—

3.8

    [Enter] Mosca, *[bleeding]*
MOSCA Where shall I run, most wretched shame of men,
  To beat out my unlucky brains?
VOLPONE   Here, here.
  What? Dost thou bleed?
MOSCA   O, that his well-driven sword
  Had been so courteous to have cleft me down
  Unto the navel, ere I lived to see   5
  My life, my hopes, my spirits, my patron, all
  Thus desperately engagèd by my error.
VOLPONE Woe on thy fortune.
MOSCA   And my follies, sir.
VOLPONE Th'hast made me miserable.
MOSCA   And myself, sir.
  Who would have thought he would have harkened so?   10
VOLPONE What shall we do?
MOSCA   I know not; if my heart
  Could expiate the mischance, I'd pluck it out.
  Will you be pleased to hang me? Or cut my throat?
  And I'll requite you, sir. Let's die like Romans,°
  Since we have lived like Grecians.
    They knock without
VOLPONE   Hark, who's there?°   15
  I hear some footing—officers, the *Saffi*,
  Come to apprehend us! I do feel the brand
  Hissing already at my forehead: now,
  Mine ears are boring.
MOSCA   To your couch, sir; you
    [Volpone jumps into bed]
  Make that place good, however. Guilty men°   20
  Suspect what they deserve still. Signor Corbaccio!

3.9

[*Enter*] *Corbaccio*

CORBACCIO Why! How now? Mosca!

[*Enter Voltore, unseen*]

MOSCA   O, undone, amazed, sir.
Your son—I know not by what accident—
Acquainted with your purpose to my patron
Touching your will, and making him your heir,
Entered our house with violence, his sword drawn,   5
Sought for you, called you wretch, unnatural,
Vowed he would kill you.

CORBACCIO   Me?

MOSCA   Yes, and my patron.

CORBACCIO This act shall disinherit him indeed;
Here is the will.

MOSCA   'Tis well, sir.

CORBACCIO   Right and well.
Be you as careful now for me.

MOSCA   My life, sir,   10
Is not more tendered, I am only yours.

CORBACCIO How does he? Will he die shortly, thinkst thou?

MOSCA   I fear
He'll outlast May.

MOSCA   Today?

CORBACCIO   No, last out May, sir.

CORBACCIO Couldst thou not gi' him a dram?

MOSCA   O, by no means, sir.

CORBACCIO Nay, I'll not bid you.

          [*He retires*]

VOLTORE [*aside*]   This is a knave, I see.   15

MOSCA How, Signor Voltore! [*Aside*] Did he hear me?

VOLTORE   Parasite.

MOSCA Who's that? Oh, sir, most timely welcome—

VOLTORE   Scarce,
To the discovery of your tricks, I fear.
You are his, only? And mine, also? Are you not?

MOSCA Who? I, sir?

VOLTORE   You, sir. What device is this   20
About a will?

MOSCA   A plot for you, sir.
VOLTORE   Come,
  Put not your foists upon me, I shall scent 'em.°
MOSCA Did you not hear it?
VOLTORE   Yes, I hear, Corbaccio
  Hath made your patron there his heir.
MOSCA   'Tis true,
  By my device, drawn to it by my plot,   25
  With hope—
VOLTORE   Your patron should reciprocate?
  And you have promised?
MOSCA   For your good, I did, sir.
  Nay more, I told his son, brought, hid him here,
  Where he might hear his father pass the deed;
  Being persuaded to it by this thought, sir,   30
  That the unnaturalness, first, of the act,
  And then his father's oft disclaiming in him°—
  Which I did mean to help on—would sure enrage him
  To do some violence upon his parent.
  On which the law should take sufficient hold,   35
  And you be stated in a double hope.
  Truth be my comfort and my conscience,
  My only aim was to dig you a fortune
  Out of these two old rotten sepulchres—
VOLTORE I cry thee mercy, Mosca.
MOSCA   —worth your patience,   40
  And your great merit, sir. And see the change!
VOLTORE Why? What success?
MOSCA   Most hapless! You must help, sir.
  Whilst we expected th'old raven, in comes
  Corvino's wife, sent hither by her husband—
VOLTORE What, with a present?
MOSCA   No, sir, on visitation   45
  (I'll tell you how, anon) and, staying long,
  The youth, he grows impatient, rushes forth,
  Seizeth the lady, wounds me, makes her swear—
  Or he would murder her, that was his vow—
  T' affirm my patron to have done her rape,   50
  Which how unlike it is, you see! And hence,
  With that pretext, he's gone, t' accuse his father,
  Defame my patron, defeat you—

VOLTORE   Where's her husband?
    Let him be sent for straight.
MOSCA   Sir, I'll go fetch him.
VOLTORE Bring him to the *Scrutineo*.
MOSCA   Sir, I will.   55
VOLTORE This must be stopped.
MOSCA   O, you do nobly, sir.
    Alas, 'twas laboured all, sir, for your good;
    Nor was there want of counsel in the plot.
    But fortune can at any time o'erthrow
    The projects of a hundred learned clerks, sir.   60
CORBACCIO [*overhearing*] What's that?
VOLTORE   Wilt please you, sir, to go
    along?
        [*Exit Voltore with Corbaccio*]
MOSCA Patron, go in and pray for our success.
VOLPONE Need makes devotion; heaven your labour bless.
        [*Exeunt*]

4.1

[Enter] Sir Politic Would-be [and] Peregrine

SIR POLITIC I told you, sir, it was a plot; you see
    What observation is. You mentioned me
    For some instructions: I will tell you, sir,°
    Since we are met here in this height of Venice,
    Some few particulars I have set down,   5
    Only for this meridian; fit to be known
    Of your crude traveller, and they are these.
    I will not touch, sir, at your phrase, or clothes,
    For they are old.
PEREGRINE   Sir, I have better.
SIR POLITIC   Pardon,
    I meant, as they are themes.
PEREGRINE   O, sir, proceed   10
    I'll slander you no more of wit, good sir.
SIR POLITIC First, for your garb, it must be grave and serious;
    Very reserved and locked; not tell a secret,
    On any terms, not to your father; scarce
    A fable but with caution; make sure choice   15
    Both of your company and discourse; beware
    You never speak a truth—
PEREGRINE   How!
SIR POLITIC   Not to strangers,
    For those be they you must converse with most;
    Others I would not know, sir, but at distance,
    So as I still might be a saver in 'em:°   20
    You shall have tricks else, passed upon you hourly.
    And then, for your religion, profess none,
    But wonder at the diversity of all;
    And for your part protest, were there no other
    But simply the laws o' th'land, you could content you;   25
    Nick Machiavel and Monsieur Bodin both
    Were of this mind. Then must you learn the use°
    And handling of your silver fork at meals,°
    The mettle of your glass—these are main matters°
    With your Italian—and to know the hour   30
    When you must eat your melons and your figs.

PEREGRINE Is that a point of state too?
SIR POLITIC   Here it is.
    For your Venetian, if he see a man
    Preposterous in the least, he has him straight;
    He has: he strips him. I'll acquaint you, sir,   35
    I now have lived here, 'tis some fourteen months;
    Within the first week of my landing here,
    All took me for a citizen of Venice,
    I knew the forms, so well—
PEREGRINE [aside]   And nothing else.
SIR POLITIC I had read Contarine, took me a house,°   40
    Dealt with my Jews, to furnish it with movables—°
    Well, if I could but find one man, one man,
    To mine own heart, whom I durst trust, I would—
PEREGRINE What? What, sir?
SIR POLITIC   Make him rich; make him a fortune:
    He should not think again. I would command it.   45
PEREGRINE As how?
SIR POLITIC   With certain projects that I have:
    Which, I may not discover.
PEREGRINE [aside]   If I had
    But one to wager with, I would lay odds now
    He tells me instantly.
SIR POLITIC   One is (and that
    I care not greatly who knows) to serve the state   50
    Of Venice with red herrings for three years,
    And at a certain rate, from Rotterdam,
    Where I have correspondence. There's a letter, [shows a letter]
    Sent me from one o' the States, and to that purpose;°
    He cannot write his name, but that's his mark.   55
PEREGRINE He is a chandler?
SIR POLITIC   No, a cheesemonger.°
    There are some other too with whom I treat
    About the same negotiation;
    And I will undertake it; for, 'tis thus,
    I'll do't with ease, I've cast it all. Your hoy   60
    Carries but three men in her, and a boy;
    And she shall make me three returns a year;
    So, if there come but one of three, I save,
    If two, I can defalk. But this is now
    If my main project fail.

PEREGRINE   Then you have others?   65
SIR POLITIC I should be loath to draw the subtle air
   Of such a place without my thousand aims.
   I'll not dissemble, sir; where'er I come,
   I love to be considerative; and 'tis true,
   I have at my free hours thought upon   70
   Some certain goods unto the state of Venice,
   Which I do call my cautions; and, sir, which
   I mean (in hope of pension) to propound
   To the Great Council, then unto the forty,
   So to the Ten. My means are made already—°   75
PEREGRINE By whom?
SIR POLITIC   Sir, one, that though his place be obscure,
   Yet he can sway, and they will hear him. He's
   A commendatore.
PEREGRINE   What, a common sergeant?
SIR POLITIC Sir, such as they are, put it in their mouths
   What they should say, sometimes, as well as greater.   80
   I think I have my notes to show you—
      [*Searching his pockets*]
PEREGRINE   Good, sir.
SIR POLITIC But you shall swear unto me, on your gentry,
   Not to anticipate—
PEREGRINE   I, sir?
SIR POLITIC   Nor reveal
   A circumstance—My paper is not with me.
PEREGRINE O, but you can remember, sir.
SIR POLITIC   My first is   85
   Concerning tinder-boxes. You must know,
   No family is, here, without its box.
   Now, sir, it being so portable a thing,
   Put case, that you or I were ill affected
   Unto the state; sir, with it in our pockets,   90
   Might not I go into the *Arsenale*?°
   Or you? Come out again? And none the wiser?
PEREGRINE Except yourself, sir.
SIR POLITIC   Go to, then. I therefore
   Advèrtise to the state, how fit it were,
   That none but such as were known patriots,   95
   Sound lovers of their country, should be suffered
   To enjoy them in their houses; and even those;

Sealed at some office, and at such a bigness,
As might not lurk in pockets.
PEREGRINE   Admirable!
SIR POLITIC My next is, how to enquire and be resolved   100
By present demonstration, whether a ship,
Newly arrivèd from *Soria*, or from
Any suspected part of all the Levant,
Be guilty of the plague; and where they use,
To lie out forty, fifty days, sometimes,   105
About the *Lazaretto* for their trial,°
I'll save that charge and loss unto the merchant,
And in an hour clear the doubt.
PEREGRINE   Indeed, sir?
SIR POLITIC Or—I will lose my labour.
PEREGRINE   My faith, that's much.
SIR POLITIC Nay, sir, conceive me. 'Twill cost me, in onions,°   110
Some thirty *livres*—
PEREGRINE   Which is one pound sterling.
SIR POLITIC Beside my waterworks; for this I do, sir.
First, I bring in your ship 'twixt two brick walls
(But those the state shall venture); on the one
I strain me a fair tarpaulin; and in that   115
I stick my onions, cut in halves; the other
Is full of loopholes, out at which I thrust
The noses of my bellows; and those bellows
I keep with waterworks in perpetual motion°
(Which is the easiest matter of a hundred).   120
Now, sir, your onion, which doth naturally
Attract th'infection, and your bellows blowing
The air upon him, will show instantly
By his changed colour, if there be contagion;
Or else remain as fair as at the first.   125
Now 'tis known, 'tis nothing.
PEREGRINE   You are right, sir.
SIR POLITIC I would I had my note.
PEREGRINE   Faith, so would I;
But you ha' done well for once, sir.
SIR POLITIC   Were I false,
Or would be made so, I could show you reasons,
How I could sell this state, now, to the Turk;°   130
Spite of their galleys, or their—

[*Searching his pockets again*]

PEREGRINE   Pray you, Sir Pol.

SIR POLITIC I have 'em not about me.

PEREGRINE   That I feared.
They're there, sir?

          [*Points to a book*]

SIR POLITIC   No, this is my diary.
Wherein I note my actions of the day.

PEREGRINE Pray you, let's see, sir. What is here? *Notandum*,   135
A rat had gnawn my spur-leathers; notwithstanding,
I put on new, and did go forth; but first
I threw three beans over the threshold. *Item*,°
I went and bought two toothpicks, whereof one°
I burst immediately, in a discourse   140
With a Dutch merchant 'bout *ragion' del stato*.°
From him I went and paid a *mocenigo*,
For piecing my silk stockings; by the way,
I cheapened sprats; and at St Mark's I urined.
Faith, these are politic notes!

SIR POLITIC   Sir, I do slip   145
No action of my life, thus but I quote it.

PEREGRINE Believe me it is wise!

SIR POLITIC   Nay, sir, read forth.

4.2

          [*Enter*] *Lady Would-be, Nano* [*and two*] *Women*

LADY WOULD-BE Where should this loose knight be, trow? Sure,
     he's housed.

NANO Why, then he's fast.

LADY WOULD-BE   Aye, he plays both with me.°
I pray you, stay. This heat will do more harm
To my complexion than his heart is worth.
I do not care to hinder, but to take him.   5

     [*Rubbing her cheek*]
How it comes off!

WOMAN   My master's yonder.

LADY WOULD-BE   Where?°

WOMAN With a young gentleman.

LADY WOULD-BE   That same's the party!
  In man's apparel. [*To Nano*] Pray you, sir, jog my knight:
  I will be tender to his reputation,
  How ever he demerit.
SIR POLITIC [*seeing her*] My lady!
PEREGRINE   Where?   10
SIR POLITIC 'Tis she indeed, sir, you shall know her. She is,
  Were she not mine, a lady of that merit
  For fashion, and behaviour; and for beauty
  I durst compare—
PEREGRINE   It seems you are not jealous,
  That dare commend her.
SIR POLITIC   Nay, and for discourse—   15
PEREGRINE Being your wife, she cannot miss that.
SIR POLITIC [*introducing Peregrine*]   Madam,
  Here is a gentleman, pray you, use him fairly,
  He seems a youth, but he is—
LADY WOULD-BE   None?
SIR POLITIC   Yes, one
  Has put his face as soon into the world—
LADY WOULD-BE You mean, as early? But today?
SIR POLITIC   How's this!°   20
LADY WOULD-BE Why, in this habit, sir, you apprehend me.
  Well, Master Would-be, this doth not become you;
  I had thought the odour, sir, of your good name
  Had been more precious to you; that you would not
  Have done this dire massàcre on your honour;   25
  One of your gravity and rank besides!
  But, knights, I see, care little for the oath
  They make to ladies—chiefly their own ladies.
SIR POLITIC Now, by my spurs, the symbol of my knighthood—
PEREGRINE [*aside*] Lord! How his brain is humbled for an oath.   30
SIR POLITIC I reach you not.
LADY WOULD-BE   Right, sir, your polity
  May bear it through thus. [*To Peregrine*] Sir, a word with you.
  I would be loath to contest publicly
  With any gentlewoman; or to seem
  Froward, or violent; as *The Courtier* says,°   35
  It comes too near rusticity in a lady,
  Which I would shun by all means; and however
  I may deserve from Master Would-be, yet,

To have one fair gentlewoman thus be made
Th'unkind instrument to wrong another,   40
And one she knows not, aye, and to persèvere,
In my poor judgement is not warranted
From being a solecism in our sex,
If not in manners.
PEREGRINE   How is this?
SIR POLITIC   Sweet madam,
Come nearer to your aim.
LADY WOULD-BE   Marry, and will, sir.   45
Since you provoke me with your impudence
And laughter of your light land-siren here,°
Your Sporus, your hermaphrodite—
PEREGRINE [*aside*]   What's here?°
Poetic fury and historic storms!°
SIR POLITIC The gentleman, believe it, is of worth,   50
And of our nation.
LADY WOULD-BE   Aye, your Whitefriars' nation?°
Come, I blush for you, Master Would-be, ay;
And am ashamed you should ha' no more forehead,
Than thus to be the patron or St George°
To a lewd harlot, a base fricatrice,   55
A female devil in a male outside.
SIR POLITIC [*to Peregrine*]   Nay,
An you be such a one, I must bid *adieu*
To your delights. The case appears too liquid.
LADY WOULD-BE Aye, you may carry't clear, with your state-face!
But for your carnival concupiscence,°   60
Who here is fled for liberty of conscience,°
From furious persecution of the marshal,
Her will I disple.
      [*Exit Sir Politic*]
PEREGRINE   This is fine, i'faith!
And do you use this often? Is this part
Of your wit's exercise, 'gainst you have occasion?°   65
Madam—
LADY WOULD-BE
      Go to, sir.
      [*She snatches Peregrine's shirt as if she were uncovering a
      disguise*]
PEREGRINE   Do you hear me, lady?°
Why, if your knight have set you to beg shirts,

Or to invite me home, you might have done it°
A nearer way by far.

LADY WOULD-BE   This cannot work you
Out of my snare.

PEREGRINE   Why? Am I in it then?   70
Indeed, your husband told me you were fair,
And so you are; only your nose inclines—
That side, that's next the sun—to the queen-apple.

LADY WOULD-BE This cannot be endured by any patience.

4.3

[Enter] Mosca

MOSCA What's the matter, madam?

LADY WOULD-BE   If the Senate
Right not my quest in this, I will protest 'em
To all the world no aristocracy.°

MOSCA What is the injury, lady?

LADY WOULD-BE   Why, the callet
You told me of, here I have ta'en disguised.   5

MOSCA Who? This? What means your ladyship? The creature
I mentioned to you is apprehended now,
Before the Senate, you shall see her—

LADY WOULD-BE   Where?

MOSCA I'll bring you to her. This young gentleman
I saw him land this morning, at the port.   10

LADY WOULD-BE Is't possible? How has my judgement wandered!
Sir, I must, blushing, say to you I have erred:
And plead your pardon.

PEREGRINE   What? More changes yet?

LADY WOULD-BE I hope you ha' not the malice to remember
A gentlewoman's passion. If you stay   15
In Venice here, please you to use me, sir—

MOSCA Will you go, madam?

LADY WOULD-BE   Pray you, sir, use me. In faith,
The more you see me, the more I shall conceive,°
You have forgot our quarrel.

          [Exeunt all except Peregrine]

PEREGRINE   This is rare!
Sir Politic Would-be? No, Sir Politic Bawd!   20

To bring me thus acquainted with his wife!
Well, wise Sir Pol, since you have practised thus
Upon my freshmanship, I'll try your salt-head,°
What proof it is against a counter-plot.
    [*Exit*]

4.4

    [*Enter*] *Voltore, Corbaccio, Corvino* [*and*] *Mosca*
VOLTORE Well, now you know the carriage of the business,°
    Your constancy is all that is required
    Unto the safety of it.
MOSCA   Is the lie
    Safely conveyed amongst us? Is that sure?
    Knows every man his burden?
CORVINO   Yes.
MOSCA   Then shrink not.   5
CORVINO [*Aside to Mosca*] But knows the advocate the truth?
MOSCA   O, sir,°
    By no means. I devised a formal tale,
    That salved your reputation. But be valiant, sir.
CORVINO I fear no one but him; that this his pleading
    Should make him stand for a co-heir—
MOSCA   Co-halter,   10
    Hang him! We will but use his tongue, his noise,
    As we do croaker's here.
        [*Pointing to Corbaccio*]
CORVINO   Aye, what shall he do?°
MOSCA When we ha' done, you mean?
CORVINO   Yes.
MOSCA   Why, we'll think—
    Sell him for *mummia*, he's half dust already.°
        To Voltore
    Do not you smile to see this buffalo,°   15
        [*Pointing to Corvino*]
    How he doth sport it with his head?—
        [*Aside*]   I should,
    If all were well and past. (*To Corbaccio*) Sir, only you
    Are he, that shall enjoy the crop of all,

And these not know for whom they toil.

CORBACCIO   Aye, peace.

MOSCA (*to Corvino*) But you shall eat it. [*Aside*] Much! (*Then to*
   Voltore again) Worshipful sir,   20
   Mercury sit upon your thundering tongue,
   Or the French Hercules, and make your language°
   As conquering as his club, to beat along,
   As with a tempest, flat, our adversaries;
   But much more yours, sir.

VOLTORE   Here they come, ha' done.   25

MOSCA I have another witness, if you need, sir,
   I can produce.

VOLTORE   Who is it?

MOSCA   Sir, I have her.°

4.5

[*Enter*] 4 *Avvocati, Bonario, Celia, Notaro, Commendatori*
[*and other court officials*]

1ST AVVOCATO The like of this the Senate never heard of.

2ND AVVOCATO 'Twill come most strange to them when we report it.

4TH AVVOCATO The gentlewoman has been ever held
   Of unreprovèd name.

3RD AVVOCATO   So the young man.

4TH AVVOCATO The more unnatural part that of his father.   5

2ND AVVOCATO More of the husband.

1ST AVVOCATO   I not know to give
   His act a name, it is so monstrous!°

4TH AVVOCATO But the impostor, he is a thing created
   T'exceed example!

1ST AVVOCATO   And all after times!

2ND AVVOCATO I never heard a true voluptuary   10
   Described but him.

3RD AVVOCATO   Appear yet those were cited?

NOTARO All but the old magnifico, Volpone.

1ST AVVOCATO Why is not he here?

MOSCA   Please your fatherhoods,
   Here is his advocate. Himself's so weak,
   So feeble—

4TH AVVOCATO What are you?
BONARIO   His parasite,   15
   His knave, his pander. I beseech the court,
   He may be forced to come, that your grave eyes
   May bear strong witness of his strange impostures.
VOLTORE Upon my faith and credit with your virtues,
   He is not able to endure the air.   20
2ND AVVOCATO Bring him, however.
3RD AVVOCATO   We will see him.
4TH AVVOCATO   Fetch him.
        [*Exeunt Commendatori*]
VOLTORE Your fatherhoods' fit pleasures be obeyed,
   But sure, the sight will rather move your pities
   Than indignation: may it please the court,
   In the meantime, he may be heard in me.   25
   I know this place most void of prejudice,
   And therefore crave it, since we have no reason
   To fear our truth should hurt our cause.
3RD AVVOCATO   Speak free.
VOLTORE Then know, most honoured fathers, I must now
   Discover to your strangely abusèd ears   30
   The most prodigious, and most frontless piece
   Of solid impudence and treachery
   That ever vicious nature yet brought forth
   To shame the state of Venice. This lewd woman, [*points to Celia*]
   That wants no artificial looks or tears   35
   To help the visor she has now put on,
   Hath long been known a close adulteress
   To that lascivious youth there [*points to Bonario*]; not suspected,
   I say, but known; and taken in the act
   With him; and by this man, the easy husband, [*points to Corvino*]   40
   Pardoned; whose timeless bounty makes him now
   Stand here, the most unhappy, innocent person
   That ever man's own goodness made accused.
   For these, not knowing how to owe a gift
   Of that dear grace, but with their shame—being placed   45
   So above all powers of their gratitude—
   Began to hate the benefit; and in place
   Of thanks, devise t'extirp the memory
   Of such an act. Wherein, I pray your fatherhoods
   T'observe the malice, yea, the rage of creatures   50

Discovered in their evils; and what heart
Such take, even from their crimes. But that, anon,
Will more appear. This gentleman, the father, [*points to Corbaccio*]
Hearing of this foul fact, with many others,
Which daily struck at his too tender ears,   55
And grieved in nothing more than that he could not
Preserve himself a parent (his son's ills
Growing to that strange flood) at last decreed
To disinherit him.
1ST AVVOCATO   These be strange turns!
2ND AVVOCATO The young man's fame was ever fair and honest.   60
VOLTORE So much more full of danger is his vice,
That can beguile so, under shade of virtue.
But as I said, my honoured sires, his father
Having this settled purpose (by what means
To him betrayed, we know not) and this day°   65
Appointed for the deed; that parricide
(I cannot style him better) by confederacy
Preparing this his paramour to be there,
Entered Volpone's house (who was the man
Your fatherhoods must understand, designed   70
For the inheritance), there sought his father.
But with what purpose sought he him, my lords?
I tremble to pronounce it, that a son
Unto a father, and to such a father
Should have so foul, felonious intent.   75
It was, to murder him. When, being prevented
By his more happy absence, what then did he?
Not check his wicked thoughts; no, now new deeds—
Mischief doth ever end, where it begins—°
An act of horror, fathers! He dragged forth   80
The agèd gentleman, that had there lain bed-rid
Three years and more, out of his innocent couch,
Naked, upon the floor, there left him; wounded
His servant in the face; and with this strumpet,
The stale to his forged practice, who was glad°   85
To be so active (I shall here desire
Your fatherhoods to note but my collections,
As most remarkable), thought at once to stop
His father's ends, discredit his free choice,
In the old gentleman, redeem themselves°   90

By laying infamy upon this man,
　　[*Points to Corvino*]
To whom, with blushing, they should owe their lives.

1ST AVVOCATO What proofs have you of this?

BONARIO   Most honoured fathers,
I humbly crave there be no credit given
To this man's mercenary tongue.

2ND AVVOCATO   Forbear.   95

BONARIO His soul moves in his fee.

3RD AVVOCATO   O, sir.

BONARIO   This fellow,
For six *sols* more, would plead against his maker.

4TH AVVOCATO You do forget yourself.

VOLTORE   Nay, nay, grave fathers,
Let him have scope. Can any man imagine
That he will spare his accuser, that would not   100
Have spared his parent?

1ST AVVOCATO   Well, produce your proofs.

CELIA I would I could forget I were a creature.°

VOLTORE Signor Corbaccio.

4TH AVVOCATO   What is he?

VOLTORE   The father.

2ND AVVOCATO Has he had an oath?

NOTARO   Yes.

CORBACCIO   What must I do now?

NOTARO Your testimony's craved.

CORBACCIO   Speak to the knave?   105
I'll ha' my mouth first stopped with earth; my heart
Abhors his knowledge; I disclaim in him.°

1ST AVVOCATO But for what cause?

CORBACCIO   The mere portent of nature.
He is an utter stranger to my loins.

BONARIO Have they made you to this?

CORBACCIO   I will not hear thee,   110
Monster of men, swine, goat, wolf, parricide,
Speak not, thou viper.

BONARIO   Sir, I will sit down,
And rather wish my innocence should suffer
Than I resist the authority of a father.

VOLTORE Signor Corvino!

2ND AVVOCATO   This is strange!

1ST AVVOCATO	Who's this?	115

NOTARO The husband.

4TH AVVOCATO   Is he sworn?

NOTARO   He is.

3RD AVVOCATO   Speak then.

CORVINO This woman, please your fatherhoods, is a whore
    Of most hot exercise, more than a partridge,
    Upon recòrd—

1ST AVVOCATO No more.

CORVINO   Neighs like a jennet.°

NOTARO Preserve the honour of the court.

CORVINO   I shall,   120
    And modesty of your most reverend ears.
    And yet I hope that I may say, these eyes
    Have seen her glued unto that piece of cedar,°
        [Indicating° Bonario]
    That fine well-timbered gallant: and that, here,
    The letters may be read, thorough the horn,°   125
    That make the story perfect.

MOSCA [aside to Corvino]   Excellent, sir!

CORVINO [to Mosca] There is no shame in this now, is there?

MOSCA [to Corvino]   None.

CORVINO Or if I said, I hoped that she were onward
    To her damnation, if there be a hell
    Greater than whore and woman; a good Catholic°   130
    May make the doubt.

3RD AVVOCATO   His grief hath made him frantic.

1ST AVVOCATO Remove him hence.

2ND AVVOCATO   Look to the woman. (She swoons)

CORVINO   Rare!
    Prettily feigned! Again!

4TH AVVOCATO   Stand from about her.

1ST AVVOCATO Give her the air.

3RD AVVOCATO   What can you say?

MOSCA   My wound,
    May't please your wisdoms, speaks for me, received   135
    In aid of my good patron, when he missed
        [Points to Bonario]
    His sought-for father, when that well-taught dame
    Had her cue given her to cry out a rape.

BONARIO O, most laid impudence! Fathers—

3RD AVVOCATO   Sir, be silent,
   You had your hearing free, so must they theirs.   140
2ND AVVOCATO I do begin to doubt th'imposture here.
4TH AVVOCATO This woman has too many moods.
VOLTORE   Grave fathers,
   She is a creature of a most professed
   And prostituted lewdness.
CORVINO   Most impetuous!
   Unsatisfied, grave fathers!
VOLTORE   May her feignings   145
   Not take your wisdoms; but this day she baited
   A stranger, a grave knight, with her loose eyes,
   And more lascivious kisses. This man saw 'em
      [*Points to Mosca*]
   Together on the water in a gondola.
MOSCA Here is the lady herself, that saw 'em too,   150
   Without; who then had in the open streets
   Pursued them, but for saving her knight's honour.
1ST AVVOCATO Produce that lady.
2ND AVVOCATO   Let her come.
      [*Exit Mosca*]
4TH AVVOCATO   These things,
   They strike with wonder!
3RD AVVOCATO   I am turned a stone!

4.6

     [*Enter*] *Mosca* [*and*] *Lady Would-be*
MOSCA Be resolute, madam.
LADY WOULD-BE
     [*Pointing to Celia*]
              Aye, this same is she.
   Out, thou chameleon harlot! Now thine eyes°
   Vie tears with the hyena. Dar'st thou look°
   Upon my wrongèd face? I cry your pardons.
   I fear I have forgettingly transgressed   5
   Against the dignity of the court—
2ND AVVOCATO   No, madam.
LADY WOULD-BE And been exorbitant—

2ND AVVOCATO   You have not, lady.°
4TH AVVOCATO These proofs are strong.
LADY WOULD-BE   Surely I had no purpose°
  To scandalize your honours, or my sex's.
3RD AVVOCATO We do believe it.
LADY WOULD-BE   Surely, you may believe it.   10
2ND AVVOCATO Madam, we do.
LADY WOULD-BE   Indeed, you may; my breeding
  Is not so coarse—
4TH AVVOCATO   We know it.
LADY WOULD-BE   To offend
  With pertinacy—
3RD AVVOCATO   Lady.
LADY WOULD-BE   Such a presence;
  No, surely.
1ST AVVOCATO We well think it.
LADY WOULD-BE   You may think it.
1ST AVVOCATO Let her o'ercome. [*To Bonario*] What witnesses
  have you,   15
  To make good your report?
BONARIO   Our consciences.
CELIA And heaven, that never fails the innocent.
4TH AVVOCATO These are no testimonies.
BONARIO   Not in your courts,
  Where multitude and clamour overcomes.
1ST AVVOCATO Nay, then you do wax insolent.
          Volpone is brought in [by the Commendatori] as impotent [Lady
          Would-be kisses him°]
VOLTORE   Here, here,   20
  The testimony comes, that will convince,°
  And put to utter dumbness their bold tongues.
  See here, grave fathers, here's the ravisher,
  The rider on men's wives, the great impostor,
  The grand voluptuary! Do you not think,   25
  These limbs should affect venery? Or these eyes
  Covet a concubine? Pray you, mark these hands—
  Are they not fit to stroke a lady's breasts?
  Perhaps he doth dissemble?
BONARIO   So he does.
VOLTORE Would you ha' him tortured?
BONARIO   I would have him proved.   30

87

VOLTORE Best try him then with goads, or burning irons;
    Put him to the strappado; I have heard°
    The rack hath cured the gout, faith, give it him,
    And help him of a malady; be courteous.°
    I'll undertake, before these honoured fathers,   35
    He shall have yet as many left diseases,
    As she has known adulterers, or thou strumpets.
    O, my most equal hearers, if these deeds,
    Acts of this bold and most exorbitant strain,
    May pass with sufferance, what one citizen,   40
    But owes the forfeit of his life, yea fame,
    To him that dares traduce him? Which of you
    Are safe, my honoured fathers? I would ask
    (With leave of your grave fatherhoods) if their plot
    Have any face or colour like to truth?   45
    Or if, unto the dullest nostril here,
    It smell not rank and most abhorrèd slander?
    I crave your care of this good gentleman,
    Whose life is much endangered by their fable;
    And as for them, I will conclude with this: 50
    That vicious persons when they are hot, and fleshed°
    In impious acts, their constancy abounds:
    Damned deeds are done with greatest confidence.
1ST AVVOCATO Take 'em to custody, and sever them.
    [Celia and Bonario are taken out]
2ND AVVOCATO 'Tis pity two such prodigies should live.   55
1ST AVVOCATO Let the old gentleman be returned with care;
    I'm sorry our credulity wronged him.
    [Volpone is carried off by the Commendatori]
4TH AVVOCATO These are two creatures!
3RD AVVOCATO   I have an earthquake in
    me!
2ND AVVOCATO Their shame, even in their cradles, fled their
    faces.
4TH AVVOCATO *[to Voltore]* You've done a worthy service to the
    state, sir,   60
    In their discovery.
1ST AVVOCATO   You shall hear ere night
    What punishment the court decrees upon 'em.
VOLTORE We thank your fatherhoods.
    [Exeunt Avvocati, Notaro and other court officials]

       How like you it?

MOSCA   Rare.
 I'd ha' your tongue, sir, tipped with gold for this;
 I'd ha' you be the heir to the whole city;   65
 The earth I'd have want men, ere you want living.°
 They're bound to erect your statue in St Mark's.
 Signor Corvino, I would have you go,
 And show yourself, that you have conquered.

CORVINO   Yes.

MOSCA It was much better, that you should profess   70
 Yourself a cuckold thus, than that the other°
 Should have been proved.

CORVINO   Nay, I considered that;
 Now, it is her fault.

MOSCA   Then, it had been yours.

CORVINO True. I do doubt this advocate still.

MOSCA   I'faith,
 You need not; I dare ease you of that care.   75

CORVINO I trust thee, Mosca.

MOSCA   As your own soul, sir.

   [Exit Corvino]

CORBACCIO   Mosca!

MOSCA Now for your business, sir.

CORBACCIO   How? Ha' you business?

MOSCA Yes, yours, sir.

CORBACCIO   O, none else?

MOSCA   None else, not I.

CORBACCIO Be careful then.

MOSCA   Rest you with both your eyes, sir.

CORBACCIO Dispatch it.

MOSCA   Instantly.

CORBACCIO   And look that all,   80
 Whatever, be put in: jewels, plate, moneys,°
 Household stuff, bedding, curtains.

MOSCA   Curtain-rings, sir.
 Only, the advocate's fee must be deducted.

CORBACCIO I'll pay him now; you'll be too prodigal.

MOSCA Sir, I must tender it.

CORBACCIO   Two sequins is well?   85

MOSCA No, six, sir.

CORBACCIO   'Tis too much.

MOSCA   He talked a great while,
  You must consider that, sir.
CORBACCIO   Well, there's three—
    · [*Gives him money*]
MOSCA I'll give it him.
CORBACCIO
      [*Gives him money*]
                        Do so, and there's for thee.
      [*Exit Corbaccio*]
MOSCA Bountiful bones! What horrid strange offence
  Did he commit 'gainst nature in his youth,   90
  Worthy this age? [*To Voltore*] You see, sir, how I work
  Unto your ends; take you no notice.
VOLTORE   No,°
  I'll leave you.
      [*Exit Voltore*]
MOSCA   All is yours—the devil and all,
  Good advocate. [*To Lady Would-be*] Madam, I'll bring you home.
LADY WOULD-BE No, I'll go see your patron.
MOSCA   That you shall not.   95
  I'll tell you why: my purpose is to urge
  My patron to reform his will; and for
  The zeal you've shown today, whereas before
  You were but third or fourth, you shall be now
  Put in the first; which would appear as begged,   100
  If you were present. Therefore—
LADY WOULD-BE   You shall sway me.
      [*Exeunt*]

5.1

[Enter] Volpone

VOLPONE Well, I am here; and all this brunt is past.
I ne'er was in dislike with my disguise
Till this fled moment; here 'twas good, in private,°
But in your public, *cavé*, whilst I breathe.
'Fore God, my left leg 'gan to have the cramp;   5
And I apprended, straight, some power had struck me
With a dead palsy. Well, I must be merry,
And shake it off. A many of these fears°
Would put me into some villainous disease,
Should they come thick upon me. I'll prevent 'em.   10
Give me a bowl of lusty wine, to fright
This humour from my heart: Hum, hum, hum. (*He drinks*)
'Tis almost gone, already; I shall conquer.
Any device, now, of rare, ingenious knavery,
That would possess me with a violent laughter,   15
Would make me up again! So, so, so, so.° (*Drinks again*)
This heat is life; 'tis blood, by this time! Mosca!

5.2

[Enter] Mosca

MOSCA How now, sir? Does the day look clear again?
Are we recovered? And wrought out of error
Into our way? To see our path before us?°
Is our trade free once more?
VOLPONE   Exquisite Mosca!
MOSCA Was it not carried learnedly?
VOLPONE   And stoutly.   5
Good wits are greatest in extremities.
MOSCA It were a folly beyond thought to trust
Any grand act unto a cowardly spirit:
You are not taken with it enough, methinks?
VOLPONE O, more than if I had enjoyed the wench;   10
The pleasure of all womankind's not like it.

MOSCA Why, now you speak, sir. We must here be fixed;
　　Here we must rest; this is our masterpiece.
　　We cannot think to go beyond this.
VOLPONE   True,
　　Thou'st played thy prize, my precious Mosca.
MOSCA   Nay, sir,   15
　　To gull the court—
VOLPONE   And quite divert the torrent
　　Upon the innocent.
MOSCA   Yes, and to make
　　So rare a music out of discords—
VOLPONE   Right.
　　That yet to me's the strangest! How thou'st borne it!
　　That these (being so divided 'mongst themselves)   20
　　Should not scent somewhat, or in me or thee,
　　Or doubt their own side.
MOSCA   True, they will not see't.
　　Too much light blinds 'em, I think. Each of 'em
　　Is so possessed, and stuffed with his own hopes,
　　That anything unto the contrary,   25
　　Never so true, or never so apparent,
　　Never so palpable, they will resist it—
VOLPONE Like a temptation of the devil.
MOSCA   Right, sir.
　　Merchants may talk of trade, and your great signors
　　Of land that yields well; but if Italy   30
　　Have any glebe more fruitful than these fellows,
　　I am deceived. Did not your advocate rare?°
VOLPONE O—'My most honoured fathers, my grave fathers,
　　Under correction of your fatherhoods,
　　What face of truth is here? If these strange deeds   35
　　May pass, most honoured fathers'—I had much ado
　　To forbear laughing.
MOSCA   'T seemed to me you sweat, sir.
VOLPONE In troth, I did a little.
MOSCA   But confess, sir,
　　Were you not daunted?
VOLPONE   In good faith, I was
　　A little in a mist; but not dejected—   40
　　Never, but still myself.
MOSCA   I think it, sir.

Now, so truth help me, I must needs say this, sir,
And, out of conscience, for your advocate:
He's taken pains, in faith, sir, and deserved,
(In my poor judgement, I speak it, under favour,°   45
Not to contrary you, sir) very richly—
Well—to be cozened.

VOLPONE   Troth, and I think so too,
By that I heard him, in the latter end.°

MOSCA O, but before, sir; had you heard him first,
Draw it to certain heads, then aggravate,°   50
Then use his vehement figures—I looked still,°
When he would shift a shirt; and doing this°
Out of pure love, no hope of gain—

VOLPONE   'Tis right.
I cannot answer him, Mosca, as I would,
Not yet; but for thy sake, at thy entreaty,   55
I will begin e'en now to vex 'em all,
This very instant.

MOSCA   Good, sir.

VOLPONE   Call the dwarf
And eunuch forth.

MOSCA   Castrone, Nano.
        [*Enter Nano, Castrone*]

NANO   Here.

VOLPONE Shall we have a jig now?

MOSCA   What you please, sir.

VOLPONE   Go,
Straight, give out about the streets, you two,   60
That I am dead; do it with constancy,
Sadly, do you hear? Impute it to the grief
Of this late slander.
        [*Exeunt Nano, Castrone*]

MOSCA   What do you mean, sir?

VOLPONE   O,
I shall have instantly my vulture, crow,
Raven, come flying hither on the news   65
To peck for carrion, my she-wolf and all,
Greedy, and full of expectation—

MOSCA And then to have it ravished from their mouths?

VOLPONE 'Tis true. I will ha' thee put on a gown°
And take upon thee as thou wert mine heir;°   70

Show 'em a will—open that chest, and reach
Forth one of those that has the blanks. I'll straight
Put in thy name.
MOSCA   It will be rare, sir.
    [*Gives Volpone a will*]
VOLPONE   Aye,
When they e'en gape, and find themselves deluded—
MOSCA Yes.
VOLPONE   And thou use them scurvily. Dispatch,   75
    Get on thy gown.
MOSCA   But, what, sir, if they ask
    After the body?
VOLPONE   Say it was corrupted.
MOSCA I'll say it stunk, sir; and was fain t'have it
    Coffined up instantly, and sent away.
VOLPONE Anything, what thou wilt. Hold, here's my will.   80
    Get thee a cap, a count-book, pen and ink,°
    Papers afore thee; sit as thou wert taking
    An inventory of parcels. I'll get up
    Behind the curtain on a stool, and hearken;
    Sometime peep over; see how they do look;   85
    With what degrees their blood doth leave their faces!
    O, 'twill afford me a rare meal of laughter.
MOSCA Your advocate will turn stark dull upon it.°
VOLPONE It will take off his oratory's edge.
MOSCA But your *clarissimo*, old round-back, he°   90
    Will crump you like a hog-louse with the touch.°
VOLPONE And what Corvino?
MOSCA   O, sir, look for him
    Tomorrow morning, with a rope and a dagger,°
    To visit all the streets; he must run mad.
    My lady too, that came into the court,   95
    To bear false witness for your worship—
VOLPONE   Yes,
    And kissed me 'fore the fathers; when my face
    Flowed all with oils.
MOSCA   And sweat, sir. Why, your gold
    Is such another medicine, it dries up
    All those offensive savours! It transforms   100
    The most deformèd, and restores 'em lovely,
    As 'twere the strange poetical girdle. Jove°

Could not invent t'himself a shroud more subtle,
To pass Acrisius' guards. It is the thing°
Makes all the world her grace, her youth, her beauty.° 105
VOLPONE I think she loves me.
MOSCA   Who? The lady, sir?°
She's jealous of you.
VOLPONE   Dost thou say so?
            [*Knocking from offstage*]
MOSCA   Hark,°
There's some already.
VOLPONE   Look.
MOSCA   It is the vulture;
He has the quickest scent.
VOLPONE   I'll to my place,
Thou, to thy posture.
MOSCA   I am set.
VOLPONE   But Mosca, 110
Play the artificer now, torture 'em rarely.°
            [*He conceals himself*]

5.3

            [*Enter*] *Voltore*
VOLTORE How now, my Mosca?
MOSCA [*writing*]   Turkey carpets, nine—
VOLTORE Taking an inventory? That is well.
MOSCA Two suits of bedding, tissue—
VOLTORE   Where's the will?°
Let me read that the while.
            [*Enter servants with Corbaccio in a chair*]
CORBACCIO   So, set me down.
And get you home.
            [*Exeunt servants*]
VOLTORE   Is he come now to trouble us? 5
MOSCA Of cloth of gold, two more—
CORBACCIO   Is it done, Mosca?
MOSCA Of several velvets, eight—
VOLTORE   I like his care.
CORBACCIO Dost thou not hear?

[*Enter Corvino*]

CORVINO   Ha? Is the hour come, Mosca?
(*Volpone peeps from behind a traverse*)
VOLPONE [*aside*] Aye, now they muster.
CORVINO   What does the advocate here?
  Or this Corbaccio?
CORBACCIO   What do these here?
         [*Enter Lady Would-be*]
LADY WOULD-BE   Mosca?   10
  Is his thread spun?
MOSCA   Eight chests of linen—
VOLPONE [*aside*]   O,°
  My fine Dame Would-be too!
CORVINO   Mosca, the will,
  That I may show it these, and rid 'em hence.
MOSCA Six chests of diaper, four of damask—There.
         [*Points to the will, which is read by Corvino, Voltore, and Lady
         Would-be*]
CORBACCIO Is that the will?
MOSCA   Down-beds, and bolsters—
VOLPONE [*aside*]   Rare!   15
  Be busy still. Now they begin to flutter;
  They never think of me. Look, see, see, see!
  How their swift eyes run over the long deed
  Unto the name, and to the legacies,
  What is bequeathed them there—
MOSCA   Ten suits of hangings—   20
VOLPONE [*aside*] Aye, i'their garters, Mosca. Now their hopes°
  Are at the gasp.
VOLTORE   Mosca the heir!
CORBACCIO   What's that?°
VOLPONE [*aside*] My advocate is dumb, look to my merchant
  He has heard of some strange storm, a ship is lost,
  He faints. My lady will swoon. Old glazen-eyes,°   25
  He hath not reached his despair yet.
CORBACCIO [*taking the will*]   All these
  Are out of hope, I'm sure the man.
CORVINO   But, Mosca—
MOSCA Two cabinets—
CORVINO   Is this in earnest?

MOSCA   One
  Of ebony.—

CORVINO   Or do you but delude me?

MOSCA The other, mother of pearl—[*to Corvino*] I am very busy.   30
  Good faith, it is a fortune thrown upon me—
  Item, one salt of agate—[*to Corvino*] not my seeking.

LADY WOULD-BE Do you hear, sir?

MOSCA   A perfumed box—[*to Lady*
    Would-be] pray you forbear,
  You see I am troubled—made of an onyx—

LADY WOULD-BE   How!

MOSCA Tomorrow, or next day, I shall be at leisure   35
  To talk with you all.

CORVINO   Is this my large hope's issue?

LADY WOULD-BE Sir, I must have a fairer answer.

MOSCA   Madam!
  Marry, and shall: 'pray you, fairly quit my house.
  Nay, raise no tempest with your looks; but hark you:
  Remember what your ladyship offered me,°   40
  To put you in an heir; go to, think on't;
  And what you said e'en your best madams did
  For maintenance, and why not you? Enough!
  Go home, and use the poor Sir Pol, your knight, well,
  For fear I tell some riddles. Go, be melancholic.   45
      [*Exit Lady Would-be*]

VOLPONE [*aside*] Oh, my fine devil!

CORVINO   Mosca, pray you a word.

MOSCA Lord! Will not you take your despatch hence yet?
  Methinks, of all, you should have been th'example.
  Why should you stay here? With what thought? What promise?
  Hear you, do not you know I know you an ass?   50
  And that you would most fain have been a wittol,
  If fortune would have let you? That you are
  A declared cuckold, on good terms? This pearl,°
  You'll say, was yours? Right. This diamond?
  I'll not deny it, but thank you. Much here else?   55
  It may be so. Why, think that these good works
  May help to hide your bad. I'll not betray you;
  Although you be but extraordinary,
  And have it only in title, it sufficeth.°

Go home, be melancholic too, or mad. 60
　　　[*Exit Corvino*]
VOLPONE [*aside*] Rare, Mosca! How his villainy becomes him!
VOLTORE Certain he doth delude all these for me.
CORBACCIO Mosca, the heir?
VOLPONE [*aside*]　　　　　　　Oh, his four eyes have found it!
CORBACCIO I'm cozened, cheated, by a parasite-slave;
　　Harlot, th'ast gulled me.
MOSCA　　　　　　　　Yes, sir. Stop your mouth, 65
　　Or I shall draw the only tooth is left.
　　Are not you he, that filthy covetous wretch,
　　With the three legs, that here, in hope of prey,°
　　Have, any time this three year, snuffed about,
　　With your most grovelling nose; and would have hired 70
　　Me to the poisoning of my patron? Sir?
　　Are not you he that have today in court
　　Professed the disinheriting of your son?
　　Perjured yourself? Go home, and die, and stink;
　　If you but croak a syllable, all comes out. 75
　　Away and call your porters! Go, go, stink!
　　　[*Exit Corbaccio*]
VOLPONE [*aside*] Excellent varlet!
VOLTORE　　　　　　　　Now, my faithful Mosca,
　　I find thy constancy—
MOSCA　　　　　　Sir?
VOLTORE　　　　　　Sincere.
MOSCA　　　　　　　　A table
　　Of porphyry—I mar'l, you'll be thus troublesome.
VOLTORE Nay, leave off now, they are gone.
MOSCA　　　　　　　　　　Why? Who are you? 80
　　What? Who did send for you? O, cry you mercy,
　　Reverend sir! Good faith, I am grieved for you,
　　That any chance of mine should thus defeat
　　Your (I must needs say) most deserving travails:
　　But, I protest, sir, it was cast upon me, 85
　　And I could, almost, wish to be without it,
　　But that the will o' the dead must be observed.
　　Marry, my joy is that you need it not;
　　You have a gift, sir (thank your education),
　　Will never let you want, while there are men 90
　　And malice to breed causes. Would I had
　　But half the like, for all my fortune, sir.

If I have any suits (as I do hope,
Things being so easy, and direct, I shall not)
I will make bold with your obstreperous aid—   95
Conceive me, for your fee, sir. In meantime,°
You that have so much law, I know ha' the conscience,
Not to be covetous of what is mine.
Good sir, I thank you for my plate; 'twill help
To set up a young man. Good faith, you look   100
As you were costive; best go home, and purge, sir.°
          [*Exit Voltore*]
VOLPONE [*coming out of hiding*] Bid him eat lettuce well. My witty
    mischief,°
Let me embrace thee. O, that I could now
Transform thee to a Venus—Mosca, go,
Straight take my habit of *clarissimo*,°   105
And walk the streets; be seen, torment 'em more;
We must pursue, as well as plot. Who would
Have lost this feast?
MOSCA   I doubt it will lose them.
VOLPONE O, my recovery shall recover all.
That I could now but think on some disguise,   110
To meet 'em in, and ask 'em questions.
How I would vex 'em still at every turn!
MOSCA Sir, I can fit you.
VOLPONE   Canst thou?
MOSCA   Yes, I know
One o' the *commendatori*, sir, so like you
Him will I straight make drunk, and bring you his habit.   115
VOLPONE A rare disguise, and answering thy brain!
O, I will be a sharp disease unto 'em.
MOSCA Sir, you must look for curses—
VOLPONE   Till they burst;
The fox fares ever best when he is cursed.°
          [*Exeunt*]

5.4

          [*Enter*] Peregrine [*disguised, and*] three Merchants
PEREGRINE Am I enough disguised?
1ST MERCHANT   I warrant you.

PEREGRINE All my ambition is to fright him only.

2ND MERCHANT If you could ship him away, 'twere excellent.

3RD MERCHANT To Zant, or to Aleppo?

PEREGRINE   Yes, and ha' his°
   Adventures put i' the *Book of Voyages*,°   5
   And his gulled story registered, for truth?°
   Well, gentlemen, when I am in a while,
   And that you think us warm in our discourse,
   Know your approaches.

1ST MERCHANT   Trust it to our care.°
      [Exeunt Merchants. Enter Woman]

PEREGRINE Save you, fair lady. Is Sir Pol within?   10

WOMAN I do not know, sir.

PEREGRINE   Pray you say unto him,
   Here is a merchant, upon earnest business,
   Desires to speak with him.

WOMAN   I will see, sir.
      [Exit Woman]

PEREGRINE   Pray you.
   I see the family is all female here.°
      [Enter Woman]

WOMAN He says, sir, he has weighty affairs of state   15
   That now require him whole; some other time°
   You may possess him.

PEREGRINE   Pray you, say again,
   If those require him whole, these will exact him,
   Whereof I bring him tidings.
      [Exit Woman]

                     What might be
   His grave affair of state now? How to make   20
   Bolognan sausages here in Venice, sparing°
   One o' the ingredients?
      [Enter Woman]

WOMAN   Sir, he says, he knows
   By your word 'tidings' that you are no statesman,°
   And therefore wills you stay.

PEREGRINE   Sweet, pray you return him:°
   I have not read so many proclamations,   25
   And studied them for words, as he has done,
   But—Here he deigns to come.
      [Exit Woman. Enter Sir Politic Would-be]

SIR POLITIC   Sir, I must crave
   Your courteous pardon. There hath chanced today
   Unkind disaster 'twixt my lady and me,
   And I was penning my apology   30
   To give her satisfaction, as you came now.
PEREGRINE Sir, I am grieved I bring you worse disaster;
   The gentleman you met at th' port, today,
   That told you he was newly arrived—
SIR POLITIC   Aye, was
   A fugitive punk?
PEREGRINE   No, sir, a spy set on you;   35
   And he has made relation to the Senate,
   That you professed to him to have a plot
   To sell the state of Venice to the Turk.
SIR POLITIC O me!
PEREGRINE   For which, warrants are signed by this time,
   To apprehend you, and to search your study   40
   For papers—
SIR POLITIC   Alas, sir. I have none, but notes
   Drawn out of play-books—
PEREGRINE   All the better, sir.°
SIR POLITIC And some essays. What shall I do?
PEREGRINE   Sir, best°
   Convey yourself into a sugar-chest,
   Or, if you could lie round, a frail were rare: 45
   And I could send you aboard.
SIR POLITIC   Sir, I but talked so,
   For discourse sake, merely.
                                (*They knock without*)
PEREGRINE   Hark, they are there.
SIR POLITIC I am a wretch, a wretch!
PEREGRINE   What will you do, sir?
   Ha' you ne'er a currant-butt to leap into?
   They'll put you to the rack; you must be sudden.   50
SIR POLITIC Sir, I have an engine—
3RD MERCHANT [*offstage*]   Sir Politic Would-be?
2ND MERCHANT [*offstage*] Where is he?
SIR POLITIC   —that I have thought upon before time.
PEREGRINE What is it?
SIR POLITIC   (I shall ne'er endure the torture!)
   Marry, it is, sir, of a tortoise-shell,

Fitted for these extremities: pray you sir, help me.°   55
    [Climbing into shell]
Here I've a place, sir, to put back my legs;
Please you to lay it on, sir; with this cap,
And my black gloves, I'll lie, sir, like a tortoise,
Till they are gone.
PEREGRINE   And call you this an engine?
SIR POLITIC Mine own device—good sir, bid my wife's women°   60
    To burn my papers.
        [Exit Peregrine. The three Merchants rush in]
1ST MERCHANT   Where's he hid?
3RD MERCHANT   We must,
    And will, sure, find him.
2ND MERCHANT   Which is his study?
      [Smoke° drifts on to the stage]
1ST MERCHANT *[to Peregrine, entering]*   What
    Are you, sir?
PEREGRINE   I'm a merchant, that came here
    To look upon this tortoise.
3RD MERCHANT   How?
1ST MERCHANT   St Mark!
    What beast is this?
PEREGRINE   It is a fish.
2ND MERCHANT
      [striking the shell]
                      Come out here.   65
PEREGRINE Nay, you may strike him, sir, and tread upon him:
    He'll bear a cart.
1ST MERCHANT   What, to run over him?
PEREGRINE   Yes.
3RD MERCHANT Let's jump upon him.
2ND MERCHANT   Can he not go?
PEREGRINE   He creeps, sir.
1ST MERCHANT Let's see him creep.
      [Prods with his sword]
PEREGRINE   No, good sir, you will hurt him.
2ND MERCHANT Heart, I'll see him creep; or prick his guts.   70
3RD MERCHANT Come out here!
PEREGRINE *[aside to Sir Politic]* Pray you sir creep a little.
1ST MERCHANT   Forth.
2ND MERCHANT Yet further.
PEREGRINE *[to Sir Politic]*   Good sir, creep.

2ND MERCHANT   We'll see his legs.

3RD MERCHANT God's so, he has garters!

They pull off the shell and discover him

1ST MERCHANT   Aye, and gloves!

2ND MERCHANT   Is this
Your fearful tortoise?

PEREGRINE
    [*removing his diguise*]
                    Now, Sir Pol, we are even;°   75
For your next project, I shall be prepared.
I am sorry for the funeral of your notes, sir.

1ST MERCHANT 'Twere a rare motion to be seen in Fleet Street!

2ND MERCHANT Aye, i'the term.

1ST MERCHANT   Or Smithfield, in the fair.°

3RD MERCHANT Methinks 'tis but a melancholic sight!   80

PEREGRINE Farewell, most politic tortoise.
    [*Exeunt Peregrine and Merchants*]

SIR POLITIC   Where's my lady?
    [*Enter Woman*]
Knows she of this?

WOMAN   I know not, sir.

SIR POLITIC   Enquire.
    [*Exit Woman*]
O, I shall be the fable of all feasts,
The freight of the *gazzette*, ship–boys' tale;
And, which is worst, even talk for ordinaries.   85
    [*Enter Woman*]

WOMAN My lady's come most melancholic home,
And says, sir, she will straight to sea, for physic.

SIR POLITIC And I, to shun this place and clime for ever,
Creeping with house on back; and think it well,
To shrink my poor head in my politic shell.
    [*Exeunt*]

5.5

    [*Enter*] Volpone, Mosca, *the first in the habit of a commendatore,
    the other, of a clarissimo*

VOLPONE Am I then like him?

MOSCA   O, sir, you are he;°
    No man can sever you.
VOLPONE   Good.
MOSCA   But what am I?
VOLPONE 'Fore heav'n, a brave *clarissimo*, thou becom'st it!
    Pity thou wert not born one.
MOSCA   If I hold
    My made one, 'twill be well.
VOLPONE   I'll go and see   5
    What news, first, at the court.
          [*Exit Volpone*]
MOSCA   Do so. My Fox
    Is out on his hole, and ere he shall re-enter°
    I'll make him languish in his borrowed case,
    Except he come to composition with me.
    Androgino, Castrone, Nano!
          [*Enter Androgino, Castrone, Nano*]
ALL   Here.   10
MOSCA Go recreate yourselves abroad; go, sport.
          [*Exeunt Androgino, Castrone, Nano*]
    So, now I have the keys, and am possessed.
    Since he will needs be dead afore his time,°
    I'll bury him, or gain by him. I'm his heir,
    And so will keep me, till he share at least.   15
    To cozen him of all were but a cheat
    Well placed; no man would construe it a sin:
    Let his sport pay for't, this is called the Fox-trap.
          [*Exit*]

5.6

          [*Enter*] Corbaccio [*and*] Corvino
CORBACCIO They say the court is set.
CORVINO   We must maintain
    Our first tale good, for both our reputations.
CORBACCIO Why? Mine's no tale; my son would there have killed
    me.
CORVINO That's true, I had forgot; mine is, I am sure.
    But for your will, sir.
CORBACCIO   Aye, I'll come upon him°   5
    For that hereafter, now his patron's dead.

[*Enter Volpone, disguised*]

VOLPONE Signor Corvino! And Corbaccio! Sir,
　Much joy unto you.

CORVINO   Of what?

VOLPONE   The sudden good,
　Dropped down upon you—

CORBACCIO   Where?

VOLPONE   —And none knows how—
　From old Volpone, sir.

CORBACCIO   Out, arrant knave!   10

VOLPONE Let not your too much wealth, sir, make you furious.

CORBACCIO Away, thou varlet!

VOLPONE   Why sir?

CORBACCIO   Dost thou mock me?

VOLPONE You mock the world, sir; did you not change wills?

CORBACCIO Out, harlot!

VOLPONE   O! Belike you are the man,
　Signor Corvino? Faith, you carry it well;   15
　You grow not mad withal; I love your spirit.
　You are not over-leavened with your fortune.
　You should ha' some would swell now like a wine-vat,
　With such an autumn—Did he gi' you all, sir?°

CORVINO Avoid, you rascal!

VOLPONE   Troth, your wife has shown   20
　Herself a very woman; but you are well,
　You need not care, you have a good estate
　To bear it out, sir, better by this chance.
　Except Corbaccio have a share?

CORBACCIO   Hence, varlet!

VOLPONE You will not be a 'known, sir; why, 'tis wise.   25
　Thus do all gamesters, at all games, dissemble;
　No man will seem to win.

　　　[*Exeunt Corbaccio and Corvino*]

　　　　　　　　　Here comes my vulture,
　Heaving his beak up i' the air, and snuffing.

5.7

[*Enter*] *Voltore*

VOLTORE Outstripped thus, by a parasite? A slave?
　Would run on errands? And make legs for crumbs?°

Well, what I'll do—
VOLPONE   The court stays for your worship.
  I e'en rejoice, sir, at your worship's happiness,
  And that it fell into so learnèd hands,   5
  That understand the fingering—
VOLTORE   What do you mean?
VOLPONE I mean to be a suitor to your worship,
  For the small tenement, out of reparations;°
  That, at the end of your long row of houses,
  By the *pescheria*: it was in Volpone's time,   10
  Your predecessor, ere he grew diseased,
  A handsome, pretty, customed bawdy-house
  As any was in Venice—none dispraised—
  But fell with him; his body and that house
  Decayed together.
VOLTORE   Come, sir, leave your prating.   15
VOLPONE Why, if your worship give me but your hand,
  That I may ha' the refusal, I have done.
  'Tis a mere toy to you, sir—candle-rents.
  As your learn'd worship knows—
VOLTORE   What do I know?
VOLPONE Marry, no end of your wealth, sir, God decrease it!°   20
VOLTORE Mistaking knave! What, mock'st thou my misfortune?
VOLPONE His blessing on your heart, sir, would 'twere more.
    [*Exit Voltore*]
Now to my first again; at the next corner.

5.8

    [*Enter*] *Corbaccio, Corvino* (*Mosca, passant*)
CORBACCIO See, in our habit! See the impudent varlet!
CORVINO That I could shoot mine eyes at him, like gun-stones.
    [*Exit Mosca*]
VOLPONE But is this true, sir, of the parasite?
CORBACCIO Again, t'afflict us? Monster!
VOLPONE   In good faith, sir,
  I'm heartily grieved a beard of your grave length   5
  Should be so over-reached. I never brooked
  That parasite's hair, methought his nose should cozen;

There still was somewhat in his look did promise
The bane of a *clarissimo*.
CORBACCIO   Knave—
VOLPONE   Methinks
   Yet you, that are so traded i' the world,   10
   A witty merchant, the fine bird, Corvino,
   That have such moral emblems on your name,°
   Should not have sung your shame and dropped your cheese,
   To let the Fox laugh at your emptiness.°
CORVINO Sirrah, you think the privilege of the place,°   15
   And your red saucy cap, that seems to me
   Nailed to your jolt-head, with those two sequins,°
   Can warrant your abuses; come you hither—
   You shall perceive, sir, I dare beat you. Approach.
VOLPONE No haste, sir, I do know your valour well,   20
   Since you durst publish what you are, sir.
CORVINO   Tarry,
   I'd speak with you.
VOLPONE   Sir, sir, another time—
CORVINO Nay, now.
VOLPONE   O God, sir! I were a wise man,
   Would stand the fury of a distracted cuckold.°
CORBACCIO What? Come again?
         Mosca walks by 'em   25
VOLPONE   Upon 'em, Mosca; save me.
CORBACCIO The air's infected where he breathes.
CORVINO   Let's fly him.
      [*Exeunt Corbaccio and Corvino*]
VOLPONE Excellent basilisk! Turn upon the vulture.

5.9

      [*Enter*] *Voltore*
VOLTORE Well, flesh-fly, it is summer with you now;°
   Your winter will come on.
MOSCA   Good advocate,
   Pray thee not rail, nor threaten out of place thus;
   Thou'lt make a solecism, as madam says.
   Get you a biggin more—your brain breaks loose.   5
      [*Exit Mosca*]

VOLTORE Well, sir.
VOLPONE   Would you ha' me beat the insolent slave?
  Throw dirt upon his first good clothes?
VOLTORE   This same
  Is doubtless some familiar!
VOLPONE   Sir, the court,
  In troth, stays for you. I am mad, a mule°.
  That never read Justinian should get up°   10
  And ride an advocate. Had you no quirk,
  To avoid gullage, sir, by such a creature?
  I hope you do but jest; he has not done't;
  This's but confederacy, to blind the rest.
  You are the heir?
VOLTORE   A strange, officious,   15
  Troublesome knave! Thou dost torment me.
VOLPONE   I know—°
  It cannot be, sir, that you should be cozened;
  'Tis not within the wit of man to do it.
  You are so wise, so prudent, and 'tis fit
        [*Leaving with Voltore*]
  That wealth and wisdom still should go together.   20
        [*Exeunt*]

5.10

        [*Enter*] four Avvocati, Notaro, Commendatori, Bonario, Celia,
        Corbaccio [*and*] Corvino
1ST AVVOCATO Are all the parties here?
NOTARO   All but the advocate.
2ND AVVOCATO And here he comes.
        [*Enter Voltore, Volpone*]
1ST AVVOCATO   Then bring 'em forth to
  sentence.
VOLTORE O, my most honoured fathers, let your mercy
  Once win upon your justice, to forgive—°
  I am distracted—
VOLPONE [*aside*] What will he do now?
VOLTORE   O,   5
  I know not which t'address myself to first,

Whether your fatherhoods, or these innocents—
CORVINO [*aside*] Will he betray himself?
VOLTORE   Whom equally
    I have abused, out of most covetous ends—
CORVINO
    [*aside to Corbaccio*]
    The man is mad!
CORBACCIO [*to Corvino*] What's that?
CORVINO [*to Corbaccio*]   He is possessed.°   10
VOLTORE For which, now struck in conscience, here I prostrate
    Myself at your offended feet for pardon. [*He kneels*]
1ST and 2ND AVVOCATI Arise.
CELIA   O heav'n, how just thou art!
VOLPONE [*aside*]   I'm
    caught
    I' mine own noose—
CORVINO [*to Corbaccio*] Be constant, sir; naught now
    Can help but impudence.
1ST AVVOCATO [*to Voltore*] Speak forward.
COMMENDATORE [*to the Courtroom*]   Silence!°   15
VOLTORE It is not passion in me, reverend fathers,
    But only conscience, conscience, my good sires,
    That makes me now tell truth. That parasite,
    That knave, hath been the instrument of all.
1ST AVVOCATO Where is that knave? Fetch him.
VOLPONE   I go.
        [*Exit Volpone*]
CORVINO   Grave fathers,   20
    This man's distracted; he confessed it now:
    For, hoping to be old Volpone's heir,
    Who now is dead—
3RD AVVOCATO   How?
2ND AVVOCATO   Is Volpone dead?
CORVINO Dead since, grave fathers—
BONARIO   O, sure vengeance!
1ST AVVOCATO   Stay—
    Then he was no deceiver?
VOLTORE   O no, none;   25
    The parasite, grave fathers.
CORVINO   He does speak,
    Out of mere envy, 'cause the servant's made

The thing he gaped for; please your fatherhoods,
This is the truth; though, I'll not justify
The other, but he may be some-deal faulty.°   30
VOLTORE Aye, to your hopes, as well as mine, Corvino;
But I'll use modesty. Pleaseth your wisdoms
To view these certain notes, and but confer them;
    [*Gives them papers*]
As I hope favour, they shall speak clear truth.
CORVINO The devil has entered him!
BONARIO   Or bides in you.   35
4TH AVVOCATO We have done ill, by a public officer
To send for him, if he be heir.
2ND AVVOCATO   For whom?
4TH AVVOCATO Him that they call the parasite.
3RD AVVOCATO   'Tis true;
He is a man of great estate now left.
4TH AVVOCATO [*to Notaro*] Go you and learn his name, and say
    the court   40
Entreats his presence here; but to the clearing
Of some few doubts.
    [*Exit Notaro*]
2ND AVVOCATO   This same's a labyrinth!
1ST AVVOCATO
    [*to Corvino*]
Stand you unto your first report?
CORVINO   My state,
My life, my fame—
BONARIO   Where is't?
CORVINO   Are at the stake.
1ST AVVOCATO
    [*to Corbaccio*]
Is yours so too?
CORBACCIO   The advocate's a knave,   45
And has a forkèd tongue—
2ND AVVOCATO   Speak to the point.
CORBACCIO So is the parasite too.
1ST AVVOCATO   This is confusion.
VOLTORE I do beseech your fatherhoods, read but those.
    [*Points to his papers*]
CORVINO And credit nothing the false spirit hath writ;
It cannot be but he is possessed, grave fathers.   50
    [*Exeunt*]

5.11

[*Enter*] *Volpone*

VOLPONE To make a snare for mine own neck! And run
My head into it wilfully! With laughter!
When I had newly 'scaped, was free and clear!
Out of mere wantonness! O, the dull devil°
Was in this brain of mine when I devised it,   5
And Mosca gave it second; he must now
Help to sear up this vein, or we bleed dead.
    [*Enter Nano, Androgino, Castrone*]
How now! Who let you loose? Whither go you now?
What? To buy gingerbread? Or to drown kitlings?
NANO Sir, Master Mosca called us out of doors,   10
And bids us all go play, and took the keys.
ANDROGINO   Yes.
VOLPONE Did Master Mosca take the keys? Why, so!
I am farther in. These are my fine conceits!
I must be merry, with a mischief to me!
What a vile wretch was I, that could not bear   15
My fortune soberly? I must ha' my crotchets!
And my conundrums! Well, go you and seek him—
His meaning may be truer than my fear.
Bid him, he straight come to me, to the court;
Thither will I, and if 't be possible,   20
Unscrew my advocate upon new hopes:°
When I provoked him, then I lost myself.
    [*Exeunt*]

5.12

[*Enter four Avvocati, Notaro,° Commendatori, Bonario, Celia,
Corbaccio, Corvino*]

1ST AVVOCATO These things can ne'er be reconciled. He, here,°
Professeth that the gentleman was wronged;
And that the gentlewoman was brought thither,°
Forced by her husband, and there left.
VOLTORE   Most true.
CELIA How ready is heaven to those that pray!

1ST AVVOCATO   But that   5
    Volpone would have ravished her, he holds
    Utterly false, knowing his impotence.
CORVINO Grave fathers, he is possessed; again I say,
    Possessed; nay, if there be possession
    And obsession, he has both.
3RD AVVOCATO   Here comes our officer.°   10
       [Enter Volpone, disguised]
VOLPONE The parasite will straight be here, grave fathers.
4TH AVVOCATO You might invent some other name, sir varlet.
3RD AVVOCATO Did not the notary meet him?
VOLPONE   Not that I know.
4TH AVVOCATO His coming will clear all.
2ND AVVOCATO   Yet it is misty.
VOLTORE May't please your fatherhoods—
VOLPONE (whispers [to] the Advocate)   Sir, the parasite   15
    Willed me to tell you that his master lives;
    That you are still the man; your hopes the same;
    And this was only a jest—
VOLTORE   How?
VOLPONE   Sir, to try
    If you were firm, and how you stood affected.°
VOLTORE Art sure he lives?
VOLPONE   Do I live, sir?
VOLTORE   O me!°   20
    I was too violent.
VOLPONE   Sir, you may redeem it,
    They said you were possessed; fall down, and seem so:
    I'll help to make it good.
        (Voltore falls)
             God bless the man!
    [To Voltore] Stop your wind hard, and swell—[to the Court] see,
      see, see, see!
    He vomits crooked pins! His eyes are set   25
    Like a dead hare's, hung in a poulter's shop!
    His mouth's running away! [To Corvino] Do you see, signor?°
    Now, 'tis in his belly.
CORVINO   Aye, the devil!
VOLPONE Now, in his throat.
CORVINO   Aye, I perceive it plain.
VOLPONE 'Twill out, 'twill out; stand clear. See, where it flies!   30

In shape of a blue toad, with a bat's wings!°
[*To Corvino*] Do not you see it, sir?
CORBACCIO   What? I think I do.
CORVINO 'Tis too manifest.
VOLPONE   Look! He comes t'himself!
VOLTORE Where am I?
VOLPONE   Take good heart, the worst is past, sir.
You are dispossessed.
1ST AVVOCATO   What accident is this?   35
2ND AVVOCATO Sudden, and full of wonder!
3RD AVVOCATO   If he were
Possessed, as it appears, all this is nothing.
CORVINO He has been often subject to these fits.
1ST AVVOCATO Show him that writing. [*To Voltore*] Do you know
it, sir?
VOLPONE [*aside to Voltore*] Deny it, sir, forswear it, know it not.   40
VOLTORE Yes, I do know it well, it is my hand;
But all that it contains is false.
BONARIO   O practice!
2ND AVVOCATO What maze is this?
1ST AVVOCATO   Is he not guilty then,
Whom you there name the parasite?
VOLTORE   Grave fathers,
No more than his good patron, old Volpone.   45
4TH AVVOCATO Why, he is dead?
VOLTORE   O no, my honoured fathers.
He lives—
1ST AVVOCATO How! Lives?
VOLTORE   Lives.
2ND AVVOCATO   This is subtler yet!
3RD AVVOCATO You said he was dead?
VOLTORE   Never.
3RD AVVOCATO [*to Corvino*]   You said so?
CORVINO   I heard
so.
4TH AVVOCATO Here comes the gentleman; make him way.
      [*Enter Mosca in the dress of a clarissimo*]
3RD AVVOCATO   A stool.°
4TH AVVOCATO [*aside*] A proper man! And were Volpone dead,   50
A fit match for my daughter.
3RD AVVOCATO   Give him way.

VOLPONE [*aside*] Mosca, I was almost lost; the advocate
  Had betrayed all; but now it is recovered.
  All's o' the hinge again—say I am living.°
MOSCA What busy knave is this? Most reverend fathers,   55
  I sooner had attended your grave pleasures,
  But that my order for the funeral
  Of my dear patron did require me—
VOLPONE [*aside*]   Mosca!
MOSCA Whom I intend to bury, like a gentleman.
VOLPONE [*aside*] Aye, quick, and cozen me of all.
2ND AVVOCATO   Still stranger!   60
  More intricate!
1ST AVVOCATO And come about again!°
4TH AVVOCATO [*aside*] It is a match, my daughter is bestowed.
MOSCA [*aside to Volpone*]
  Will you gi' me half?
VOLPONE [*aside to Mosca*] First, I'll be hanged.
MOSCA [*aside to Volpone*]   I know;
  Your voice is good, cry not so loud.
1ST AVVOCATO   Demand
  The advocate. Sir, did not you affirm°   65
  Volpone was alive?
VOLPONE   Yes, and he is;
  This gent'man [*points to Mosca*] told me so. [*Aside to Mosca*] Thou
    shalt have half.
MOSCA Whose drunkard is this same? Speak some, that know him:
  I never saw his face [*Aside to Volpone*] I cannot now
  Afford it you so cheap.
VOLPONE [*aside to Mosca*] No?
1ST AVVOCATO [*to Voltore*]   What say you?   70
VOLTORE The officer told me.
VOLPONE   I did, grave fathers,
  And will maintain he lives, with mine own life.
  And that this creature [*points to Mosca*] told me. [*Aside*] I was born,
  With all good stars my enemies.
MOSCA   Most grave fathers,
  If such an insolence as this must pass°   75
  Upon me, I am silent: 'twas not this;
  For which you sent, I hope.
2ND AVVOCATO   Take him away.
VOLPONE [*aside*]
  Mosca!

3RD AVVOCATO Let him be whipped—
VOLPONE [*aside to Mosca*]   Wilt thou betray me?
   Cozen me?
3RD AVVOCATO —and taught to bear himself
   Toward a person of his rank.
4TH AVVOCATO   Away.   80
       [*Volpone is seized*]
MOSCA I humbly thank your fatherhoods.
VOLPONE [*aside*]   Soft, soft. Whipped?
   And lose all that I have? If I confess,
   It cannot be much more.
4TH AVVOCATO [*to Mosca*] Sir, are you married?
VOLPONE [*aside*] They'll be allied anon; I must be resolute.°
   The Fox shall here uncase.
       He puts off his disguise
MOSCA [*aside*]   Patron!
VOLPONE   Nay, now   85
   My ruins shall not come alone; your match
   I'll hinder sure: my substance shall not glue you,
   Nor screw you, into a family.
MOSCA   Why, patron!
VOLPONE I am Volpone, and this [*points to Mosca*] is my knave;
   This, [*to Voltore*] his own knave; this, [*to Corbaccio*] avarice's fool; 90
   This, [*to Corvino*] a chimera of wittol, fool, and knave;
   And, reverend fathers, since we all can hope
   Naught but a sentence, let's not now despair it.°
   You hear me brief.
CORVINO   May it please your fatherhoods—
COMMENDATORE   Silence!
1ST AVVOCATO The knot is now undone, by miracle!°   95
2ND AVVOCATO Nothing can be more clear.
3RD AVVOCATO   Or can more prove
   These innocent.
1ST AVVOCATO   Give 'em their liberty.
BONARIO Heaven could not long let such gross crimes be hid.
2ND AVVOCATO If this be held the highway to get riches,
   May I be poor.
3RD AVVOCATO This 's not the gain, but torment.   100
1ST AVVOCATO These possess wealth, as sick men possess fevers,
   Which trulier may be said to possess them.
2ND AVVOCATO Disrobe that parasite.
CORVINO, MOSCA   Most honoured fathers—

1ST AVVOCATO Can you plead aught to stay the course of justice?
  If you can, speak.
CORVINO, VOLTORE We beg favour.
CELIA   And mercy.   105
1ST AVVOCATO You hurt your innocence, suing for the guilty.
  Stand forth; and, first, the parasite. You appear
  T'have been the chiefest minister, if not plotter,
  In all these lewd impostures; and now, lastly,
  Have with your impudence abused the court,   110
  And habit of a gentleman of Venice,
  Being a fellow of no birth or blood
  For which our sentence is, first thou be whipped;
  Then live perpetual prisoner in our galleys.
VOLPONE I thank you for him.
MOSCA   Bane to thy wolfish nature.°   115
1ST AVVOCATO Deliver him to the *Saffi*.
      [*Mosca is taken aside*]
                                            Thou, Volpone,
  By blood and rank a gentleman, canst not fall
  Under like censure; but our judgement on thee
  Is that thy substance all be straight confiscate
  To the hospital of the *Incurabili*:°   120
  And since the most was gotten by imposture,
  By feigning lame, gout, palsy, and such diseases,
  Thou art to lie in prison cramped with irons,
  Till thou be'st sick and lame indeed. Remove him.
VOLPONE This is called mortifying of a Fox.°   125
      [*He is taken aside*]
1ST AVVOCATO Thou, Voltore, to take away the scandal
  Thou hast given all worthy men of thy profession,
  Art banished from their fellowship, and our state.
  Corbaccio—bring him near—we here possess
  Thy son of all thy state; and confine thee   130
  To the monastery of *San Spirito*°
  Where, since thou knew'st not how to live well here,
  Thou shalt be learned to die well.
CORBACCIO   Ha! What said he?
COMMENDATORE
      [*taking him aside*]
  You shall know anon, sir.
1ST AVVOCATO   Thou, Corvino, shalt
  Be straight embarked from thine own house, and rowed   135

Round about Venice, through the Grand Canal,°
Wearing a cap with fair long ass's ears,
Instead of horns; and a so to mount (a paper
Pinned on thy breast) to the *berlina*—
CORVINO   Yes,
And have mine eyes beat out with stinking fish,   140
Bruised fruit and rotten eggs—'Tis well. I'm glad,
I shall not see my shame yet.
1ST AVVOCATO   And to expiate
Thy wrongs done to thy wife, thou art to send her
Home to her father with her dowry trebled
    [*Corvino and Voltore are taken aside*]
And these are all your judgements.
ALL   Honoured fathers.   145
1ST AVVOCATO Which may not be revoked. Now you begin,
When crimes are done and past and to be punished,
To think what your crimes are. Away with them!
Let all that see these vices thus rewarded
Take heart, and love to study 'em. Mischiefs feed   150
Like beasts till they be fat, and then they bleed.
    [*Exeunt all. Volpone re-enters*]
VOLPONE The seasoning of a play is the applause.
Now, though the Fox be punished by the laws,
He yet doth hope there is no suffering due
For any fact which he hath done 'gainst you;   155
If there be, censure him—here he doubtful stands.
If not, fare jovially, and clap your hands.°

This comedy was first
acted in the year
1605°
By the King's Majesty's Servants.
The principal comedians° were
Richard Burbage   John Heminges
Henry Condell   John Lowin
William Sly   Alexander Cooke
With the allowance° of the Master of the Revels

EPICENE

or

THE SILENT WOMAN

TO THE TRULY NOBLE,
BY ALL TITLES,
Sir Francis Stuart:°

Sir,

My hope is not so nourished by example, as it will conclude this   5
dumb piece° should please you, by cause it hath pleased others before,
but by trust, that when you have read it, you will find it worthy to
have displeased none. This makes that I now number you not only in
the names of favour, but the names of justice, to what I write; and do
presently call you to the exercise of that noblest and manliest virtue: 10
as coveting rather to be freed in my fame by the authority of a judge
than the credit of an undertaker. Read therefore, I pray you, and
censure. There is not a line or syllable in it changed from the
simplicity of the first copy. And when you shall consider, through
the certain hatred of some, how much a man's innocency may be   15
endangered by an uncertain accusation,° you will, I doubt not, so
begin to hate the iniquity of such natures, as I shall love the
contumely done me, whose end was so honourable, as to be wiped off
by your sentence.

Your unprofitable but true lover,   20
BEN. JONSON

THE PERSONS OF THE PLAY

MOROSE,° a gentleman *that loves no noise*
[SIR] DAUPHINE EUGENIE,° a knight, his nephew
[NED] CLERIMONT,° a gentleman, his friend
TRUEWIT, another friend
EPICENE,° a young gentleman, supposed the Silent Woman
[SIR] JOHN DAW,° a knight, her servant
[SIR] AMOROUS LA FOOLE,° a knight also
THOMAS OTTER,° a land and sea captain
CUTBEARD, a barber
MUTE, one of Morose his servants
MADAM HAUGHTY
MADAM CENTAURE° } Ladies Collegiates°
MISTRESS [DOL] MAVIS°
MISTRESS TRUSTY, the Lady Haughty's woman } Pretenders
MISTRESS OTTER, the captain's wife
PARSON
BOY
PAGES
SERVANTS
[MUSICIANS]

THE SCENE

London

Prologue

Truth says, of old the art of making plays
    Was to content the people; and their praise
    Was to the poet money, wine, and bays.°
But in this age, a sect of writers are,
    That only for particular likings care,°   5
    And will taste nothing that is popular.
With such we mingle neither brains nor breasts;°
    Our wishes, like to those make public feasts°
    Are not to please the cooks' tastes, but the guests'.
Yet if those cunning palates hither come,   10
    They shall find guests' entreaty, and good room;
    And though all relish not, sure there will be some
That, when they leave their seats, shall make 'em say,
    'Who wrote that piece, could so have wrote a play,
    But that he knew this was the better way.'   15
For to present all custard or all tart,
    And have no other meats to bear a part,
    Or to want bread and salt, were but coarse art.
The poet prays you then with better thought
    To sit; and when his cates are all in brought,   20
    Though there be none far fet there will dear-bought
Be fit for ladies: some for lords, knights, squires,
    Some for your waiting wench, and city-wires,°
    Some for your men, and daughters of Whitefriars.°
Nor is it only while you keep your seat   25
Here, that his feast will last; but you shall eat
    A week at ord'naries, on his broken meat:°
            If his Muse be true,
            Who commends her to you.

Another
Occasioned by some person's impertinent exception
The ends of all who for the scene do write,
    Are, or should be, to profit and delight.°
And still 't hath been the praise of all best times,

So persons were not touched, to tax the crimes.
Then in this play which we present tonight, 5
   And make the object of your ear and sight,
On forfeit of yourselves, think nothing true,
   Lest so you make the maker to judge you.
For he knows poet never credit gained
   By writing truths, but things (like truths) well feigned. 10
If any yet will (with particular sleight
   Of application) wrest what he doth write,°
And that he meant or him or her will say:
   They make a libel which he made a play.

1.1

[Enter] Clerimont (he comes out making himself ready°), Boy

CLERIMONT Ha' you got the song yet perfect° I ga' you, boy?

BOY Yes, sir.

CLERIMONT Let me hear it.

BOY You shall, sir, but i'faith let nobody else.

CLERIMONT Why, I pray?   5

BOY It will get you the dangerous name of a poet in town, sir, besides
me a perfect deal of ill-will at the mansion you wot of, whose lady
is the argument of it; where now I am the welcomest thing under
a man that comes there.

CLERIMONT I think, and above a man too, if the truth were racked   10
out of you.

BOY No faith, I'll confess before, sir. The gentlewomen play with me
and throw me o' the bed and carry me in to my lady; and she kisses
me with her oiled face and puts a peruke o' my head and asks me
an I will wear her gown; and I say, 'no': and then she hits me a   15
blow o' the ear and calls me innocent and lets me go.

CLERIMONT No marvel if the door be kept shut against your master,
when the entrance is so easy to you—well, sir, you shall go there
no more, lest I be fain to seek your voice in my lady's rushes°
a fortnight hence. Sing, sir.   20

Boy sings°. [Enter Truewit]

TRUEWIT Why, here's the man that can melt away his time and never
feels it! What, between his mistress abroad and his ingle at home,
high fare, soft lodging, fine clothes, and his fiddle, he thinks the
hours ha' no wings or the day no post-horse.° Well, sir gallant,
were you struck with the plague this minute or condemned to any   25
capital punishment tomorrow, you would begin then to think and
value every article o' your time,° esteem it at the true rate and give
all for't.

CLERIMONT Why, what should a man do?

TRUEWIT Why, nothing, or that which, when 'tis done, is as idle.   30
Hearken after the next horse race, or hunting match; lay wagers,
praise Puppy, or Peppercorn, Whitefoot, Franklin; swear upon
Whitemane's° party; spend aloud° that my lords may hear
you; visit my ladies at night and be able to give 'em the character
of every bowler or bettor o' the green. These be the things   35

wherein your fashionable men exercise themselves, and I for company.

CLERIMONT Nay, if I have thy authority, I'll not leave yet. Come, the other are considerations when we come to have grey heads and weak hams, moist eyes and shrunk members. We'll think on 'em   40 then; then we'll pray and fast.

TRUEWIT Aye, and destine only that time of age to goodness, which our want of ability will not let us employ in evil?

CLERIMONT Why, then 'tis time enough.

TRUEWIT Yes; as if a man should sleep all the term and think to   45 effect his business the last day. O, Clerimont, this time, because it is an incorporeal thing and not subject to sense, we mock ourselves the fineliest out of it, with vanity and misery indeed, not seeking an end of wretchedness, but only changing the matter still.   50

CLERIMONT Nay, thou'lt not leave now—

TRUEWIT See but our common disease!° With what justice can we complain that great men will not look upon us nor be at leisure to give our affairs such despatch as we expect, when we will never do it to ourselves, nor hear nor regard ourselves.   55

CLERIMONT Foh, thou hast read Plutarch's *Morals*, now, or some such tedious fellow;° and it shows so vilely with thee, 'fore God, 'twill spoil thy wit utterly. Talk me of pins and feathers and ladies, and rushes and such things; and leave this Stoicity alone till thou mak'st sermons.   60

TRUEWIT Well, sir, if it will not take, I have learned to lose as little of my kindness as I can. I'll do good to no man against his will, certainly. When were you at the college?

CLERIMONT What college?

TRUEWIT As if you knew not!   65

CLERIMONT No, faith, I came but from court yesterday.

TRUEWIT Why, is it not arrived there yet, the news? A new foundation, sir, here i' the town, of ladies that call themselves the Collegiates, an order between courtiers and country madams,° that live from° their husbands and give entertainment to all the Wits   70 and Braveries o' the time, as they call 'em: cry down or up what they like or dislike in a brain or a fashion with most masculine or rather hermaphroditical authority, and every day gain to their college some new probationer.

CLERIMONT Who is the president?   75

TRUEWIT The grave and youthful matron, the Lady Haughty.

CLERIMONT A pox of her autumnal face, her pieced beauty: there's
no man can be admitted till she be ready nowadays, till she has
painted and perfumed and washed and scoured, but the boy here;
and him she wipes her oiled lips upon, like a sponge. I have made   80
a song, I pray thee hear it, o' the subject.

[*Boy sings again*]

SONG

Still to be neat, still to be dressed,
As you were going to a feast;
Still to be powdered, still perfumed:
Lady, it is to be presumed,   85
Though art's hid causes are not found,
All is not sweet, all is not sound.
Give me a look, give me a face,
That makes simplicity a grace;
Robes loosely flowing, hair as free: 90
Such sweet neglect more taketh me,
Than all th'adulteries of art.
They strike mine eyes, but not my heart.

TRUEWIT And I am clearly o' the other side: I love a good dressing
before any beauty o' the world. O, a woman is then like a delicate   95
garden; nor is there one kind of it: she may vary every hour, take
often counsel of her glass and choose the best. If she have good
ears, show 'em; good hair, lay it out; good legs, wear short clothes;
a good hand, discover it often; practise any art to mend breath,
cleanse teeth, repair eyebrows, paint, and profess it.   100

CLERIMONT How? Publicly?

TRUEWIT The doing of it, not the manner: that must be private.
Many things that seem foul i' the doing do please, done. A lady
should indeed study her face when we think she sleeps; nor
when the doors are shut should men be enquiring; all is sacred   105
within then. Is it for us to see their perukes put on, their false
teeth, their complexion, their eyebrows, their nails? You see gilders
will not work but enclosed. They must not discover how little
serves with the help of art to adorn a great deal. How long did the
canvas hang afore Aldgate?° Were the people suffered to see the   110
city's *Love* and *Charity* while they were rude stone, before they
were painted and burnished? No. No more should servants
approach their mistresses, but when they are complete and
finished.

CLERIMONT Well said, my Truewit.   115

TRUEWIT And a wise lady will keep a guard always upon the place, that she may do things securely. I once followed a rude fellow into a chamber, where the poor madam, for haste, and troubled, snatched at her peruke to cover her baldness and put it on the wrong way.   120

CLERIMONT O prodigy!

TRUEWIT And the unconscionable knave held her in compliment an hour, with that reversed face, when I still looked when she should talk from the t'other side.

CLERIMONT Why, thou shouldst ha' relieved her.   125

TRUEWIT No faith, I let her alone, as we'll let this argument, if you please, and pass to another. When saw you Dauphine Eugenie?

CLERIMONT Not these three days. Shall we go to him this morning? He is very melancholic, I hear.

TRUEWIT Sick o' the uncle,° is he? I met that stiff piece of formality,   130 his uncle, yesterday, with a huge turban of nightcaps on his head, buckled over his ears.

CLERIMONT O, that's his custom when he walks abroad. He can endure no noise, man.

TRUEWIT So I have heard. But is the disease so ridiculous in him as   135 it is made? They say he has been upon divers° treaties with the fishwives, and orange-women; and articles propounded between them. Marry, the chimney-sweepers will not be drawn in.

CLERIMONT No, nor the broom-men: they stand out stiffly. He cannot endure a costermonger; he swoons if he hear one.   140

TRUEWIT Methinks a smith should be ominous.

CLERIMONT Or any hammerman. A brazier is not suffered to dwell in the parish, nor an armourer. He would have hanged a pewterer's 'prentice once upon a Shrove Tuesday's° riot, for being o' that trade, when the rest were quit.   145

TRUEWIT A trumpet should fright him terribly, or the hautboys?

CLERIMONT Out of his senses. The waits of the city have a pension of him not to come near that ward. This youth [*indicating the Boy*] practised on him one night like the bellman;° and never left till he had brought him down to the door with a long sword, and there   150 left him flourishing with the air.

BOY Why, sir, he hath chosen a street to lie in so narrow at both ends that it will receive no coaches, nor carts, nor any of these common noises: and therefore we that love him devise to bring him in such as we may, now and then, for his exercise, to breathe him. He   155 would grow resty else in his ease. His virtue would rust without

action. I entreated a bearward one day to come down with the dogs
of some four parishes that way, and I thank him, he did; and cried
his games° under Master Morose's window till he was sent crying
away with his head made a most bleeding spectacle to the   160
multitude. And another time a fencer, marching to his prize, had
his drum most tragically run through, for taking that street in his
way, at my request.

TRUEWIT A good wag. How does he for the bells?

CLERIMONT O, i' the Queen's time he was wont to go out of town   165
every Saturday at ten o'clock, or on holiday eves. But now, by
reason of the sickness, the perpetuity of ringing° has made him
devise a room with double walls and treble ceilings, the windows
close shut and caulked, and there he lives by candlelight. He
turned away a man° last week for having a pair of new shoes that   170
creaked. And this fellow waits on him now in tennis-court socks,
or slippers soled with wool, and they talk each to other in a trunk.
See who comes here!

1.2

[Enter] Dauphine

DAUPHINE How now! What ail you, sirs? Dumb?

TRUEWIT Struck into stone, almost, I am here,° with tales o' thine
uncle! There was never such a prodigy heard of.

DAUPHINE I would you would once lose this subject, my masters, for
my sake. They are such as you are that have brought me into that   5
predicament I am with him.

TRUEWIT How is that?

DAUPHINE Marry, that he will disinherit me, no more. He thinks I
and my company are authors of all the ridiculous acts and
monuments° are told of him.   10

TRUEWIT 'Slid, I would be the author of more to vex him; that
purpose deserves it: it gives thee law of° plaguing him. I'll tell
thee what I would do. I would make a false almanac, get it printed,
and then ha' him drawn out on a coronation day to the Tower
Wharf,° and kill him with the noise of the ordnance. Disinherit   15
thee! He cannot, man. Art not thou next of blood, and his sister's
son?

DAUPHINE Aye, but he will thrust me out of it, he vows, and marry.

TRUEWIT How? That's a more portent. Can he endure no noise, and
   will venture on a wife?   20

CLERIMONT Yes. Why, thou art a stranger, it seems, to his best trick
   yet. He has employed a fellow this half year, all over England, to
   hearken him out a dumb woman, be she of any form or any quality,
   so she be able to bear children; her silence is dowry enough, he
   says.   25

TRUEWIT But I trust to God he has found none.

CLERIMONT No, but he has heard of one that's lodged i' the next
   street to him, who is exceedingly soft-spoken; thrifty of her speech,
   that spends but six words a day. And her he's about now, and shall
   have her.   30

TRUEWIT Is't possible? Who is his agent i' the business?

CLERIMONT Marry, a barber, one Cutbeard: an honest fellow, one
   that tells Dauphine all here.

TRUEWIT Why, you oppress me with wonder! A woman and a
   barber, and love no noise!   35

CLERIMONT Yes, faith. The fellow trims him silently and has not the
   knack with his shears or his fingers; and that continence in a barber
   he thinks so eminent a virtue, as it has made him chief of his
   counsel.

TRUEWIT Is the barber to be seen? Or the wench?   40

CLERIMONT Yes, that they are.

TRUEWIT I pray thee, Dauphine, let's go thither.

DAUPHINE I have some business now; I cannot i' faith.

TRUEWIT You shall have no business shall make you neglect this, sir.
   We'll make her talk, believe it; or if she will not, we can give out 45
   at least so much as shall interrupt the treaty: we will break it. Thou
   art bound in conscience, when he suspects thee without cause, to
   torment him.

DAUPHINE Not I, by any means. I'll give no suffrage to't. He shall
   never ha' that plea against me that I opposed the least fancy of his. 50
   Let it lie upon my stars° to be guilty, I'll be innocent.

TRUEWIT Yes, and be poor and beg; do, innocent, when some groom
   of his has got him an heir, or this barber, if he himself cannot.
   Innocent! I pray thee, Ned, where lies she? Let him be innocent
   still.   55

CLERIMONT Why, right over against the barber's, in the house where
   Sir John Daw lies.

TRUEWIT You do not mean to confound me!

CLERIMONT Why?

TRUEWIT Does he that would marry her know so much?   60
CLERIMONT I cannot tell.
TRUEWIT 'Twere enough of imputation to her, with him.
CLERIMONT Why?
TRUEWIT The only talking sir i' the town! Jack Daw! And he teach
her not to speak—God b'w'you. I have some business too.   65
CLERIMONT Will you not go thither then?
TRUEWIT Not with the danger to meet Daw, for mine ears.
CLERIMONT Why? I thought you two had been upon very good
terms.
TRUEWIT Yes, of keeping distance.   70
CLERIMONT They say he is a very good scholar.
TRUEWIT Aye, and he says it first. A pox on him, a fellow that
pretends only to learning, buys titles, and nothing else of books in
him.
CLERIMONT The world reports him to be very learned.   75
TRUEWIT I am sorry the world should so conspire to belie him.
CLERIMONT Good faith, I have heard very good things come from
him.
TRUEWIT You may. There's none so desperately ignorant to deny
that: would they were his own. God b'w'you, gentlemen.   80
        [*Exit Truewit*]
CLERIMONT This is very abrupt!

1.3

DAUPHINE Come, you are a strange open man to tell everything
thus.
CLERIMONT Why, believe it, Dauphine, Truewit's a very honest
fellow.
DAUPHINE I think no other, but this frank nature of his is not for   5
secrets.
CLERIMONT Nay, then you are mistaken, Dauphine. I know where
he has been well trusted, and discharged the trust very truly and
heartily.
DAUPHINE I contend not, Ned, but with the fewer a business is   10
carried, it is ever the safer. Now we are alone, if you'll go thither,
I am for you.

CLERIMONT When were you there?

DAUPHINE Last night—and such a *Decameron*° of sport fallen out!
  Boccace never thought of the like. Daw does nothing but court her,   15
  and the wrong way. He would lie with her and praises her
  modesty; desires that she would talk and be free, and commends her silence in verses, which he reads and swears are the best
  that ever man made. Then rails at his fortunes, stamps, and
  mutines why° he is not made a councillor and called to affairs of   20
  state.

CLERIMONT I pray thee let's go. I would fain partake this. Some
  water,° boy.
    [*Exit Boy*]

DAUPHINE We are invited to dinner together, he and I, by one that
  came thither to him, Sir La Foole.   25

CLERIMONT O, that's a precious manikin!

DAUPHINE Do you know him?

CLERIMONT Aye, and he will know you too, if e'er he saw you but
  once, though you should meet him at church in the midst of
  prayers. He is one of the Braveries, though he be none o' the Wits.   30
  He will salute a judge upon the bench and a bishop in the pulpit,
  a lawyer when he is pleading at the bar, and a lady when she is
  dancing in a masque, and put her out.° He does give plays° and
  suppers, and invites his guests to 'em aloud, out of his window as
  they ride by in coaches. He has a lodging in the Strand° for the   35
  purpose. Or to watch when ladies are gone to the china-houses or
  the Exchange,° that he may meet 'em by chance and give 'em
  presents, some two or three hundred pounds' worth of toys, to be
  laughed at. He is never without a spare banquet, or sweetmeats in
  his chamber, for their women° to alight at and come up to for a   40
  bait.

DAUPHINE Excellent! He was a fine youth last night, but now he is
  much finer! What is his Christian name? I ha' forgot.

CLERIMONT Sir Amorous La Foole.
    [*Enter Boy*]

BOY The gentleman is here below that owns that name.   45

CLERIMONT Heart, he's come to invite me to dinner, I hold my life.

DAUPHINE Like enough. Pray thee, let's ha' him up.

CLERIMONT Boy, marshal him.°

BOY With a truncheon,° sir?

CLERIMONT Away, I beseech you.   50

[*Exit Boy*]

I'll make him tell us his pedigree now, and what meat he has to dinner, and who are his guests, and the whole course of his fortunes—with a breath.

1.4

[*Enter Sir Amorous*] *La Foole*

LA FOOLE 'Save, dear Sir Dauphine, honoured Master Clerimont.

CLERIMONT Sir Amorous! You have very much honested my lodging with your presence.

LA FOOLE Good faith, it is a fine lodging, almost as delicate a lodging as mine.   5

CLERIMONT Not so, sir.

LA FOOLE Excuse me, sir, if it were i' the Strand, I assure you. I am come, Master Clerimont, to entreat you wait upon two or three ladies to dinner today.

CLERIMONT How, sir! Wait upon 'em? Did you ever see me carry   10
dishes?

LA FOOLE No, sir, dispense with° me; I meant to bear 'em company .

CLERIMONT O, that I will, sir. The doubtfulness o' your phrase, believe it, sir, would breed you a quarrel once an hour with the   15
terrible boys,° if you should but keep 'em fellowship a day.

LA FOOLE It should be extremely against my will, sir, if I contested with any man.

CLERIMONT I believe it, sir. Where hold you your feast?

LA FOOLE At Tom Otter's, sir.   20

DAUPHINE Tom Otter? What's he?

LA FOOLE Captain Otter, sir. He is a kind of gamester, but he has had command both by sea and by land.

DAUPHINE O, then he is *animal amphibium*?°

LA FOOLE Aye, sir. His wife was the rich china-woman° that the   25
courtiers visited so often, that gave the rare entertainment. She commands all at home.

CLERIMONT Then she is Captain Otter?

LA FOOLE You say very well, sir. She is my kinswoman, a La Foole by the mother side, and will invite any great ladies for my sake.   30

DAUPHINE Not of the La Fooles of Essex?

LA FOOLE No, sir, the La Fooles of London.

CLERIMONT [*aside to Dauphine*] Now, h'is in.

LA FOOLE They all come out of our house, the La Fooles o' the north, the La Fooles of the west, the La Fooles of the east, and south—we are as ancient a family as any is in Europe—but I myself am descended lineally of the French La Fooles—and we do bear for our coat° yellow or or, chequered azure and gules,° and some three or four colours more, which is a very noted coat and has sometimes been solemnly worn by divers nobility of our house—but let that go, antiquity is not respected now—I had a brace of fat does sent me, gentlemen, and half a dozen of pheasants, a dozen or two of godwits, and some other fowl, which I would have eaten while they are good, and in good company— there will be a great lady or two, my Lady Haughty, my Lady Centaure, Mistress Dol Mavis—and they come a' purpose to see the silent gentlewoman, Mistress Epicene, that honest Sir John Daw has promised to bring thither—and then Mistress Trusty, my lady's woman, will be there too, and this honourable knight, Sir Dauphine, with yourself, Master Clerimont—and we'll be very merry, and have fiddlers and dance—I have been a mad wag in my time and have spent some crowns since I was a page in court to my Lord Lofty, and after, my lady's gentleman-usher, who got me knighted in Ireland,° since it pleased my elder brother to die—I had as fair a gold jerkin on that day as any was worn in the Island voyage,° or at Caliz,° none dispraised, and I came over in it hither, showed myself to my friends in court and after went down to my tenants in the country and surveyed my lands, let new leases, took their money, spent it in the eye° o' the land here, upon ladies—and now I can take up° at my pleasure.

DAUPHINE Can you take up ladies, sir?

CLERIMONT O, let him breathe, he has not recovered.

DAUPHINE Would I were your half in that commodity°—

LA FOOLE No, sir, excuse me: I meant money, which can take up anything. I have another guest or two to invite and say as much to, gentlemen. I'll take my leave abruptly, in hope you will not fail—Your servant.

[*Exit La Foole*]

DAUPHINE We will not fail you, Sir precious La Foole; but she shall that your ladies come to see, if I have credit afore° Sir Daw.

CLERIMONT Did you ever hear such a wind-fucker as this?

DAUPHINE Or such a rook as the other, that will betray his mistress to be seen. Come, 'tis time we prevented it.

CLERIMONT Go.

[*Exeunt*]

2.1

[Enter] Morose [and] Mute

MOROSE Cannot I yet find out a more compendious method than by
this trunk to save my servants the labour of speech and mine ears
the discord of sounds? Let me see: all discourses but mine own
afflict me; they seem harsh, impertinent and irksome. Is it not
possible that thou shouldst answer me by signs and I apprehend   5
thee, fellow? Speak not, though I question you. You have taken
the ring off from the street door as I bade you? Answer me not by
speech, but by silence; unless it be otherwise. (*At the breaches, still
the fellow makes legs or signs*)°—*[Mute nods]*. Very good. And you
have fastened on a thick quilt or flock-bed on the outside of the   10
door, that if they knock with their daggers or with brickbats, they
can make no noise? But with your leg, your answer, unless it be
otherwise—very good. This is not only fit modesty in a servant,
but good state and discretion in a master. And you have been with
Cutbeard, the barber, to have him come to me?—Good. And he   15
will come presently? Answer me not but with your leg, unless it
be otherwise: if it be otherwise, shake your head, or shrug.—So.
Your Italian and Spaniard are wise in these! And it is a frugal and
comely gravity. How long will it be ere Cutbeard come? Stay, if
an hour, hold up your whole hand; if half an hour, two fingers; if   20
a quarter, one;—Good: half a quarter? 'Tis well. And have you
given him a key, to come in without knocking?—Good. And is the
lock oiled, and the hinges, today?—Good. And the quilting of the
stairs nowhere worn out and bare?—Very good. I see by much
doctrine and impulsion it may be effected. Stand by. The Turk in   25
this divine discipline is admirable, exceeding all the potentates of
the earth; still waited on by mutes, and all his commands so
executed, yea, even in the war (as I have heard) and in his marches,
most of his charges and directions given by signs and with silence:
an exquisite art! And I am heartily ashamed and angry oftentimes   30
that the princes of Christendom should suffer a barbarian to
transcend 'em in so high a point of felicity. I will practise it
hereafter. (*One winds a horn without*)° How now? O! O! What
villain? What prodigy of mankind is that? Look.

[Exit Mute. Horn sounds (again)]

O! Cut his throat, cut his throat! What murderer, hell-hound, devil   35
can this be?

[*Enter Mute*]

MUTE It is a post from the court—

MOROSE Out, rogue, and must thou blow thy horn too?

MUTE Alas, it is a post from the court, sir, that says he must speak
with you, pain of death—   40

MOROSE Pain of thy life, be silent.

2.2

[*Enter*] *Truewit* [*with a posthorn and halter*]

TRUEWIT By your leave, sir—I am a stranger here—is your name
Master Morose? Is your name Master Morose? Fishes!° Pytha-
goreans° all! This is strange! What say you, sir, nothing? Has
Harpocrates been here with his club° among you? Well, sir, I will
believe you to be the man at this time; I will venture upon you,   5
sir. Your friends at court commend 'em to you, sir—

MOROSE [*aside*] O men! O manners!° Was there ever such
impudence?

TRUEWIT And are extremely solicitous for you, sir.

MOROSE Whose knave are you?   10

TRUEWIT Mine own knave and your compeer, sir.

MOROSE Fetch me my sword—

TRUEWIT You shall taste the one half of my dagger, if you do,
groom, and you, the other, if you stir, sir. Be patient, I charge you
in the King's name, and hear me without insurrection. They say   15
you are to marry? To marry! Do you mark, sir?

MOROSE How then, rude companion!

TRUEWIT Marry, your friends do wonder, sir, the Thames being so
near, wherein you may drown so handsomely; or London Bridge
at a low fall° with a fine leap, to hurry you down the stream; or   20
such a delicate steeple i' the town as Bow,° to vault from; or a
braver height, as Paul's;° or if you affected to do it nearer home
and a shorter way, an excellent garret window into the street; or a
beam in the said garret, with this halter (*he shows him a halter*);
which they have sent, and desire that you would sooner commit   25
your grave head to this knot than to the wedlock noose; or take a
little sublimate and go out of the world like a rat; or a fly (as one
said) with a straw i' your arse:° any way rather than to follow this
goblin matrimony. Alas, sir, do you ever think to find a chaste wife
in these times? Now? When there are so many masques, plays,   30

Puritan preachings,° mad folks,° and other strange sights to be
seen daily, private and public? If you had lived in King Ethelred's
time, sir, or Edward° the Confessor's, you might perhaps have
found in some cold country hamlet, then, a dull frosty wench
would have been contented with one man: now they will as soon   35
be pleased with one leg or one eye. I'll tell you, sir, the monstrous
hazards you shall run with a wife.

MOROSE Good sir! Have I ever cozened any friends of yours of their
land? Bought their possessions? Taken forfeit of their mortgage?
Begged a reversion from 'em?° Bastarded their issue? What have I   40
done that may deserve this?

TRUEWIT Nothing, sir, that I know, but your itch of marriage.

MOROSE Why, if I had made an assassinate upon your father, vitiated
your mother, ravished your sisters—

TRUEWIT I would kill you, sir, I would kill you if you had.   45

MOROSE Why, you do more in this, sir. It were a vengeance centuple,
for all facinorous acts that could be named, to do that you do—

TRUEWIT Alas, sir, I am but a messenger: I but tell you what you
must hear. It seems your friends are careful after your soul's
health, sir, and would have you know the danger (but you may do   50
your pleasure for all them, I persuade not, sir). If after you are
married your wife do run away with a vaulter or the Frenchman
that walks upon ropes or him that dances the jig or a fencer for his
skill at his weapon, why it is not their fault; they have discharged
their consciences when you know what may happen. Nay, suffer   55
valiantly, sir, for I must tell you all the perils that you are
obnoxious to. If she be fair, young, and vegetous, no sweetmeats
ever drew more flies; all the yellow doublets and great roses° i' the
town will be there. If foul and crooked, she'll be with them and
buy those doublets and roses, sir. If rich, and that you marry her   60
dowry, not her, she'll reign in your house as imperious as a widow.
If noble, all her kindred will be your tyrants. If fruitful, as proud
as May and humorous as April; she must have her doctors, her
midwives, her nurses, her longings every hour, though it be for the
dearest morsel of man. If learned, there was never such a parrot;   65
all your patrimony will be too little for the guests that must be
invited to hear her speak Latin and Greek, and you must lie with
her in those languages too, if you will please her. If precise, you
must feast all the silenced brethren,° once in three days; salute the
sister; entertain the whole family° or wood of 'em; and hear   70
long-winded exercises, singings and catechizings, which you are

not given to, and yet must give for, to please the zealous° matron
your wife, who for the holy cause° will cozen you over and above.
You begin to sweat, sir? But this is not half, i' faith; you may do
your pleasure notwithstanding, as I said before, I come not to   75
persuade you. (*The Mute is stealing away*) Upon my faith, master
servingman, if you do stir, I will beat you.

MOROSE O, what is my sin! What is my sin?

TRUEWIT Then if you love your wife, or rather dote on her, sir, o,
how she'll torture you and take pleasure i' your torments! You   80
shall lie with her but when she lists; she will not hurt her beauty,
her complexion; or it must be for that jewel or that pearl when she
does; every half hour's pleasure must be bought anew, and with
the same pain and charge you wooed her at first. Then you must
keep what servants she please; what company she will; that friend   85
must not visit you without her licence; and him she loves most she
will seem to hate eagerliest, to decline your jealousy; or feign to be
jealous of you first, and for that cause go live with her she-friend
or cousin° at the college, that can instruct her in all the mysteries
of writing letters, corrupting servants, taming spies; where she   90
must have that rich gown for such a great day, a new one for the
next, a richer for the third; be served in silver; have the chamber
filled with a succession of grooms, footmen, ushers, and other
messengers, besides embroiderers, jewellers, tire-women, semp-
sters, feathermen, perfumers; while she feels not how the land drops   95
away, nor the acres melt, nor foresees the change when the mercer
has your woods for her velvets; never weighs what her pride
costs, sir, so she may kiss a page or a smooth chin that has the
despair of a beard; be a stateswoman, know all the news: what was
done at Salisbury,° what at the Bath,° what at court, what in   100
progress; or so she may censure poets and authors and styles, and
compare 'em, Daniel with Spenser,° Jonson with the t'other
youth,° and so forth; or be thought cunning in controversies, or
the very knots of divinity, and have often in her mouth the state
of the question,° and then skip to the mathematics and demonstra-   105
tion; and answer in religion to one, in state to another, in bawdry
to a third.

MOROSE O, o!

TRUEWIT All this is very true, sir. And then her going in disguise to
that conjurer and this cunning woman, where the first question is,   110
how soon you shall die? Next, if her present servant love her? Next
that, if she shall have a new servant? And how many? Which of

her family would make the best bawd, male or female? What precedence she shall have by her next match? And sets down the answers, and believes 'em above the scriptures. Nay, perhaps she'll   115
study the art.

MOROSE Gentle sir, ha' you done? Ha' you had your pleasure o' me? I'll think of these things.

TRUEWIT Yes, sir; and then comes reeking home of vapour and sweat with going afoot, and lies in a month of a new face, all oil and   120
birdlime; and rises° in asses' milk, and is cleansed with a new fucus; God b'w'you, sir. One thing more (which I had almost forgot). This too, with whom you are to marry, may have made a conveyance of her virginity aforehand, as your wise widows do of their states before they marry, in trust to some friend, sir: who can   125
tell? Or if she have not done it yet, she may do, upon the wedding day or the night before, and antedate you cuckold. The like has been heard of in nature. 'Tis no devised impossible thing, sir. God b'w'you. I'll be bold to leave this rope with you, sir, for a remembrance. Farewell, Mute.

        [Exit Truewit]   130

MOROSE Come, ha' me to my chamber, but first shut the door. (The horn again) O shut the door, shut the door. Is he come again?

        [Enter Cutbeard]

CUTBEARD 'Tis I, sir, your barber.

MOROSE O, Cutbeard, Cutbeard, Cutbeard! Here has been a cut-throat with me; help me in to my bed, and give me physic° with   135
thy counsel.

        [Exeunt]

2.3

        [Enter] Daw, Clerimont, Dauphine [and] Epicene

DAW Nay, and she will, let her refuse at her own charges; 'tis nothing to me, gentlemen. But she will not be invited to the like feasts or guests every day.

CLERIMONT O, by no means, she may not refuse (They dissuade her, privately)—to stay at home if you love your reputation. 'Slight, you   5
are invited thither o' purpose to be seen and laughed at by the lady of the college and her shadows. This trumpeter [indicating Daw] hath proclaimed you.

DAUPHINE You shall not go; let him be laughed at in your stead, for
not bringing you, and put him to his extemporal faculty of fooling   10
and talking loud to satisfy the company.

CLERIMONT He will suspect us, talk aloud—Pray, Mistress Epicene,
let's see your verses; we have Sir John Daw's leave; do not conceal
your servant's merit and your own glories.

EPICENE They'll prove my servant's glories if you have his leave so   15
soon.

DAUPHINE [aside] His vainglories, lady!

DAW Show 'em, show 'em, mistress, I dare own 'em.

EPICENE Judge you, what glories?

DAW Nay, I'll read 'em myself too; an author must recite his own   20
works. It is a madrigal of modesty.

> Modest and fair, for fair and good are near
> Neighbours, howe'er—

DAUPHINE Very good.

CLERIMONT Aye, is't not?   25

DAW   *No noble virtue ever was alone,*
> *But two in one.*

DAUPHINE Excellent!

CLERIMONT That again, I pray, Sir John.

DAUPHINE It has something in't like rare wit and sense.   30

CLERIMONT Peace.

DAW   *No noble virtue ever was alone,*
> *But two in one.*
> *Then when I praise sweet modesty, I praise*
> *Bright beauty's rays:*   35
> *And having praised both beauty, and modesty,*
> *I have praised thee.*

DAUPHINE Admirable!

CLERIMONT How it chimes, and cries tink i' the close,° divinely!

DAUPHINE Aye, 'tis Seneca.   40

CLERIMONT No, I think 'tis Plutarch.°

DAW The dor on° Plutarch and Seneca, I hate it: they are mine own
imaginations, by that light.° I wonder those fellows have such
credit with gentlemen!

CLERIMONT They are very grave authors.   45

DAW Grave asses! Mere essayists! A few loose sentences and
that's all. A man would talk so his whole age: I do utter as good
things every hour, if they were collected and observed, as either of
'em.

DAUPHINE Indeed, Sir John!   50

CLERIMONT He must needs, living among the Wits and Braveries
too.

DAUPHINE Aye, and being president of 'em as he is.

DAW There's Aristotle, a mere commonplace fellow; Plato, a dis-
courser; Thucydides and Livy, tedious and dry; Tacitus, an entire   55
knot, sometimes worth the untying, very seldom.

CLERIMONT What do you think of the poets, Sir John?

DAW Not worthy to be named for authors. Homer, an old tedious
prolix ass, talks of curriers and chines° of beef. Virgil, of dunging
of land, and bees.° Horace, of I know not what.   60

CLERIMONT I think so.

DAW And so Pindarus, Lycophron, Anacreon, Catullus, Seneca the
tragedian, Lucan, Propertius, Tibullus, Martial, Juvenal, Auso-
nius, Statius, Politian, Valerius Flaccus, and the rest°—

CLERIMONT What a sack full of their names he has got!   65

DAUPHINE And how he pours 'em out! Politian with Valerius
Flaccus!

CLERIMONT Was not the character right of him?

DAUPHINE As could be made, i' faith.

DAW And Persius, a crabbed coxcomb not to be endured.   70

DAUPHINE Why, whom do you account for authors, Sir John Daw?

DAW *Syntagma juris civilis, Corpus juris civilis, Corpus juris canonici,*
the King of Spain's Bible.°

DAUPHINE Is the King of Spain's Bible an author?

CLERIMONT Yes, and Syntagma.   75

DAUPHINE What was that Syntagma, sir?

DAW A civil lawyer, a Spaniard.

DAUPHINE Sure, Corpus was a Dutchman.

CLERIMONT Aye, both the Corpusses, I knew 'em: they were very
corpulent authors.   80

DAW And then there's Vatablus, Pomponatius, Symancha;° the other
are not to be received within the thought of a scholar.

DAUPHINE 'Fore God, you have a simple learned servant, lady, in
titles.

CLERIMONT I wonder that he is not called to the helm and made a   85
councillor!

DAUPHINE He is one extraordinary.

CLERIMONT Nay, but in ordinary!° To say truth, the state wants
such.

DAUPHINE Why, that will follow.   90

CLERIMONT I muse a mistress can be so silent to the dotes of such a servant.

DAW 'Tis her virtue, sir. I have written somewhat of her silence too.

DAUPHINE In verse, Sir John?   95

CLERIMONT What else?

DAUPHINE Why, how can you justify your own being of a poet, that so slight all the old poets?

DAW Why, every man that writes in verse is not a poet; you have of the Wits that write verses and yet are no poets: they are poets that   100
live by it, the poor fellows that live by it.

DAUPHINE Why, would not you live by your verses, Sir John?

CLERIMONT No, 'twere pity he should. A knight live by his verses? He did not make 'em to that end, I hope.

DAUPHINE And yet the noble Sidney lives by his, and the noble   105
family° not ashamed.

CLERIMONT Aye, he professed himself; but Sir John Daw has more caution: he'll not hinder his own rising i' the state so much! Do you think he will? Your verses, good Sir John, and no poems.   110

DAW   *Silence in woman is like speech in man,*
                Deny't who can.'

DAUPHINE Not I, believe it; your reason, sir.

DAW   *'Nor is't a tale,*
                That female vice should be a virtue male,   115
                Or masculine vice, a female virtue be:
                    You shall it see
                    Proved with increase,
                I know to speak, and she to hold her peace.

Do you conceive me, gentlemen?   120

DAUPHINE No faith, how mean you 'with increase', Sir John?

DAW Why, 'with increase' is when I court her for the common cause of mankind and she says nothing but *consentire videtur*, and in time is *gravida*.°

DAUPHINE Then this is a ballad of procreation?   125

CLERIMONT A madrigal of procreation, you mistake.

EPICENE Pray give me my verses again, servant.

DAW If you'll ask 'em aloud, you shall.

        [*Epicene and Daw walk aside*]

CLERIMONT See, here's Truewit again!

2.4

[Enter] Truewit [with his post-horn]

CLERIMONT Where hast thou been, in the name of madness, thus
accoutred with thy horn?

TRUEWIT Where the sound of it might have pierced your senses with
gladness, had you been in ear-reach of it. Dauphine, fall down and
worship me: I have forbid the banns, lad. I have been with thy   5
virtuous uncle and have broke the match.

DAUPHINE You ha' not, I hope.

TRUEWIT Yes faith, an thou shouldst hope otherwise, I should repent
me; this horn got me entrance—kiss it. I had no other way to get
in but by feigning to be a post; but when I got in once, I proved   10
none, but rather the contrary, turned him into a post or a stone or
what is stiffer, with thundering into him the incommodities of a
wife and the miseries of marriage. If ever Gorgon were seen in the
shape of a woman, he hath seen her in my description. I have put
him off o' that scent for ever. Why do you not applaud and adore   15
me, sirs? Why stand you mute? Are you stupid? You are not
worthy o' the benefit.

DAUPHINE Did not I tell you? Mischief!—

CLERIMONT I would you had placed this benefit somewhere else.

TRUEWIT Why so?   20

CLERIMONT 'Slight, you have done the most inconsiderate, rash,
weak thing that ever man did to his friend.

DAUPHINE Friend! If the most malicious enemy I have had studied
to inflict an injury upon me, it could not be a greater.

TRUEWIT Wherein, for God's sake? Gentlemen; come to yourselves   25
again.

DAUPHINE But I presaged thus much afore to you.

CLERIMONT Would my lips had been soldered when I spake on 't.
'Slight, what moved you to be thus impertinent?

TRUEWIT My masters, do not put on this strange face to pay my   30
courtesy; off with this visor. Have good turns done you and thank
'em this way?

DAUPHINE 'Fore heaven, you have undone me. That which I have
plotted for and been maturing now these four months, you have
blasted in a minute; now I am lost, I may speak. This gentlewoman   35
was lodged here by me o' purpose, and, to be put upon my uncle,
hath professed this obstinate silence for my sake, being my entire

friend, and one that for the requital of such a fortune as to marry him, would have made me very ample conditions: where now, all my hopes are utterly miscarried by this unlucky accident. 40

CLERIMONT Thus 'tis when a man will be ignorantly officious, do services and not know his why. I wonder what courteous itch possessed you! You never did absurder part i' your life nor a greater trespass to friendship, to humanity.

DAUPHINE Faith, you may forgive it, best; 'twas your cause princi- 45 pally.

CLERIMONT I know it; would it had not.

[*Enter Cutbeard*]

DAUPHINE How now, Cutbeard, what news?

CUTBEARD The best, the happiest that ever was, sir. There has been a mad gentleman with your uncle this morning—[*noticing Truewit*] I 50 think this be the gentleman—that has almost talked him out of his wits, with threatening him from marriage—

DAUPHINE On, I pray thee.

CUTBEARD And your uncle, sir, he thinks 'twas done by your procurement; therefore he will see the party you wot of presently, 55 and if he like her, he says, and that she be so inclining to dumb as I have told him, he swears he will marry her today, instantly, and not defer it a minute longer.

DAUPHINE Excellent! Beyond our expectation!

TRUEWIT Beyond your expectation? By this light, I knew it would 60 be thus.

DAUPHINE Nay, sweet Truewit, forgive me.

TRUEWIT No, I was 'ignorantly officious, impertinent': this was the 'absurd, weak part'.

CLERIMONT Wilt thou ascribe that to merit, now was mere fortune? 65

TRUEWIT Fortune? Mere providence.° Fortune had not a finger in't. I saw it must necessarily in nature fall out so; my genius is never false to me in these things. Show me how it could be otherwise.

DAUPHINE Nay, gentlemen, contend not, 'tis well now.

TRUEWIT Alas, I let him go on with 'inconsiderate' and 'rash', and 70 what he pleased.

CLERIMONT Away thou strange justifier of thyself, to be wiser than thou wert by the event.

TRUEWIT Event! By this light, thou shalt never persuade me but I foresaw it as well as the stars themselves. 75

DAUPHINE Nay, gentlemen, 'tis well now; do you two entertain Sir John Daw with discourse while I send her away with instructions.

TRUEWIT I'll be acquainted with her first, by your favour.
    [Epicene and Daw come forward]

CLERIMONT Master Truewit, lady, a friend of ours.

TRUEWIT I am sorry I have not known you sooner, lady, to celebrate   80
this rare virtue of your silence.

CLERIMONT Faith, an you had come sooner, you should ha' seen and
heard her well celebrated in Sir John Daw's madrigals.
    [Exeunt Dauphine, Epicene, Cutbeard]

TRUEWIT Jack Daw, God save you, when saw you La Foole?

DAW Not since last night, Master Truewit.   85

TRUEWIT That's miracle! I thought you two had been inseparable.

DAW He's gone to invite his guests.

TRUEWIT Gods so, 'tis true! What a false memory have I towards
that man! I am one;° I met him e'en now, upon that he calls his
delicate fine black horse, rid into a foam with posting from place   90
to place and person to person to give 'em the cue—

CLERIMONT Lest they should forget?

TRUEWIT Yes, there was never poor captain took more pains at a
muster to show men than he at this meal to show friends.

DAW It is his quarter-feast,° sir.   95

CLERIMONT What, do you say so, Sir John?

TRUEWIT Nay, Jack Daw will not be out, at the best friends he has,
to the talent of his wit.° Where's his mistress, to hear and applaud
him? Is she gone?

DAW Is Mistress Epicene gone?   100

CLERIMONT Gone afore with Sir Dauphine, I warrant, to the place.

TRUEWIT Gone afore! That were a manifest injury, a disgrace and a
half, to refuse him at such a festival time as this, being a Bravery
and a Wit too.

CLERIMONT Tut, he'll swallow it like cream: he's better read *in jure*   105
civili° than to esteem anything a disgrace is offered him from a
mistress.

DAW Nay, let her e'en go; she shall sit alone and be dumb in her
chamber a week together, for John Daw, I warrant her. Does she
refuse me?   110

CLERIMONT No, sir, do not take it so to heart: she does not refuse
you, but a little neglect you. Good faith, Truewit, you were to
blame to put it into his head that she does refuse him.

TRUEWIT She does refuse him, sir, palpably, however you mince it.
An I were as he, I would swear to speak ne'er a word to her today   115
for't.

DAW By this light, no more I will not.

TRUEWIT Nor to anybody else, sir.

DAW Nay, I will not say so, gentlemen.

CLERIMONT [aside to Truewit] It had been an excellent happy   120
condition for the company if you could have drawn him to it.

DAW I'll be very melancholic, i' faith.

CLERIMONT As a dog, if I were as you, Sir John.

TRUEWIT Or a snail or a hog-louse: I would roll myself up for this
day; in troth, they should not unwind me.   125

DAW By this pick-tooth, so I will.

CLERIMONT [aside to Truewit] 'Tis well done; he begins already to
be angry with his teeth.

DAW Will you go, gentlemen?

CLERIMONT Nay, you must walk alone if you be right melancholic,   130
Sir John.

TRUEWIT Yes, sir, we'll dog you; we'll follow you afar off.

    [Exit Daw]

CLERIMONT Was there ever such a two yards of knighthood
measured out by time to be sold to laughter?

TRUEWIT A mere talking mole!° Hang him, no mushroom was ever   135
so fresh.° A fellow so utterly nothing, as he knows not what he
would be.

CLERIMONT Let's follow him, but first, let's go to Dauphine; he's
hovering about the house, to hear what news.

TRUEWIT Content.   140

    [Exeunt]

2.5

    [Enter] Morose, Epicene, Cutbeard [and] Mute

MOROSE Welcome, Cutbeard; draw near with your fair charge: and
in her ear, softly entreat her to unmask—[Cutbeard whispers to
Epicene, who unmasks] So. Is the door shut?—[Mute makes a leg]
Enough. Now, Cutbeard, with the same discipline I use to my
family, I will question you. As I conceive, Cutbeard, this gentlewo-   5
man is she you have provided and brought in hope she will fit
me in the place and person of a wife? Answer me not but with
your leg, unless it be otherwise:—Very well done, Cutbeard. I
conceive besides, Cutbeard, you have been pre-acquainted with her

birth, education, and qualities, or else you would not prefer her to   10
my acceptance, in the weighty consequence of marriage.—This
I conceive, Cutbeard. Answer me not but with your leg, unless it
be otherwise.—Very well done, Cutbeard. Give aside now a little,
and leave me to examine her condition and aptitude to my
affection. (*He goes about her and views her*) She is exceeding fair   15
and of a special good favour; a sweet composition or harmony of
limbs; her temper of beauty has the true height of my blood.° The
knave hath exceedingly well fitted me without; I will now try her
within. Come near, fair gentlewoman: let not my behaviour seem
rude, though unto you, being rare, it may haply appear strange.   20
(*She curtsies*) Nay, lady, you may speak, though Cutbeard and my
man might not, for of all sounds only the sweet voice of a fair lady
has the just length of mine ears. I beseech you, say, lady, out of
the first fire of meeting eyes (they say) love is stricken: do you feel
any such motion suddenly shot into you from any part you see in   25
me? Ha, lady? (*Curtsy*) Alas, lady, these answers by silent curtsies,
from you are too courtless and simple. I have ever had my breeding
in court, and she that shall be·my wife must be accomplished with
courtly and audacious ornaments. Can you speak, lady?

EPICENE (*she speaks softly*) Judge you, forsooth.   30

MOROSE What say you, lady? Speak out, I beseech you.

EPICENE Judge you, forsooth.

MOROSE O' my judgement, a divine softness! But can you naturally,
lady, as I enjoin these [*indicates Cutbeard and Mute*] by doctrine
and industry, refer yourself to the search of my judgement,   35
and—not taking pleasure in your tongue, which is a woman's
chiefest pleasure—think it plausible to answer me by silent gestures, so long as my speeches jump right° with what you conceive?
(*Curtsy*) Excellent! Divine! If it were possible she should hold out
thus! Peace, Cutbeard, thou art made forever, as thou has made   40
me, if this felicity have lasting; but I will try her further. Dear
lady, I am courtly, I tell you, and I must have mine ears banqueted
with pleasant and witty conferences, pretty girds, scoffs, and
dalliance in her that I mean to choose for my bedfere. The ladies
in court think it a most desperate impair to their quickness of wit   45
and good carriage if they cannot give occasion for a man to court
'em, and when an amorous discourse is set on foot, minister as
good matter to continue it, as himself; and do you alone so much
differ from all them, that what they with so much circumstance
affect and toil for, to seem learned, to seem judicious, to seem   50

sharp and conceited, you can bury in yourself with silence, and
rather trust your graces to the fair conscience of virtue than to the
world's or your own proclamation?

EPICENE I should be sorry else.

MOROSE What say you, lady? Good lady, speak out.   55

EPICENE I should be sorry, else.

MOROSE That sorrow doth fill me with gladness! O Morose, thou art
happy above mankind! Pray that thou mayest contain thyself. I will
only put her to it once more, and it shall be with the utmost touch
and test of their sex. But hear me, fair lady, I do also love to see   60
her whom I shall choose for my heifer to be the first and principal
in all fashions; precede all the dames at court by a fortnight; have
her council of tailors, lineners, lace-women, embroiderers, and sit
with 'em sometimes twice a day upon French intelligences;° and
then come forth varied like Nature, or oftener than she, and better   65
by the help of Art, her emulous servant. This do I affect. And how
will you be able, lady, with this frugality of speech, to give the
manifold (but necessary) instructions for that bodice, these sleeves,
those skirts, this cut, that stitch, this embroidery, that lace, this
wire, those knots, that ruff, those roses, this girdle, that fan, the   70
t'other scarf, these gloves? Ha! What say you, lady?

EPICENE I'll leave it to you, sir.

MOROSE How, lady? Pray you, rise a note.

EPICENE I leave it to wisdom, and you, sir.

MOROSE Admirable creature! I will trouble you no more; I will not   75
sin against so sweet a simplicity. Let me now be bold to print on
those divine lips the seal of being mine [*kisses her*]. Cutbeard, I give
thee the lease of thy house free; thank me not, but with thy
leg—[*Cutbeard makes a leg*] I know what thou wouldst say, she's
poor, and her friends deceased; she has brought a wealthy dowry   80
in her silence, Cutbeard, and in respect of her poverty, Cutbeard,
I shall have her more loving and obedient, Cutbeard. Go thy ways
and get me a minister presently, with a soft, low voice to marry
us, and pray him he will not be impertinent, but brief as he can;
away: softly, Cutbeard.   85

     [*Exit Cutbeard*]

Sirrah, conduct your mistress into the dining room, your now-
mistress.

     [*Exeunt Mute and Epicene*]

Oh my felicity! How I shall be revenged on mine insolent kinsman
and his plots to fright me from marrying! This night I will get an

heir, and thrust him out of my blood like a stranger; he would be   90
knighted, forsooth, and thought by that means to reign over me,
his title must do it: no, kinsman, I will now make you bring me
the tenth lord's and the sixteenth lady's letter,° kinsman and it
shall do you no good, kinsman. Your knighthood itself shall come
on its knees, and it shall be rejected; it shall be sued for its fees to   95
execution and not be redeemed; it shall cheat at the twelvepenny
ordinary, it° knighthood, for its diet all the term time, and tell tales
for it in the vacation, to the hostess; or it knighthood shall do
worse—take sanctuary in Coleharbour,° and fast. It shall fright all
it friends with borrowing letters, and when one of the fourscore   100
hath brought it knighthood ten shillings, it knighthood shall go to
the Cranes,° or the Bear° at the Bridge foot, and be drunk in fear;
it shall not have money to discharge one tavern reckoning, to invite
the old creditors to forbear it knighthood, or the new that should
be, to trust it knighthood. It shall be the tenth name in the   105
bond,° to take up the commodity° of pipkins and stone jugs, and
the part thereof shall not furnish it knighthood forth for the
attempting of a baker's widow, a brown° baker's widow. It shall give
it knighthood's name for a stallion to all gamesome citizens' wives,
and be refused, when the master of a dancing school, or—How° do   110
you call him—the worst reveller in the town is taken; it shall want
clothes, and by reason of that, wit to fool to lawyers. It shall not
have hope to repair itself by Constantinople, Ireland, or Virginia;°
but the best and last fortune to it knighthood shall be to make Doll
Tearsheet or Kate Common° a lady, and so it knighthood may eat.°   115

    [*Exit*]

2.6

    [*Enter*] *Truewit, Dauphine* [*and*] *Clerimont*

TRUEWIT Are you sure he is not gone by?

DAUPHINE No, I stayed in the shop ever since.

CLERIMONT But he may take the other end of the lane.

DAUPHINE No, I told him I would be here at this end; I appointed
    him hither.°   5

TRUEWIT What a barbarian it is to stay then!

DAUPHINE Yonder he comes.

    [*Enter Cutbeard*]

CLERIMONT And his charge left behind him, which is a very good
sign, Dauphine.

DAUPHINE How now, Cutbeard, succeeds it or no?   10

CUTBEARD Past imagination, sir, *omnia secunda*; you could not have
prayed to have had it so well: *saltat senex*,° as it is i' the proverb,
he does triumph in his felicity; admires the party! He has given
me the lease of my house too! And I am now going for a silent
minister to marry 'em, and away.   15

TRUEWIT 'Slight, get one o' the silenced ministers,° a zealous brother
would torment him purely.°

CUTBEARD *Cum privilegio*,° sir.

DAUPHINE O, by no means, let's do nothing to hinder it now;
when 'tis done and finished, I am for you, for any device of   20
vexation.

CUTBEARD And that shall be within this half hour, upon my dexterity,
gentlemen. Contrive what you can in the meantime, *bonis avibus*.°
    [*Exit Cutbeard*]

CLERIMONT How the slave doth Latin it!

TRUEWIT It would be made a jest to posterity, sirs, this day's mirth, 25
if ye will.

CLERIMONT Beshrew his heart that will not, I pronounce.

DAUPHINE And for my part. What is't?

TRUEWIT To translate all La Foole's company and his feast hither
today, to celebrate this bride-ale.   30

DAUPHINE Aye, marry, but how will't be done?

TRUEWIT I'll undertake the directing of all the lady guests thither,
and then the meat must follow.

CLERIMONT For God's sake, let's effect it; it will be an excellent
comedy of affliction, so many several noises.   35

DAUPHINE But are they not at the other place° already, think you?

TRUEWIT I'll warrant you for the college honours: one o' their faces
has not the priming colour laid on yet, nor the other her smock
sleeked.

CLERIMONT O, but they'll rise earlier than ordinary to a feast.   40

TRUEWIT Best go see and assure ourselves.

CLERIMONT Who knows the house?

TRUEWIT I'll lead you; were you never there yet?

DAUPHINE Not I.

CLERIMONT Nor I.   45

TRUEWIT Where ha' you lived then? Not know Tom Otter?

CLERIMONT No. For God's sake, what is he?

TRUEWIT An excellent animal, equal with your Daw, or La Foole, if not transcendent, and does Latin it as much as your barber; he is his wife's subject, he calls her princess, and at such times as these, follows her up and down the house like a page, with his hat off, partly for heat, partly for reverence. At this instant, he is marshalling of his bull, bear, and horse.

DAUPHINE What be those, in the names of Sphinx?°

TRUEWIT Why, sir, he has been a great man at the Bear Garden° in his time, and from that subtle sport has ta'en the witty denomination of his chief carousing cups.° One he calls his bull, another his bear, another his horse. And then he has his lesser glasses that he calls his deer and his ape, and several degrees of 'em too, and never is well nor thinks any entertainment perfect, till these be brought out and set o' the cupboard.

CLERIMONT For God's love! We should miss this if we should not go.

TRUEWIT Nay, he has a thousand things as good that will speak him° all day. He will rail on his wife with certain commonplaces behind her back, and to her face—

DAUPHINE No more of him. Let's go see him, I petition you.

 [*Exeunt*]

3.1

[*Enter*] *Otter, Mistress Otter; Truewit, Clerimont* [*and*]
Dauphine [*follow, unobserved*]

OTTER Nay, good princess, hear me *pauca verba.*°

MISTRESS OTTER By that light, I'll ha' you chained up with your
bull-dogs and bear-dogs, if you be not civil the sooner. I'll send
you to kennel, i'faith. You were best bait me with your bull, bear
and horse! Never a time that the courtiers or collegiates come to   5
the house, but you make it a Shrove Tuesday!° I would have you
get your Whitsuntide velvet cap, and your staff° i' your hand to
entertain 'em; yes in troth, do.

OTTER Not so, princess, neither, but under correction, sweet princess, gi' me leave—these things I am known to the courtiers by. It   10
is reported to them for my humour, and they receive it so, and do
expect it. Tom Otter's bull, bear and horse is known all over
England, *in rerum natura.*°

MISTRESS OTTER 'Fore me, I will *na-ture* 'em over to Paris Garden,
and *na-ture* you thither too, if you pronounce 'em again. Is a bear   15
a fit beast, or a bull, to mix in society with great ladies? Think i'
your discretion, in any good polity?

OTTER The horse then, good princess.

MISTRESS OTTER Well, I am contented for the horse; they love to be
well horsed, I know. I love it myself.   20

OTTER And it is a delicate fine horse this. *Poetarum Pegasus.*° Under
correction, princess, Jupiter did turn himself into a—*taurus*° or
bull, under correction, good princess.

MISTRESS OTTER By my integrity, I'll send you over to the Bankside, I'll commit you to the Master of the Garden, if I hear but a   25
syllable more. Must my house or my roof be polluted with the
scent of bears and bulls, when it is perfumed for great ladies? Is
this according to the instrument, when I married you? That I
would be princess, and reign in mine own house, and you would
be my subject, and obey me? What did you bring me, should make   30
you thus peremptory? Do I allow you your half-crown a day to
spend where you will among your gamesters, to vex and torment
me at such times as these? Who gives you your maintenance, I pray
you? Who allows you your horse meat, and man's meat? Your
three suits° of apparel a year? Your four pair of stockings, one silk,   35

three worsted? Your clean linen, your bands and cuffs when I can
get you to wear 'em? 'Tis mar'l you ha' 'em on now. Who graces
you with courtiers or great personages to speak to you out of their
coaches and come home to your house? Were you ever so much as
looked upon by a lord or a lady before I married you, but on the   40
Easter or Whitsun holidays, and then out at the Banqueting House
window, when Ned Whiting or George Stone were at the stake?

TRUEWIT [aside] For God's sake let's go stave her off him.

MISTRESS OTTER Answer me to that. And did not I take you up
from thence in an old greasy buff-doublet, with points and green   45
velvet sleeves out at the elbows? You forget this.

TRUEWIT [aside] She'll worry him if we help not in time.

MISTRESS OTTER O, here are some o' the gallants! Go to, behave
yourself distinctly and with good morality, or I protest, I'll take
away your exhibition.   50

3.2

Truewit, Clerimont [and] Dauphine [come forward]

TRUEWIT By your leave, fair Mistress Otter, I'll be bold to enter
these gentlemen in your acquaintance.

MISTRESS OTTER It shall not be obnoxious or difficil,° sir.

TRUEWIT How does my noble Captain? Is the bull, bear, and horse,
in rerum natura° still?   5

OTTER Sir, *sic visum superis.*°

MISTRESS OTTER I would you would but intimate 'em,° do. Go your
ways in, and get toasts and butter° made for the woodcocks. That's
a fit province for you.

[*Exit Otter*]

CLERIMONT [*aside to Truewit and Dauphine*] Alas, what a tyranny is   10
this poor fellow married to.

TRUEWIT O, but the sport will be anon, when we get him loose.

DAUPHINE Dares he ever speak?

TRUEWIT No Anabaptist° ever railed with the like licence:° but mark
her language in the meantime, I beseech you.   15

MISTRESS OTTER Gentlemen, you are very aptly come. My cousin,
Sir Amorous, will be here briefly.

TRUEWIT In good time, lady. Was not Sir John Daw here to ask for
him and the company?

MISTRESS OTTER I cannot assure you, Master Truewit. Here was a   20
    very melancholy knight in a ruff, that demanded my subject° for
    somebody, a gentleman, I think.

CLERIMONT Aye, that was he, lady.

MISTRESS OTTER But he departed straight, I can resolve you.

DAUPHINE What an excellent choice phrase this lady expresses in!   25

TRUEWIT O, sir, she is the only authentical courtier that is not
    naturally bred one, in the city.

MISTRESS OTTER You have taken that report upon trust, gentlemen.

TRUEWIT No, I assure you, the court governs it so, lady, in your
    behalf.   30

MISTRESS OTTER I am the servant of the court and courtiers, sir.

TRUEWIT They are rather your idolaters.

MISTRESS OTTER Not so, sir.
    [*Enter Cutbeard, to whom Dauphine, Truewit and Clerimont
    speak apart*]

DAUPHINE How now, Cutbeard? Any cross?

CUTBEARD O no, sir, *omnia bene*.° 'Twas never better o' the hinges,°   35
    all's sure. I have so pleased him with a curate that he's gone to't
    almost with the delight he hopes for soon.

DAUPHINE What is he, for a vicar?°

CUTBEARD One that has catched a cold, sir, and can scarce be heard
    six inches off, as if he spoke out of a bulrush that were not picked,°   40
    or his throat were full of pith: a fine quick fellow and an excellent
    barber of prayers. I came to tell you, sir, that you might *omnem
    movere lapidem*° (as they say), be ready with your vexation.

DAUPHINE Gramercy, honest Cutbeard, be thereabouts with thy key
    to let us in.   45

CUTBEARD I will not fail you, sir: *ad manum.*°
    [*Exit Cutbeard*]

TRUEWIT Well, I'll go watch my coaches.

CLERIMONT Do, and we'll send Daw to you, if you meet him not.
    [*Exit Truewit*]

MISTRESS OTTER Is Master Truewit gone?

DAUPHINE Yes, lady, there is some unfortunate business fallen out.   50

MISTRESS OTTER So I judged by the physiognomy of the fellow that
    came in; and I had a dream last night too of the new pageant° and
    my Lady Mayoress, which is always very ominous to me. I told it
    my Lady Haughty t'other day, when her honour came hither to see
    some China stuffs,° and she expounded it out of Artemidorus,° and   55
    I have found it since very true. It has done me many affronts.

CLERIMONT Your dream, lady?

MISTRESS OTTER Yes, sir, anything I do but dream o' the city. It
stained me a damask tablecloth, cost me eighteen pound at one
time, and burnt me a black satin gown as I stood by the fire at my   60
Lady Centaure's chamber in the college another time. A third
time, at the lord's masque, it dropped all my wire and my ruff with
wax candle, that I could not go up to the banquet. A fourth time,
as I was taking coach to go to Ware° to meet a friend, it dashed
me a new suit all over (a crimson satin doublet° and black velvet   65
skirts) with a brewer's horse, that I was fain to go in and shift me,
and kept my chamber a leash of° days for the anguish of it.

DAUPHINE These were dire mischances, lady.

CLERIMONT I would not dwell in the city, an 'twere so fatal to me.

MISTRESS OTTER Yes, sir, but I do take advice of my doctor to   70
dream of it as little as I can.

DAUPHINE You do well, Mistress Otter.

[*Enter Daw; Clerimont takes him aside*]

MISTRESS OTTER Will it please you to enter the house farther,
gentlemen?

DAUPHINE And your favour,° lady; but we stay to speak with a   75
knight, Sir John Daw, who is here come. We shall follow you, lady.

MISTRESS OTTER At your own time, sir. It is my cousin Sir Amorous
his feast.—

DAUPHINE I know it, lady.

MISTRESS OTTER And mine together. But it is for his honour, and   80
therefore I take no name of it, more than of the place.°

DAUPHINE You are a bounteous kinswoman.

MISTRESS OTTER Your servant, sir.

[*Exit Mistress Otter*]

3.3

Clerimont [*and*] *Daw* [*come forward*]

CLERIMONT Why, do not you know it, Sir John Daw?

DAW No, I am a rook if I do.

CLERIMONT I'll tell you then, she's married by this time! And
whereas you were put i' the head that she was gone with Sir
Dauphine, I assure you Sir Dauphine has been the noblest,   5
honestest friend to you that ever gentleman of your quality could

boast of. He has discovered the whole plot, and made your mistress
so acknowledging and indeed so ashamed of her injury to you that
she desires you to forgive her and but grace her wedding with your
presence today—she is to be married to a very good fortune, she   10
says, his uncle, old Morose; and she willed me in private to tell
you that she shall be able to do you more favours, and with more
security now, than before.

DAW Did she say so, i' faith?

CLERIMONT Why, what do you think of me, Sir John? Ask Sir   15
Dauphine.

DAW Nay, I believe you. Good Sir Dauphine, did she desire me to
forgive her?

DAUPHINE I assure you, Sir John, she did.

DAW Nay then, I do with all my heart, and I'll be jovial.   20

CLERIMONT Yes, for look you, sir, this was the injury to you. La
Foole intended this feast to honour her bridal day, and made you
the property to invite the college ladies and promise to bring her;
and then at the time she should have appeared (as his friend) to
have given you the dor.° Whereas now, Sir Dauphine has brought   25
her to a feeling of it, with this kind of satisfaction, that you shall
bring all the ladies to the place where she is, and be very jovial;
and there she will have a dinner which shall be in your name, and
so disappoint La Foole, to make you good again and (as it were) a
saver i' the man.°   30

DAW As I am a knight, I honour her and forgive her heartily.

CLERIMONT About it then presently. Truewit is gone before to
confront the coaches and to acquaint you with so much if he meet
you. Join with him and 'tis well.

     [*Enter La Foole*]

See, here comes your antagonist, but take you no notice, but be   35
very jovial.

LA FOOLE Are the ladies come, Sir John Daw, and your mistress?
Sir Dauphine! You are exceeding welcome, and honest Master
Clerimont. Where's my cousin? Did you see no collegiates,
gentlemen?   40

     [*Exit Daw*]

DAUPHINE Collegiates! Do you not hear, Sir Amorous, how you are
abused?

LA FOOLE How, sir?

CLERIMONT Will you speak so kindly to Sir John Daw, that has done
you such an affront?   45

LA FOOLE Wherein, gentlemen? Let me be a suitor to you to know, I beseech you!

CLERIMONT Why, sir, his mistress is married today to Sir Dauphine's uncle, your cousin's neighbour, and he has diverted all the ladies and all your company thither, to frustrate your provision and stick a disgrace upon you. He was here now to have enticed us away from you too, but we told him his own,° I think.   50

LA FOOLE Has Sir John Daw wronged me so inhumanly?

DAUPHINE He has done it, Sir Amorous, most maliciously and treacherously; but if you'll be ruled by us, you shall quit him i'faith.   55

LA FOOLE Good gentlemen! I'll make one,° believe it. How, I pray?

DAUPHINE Marry, sir, get me your pheasants and your godwits and your best meat, and dish it in silver dishes of your cousin's presently, and say nothing, but clap me a clean towel about you, like a sewer, and bare-headed° march afore it with a good confidence—'tis but over the way, hard by—and we'll second you, where you shall set it o' the board, and bid 'em welcome to't, which shall show 'tis yours and disgrace his preparation utterly; and for your cousin, whereas she should be troubled here at home with care of making and giving welcome, she shall transfer all that labour thither and be a principal guest herself, sit ranked with the college-honours, and be honoured and have her health drunk as often, as bare,° and as loud as the best of 'em.   60   65

LA FOOLE I'll go tell her presently. It shall be done, that's resolved.   70
     [Exit La Foole]

CLERIMONT I thought he would not hear it out, but 'twould take him.

DAUPHINE Well, there be guests and meat now; how shall we do for music?

CLERIMONT The smell of the venison going through the street will invite one noise of fiddlers or other.   75

DAUPHINE I would it would call the trumpeters thither.

CLERIMONT Faith, there is hope; they have intelligence of all feasts. There's good correspondence betwixt them and the London cooks. 'Tis twenty to one but we have 'em.

DAUPHINE 'Twill be a most solemn day for my uncle, and an excellent fit of mirth for us.   80

CLERIMONT Aye, if we can hold up the emulation betwixt Foole and Daw, and never bring them to expostulate.

DAUPHINE Tut, flatter 'em both (as Truewit says) and you may take their understandings in a purse-net. They'll believe them-   85

selves to be just such men as we make 'em, neither more nor
less. They have nothing, not the use of their senses, but by
tradition.°

CLERIMONT See! Sir Amorous has his towel on already. Have you
persuaded your cousin?   90
    La Foole enters like a sewer

LA FOOLE Yes, 'tis very feasible; she'll do anything she says, rather
than the La Fooles shall be disgraced.

DAUPHINE She is a noble kinswoman. It will be such a pestling
device, Sir Amorous! It will pound all your enemy's practices to
powder and blow him up with his own mine, his own train.   95

LA FOOLE Nay, we'll give fire, I warrant you.

CLERIMONT But you must carry it privately, without any noise, and
take no notice by any means—
    [*Enter Otter*]

OTTER Gentlemen, my Princess says you shall have all her silver
dishes, *festinate*° and she's gone to alter her tire a little, and go with   100
you—

CLERIMONT And yourself too, Captain Otter.

DAUPHINE By any means, sir.

OTTER Yes, sir, I do mean it; but I would entreat my cousin Sir
Amorous, and you gentlemen, to be suitors to my princess, that I   105
may carry my bull and my bear, as well as my horse.

CLERIMONT That you shall do, Captain Otter.

LA FOOLE My cousin will never consent, gentlemen.

DAUPHINE She must consent, Sir Amorous, to reason.

LA FOOLE Why, she says they are no *decorum* among ladies.   110

OTTER But they are *decora*,° and that's better, sir.

CLERIMONT 'Aye, she must hear argument. Did not Pasiphaë,° who
was a queen, love a bull? And was not Callisto,° the mother of
Arcas, turned into a bear, and made a star, Mistress Ursula,° i' the
heavens?   115

OTTER O God, that I could ha' said as much! I will have these stories
painted i' the Bear Garden, *ex Ovidii Metamorphosi.*°

DAUPHINE Where is your princess, Captain? Pray be our leader.

OTTER That I shall, sir.

CLERIMONT Make haste, good Sir Amorous.   120
    [*Exeunt*]

3.4

[Enter] Morose, Epicene, Parson [and] Cutbeard

MOROSE *[to Parson]* Sir, there's an angel for yourself, and a brace of angels for your cold. Muse not at this manage of my bounty. It is fit we should thank fortune, double to nature, for any benefit she confers upon us; besides, it is your imperfection, but my solace.   5

PARSON *(the parson speaks, as having a cold)*° I thank your worship, so is it mine, now.

MOROSE What says he, Cutbeard?

CUTBEARD He says, *praesto*, sir, whensoever your worship needs him, he can be ready with the like. He got this cold with sitting   10
up late and singing catches with cloth-workers.°

MOROSE No more. I thank him.

PARSON God keep your worship and give you much joy with your fair spouse. *(He coughs)* Umh, umh.

MOROSE O, o, stay, Cutbeard! Let him give me five shillings of my   15
money back. As it is bounty to reward benefits, so is it equity to mulct injuries. I will have it. What says he?

CUTBEARD He cannot change it, sir.

MOROSE It must be changed.

CUTBEARD *[aside to Parson]* Cough again.   20

MOROSE What says he?

CUTBEARD He will cough out the rest, sir.

PARSON *(again)* Umh, umh, umh.

MOROSE Away, away with him, stop his mouth, away, I forgive it.—
[Exit Cutbeard, forcing Parson offstage]

EPICENE Fie, Master Morose, that you will use this violence to a man   25
of the church.

MOROSE How!

EPICENE It does not become your gravity or breeding—as you pretend in court—to have offered this outrage on a waterman or any more boisterous creature, much less on a man of his civil coat.°   30

MOROSE You can speak then!

EPICENE Yes, sir.

MOROSE Speak out, I mean.

EPICENE Aye, sir. Why, did you think you had married a statue? Or a motion only? One of the French puppets with the eyes turned   35
with a wire? Or some innocent out of the Hospital° that would

stand with her hands thus,° and a plaice mouth,° and look upon
you?

MOROSE O immodesty! A manifest woman! What, Cutbeard?

EPICENE Nay, never quarrel with Cutbeard, sir it is too late now. I   40
confess, it doth bate somewhat of the modesty I had when I writ
simply maid; but I hope I shall make it a stock still competent° to
the estate and dignity of your wife.

MOROSE She can talk!

EPICENE Yes indeed, sir.   45

MOROSE What, sirrah. None of my knaves, there?

[Enter Mute]

Where is this impostor, Cutbeard?

[Mute makes signs]

EPICENE Speak to him, fellow, speak to him. I'll have none of this
coacted, unnatural dumbness in my house, in a family where I
govern.   50

[Exit Mute]

MOROSE She is my regent already! I have married a Penthesilea,° a
Semiramis,° sold my liberty to a distaff!°

3.5

[Enter] Truewit

TRUEWIT Where's Master Morose?

MOROSE Is he come again? Lord have mercy upon me.

TRUEWIT I wish you all joy, Mistress Epicene, with your grave and
honourable match.

[Kisses her]

EPICENE I return you the thanks, Master Truewit, so friendly a wish   5
deserves.

[Kisses him]

MOROSE She has acquaintance too!

TRUEWIT God save you, sir, and give you all contentment in your
fair choice here. Before I was the bird of night to you, the owl,°
but now I am the messenger of peace, a dove, and bring you the   10
glad wishes of many friends, to the celebration of this good hour.

MOROSE What hour, sir?

TRUEWIT Your marriage hour, sir. I commend your resolution, that
(notwithstanding all the dangers I laid afore you in the voice of a

night-crow°) would yet go on and be yourself. It shows you are a   15
man constant to your own ends, and upright to your purposes, that
would not be put off with left-handed° cries.

MOROSE How should you arrive at the knowledge of so much?

TRUEWIT Why, did you ever hope, sir, committing the secrecy of it
to a barber, that less than the whole town should know it? You   20
might as well ha' told it the conduit or the bakehouse° or the
infantry that follow the court,° and with more security. Could your
gravity forget so old and noted a remnant as *lippis et tonsoribus
notum*?° Well, sir, forgive it yourself now, the fault, and be
communicable with your friends. Here will be three or four   25
fashionable ladies from the college to visit you presently, and their
train of minions and followers.

MOROSE Bar my doors! Bar my doors! Where are all my eaters, my
mouths now?

    [Enter servants]

Bar up my doors, you varlets.   30

EPICENE He is a varlet that stirs to such an office. Let 'em stand
open. I would see him that dares move his eyes toward it. Shall I
have a barricado made against my friends, to be barred of any
pleasure they can bring in to me with honourable visitation?

MOROSE O Amazonian impudence!   35

TRUEWIT Nay faith, in this, sir, she speaks but reason, and methinks
is more continent than you. Would you go to bed so presently, sir,
afore noon? A man of your head and hair should owe more to that
reverend ceremony, and not mount the marriage-bed like a town
bull,° or a mountain goat,° but stay the due season and ascend it   40
then with religion and fear. Those delights are to be steeped in
the humour and silence of the night; and give the day to other
open pleasures and jollities of feast, of music, of revels, of
discourse: we'll have all, sir, that may make your Hymen high and
happy.   45

MOROSE O, my torment, my torment!

TRUEWIT Nay, if you endure the first half hour, sir, so tediously, and
with this irksomeness; what comfort or hope can this fair gentlewoman make to herself° hereafter, in the consideration of so many
years as are to come—   50

MOROSE Of my affliction. Good sir, depart and let her do it alone.

TRUEWIT I have done, sir.

MOROSE That cursed barber!

TRUEWIT Yes faith, a cursed wretch indeed, sir.

MOROSE I have married his cittern,° that's common to all men. Some   55
plague, above the plague—

TRUEWIT All Egypt's ten plagues.°

MOROSE Revenge me on him.

TRUEWIT 'Tis very well, sir. If you laid on a curse or two more, I'll
assure you he'll bear 'em. As, that he may get the pox with seeking   60
to cure it, sir? Or that while he is curling another man's hair,° his
own may drop off? Or for burning some male bawd's lock, he may
have his brain beat out with the curling iron?

MOROSE No, let the wretch live wretched. May he get the itch, and
his shop so lousy as no man dare come at him, nor he come at no   65
man.

TRUEWIT Aye, and if he would swallow all his balls° for pills, let not
them purge him.

MOROSE Let his warming pan be ever cold.

TRUEWIT A perpetual frost underneath it, sir.   70

MOROSE Let him never hope to see fire again.

TRUEWIT But in hell, sir.

MOROSE His chairs be always empty, his scissors rust, and his combs
mould in their cases.

TRUEWIT Very dreadful that! And may he lose the invention, sir, of   75
carving lanterns in paper.°

MOROSE Let there be no bawd carted that year to employ a basin°
of his but let him be glad to eat his sponge for bread.

TRUEWIT And drink lotium° to it, and much good do him.

MOROSE Or for want of bread—   80

TRUEWIT Eat ear-wax, sir. I'll help you. Or draw his own teeth and
add them to the lute string.°

MOROSE No, beat the old ones to powder, and make bread of them.

TRUEWIT Yes, make meal o' the millstones.°

MOROSE May all the botches and burns that he has cured on others   85
break out upon him.

TRUEWIT And he now forget the cure of 'em in himself, sir; or if he
do remember it, let him ha' scraped all his linen into lint for 't,
and have not a rag left him to set up° with.

MOROSE Let him never set up again, but have the gout in his hands   90
forever. Now, no more, sir.

TRUEWIT O that last was too high set!° You might go less with him
i' faith, and be revenged enough; as, that he be never able to
new-paint his pole—

MOROSE Good sir, no more. I forgot myself.   95

TRUEWIT Or want credit to take up with a comb-maker—

MOROSE No more, sir.

TRUEWIT Or having broken his glass in a former despair, fall now into a much greater, of ever getting another—

MOROSE I beseech you, no more.   100

TRUEWIT Or that he never be trusted with trimming of any but chimney-sweepers—

MOROSE Sir—

TRUEWIT Or may he cut a collier's° throat with his razor, by chance-medley,° and yet hang for't.   105

MOROSE I will forgive him, rather than hear any more. I beseech you, sir.

3.6

[*Enter*] *Daw, Haughty, Centaure, Mavis* [*and*] *Trusty*

DAW This way, madam.

MOROSE O, the sea breaks in upon me! Another flood!° An inundation! I shall be o'erwhelmed with noise. It beats already at my shores. I feel an earthquake in myself for't.

DAW [*to Epicene*] 'Give you joy, mistress.   5

MOROSE Has she servants too!

DAW I have brought some ladies here to see and know you. (*She kisses them severally as he presents them*) My Lady Haughty, this my Lady Centaure, Mistress Dol Mavis, Mistress Trusty my Lady Haughty's woman. Where's your husband? Let's see him: can he   10
endure no noise? Let me come to him.

MOROSE What nomenclator is this?

TRUEWIT Sir John Daw, sir, your wife's servant, this.

MOROSE A Daw, and her servant! O, 'tis decreed, 'tis decreed of me,° an she have such servants.   15

[*Morose starts to leave*]

TRUEWIT Nay, sir, you must kiss the ladies, you must not go away now; they come toward you to seek you out.

HAUGHTY I' faith, Master Morose, would you steal a marriage° thus, in the midst of so many friends, and not acquaint us? Well, I'll kiss you, notwithstanding the justice of my quarrel; you shall give me   20
leave, mistress, to use a becoming familiarity with your husband.

[*Kisses him*]

EPICENE Your ladyship does me an honour in it, to let me know he

is so worthy your favour; as you have done both him and me grace
to visit so unprepared a pair to entertain you.

MOROSE Compliment! Compliment!   25

EPICENE But I must lay the burden of that upon my servant here.

HAUGHTY It shall not need, Mistress Morose, we will all bear° rather
than one shall be oppressed.°

MOROSE I know it, and you will teach her the faculty, if she be to
learn it.°   30
          [*Walks aside*]

HAUGHTY Is this the silent woman?

CENTAURE Nay, she has found her tongue since she was married,
Master Truewit says.

HAUGHTY O, Master Truewit! 'Save you. What kind of creature is
your bride here? She speaks, methinks!   35

TRUEWIT Yes, madam, believe it, she is a gentlewoman of very
absolute behaviour and of a good race.

HAUGHTY And Jack Daw told us she could not speak.

TRUEWIT So it was carried in plot, madam, to put her upon this old
fellow, by Sir Dauphine, his nephew, and one or two more of us;   40
but she is a woman of an excellent assurance, and an extraordinary
happy wit and tongue. You shall see her make rare sport with Daw
ere night.

HAUGHTY And he brought us to laugh at her!

TRUEWIT That falls out often, madam, that he that thinks himself   45
the master-wit is the master-fool. I assure your ladyship, ye cannot
laugh at her.

HAUGHTY No, we'll have her to the college; an she have wit, she
shall be one of us! Shall she not, Centaure? We'll make her a
collegiate.   50

CENTAURE Yes, faith, madam, and Mavis and she will set up a side.°

TRUEWIT Believe it, madam, and Mistress Mavis, she will sustain her
part.

MAVIS I'll tell you that when I have talked with her and tried her.

HAUGHTY Use her very civilly, Mavis.   55

MAVIS So I will, madam.
          [*Walks aside with Epicene*]

MOROSE Blessed minute, that they would whisper thus ever.

TRUEWIT In the meantime, madam, would but your ladyship help to
vex him a little: you know his disease, talk to him about the
wedding ceremonies or call for your gloves or—   60

HAUGHTY Let me alone.° Centaure, help me. Master bridegroom,
where are you?

MOROSE O, it was too miraculously good to last!

HAUGHTY We see no ensigns of a wedding here, no character of a
bride-ale: where be our scarfs and our gloves?° I pray you, give   65
'em us. Let's know your bride's colours° and yours at least.

CENTAURE Alas, madam, he has provided none.

MOROSE Had I known your ladyship's painter, I would.

HAUGHTY He has given it you, Centaure, i'faith. But do you hear,
Master Morose, a jest will not absolve you in this manner. You   70
that have sucked the milk of the court, and from thence have been
brought up to the very strong meats° and wine of it, been a
courtier from the biggin to the night-cap (as we may say), and you
to offend in such a high point of ceremony as this, and let your
nuptials want all marks of solemnity! How much plate have you   75
lost today—if you had but regarded your profit—what gifts, what
friends, through your mere rusticity?°

MOROSE Madam—

HAUGHTY Pardon me, sir, I must insinuate your errors to you.
No gloves? No garters?° No scarfs? No epithalamium? No   80
masque?

DAW Yes, madam, I'll make an epithalamium, I promised my
mistress, I have begun it already: will your ladyship hear it?

HAUGHTY Aye, good Jack Daw.

MOROSE [to Madam Haughty] Will it please your ladyship command   85
a chamber and be private with your friend?° You shall have your
choice of rooms to retire to after: my whole house is yours. I know
it° hath been your ladyship's errand into the city at other times,
however now you have been unhappily diverted upon me: but I
shall be loath to break any honourable custom of your ladyship's.   90
And therefore, good madam—

EPICENE Come, you are a rude bridegroom to entertain ladies of
honour in this fashion.

CENTAURE He is a rude groom,° indeed.

TRUEWIT By that light, you deserve to be grafted° and have your   95
horns reach from one side of the island to the other. [Aside, to
Morose] Do not mistake me, sir; I but speak this to give the ladies
some heart again, not for any malice to you.

MOROSE Is this your bravo, ladies?

TRUEWIT As God help me, if you utter such another word, I'll take   100
mistress bride in and begin to you in a very sad cup,° do you see?
Go to, know your friends and such as love you.

3.7

[Enter] Clerimont [and musicians]

CLERIMONT By your leave, ladies. Do you want any music? I have
brought you variety of noises. Play, sirs, all of you.

Music of all sorts

MOROSE O, a plot, a plot, a plot, a plot upon me! This day I shall
be their anvil to work on, they will grate me asunder. 'Tis worse
than the noise of a saw.   5

CLERIMONT No, they are hair, rosin and guts.° I can give you the
receipt.

TRUEWIT Peace, boys.

CLERIMONT Play, I say.

TRUEWIT Peace, rascals. [*To Morose*] You see who's your friend now,   10
sir? Take courage, put on a martyr's resolution. Mock down all
their attemptings with patience. 'Tis but a day, and I would suffer
heroically. Should an ass° exceed me in fortitude? No. You betray
your infirmity with your hanging dull ears,° and make them insult:
bear up bravely and constantly. Look you here, sir, what honour   15
is done you unexpected by your nephew; a wedding dinner come,
and a knight-sewer before it, for the more reputation°

*La Foole passes over sewing the meat [with Mistress Otter and
servants°]*

and fine Mistress Otter, your neighbour, in the rump or tail of it.

MOROSE Is that Gorgon, that Medusa come? Hide me, hide me!

TRUEWIT I warrant you, sir, she will not transform you. Look upon   20
her with a good courage. Pray you entertain her and conduct your
guests in. No? Mistress bride, will you entreat in the ladies? Your
bridegroom is so shamefaced, here—

EPICENE Will it please your ladyship, madam?

HAUGHTY With the benefit of your company, mistress.   25

EPICENE Servant, pray you perform your duties.

DAW And glad to be commanded, mistress.

CENTAURE How like you her wit, Mavis?

MAVIS Very prettily, absolutely well.

MISTRESS OTTER [*trying to take precedence*] 'Tis my place.   30

MAVIS You shall pardon me, Mistress Otter.

MISTRESS OTTER Why I am a collegiate.

MAVIS But not in ordinary.°

MISTRESS OTTER But I am.

MAVIS We'll dispute that within.   35
         [Exeunt Daw, Ladies]
CLERIMONT Would this had lasted a little longer.
TRUEWIT And that they had sent for the heralds.°
         [Enter Otter]
    Captain Otter, what news?
OTTER I have brought my bull, bear and horse, in private, and
    yonder are the trumpeters without, and the drum, gentlemen.   40
MOROSE O, o, o!
         The drum and trumpets sound
OTTER And we will have a rouse in each of 'em anon, for bold
    Britons, i'faith.
         [They sound again]
MOROSE O, o, o!
         [Exit Morose]
ALL Follow, follow, follow   45
         [Exeunt]

4.1

[Enter] Truewit *[and]* Clerimont

TRUEWIT Was there ever poor bridegroom so tormented? Or man indeed?

CLERIMONT I have not read of the like in the chronicles of the land.

TRUEWIT Sure, he cannot but go to a place of rest after all this purgatory. 5

CLERIMONT He may presume it, I think.

TRUEWIT The spitting, the coughing, the laughter, the neezing, the farting, dancing, noise of the music, and her masculine and loud commanding and urging the whole family, makes him think he has married a Fury. 10

CLERIMONT And she carries it up bravely.

TRUEWIT Aye, she takes any occasion to speak: that's the height on't.

CLERIMONT And how soberly Dauphine labours to satisfy him that it was none of his plot!

TRUEWIT And has almost brought him to the faith, i' the article.° 15
Here he comes.

[Enter Dauphine]

Where is he now? What's become of him, Dauphine?

DAUPHINE O, hold me up a little, I shall go away i' the jest° else. He has got on his whole nest of nightcaps,° and locked himself up i' the top o' the house, as high as ever he can climb from the noise. 20
I peeped in at a cranny and saw him sitting over a cross-beam o' the roof, like him o' the saddler's horse° in Fleet Street, upright; and he will sleep there.

CLERIMONT But where are your collegiates?

DAUPHINE Withdrawn with the bride in private. 25

TRUEWIT O, they are instructing her i' the college grammar. If she have grace with them, she knows all their secrets instantly.

CLERIMONT Methinks the Lady Haughty looks well today, for all my dispraise of her i' the morning. I think I shall come about to thee° again, Truewit. 30

TRUEWIT Believe it, I told you right. Women ought to repair the losses time and years have made i' their features, with dressings. And an intelligent woman, if she know by herself the least defect, will be most curious to hide it; and it becomes her. If she be short,

167

let her sit much, lest when she stands she be thought to sit. If she   35
have an ill foot, let her wear her gown the longer and her shoe the
thinner. If a fat hand and scald nails, let her carve the less, and
act° in gloves. If a sour breath, let her never discourse fasting,
and always talk at her distance. If she have black and rugged teeth,
let her offer the less at laughter, especially if she laugh wide and   40
open.

CLERIMONT O, you shall have some women, when they laugh, you
would think they brayed, it is so rude, and—

TRUEWIT Aye, and others that will stalk i' their gait like an ostrich,
and take huge strides. I cannot endure such a sight. I love measure   45
i' the feet and number i' the voice:° they are gentlenesses that
oft-times draw no less than the face.

DAUPHINE How cam'st thou to study these creatures so exactly? I
would thou wouldst make me a proficient.

TRUEWIT Yes, but you must leave to live i' your chamber then a   50
month together upon *Amadis de Gaule*° or *Don Quixote*,° as you are
wont; and come abroad where the matter is frequent, to court, to
tiltings, public shows and feasts, to plays, and church sometimes:
thither they come to show their new tires too, to see and to be
seen. In these places a man shall find whom to love, whom to play   55
with, whom to touch once, whom to hold ever. The variety arrests
his judgement. A wench to please a man comes not down dropping
from the ceiling, as he lies on his back droning° a tobacco pipe.
He must go where she is.

DAUPHINE Yes, and be never the near.°   60

TRUEWIT Out, heretic! That diffidence makes thee worthy it should
be so.

CLERIMONT He says true to you, Dauphine.

DAUPHINE Why?

TRUEWIT A man should not doubt to° overcome any woman. Think   65
he can vanquish 'em, and he shall; for though they deny, their
desire is to be tempted. Penelope° herself cannot hold out long.
Ostend,° you saw, was taken at last. You must persevere and hold
to your purpose. They would solicit us, but that they are afraid.
Howsoever, they wish in their hearts we should solicit them. Praise   70
'em, flatter 'em, you shall never want eloquence or trust; even the
chastest delight to feel themselves that way rubbed. With praises
you must mix kisses too. If they take them, they'll take more.
Though they strive, they would be overcome.

CLERIMONT O, but a man must beware of force.   75

TRUEWIT It is to them an acceptable violence, and has oft-times the
place of the greatest courtesy. She that might have been forced,
and you let her go free without touching, though she then seem to
thank you, will ever hate you after; and glad i' the face, is assuredly
sad at the heart.   80

CLERIMONT But all women are not to be taken all ways.

TRUEWIT 'Tis true. No more than all birds or all fishes. If you appear
learned to an ignorant wench, or jocund to a sad, or witty to a
foolish, why she presently begins to mistrust herself. You must
approach them i' their own height, their own line;° for the contrary   85
makes many that fear to commit themselves to noble and worthy
fellows run into the embraces of a rascal. If she love wit, give
verses, though you borrow 'em of a friend, or buy 'em, to have
good. If valour, talk of your sword and be frequent in the mention
of quarrels, though you be staunch in fighting. If activity, be seen   90
o' your barbary often, or leaping over stools for the credit of your
back.° If she love good clothes or dressing, have your learned
counsel about you every morning, your French tailor, barber,
linener, *et cetera*. Let your powder, your glass and your comb be
your dearest acquaintance. Take more care for the ornament of   95
your head than the safety,° and wish the commonwealth rather
troubled than a hair about you. That will take her. Then if she be
covetous and craving, do you promise anything, and perform
sparingly; so shall you keep her in appetite still. Seem as you
would give, but be like a barren field that yields little, or unlucky   100
dice to foolish and hoping gamesters. Let your gifts be slight and
dainty rather than precious. Let cunning be above cost. Give
cherries at time of year, or apricots; and say they were sent you
out o' the country, though you bought 'em in Cheapside. Admire
her tires; like her in all fashions; compare her in every habit to   105
some deity; invent excellent dreams to flatter her, and riddles; or,
if she be a great one, perform always the second parts° to her: like
what she likes, praise whom she praises, and fail not to make the
household and servants yours, yea the whole family, and salute 'em
by their names—'tis but light cost if you can purchase 'em so and   110
make her physician your pensioner, and her chief woman. Nor will
it be out of your gain to make love to hɛr° too, so she follow, not
usher, her lady's pleasure. All blabbing is taken away when she
comes to be a part of the crime.

DAUPHINE On what courtly lap hast thou late slept, to come forth   115
so sudden and absolute a courtling?

TRUEWIT Good faith, I should rather question you, that are so hearkening after these mysteries. I begin to suspect your diligence, Dauphine. Speak, art thou in love in earnest?

DAUPHINE Yes, by my troth am I; 'twere ill dissembling before thee.   120

TRUEWIT With which of 'em, I pray thee?

DAUPHINE With all the collegiates.

CLERIMONT Out on thee. We'll keep you at home, believe it, i' the stable, an you be such a stallion.

TRUEWIT No. I like him well. Men should love wisely, and all   125
women: someone for the face, and let her please the eye; another for the skin, and let her please the touch; a third for the voice, and let her please the ear; and where the objects mix, let the senses so too. Thou wouldst think it strange if I should make 'em all in love with thee afore night!   130

DAUPHINE I would say thou hadst the best philtre i' the world, and couldst do more than Madam Medea,° or Doctor Forman.°

TRUEWIT If I do not, let me play the mountebank for my meat while I live, and the bawd for my drink.

DAUPHINE So be it, I say.   135

4.2

[Enter] Otter [carrying his cups], Daw [and] La Foole

OTTER O lord, gentlemen, how my knights and I have missed you here!

CLERIMONT Why, Captain, what service? What service?

OTTER To see me bring up my bull, bear, and horse to fight.

DAW Yes faith, the captain says we shall be his dogs to bait 'em.   5

DAUPHINE A good employment.

TRUEWIT Come on, let's see a course° then.

LA FOOLE I am afraid my cousin will be offended if she come.

OTTER Be afraid of nothing. Gentlemen, I have placed the drum and the trumpets, and one to give 'em the sign when you are ready.   10
[Brings out cups] Here's my bull for myself, and my bear for Sir John Daw, and my horse for Sir Amorous. Pray set your foot to mine, and yours to his,° and—

LA FOOLE Pray God my cousin come not.

OTTER St George and St Andrew, fear no cousins. Come, sound,   15
sound. *Et rauco strepuerunt cornua cantu.*°

[Drums and trumpets sound; they drink]

TRUEWIT Well said,° Captain, i'faith well fought at the bull.

CLERIMONT Well held at the bear.

TRUEWIT Loo, loo, captain.

DAUPHINE O, the horse has kicked off his dog already.   20

LA FOOLE I cannot drink it, as I am a knight.

TRUEWIT Gods so, off with his spurs,° somebody.

LA FOOLE It goes again my conscience. My cousin will be angry with
it.

DAW I ha' done mine.   25

TRUEWIT You fought high and fair, Sir John.

CLERIMONT At the head.

DAUPHINE Like an excellent bear-dog.

CLERIMONT *[aside to Daw]* You take no notice of the business, I
hope.   30

DAW *[aside to Clerimont]* Not a word, sir, you see we are jovial.

OTTER Sir Amorous, you must not equivocate. It must be pulled
down, for all my cousin.

CLERIMONT *[aside to La Foole]* 'Sfoot, if you take not your drink,
they'll think you are discontented with something: you'll betray all,   35
if you take the least notice.

LA FOOLE *[aside to Clerimont]* Not I, I'll both drink and talk then.

OTTER You must pull the horse on his knees, Sir Amorous: fear no
cousins. *Iacta est alea.*°

TRUEWIT *[aside to Dauphine and Clerimont]* O, now he's in his vein,   40
and bold. The least hint given him of his wife now will make him
rail desperately.

CLERIMONT Speak to him of her.

TRUEWIT Do you, and I'll fetch her to the hearing of it.

[Exit Truewit]

DAUPHINE Captain he-Otter, your she-Otter is coming, your wife.   45

OTTER Wife! Buzz. *Titivilitium.* There's no such thing in nature. I
confess, gentlemen, I have a cook, a laundress, a house-drudge,
that serves my necessary turns, and goes under that title. But he's
an ass that will be so uxorious to tie his affections to one circle.°
Come, the name dulls appetite. Here, replenish again: another   50
bout. Wives are nasty sluttish animals.

[Fills the cups]

DAUPHINE O, captain.

OTTER As ever the earth bare, *tribus verbis.*° Where's Master Truewit?

DAW He's slipped aside, sir.

CLERIMONT But you must drink and be jovial.   55
DAW Yes, give it me.
LA FOOLE And me too.
DAW Let's be jovial.
LA FOOLE As jovial as you will.
OTTER Agreed. Now you shall ha' the bear, cousin, and Sir John   60
   Daw the horse, and I'll ha' the bull still. Sound Tritons° o' the
   Thames. *Nunc est bibendum, nunc pede libero°*—
        (*Morose speaks from above,° the trumpets sounding*)
MOROSE Villains, murderers, sons of the earth,° and traitors, what
   do you there?
CLERIMONT O, now the trumpets have waked him, we shall have his   65
   company.
OTTER A wife is a scurvy clogdogdo;° an unlucky thing, a very
   foresaid bear-whelp, without any good fashion or breeding: *mala
   bestia.°*
        His wife is brought out [by Truewit] to hear him [unobserved]
DAUPHINE Why did you marry one then, Captain?   70
OTTER A pox—I married with six thousand pound, I. I was in love
   with that. I ha' not kissed my Fury these forty weeks.
CLERIMONT The more to blame you, captain.
TRUEWIT Nay, Mistress Otter, hear him a little first.
OTTER She has a breath worse than my grandmother's, *profecto.*   75
MISTRESS OTTER O treacherous liar. Kiss me, sweet Master Truewit,
   and prove him a slandering knave.
TRUEWIT I'll rather believe you, lady.
OTTER And she has a peruke that's like a pound of hemp made up
   in shoe-threads.   80
MISTRESS OTTER O viper,° mandrake!°
OTTER A most vile face! And yet she spends me forty pound a year
   in mercury and hogs'-bones.° All her teeth were made i' the
   Blackfriars, both her eyebrows i' the Strand, and her hair in Silver
   Street. Every part o' the town owns a piece of her.   85
MISTRESS OTTER I cannot hold.
OTTER She takes herself asunder still when she goes to bed, into
   some twenty boxes, and about next day noon is put together again,
   like a great German clock;° and so comes forth and rings a tedious
   larum to the whole house, and then is quiet again for an hour, but   90
   for her quarters.° Ha' you done me right,° gentlemen?
MISTRESS OTTER No, sir, I'll do you right with my quarters, with
   my quarters.
        (*She falls upon him and beats him*)

OTTER O, hold, good princess.

TRUEWIT Sound, sound.   95

    [Drum and trumpets sound]

CLERIMONT A battle, a battle!

MISTRESS OTTER You notorious stinkardly bear-ward, does my
    breath smell?

OTTER Under correction, dear princess. Look to my bear, and my
    horse, gentlemen.   100

MISTRESS OTTER Do I want teeth and eyebrows, thou bulldog?

TRUEWIT Sound, sound still.

    [They sound again]

OTTER No, I protest, under correction—

MISTRESS OTTER Aye, now you are under correction, you protest:
    but you did not protest before correction, sir. Thou Judas, to offer   105
    to betray thy princess! I'll make thee an example—

    Morose descends° with a long sword

MOROSE I will have no such examples in my house, Lady Otter.

MISTRESS OTTER Ah—

MOROSE Mistress Mary Ambree,° your examples are dangerous.
    Rogues, hellhounds, stentors,° out of my doors, you sons of noise   110
    and tumult, begot on an ill May Day,° or when the galley-foist° is
    afloat to Westminster! A trumpeter could not be conceived but
    then!

    [Exeunt Mistress Otter, Daw, La Foole, musicians]

DAUPHINE What ails you, sir?

MOROSE They have rent my roof, walls, and all my windows asunder   115
    with their brazen throats.

    [Exit Morose]

TRUEWIT Best follow him, Dauphine.

DAUPHINE So I will.

    [Exit Dauphine]

CLERIMONT Where's Daw and La Foole?

OTTER They are both run away, sir. Good gentlemen, help to pacify   120
    my princess, and speak to the great ladies for me. Now must I go
    lie with the bears this fortnight, and keep out o' the way till my
    peace be made, for this scandal she has taken. Did you not see my
    bullhead, gentlemen?

CLERIMONT Is 't not on, Captain?   125

TRUEWIT No, but he may make a new one, by that, is on.°

OTTER O, here 'tis. An you come over, gentlemen, and ask for Tom
    Otter, we'll go down to Ratcliffe° and have a course i'faith, for all
    these disasters. There's *bona spes*° left.

TRUEWIT Away, Captain, get off while you are well.   130
    [Exit Otter]
CLERIMONT I am glad we are rid of him.
TRUEWIT You had never been, unless we had put his wife upon him.
  His humour is as tedious at last as it was ridiculous at first.

4.3

[Enter] Haughty, Mistress Otter, Mavis, Daw, La Foole,
Centaure, Epicene. [Truewit and Clerimont move aside to
observe]

HAUGHTY We wondered why you shrieked so, Mistress Otter.
MISTRESS OTTER O God, madam, he came down with a huge long
  naked weapon in both his hands, and looked so dreadfully! Sure,
  he's beside himself.
MAVIS Why, what made you° there, Mistress Otter?   5
MISTRESS OTTER Alas, Mistress Mavis, I was chastising my subject,
  and thought nothing of him.
DAW Faith, mistress, you must do so too. Learn to chastise. Mistress
  Otter corrects her husband so, he dares not speak but under
  correction.   10
LA FOOLE And with his hat off to her: 'twould do you good to see.
HAUGHTY In sadness 'tis good and mature counsel: practise it,
  Morose. I'll call you Morose° still now, as I call Centaure and
  Mavis: we four will be all one.
CENTAURE And you'll come to the college and live with us?   15
HAUGHTY Make him give milk and honey.°
MAVIS Look how you manage him at first, you shall have him ever
  after.
CENTAURE Let him allow you your coach and four horses, your
  woman, your chambermaid, your page, your gentleman-usher,   20
  your French cook, and four grooms.
HAUGHTY And go with us to Bedlam, to the china houses, and to
  the Exchange.
CENTAURE It will open the gate to your fame.
HAUGHTY Here's Centaure has immortalized herself with taming of   25
  her wild male.
MAVIS Aye, she has done the miracle of the kingdom.
EPICENE But, ladies, do you count it lawful to have such plurality of
  servants, and do 'em all graces?

HAUGHTY Why not? Why should women deny their favours to men? 30
  Are they the poorer or the worse?

DAW Is the Thames the less for the dyers' water, mistress?

LA FOOLE Or a torch for lighting many torches?

TRUEWIT [aside] Well said, La Foole; what a new one° he has got!

CENTAURE They are empty losses women fear in this kind. 35

HAUGHTY Besides, ladies should be mindful of the approach of age,
  and let no time want his due use. The best of our days pass first.

MAVIS We are rivers that cannot be called back, madam: she that now
  excludes her lovers may live to lie a forsaken beldame in a frozen
  bed. 40

CENTAURE 'Tis true, Mavis; and who will wait on us to coach then?
  Or write or tell us the news then? Make anagrams of our names,
  and invite us to the Cockpit,° and kiss our hands all the playtime,
  and draw their weapons for our honours?

HAUGHTY Not one. 45

DAW Nay, my mistress is not altogether unintelligent of these things;
  here be in presence have tasted of her favours.

CLERIMONT [aside] What a neighing hobby-horse is this!

EPICENE But not with intent to boast 'em again, servant. And have
  you those excellent receipts, madam, to keep yourselves from 50
  bearing of children?

HAUGHTY O yes, Morose. How should we maintain our youth and
  beauty else? Many births of a woman make her old, as many crops
  make the earth barren.

4.4

[Enter] Morose [and] Dauphine; [they speak apart]

MOROSE O my cursed angel, that instructed me to this fate!

DAUPHINE Why, sir?

MOROSE That I should be seduced by so foolish a devil as a barber
  will make!

DAUPHINE I would I had been worthy, sir, to have partaken your 5
  counsel; you should never have trusted it to such a minister.

MOROSE Would I could redeem it with the loss of an eye, nephew,
  a hand, or any other member.

DAUPHINE Marry, God forbid, sir, that you should geld yourself to
  anger your wife. 10

MOROSE So it would rid me of her! And that I did supererogatory°
penance in a belfry, at Westminster Hall,° i' the Cockpit, at the
fall of a stag,° the Tower Wharf°—what place is there else?—
London Bridge,° Paris Garden, Billingsgate,° when the noises are
at their height and loudest. Nay, I would sit out a play that were   15
nothing but fights at sea, drum, trumpet, and target!

DAUPHINE I hope there shall be no such need, sir. Take patience,
good uncle. This is but a day, and 'tis well worn too now.

MOROSE O, 'twill be so forever, nephew, I foresee it, forever. Strife
and tumult are the dowry that comes with a wife.   20

TRUEWIT I told you so, sir, and you would not believe me.

MOROSE Alas, do not rub those wounds, Master Truewit, to blood
again; 'twas my negligence. Add not affliction to affliction. I have
perceived the effect of it, too late, in Madam Otter.

EPICENE [coming forward] How do you, sir?   25

MOROSE Did you ever hear a more unnecessary question? As if she
did not see! Why, I do as you see, empress, empress.

EPICENE You are not well, sir! You look very ill! Something has
distempered you.

MOROSE O horrible, monstrous impertinencies! Would not one of   30
these have served? Do you think, sir? Would not one of these have
served?

TRUEWIT Yes, sir, but these are but notes of female kindness,° sir:
certain tokens that she has a voice, sir.

MOROSE O, is't so? Come, an't be no otherwise—what say you?   35

EPICENE How do you feel yourself, sir?

MOROSE Again that!

TRUEWIT Nay, look you, sir: you would be friends with your wife
upon unconscionable terms, her silence—

EPICENE They say you are run mad, sir.   40

MOROSE Not for love, I assure you, of you; do you see?

EPICENE O lord, gentlemen! Lay hold on him for God's sake: what
shall I do? Who's his physician—can you tell—that knows the state
of his body best, that I might send for him? Good sir, speak. I'll
send for one of my doctors else.   45

MOROSE What, to poison me, that I might die intestate and leave you
possessed of all?

EPICENE Lord, how idly he talks, and how his eyes sparkle! He
looks green about the temples! Do you see what blue spots he
has?°   50

CLERIMONT Aye, it's melancholy.

EPICENE Gentlemen, for heaven's sake counsel me. Ladies! Servant,
you have read Pliny° and Paracelsus:° ne'er a word now to comfort
a poor gentlewoman? Aye me! What fortune had I to marry a
distracted man?   55

DAW I'll tell you, mistress—

TRUEWIT [aside] How rarely she holds it up!

MOROSE What mean you, gentlemen?

EPICENE What will you tell me, servant?

DAW The disease in Greek is called *mania*, in Latin, *insania, furor,*   60
vel ecstasis melancholica, that is, *egressio*, when a man *ex melancholico
evadit fanaticus*.°

MOROSE Shall I have a lecture read upon me alive?°

DAW But he may be but *phreneticus*, yet, mistress and *phrenetis* is only
delirium, or so—   65

EPICENE Aye, that is for the disease, servant; but what is this to the
cure? We are sure enough of the disease.

MOROSE Let me go.

TRUEWIT Why, we'll entreat her to hold her peace, sir.

MOROSE O, no. Labour not to stop her. She is like a conduit-pipe   70
that will gush out with more force when she opens again.

HAUGHTY I'll tell you, Morose, you must talk divinity to him
altogether, or moral philosophy.

LA FOOLE Aye, and there's an excellent book of moral philosophy,
madam, of Reynard the Fox and all the beasts, called *Doni's*   75
Philosophy.°

CENTAURE There is, indeed, Sir Amorous La Foole.

MOROSE O misery!

LA FOOLE I have read it, my Lady Centaure, all over to my cousin
here.   80

MISTRESS OTTER Aye, and 'tis a very good book as any is of the
moderns.

DAW Tut, he must have Seneca read to him, and Plutarch,° and the
ancients; the moderns are not for this disease.

CLERIMONT Why, you discommended them too, today, Sir John.   85

DAW Aye, in some cases; but in these they are best, and Aristotle's
Ethics.°

MAVIS Say you so, Sir John? I think you are deceived: you took it
upon trust.

HAUGHTY Where's Trusty, my woman? I'll end this difference. I   90
prithee, Otter, call her. Her father and mother were both mad
when they put her to me.

[Exit Mistress Otter]

MOROSE I think so. Nay, gentlemen, I am tame. This is but an exercise,° I know, a marriage ceremony, which I must endure.

HAUGHTY And one of 'em (I know not which) was cured with *The* 95 *Sick Man's Salve*;° and the other with *Greene's Groat's Worth of Wit*.°

TRUEWIT A very cheap cure, madam.

HAUGHTY Aye, it's very feasible.

[Enter Mistress Otter, Trusty]

MISTRESS OTTER My lady called for you, Mistress Trusty: you must 100 decide a controversy.

HAUGHTY O Trusty, which was it you said, your father or your mother, that was cured with *The Sick Man's Salve*?

TRUSTY My mother, madam, with the *Salve*.

TRUEWIT Then it was *The Sick Woman's Salve*. 105

TRUSTY And my father with the *Groat's Worth of Wit*. But there was other means used: we had a preacher that would preach folk asleep still; and so they were prescribed to go to church, by an old woman that was their physician, thrice a week—

EPICENE To sleep? 110

TRUSTY Yes forsooth: and every night they read themselves asleep on those books.

EPICENE Good faith, it stands with great reason. I would I knew where to procure those books.

MOROSE O! 115

LA FOOLE I can help you with one of 'em, Mistress Morose, the *Groat's Worth of Wit*.

EPICENE But I shall disfurnish you,° Sir Amorous: can you spare it?

LA FOOLE O, yes, for a week or so; I'll read it myself to him.

EPICENE No, I must do that, sir; that must be my office. 120

MOROSE O, o!

EPICENE Sure, he would do well enough if he could sleep.

MOROSE No, I should do well enough if you could sleep. Have I no friend that will make her drunk? Or give her a little laudanum? Or opium? 125

TRUEWIT Why, sir, she talks ten times worse in her sleep.

MOROSE How!

CLERIMONT Do you not know that, sir? Never ceases all night.

TRUEWIT And snores like a porpoise.

MOROSE O, redeem me, fate, redeem me, fate. For how many causes 130 may a man be divorced, nephew?

DAUPHINE I know not truly, sir.

TRUEWIT Some divine must resolve you in that, sir, or canon lawyer.°

MOROSE I will not rest, I will not think of any other hope or comfort 135
till I know.

    [*Exeunt Morose and Dauphine*]

CLERIMONT Alas, poor man.

TRUEWIT You'll make him mad indeed, ladies, if you pursue this.

HAUGHTY No, we'll let him breathe now a quarter of an hour or so.

CLERIMONT By my faith, a large truce. 140

HAUGHTY Is that his keeper, that is gone with him?

DAW It is his nephew, madam.

LA FOOLE Sir Dauphine Eugenie.

CENTAURE He looks like a very pitiful knight—

DAW As can be. This marriage has put him out of all. 145

LA FOOLE He has not a penny in his purse, madam—

DAW He is ready to cry all this day.

LA FOOLE A very shark, he set me i' the nick° t'other night at primero.

TRUEWIT [*aside*] How these swabbers talk!

CLERIMONT Aye, Otter's wine has swelled their humours above a 150
spring tide.

HAUGHTY Good Morose, let's go in again. I like your couches
exceeding well: we'll go lie and talk there.

EPICENE I wait on you, madam.

    [*Exeunt Mistress Otter, Haughty, Centaure, Mavis, Trusty, La
Foole, Daw*]

TRUEWIT 'Slight, I will have 'em as silent as signs, and their posts 155
too, ere I ha' done. Do you hear, lady bride? I pray thee now, as
thou art a noble wench, continue this discourse of Dauphine
within: but praise him exceedingly. Magnify him with all the
height of affection thou canst (I have some purpose in't) and but
beat off these two rooks, Jack Daw and his fellow, with any 160
discontentment hither, and I'll honour thee for ever.

EPICENE I was about it here. It angered me to the soul, to hear 'em
begin to talk so malapert.

TRUEWIT Pray thee perform it, and thou win'st me an idolater to
thee everlasting. 165

EPICENE Will you go in and hear me do it?

TRUEWIT No, I'll stay here. Drive 'em out of your company, 'tis all
I ask, which cannot be any way better done than by extolling
Dauphine, whom they have so slighted.

EPICENE I warrant you; you shall expect one of 'em presently.
    [*Exit Epicene*]

CLERIMONT What a cast of kestrels are these, to hawk after ladies
    thus?

TRUEWIT Aye, and strike at such an eagle as Dauphine.

CLERIMONT He will be mad when we tell him. Here he comes.   175

4.5

    [*Enter*] *Dauphine*

CLERIMONT O sir, you are welcome.

TRUEWIT Where's thine uncle?

DAUPHINE Run out o' door in's nightcaps to talk with a casuist about
    his divorce. It works admirably.

TRUEWIT Thou wouldst ha' said so and thou hadst been here! The   5
    ladies have laughed at thee most comically since thou went'st,
    Dauphine.

CLERIMONT And asked if thou wert thine uncle's keeper?°

TRUEWIT And the brace of baboons answered 'yes', and said thou
    wert a pitiful poor fellow and didst live upon posts,° and hadst   10
    nothing but three suits° of apparel and some few benevolences that
    lords ga' thee to fool to 'em and swagger.

DAUPHINE Let me not live, I'll beat 'em. I'll bind 'em both to grand
    madam's bed-posts and have 'em baited with monkeys.

TRUEWIT Thou shalt not need, they shall be beaten to thy hand,°   15
    Dauphine. I have an execution to serve upon 'em I warrant thee
    shall serve; trust my plot.

DAUPHINE Aye, you have many plots! So you had one to make all
    the wenches in love with me.

TRUEWIT Why, if I do not yet afore night, as near as 'tis, and that   20
    they do not every one invite thee and be ready to scratch for thee,
    take the mortgage of my wit.

CLERIMONT 'Fore God, I'll be his witness; thou shalt have it,
    Dauphine thou shalt be his fool for ever if thou dost not.

TRUEWIT Agreed. Perhaps 'twill be the better estate. Do you observe   25
    this gallery, or rather lobby, indeed? Here are a couple of studies,° at
    each end one: here will I act such a tragicomedy between the
    Guelphs and the Ghibellines,° Daw and La Foole—which of 'em
    comes out first, will I seize on. You two shall be the chorus behind

the arras, and whip out between the acts and speak. If I do not   30
make 'em keep the peace for this remnant of the day, if not of the
year, I have failed once—I hear Daw coming. Hide, and do not
laugh, for God's sake.

    [They hide. Enter Daw]

DAW Which is the way into the garden, trow?

TRUEWIT O, Jack Daw! I am glad I have met with you. In good faith,   35
    I must have this matter go no further between you. I must ha' it
    taken up.°

DAW What matter, sir? Between whom?

TRUEWIT Come, you disguise it—Sir Amorous and you. If you love
    me, Jack, you shall make use of your philosophy now, for this once,   40
    and deliver me your sword. This is not the wedding the centaurs
    were at,° though there be a she-one° here. The bride has entreated
    me I will see no blood shed at her bridal; you saw her whisper me
    erewhile.

    [Takes his sword]

DAW As I hope to finish Tacitus, I intend no murder.   45

TRUEWIT Do you not wait for Sir Amorous?

DAW Not I, by my knighthood.

TRUEWIT And your scholarship too?

DAW And my scholarship too.

TRUEWIT Go to, then I return you your sword and ask you   50
    mercy; but put it not up,° for you will be assaulted. I understood
    that you had apprehended it, and walked here to brave him,
    and that you had held your life contemptible in regard of your
    honour.

DAW No, no, no such thing I assure you. He and I parted now as   55
    good friends as could be.

TRUEWIT Trust not you to that visor. I saw him since dinner with
    another face: I have known many men in my time vexed with
    losses, with deaths and with abuses, but so offended a wight as Sir
    Amorous did I never see or read of. For taking away his guests,   60
    sir, today, that's the cause, and he declares it behind your back,
    with such threatenings and contempts—he said to Dauphine, you
    were the arrantest ass—

DAW Aye, he may say his pleasure.

TRUEWIT And swears you are so protested a coward that he knows   65
    you will never do him any manly or single right,° and therefore he
    will take his course.

DAW I'll give him any satisfaction, sir—but fighting.

TRUEWIT Aye, sir, but who knows what satisfaction he'll take? Blood
he thirsts for, and blood he will have: and whereabouts on you he   70
will have it, who knows but himself?

DAW I pray you, Master Truewit, be you a mediator.

TRUEWIT Well sir, conceal yourself then in this study till I return.
(*He puts him up*) Nay, you must be content to be locked in; for,
for mine own reputation I would not have you seen to receive a   75
public disgrace, while I have the matter in managing. Gods so,
here he comes: keep your breath close that he do not hear you sigh.
In good faith, Sir Amorous, he is not this way; I pray you be
merciful, do not murder him; he is a Christian as good as you; you
are armed as if you sought a revenge on all his race. Good   80
Dauphine, get him away from this place. I never knew a man's
choler so high, but he would speak to his friends, he would hear
reason. Jack Daw. Jack Daw! Asleep?

DAW [*within*] Is he gone, Master Truewit?

TRUEWIT Aye, did you hear him?   85

DAW O God, yes.

TRUEWIT [*aside*] What a quick ear fear has!

DAW But is he so armed, as you say?
      [*He comes out of the study*]

TRUEWIT Armed? Did you ever see a fellow set out to take possession?°   90

DAW Aye, sir.

TRUEWIT That may give you some light to conceive of him, but 'tis
nothing to the principal.° Some false brother° i' the house has
furnished him strangely. Or if it were out o' the house, it was Tom
Otter.   95

DAW Indeed, he's a captain, and his wife is his kinswoman.

TRUEWIT He has got somebody's old two-hand sword, to mow you
off at the knees. And that sword hath spawned such a dagger!—but
then he is so hung with pikes, halberds, petronels, calivers, and
muskets, that he looks like a justice of peace's hall:° a man of two   100
thousand a year is not 'sessed° at so many weapons as he has on.
There was never fencer challenged at so many several foils.° You
would think he meant to murder all St Pulchre's° parish. If he
could but victual himself for half a year in his breeches,° he is
sufficiently armed to overrun a country.   105

DAW Good lord, what means he, sir! I pray you, Master Truewit, be
you a mediator.

TRUEWIT Well, I'll try if he will be appeased with a leg or an arm;
if not, you must die once.

DAW I would be loath to lose my right arm, for writing madrigals.   110

TRUEWIT Why, if he will be satisfied with a thumb or a little finger,
all's one to me. You must think I'll do my best.

DAW Good sir, do.

> *He puts him up again, and then [Clerimont and Dauphine] come
> forth*

CLERIMONT What hast thou done?

TRUEWIT He will let me do nothing, man, he does all afore me; he   115
offers his left arm.

CLERIMONT His left wing, for a Jack Daw.

DAUPHINE Take it, by all means.

TRUEWIT How! Maim a man forever for a jest? What a conscience
hast thou?   120

DAUPHINE 'Tis no loss to him: he has no employment for his arms
but to eat spoon-meat. Beside, as good maim his body as his
reputation.

TRUEWIT He is a scholar and a wit, and yet he does not think so.
But he loses no reputation with us, for we all resolved him° an ass   125
before. To your places again.

CLERIMONT I pray thee let me be in at the other a little.

TRUEWIT Look, you'll spoil all: these be ever your tricks.

CLERIMONT No, but I could hit of some things that thou wilt miss,
and thou wilt say are good ones.   130

TRUEWIT I warrant you. I pray forbear, I'll leave it off else.

DAUPHINE Come away, Clerimont.

> *[They hide. Enter La Foole]*

TRUEWIT Sir Amorous!

LA FOOLE Master Truewit.

TRUEWIT Whither were you going?   135

LA FOOLE Down into the court to make water.

TRUEWIT By no means, sir, you shall rather tempt your breeches.°

LA FOOLE Why, sir?

TRUEWIT Enter here, if you love your life.

> *[He opens the door of the other study]*

LA FOOLE Why! Why!   140

TRUEWIT Question till your throat be cut, do; dally till the enraged
soul find you.

LA FOOLE Who's that?

TRUEWIT Daw it is; will you in?   145

LA FOOLE Aye, aye, I'll in; what's the matter?

TRUEWIT Nay, if he had been cool enough to tell us that, there had been some hope to atone you, but he seems so implacably enraged.

LA FOOLE 'Slight, let him rage. I'll hide myself.

TRUEWIT Do, good sir. But what have you done to him within that   150
should provoke him thus? You have broke some jest upon him afore the ladies—

LA FOOLE Not I, never in my life broke jest upon any man. The bride was praising Sir Dauphine, and he went away in snuff,° and I followed him, unless he took offence at me in his drink erewhile,   155
that I would not pledge all the horse full.

TRUEWIT By my faith, and that may be, you remember well; but he walks the round up and down,° through every room o' the house, with a towel in his hand, crying 'Where's La Foole? Who saw La Foole'? And when Dauphine and I demanded the cause, we can   160
force no answer from him, but 'o revenge, how sweet art thou! I will strangle him in this towel'—which leads us to conjecture that the main cause of his fury is for bringing your meat today, with a towel about you, to his discredit.

LA FOOLE Like enough. Why, an he be angry for that, I'll stay here   165
till his anger be blown over.

TRUEWIT A good becoming resolution, sir. If you can put it on° o' the sudden.

LA FOOLE Yes, I can put it on. Or I'll away into the country presently.   170

TRUEWIT How will you get out o' the house, sir? He knows you are i' the house, and he'll watch you this sennight but he'll have you. He'll outwait a sergeant for you.

LA FOOLE Why, then I'll stay here.

TRUEWIT You must think how to victual yourself in time then.   175

LA FOOLE Why, sweet Master Truewit, will you entreat my cousin Otter to send me a cold venison pasty, a bottle or two of wine, and a chamber pot?

TRUEWIT A stool were better, sir, of Sir A–jax° his invention.

LA FOOLE Aye, that will be better indeed; and a pallet to lie on.   180

TRUEWIT O, I would not advise you to sleep by any means.

LA FOOLE Would you not, sir? Why then I will not.

TRUEWIT Yet there's another fear—

LA FOOLE Is there, sir? What is't?

TRUEWIT No, he cannot break open this door with his foot, sure.   185

LA FOOLE I'll set my back against it, sir. I have a good back.

TRUEWIT But then if he should batter.

LA FOOLE Batter! If he dare, I'll have an action of battery against him.

TRUEWIT Cast you the worst. He has sent for powder already, and what he will do with it no man knows: perhaps blow up the corner o' the house, where he suspects you are. Here he comes! In, quickly!

He feigns as if one were present, to fright the other, who is run in to hide himself

I protest, Sir John Daw, he is not this way. What will you do? Before God, you shall hang no petard here. I'll die rather. Will you not take my word? I never knew one but would be satisfied. Sir Amorous, there's no standing out. He has made a petard of an old brass pot, to force your door. Think upon some satisfaction or terms to offer him.

LA FOOLE [*within*] Sir, I'll give him any satisfaction. I dare give any terms.

TRUEWIT You'll leave it to me then?

LA FOOLE Aye, sir. I'll stand to any conditions.

TRUEWIT (*he calls forth Clerimont and Dauphine*) How now, what think you, sirs? Were't not a difficult thing to determine which of these two feared most?

CLERIMONT Yes, but this fears the bravest: the other a whindling dastard, Jack Daw! But La Foole, a brave heroic coward! And is afraid in a great look and a stout accent. I like him rarely.

TRUEWIT Had it not been pity these two should ha' been concealed?

CLERIMONT Shall I make a motion?

TRUEWIT Briefly. For I must strike while 'tis hot.

CLERIMONT Shall I go fetch the ladies to the catastrophe?

TRUEWIT Umh? Aye, by my troth.

DAUPHINE By no mortal means. Let them continue in the state of ignorance, and err still; think 'em wits and fine fellows, as they have done. 'Twere sin to reform them.

TRUEWIT Well, I will have 'em fetched, now I think on't, for a private purpose of mine; do, Clerimont, fetch 'em, and discourse to 'em all that's passed, and bring 'em into the gallery here.

DAUPHINE This is thy extreme vanity now; thou think'st thou wert undone if every jest thou mak'st were not published.

TRUEWIT Thou shalt see how unjust thou art, presently. Clerimont, say it was Dauphine's plot.

[*Exit Clerimont*]

Trust me not if the whole drift be not for thy good. There's a carpet i' the next room: put it on, with this scarf over thy face and a cushion o' thy head, and be ready when I call Amorous. Away—

[*Exit Dauphine*]

John Daw.

DAW [*coming out of hiding*] What good news, sir?   230

TRUEWIT Faith, I have followed and argued with him hard for you. I told him you were a knight and a scholar, and that you knew fortitude did consist *magis patiendo quam faciendo, magis ferendo quam feriendo*.°

DAW It doth so indeed, sir.   235

TRUEWIT And that you would suffer, I told him; so at first he demanded, by my troth, in my conceit, too much.

DAW What was it, sir?

TRUEWIT Your upper lip, and six o' your fore-teeth.

DAW 'Twas unreasonable.   240

TRUEWIT Nay, I told him plainly, you could not spare 'em all. So after long argument—*pro* and *con*, as you know—I brought him down to your two butter-teeth, and them he would have.

DAW O, did you so? Why, he shall have 'em.

TRUEWIT But he shall not, sir, by your leave. The conclusion is this,   245
sir: because you shall be very good friends hereafter, and this never to be remembered or upbraided—besides that he may not boast he has done any such thing to you in his own person—he is to come here in disguise, give you five kicks in private, sir, take your sword from you and lock you up in that study, during   250
pleasure. Which will be but a little while, we'll get it released presently.

DAW Five kicks? He shall have six, sir, to be friends.

TRUEWIT Believe me, you shall not overshoot yourself to send him that word by me.   255

DAW Deliver it, sir. He shall have it with all my heart, to be friends.

TRUEWIT Friends? Nay, an he should not be so, and heartily too, upon these terms, he shall have me to enemy while I live. Come, sir, bear it bravely.

DAW O God, sir, 'tis nothing.   260

TRUEWIT True. What's six kicks to a man that reads Seneca?°

DAW I have had a hundred, sir.

TRUEWIT Sir Amorous. No speaking one to another, or rehearsing old matters.

[*Enter above Haughty, Centaure, Mavis, Mistress Otter, Epicene, Trusty, Clerimont*] *Dauphine comes forth [disguised] and kicks him*

DAW One, two, three, four, five. I protest, Sir Amorous, you shall have six.   265

TRUEWIT Nay, I told you, you should not talk. Come, give him six, an he will needs. [*Dauphine kicks him again*] Your sword. [*Daw gives his sword to Truewit*] Now return to your safe custody: you shall presently meet afore the ladies, and be the dearest friends one to another—   270

[*Exit Daw*]

Give me the scarf; now thou shalt beat the other bare-faced. Stand by—

[*Exit Dauphine*]

Sir Amorous.

[*Enter La Foole*]

LA FOOLE What's here? A sword.   275

TRUEWIT I cannot help it, without I should take the quarrel upon myself; here he has sent you his sword—

LA FOOLE I'll receive none on't.

TRUEWIT And he wills you to fasten it against a wall, and break your head in some few several places against the hilts.   280

LA FOOLE I will not: tell him roundly. I cannot endure to shed my own blood.

TRUEWIT Will you not?

LA FOOLE No. I'll beat it against a fair flat wall, if that will satisfy him: if not, he shall beat it himself for Amorous.   285

TRUEWIT Why, this is strange starting off° when a man undertakes for you! I offered him another condition: will you stand to that?

LA FOOLE Aye, what is't?

TRUEWIT That you will be beaten in private.

LA FOOLE Yes. I am content, at the blunt.°   290

TRUEWIT Then you must submit yourself to be hoodwinked in this scarf, and be led to him, where he will take your sword from you, and make you bear a blow over the mouth, *gules*, and tweaks by the nose, *sans nombre*.°

LA FOOLE I am content. But why must I be blinded?   295

TRUEWIT That's for your good, sir; because—if he should grow insolent, upon this and publish it hereafter to your disgrace— which I hope he will not do—you might swear safely and protest he never beat you, to your knowledge.

LA FOOLE O, I conceive.   300

TRUEWIT I do not doubt but you'll be perfect good friends upon't,
and not dare to utter an ill thought one of another in future.

LA FOOLE Not I, as God help me, of him.

TRUEWIT Nor he of you, sir. If he should—[*Blindfolds him*] Come,
sir. All hid,° Sir John.   305

> *Dauphine enters to tweak him*

LA FOOLE O, Sir John, Sir John. O, oooooh! O—

> [*Dauphine takes his sword*]

TRUEWIT Good Sir John, leave tweaking, you'll blow his nose off.

> [*Exit Dauphine with swords*]

'Tis Sir John's pleasure you should retire into the study. [*Takes off
the blindfold*] Why, now you are friends. All bitterness between
you, I hope, is buried; you shall come forth by and by, Damon and   310
Pythias° upon 't, and embrace with all the rankness of friendship
that can be.

> [*Exit La Foole*]

I trust we shall have 'em tamer i' their language hereafter.

> [*Enter Dauphine*]

Dauphine, I worship thee. God's will, the ladies have surprised us!

4.6

> [*Enter below*] *Haughty, Centaure, Mavis, Mistress Otter,*
> *Epicene, Trusty* [*and*] *Clerimont, having discovered part of the*
> *past scene above*

HAUGHTY Centaure, how our judgements were imposed on by these
adulterate knights!

CENTAURE Nay, madam, Mavis was more deceived than we; 'twas
her commendation uttered 'em in the college.

MAVIS I commended but their wits, madam, and their braveries. I   5
never looked toward their valours.

HAUGHTY Sir Dauphine is valiant, and a wit too, it seems.

MAVIS And a bravery too.

HAUGHTY Was this his project?

MISTRESS OTTER So Master Clerimont intimates, madam.   10

HAUGHTY Good Morose, when you come to the college, will you
bring him with you? He seems a very perfect gentleman.

EPICENE He is so, madam, believe it.

CENTAURE But when will you come, Morose?

EPICENE Three or four days hence, madam, when I have got me a   15
coach and horses.

HAUGHTY No, tomorrow, good Morose, Centaure shall send you her
coach.

MAVIS Yes faith, do, and bring Sir Dauphine with you.

HAUGHTY She has promised that, Mavis.   20

MAVIS He is a very worthy gentleman in his exteriors, madam.

HAUGHTY Aye, he shows he is judicial in his clothes.

CENTAURE And yet not so superlatively neat as some, madam, that
have their faces set in a brake!°

HAUGHTY Aye, and have every hair in form!°   25

MAVIS That wear purer linen than ourselves, and profess more
neatness than the French hermaphrodite!°

EPICENE Aye, ladies, they, what they tell one of us, have told a
thousand, and are the only thieves of our fame, that think to take
us with that perfume or with that lace, and laugh at us unconscion-   30
ably when they have done.

HAUGHTY But Sir Dauphine's carelessness becomes him.

CENTAURE I could love a man for such a nose!

MAVIS Or such a leg!

CENTAURE He has an exceeding good eye, madam!   35

MAVIS And a very good lock!

CENTAURE Good Morose, bring him to my chamber first.

MISTRESS OTTER Please your honours to meet at my house, madam?

TRUEWIT [aside to Dauphine] See how they eye thee, man! They are
taken, I warrant thee.   40

HAUGHTY [joining Truewit and Dauphine] You have unbraced our
brace of knights, here, Master Truewit.

TRUEWIT Not I, madam, it was Sir Dauphine's engine: who, if he
have disfurnished your ladyship of any guard or service by it, is
able to make the place good again in himself.   45

HAUGHTY There's no suspicion of that, sir.

CENTAURE Gods so, Mavis, Haughty is kissing.

MAVIS Let us go too and take part.

HAUGHTY But I am glad of the fortune—beside the discovery of two
such empty caskets—to gain the knowledge of so rich a mine of   50
virtue as Sir Dauphine.

    [Centaure and Mavis come forward]

CENTAURE We would be all glad to style him of our friendship, and
see him at the college.

MAVIS He cannot mix with a sweeter society, I'll prophesy, and I hope he himself will think so.

DAUPHINE I should be rude to imagine otherwise, lady.   55

TRUEWIT [*aside to Dauphine*] Did not I tell thee, Dauphine? Why, all their actions are governed by crude opinion, without reason or cause; they know not why they do anything; but as they are informed, believe, judge, praise, condemn, love, hate, and in   60 emulation one of another, do all these things alike. Only, they have a natural inclination sways 'em generally to the worst, when they are left to themselves. But pursue it, now thou hast 'em.

HAUGHTY Shall we go in again, Morose?

EPICENE Yes, madam.   65

CENTAURE We'll entreat Sir Dauphine's company.

TRUEWIT Stay, good madam, the interview of the two friends, Pylades and Orestes:° I'll fetch 'em out to you straight.

HAUGHTY Will you, Master Truewit?

DAUPHINE Aye, but noble ladies, do not confess in your countenance   70 or outward bearing to 'em any discovery of their follies, that we may see how they will bear up again, with what assurance, and erection.

HAUGHTY We will not, Sir Dauphine.

CENTAURE, MAVIS Upon our honours, Sir Dauphine.   75

TRUEWIT [*at the first door*] Sir Amorous, Sir Amorous. The ladies are here.

LA FOOLE [*within*] Are they?

TRUEWIT Yes, but slip out by and by as their backs are turned and meet Sir John here, as by chance, when I call you. [*Goes to second   80 door*] Jack Daw.

DAW [*within*] What say you, sir?

TRUEWIT Whip out behind me suddenly: and no anger i' your looks to your adversary. Now, now.

[*Enter La Foole, Daw*]

LA FOOLE Noble Sir John Daw! Where ha' you been?   85

DAW To seek you, Sir Amorous.

LA FOOLE Me! I honour you.

DAW I prevent you, sir.

CLERIMONT They have forgot their rapiers!

TRUEWIT O, they meet in peace, man.

DAUPHINE Where's your sword, Sir John?   90

CLERIMONT And yours, Sir Amorous?

DAW Mine! My boy had it forth° to mend the handle, e'en now.

LA FOOLE And my gold handle was broke too, and my boy had it
forth.   95

DAUPHINE Indeed, sir? How their excuses meet!

CLERIMONT What a consent there is i' the handles?

TRUEWIT Nay, there is so i' the points too, I warrant you.

MISTRESS OTTER O, me! Madam, he comes again, the madman.
Away!   100

     [*Exeunt Ladies, La Foole, Daw*]

4.7

     [*Enter*] *Morose* [*with a sword in each hand.*] *He had found the
two swords drawn within*

MOROSE What make these naked weapons here, gentlemen?

TRUEWIT O, sir! Here hath like to been murder since you went! A
couple of knights fallen out about the bride's favours. We were fain
to take away their weapons, your house had been begged° by this
time else—   5

MOROSE For what?

CLERIMONT For manslaughter, sir, as being accessory.

MOROSE And for her favours?

TRUEWIT Aye, sir, heretofore, not present. Clerimont, carry 'em
their swords now. They have done all the hurt they will do.   10

     [*Exit Clerimont with the swords*]

DAUPHINE Ha' you spoke with a lawyer, sir?

MOROSE O no! There is such a noise i' the court that they have
frighted me home with more violence than I went! Such speaking
and counter-speaking, with their several voices of citations, appel-
lations, allegations, certificates, attachments, intergatories, references,   15
convictions, and afflictions indeed among the doctors and proctors!
That the noise here is silence to 't! A kind of calm midnight!

TRUEWIT Why, sir, if you would be resolved° indeed, I can bring
you hither a very sufficient lawyer, and a learned divine, that shall
inquire into every least scruple for you.   20

MOROSE Can you, Master Truewit?

TRUEWIT Yes, and are very sober grave persons, that will dispatch it
in a chamber, with a whisper or two.

MOROSE Good sir, shall I hope this benefit from you, and trust
myself into your hands?   25

TRUEWIT Alas, sir! Your nephew and I have been ashamed, and
oft-times mad since you went, to think how you are abused. Go
in, good sir, and lock yourself up till we call you; we'll tell you
more anon, sir.

MOROSE Do your pleasure with me, gentlemen; I believe in you, and   30
that deserves no delusion—

TRUEWIT You shall find none, sir
      [*Exit Morose*]
—but heaped, heaped plenty of vexation.

DAUPHINE What wilt thou do now, wit?

TRUEWIT Recover me hither Otter and the barber if you can, by any   35
means, presently.

DAUPHINE Why? To what purpose?

TRUEWIT O, I'll make the deepest divine and gravest lawyer out o'
them two, for him—

DAUPHINE Thou canst not man; these are waking dreams.   40

TRUEWIT Do not fear me. Clap but a civil gown with a welt° o' the
one, and a canonical cloak with sleeves° o' the other, and give 'em
a few terms i' their mouths, if there come not forth as able a doctor
and complete a parson for this turn as may be wished, trust not
my election. And I hope, without wronging the dignity of either   45
profession, since they are but persons put on, and for mirth's
sake,° to torment him. The barber smatters Latin, I remember.

DAUPHINE Yes, and Otter too.

TRUEWIT Well then, if I make 'em not wrangle out this case to his
no comfort, let me be thought a Jack Daw or La Foole, or anything   50
worse. Go you to your ladies, but first send for them.

DAUPHINE I will.
      [*Exeunt*]

5.1

[*Enter*] *La Foole, Clerimont* [*and*] *Daw*

LA FOOLE Where had you our swords, Master Clerimont?

CLERIMONT Why, Dauphine took 'em from the madman.

LA FOOLE And he took 'em from our boys, I warrant you?

CLERIMONT Very like, sir.

LA FOOLE Thank you, good Master Clerimont. Sir John Daw and I   5
are both beholden to you.

CLERIMONT Would I knew how to make you so, gentlemen.

DAW Sir Amorous and I are your servants, sir.

[*Enter Mavis*]

MAVIS Gentlemen, have any of you a pen and ink? I would fain write
out a riddle in Italian for Sir Dauphine to translate.   10

CLERIMONT Not I, in troth, lady, I am no scrivener.

DAW I can furnish you, I think, lady.

[*Exit Daw with Mavis*]

CLERIMONT He has it in the haft of a knife, I believe!

LA FOOLE No, he has his box of instruments.

CLERIMONT Like a surgeon!   15

LA FOOLE For the mathematics: his square, his compasses, his brass
pens, and black lead, to draw maps of every place and person
where he comes.

CLERIMONT How, maps of persons?

LA FOOLE Yes, sir, of Nomentack,° when he was here, and of the   20
Prince of Moldavia, and of his mistress,° Mistress Epicene.

CLERIMONT Away! He has not found out her latitude,° I hope.

LA FOOLE You are a pleasant gentleman, sir.

[*Enter Daw*]

CLERIMONT Faith, now we are in private, let's wanton it a little, and
talk waggishly. Sir John, I am telling Sir Amorous here that you   25
two govern the ladies; where'er you come, you carry the feminine
gender afore you.°

DAW They shall rather carry us afore them, if they will, sir.

CLERIMONT Nay, I believe that they do, withal; but that you are the
prime-men in their affections, and direct all their actions—   30

DAW Not I; Sir Amorous is.

LA FOOLE I protest, Sir John is.

DAW As I hope to rise i' the state, Sir Amorous, you ha' the person.

LA FOOLE Sir John, you ha' the person and the discourse too.

DAW Not I, sir. I have no discourse—and then you have activity   35
beside.

LA FOOLE I protest, Sir John, you come as high from Tripoli° as I
do every whit and lift as many joined stools, and leap over 'em, if
you would use it—

CLERIMONT Well, agree on't together, knights; for between you, you   40
divide the kingdom or commonwealth of ladies' affections: I see it
and can perceive a little how they observe you and fear you,
indeed. You could tell strange stories, my masters, if you would, I
know.

DAW Faith, we have seen somewhat, sir.   45

LA FOOLE That we have—velvet petticoats, and wrought smocks, or
so.

DAW Aye, and—

CLERIMONT Nay, out with it, Sir John; do not envy your friend the
pleasure of hearing, when you have had the delight of tasting.   50

DAW Why—a—do you speak, Sir Amorous.

LA FOOLE No, do you, Sir John Daw.

DAW I' faith, you shall.

LA FOOLE I' faith, you shall.

DAW Why, we have been—   55

LA FOOLE In the great bed at Ware° together in our time. On, Sir
John.

DAW Nay, do you, Sir Amorous.

CLERIMONT And these ladies with you, knights?

LA FOOLE No, excuse us, sir.   60

DAW We must not wound reputation.

LA FOOLE No matter—they were these, or others. Our bath° cost us
fifteen pound, when we came home.

CLERIMONT Do you hear, Sir John, you shall tell me but one thing
truly, as you love me.   65

DAW If I can, I will, sir.

CLERIMONT You lay in the same house with the bride, here?

DAW Yes, and conversed with her hourly, sir.

CLERIMONT And what humour is she of? Is she coming and open,
free?   70

DAW O, exceeding open, sir. I was her servant, and Sir Amorous was
to be.

CLERIMONT Come, you have both had favours from her? I know and
have heard so much.

DAW O no, sir.   75

LA FOOLE You shall excuse us, sir: we must not wound reputation.

CLERIMONT Tut, she is married now, and you cannot hurt her with
   any report, and therefore speak plainly: how many times, i' faith?
   Which of you led first? Ha?

LA FOOLE Sir John had her maidenhead, indeed.   80

DAW O, it pleases him to say so, sir, but Sir Amorous knows what's
   what, as well.

CLERIMONT Dost thou i' faith, Amorous?

LA FOOLE In a manner, sir.

CLERIMONT Why, I commend you lads. Little knows Don Bride-   85
   groom of this. Nor shall he, for me.

DAW Hang him, mad ox.

CLERIMONT Speak softly: here comes his nephew, with the Lady
   Haughty. He'll get the ladies from you, sirs, if you look not to him
   in time.   90

LA FOOLE Why, if he do, we'll fetch 'em home again, I warrant you.
   [*Exeunt*]

5.2

[Enter] Haughty [and] Dauphine

HAUGHTY I assure you, Sir Dauphine, it is the price and estimation
   of your virtue only that hath embarked me to this adventure, and
   I could not but make out° to tell you so; nor can I repent me of
   the act, since it is always an argument of some virtue in ourselves
   that we love and affect it so in others.   5

DAUPHINE Your ladyship sets too high a price on my weakness.

HAUGHTY Sir, I can distinguish gems from pebbles—

DAUPHINE Are you so skilful in stones?

HAUGHTY And howsoever I may suffer in such a judgement as
   yours, by admitting equality of rank or society with Centaure or   10
   Mavis—

DAUPHINE You do not, madam; I perceive they are your mere
   foils.

HAUGHTY Then are you a friend to truth, sir. It makes me love you
   the more. It is not the outward but the inward man that I affect.   15
   They are not apprehensive of an eminent perfection, but love flat
   and dully.

CENTAURE [*within*] Where are you, my Lady Haughty?

HAUGHTY I come presently, Centaure. My chamber, sir, my page
shall show you; and Trusty, my woman, shall be ever awake for   20
you; you need not fear to communicate anything with her, for she
is a Fidelia.° I pray you wear this jewel for my sake, Sir Dauphine.
    [*Enter Centaure*]
Where's Mavis, Centaure?

CENTAURE Within, madam, a-writing. I'll follow you presently. I'll
but speak a word with Sir Dauphine.   25
    [*Exit Haughty*]

DAUPHINE With me, madam?

CENTAURE Good Sir Dauphine, do not trust Haughty, nor make any
credit to° her, whatever you do besides. Sir Dauphine, I give you
this caution: she is a perfect courtier, and loves nobody, but for
her uses; and for her uses, she loves all. Besides, her physicians   30
give her out to be none o' the clearest—whether she pay 'em or
no, heaven knows; and she's above fifty too, and pargets!° See her
in a forenoon. Here comes Mavis, a worse face than she! You
would not like this, by candlelight. If you'll come to my chamber
one o' these mornings early, or late in an evening, I'll tell you   35
more.
    [*Enter Mavis*]
Where's Haughty, Mavis?

MAVIS Within, Centaure.

CENTAURE What ha' you there?

MAVIS An Italian riddle for Sir Dauphine—(you shall not see it i'   40
faith, Centaure). Good Sir Dauphine, solve it for me. I'll call for
it anon.
    [*Exeunt Mavis, Centaure. Enter Clerimont*]

CLERIMONT How now, Dauphine? How dost thou quit thyself of
these females?

DAUPHINE 'Slight, they haunt me like fairies, and give me jewels   45
here, I cannot be rid of 'em.

CLERIMONT O, you must not tell° though.

DAUPHINE Mass, I forgot that; I was never so assaulted. One loves
for virtue, and bribes me with this [*indicates jewel*]. Another loves
me with caution,° and so would possess me. A third brings me a   50
riddle here, and all are jealous and rail each at other.

CLERIMONT A riddle? Pray let me see't? (*He reads the paper*) 'Sir
Dauphine, I chose this way of intimation for privacy. The ladies
here, I know, have both hope and purpose to make a collegiate and
servant of you. If I might be so honoured as to appear at any end   55

of so noble a work, I would enter into a fame of taking physic°
tomorrow, and continue it four or five days or longer, for your
visitation. Mavis.' By my faith, a subtle one! Call you this a riddle?
What's their plain dealing, trow?

DAUPHINE We lack Truewit to tell us that.   60

CLERIMONT We lack him for somewhat else too: his knights *reformados*° are wound up as high and insolent as ever they were.

DAUPHINE You jest.

CLERIMONT No drunkards, either with wine or vanity, ever confessed such stories of themselves. I would not give a fly's leg in   65
balance against all the women's reputations here, if they could be
but thought to speak truth; and for the bride, they have made their
affidavit against her directly—

DAUPHINE What, that they have lain with her?

CLERIMONT Yes, and tell times and circumstances, with the cause   70
why and the place where. I had almost brought 'em to affirm that
they had done it today.

DAUPHINE Not both of 'em.

CLERIMONT Yes faith with a sooth or two more° I had effected it.
They would ha' set it down under their hands.°   75

DAUPHINE Why, they will be our sport, I see, still! Whether we will
or no.

5.3

[*Enter*] *Truewit*

TRUEWIT O, are you here? Come, Dauphine. Go, call your uncle
presently. I have fitted my divine and my canonist, dyed their
beards and all; the knaves do not know themselves, they are so
exalted and altered. Preferment changes any man. Thou shalt keep
one door, and I another, and then Clerimont in the midst, that he   5
may have no means of escape from their cavilling when they grow
hot once. And then the women (as I have given the bride her
instructions) to break in upon him, i' the *l'envoy*.° O, 'twill be full
and twanging! Away, fetch him.

[*Exit Dauphine. Enter Cutbeard disguised as a canon lawyer,
Otter as a divine*]

Come, master doctor, and master parson, look to your parts now, and   10
discharge 'em bravely; you are well set forth, perform it as well. If
you chance to be out,° do not confess it with standing still or

humming or gaping one at another, but go on and talk aloud and
eagerly, use vehement action, and only remember your terms, and
you are safe. Let the matter go where it will: you have many will   15
do so. But at first, be very solemn and grave like your garments,
though you loose yourselves after and skip out like a brace of
jugglers on a table. Here he comes! Set your faces, and look
superciliously while I present you.

    [*Enter Dauphine, Morose*]

MOROSE Are these the two learned men?   20

TRUEWIT Yes, sir; please you salute 'em?

MOROSE Salute 'em? I had rather do anything than wear out time so
unfruitfully, sir. I wonder how these common forms, as 'God save
you' and 'you are welcome', are come to be a habit in our lives!
Or, 'I am glad to see you!' when I cannot see what the profit can   25
be of these words, so long as it is no whit better with him whose
affairs are sad and grievous, that he hears this salutation.

TRUEWIT 'Tis true, sir, we'll go to the matter then. Gentlemen,
master doctor and master parson, I have acquainted you sufficiently with the business for which you are come hither. And you are   30
not now to inform yourselves in the state of the question, I know.
This is the gentleman who expects your resolution, and therefore,
when you please, begin.

OTTER Please you, master doctor.

CUTBEARD Please you, good master parson.   35

OTTER I would hear the canon law speak first.

CUTBEARD It must give place to positive divinity,° sir.

MOROSE Nay, good gentlemen, do not throw me into circumstances.
Let your comforts arrive quickly at me, those that are. Be swift in
affording me my peace, if so I shall hope any. I love not your   40
disputations or your court tumults. And that it be not strange to
you, I will tell you. My father, in my education, was wont to advise
me that I should always collect and contain my mind, not suffering
it to flow loosely; that I should look to what things were necessary
to the carriage of my life, and what not, embracing the one and   45
eschewing the other. In short, that I should endear myself to rest
and avoid turmoil, which now is grown to be another nature to me.
So that I come not to your public pleadings or your places of noise;
not that I neglect those things that make for the dignity of the
commonwealth but for the mere avoiding of clamours, and imper-   50
tinencies of orators that know not how to be silent. And for the
cause of noise am I now a suitor to you. You do not know in what

a misery I have been exercised this day, what a torrent of evil! My
very house turns round with the tumult! I dwell in a windmill! The
perpetual motion is here, and not at Eltham.°   55

TRUEWIT Well, good master doctor, will you break the ice? Master
parson will wade after.

CUTBEARD Sir, though unworthy and the weaker, I will presume.

OTTER 'Tis no presumption, *domine* doctor.

MOROSE Yet again!   60

CUTBEARD Your question is, for how many causes a man may have
divortium legitimum, a lawful divorce. First, you must understand
the nature of the word divorce, *à divertendo*°—

MOROSE No excursions upon words, good doctor; to the question
briefly.   65

CUTBEARD I answer then, the canon law affords divorce but in few
cases, and the principal is in the common case, the adulterous case.
But there are *duodecim impedimenta*, twelve impediments (as we call
'em) all which do not *dirimere contractum*, but *irritum reddere
matrimonium*, as we say in the canon law, not take away the bond,   70
but cause a nullity therein

MOROSE I understood you before; good sir, avoid your impertinency
of translation.

OTTER He cannot open this too much, sir, by your favour.

MOROSE Yet more!   75

TRUEWIT O, you must give the learned men leave, sir. To your
impediments, master doctor.

CUTBEARD The first is *impedimentum erroris*.°

OTTER Of which there are several species.

CUTBEARD Aye, as *error personae*.°   80

OTTER If you contract yourself to one person, thinking her another.

CUTBEARD Then, *error fortunae*.°

OTTER If she be a beggar, and you thought her rich.

CUTBEARD Then, *error qualitatis*.°

OTTER If she prove stubborn or headstrong, that you thought   85
obedient.

MOROSE How? Is that, sir, a lawful impediment? One at once, I pray
you gentlemen.

OTTER Aye, *ante copulam*, but not *post copulam*,° sir.

CUTBEARD Master parson says right. *Nec post nuptiarum benedic-*   90
tionem.° It doth indeed but *irrita reddere sponsalia*, annul the contract;° after marriage it is of no obstancy.

TRUEWIT Alas, sir, what a hope are we fallen from, by this time!

CUTBEARD The next is *conditio*: if you thought her free born and she
prove a bond-woman, there is impediment of estate and condi-   95
tion.°

OTTER Aye, but master doctor, those servitudes are *sublatae* now,
among us Christians.°

CUTBEARD By your favour, master parson—

OTTER You shall give me leave, master doctor.   100

MOROSE Nay, gentlemen, quarrel not in that question; it concerns
not my case: pass to the third.

CUTBEARD Well then, the third is *votum*. If either party have made
a vow of chastity. But that practice, as master parson said of the
other, is taken away among us, thanks be to discipline.° The fourth   105
is *cognatio*: if the persons be of kin within the degrees.

OTTER Aye. Do you know what the degrees° are, sir?

MOROSE No, nor I care not, sir; they offer me no comfort in the
question, I am sure.

CUTBEARD But there is a branch of this impediment may, which is   110
cognatio spiritualis.° If you were her godfather, sir, then the
marriage is incestuous.

OTTER That comment is absurd and superstitious,° master doctor. I
cannot endure it. Are we not all brothers and sisters, and as much
akin in that as godfathers and goddaughters?   115

MOROSE O me! To end the controversy, I never was a godfather, I
never was a godfather in my life, sir. Pass to the next.

CUTBEARD The fifth is *crimen adulterii*:° the known case. The sixth,
cultus disparitas, difference of religion: have you ever examined her
what religion she is of?   120

MOROSE No, I would rather she were of none, than be put to the
trouble of it!

OTTER You may have it done for you,° sir.

MOROSE By no means, good sir; on to the rest. Shall you ever come
to an end, think you?   125

TRUEWIT Yes, he has done half, sir—On to the rest. Be patient and
expect, sir.

CUTBEARD The seventh is *vis*: if it were upon compulsion or force.

MOROSE O no, it was too voluntary, mine, too voluntary.

CUTBEARD The eighth is *ordo*: if ever she have taken holy orders.°   130

OTTER That's superstitious, too.

MOROSE No matter, master parson: would she would go into a
nunnery yet.

CUTBEARD The ninth is *ligamen*: if you were bound, sir, to any other
before.°   135

MOROSE I thrust myself too soon into these fetters.

CUTBEARD The tenth is *publica honestas*, which is *inchoata quaedam
affinitas*.°

OTTER Aye, or *affinitas orta ex sponsalibus*, and is but *leve impedimentum*.°   140

MOROSE I feel no air of comfort blowing to me in all this.

CUTBEARD The eleventh is *affinitas ex fornicatione*.°

OTTER Which is no less *vera affinitas*° than the other, master
doctor.

CUTBEARD True, *quae oritur ex legitimo matrimonio*.°   145

OTTER You say right, venerable doctor. And, *nascitur ex eo, quod per
coniugium duae personae efficiuntur una caro*°—

MOROSE Heyday, now they begin.

CUTBEARD I conceive you, master parson. *Ita per fornicationem aeque
est verus pater, qui sic generat*°—   150

OTTER *Et vere filius qui sic generatur*°—

MOROSE What's all this to me?

CLERIMONT [*aside*] Now it grows warm.

CUTBEARD The twelfth and last is *si forte coire nequibis*.°

OTTER Aye, that is *impedimentum gravissimum*.° It doth utterly annul   155
and annihilate, that. If you have *manifestam frigiditatem*,° you are
well, sir.

TRUEWIT Why, there is comfort come at length, sir. Confess yourself
but a man unable, and she will sue to be divorced first.

OTTER Aye, or if there be *morbus perpetuus et insanabilis*,° as *paralysis*,   160
elephantiasis, or so—

DAUPHINE O, but *frigiditas* is the fairer way, gentlemen.

OTTER You say troth, sir, and as it is in the canon, master doctor.

CUTBEARD I conceive you, sir.   165

CLERIMONT [*aside*] Before he speaks.

OTTER That 'a boy, or child, under years, is not fit for marriage,
because he cannot *reddere debitum*'.° So your *omnipotentes*°—

TRUEWIT [*aside to Otter*] Your *impotentes*, you whoreson lobster.°

OTTER Your *impotentes*, I should say, are *minime apti ad contrahenda*   170
matrimonium.°

TRUEWIT [*aisde to Otter*] *Matrimonium*? We shall have most unmatri-
monial° Latin with you: *matrimonia*, and be hanged.

DAUPHINE [*aside to Truewit*] You put 'em out, man.

CUTBEARD But then there will arise a doubt, master parson, in our   175
case, *post matrimonium*:° that *frigiditate praeditus*°—do you conceive
me, sir?

OTTER Very well, sir.

CUTBEARD Who cannot *uti uxore pro uxore*, may *habere eam pro
sorore*.°   180

OTTER Absurd, absurd, absurd, and merely apostatical.°

CUTBEARD You shall pardon me, master parson, I can prove it.

OTTER You can prove a will, master doctor, you can prove nothing
else. Does not the verse of your own canon say, *Haec socianda
vetant conubia, facta retractant*°—   185

CUTBEARD I grant you, but how do they *retractare*, master parson?

MOROSE O, this was it I feared.

OTTER *In aeternum*,° sir.

CUTBEARD That's false in divinity, by your favour.

OTTER 'Tis false in humanity, to say so. Is he not *prorsus inutilis ad*   190
torum?° Can he *praestare fidem datam*?° I would fain know.

CUTBEARD Yes: how if he do *convalere*?°

OTTER He cannot *convalere*, it is impossible.

TRUEWIT [*to Morose*] Nay, good sir, attend the learned men, they'll
think you neglect 'em else.   195

CUTBEARD Or if he do *simulare* himself *frigidum, odio uxoris*,° or so?

OTTER I say he is *adulter manifestus*° then.

DAUPHINE They dispute it very learnedly, i' faith.

OTTER And *prostitutor uxoris*,° and this is positive.

MOROSE Good sir, let me escape.   200

TRUEWIT You will not do me that wrong, sir?

OTTER And therefore, if he be *manifeste frigidus*,° sir—

CUTBEARD Aye, if he be *manifeste frigidus*, I grant you—

OTTER Why, that was my conclusion.

CUTBEARD And mine too.   205

TRUEWIT Nay, hear the conclusion, sir.

OTTER Then, *frigiditatis causa*°—

CUTBEARD Yes, *causa frigiditatis*—

MOROSE O, mine ears!

OTTER She may have *libellum divortii*° against you.   210

CUTBEARD Aye, *divortii libellum* she will sure have.

MOROSE Good echoes, forbear.

OTTER If you confess it.

CUTBEARD Which I would do, sir—

MOROSE I will do anything—   215
OTTER And clear myself *in foro conscientiae*°—
CUTBEARD Because you want indeed—
MOROSE Yet more?
OTTER *Exercendi potestate.*°

5.4

[Enter] Epicene, Haughty, Centaure, Mavis, Mistress Otter,
Daw [and] La Foole

EPICENE I will not endure it any longer. Ladies, I beseech you help
me. This is such a wrong as never was offered to poor bride before.
Upon her marriage day, to have her husband conspire against her,
and a couple of mercenary companions to be brought in for form's
sake to persuade a separation! If you had blood or virtue in you,   5
gentlemen, you would not suffer such earwigs about a husband, or
scorpions to creep between man and wife—

MOROSE O, the variety and changes° of my torment!
HAUGHTY Let 'em be cudgelled out of doors by our grooms.
CENTAURE I'll lend you my footman.   10
MAVIS We'll have our men blanket 'em i' the hall.
MISTRESS OTTER As there was one° at our house, madam, for
peeping in at the door.
DAW Content, i'faith.
TRUEWIT Stay, ladies and gentlemen, you'll hear before you pro-   15
ceed?
MAVIS I'd ha' the bridegroom blanketed too.
CENTAURE Begin with him first.
HAUGHTY Yes, by my troth.
MOROSE O, mankind generation!   20
DAUPHINE Ladies, for my sake forbear.
HAUGHTY Yes, for Sir Dauphine's sake.
CENTAURE He shall command us.
LA FOOLE He is as fine a gentleman of his inches,° madam, as any
is about the town, and wears as good colours when he list.   25
TRUEWIT *[aside to Morose]* Be brief, sir, and confess your infirmity,
she'll be afire to be quit of you; if she but hear that named once,
you shall not entreat her to stay. She'll fly you like one that had
the marks upon him.
MOROSE Ladies, I must crave all your pardons—   30

TRUEWIT Silence, ladies.

MOROSE For a wrong I have done to your whole sex in marrying this
fair and virtuous gentlewoman—

CLERIMONT Hear him, good ladies.

MOROSE Being guilty of an infirmity which, before I conferred with   35
these learned men, I thought I might have concealed—

TRUEWIT But now being better informed in his conscience by them, he
is to declare it and give satisfaction by asking your public forgiveness.

MOROSE I am no man, ladies.

ALL How!   40

MOROSE Utterly unabled in nature, by reason of frigidity, to perform
the duties or any the least office of a husband.

MAVIS Now, out upon him, prodigious creature!

CENTAURE Bridegroom uncarnate.°

HAUGHTY And would you offer it° to a young gentlewoman?   45

MISTRESS OTTER A lady of her longings?

EPICENE Tut, a device, a device, this, it smells rankly, ladies. A mere
comment of his own.

TRUEWIT Why, if you suspect that, ladies, you may have him
searched.   50

DAW As the custom is, by a jury of physicians.

LA FOOLE Yes faith, 'twill be brave.

MOROSE O me, must I undergo that?

MISTRESS OTTER No, let women search him, madam: we can do it
ourselves.   55

MOROSE Out on me, worse!

EPICENE No, ladies, you shall not need, I'll take him with all his
faults.

MOROSE Worst of all!

CLERIMONT Why, then 'tis no divorce, doctor, if she consent not?   60

CUTBEARD No, if the man be *frigidus*, it is *de parte uxoris*° that we
grant *libellum divortii* in the law.

OTTER Aye, it is the same in theology.

MOROSE Worse, worse than worst!

TRUEWIT Nay, sir, be not utterly disheartened; we have yet a small   65
relic of hope left, as near as our comfort is blown out. [*Aside to
Clerimont*] Clerimont, produce your brace of knights. [*Aloud to
Otter*] What was that, master parson, you told me *in errore
qualitatis*,° e'en now? [*Aside to Dauphine*] Dauphine, whisper the
bride that she carry it° as if she were guilty and ashamed.   70

OTTER Marry sir, *in errore qualitatis* (which master doctor did forbear to urge) if she be found *corrupta*, that is, vitiated or broken up, that was *pro virgine desponsa*, espoused for a maid—

MOROSE What then, sir?

OTTER It doth *dirimere contractum* and *irritum reddere°* too. 75

TRUEWIT If this be true, we are happy again, sir, once more. Here are an honourable brace of knights that shall affirm so much.

DAW Pardon us, good Master Clerimont.

LA FOOLE You shall excuse us, Master Clerimont.

CLERIMONT Nay, you must make it good now, knights; there is no 80 remedy; I'll eat no words for you, nor no men: you know you spoke it to me?

DAW Is this gentleman-like, sir?

TRUEWIT [*aside to Daw*] Jack Daw, he's worse than Sir Amorous: fiercer a great deal. [*Aside to La Foole*] Sir Amorous, beware, there 85 be ten Daws in this Clerimont.

LA FOOLE I'll confess it, sir.

DAW Will you, Sir Amorous? Will you wound reputation?

LA FOOLE I am resolved.

TRUEWIT So should you be too, Jack Daw: what should keep you 90 off? She is but a woman, and in disgrace. He'll be glad on't.

DAW Will he? I thought he would ha' been angry.

CLERIMONT You will dispatch, knights; it must be done, i'faith.

TRUEWIT Why, an it must it shall, sir, they say. They'll ne'er go back. [*aside to Daw and La Foole*] Do not tempt his patience. 95

DAW It is true indeed, sir.

LA FOOLE Yes, I assure you, sir.

MOROSE What is true, gentlemen? What do you assure me?

DAW That we have known your bride, sir—

LA FOOLE In good fashion. She was our mistress, or so— 100

CLERIMONT Nay, you must be plain, knights, as you were to me.

OTTER Aye, the question is, if you have *carnaliter*, or no.

LA FOOLE *Carnaliter*? What else, sir?

OTTER It is enough: a plain nullity.

EPICENE I am undone, I am undone! 105

MOROSE O, let me worship and adore you, gentlemen!

EPICENE I am undone!

MOROSE Yes, to my hand,° I thank these knights: master parson, let me thank you otherwise.

    [*Gives him money*]

CENTAURE And ha' they confessed?   110

MAVIS Now out upon 'em, informers!

TRUEWIT You see what creatures you may bestow your favours on,
madams.

HAUGHTY I would except against 'em as beaten knights,° wench, and
not good witnesses in law.   115

MISTRESS OTTER Poor gentlewoman, how she takes it!

HAUGHTY Be comforted, Morose; I love you the better for't.

CENTAURE So do I, I protest.

CUTBEARD But gentlemen, you have not known her since *matrimonium*?   120

DAW Not today, master doctor.

LA FOOLE No, sir, not today.

CUTBEARD Why, then I say, for any act before, the *matrimonium* is
good and perfect, unless the worshipful bridegroom did precisely,
before witness, demand if she were *virgo ante nuptias*.°   125

EPICENE No, that he did not, I assure you, master doctor.

CUTBEARD If he cannot prove that, it is *ratum coniugium*,° notwithstanding the premises. And they do no way *impedire*. And this is
my sentence, this I pronounce.

OTTER I am of master doctor's resolution too, sir: if you made not   130
that demand *ante nuptias*.

MOROSE O my heart! Wilt thou break? Wilt thou break? This is
worst of all worst worsts that hell could have devised! Marry a
whore! And so much noise!

DAUPHINE Come, I see now plain confederacy in this doctor and this   135
parson, to abuse a gentleman. You study his affliction. I pray be
gone, companions. And gentlemen, I begin to suspect you for
having parts with 'em. Sir, will it please you hear me?

MOROSE O, do not talk to me; take not from me the pleasure of dying
in silence, nephew.   140

DAUPHINE Sir, I must speak to you. I have been long your poor
despised kinsman, and many a hard thought has strengthened you
against me; but now it shall appear if either I love you or your
peace, and prefer them to all the world beside. I will not be long
or grievous to you, sir. If I free you of this unhappy match   145
absolutely and instantly after all this trouble, and almost in your
despair, now—

MOROSE It cannot be.

DAUPHINE Sir, that you be never troubled with a murmur of it more,
what shall I hope for or deserve of you?   150

MOROSE O, what thou wilt, nephew! Thou shalt deserve me and have me.

DAUPHINE Shall I have your favour perfect to me, and love hereafter?

MOROSE That, and anything beside. Make thine own conditions. My   155
whole estate is thine. Manage it, I will become thy ward.

DAUPHINE Nay, sir, I will not be so unreasonable.

EPICENE Will Sir Dauphine be mine enemy too?

DAUPHINE You know I have been long a suitor to you, uncle, that
out of your estate, which is fifteen hundred a year, you would allow   160
me but five hundred during life, and assure the rest upon me after:
to which I have often by myself and friends tendered you a writing
to sign, which you would never consent or incline to. If you please
but to effect it now—

MOROSE Thou shalt have it, nephew, I will do it, and more.   165

DAUPHINE If I quit you not presently and forever of this cumber,
you shall have power instantly, afore all these, to revoke your act,
and I will become whose slave you will give me to, forever.

MOROSE Where is the writing? I will seal to it, that, or to a blank,
and write thine own conditions.   170

EPICENE O me, most unfortunate wretched gentlewoman!

HAUGHTY Will Sir Dauphine do this?

EPICENE Good sir, have some compassion on me.

MOROSE O, my nephew knows you belike: away, crocodile.

CENTAURE He does it not, sure, without good ground.   175

DAUPHINE Here, sir.

    [He gives Morose the document]

MOROSE Come, nephew: give me the pen. I will subscribe to
anything, and seal to what thou wilt, for my deliverance. Thou art
my restorer. Here, I deliver it thee as my deed. [*Returns the
document*] If there be a word in it lacking, or writ with false   180
orthography, I protest before°—I will not take the advantage.

DAUPHINE Then here is your release, sir (*he takes off Epicene's
peruke*)—you have married a boy: a gentleman's son that I have
brought up this half year, at my great charges, and for this
composition which I have now made with you. What say you,   185
master doctor? This is *iustum impedimentum,*° I hope, *error personae*?

OTTER Yes sir, *in primo gradu.*°

CUTBEARD *In primu gradu.*

DAUPHINE I thank you, good Doctor Cutbeard, and Parson Otter.
(*He pulls off their beards and disguise*) You are beholden to 'em, sir,   190

that have taken this pains for you; and my friend, Master Truewit,
who enabled 'em for the business. Now you may go in and rest;
be as private as you will, sir. I'll not trouble you till you trouble
me with your funeral, which I care not how soon it come.

    [*Exit Morose*]

Cutbeard, I'll make your lease good. Thank me not but with your   195
leg, Cutbeard. And Tom Otter, your princess shall be reconciled
to you. How now, gentlemen! Do you look at me?

CLERIMONT A boy.

DAUPHINE Yes, Mistress Epicene.

TRUEWIT Well, Dauphine, you have lurched your friends of the   200
better half of the garland,° by concealing this part of the plot! But
much good do it thee, thou deserv'st it, lad. And Clerimont, for
thy unexpected bringing in these two to confession, wear my part
of it freely. Nay, Sir Daw and Sir La Foole, you see the
gentlewoman that has done you the favours! We are all thankful to   205
you, and so should the womankind here, specially for lying on°
her, though not with her! You meant so, I am sure? But that we
have stuck it upon° you today, in your own imagined persons, and
so lately, this Amazon,° the champion of the sex, should beat you
now thriftily for the common slanders which ladies receive from   210
such cuckoos as you are. You are they, that when no merit or
fortune can make you hope to enjoy their bodies, will yet lie with
their reputations and make their fame suffer. Away you common
moths of these and all ladies' honours. Go, travel to make legs and
faces,° and come home with some new matter to be laughed at: 215
you deserve to live in an air as corrupted as that wherewith you
feed rumour.

    [*Exeunt Daw, La Foole*]

Madams, you are mute upon this new metamorphosis! But here
stands she that has vindicated your fames. Take heed of such   220
insectae° hereafter. And let it not trouble you that you have
discovered any mysteries to this young gentleman. He is almost of
years,° and will make a good visitant within this twelve month. In
the meantime, we'll all undertake for his secrecy, that can speak so
well of his silence. [*Coming forward*] Spectators, if you like this   225
comedy, rise cheerfully, and now Morose is gone in, clap your
hands. It may be that noise will cure him, at least please him.

    [*Exeunt*]

This comedy was first
acted in the year
1609
By the Children of Her Majesty's
Revels°
The principal comedians° were
Nathan Field   William Barkstead
Giles Carey   William Penn
Hugh Attwell   Richard Allin
John Smith   John Blaney
With the allowance of the Master of Revels

THE ALCHEMIST

TO THE LADY MOST DESERVING
HER NAME AND BLOOD:
Mary, Lady Wroth°

Madam,

In the age of sacrifices, the truth of religion was not in the greatness   5
and fat of the offerings, but in the devotion and zeal of the sacrificers:
else, what could a handful of gums have done in the sight of a
hecatomb?° Or how might I appear at this altar, except with those
affections that no less love the light and witness than they have the
conscience of your virtue? If what I offer bear an acceptable odour,   10
and hold the first strength, it is your value of it which remembers
where, when, and to whom it was kindled. Otherwise, as the times
are, there comes rarely forth that thing so full of authority or example
but by assiduity and custom grows less, and loses. This yet safe in
your judgement (which is a Sidney's) is forbidden to speak more, lest   15
it talk or look like one of the ambitious Faces of the time, who, the
more they paint, are the less themselves.

Your Ladyship's
true honourer,
BEN JONSON   20

TO THE READER

If thou beest more, thou art an understander, and then I trust thee. If thou art one that tak'st up, and but a pretender, beware at what hands thou receiv'st thy commodity; for thou wert never more fair in the way to be cozened than in this age in poetry, especially in plays: wherein now the concupiscence of dances and antics so reigneth, as to run away from Nature and be afraid of her is the only point of art that tickles the spectators. But how out of purpose and place do I name art, when the professors are grown so obstinate contemners of it, and presumers on their own naturals,° as they are deriders of all diligence that way, and by simple mocking at the terms, when they understand not the things, think to get off wittily with their ignorance? Nay, they are esteemed the more learned and sufficient for this by the many, through their excellent vice° of judgement. For they commend writers as they do fencers or wrestlers, who if they come in robustuously, and put for it with a great deal of violence, are received for the braver fellows, when many times their own rudeness is the cause of their disgrace, and a little touch of their adversary gives all that boisterous force the foil. I deny not, but that these men, who always seek to do more than enough, may sometime happen on something that is good and great; but very seldom: and when it comes it doth not recompense the rest of their ill. It sticks out perhaps, and is more eminent, because all is sordid and vile about it, as lights are more discerned in a thick darkness than a faint shadow. I speak not this out of a hope to do good on any man against his will, for I know, if it were put to the question of theirs and mine, the worse would find more suffrages, because the most favour common errors. But I give thee this warning, that there is a great difference between those that (to gain the opinion of copy) utter all they can, however unfitly, and those that use election and a mean. For it is only the disease of the unskilful to think rude things greater than polished, or scattered more numerous° than composed.

THE PERSONS OF THE PLAY

SUBTLE, the alchemist
FACE, the housekeeper
DOLL COMMON, their colleague
DAPPER, a clerk
[ABEL] DRUGGER, a tobacco-man
LOVEWIT,° master of the house
[SIR] EPICURE MAMMON, a knight
[PERTINAX°] SURLY, a gamester

TRIBULATION [WHOLESOME], a
    pastor of Amsterdam
ANANIAS,° a deacon there
KESTREL,° the angry boy
DAME PLIANT, his sister, a widow
NEIGHBOURS
OFFICERS
MUTES°

THE SCENE

London

T he sickness hot, a master quit, for fear,°
H is house in town, and left one servant there.
E ase him corrupted, and gave means to know
A cheater and his punk, who, now brought low,   5
L eaving their narrow practice, were become°
C ozeners at large; and only wanting some
H ouse to set up, with him they here contract,
E each for a share, and all begin to act.
M uch company they draw, and much abuse,   10
I n casting figures, telling fortunes, news,
S elling of flies, flat bawdry, with the stone:°
T ill it, and they, and all in fume are gone.

Prologue

Fortune, that favours fools, these two short hours
    We wish away, both for your sakes, and ours,
Judging spectators; and desire in place
    To th' author justice, to ourselves but grace.
Our scene is London, 'cause we would make known   5
    No country's mirth is better than our own.
No clime breeds better matter for your whore,
    Bawd, squire, impostor, many persons more,
Whose manners, now called humours, feed the stage,
    And which have still been subject for the rage   10
Or spleen of comic writers. Though this pen
    Did never aim to grieve, but better men,
Howe'er the age he lives in doth endure
    The vices that she breeds, above their cure.
But when the wholesome remedies are sweet,   15
    And in their working, gain and profit meet,
He hopes to find no spirit so much diseased,
    But will, with such fair còrrectives, be pleased;
For here, he doth not fear, who can apply.°
    If there be any, that will sit so nigh   20

Unto the stream, to look what it doth run,
    They shall find things they'd think, or wish, were done;
They are so natural follies, but so shown,
    As even the doers may see, and yet not own.

1.1

[Enter] Face [with a sword], Subtle [with a small glass bottle, and] Doll Common

FACE Believe't, I will.

SUBTLE   Thy worst. I fart at thee.°

DOLL Ha' you your wits? Why gentlemen! For love—

FACE Sirrah, I'll strip you—

SUBTLE   What to do? Lick figs°

Out at my—

FACE   Rogue, rogue, out of all your sleights.°

DOLL Nay, look ye! Sovereign, General, are you madmen?   5

SUBTLE O, let the wild sheep loose. I'll gum your silks
With good strong water, an you come.

DOLL   Will you have°
The neighbours hear you? Will you betray all?
Hark, I hear somebody.

FACE   Sirrah—

SUBTLE   I shall mar
All that the tailor has made, if you approach.   10

FACE You most notorious whelp, you insolent slave,
Dare you do this?

SUBTLE   Yes faith, yes faith.

FACE   Why? Who
Am I, my mongrel? Who am I?

SUBTLE   I'll tell you,
Since you know not yourself—

FACE   Speak lower, rogue.

SUBTLE Yes. You were once—time's not long past—the good,   15
Honest, plain, livery-three-pound-thrum; that kept°
Your master's worship's house, here in the Friars,°
For the vacations—

FACE   Will you be so loud?°

SUBTLE Since, by my means, translated suburb-captain.°

FACE By your means, Doctor Dog?

SUBTLE   Within man's memory,   20
All this I speak of.

FACE   Why, I pray you, have I
Been countenanced by you? Or you by me?

Do but collect, sir, where I met you first.

SUBTLE I do not hear well.

FACE   Not of this, I think it.
But I shall put you in mind, sir, at Pie Corner,°   25
Taking your meal of steam in from cooks' stalls,
Where, like the father of hunger, you did walk
Piteously costive, with your pinched-horn nose,°
And your complexion of the Roman wash,
Stuck full of black and melancholic worms,°   30
Like powder-corns shot at the artillery yard.°

SUBTLE I wish you could advance your voice a little.

FACE When you went pinned up in the several rags
You'd raked and picked from dunghills before day,
Your feet in mouldy slippers for your kibes,   35
A felt of rug, and a thin threaden cloak°
That scarce would cover your no-buttocks—

SUBTLE   So, sir!

FACE When all your alchemy and your algebra,°
Your minerals, vegetals, and animals,
Your conjuring, cozening, and your dozen of trades,   40
Could not relieve your corpse with so much linen
Would make you tinder, but to see a fire,
I ga' you count'nance, credit for your coals,
Your stills, your glasses, your materials,
Built you a furnace, drew you customers,   45
Advanced all your black arts; lent you, beside,
A house to practise in—

SUBTLE   Your master's house!

FACE Where you have studied the more thriving skill
Of bawdry, since.

SUBTLE   Yes, in your master's house.
You and the rats, here, kept possession.   50
Make it not strange. I know yo'were one could keep
The buttery-hatch still locked, and save the chippings,
Sell the dole-beer to *aqua-vitae* men,°
The which, together with your Christmas vails,
At post and pair, your letting out of counters,°   55
Made you a pretty stock, some twenty marks,°
And gave you credit to converse with cobwebs,
Here, since your mistress' death hath broke up house.

FACE You might talk softlier, rascal.

SUBTLE   No, you scarab,
  I'll thunder you in pieces. I will teach you   60
  How to beware to tempt a fury again
  That carries tempest in his hand and voice.
FACE The place has made you valiant.
SUBTLE   No, your clothes.
  Thou vermin, have I ta'en thee out of dung,
  So poor, so wretched, when no living thing   65
  Would keep thee company but a spider or worse?
  Raised thee from brooms and dust and watering pots?
  Sublimed thee and exalted thee and fixed thee
  I' the third region, called our state of grace?°
  Wrought thee to spirit, to quintessence, with pains°   70
  Would twice have won me the philosophers' work?°
  Put thee in words and fashion? Made thee fit
  For more than ordinary fellowships?
  Given thee thy oaths, thy quarrelling dimensions?
  Thy rules, to cheat at horse-race, cock-pit, cards,   75
  Dice, or whatever gallant tincture else?
  Made thee a second in mine own great art?
  And have I this for thank? Do you rebel?
  Do you fly out i' the projection?°
  Would you be gone now?
DOLL   Gentlemen, what mean you?   80
  Will you mar all?
SUBTLE   Slave, thou hadst had no name—
DOLL Will you undo yourselves with civil war?
SUBTLE Never been known, past *equi-clibanum*,°
  The heat of horse-dung, underground in cellars,
  Or an ale-house darker than deaf John's; been lost°   85
  To all mankind but laundresses and tapsters,
  Had not I been.
DOLL   D'you know who hears you, Sovereign?
FACE Sirrah—
DOLL   Nay, General, I thought you were civil—
FACE I shall turn desperate if you grow thus loud.
SUBTLE And hang thyself, I care not.
FACE   Hang thee, collier,   90
  And all thy pots and pans, in picture I will,
  Since thou hast moved me—
DOLL [*aside*]   O, this'll o'erthrow all.

FACE Write thee up bawd, in Paul's; have all thy tricks°
    Of cozening with a hollow coal, dust, scrapings,°
    Searching for things lost, with a sieve and shears,°   95
    Erecting figures in your rows of houses,°
    And taking in of shadows with a glass,°
    Told in red letters; and a face cut for thee,
    Worse than Gamaliel Ratsey's.
DOLL   Are you sound?°
    Ha' you your senses, masters?
FACE   I will have   100
    A book, but barely reckoning thy impostures,
    Shall prove a true philosophers' stone to printers.
SUBTLE Away, you trencher-rascal.
FACE   Out, you dog-leech,
    The vomit of all prisons—
DOLL   Will you be
    Your own destructions, gentlemen?
FACE   Still spewed out   105
    For lying too heavy o' the basket.
SUBTLE   Cheater.°
FACE Bawd.
SUBTLE   Cowherd.
FACE   Conjurer.
SUBTLE   Cutpurse.
FACE   Witch.
DOLL   O me!
    We are ruined! Lost! Ha' you no more regard
    To your reputations? Where's your judgement? 'Slight,
    Have yet some care of me, o' your republic—°   110
FACE Away this brach. I'll bring thee, rogue, within
    The statute of sorcery, *tricesimo tertio*,
    Of Harry the Eight: aye, and perhaps thy neck°
    Within a noose, for laundering gold and barbing it.°
DOLL You'll bring your head within a cockscomb, will you?   115
       She catcheth out Face his sword, and breaks Subtle's glass
    And you, sir, with your menstrue, gather it up.
    'Sdeath, you abominable pair of stinkards,
    Leave off your barking, and grow one again,
    Or by the light that shines I'll cut your throats.
    I'll not be made a prey unto the marshal   120
    For ne'er a snarling dog-bolt o' you both.°

Ha' you together cozened all this while,
And all the world, and shall it now be said
Yo've made most courteous shift to cozen yourselves?
[*To Face*] You will accuse him? You will bring him in   125
Within the statute? Who shall take your word?
A whoreson, upstart, apocryphal captain
Whom not a Puritan in Blackfriars will trust
So much as for a feather! [*To Subtle*] And you, too,°
Will give the cause, forsooth? You will insult   130
And claim a primacy in the divisions?°
You must be chief? As if you only had
The powder to project with? And the work°
Were not begun out of equality?
The venture tripartite? All things in common?   135
Without priority? 'Sdeath, you perpetual curs,
Fall to your couples again, and cozen kindly°
And heartily and lovingly, as you should,
And lose not the beginning of a term,°
Or, by this hand, I shall grow factious too,   140
And take my part, and quit you.
FACE   'Tis his fault,
He ever murmurs and objects his pains,
And says the weight of all lies upon him.
SUBTLE Why, so it does.
DOLL   How does it? Do not we
Sustain our parts?
SUBTLE   Yes, but they are not equal.   145
DOLL Why, if your part exceed today, I hope
Ours may tomorrow match it.
SUBTLE   Aye, they may.
DOLL May, murmuring mastiff? Aye, and do. Death on me!
Help me to throttle him.
        [*Seizes Subtle by the throat*]
SUBTLE   Dorothy, mistress Dorothy,
'Ods precious, I'll do anything. What do you mean?°   150
DOLL Because o' your fermentation and cibation?
SUBTLE Not I, by heaven—
DOLL   Your *Sol* and *Luna*—help me.°
SUBTLE Would I were hanged then. I'll conform myself.
DOLL Will you, sir, do so then, and quickly? Swear.
SUBTLE What should I swear?

DOLL   To leave your faction, sir.   155
    And labour kindly in the common work.
SUBTLE Let me not breathe, if I meant aught beside.
    I only used those speeches as a spur
    To him.
DOLL   I hope we need no spurs, sir. Do we?
FACE 'Slid, prove today who shall shark best.
SUBTLE   Agreed.   160
DOLL Yes, and work close and friendly.
SUBTLE   'Slight, the knot
    Shall grow the stronger for this breach, with me.
        [*Doll releases him*]
DOLL Why so, my good baboons! Shall we go make
    A sort of sober, scurvy, precise neighbours,
    That scarce have smiled twice, sin' the king came in,°   165
    A feast of laughter at our follies? Rascals
    Would run themselves from breath to see me ride,°
    Or you to have but a hole to thrust your heads in,
    For which you should pay ear-rent? No, agree.°
    And may Don Provost ride a-feasting, long,°   170
    In his old velvet jerkin and stained scarfs,
    My noble Sovereign, and worthy General,
    Ere we contribute a new crewel garter
    To his most worsted worship.
SUBTLE   Royal Doll!
    Spoken like Claridiana, and thyself!°   175
FACE For which, at supper, thou shalt sit in triumph,
    And not be styled Doll Common, but Doll Proper,
    Doll Singular: the longest cut, at night,
    Shall draw thee for his Doll Particular.°
        [*A bell rings*]
SUBTLE Who's that? One rings. To the window, Doll. Pray heaven   180
    The master do not trouble us this quarter.
FACE O, fear not him. While there dies one a week
    O'the plague, he's safe from thinking toward London.
    Beside, he's busy at his hopyards now;
    I had a letter from him. If he do,   185
    He'll send such word for airing o' the house
    As you shall have sufficient time to quit it;
    Though we break up a fortnight, 'tis no matter.
SUBTLE Who is it, Doll?

DOLL   A fine young codling.
FACE   O,
   My lawyer's clerk, I lighted on last night   190
   In Holborn, at the Dagger. He would have—°
   I told you of him—a familiar
   To rifle with, at horses, and win cups.
DOLL O, let him in.
SUBTLE   Stay. Who shall do't?
FACE   Get you
   Your robes on. I will meet him, as going out.   195
DOLL And what shall I do?
FACE   Not be seen, away.
      [*Exit Doll*]
   Seem you very reserved.
SUBTLE   Enough.
      [*Exit Subtle*]
FACE   God b'w'you, sir.
   I pray you, let him know that I was here.
   His name is Dapper. I would gladly have stayed, but—

1.2

      [*Enter*] *Dapper*
DAPPER Captain, I am here.
FACE   Who's that? He's come, I think, Doctor.
   Good faith, sir, I was going away.
DAPPER   In truth,
   I'm very sorry, Captain.
FACE   But I thought
   Sure I should meet you.
DAPPER   Aye, I'm very glad.
   I had a scurvy writ or two to make,   5
   And I had lent my watch last night to one
   That dines today at the sheriff's, and so was robbed
   Of my pass-time.
      [*Enter Subtle in alchemist's robes*]
         Is this the cunning-man?
FACE This is his worship.
DAPPER   Is he a Doctor?

FACE   Yes.

DAPPER And ha' you broke with him, Captain?

FACE   Aye.

DAPPER   And how?°   10

FACE Faith, he does make the matter, sir, so dainty,
 I know not what to say—

DAPPER   Not so, good Captain.

FACE Would I were fairly rid on't, believe me.

DAPPER Nay, now you grieve me, sir. Why should you wish so?
 I dare assure you I'll not be ungrateful.   15

FACE I cannot think you will, sir. But the law
 Is such a thing—And then, he says, Read's matter°
 Falling so lately—

DAPPER   Read? He was an ass,
 And dealt, sir, with a fool.

FACE   It was a clerk, sir.

DAPPER A clerk?

FACE   Nay, hear me, sir, you know the law   20
 Better, I think—

DAPPER   I should, sir, and the danger.
 You know I showed the statute to you?

FACE   You did so.

DAPPER And will I tell, then? By this hand of flesh,
 Would it might never write good court-hand more,
 If I discover. What do you think of me,   25
 That I am a *chiaus*?

FACE   What's that?

DAPPER   The Turk, was here—°
 As one would say, do you think I am a Turk?

FACE I'll tell the Doctor so.

DAPPER   Do, good sweet Captain.

FACE Come, noble Doctor, pray thee, let's prevail;
 This is the gentleman, and he is no *chiaus*.   30

SUBTLE Captain, I have returned you all my answer.
 I would do much, sir, for your love—but this
 I neither may, nor can.

FACE   Tut, do not say so.
 You deal now with a noble fellow, Doctor,
 One that will thank you richly, and he's no *chiaus*:   35
 Let that, sir, move you.

SUBTLE   Pray you, forbear—

FACE   He has
    Four angels, here—
SUBTLE   You do me wrong, good sir.
FACE Doctor, wherein? To tempt you with these spirits?
SUBTLE To tempt my art and love, sir, to my peril.
    'Fore heaven, I scarce can think you are my friend,   40
    That so would draw me to apparent danger.
FACE I draw you? A horse draw you, and a halter,°
    You, and your flies together—
DAPPER   Nay, good Captain.
FACE That know no difference of men.
SUBTLE   Good words, sir.
FACE Good deeds, Sir Doctor Dog's-meat. 'Slight I bring you   45
    No cheating Clim-o'-the-Cloughs, or Claribels,°
    That look as big as five-and-fifty and flush,°
    And spit out secrets like hot custard—
DAPPER   Captain.
FACE Nor any melancholic underscribe,
    Shall tell the Vicar; but a special gentle,°   50
    That is the heir to forty marks a year,
    Consorts with the small poets of the time,
    Is the sole hope of his old grandmother,
    That knows the law, and writes you six fair hands,°
    Is a fine clerk, and has his ciphering perfect,   55
    Will take his oath, o' the Greek Testament,°
    If need be, in his pocket, and can court
    His mistress out of Ovid.
DAPPER   Nay, dear Captain.
FACE Did you not tell me so?
DAPPER   Yes, but I'd ha' you
    Use Master Doctor with some more respect.   60
FACE Hang him, proud stag, with his broad velvet head.°
    But for your sake, I'd choke ere I would change
    An article of breath with such a puck-fist—
    Come, let's be gone.
SUBTLE   Pray you, le' me speak with you.
DAPPER His worship calls you, Captain.
FACE   I am sorry   65
    I e'er embarked myself in such a business.
DAPPER Nay, good sir. He did call you.
FACE   Will he take, then?

SUBTLE First, hear me—
FACE   Not a syllable, 'less you take.
SUBTLE Pray ye, sir—
FACE   Upon no terms, but an *assumpsit*.°
SUBTLE Your humour must be law.
        He takes the money
FACE   Why now, sir, talk.   70
  Now I dare hear you with mine honour. Speak.
  So may this gentleman too.
SUBTLE   Why, sir—
FACE   No whispering.
SUBTLE 'Fore heaven, you do not apprehend the loss
  You do yourself in this.
FACE   Wherein? For what?
SUBTLE Marry, to be so importunate for one,   75
  That, when he has it, will undo you all;
  He'll win up all the money i' the town.
FACE How!
SUBTLE   Yes. And blow up gamester after gamester,
  As they do crackers in a puppet play.
  If I do give him a familiar,   80
  Give you him all you play for; never set him:
  For he will have it.
FACE   You're mistaken, Doctor.°
  Why, he does ask one but for cups, and horses,
  A rifling fly: none o' your great familiars.
DAPPER Yes, Captain, I would have it for all games.   85
SUBTLE I told you so.
FACE [*to Dapper*]   'Slight, that's a new business!
  I understood you, a tame bird, to fly
  Twice in a term, or so; on Friday nights,
  When you had left the office; for a nag
  Of forty or fifty shillings.
DAPPER   Aye, 'tis true, sir,   90
  But I do think, now, I shall leave the law,
  And therefore—
FACE   Why, this changes quite the case!
  D'you think that I dare move him?
DAPPER   If you please, sir,
  All's one to him, I see.
FACE   What? For that money?

I cannot with my conscience. Nor should you   95
Make the request, methinks.

DAPPER   No, sir, I mean
To add consideration.

FACE   Why then, sir,
I'll try. [*To Subtle*] Say that it were for all games, Doctor?

SUBTLE I say, then, not a mouth shall eat for him
At any ordinary, but o' the score,°   100
That is a gaming mouth, conceive me.

FACE   Indeed!

SUBTLE He'll draw you all the treasure of the realm,
If it be set him.

FACE   Speak you this from art?

SUBTLE Aye, sir, and reason too: the ground of art.
He's o' the only best complexion   105
The Queen of Fairy loves.

FACE   What? Is he?

SUBTLE   Peace.
He'll overhear you. Sir, should she but see him—

FACE What?

SUBTLE   Do not you tell him.

FACE   Will he win at cards too?

SUBTLE The spirits of dead Holland, living Isaac,°
You'd swear were in him; such a vigorous luck   110
As cannot be resisted. 'Slight, he'll put
Six o' your gallants to a cloak, indeed.°

FACE A strange success that some man shall be born to!

SUBTLE He hears you, man—

DAPPER   Sir, I'll not be ingrateful.

FACE Faith, I have a confidence in his good nature.   115
You hear, he says he will not be ingrateful.

SUBTLE Why, as you please, my venture follows yours.

FACE Troth, do it, Doctor. Think him trusty, and make him.
He may make us both happy in an hour;
Win some five thousand pound, and send us two on't.   120

DAPPER Believe it, and I will, sir.

FACE   And you shall, sir.
You have heard all?
            Face takes him aside

DAPPER   No, what was't? Nothing, I sir.

FACE Nothing?

DAPPER   A little, sir.
FACE   Well, a rare star
  Reigned at your birth.
DAPPER   At mine, sir? No.
FACE   The Doctor
  Swears that you are—
SUBTLE   Nay, Captain, you'll tell all, now.   125
FACE Allied to the Queen of Fairy.
DAPPER   Who? That I am?
  Believe it, no such matter—
FACE   Yes, and that
  You were born with a caul o' your head.
DAPPER   Who says so?
FACE   Come.°
  You know it well enough, though you dissemble it.
DAPPER I'fac, I do not. You are mistaken.
FACE   How?   130
  Swear by your fac? And in a thing so known
  Unto the Doctor? How shall we, sir, trust you
  I'the other matter? Can we ever think,
  When you have won five or six thousand pound,
  You'll send us shares in't, by this rate?
DAPPER   By Jove, sir,   135
  I'll win ten thousand pound, and send you half.
  I'fac's no oath.
SUBTLE   No, no, he did but jest.
FACE Go to. Go, thank the Doctor. He's your friend
  To take it so.
DAPPER   I thank his worship.
FACE   So?
  Another angel.
DAPPER   Must I?
FACE   Must you? 'Slight,   140
  What else is thanks? Will you be trivial?
    [*Dapper gives money*]
                    Doctor,
  When must he come for his familiar?
DAPPER Shall I not ha' it with me?
SUBTLE   O, good sir!
  There must a world of ceremonies pass,
  You must be bathed and fumigated first;   145

Besides, the Queen of Fairy does not rise
Till it be noon.
FACE   Not if she danced tonight.
SUBTLE And she must bless it.
FACE   Did you never see
Her royal Grace yet?
DAPPER   Whom?
FACE   Your aunt of Fairy?
SUBTLE Not since she kissed him in the cradle, Captain,   150
I can resolve you that.
FACE   Well, see her Grace,
Whate'er it cost you, for a thing that I know!°
It will be somewhat hard to compass; but,
However, see her. You are made, believe it,
If you can see her. Her Grace is a lone woman,
And very rich, and if she take a fancy,   155
She will do strange things. See her, at any hand.
'Slid, she may hap to leave you all she has!
It is the Doctor's fear.
DAPPER   How will't be done then?
FACE Let me alone, take you no thought. Do you
But say to me, 'Captain, I'll see her Grace.'   160
DAPPER Captain, I'll see her Grace.
        One knocks without
FACE   Enough.
SUBTLE   Who's there?
Anon. [*Aside to Face*] Conduct him forth, by the back way.
[*To Dapper*] Sir, against one o'clock, prepare yourself.
Till when you must be fasting; only, take   165
Three drops of vinegar in at your nose;
Two at your mouth; and one at either ear;
Then bathe your fingers' ends; and wash your eyes,
To sharpen your five senses; and cry 'hum'
Thrice; and then 'buzz', as often; and then, come.   170
        [*Exit Subtle*]
FACE Can you remember this?
DAPPER   I warrant you.
FACE Well, then, away. 'Tis but your bestowing
Some twenty nobles 'mong her Grace's servants;
And put on a clean shirt. You do not know
What grace her Grace may do you in clean linen.   175
        [*Exeunt Dapper and Face*]

1.3

[*Enter*] *Drugger* [*and Subtle from opposite sides*]

SUBTLE Come in—[*addressing imaginary women offstage*] good
   wives, I pray you forbear me now.
   Troth I can do you no good, till afternoon—
   What is your name, say you, Abel Drugger?

DRUGGER   Yes, sir.

SUBTLE A seller of tobacco?

DRUGGER   Yes, sir.

SUBTLE   Umh.
   Free of the Grocers?

DRUGGER   Aye, an't please you.

SUBTLE   Well—°   5
   Your business, Abel?

DRUGGER   This, an't please your worship,
   I am a young beginner, and am building
   Of a new shop, an't like your worship; just
   At corner of a street—here's the plot on't—°
   And I would know by art, sir, of your worship,   10
   Which way I should make my door, by necromancy.
   And where my shelves. And which should be for boxes.
   And which for pots. I would be glad to thrive, sir.
   And I was wished to your worship by a gentleman,
   One Captain Face, that says you know men's planets,   15
   And their good angels, and their bad.

SUBTLE   I do,
   If I do see 'em—
      [*Enter Face*]

FACE   What! My honest Abel?
   Thou art well met here!

DRUGGER   Troth, sir, I was speaking,
   Just as your worship came here, of your worship.
   I pray you, speak for me to Master Doctor.   20

FACE He shall do anything. Doctor, do you hear?
   This is my friend, Abel, an honest fellow,
   He lets me have good tobacco, and he does not
   Sophisticate it with sack-lees or oil,
   Nor washes it in muscadel and grains,   25
   Nor buries it in gravel underground,

Wrapped up in greasy leather, or pissed clouts,°
But keeps it in fine lily-pots, that opened,
Smell like conserve of roses, or French beans.°
He has his maple block, his silver tongs,   30
Winchester pipes, and fire of juniper.°
A neat, spruce, honest fellow, and no goldsmith.°
SUBTLE He's a fortunate fellow, that I am sure on—
FACE Already, sir, ha' you found it? Lo thee Abel!
SUBTLE And in right way toward riches—
FACE   Sir.
SUBTLE   This summer,   35
He will be of the clothing of his Company:
And next spring, called to the scarlet. Spend what he can.°
FACE What, and so little beard?
SUBTLE   Sir, you must think,
He may have a receipt to make hair come.
But he'll be wise, preserve his youth, and fine for't;°   40
His fortune looks for him another way.
FACE 'Slid, Doctor, how canst thou know this so soon?
I'm amused, at that!
SUBTLE   By a rule, Captain,
In metoposcopy, which I do work by,
A certain star i'the forehead, which you see not.   45
Your chestnut or your olive-coloured face
Does never fail, and your long ear doth promise.
I knew't by certain spots too, in his teeth,
And on the nail of his mercurial finger.
FACE Which finger's that?
SUBTLE   His little finger. Look.   50
You were born upon a Wednesday?
DRUGGER   Yes, indeed, sir.
SUBTLE The thumb, in chiromancy, we give Venus;
The forefinger to Jove; the midst, to Saturn;
The ring to Sol; the least, to Mercury:
Who was the lord, sir, of his horoscope,   55
His house of life being Libra, which foreshowed,°
He should be a merchant, and should trade with balance.
FACE Why, this is strange! Is't not, honest Nab?
SUBTLE There is a ship now, coming from Ormus,°
That shall yield him such a commodity   60
Of drugs—This is the west, and this the south?

DRUGGER Yes, sir.

SUBTLE   And those are your two sides?

DRUGGER   Aye, sir.

SUBTLE Make me your door, then, south; your broad side, west:
And on the east side of your shop, aloft,
Write *Mathlai, Tarmiel,* and *Baraborat*;   65
Upon the north part, *Rael, Velel, Thiel.*°
They are the names of those Mercurial spirits,
That do fright flies from boxes.

DRUGGER   Yes, sir.

SUBTLE   And
Beneath your threshold, bury me a lodestone
To draw in gallants that wear spurs; the rest,   70
They'll seem to follow.

FACE   That's a secret, Nab!

SUBTLE And on your stall a puppet with a vice,
And a court-fucus to call city-dames.
You shall deal much with minerals.

DRUGGER   Sir, I have,
At home, already—

SUBTLE   Aye, I know, you've arsenic,   75
Vitriol, sal-tartar, argaile, alkali,
Cinoper: I know all. This fellow, Captain,
Will come, in time, to be a great distiller,
And give a say (I will not say directly,°
But very fair) at the philosophers' stone.   80

FACE Why, how now, Abel! Is this true?

DRUGGER   Good Captain,
What must I give?

FACE   Nay, I'll not counsel thee.
Thou hear'st, what wealth (he says, spend what thou canst)
Th'art like to come to.

DRUGGER   I would gi' him a crown.

FACE A crown! And toward such a fortune? Heart,   85
Thou shalt rather gi' him thy shop. No gold about thee?

DRUGGER Yes, I have a portague I ha' kept this half year.

FACE Out on thee, Nab; 'Slight, there was such an offer—
'Shalt keep 't no longer, I'll gi' it him for thee?
        [*Gives coin to Subtle*]
Doctor, Nab prays your worship to drink this, and swears   90
He will appear more grateful, as your skill

Does raise him in the world.

DRUGGER   I would entreat
Another favour of his worship.

FACE   What is't, Nab?

DRUGGER But to look over, sir, my almanac,
And cross out my ill-days, that I may neither   95
Bargain, nor trust upon them.

FACE   That he shall, Nab.
Leave it, it shall be done 'gainst afternoon.

SUBTLE And a direction for his shelves.

FACE   Now, Nab?
Art thou well pleased, Nab?

DRUGGER   Thank sir, both your worships.

FACE. Away.
      [*Exit Drugger*]
Why, now, you smoky persecuter of nature!   100
Now do you see that something's to be done,
Beside your beech-coal and your corsive waters,
Your crosslets, crucibles, and cucurbites?
You must have stuff brought home to you to work on?
And yet you think I am at no expense,   105
In searching out these veins, then following 'em,
Then trying 'em out. 'Fore God, my intelligence
Costs me more money than my share oft comes to,
In these rare works.

SUBTLE   You're pleasant, sir. How now?

1.4

      [*Enter*] Doll [*Common*]

SUBTLE What says my dainty Dolkin?

DOLL   Yonder fishwife
Will not away. And there's your giantess,
The bawd of Lambeth.

SUBTLE   Heart, I cannot speak with 'em.

DOLL Not afore night, I have told 'em, in a voice
Thorough the trunk, like one of your familiars.   5
But I have spied Sir Epicure Mammon—

SUBTLE   Where?

DOLL Coming along, at far end of the lane,
   Slow of his feet but earnest of his tongue,
   To one that's with him.
SUBTLE   Face, go you and shift.
     [*Exit Face*]
   Doll, you must presently make ready too—   10
DOLL Why, what's the matter?
SUBTLE   O, I did look for him
   With the sun's rising: 'marvel he could sleep!
   This is the day I am to perfect for him
   The *magisterium*, our great work, the stone;°
   And yield it, made, into his hands: of which   15
   He has this month talked as he were possessed.
   And now he's dealing pieces on't away.
   Methinks I see him entering ordinaries,
   Dispensing for the pox; and plaguy houses,
   Reaching his dose; walking Moorfields for lepers;°   20
   And offering citizens' wives pomander-bracelets°
   As his preservative, made of the elixir;
   Searching the spittle, to make old bawds young;
   And the highways for beggars to make rich.
   I see no end of his labours. He will make   25
   Nature ashamed of her long sleep, when art,
   Who's but a stepdame, shall do more than she,
   In her best love to mankind, ever could.
   If his dream last, he'll turn the age to gold.
     [*Exeunt*]

2.1

[Enter Sir Epicure] Mammon [and] Surly

MAMMON Come on, sir. Now you set your foot on shore
In novo orbe; here's the rich Peru;°
And there within, sir, are the golden mines,
Great Solomon's Ophir! He was sailing to't°
Three years, but we have reached it in ten months.   5
This is the day wherein to all my friends,
I will pronounce the happy word, 'be rich'.
This day you shall be *spectatissimi*.°
You shall no more deal with the hollow die,°
Or the frail card. No more be at charge of keeping   10
The livery-punk, for the young heir that must
Seal, at all hours, in his shirt. No more,
If he deny, ha' him beaten to't, as he is
That brings him the commodity. No more°
Shall thirst of satin or the covetous hunger   15
Of velvet entrails for a rude-spun cloak,
To be displayed at Madam Augusta's, make°
The sons of sword and hazard fall before°
The golden calf, and on their knees, whole nights,°
Commit idolatry with wine and trumpets,   20
Or go a-feasting, after drum and ensign.°
No more of this. You shall start up young viceroys,°
And have your punks and punkettees, my Surly.
And unto thee I speak it first, 'be rich'.
Where is my Subtle, there? Within, ho?
FACE (*within*)   Sir.   25
He'll come to you by and by.
MAMMON   That's his fire-drake,°
His lungs, his Zephyrus, he that puffs his coals,
Till he firk nature up in her own centre.
You are not faithful, sir. This night I'll change
All that is metal in my house to gold.   30
And early in the morning will I send
To all the plumbers and the pewterers,
And buy their tin and lead up; and to Lothbury,°
For all the copper.

SURLY   What, and turn that too?

MAMMON Yes, and I'll purchase Devonshire and Cornwall,°   35
  And make them perfect Indies! You admire now?

SURLY No, faith.

MAMMON   But when you see th' effects of the great medicine,
  Of which one part projected on a hundred
  Of Mercury or Venus or the Moon,
  Shall turn it to as many of the Sun;°   40
  Nay, to a thousand, so *ad infinitum*:°
  You will believe me.

SURLY   Yes, when I see't, I will.
  But if my eyes do cozen me so (and I
  Giving 'em no occasion) sure, I'll have
  A whore, shall piss 'em out, next day.

MAMMON   Ha! Why?   45
  Do you think I fable with you? I assure you,
  He that has once the flower of the sun,
  The perfect ruby, which we call elixir,°
  Not only can do that, but by its virtue
  Can confer honour, love, respect, long life,   50
  Give safety, valour—yea, and victory,
  To whom he will. In eight and twenty days,
  I'll make an old man of fourscore a child.

SURLY No doubt, he's that already.

MAMMON   Nay, I mean
  Restore his years, renew him like an eagle,°   55
  To the fifth age; make him get sons and daughters,°
  Young giants; as our philosophers have done
  (The ancient patriarchs afore the flood)°
  But taking, once a week, on a knife's point,
  The quantity of a grain of mustard of it;   60
  Become stout Marses, and beget young Cupids.

SURLY The decayed vestals of Pict-hatch would thank you,°
  That keep the fire alive there.

MAMMON   'Tis the secret
  Of nature naturized 'gainst all infections,°
  Cures all diseases coming of all causes,   65
  A month's grief in a day; a year's in twelve;
  And of what age soever, in a month,
  Past all the doses of your drugging doctors.
  I'll undertake, withal, to fright the plague

Out o' the kingdom, in three months.

SURLY   And I'll   70
Be bound, the players shall sing your praises then,°
Without their poets.

MAMMON   Sir, I'll do't. Meantime,
I'll give away so much unto my man,
Shall serve th' whole city with preservative,
Weekly, each house his dose, and at the rate—   75

SURLY As he that built the waterwork does with water?°

MAMMON You are incredulous.

SURLY   Faith, I have a humour,
I would not willingly be gulled. Your stone
Cannot transmute me.

MAMMON   Pertinax, Surly,
Will you believe antiquity? Records?   80
I'll show you a book where Moses and his sister
And Solomon have written of the art;
Aye, and a treatise penned by Adam.°

SURLY   How!

MAMMON O' the philosophers' stone, and in High Dutch.°

SURLY Did Adam write, sir, in High Dutch?

MAMMON   He did,   85
Which proves it was the primitive tongue. .

SURLY   What paper?

MAMMON On cedar board.

SURLY   O that indeed (they say)
Will last 'gainst worms.

MAMMON   'Tis like your Irish wood°
'Gainst cobwebs. I have a piece of Jason's fleece, too,°
Which was no other than a book of alchemy,   90
Writ in large sheepskin, a good fat ram-vellum.
Such was Pythagoras' thigh, Pandora's tub,°
And all that fable of Medea's charms,
The manner of our work: the bulls, our furnace,
Still breathing fire; our argent-vive, the dragon;   95
The dragon's teeth, mercury sublimate,°
That keeps the whiteness, hardness, and the biting;
And they are gathered into Jason's helm°
(Th' alembic) and then sowed in Mars his field,°
And thence sublimed so often, till they are fixed.°   100
Both this, th' Hesperian garden, Cadmus' story,°

Jove's shower, the boon of Midas, Argus' eyes,°
Boccace his Demogorgon, thousands more,°
All abstract riddles of our stone. How now?°

2.2

[Enter] Face [dressed as an alchemist's assistant]

MAMMON Do we succeed? Is our day come? And holds it?

FACE The evening will set red upon you, sir;
You have colour for it, crimson: the red ferment°
Has done his office. Three hours hence, prepare you
To see projection.

MAMMON   Pertinax, my Surly,   5
Again I say to thee aloud: 'be rich'.
This day thou shalt have ingots, and tomorrow
Give lords th' affront. Is it, my Zephyrus, right?°
Blushes the bolt's-head?

FACE   Like a wench with child, sir,°
That were but now discovered to her master.   10

MAMMON Excellent witty Lungs! My only care is
Where to get stuff enough now; to project on;
This town will not half serve me.

FACE   No, sir? Buy
The covering off o' churches.

MAMMON   That's true.

FACE   Yes,
Let 'em stand bare, as do their auditory.   15
Or cap 'em new with shingles.

MAMMON   No, good thatch:°
Thatch will lie light upo' the rafters, Lungs.
Lungs, I will manumit thee from the furnace;
I will restore thee thy complexion, Puff,
Lost in the embers; and repair this brain,   20
Hurt wi' the fume o'the metals.

FACE   I have blown, sir,
Hard, for your worship; thrown by many a coal
When 'twas not beech; weighed those I put in, just,
To keep your heat still even. These bleared eyes
Have waked to read your several colours, sir,   25

Of the pale citron, the green lion, the crow,
The peacock's tail, the plumèd swan.

MAMMON   And lastly,
Thou hast descried the flower, the *sanguis agni?*°

FACE Yes, sir.

MAMMON   Where's master?

FACE   At's prayers, sir, he,
Good man, he's doing his devotions,   30
For the success.

MAMMON   Lungs, I will set a period,
To all thy labours: thou shalt be the master
Of my seraglio.

FACE   Good, sir.

MAMMON   But do you hear?°
I'll geld you, Lungs.

FACE   Yes, sir.

MAMMON   For I do mean
To have a list of wives and concubines   35
Equal with Solomon, who had the stone°
Alike with me; and I will make me a back
With the elixir that shall be as tough
As Hercules, to encounter fifty a night.°
Th'art sure thou saw'st it blood?

FACE   Both blood and spirit, sir.°   40

MAMMON I will have all my beds blown up, not stuffed;
Down is too hard. And then mine oval room
Filled with such pictures as Tiberius took
From Elephantis, and dull Aretine
But coldly imitated. Then, my glasses°   45
Cut in more subtle angles, to disperse
And multiply the figures as I walk
Naked between my *succubae*. My mists°
I'll have of perfume, vapoured 'bout the room,
To loose ourselves in; and my baths like pits   50
To fall into, from whence we will come forth
And roll us dry in gossamer and roses.—
Is it arrived at ruby?—Where I spy
A wealthy citizen, or rich lawyer,
Have a sublimed pure wife, unto that fellow   55
I'll send a thousand pound to be my cuckold.

FACE And I shall carry it?

MAMMON   No. I'll ha' no bawds
  But fathers and mothers. They will do it best.
  Best of all others. And my flatterers
  Shall be the pure and gravest of divines   60
  That I can get for money. My mere fools,
  Eloquent burgesses, and then my poets,
  The same that writ so subtly of the fart,°
  Whom I will entertain, still, for that subject.
  The few that would give out themselves to be   65
  Court and town stallions, and eachwhere belie
  Ladies, who are known most innocent, for them;°
  Those will I beg to make me eunuchs of,
  And they shall fan me with ten ostrich tails
  Apiece, made in a plume to gather wind.   70
  We will be brave, Puff, now we ha' the medicine.
  My meat shall all come in in Indian shells,
  Dishes of agate, set in gold, and studded
  With emeralds, sapphires, hyacinths and rubies.
  The tongues of carps, dormice and camels' heels,   75
  Boiled i' the spirit of Sol, and dissolved pearl°
  (Apicius' diet, 'gainst the epilepsy);°
  And I will eat these broths with spoons of amber,
  Headed with diamond and carbuncle.
  My footboy shall eat pheasants, calvered salmons,   80
  Knots, godwits, lampreys. I myself will have
  The beards of barbels, served instead of salads;
  Oiled mushrooms; and the swelling unctuous paps
  Of a fat pregnant sow, newly cut off,
  Dressed with an exquisite and poignant sauce;   85
  For which, I'll say unto my cook, 'there's gold,
  Go forth, and be a knight.'
FACE   Sir, I'll go look
  A little, how it heightens.
MAMMON   Do.
    [*Exit Face*]
                          My shirts
  I'll have of taffeta-sarsnet, soft and light
  As cobwebs; and for all my other raiment   90
  It shall be such as might provoke the Persian,°
  Were he to teach the world riot anew.
  My gloves of fishes' and birds' skins, perfumed

With gums of paradise, and eastern air—°

SURLY And do you think to have the stone, with this? 95

MAMMON No, I do think to have all this with the stone.

SURLY Why, I have heard he must be *homo frugi*,°
    A pious, holy and religious man,
    One free from mortal sin, a very virgin.

MAMMON That makes it, sir, he is so. But I buy it.° 100
    My venture brings it me. He, honest wretch,
    A notable, superstitious, good soul,
    Has worn his knees bare and his slippers bald,
    With prayer and fasting for it; and, sir, let him
    Do it alone, for me, still. Here he comes, 105
    Not a profane word afore him! 'Tis poison.

2.3

[Enter] Subtle

MAMMON Good morrow, father.

SUBTLE   Gentle son, good morrow,
    And to your friend there. What is he, is with you?

MAMMON An heretic that I did bring along
    In hope, sir, to convert him.

SUBTLE   Son, I doubt
    You're covetous, that thus you meet your time 5
    I' the just point, prevent your day, at morning.
    This argues something worthy of a fear
    Of importune and carnal appetite.
    Take heed you do not cause the blessing leave you,
    With your ungoverned haste. I should be sorry 10
    To see my labours, now e'en at perfection,
    Got by long watching and large patience,
    Not prosper where my love and zeal hath placed 'em.
    Which (heaven I call to witness, with yourself,
    To whom I have poured my thoughts) in all my ends, 15
    Have looked no way but unto public good,
    To pious uses, and dear charity,
    Now grown a prodigy with men. Wherein
    If you, my son, should now prevaricate,
    And to your own particular lusts employ 20

So great and catholic a bliss, be sure
A curse will follow, yea, and overtake
Your subtle and most secret ways.

MAMMON   I know, sir,
You shall not need to fear me. I but come
To ha' you confute this gentleman.

SURLY   Who is,   25
Indeed, sir, somewhat costive of belief
Toward your stone; would not be gulled.

SUBTLE   Well, son,
All that I can convince him in, is this,
The work is done; bright Sol is in his robe.
We have a medicine of the triple soul,   30
The glorified spirit. Thanks be to heaven,°
And make us worthy of it. Ulenspiegel!°

FACE [within] Anon, sir.
          [Enter Face]

SUBTLE   Look well to the register,
And let your heat still lessen by degrees,
To the aludels.

FACE   Yes, sir.

SUBTLE   Did you look   35
O'the bolt's-head yet?

FACE   Which, on D, sir?

SUBTLE   Aye.
What's the complexion?

FACE   Whitish.

SUBTLE   Infuse vinegar,
To draw his volatile substance and his tincture,
And let the water in glass E be filtered,
And put into the gripe's egg. Lute him well;°   40
And leave him closed in balneo.

FACE   I will, sir.°
          [Exit Face]

SURLY What a brave language here is, next to canting!

SUBTLE I have another work you never saw, son,
That three days since passed the philosophers' wheel,°
In the lent heat of athanor, and's become   45
Sulphur o' nature.

MAMMON   But 'tis for me?

SUBTLE   What need you?°

You have enough in that is perfect.

MAMMON   O, but—

SUBTLE   Why, this is covetise!

MAMMON   No, I assure you,°
   I shall employ it all in pious uses,
   Founding of colleges and grammar schools,   50
   Marrying young virgins, building hospitals,
   And now and then a church.
       [Enter Face]

SUBTLE   How now?

FACE   Sir, please you,
   Shall I not change the filter?

SUBTLE   Marry, yes.
   And bring me the complexion of glass B.
       [Exit Face]

MAMMON   Ha' you another?

SUBTLE   Yes, son, were I assured   55
   Your piety were firm, we would not want
   The means to glorify it. But I hope the best;
   I mean to tinct C in sand-heat tomorrow,
   And give him imbibition.

MAMMON   Of white oil?

SUBTLE   No, sir, of red. F is come over the helm too,   60
   I thank my Maker, in St Mary's bath,°
   And shows *lac virginis*. Blessed be heaven.°
   I sent you of his faeces there, calcined.
   Out of that calx, I' ha' won the salt of Mercury.°

MAMMON   By pouring on your rectified water?   65

SUBTLE   Yes, and reverberating in athanor.
       [Enter Face]
   How now? What colour says it?

FACE   The ground black, sir.

MAMMON   That's your crow's head?

SURLY   Your cockscomb's, is it not?°

SUBTLE   No, 'tis not perfect; would it were the crow.
   That work wants something.

SURLY [*aside*]   O, I looked for this.   70
   The hay is a-pitching.

SUBTLE   Are you sure you loosed 'em°
   I' their own menstrue?

FACE   Yes, sir, and then married 'em,

And put 'em in a bolt's-head, nipped to digestion,°
According as you bade me; when I set
The liquor of Mars to circulation,°   75
In the same heat.
SUBTLE   The process, then, was right.
FACE Yes, by the token, sir, the retort brake,
And what was saved was put into the pelican,
And signed with Hermes' seal.
SUBTLE   I think 'twas so.°
We should have a new amalgama.
SURLY [*aside*]   O, this ferret   80
Is rank as any polecat.
SUBTLE   But I care not.
Let him e'en die; we have enough beside,°
In embrion. H has his white shirt on?
FACE   Yes, sir,°
He's ripe for inceration; he stands warm
In his ash-fire. I would not you should let   85
Any die now, if I might counsel, sir,
For luck's sake to the rest. It is not good.
MAMMON He says right.
SURLY [*aside*]   Aye, are you bolted?
FACE   Nay, I know't, sir,
I've seen the ill fortune. What is some three ounces
Of fresh materials?
MAMMON   Is't no more?
FACE   No more, sir,   90
Of gold t' amalgam with some six of mercury.
MAMMON Away, here's money. What will serve?
FACE [*pointing to Subtle*]   Ask him, sir.
MAMMON How much?
SUBTLE   Give him nine pound; you may gi' him ten.
SURLY [*aside*] Yes, twenty, and be cozened, do.
MAMMON [*gives money*]   There 'tis.
SUBTLE This needs not. But that you will have it, so,   95
To see conclusions of all. For two
Of our inferior works are at fixation.
A third is in ascension. Go your ways.
Ha' you set the oil of Luna *in kemia*?°
FACE Yes, sir.
SUBTLE   And the philosophers' vinegar?

FACE   Aye.°   100
  [*Exit Face*]
SURLY We shall have a salad.
MAMMON   When do you make projection?
SUBTLE Son, be not hasty, I exalt our medicine,
  By hanging him *in balneo vaporoso*;°
  And giving him solution; then congeal him;
  And then dissolve him; then again congeal him;   105
  For look, how oft I iterate the work,
  So many times I add unto his virtue.
  As, if at first, one ounce convert a hundred,
  After his second loose, he'll turn a thousand;
  His third solution, ten; his fourth, a hundred.   110
  After his fifth, a thousand thousand ounces
  Of any imperfect metal, into pure
  Silver or gold, in all examinations
  As good as any of the natural mine.
  Get you your stuff here, against afternoon,   115
  Your brass, your pewter, and your andirons.
MAMMON Not those of iron?
SUBTLE   Yes. You may bring them, too.
  We'll change all metals.
SURLY   I believe you in that.
MAMMON Then I may send my spits?
SUBTLE   Yes, and your racks.
SURLY And dripping-pans and pot-hangers and hooks?   120
  Shall he not?
SUBTLE   If he please.
SURLY   To be an ass.
SUBTLE How, sir!
MAMMON   This gent'man you must bear withal.
  I told you he had no faith.
SURLY   And little hope, sir,
  But much less charity, should I gull myself.
SUBTLE Why, what have you observed, sir, in our art,   125
  Seems so impossible?
SURLY   But your whole work, no more.
  That you should hatch gold in a furnace, sir,
  As they do eggs in Egypt!
SUBTLE   Sir, do you°
  Believe that eggs are hatched so?

SURLY   If I should?

SUBTLE Why, I think that the greater miracle.   130
No egg, but differs from a chicken more,
Than metals in themselves.

SURLY   That cannot be.
The egg's ordained by nature to that end,
And is a chicken *in potentia*.°

SUBTLE The same we say of lead and other metals,   135
Which would be gold if they had time.

MAMMON   And that
Our art doth further.

SUBTLE   Aye, for 'twere absurd
To think that nature in the earth bred gold
Perfect, i'the instant. Something went before.
There must be remote matter.

SURLY   Aye, what is that?°   140

SUBTLE Marry, we say—

MAMMON   Aye, now it heats; stand, father.
Pound him to dust—

SUBTLE   It is, of the one part,
A humid exhalation, which we call
Materia liquida, or the unctuous water;°
On the other part, a certain crass and viscous   145
Portion of earth; both which, concorporate,
Do make the elementary matter of gold,
Which is not yet *propria materia*,°
But common to all metals and all stones.
For where it is forsaken of that moisture,   150
And hath more dryness, it becomes a stone;
Where it retains more of the humid fatness,
It turns to sulphur, or to quicksilver,
Who are the parents of all other metals.
Nor can this remote matter suddenly   155
Progress so from extreme unto extreme,
As to grow gold, and leap o'er all the means.°
Nature doth first beget the imperfect; then
Proceeds she to the perfect. Of that airy
And oily water, mercury is engendered;   160
Sulphur o'the fat and earthy part: the one
(Which is the last) supplying the place of male,
The other of the female, in all metals.

Some do believe hermaphrodeity,
That both do act and suffer. But these two   165
Make the rest ductile, malleable, extensive.
And even in gold, they are; for we do find
Seeds of them, by our fire, and gold in them,
And can produce the species of each metal
More perfect thence than nature doth in earth.   170
Beside, who doth not see in daily practice
Art can beget bees, hornets, beetles, wasps,
Out of the carcasses and dung of creatures;°
Yea, scorpions, of an herb, being ritely placed?
And these are living creatures, far more perfect   175
And excellent than metals.

MAMMON   Well said, father!
Nay, if he take you in hand, sir, with an argument,
He'll bray you in a mortar.

SURLY   Pray you, sir, stay.
Rather than I'll be brayed, sir, I'll believe,
That alchemy is a pretty kind of game,   180
Somewhat like tricks o'the cards, to cheat a man
With charming.

SUBTLE   Sir?

SURLY   What else are all your terms,
Whereon no one o' your writers 'grees with other?
Of your elixir, your *lac virginis*,
Your stone, your medicine, and your chrysosperm,   185
Your sal, your sulphur, and your mercury,°
Your oil of height, your tree of life, your blood,°
Your marcasite, your tutty, your magnesia,
Your toad, your crow, your dragon, and your panther,°
Your sun, your moon, your firmament, your adrop,°   190
Your lato, azoth, zarnich, kibrit, heautarit,
And then, your red man, and your white woman,°
With all your broths, your menstrues, and materials
Of piss, and egg-shells, women's terms, man's blood,
Hair o' the head, burnt clouts, chalk, merds, and clay,   195
Powder of bones, scalings of iron, glass,
And worlds of other strange ingredients,
Would burst a man to name?

SUBTLE   And all these, named,
Intending but one thing: which art our writers

Used to obscure their art.

MAMMON   Sir, so I told him,   200
Because the simple idiot should not learn it,
And make it vulgar.

SUBTLE   Was not all the knowledge
Of the Egyptians writ in mystic symbols?°
Speak not the Scriptures oft in parables?
Are not the choicest fables of the poets,   205
That were the fountains and first springs of wisdom,
Wrapped in perplexèd allegories?

MAMMON   I urged that,
And cleared to him that Sisyphus was damned°
To roll the ceaseless stone only because
He would have made ours common.   210
        Doll is seen
Who is this?

SUBTLE God's precious—What do you mean? Go in, good lady,
Let me entreat you.
        [*Exit Doll*]
Where's this varlet?
        [*Enter Face*]

FACE   Sir?

SUBTLE You very knave! Do you use me thus?

FACE   Wherein, sir?   215

SUBTLE Go in and see, you traitor. Go!
        [*Exit Face*]

MAMMON   Who is it, sir?

SUBTLE Nothing, sir. Nothing.

MAMMON   What's the matter? Good sir!
I have not seen you thus distempered. Who is't?

SUBTLE All arts have still had, sir, their adversaries,
But ours the most ignorant.   220
        Face returns
What now?

FACE 'Twas not my fault, sir, she would speak with you.

SUBTLE Would she, sir? Follow me.
        [*Exit Subtle*]

MAMMON   Stay, Lungs.

FACE   I dare not, sir.

MAMMON Stay man; what is she?

FACE   A lord's sister, sir.

MAMMON How! Pray thee, stay!

FACE   She's mad, sir, and sent hither—   225
  He'll be mad too.

MAMMON   I warrant thee. Why sent hither?

FACE Sir, to be cured.

SUBTLE [*within*]   Why, rascal!

FACE   Lo you. Here, sir.

> *He goes out*

MAMMON 'Fore God, a Bradamante, a brave piece.°

SURLY Heart, this is a bawdy house! I'll be burnt else.

MAMMON O, by this light, no. Do not wrong him. He's   230
  Too scrupulous that way. It is his vice.
  No, he's a rare physician, do him right.
  An excellent Paracelsian! And has done
  Strange cures with mineral physic. He deals all
  With spirits, he. He will not hear a word   235
  Of Galen, or his tedious recipes.°
  How now, Lungs!

> *[Enter] Face again*

FACE   Softly, sir, speak softly. I meant.
  To ha' told your worship all. This must not hear.°

MAMMON No, he will not be gulled; let him alone.

FACE You're very right, sir; she is a most rare scholar,   240
  And is gone mad with studying Broughton's works.°
  If you but name a word touching the Hebrew,
  She falls into her fit, and will discourse
  So learnedly of genealogies,
  As you would run mad, too, to hear her, sir.   245

MAMMON How might one do t' have conference with her, Lungs?

FACE O, divers have run mad upon the conference.
  I do not know, sir; I am sent in haste
  To fetch a vial.

SURLY   Be not gulled, Sir Mammon.

MAMMON Wherein? Pray ye, be patient.

SURLY   Yes, as you are.   250
  And trust confederate knaves, and bawds and whores.

MAMMON You are too foul, believe it. Come, here, Ulen.
  One word.

FACE   I dare not, in good faith.

> *[Going]*

MAMMON   Stay, knave.

FACE He's extreme angry that you saw her, sir.

MAMMON Drink that. [*Gives money*] What is she when she's out   255
   of her fit?

FACE O, the most affablest creature, sir! So merry!
   So pleasant! She'll mount you up, like quick-silver,
   Over the helm; and circulate like oil,
   A very vegetal; discourse of state,   260
   Of mathematics, bawdry, anything—

MAMMON Is she no way accessible? No means,
   No trick, to give a man a taste of her—wit—
   Or so?—

SUBTLE [*within*] Ulen!

FACE   I'll come to you again, sir.   265
   [*Exit Face*]

MAMMON Surly, I did not think one o' your breeding
   Would traduce personages of worth.

SURLY [*bowing*]   Sir Epicure,
   Your friend to use; yet still loath to be gulled.
   I do not like your philosophical bawds.
   Their stone is lechery enough to pay for,   270
   Without this bait.

MAMMON   'Heart, you abuse yourself.
   I know the lady, and her friends, and means,
   The original of this disaster. Her brother
   Has told me all.

SURLY   And yet you ne'er saw her
   Till now?   275

MAMMON O, yes, but I forgot. I have (believe it)
   One o'the treacherou'st memories, I do think,
   Of all mankind.

SURLY   What call you her—brother?

MAMMON   My lord—
   He wi'not have his name known, now I think on't.

SURLY A very treacherous memory!

MAMMON   O' my faith—   280

SURLY Tut, if you ha' it not about you, pass it
   Till we meet next.

MAMMON   Nay, by this hand, 'tis true.
   He's one I honour, and my noble friend,
   And I respect his house.

SURLY   Heart! Can it be,

That a grave sir, a rich, that has no need,   285
A wise sir, too, at other times, should thus
With his own oaths and arguments make hard means
To gull himself? An this be your elixir,
Your *lapis mineralis*, and your lunary,°
Give me your honest trick, yet, at primero,   290
Or gleek; and take your *lutum sapientis*,°
Your *menstruum simplex*; I'll have gold before you°
And with less danger of the quick-silver,
Or the hot sulphur.
          [*Enter Face*]
FACE [*to Surly*]   Here's one from Captain Face, sir,°
Desires you meet him i'the Temple Church°   295
Some half hour hence, and upon earnest business.
          He whispers Mammon
Sir, if you please to quit us now, and come
Again within two hours, you shall have
My master busy examining o' the works;
And I will steal you in unto the party,   300
That you may see her converse. [*Aside to Surly*] Sir, shall I say
You'll meet the Captain's worship?
SURLY   Sir, I will.
[*Aside*] But by attorney, and to a second purpose.°
Now I am sure it is a bawdy-house;
I'll swear it, were the marshal here to thank me;   305
The naming this commander doth confirm it.
Don Face! Why, he's the most authentic dealer
I' these commodities! The superintendent
To all the quainter traffickers in town.°
He is their visitor, and does appoint   310
Who lies with whom, and at what hour, what price,
Which gown, and in what smock, what fall, what tire.
Him will I prove, by a third person, to find
The subtleties of this dark labyrinth;
Which if I do discover, dear Sir Mammon,   315
You'll give your poor friend leave, though no philosopher,
To laugh; for you that are, 'tis thought, shall weep.°
FACE [*aside, to Surly*] Sir, he does pray you'll not forget.
SURLY   I will not, sir.—
Sir Epicure, I shall leave you?
MAMMON   I follow you straight.

[*Exit Surly*]

FACE But do so, good sir, to avoid suspicion.   320

This gent'man has a parlous head.

MAMMON   But wilt thou, Ulen.

Be constant to thy promise?

FACE   As my life, sir.

MAMMON And wilt thou insinuate what I am? And praise me?

And say I am a noble fellow?

FACE   O, what else, sir?

And that you'll make her royal with the stone,   325

An empress; and yourself king of Bantam.°

MAMMON Wilt thou do this?

FACE   Will I, sir?

MAMMON   Lungs, my Lungs!

I love thee.

FACE   Send your stuff, sir, that my master

May busy himself about projection.

MAMMON Th'hast witched me, rogue; take, go.

        [*Gives money*]

FACE   Your jack and all, sir.   330

MAMMON Thou art a villain—I will send my jack,

And the weights too. Slave, I could bite thine ear.°

Away, thou dost not care for me.

FACE   Not I, sir?

MAMMON Come, I was born to make thee, my good weasel,

Set thee on a bench, and ha' thee twirl a chain°   335

With the best lord's vermin, of 'em all.

FACE   Away, sir.°

MAMMON A Count, nay, a Count Palatine—

FACE   Good sir, go.°

MAMMON Shall not advance thee better; no, nor faster.

        [*Exit Sir Epicure Mammon*]

2.4

[*Enter*] *Subtle* [*and*] *Doll*

SUBTLE Has he bit? Has he bit?

FACE   And swallowed too, my Subtle.

I ha' given him line, and now he plays, i'faith.

SUBTLE And shall we twitch him?

FACE   Thorough both the gills.
A wench is a rare bait, with which a man
No sooner's taken, but he straight firks mad.°   5

SUBTLE Doll, my Lord What's hum's'sister, you must now
Bear yourself *statelijh*.

DOLL   O, let me alone.
I'll not forget my race, I warrant you.
I'll keep my distance, laugh, and talk aloud;
Have all the tricks of a proud scurvy lady,   10
And be as rude as her woman.

FACE   Well said, Sanguine.

SUBTLE But will he send his andirons?

FACE   His jack too;
And's iron shoeing-horn; I ha' spoke to him. Well,
I must not lose my wary gamester, yonder.

SUBTLE O Monsieur Caution, that will not be gulled?   15

FACE Aye, if I can strike a fine hook into him, now;
The Temple Church, there I have cast mine angle.
Well, pray for me. I'll about it.
      One knocks

SUBTLE   What, more gudgeons!°
Doll, scout, scout [*Doll looks out of window*]; stay Face, you must
go to the door;   20
Pray God it be my Anabaptist. Who is't, Doll?°

DOLL I know him not. He looks like a gold-end man.

SUBTLE Gods so! 'Tis he, he said he would send. What call you him?
The sanctified elder, that should deal
For Mammon's jack and andirons! Let him in.   25
Stay, help me off, first, with my gown.
      [*Exit Face with gown*]
Away Madam, to your withdrawing chamber.
      [*Exit Doll*]
                              Now,
In a new tune, new gesture, but old language.
This fellow is sent from one negotiates with me
About the stone, too; for the holy brethren
Of Amsterdam, the exiled saints that hope°   30
To raise their discipline by it. I must use him
In some strange fashion now, to make him admire me.

2.5

[*Enter*] *Ananias*

SUBTLE   Where is my drudge?

    [*Enter Face*]

FACE   Sir.

SUBTLE   Take away the recipient,

  And rectify your menstrue from the phlegma.

  Then pour it o' the *Sol*, in the cucurbit,

  And let 'em macerate together.

FACE   Yes, sir.

  And save the ground?

SUBTLE   No. *Terra damnata*°   5

  Must not have entrance in the work. Who are you?

ANANIAS   A faithful brother, if it please you.

SUBTLE   What's that?

  A Lullianist? A Ripley? *Filius artis?*°

  Can you sublime and dulcify? Calcine?

  Know you the sapor pontic? Sapor stiptic?°   10

  Or what is homogene, or heterogene?

ANANIAS   I understand no heathen language, truly.

SUBTLE   Heathen, you Knipperdollink? Is *ars sacra*,°

  Or *chrysopoeia*, or *spagyrica*,

  Or the pamphysic, or panarchic knowledge,°   15

  A heathen language?

ANANIAS   Heathen Greek, I take it.

SUBTLE   How? Heathen Greek?

ANANIAS   All's heathen but the Hebrew.°

SUBTLE   Sirrah, my varlet, stand you forth and speak to him

  Like a philosopher; answer i'the language.

  Name the vexations, and the martyrizations   20

  Of metals in the work.

FACE   Sir, putrefaction,

  Solution, ablution, sublimation,

  Cohobation, calcination, ceration, and

  Fixation.

SUBTLE   This is heathen Greek to you now?

  And when comes vivification?

FACE   After mortification.   25

SUBTLE   What's cohobation?

FACE   'Tis the pouring on

Your *aqua regis*, and then drawing him off,°
To the trine circle of the seven spheres.°
SUBTLE What's the proper passion of metals?
FACE   Malleation.°
SUBTLE What's your *ultimum supplicium auri*?
FACE   Antimonium.°   30
SUBTLE This's heathen Greek to you? And what's your mercury?
FACE A very fugitive; he will be gone, sir.°
SUBTLE How know you him?
FACE   By his viscosity,
   His oleosity, and his suscitability.
SUBTLE How do you sublime him?
FACE   With the calx of eggshells,   35
   White marble, talc.
SUBTLE   Your *magisterium*, now?
   What's that?
FACE   Shifting, sir, your elements,
   Dry into cold, cold into moist, moist into hot, hot into dry.
SUBTLE   This's heathen Greek to you, still?
   Your *lapis philosophicus*?
FACE   'Tis a stone, and not   40
   A stone; a spirit, a soul, and a body,°
   Which if you do dissolve, it is dissolved;
   If you coagulate, it is coagulated;
   If you make it to fly, it flieth.
SUBTLE   Enough.
      [*Exit Face*]
   This's heathen Greek to you? What are you, sir?   45
ANANIAS Please you, a servant of the exiled brethren,
   That deal with widow's and with orphans' goods,
   And make a just account unto the saints:
   A deacon.
SUBTLE   O, you are sent from Master Wholesome,
   Your teacher?
ANANIAS   From Tribulation Wholesome,   50
   Our very zealous pastor.
SUBTLE   Good. I have
   Some orphans' goods to come here.
ANANIAS   Of what kind, sir?
SUBTLE Pewter and brass, andirons and kitchenware,
   Metals that we must use our medicine on,
   Wherein the brethren may have a penn'orth,   55

For ready money.

ANANIAS   Were the orphans' parents
Sincere professors?

SUBTLE   Why do you ask?

ANANIAS   Because
We then are to deal justly, and give, in truth,
Their utmost value.

SUBTLE   'Slid, you'd cozen, else,
An if their parents were not of the faithful?   60
I will not trust you, now I think on't,
Till I ha' talked with your pastor. Ha' you brought money
To buy more coals?

ANANIAS   No, surely.

SUBTLE   No? How so?

ANANIAS The brethren bid me say unto you, sir,
Surely they will not venture any more,   65
Till they may see projection.

SUBTLE   How!

ANANIAS   You've had
For the instruments, as bricks, and loam, and glasses,
Already thirty pound; and for materials,
They say, some ninety more; and they have heard, since,
That one at Heidelberg made it of an egg,   70
And a small paper of pin-dust.

SUBTLE   What's your name?°

ANANIAS My name is Ananias.

SUBTLE   Out, the varlet
That cozened the Apostles! Hence, away,°
Flee, Mischief! Had your holy consistory
No name to send me of another sound   75
Than wicked Ananias? Send your elders
Hither to make atonement for you, quickly.
And gi' me satisfaction, or out goes
The fire, and down th' alembics and the furnace,
Piger Henricus, or what not. Thou wretch,°   80
Both sericon and bufo shall be lost,°
Tell 'em. All hope of rooting out the bishops,
Or the antichristian hierarchy shall perish,°
If they stay threescore minutes. The aqueity,
Terreity, and sulphureity   85
Shall run together again, and all be annulled,°

Thou wicked Ananias.

  [*Exit Ananias*]
        This will fetch 'em,
And make 'em haste towards their gulling more.
A man must deal like a rough nurse, and fright
Those that are froward to an appetite.   90

2.6

  [*Enter*] *Face* [*and*] *Drugger*

FACE He's busy with his spirits, but we'll upon him.
SUBTLE How now! What mates? What Bayards ha' we here?°
FACE I told you he would be furious. Sir, here's Nab,
  Has brought you another piece of gold to look on
  [*Aside to Drugger*] We must appease him. Give it me—and prays you, 5
  You would devise—[*to Drugger*] what is it Nab?
DRUGGER   A sign, sir.
FACE Aye, a good lucky one, a thriving sign, Doctor.
SUBTLE I was devising now.
FACE [*aside to Subtle*]   —Slight, do not say so,
  He will repent he ga' you any more—
  What say you to his constellation, Doctor?   10
  The Balance?
SUBTLE   No, that way is stale and common.
  A townsman born in Taurus gives the bull,
  Or the bull's head; in Aries, the ram.
  A poor device. No, I will have his name
  Formed in some mystic character, whose *radii*,   15
  Striking the senses of the passers-by,
  Shall, by a virtual influence, breed affections,
  That may result upon the party owns it;
  As thus—
FACE   Nab!
SUBTLE   He first shall have a bell, that's Abel;
  And by it standing one whose name is Dee,°   20
  In a rug gown; there's D and rug, that's Drug:
  And right anenst him a dog snarling, 'er';
  There's Drugger, Abel Drugger. That's his sign.
  And here's now mystery and hieroglyphic!°

FACE Abel, thou art made.

DRUGGER [*bowing*]   Sir, I do thank his worship.   25

FACE Six o' thy legs more will not do it, Nab.
   He has brought you a pipe of tobacco, Doctor.

DRUGGER   Yes, sir.
   I have another thing I would impart—

FACE Out with it, Nab.

DRUGGER   Sir, there is lodged, hard by me,
   A rich young widow—

FACE   Good! A bona-roba?   30

DRUGGER But nineteen, at the most.

FACE   Very good, Abel.

DRUGGER Marry, she's not in fashion, yet; she wears
   A hood, but 't stands a cop.

FACE   No matter, Abel.°

DRUGGER And I do now and then give her a fucus—

FACE What? Dost thou deal, Nab?

SUBTLE   I did tell you, Captain.   35

DRUGGER And physic too sometime, sir—for which she trusts me
   With all her mind. She's come up here of purpose
   To learn the fashion.

FACE   Good—[*aside*] his match too!—On, Nab.

DRUGGER And she does strangely long to know her fortune.

FACE God's lid, Nab, send her to the Doctor, hither.   40

DRUGGER Yes, I have spoke to her of his worship already;
   But she's afraid it will be blown abroad,°
   And hurt her marriage.

FACE   Hurt it? 'Tis the way
   To heal it, if 'twere hurt; to make it more
   Followed and sought. Nab, thou shalt tell her this.   45
   She'll be more known, more talked of, and your widows
   Are ne'er of any price till they be famous;
   Their honour is their multitude of suitors.
   Send her, it may be thy good fortune. [*Drugger shakes his head*] What?
   Thou dost not know.

DRUGGER   No, sir, she'll never marry   50
   Under a knight. Her brother has made a vow.

FACE What, and dost thou despair, my little Nab,
   Knowing what the Doctor has set down for thee,
   And seeing so many o'the city dubbed?
   One glass o' thy water, with a madam I know,°   55

Will have it done, Nab. What's her brother? A knight?

DRUGGER No, sir, a gentleman, newly warm in his land, sir.
Scarce cold in his one-and-twenty, that does govern
His sister here; and is a man himself
Of some three thousand a year, and is come up   60
To learn to quarrel, and to live by his wits,
And will go down again, and die i'the country.

FACE How! To quarrel?

DRUGGER   Yes, sir, to carry quarrels,
As gallants do, and manage 'em by line.°

FACE 'Slid, Nab! The Doctor is the only man   65
In Christendom for him. He has made a table,
With mathematical demonstrations,
Touching the art of quarrels. He will give him
An instrument to quarrel by. Go, bring 'em both,
Him, and his sister. And, for thee, with her   70
The Doctor haply may persuade. Go to.
'Shalt give his worship a new damask suit
Upon the premises.

SUBTLE   O, good Captain!

FACE   He shall,
He is the honestest fellow, Doctor. Stay not,
No offers, bring the damask, and the parties.   75

DRUGGER I'll try my power, sir.

FACE   And thy will too, Nab.

SUBTLE 'Tis good tobacco this! What is't an ounce?

FACE He'll send you a pound, Doctor.

SUBTLE   O, no.

FACE   He will do't.
It is the goodest soul. [*Aside to Drugger*] Abel, about it.
Thou shalt know more anon. Away, be gone.   80
        [*Exit Drugger*]
A miserable rogue, and lives with cheese,
And has the worms. That was the cause indeed
Why he came now. He dealt with me in private
To get a medicine for 'em.

SUBTLE   And shall, sir. This works.

FACE A wife, a wife, for one on us, my dear Subtle   85
We'll e'en draw lots, and he that fails shall have
The more in goods, the other has in tail.°

SUBTLE Rather the less. For she may be so light

She may want grains.

FACE   Aye, or be such a burden,°

A man would scarce endure her for the whole.   90

SUBTLE Faith, best let's see her first, and then determine.

FACE Content. But Doll must ha' no breath on't.

SUBTLE   Mum.

Away you to your Surly yonder; catch him.

FACE Pray God I ha' not stayed too long.

SUBTLE   I fear it.

    [Exeunt]

3.1

[Enter] Tribulation [Wholesome and Ananias]

TRIBULATION These chastisements are common to the saints,
    And such rebukes we of the separation
    Must bear, with willing shoulders, as the trials
    Sent forth to tempt our frailties.

ANANIAS   In pure zeal,
    I do not like the man; he is a heathen,   5
    And speaks the language of Canaan, truly.°

TRIBULATION I think him a profane person indeed.

ANANIAS   He bears
    The visible mark of the Beast in his forehead.°
    And for his stone, it is a work of darkness,
    And with philosophy blinds the eyes of man.   10

TRIBULATION Good brother, we must bend unto all means
    That may give furtherance to the holy cause.

ANANIAS Which his cannot: the sanctified cause
    Should have a sanctified course.

TRIBULATION   Not always necessary.
    The children of perdition are oft-times   15
    Made instruments even of the greatest works.
    Beside, we should give somewhat to man's nature,
    The place he lives in, still about the fire,
    And fume of metals, that intoxicate
    The brain of man, and make him prone to passion.   20
    Where have you greater atheists than your cooks?
    Or more profane or choleric than your glass-men?
    More antichristian than your bell-founders?°
    What makes the devil so devilish, I would ask you,
    Satan, our common enemy, but his being   25
    Perpetually about the fire, and boiling
    Brimstone and arsenic? We must give, I say,
    Unto the motives, and the stirrers up°
    Of humours in the blood. It may be so,
    When as the work is done, the stone is made,   30
    This heat of his may turn into a zeal,
    And stand up for the beauteous discipline
    Against the menstruous cloth and rag of Rome.°

We must await his calling, and the coming
Of the good spirit. You did fault, t'upbraid him   35
With the brethren's blessing of Heidelberg, weighing°
What need we have to hasten on the work,
For the restoring of the silenced saints,°
Which ne'er will be but by the philosophers' stone.
And so a learned elder, one of Scotland,°   40
Assured me; *aurum potabilè* being°
The only medicine, for the civil magistrate,
T'incline him to a feeling of the cause,
And must be daily used in the disease.

ANANIAS I have not edified more, truly, by man,   45
    Not since the beautiful light first shone on me;
    And I am sad my zeal hath so offended.

TRIBULATION Let us call on him then.

ANANIAS   The motion's good,
    And of the spirit; I will knock first. [*Knocks*] Peace be within.

3.2

[*Enter*] *Subtle*

SUBTLE O, are you come? 'Twas time. Your threescore minutes
    Were at the last thread, you see, and down had gone
    Furnus acediae, turris circulatorius:°
    Limbeck, bolt's-head, retort, and pelican
    Had all been cinders.—Wicked Ananias!   5
    Art thou returned? Nay then, it goes down yet.

TRIBULATION Sir, be appeased, he is come to humble
    Himself in spirit, and to ask your patience,
    If too much zeal hath carried him aside
    From the due path.

SUBTLE   Why, this doth qualify!   10

TRIBULATION The brethren had no purpose, verily,
    To give you the least grievance, but are ready
    To lend their willing hands to any project
    The spirit and you direct.

SUBTLE   This qualifies more!

TRIBULATION And for the orphans' goods, let them be valued,   15
    Or what is needful else to the holy work,

It shall be numbered; here, by me, the saints
Throw down their purse before you.

SUBTLE   This qualifies most!
Why, thus it should be; now you understand.
Have I discoursed so unto you; of our stone?   20
And of the good that it shall bring your cause?
Showed you (beside the main of hiring forces
Abroad, drawing the Hollanders, your friends,
From the Indies, to serve you, with all their fleet)°
That even the med'cinal use shall make you a faction,   25
And party in the realm? As, put the case,
That some great man in state, he have the gout,
Why, you but send three drops of your elixir,
You help him straight: there you have made a friend.
Another has the palsy or the dropsy,   30
He takes of your incombustible stuff,°
He's young again: there you have made a friend.
A lady that is past the feat of body,°
Though not of mind, and hath her face decayed
Beyond all cure of paintings, you restore   35
With the oil of talc: there you have made a friend,
And all her friends. A lord that is a leper,
A knight that has the bone-ache, or a squire
That hath both these, you make 'em smooth and sound,
With a bare fricace of your medicine: still   40
You increase your friends.

TRIBULATION   Aye, 'tis very pregnant.
SUBTLE And then the turning of this lawyer's pewter
To plate, at Christmas—
ANANIAS   Christ-tide, I pray you.°
SUBTLE Yet, Ananias?
ANANIAS   I have done.
SUBTLE   Or changing
His parcel-gilt to massy gold. You cannot   45
But raise you friends. Withal, to be of power
To pay an army in the field, to buy
The king of France out of his realms, or Spain
Out of his Indies. What can you not do,°
Against lords spiritual or temporal°   50
That shall oppone you?
TRIBULATION   Verily, 'tis true.

We may be temporal lords ourselves, I take it.°
SUBTLE You may be anything, and leave off to make
 Long-winded exercises, or suck up°
 Your 'ha' and 'hum' in a tune. I not deny°   55
 But such as are not gracèd in a state
 May, for their ends, be adverse in religion,
 And get a tune to call the flock together;
 For, to say sooth, a tune does much with women
 And other phlegmatic people; it is your bell.   60
ANANIAS Bells are profane; a tune may be religious.
SUBTLE No warning with you? Then farewell my patience.
 'Slight, it shall down; I will not be thus tortured.°
TRIBULATION I pray you, sir.
SUBTLE   All shall perish. I have spoke it.
TRIBULATION Let me find grace, sir, in your eyes; the man   65
 He stands corrected; neither did his zeal
 (But as yourself) allow a tune somewhere,
 Which now, being toward the stone, we shall not need.
SUBTLE No, nor your holy vizard to win widows
 To give you legacies; or make zealous wives   70
 To rob their husbands for the common cause;
 Nor take the start of bonds, broke but one day,
 And say they were forfeited by providence.
 Nor shall you need o'er night to eat huge meals,
 To celebrate your next day's fast the better,   75
 The whilst the brethren and the sisters, humbled,
 Abate the stiffness of the flesh. Nor cast
 Before your hungry hearers scrupulous bones,°
 As whether a Christian may hawk or hunt,
 Or whether matrons of the holy assembly   80
 May lay their hair out, or wear doublets,°
 Or have that idol, Starch, about their linen.
ANANIAS It is, indeed, an idol.
TRIBULATION   Mind him not, sir.
 I do command thee, spirit (of zeal, but trouble)
 To peace within him. Pray you, sir, go on.   85
SUBTLE Nor shall you need to libel 'gainst the prelates,
 And shorten so your ears against the hearing°
 Of the next wire-drawn grace. Nor of necessity
 Rail against plays to please the alderman
 Whose daily custard you devour. Nor lie   90

With zealous rage, till you are hoarse. Not one
Of these so singular arts. Nor call yourselves,
By names of Tribulation, Persecution,
Restraint, Long-Patience, and such like, affected
By the whole family, or wood of you,   95
Only for glory, and to catch the ear
Of the disciple.
TRIBULATION   Truly, sir, they are
Ways that the godly brethren have invented
For propagation of the glorious cause,
As very notable means, and whereby also   100
Themselves grow soon and profitably famous.
SUBTLE O, but the stone, all's idle to it! Nothing!
The art of angels, nature's miracle,
The divine secret that doth fly in clouds
From east to west, and whose tradition   105
Is not from men, but spirits.
ANANIAS   I hate traditions;°
I do not trust them—
TRIBULATION   Peace.
ANANIAS   They are Popish, all!
I will not peace. I will not—
TRIBULATION   Ananias.
ANANIAS Please the profane; to grieve the godly; I may not.
SUBTLE Well, Ananias, thou shalt overcome.   110
TRIBULATION It is an ignorant zeal that haunts him, sir.
But truly, else, a very faithful brother,
A botcher, and a man, by revelation,°
That hath a competent knowledge of the truth.
SUBTLE Has he a competent sum, there, i' the bag,   115
To buy the goods within? I am made guardian,
And must for charity and conscience sake,
Now see the most be made for my poor orphans,
Though I desire the brethren, too, good gainers.
There they are, within. When you have viewed and bought 'em,   120
And ta'en the inventory of what they are,
They're ready for projection; there's no more
To do: cast on the medicine, so much silver
As there is tin there, so much gold as brass,
I'll gi' it you in, by weight.
TRIBULATION   But how long time,°   125

Sir, must the saints expect, yet?

SUBTLE   Let me see,
How's the moon now? Eight, nine, ten days hence
He will be silver potate; then three days
Before he citronise: some fifteen days,
The *magisterium* will be perfected.   130

ANANIAS About the second day of the third week
In the ninth month?

SUBTLE   Yes, my good Ananias.°

TRIBULATION What will the orphans' goods arise to, think you?

SUBTLE Some hundred marks; as much as filled three cars,
Unladed now: you'll make six millions of 'em.   135
But I must ha' more coals laid in.

TRIBULATION   How!

SUBTLE   Another load,
And then we ha' finished. We must now increase
Our fire to *ignis ardens*; we are past
Fimus equinus, balnei, cineris,°
And all those lenter heats. If the holy purse   140
Should with this draught fall low, and that the saints
Do need a present sum, I have a trick
To melt the pewter you shall buy now, instantly,
And with a tincture make you as good Dutch dollars,
As any are in Holland.

TRIBULATION   Can you so?   145

SUBTLE Aye, and shall bide the third examination.

ANANIAS It will be joyful tidings to the brethren.

SUBTLE But you must carry it, secret.

TRIBULATION   Aye, but stay,
This act of coining, is it lawful?

ANANIAS   Lawful?
We know no magistrate. Or, if we did,°   150
This's foreign coin.

SUBTLE   It is no coining, sir.°
It is but casting.

TRIBULATION   Ha! You distinguish well.
Casting of money may be lawful.

ANANIAS   'Tis, sir.

TRIBULATION Truly, I take it so.

SUBTLE   There is no scruple,
Sir, to be made of it; believe Ananias;   155

This case of conscience he is studied in.°

TRIBULATION I'll make a question of it to the brethren.

ANANIAS The brethren shall approve it lawful, doubt not.
Where shall't be done?

Knock without

SUBTLE   For that we'll talk anon.
There's some to speak with me. Go in, I pray you,   160
And view the parcels. That's the inventory.
I'll come to you straight.

[Exeunt Tribulation, Ananias]
                    Who is it? Face! Appear!

3.3

[Enter] Face

SUBTLE How now? Good prize?

FACE   Good pox! Yond' costive cheater
Never came on.

SUBTLE   How then?

FACE   I ha' walked the round,°
Till now, and no such thing.

SUBTLE   And ha' you quit him?

FACE Quit him? An hell would quit him too, he were happy.
'Slight, would you have me stalk like a mill-jade,   5
All day, for one that will not yield us grains?
I know him of old.

SUBTLE   O, but to ha' gulled him,
Had been a mastery.

FACE   Let him go, black boy,°
And turn thee, that some fresh news may possess thee.
A noble Count, a Don of Spain (my dear   10
Delicious compeer, and my party-bawd)
Who is come hither, private, for his conscience,°
And brought munition with him, six great slops,
Bigger than three Dutch hoys, beside round trunks,°
Furnished with pistolets, and pieces of eight,°   15
Will straight be here, my rogue, to have thy bath—
That is the colour—and to make his battery°
Upon our Doll, our castle, our Cinque Port,

Our Dover pier, our what thou wilt. Where is she?
She must prepare perfumes, delicate linen,   20
The bath in chief, a banquet, and her wit,
For she must milk his epididymis.
Where is the doxy?

SUBTLE   I'll send her to thee;
And but dispatch my brace of little John Leidens,°
And come again myself.

FACE   Are they within then?   25

SUBTLE Numbering the sum.

FACE   How much?

SUBTLE   A hundred marks, boy.
    [*Exit Subtle*]

FACE Why, this's a lucky day! Ten pounds of Mammon!
Three o' my clerk! A portague o' my grocer!
This o' the brethren! Beside reversions,
And states to come i' the widow, and my Count!   30
My share today will not be bought for forty—
    [*Enter Doll*]

DOLL   What?

FACE Pounds, dainty Dorothy, art thou so near?

DOLL Yes, say lord General, how fares our camp?°

FACE As with the few that had entrenched themselves
Safe, by their discipline, against a world, Doll: 35
And laughed within those trenches, and grew fat
With thinking on the booties, Doll, brought in
Daily by their small parties. This dear hour,°
A doughty Don is taken with my Doll,
And thou mayst make his ransom what thou wilt,   40
My Dousabel; he shall be brought here, fettered°
With thy fair looks, before he sees thee; and thrown
In a down-bed, as dark as any dungeon;
Where thou shalt keep him waking with thy drum—
Thy drum, my Doll, thy drum—till he be tame   45
As the poor blackbirds were i' the great frost,°
Or bees are with a basin; and so hive him°
I'the swan-skin coverlid and cambric sheets,
Till he work honey and wax, my little God's-gift.°

DOLL What is he, General

FACE   An *Adelantado*,   50
A Grandee, girl. Was not my Dapper here yet?

DOLL No.

FACE   Nor my Drugger?

DOLL   Neither.

FACE   A pox on 'em,
They are so long a-furnishing! Such stinkards
Would not be seen upon these festival days.
      [*Enter Subtle*]
How now! Ha' you done?

SUBTLE   Done. They are gone. The sum   55
Is here in bank, my Face. I would we knew°
Another chapman now would buy 'em outright.

FACE 'Slid, Nab shall do't, against he ha' the widow,
To furnish household.

SUBTLE   Excellent, well thought on;
Pray God he come.

FACE   I pray he keep away   60
Till our new business be o'er-past.

SUBTLE   But, Face,
How cam'st thou by this secret Don?

FACE   A spirit
Brought me th'intelligence, in a paper, here,
      [*Shows paper*]
As I was conjuring, yonder, in my circle
For Surly: I ha' my flies abroad. Your bath   65
Is famous, Subtle, by my means. Sweet Doll,
You must go tune your virginal, no losing
O' the least time. And—do you hear?—good action.
Firk like a flounder; kiss like a scallop, close;
And tickle him with thy mother-tongue. His great°   70
Verdugoship has not a jot of language:°
So much the easier to be cozened, my Dolly.
He will come here in a hired coach, obscure,
And our own coachman, whom I have sent as guide,
No creature else (*One knocks*) Who's that?

SUBTLE   It i' not he?   75

FACE O no, not yet this hour.

SUBTLE   Who is't?

DOLL [*at the window*]   Dapper,
Your clerk.

FACE   God's will, then, Queen of Fairy,
On with your tire; and, Doctor, with your robes.

Let's dispatch him, for God's sake.

SUBTLE   'Twill be long.

FACE I warrant you, take but the cues I give you,   80
It shall be brief enough. [*Looking out*] 'Slight, here are more!
Abel, and I think the angry boy, the heir,°
That fain would quarrel.

SUBTLE   And the widow?

FACE   No,
Not that I see. Away.
      [*Exit Subtle*]
      [*Opens door*]   O, sir, you are welcome.

3.4

      [*Enter*] *Dapper*

FACE The Doctor is within, a-moving for you;
I have had the most ado to win him to it!
He swears you'll be the darling o' the dice:
He never heard her Highness dote till now (he says).
Your aunt has giv'n you the most gracious words   5
That can be thought on.

DAPPER   Shall I see her Grace?

FACE See her, and kiss her too.
      [*Enter Drugger, Kestrel*]
                              What? Honest Nab!
Has brought the damask?

DRUGGER   No, sir; here's tobacco.

FACE 'Tis well done, Nab; thou'lt bring the damask too?

DRUGGER Yes; here's the gentleman, Captain, Master Kestrel,   10
I have brought to see the Doctor.

FACE   Where's the widow?

DRUGGER Sir, as he likes, his sister (he says) shall come.

FACE O, is it so? Good time. Is your name Kestrel, sir?°

KESTREL Aye, and the best o'the Kestrels; I'd be sorry else,
By fifteen hundred a year. Where is this Doctor?   15
My mad tobacco boy here tells me of one
That can do things. Has he any skill?

FACE   Wherein, sir?

KESTREL To carry a business, manage a quarrel fairly,

Upon fit terms.

FACE   It seems, sir, you're but young
  About the town, that can make that a question!   20
KESTREL Sir, not so young but I have heard some speech
  Of the angry boys, and seen 'em take tobacco,
  And in his shop; and I can take it too.
  And I would fain be one of 'em, and go down
  And practice i'the country.
FACE   Sir, for the *duello*,   25
  The Doctor, I assure you, shall inform you
  To the least shadow of a hair; and show you
  An instrument he has, of his own making,
  Wherewith, no sooner shall you make report
  Of any quarrel, but he will take the height on't,   30
  Most instantly, and tell in what degree
  Of safety it lies in, or mortality,
  And how it may be borne, whether in a right line,
  Or a half-circle; or may else be cast
  Into an angle blunt, if not acute: 35
  All this he will demonstrate. And then, rules
  To give and take the lie by.
KESTREL   How? To take it?
FACE Yes, in oblique he'll show you, or in circle,
  But never in diameter. The whole town°
  Study his theorems and dispute them ordinarily°   40
  At the eating academies.
KESTREL   But does he teach
  Living by the wits too?
FACE   .Anything whatever.
  You cannot think that subtlety, but he reads it.
  He made me a Captain. I was a stark pimp,
  Just o' your standing, 'fore I met with him—   45
  It i' not two months since. I'll tell you his method:
  First, he will enter you at some ordinary.
KESTREL No, I'll not come there. You shall pardon me.
FACE   For why, sir?
KESTREL There's gaming there, and tricks.
FACE   Why, would you be
  A gallant, and not game?
KESTREL   Aye, 'twill spend a man.   50
FACE Spend you? It will repair you when you are spent.

How do they live by their wits, there, that have vented
Six times your fortunes?

KESTREL   What, three thousand a year!

FACE Aye, forty thousand.

KESTREL   Are there such?

FACE   Aye, sir.
And gallants, yet. Here's a young gentleman,   55
    [*Indicates Dapper*]
Is born to nothing: forty marks a year,
Which I count nothing. He's to be initiated,
And have a fly o'the Doctor. He will win you
By unresistable luck, within this fortnight,
Enough to buy a barony. They will set him   60
Upmost, at the groom-porter's, all the Christmas!°
And for the whole year through, at every place
Where there is play, present him with the chair,
The best attendance, the best drink, sometimes
Two glasses of canary, and pay nothing;   65
The purest linen, and the sharpest knife,
The partridge next his trencher, and, somewhere,
The dainty bed, in private, with the dainty.
You shall ha' your ordinaries bid for him,
As playhouses for a poet; and the master   70
Pray him aloud to name what dish he affects,
Which must be buttered shrimps; and those that drink°
To no mouth else, will drink to his, as being
The goodly president mouth of all the board.

KESTREL Do you not gull one?

FACE   'Od's my life! Do you think it?   75
You shall have a cast commander (can but get
In credit with a glover, or a spurrier,
For some two pair, of either's ware, aforehand)
Will by most swift posts dealing with him,°
Arrive at competent means to keep himself,   80
His punk, and naked boy, in excellent fashion,°
And be admired for't.

KESTREL   Will the Doctor teach this?

FACE He will do more, sir, when your land is gone,
(As men of spirit hate to keep earth long)°
In a vacation, when small money is stirring,   85
And ordinaries suspended till the term,°

He'll show a perspective, where on one side
You shall behold the faces and the persons
Of all sufficient young heirs in town,
Whose bonds are current for commodity;°   90
On th' other side, the merchants' forms, and others,
That, without help of any second broker
(Who would expect a share) will trust such parcels;
In the third square, the very street and sign
Where the commodity dwells, and does but wait   95
To be delivered, be it pepper, soap,
Hops, or tobacco, oatmeal, woad, or cheeses.
All which you may so handle to enjoy
To your own use, and never stand obliged.

KESTREL I'faith! Is he such a fellow?

FACE   Why, Nab here knows him.   100
And then for making matches for rich widows,
Young gentlewomen, heirs, the fortunat's man!
He's sent to, far and near, all over England,
To have his counsel, and to know their fortunes.

KESTREL God's will, my suster shall see him.

FACE   I'll tell you, sir,°   105
What he did tell me of Nab. It's a strange thing!
(By the way you must eat no cheese, Nab, it breeds melancholy,
And that same melancholy breeds worms. But pass it.)°
He told me honest Nab, here, was ne'er at tavern,
But once in's life.

DRUGGER   Truth, and no more I was not.   110

FACE And then he was so sick—

DRUGGER   Could he tell you that too?

FACE How should I know it?

DRUGGER   In troth we had been a-shooting,
And had a piece of fat ram-mutton to supper,
That lay so heavy o' my stomach—

FACE   And he has no head
To bear any wine; for what with the noise o'the fiddlers,   115
And care of his shop, for he dares keep no servants—

DRUGGER My head did so ache—

FACE   As he was fain to be brought home,
The Doctor told me. And then, a good old woman—

DRUGGER (Yes, faith, she dwells in Seacoal Lane) did cure me°
With sodden ale, and pellitory o'the wall:°   120
Cost me but twopence. I had another sickness,

Was worse than that.

FACE   Aye, that was with the grief
Thou took'st for being 'sessed at eighteen pence,
For the waterwork.

DRUGGER   In truth, and it was like°
T' have cost me almost my life.

FACE   Thy hair went off?   125

DRUGGER Yes, sir, 'twas done for spite.

FACE   Nay, so says the Doctor.

KESTREL Pray thee, tobacco boy, go fetch my suster,
I'll see this learned boy before I go,
And so shall she.

FACE   Sir, he is busy now,
But if you have a sister to fetch hither,   130
Perhaps your own pains may command her sooner;
And he, by that time, will be free.

KESTREL   I go.

     [*Exit Kestrel*]

FACE Drugger, she's thine: the damask.

     [*Exit Drugger*]

     [*Aside*] Subtle and I
Must wrestle for her—Come on, Master Dapper.   135
You see how I turn clients, here, away,
To give your cause dispatch. Ha' you performed
The ceremonies were enjoined you?

DAPPER   Yes, o'the vinegar,
And the clean shirt.

FACE   'Tis well; that shirt may do you
More worship than you think. Your aunt's afire,   140
But that she will not show it, t' have a sight on you.
Ha' you provided for her Grace's servants?

DAPPER Yes, here are six score Edward shillings.

FACE   Good.

DAPPER And an old Harry's sovereign.

FACE   Very good.

DAPPER And three James shillings, and an Elizabeth groat,   145
Just twenty nobles.

FACE   O, you are too just.
I would you had had the other noble in Marys.

DAPPER I have some Philip and Marys.

FACE   Aye, those same°
Are best of all. Where are they? Hark, the Doctor.

3.5

[Enter] Subtle disguised like a Priest of Fairy

SUBTLE   Is yet her Grace's cousin come?

FACE   He is come.

SUBTLE   And is he fasting?

FACE   Yes.

SUBTLE   And hath cried 'hum'?

FACE   Thrice, you must answer.

DAPPER   Thrice.

SUBTLE   And as oft 'buzz'?

FACE   If you have, say.

DAPPER   I have.

SUBTLE   Then, to her coz:

Hoping that he hath vinegared his senses,   5

As he was bid, the Fairy Queen dispenses,

By me, this robe, the petticoat of Fortune;

Which that he straight put on, she doth importune.

[They dress him in a petticoat]

And though to Fortune near be her petticoat,

Yet nearer is her smock, the Queen doth note;   10

And therefore, even of that a piece she hath sent,

Which, being a child, to wrap him in was rent;

And prays him for a scarf he now will wear it

(With as much love, as then her Grace did tear it)

About his eyes, to show he is fortunate.   15

They blind him with a rag

And trusting unto her to make his state,

He'll throw away all worldly pelf about him;

Which that he will perform, she doth not doubt him.

FACE   She need not doubt him, sir. Alas, he has nothing

But what he will part withal as willingly   20

Upon her Grace's word—throw away your purse—

[Dapper begins to empty his pockets]

As she would ask it. (Handkerchiefs and all!)

She cannot bid that thing, but he'll obey.

He throws away, as they bid him

If you have a ring about you, cast it off,

Or a silver seal, at your wrist; her Grace will send   25

Her fairies here to search you; therefore deal

Directly with her Highness. If they find

That you conceal a mite, you are undone.
DAPPER Truly, there's all.
FACE   All what?
DAPPER   My money, truly.
FACE Keep nothing that is transitory about you.   30
    [*Aside*] Bid Doll play music.
       Doll enters with a cittern
                Look, the elves are come
To pinch you, if you tell not truth. Advise you.
       They pinch him
DAPPER O, I have a papper with a spur-rial in't.
FACE   *Ti, ti,*°
    They knew't, they say.
SUBTLE   *Ti, ti, ti, ti,* he has more yet.
FACE *Ti, ti-ti-ti.* I'the t'other pocket?
SUBTLE   *Titi, titi, titi, titi.*   35
    They must pinch him or he will never confess, they say.
DAPPER O, o!
FACE   Nay, pray you hold. He is her Grace's nephew.
    Ti, ti, ti? What care you? Good faith, you shall care.
    Deal plainly, sir, and shame the fairies. Show
    You are an innocent.
DAPPER   By this good light, I ha' nothing.   40
SUBTLE *Ti ti, ti ti to ta.* He does equivocate, she says—
    Ti, ti do ti, ti ti do, ti da—and swears by the light, when he is
    blinded.
DAPPER By this good dark, I ha' nothing but a half-crown
    Of gold, about my wrist, that my love gave me;   45
    And a leaden heart I wore, sin' she forsook me.
FACE I thought 'twas something. And would you incur
    Your aunt's displeasure for these trifles? Come,
    I had rather you had thrown away twenty half-crowns.
       [*Removes gold from Dapper's wrist*]
    You may wear your leaden heart still.
       [*Doll looks out*]
       [*To Doll*]   How now?   50
SUBTLE What news, Doll?
DOLL   Yonder's your knight Sir Mammon.
FACE God's lid, we never thought of him, till now.
    Where is he?
DOLL   Here, hard by. He's at the door.

SUBTLE [*to Face*] And you are not ready now? Doll, get his suit.
    [*Exit Doll*]
  He must not be sent back.
FACE   O, by no means.   55
  What shall we do with this same puffin here,
  Now he's o'the spit?
SUBTLE   Why, lay him back a while,°
  With some device.
    [*Enter Doll with Face's disguise*]
          Ti, ti ti, ti ti ti. Would her Grace speak with me?
  I come. [*Aside*] Help, Doll.
FACE (*he speaks through the keyhole, the other knocking*) Who's there?
  Sir Epicure!   60
  My master's i'the way. Please you to walk
  Three or four turns, but till his back be turned,
  And I am for you. Quickly, Doll.
SUBTLE   Her Grace
  Commends her kindly to you, Master Dapper.
DAPPER I long to see her Grace.
SUBTLE   She now is set   65
  At dinner in her bed, and she has sent you
  From her own private trencher, a dead mouse
  And a piece of gingerbread, to be merry withal,
  And stay your stomach, lest you faint with fasting;
  Yet, if you could hold out till she saw you (she says)   70
  It would be better for you.
FACE   Sir, he shall
  Hold out, an 'twere this two hours, for her Highness;
  I can assure you that. We will not lose
  All we ha' done—
SUBTLE   He must nor see nor speak
  To anybody till then.
FACE   For that we'll put, sir,   75
  A stay in's mouth.
SUBTLE   Of what?
FACE   Of gingerbread.
  Make you it fit. He that hath pleased her Grace
  Thus far, shall not now crinkle for a little.
  [*To Dapper*] Gape sir, and let him fit you.
    [*Stuffing gingerbread into his mouth*]
SUBTLE   Where shall we now

Bestow him?
DOLL   I' the privy.
SUBTLE   Come along, sir,   80
I now must show you Fortune's privy lodgings.
FACE Are they perfumed? And his bath ready?
SUBTLE   All.
Only the fumigation's somewhat strong.
        [*Exeunt Subtle, Doll, Dapper*]
FACE Sir Epicure, I am yours, sir, by and by.

4.1

[*Enter Sir Epicure*] *Mammon*

FACE O, sir, you're come i'the only, finest time—

MAMMON Where's master?

FACE   Now preparing for projection, sir.
  Your stuff will be all changed shortly.

MAMMON   Into gold?

FACE To gold and silver, sir.

MAMMON   Silver I care not for.

FACE Yes, sir, a little to give beggars.

MAMMON   Where's the lady?   5

FACE At hand, here. I ha' told her such brave things o' you,
  Touching your bounty and your noble spirit—

MAMMON   Hast thou?

FACE As she is almost in her fit to see you.
  But, good sir, no divinity i' your conference,
  For fear of putting her in rage—

MAMMON   I warrant thee.   10

FACE Six men will not hold her down. And then,
  If the old man should hear, or see you—

MAMMON   Fear not.

FACE The very house, sir, would run mad. You know it,
  How scrupulous he is, and violent,
  'Gainst the least act of sin. Physic, or mathematics,   15
  Poetry, state, or bawdry (as I told you)
  She will endure, and never startle; but
  No word of controversy.

MAMMON   I am schooled, good Ulen.

FACE And you must praise her house, remember that,
  And her nobility.

MAMMON   Let me alone.   20
  No herald, no nor antiquary, Lungs,
  Shall do it better. Go.

FACE [*aside*]   Why, this is yet
  A kind of modern happiness, to have
  Doll Common for a great lady.
     [*Exit Face*]

MAMMON   Now, Epicure,

Heighten thyself, talk to her, all in gold;   25
Rain her as many showers as Jove did drops
Unto his Danaë; show the god a miser
Compared with Mammon. What? The stone will do't.
She shall feel gold, taste gold, hear gold, sleep gold:
Nay, we will *concumbere* gold. I will be puissant   30
And mighty in my talk to her! Here she comes.
  [*Enter Doll, Face*]

FACE [*aside*] To him, Doll, suckle him. [*Aloud*] This is the noble knight
I told your ladyship—

MAMMON   Madam, with your pardon,
I kiss your vesture.
  [*Bows low to kiss her hem*]

DOLL   Sir, I were uncivil   35
If I would suffer that; my lip to you, sir.
  [*They kiss*]

MAMMON I hope my lord your brother be in health, lady?

DOLL My lord my brother is, though I no lady, sir.

FACE [*aside*] Well said my Guinea-bird.

MAMMON   Right noble madam—°

FACE [*aside*] O, we shall have most fierce idolatry!   40

MAMMON 'Tis your prerogative.

DOLL   Rather your courtesy.

MAMMON Were there nought else t' enlarge your virtues to me,
These answers speak your breeding and your blood.

DOLL Blood we boast none, sir; a poor baron's daughter.

MAMMON Poor! And gat you? Profane not. Had your father   45
Slept all the happy remnant of his life
After the act, lain but there still, and panted,
He'd done enough to make himself, his issue,
And his posterity noble.

DOLL   Sir, although
We may be said to want the gilt and trappings,   50
The dress of honour, yet we strive to keep
The seeds and the materials.

MAMMON   I do see
The old ingredient, virtue, was not lost,
Nor the drug, money, used to make your compound.
There is a strange nobility i' your eye,   55
This lip, that chin! Methinks you do resemble

One o' the Austriac princes.

FACE [*aside*]   Very like,°
Her father was an Irish costermonger.

MAMMON The house of Valois just had such a nose.°
And such a forehead yet the Medici   60
Of Florence boast.

DOLL   Troth, and I have been likened°
To all these princes.

FACE [*aside*]   I'll be sworn, I heard it.

MAMMON I know not how! It is not any one,
But e'en the very choice of all their features.

FACE [*aside*] I'll in, and laugh.
        [*Exit Face*]

MAMMON   A certain touch, or air,   65
That sparkles a divinity beyond
An earthly beauty!

DOLL   O, you play the courtier.

MAMMON Good lady, gi' me leave—

DOLL   In faith, I may not,
To mock me, sir.

MAMMON   To burn i' this sweet flame;
The phoenix never knew a nobler death.   70

DOLL Nay, now you court the courtier, and destroy
What you would build. This art, sir, i' your words,
Calls your whole faith in question.

MAMMON   By my soul—

DOLL Nay, oaths are made o' the same air, sir.

MAMMON   Nature
Never bestowed upon mortality,   75
A more unblamed, a more harmonious feature;
She played the stepdame in all faces, else.
Sweet madam, let me be particular—

DOLL Particular, sir? I pray you, know your distance.

MAMMON In no ill sense, sweet lady, but to ask   80
How your fair graces pass the hours? I see
You're lodged here, i' the house of a rare man,
An excellent artist—but what's that to you?

DOLL Yes, sir. I study here the mathematics,
And distillation.

MAMMON   O, I cry your pardon.   85
He's a divine instructor! Can extract

The souls of all things by his art; call all
The virtues and the miracles of the sun,
Into a temperate furnace; teach dull nature
What her own forces are. A man the Emp'ror   90
Has courted—above Kelly sent his medals,°
And chains t' invite him.

DOLL   Aye, and for his physic, sir—

MAMMON Above the art of Aesculapius,
That drew the envy of the Thunderer!°
I know all this, and more.

DOLL   Troth, I am taken, sir,   95
Whole, with these studies that contemplate nature.

MAMMON It is a noble humour. But this form
Was not intended to so dark a use!
Had you been crooked, foul, of some coarse mould,
A cloister had done well; but such a feature   100
That might stand up the glory of a kingdom,
To live recluse! Is a mere solecism,°
Though in a nunnery. It must not be.
I muse my lord your brother will permit it!
You should spend half my land first, were I he.   105
Does not this diamond better on my finger
Than i' the quarry?

DOLL   Yes.

MAMMON   Why, you are like it.
You were created, lady, for the light!
Hear, you shall wear it; take it, the first pledge
Of what I speak: to bind you to believe me.   110
      [*Gives her the ring*]

DOLL In chains of adamant?

MAMMON   Yes, the strongest bands.
And take a secret, too. Here, by your side,
Doth stand, this hour, the happiest man in Europe.

DOLL You are contented, sir?

MAMMON   Nay, in true being:
The envy of princes and the fear of states.   115

DOLL Say you so, Sir Epicure?

MAMMON   Yes, and thou shalt prove it,
Daughter of honour. I have cast mine eye
Upon thy form, and I will rear this beauty
Above all styles.

DOLL You mean no treason, sir!

MAMMON No, I will take away that jealousy. 120
   I am the lord of the philosophers' stone,
   And thou the lady.

DOLL How sir! Ha' you that?

MAMMON I am the master of the mastery.
   This day, the good old wretch, here, o' the house
   Has made it for us. Now, he's at projection. 125
   Think, therefore, thy first wish, now; let me hear it,
   And it shall rain into thy lap, no shower,
   But floods of gold, whole cataracts, a deluge,
   To get a nation on thee!

DOLL You are pleased, sir,
   To work on the ambition of our sex. 130

MAMMON I'm pleased the glory of her sex should know
   This nook, here, of the Friars, is no climate
   For her to live obscurely in, to learn
   Physic and surgery for the constable's wife
   Of some odd hundred in Essex; but come forth, 135
   And taste the air of palaces; eat, drink
   The toils of emp'rics, and their boasted practice;
   Tincture of pearl, and coral, gold, and amber;
   Be seen at feasts, and triumphs; have it asked,
   What miracle she is? Set all the eyes 140
   Of court afire, like a burning glass,
   And work 'em into cinders, when the jewels
   Of twenty states adorn thee, and the light
   Strikes out the stars; that, when thy name is mentioned,
   Queens may look pale: and we but showing our love, 145
   Nero's Poppaea may be lost in story!°
   Thus will we have it.

DOLL I could well consent, sir.
   But in a monarchy, how will this be?
   The prince will soon take notice, and both seize
   You and your stone, it being a wealth unfit 150
   For any private subject.

MAMMON If he knew it.

DOLL Yourself do boast it, sir.

MAMMON To thee, my life.

DOLL O, but beware, sir! You may come to end
   The remnant of your days in a loath'd prison,

By speaking of it.

MAMMON   'Tis no idle fear!   155
We'll therefore go with all, my girl, and live
In a free state, where we will eat our mullets°
Soused in high-country wines, sup pheasants' eggs,
And have our cockles boiled in silver shells,
Our shrimps to swim again, as when they lived,   160
In a rare butter made of dolphins' milk,
Whose cream does look like opals; and with these
Delicate meats, set ourselves high for pleasure,
And take us down again, and then renew
Our youth and strength with drinking the elixir,   165
And so enjoy a perpetuity
Of life and lust. And thou shalt ha' thy wardrobe,
Richer than Nature's, still, to change thyself,
And vary oft'ner, for thy pride, than she,
Or Art, her wise and almost-equal servant.   170
        [Enter Face]

FACE Sir, you are too loud. I hear you, every word,
Into the laboratory. Some fitter place!
The garden, or great chamber above. [Aside to Mammon] How like
    you her?

MAMMON Excellent! Lungs. There's for thee.
        [Gives money]

FACE   But, do you hear?   175
Good sir, beware, no mention of the Rabbins.

MAMMON We think not on 'em.

FACE   O, it is well, sir.
        [Exeunt Doll, Mammon]

                                          Subtle!

        4.2

        [Enter] Subtle

FACE Dost thou not laugh?

SUBTLE   Yes. Are they gone?

FACE   All's clear.

SUBTLE The widow is come.

FACE   And your quarrelling disciple?

SUBTLE Aye.

FACE   I must to my captainship again then.

SUBTLE Stay, bring 'em in first.

FACE   So I meant. What is she?
  A bonnibel?

SUBTLE   I know not.

FACE   We'll draw lots,   5
  You'll stand to that?

SUBTLE   What else?

FACE   O for a suit
  To fall now, like a curtain: flap!

SUBTLE   To the door, man.°

FACE You'll ha' the first kiss, 'cause I am not ready.
        [*Goes to door*]

SUBTLE [*aside*] Yes, and perhaps hit you through both the nostrils.°
        [*Face opens door. Enter Kestrel, Dame Pliant*]

FACE Who would you speak with?

KESTREL   Where's the Captain?

FACE   Gone, sir,   10
  About some business.

KESTREL   Gone?

FACE   He'll return straight.
  But Master Doctor, his lieutenant, is here.
        [*Exit Face*]

SUBTLE Come near, my worshipful boy, my *terrae fili*,°
  That is, my boy of land; make thy approaches.
  Welcome, I know thy lusts and thy desires,   15
  And I will serve and satisfy 'em. Begin,
  Charge me from thence, or thence, or in this line;
  Here is my centre: ground thy quarrel.

KESTREL   You lie.

SUBTLE How, child of wrath and anger! The loud lie?
  For what, my sudden boy?

KESTREL   Nay, that look you to,   20
  I am aforehand.

SUBTLE   O, this's no true grammar,°
  And as ill logic! You must render causes, child,°
  Your first and second intentions, know your canons
  And your divisions, modes, degrees and differences,
  Your predicaments, substance and accident,   25
  Series extern and intern, with their causes

Efficient, material, formal, final,
And ha' your elements perfect—
KESTREL   What, is this°
The angry tongue he talks in?
SUBTLE   That false precept
Of being aforehand has deceived a number,   30
And made 'em enter quarrels, oftentimes,
Before they were aware; and afterward,
Against their wills.
KESTREL   How must I do then, sir?
SUBTLE I cry this lady mercy. She should, first,
        [*Turns to Dame Pliant*]
Have been saluted. I do call you lady,   35
Because you are to be one ere't be long,
My soft and buxom widow.
        He kisses her
KESTREL   Is she, i'faith?
SUBTLE Yes, or my art is an egregious liar.
KESTREL How know you?
SUBTLE   By inspection on her forehead,
And subtlety of her lip, which must be tasted°   40
Often, to make a judgement.
        He kisses her again
                          'Slight, she melts
Like a myrobalan! Here is yet a line°
In rivo frontis tells me he is no knight.°
PLIANT What is he then, sir?
SUBTLE   Let me see your hand.
O, your *linea fortunae* makes it plain;°   45
And *stella*, here, *in monte Veneris*:°
But, most of all, *junctura anularis*.°
He is a soldier, or a man of art, lady,
But shall have some great honour shortly.
PLIANT   Brother,
He's a rare man, believe me!
KESTREL   Hold your peace.   50
Here comes the t'other rare man.
        [*Enter Face in captain's uniform*]
                          Save you, Captain.
FACE Good Master Kestrel. Is this your sister?
KESTREL   Aye, sir.

Please you to kuss her, and be proud to know her?

FACE I shall be proud to know you, lady.

    [*Kisses her*]

PLIANT   Brother,

  He calls me lady, too.

KESTREL   Aye, peace. I heard it: 55

FACE [*to Subtle*] The Count is come.

SUBTLE   Where is he?

FACE   At the door.

SUBTLE Why, you must entertain him.

FACE   What'll you do

  With these the while?

SUBTLE   Why, have 'em up, and show 'em

  Some fustian book, or the dark glass.

FACE   'Fore God,°

  She is a delicate dabchick! I must have her.   60

    [*Exit Face*]

SUBTLE Must you? Aye, if your fortune will, you must.

  [*To Kestrel*] Come sir, the Captain will come to us presently.

  I'll ha' you to my chamber of demonstrations,

  Where I'll show you both the grammar and logic

  And rhetoric of quarrelling; my whole method   65

  Drawn out in tables; and my instrument,

  That hath the several scale upon't, shall make you

  Able to quarrel at a straw's breadth by moonlight.

  And, lady, I'll have you look in a glass,

  Some half an hour, but to clear your eyesight,   70

  Against you see your fortune; which is greater

  Than I may judge upon the sudden, trust me.

    [*Exeunt*]

4.3

    [*Enter*] Face

FACE Where are you, Doctor?

SUBTLE [*within*]   I'll come to you presently.

FACE I will ha' this same widow, now I ha' seen her,

  On any composition.

    [*Enter Subtle*]

SUBTLE   What do you say?
FACE Ha' you disposed of them?
SUBTLE   I ha' sent 'em up.
FACE Subtle, in troth, I needs must have this widow.   5
SUBTLE Is that the matter?
FACE   Nay, but hear me.
SUBTLE   Go to;
   If you rebel once, Doll shall know it all.
   Therefore be quiet, and obey your chance.
FACE Nay, thou art so violent now—do but conceive,
   Thou art old, and canst not serve—
SUBTLE   Who? Cannot I?°   10
   'Slight, I will serve her with thee, for a—
FACE   Nay,
   But understand; I'll gi' you composition.
SUBTLE I will not treat with thee; what, sell my fortune?
   'Tis better than my birthright. Do not murmur.
   Win her and carry her. If you grumble, Doll   15
   Knows it directly.
FACE   Well, sir, I am silent.
   Will you go help to fetch in Don, in state?
SUBTLE I follow you, sir.
     [*Exit Face*]
   We must keep Face in awe,
   Or he will overlook us like a tyrant.   20
   Brain of a tailor! Who comes here? Don John!°
     [*Enter*] *Surly like a Spaniard* [*with Face*]
SURLY *Señores, beso las manos, a vuestras mercedes.*°
SUBTLE Would you had stooped a little, and kissed our *anos.*
FACE Peace, Subtle.
SUBTLE   Stab me; I shall never hold, man.
   He looks in that deep ruff like a head in a platter,   25
   Served in by a short cloak upon two trestles!
FACE Or what do you say to a collar of brawn, cut down
   Beneath the souse, and wriggled with a knife?°
SUBTLE 'Slud, he does look too fat to be a Spaniard.
FACE Perhaps some Fleming, or some Hollander got him   30
   In D'Alva's time; Count Egmont's bastard.
SUBTLE   Don,°
   Your scurvy, yellow, Madrid face is welcome.
SURLY *Gracias.*

SUBTLE   He speaks out of a fortification.
    Pray God! he ha' no squibs in those deep sets.°
SURLY *¡Por Diós, señores, muy linda casa!*°   35
SUBTLE What says he?
FACE   Praises the house, I think,
    I know no more but's action.
SUBTLE   Yes, the *casa,*°
    My precious Diego, will prove fair enough,
    To cozen you in. Do you mark? You shall
    Be cozened, Diego.
FACE   Cozened, do you see?   40
    My worthy Donzel, cozened.
SURLY   *Entiendo.*
SUBTLE Do you intend it? So do we, dear Don.
    Have you brought pistolets? Or portagues?
    My solemn Don? [*To Face*] Dost thou feel any?
FACE (*he feels his pockets*)   Full.
SUBTLE You shall be emptied, Don; pumped and drawn   45
    Dry, as they say.
FACE   Milked, in troth, sweet Don.
SUBTLE See all the monsters; the great lion of all, Don.°
SURLY *¿Con licencia, se puede ver a esta señora?*°
SUBTLE What talks he now?
FACE   O'the *señora.*
SUBTLE   O, Don,
    That is the lioness, which you shall see   50
    Also, my Don.
FACE   Slid, Subtle, how shall we do?
SUBTLE For what?
FACE   Why, Doll's employed, you know.
SUBTLE   That's true!
    'Fore heaven I know not; he must stay, that's all.
FACE Stay? That he must not by no means.
SUBTLE   No? Why?
FACE Unless you'll mar all. 'Slight, he'll suspect it.   55
    And then he will not pay, not half so well.
    This is a travelled punk-master, and does know
    All the delays; a notable hot rascal,
    And looks, already, rampant.
SUBTLE   'Sdeath, and Mammon
    Must not be troubled.

FACE   Mammon, in no case!   60
SUBTLE What shall we do then?
FACE   Think: you must be sudden.
SURLY *Entiendo, que la señora es tan hermosa,*
    Que codicio tanto verla,
    Como la buena venturanza de mi vida.°
FACE *Mi vida?* 'Slid, Subtle, he puts me in mind o'the widow.   65
    What dost thou say to draw her to it? Ha?
    And tell her it is her fortune. All our venture
    Now lies upon't. It is but one man more,
    Which on's chance to have her; and, beside,°
    There is no maidenhead to be feared or lost.   70
    What dost thou think on't, Subtle?
SUBTLE   Who, I? Why—
FACE The credit of our house too is engaged.
SUBTLE You made me an offer for my share erewhile.
    What wilt thou gi' me, i'faith?
FACE   O, by that light,
    I'll not buy now. You know your doom to me: 75
    E'en take your lot, obey your chance, sir; win her,
    And wear her, out for me.
SUBTLE   'Slight. I'll not work her then.°
FACE It is the common cause; therefore bethink you.
    Doll else must know it, as you said.
SUBTLE   I care not.
SURLY *¿Señores, por qué se tarda tanto?°*   80
SUBTLE Faith, I am not fit, I am old.
FACE   That's now no reason, sir.
SURLY *Puede ser de hacer burla de mi amor.°*
FACE You hear the Don, too? By this air, I call
    And loose the hinges. Doll!
SUBTLE   A plague of hell—
FACE Will you then do?
SUBTLE   You're a terrible rogue,   85
    I'll think of this. Will you, sir, call the widow?
FACE Yes, and I'll take her too, with all her faults,
    Now I do think on't better.
SUBTLE   With all my heart, sir;
    Am I discharged o'the lot?
FACE   As you please.
SUBTLE   Hands.

[*They shake hands*]

FACE Remember now, that upon any change,   90
    You never claim her.

SUBTLE   Much good joy, and health to you, sir.
    Marry a whore? Fate, let me wed a witch first.

SURLY *Por estas honradas barbas—*

SUBTLE   He swears by his beard.°
    Dispatch, and call the brother too.

    [*Exit Face*]

SURLY   *Tengo duda, señores,*
Que no me hagan alguna traición.°   95

SUBTLE How, issue on? Yes, *presto señor.* Please you
    Enthratha the *chambratha,* worthy Don,
    Where if it please the Fates, in your *bathada,*°
    You shall be soaked, and stroked, and tubbed, and rubbed,
    And scrubbed, and fubbed, dear Don, before you go.   100
    You shall, in faith, my scurvy baboon Don,
    Be curried, clawed, and flawed, and tawed, indeed.
    I will the heartlier go about it now, ·
    And make the widow a punk, so much the sooner,
    To be revenged on this impetuous Face: 105
    The quickly doing of it is the grace.

    [*Exeunt*]

4.4

    [*Enter*] *Face, Dame Pliant* [*and*] *Kestrel*

FACE Come lady. [*To Kestrel*] I knew the Doctor would not leave,
    Till he had found the very nick of her fortune.

KESTREL To be a countess, say you?

FACE   A Spanish countess, sir.

PLIANT Why? Is that better than an English countess?

FACE Better? 'Slight, make you that a question, lady?   5

KESTREL Nay, she is a fool, Captain, you must pardon her.

FACE Ask from your courtier, to your inns-of-court man,
    To your mere milliner: they will tell you, all,
    Your Spanish jennet is the best horse; your Spanish
    Stoup is the best garb; your Spanish beard°   10
    Is the best cut, your Spanish ruffs are the best

Wear; your Spanish pavan the best dance.
Your Spanish titillation in a glove
The best perfume; and for your Spanish pike,
And Spanish blade, let your poor Captain speak.   15
Here comes the Doctor.
          [*Enter Subtle*]

SUBTLE   My most honoured lady—
    For so I am now to style you, having found
          [*Shows horoscope*]
    By this my scheme, you are to undergo
    An honourable fortune, very shortly—
    What will you say now, if some—

FACE   I ha' told her all, sir,   20
    And her right worshipful brother, here, that she shall be
    A countess; do not delay 'em, sir. A Spanish countess.

SUBTLE Still, my scarce worshipful Captain, you can keep
    No secret. Well, since he has told you, madam,
    Do you forgive him, and I do.

KESTREL   She shall do that, sir.   25
    I'll look to't; 'tis my charge.

SUBTLE   Well then. Nought rests
    But that she fit her love, now, to her fortune.

PLIANT Truly, I shall never brook a Spaniard.

SUBTLE   No?

PLIANT Never sin' eighty-eight could I abide 'em,°
    And that was some three year afore I was born, in truth.   30

SUBTLE Come, you must love him, or be miserable:
    Choose which you will.

FACE   By this good rush, persuade her;°
    She will cry strawberries else, within this twelvemonth.

SUBTLE Nay, shads and mackerel, which is worse.

FACE   Indeed, sir?°

KESTREL God's lid, you shall love him, or I'll kick you.

PLIANT   Why,   35
    I'll do as you will ha' me, brother.

KESTREL   Do,
    Or by this hand I'll maul you.

FACE   Nay, good sir,
    Be not so fierce.

SUBTLE   No, my enragèd child,
    She will be ruled. What, when she comes to taste

    The pleasures of a countess! To be courted—   40
FACE And kissed, and ruffled!
SUBTLE   Aye, behind the hangings.
FACE And then come forth in pomp!
SUBTLE   And know her state!
FACE Of keeping all th' idolaters o'the chamber
    Barer to her than at their prayers!
SUBTLE   Is served°
    Upon the knee!
FACE   And has her pages, ushers,   45
    Footmen, and coaches—
SUBTLE   Her six mares—
FACE   Nay, eight!
SUBTLE To hurry her through London, to th' Exchange,
    Bedlam, the china-houses—
FACE   Yes, and have°
    The citizens gape at her, and praise her tires!
    And my lord's goose-turd bands, that rides with her!°   50
KESTREL Most brave! By this hand, you are not my suster,
    If you refuse.
PLIANT   I will not refuse, brother.
    [*Enter Surly*]
SURLY *¿Qué es esto, señores, que no se venga?*
    ¡Esta tardanza me mata!
FACE   It is the Count come!°
    The Doctor knew he would be here, by his art.   55
SUBTLE *¡En gallanta madama, Don! ¡Gallantissima!*°
SURLY *¡Por tódos los Dioses, la más acabada*
    Hermosura, que he visto en mi vida!°
FACE Is't not a gallant language that they speak?
KESTREL An admirable language! Is't not French?   60
FACE No, Spanish, sir.
KESTREL   It goes like law French,°
    And that, they say, is the courtliest language.
FACE   List, sir.
SURLY *El sol ha perdido su lumbre, con el*
    Resplandor que tráe esta dama. ¡Válgame Diós!°
FACE He admires your sister.
KESTREL   Must not she make curtsy?   65
SUBTLE 'Ods will, she must go to him, man, and kiss him!
    It is the Spanish fashion for the women

　　To make first court.

FACE　　　　　　　　　'Tis true he tells you, sir;
　　His art knows all.

SURLY　　　　¿Por qué no se acude?°

KESTREL　He speaks to her, I think?

FACE　　　　　　　　　That he does sir.　　　　　　70

SURLY　¿ Por el amor de Diós, que és esto, que se tarda?°

KESTREL　Nay, see: she will not understand him! Gull.
　　Noddy.

PLIANT　What say you, brother?

KESTREL　　　　　　　Ass, my suster,
　　Go kuss him, as the cunning man would ha' you,
　　I'll thrust a pin i' your buttocks else.

FACE　　　　　　　　　O, no, sir.　　　　　　75

SURLY　Señora mía, mi persona muy indigna está
　　Allegar a tanta hermosura.°

FACE　Does he not use her bravely?

KESTREL　　　　　　　Bravely, i'faith!

FACE　Nay, he will use her better.

KESTREL　　　　　　　Do you think so?

SURLY　Señora, si sera servida, entremos.°　　　　80
　　　　[Exeunt Surly, Dame Pliant]

KESTREL　Where does he carry her?

FACE　　　　　　　　　Into the garden, sir;
　　Take you no thought. I must interpret for her.

SUBTLE　Give Doll the word.
　　　　[Exit Face]
　　[To Kestrel] Come, my fierce child, advance,°
　　We'll to our quarrelling lesson again.

KESTREL　　　　　　　Agreed.　　　　　　85
　　I love a Spanish boy, with all my heart.

SUBTLE　Nay, and by this means, sir, you shall be brother
　　To a great Count.

KESTREL　　　　　Aye, I knew that, at first.
　　This match will advance the house of the Kestrels.

SUBTLE　Pray God, your sister prove but pliant.

KESTREL　　　　　　　Why,　　　　　　90
　　Her name is so, by her other husband.

SUBTLE　　　　　　　How!

KESTREL　The widow Pliant. Knew you not that?

SUBTLE　　　　　　　No faith, sir.

Yet, by erection of her figure, I guessed it.°
Come, let's go practise.

KESTREL   Yes, but do you think, Doctor,
I e'er shall quarrel well?

SUBTLE   I warrant you.   95

  [*Exeunt*]

4.5

  [*Enter*] *Doll in her fit of talking* [*and Sir Epicure*] *Mammon*

DOLL For after Alexander's death—

MAMMON   Good lady—

DOLL That Perdiccas and Antigonus were slain,
The two that stood, Seleuc' and Ptolemy—°

MAMMON Madam—

DOLL   Made up the two legs, and the fourth Beast.
That was Gog-north, and Egypt-south, which after°   5
Was called Gog Iron-leg and South Iron-leg—

MAMMON   Lady—

DOLL And then Gog-hornèd. So was Egypt, too.
Then Egypt clay-leg, and Gog clay-leg—

MAMMON   Sweet madam—

DOLL And last Gog-dust, and Egypt-dust, which fall
In the last link of the fourth chain. And these°   10
Be stars in story, which none see, or look at—

MAMMON What shall I do?

DOLL   For, as he says, except
We call the Rabbins, and the heathen Greeks—

MAMMON Dear lady—

DOLL   To come from Salem and from Athens,°
And teach the people of Great Britain—
  [*Enter Face*]

FACE   What's the matter, sir?   15

DOLL To speak the tongue of Eber and Javan—°

MAMMON   O,
She's in her fit.

DOLL   We shall know nothing—

FACE   Death, sir,

We are undone!

DOLL   Where, then, a learned linguist
Shall see the ancient used communion
Of vowels and consonants—

FACE   My master will hear!°   20

DOLL A wisdom—which Pythagoras held most high—

MAMMON Sweet honourable lady—

DOLL   To comprise
All sounds of voices, in few marks of letters—

FACE Nay, you must never hope to lay her now.

          They speak together

DOLL And so we may arrive by Talmud skill,°   25
And profane Greek, to raise the building up
Of Heber's house, against the Ismaelite,°
King of Togarma, and his habergions°
Brimstony, blue, and fiery; and the force
Of King Abaddon, and the Beast of Cittim,°   30
Which Rabbi David Kimchi, Onkelos,°
And Aben-Ezra do interpret Rome.°

FACE How did you put her into't?

MAMMON   Alas, I talked
Of a fifth monarchy I would erect
With the philosophers' stone (by chance), and she   35
Falls on the other four straight.°

FACE   Out of Broughton!
I told you so. 'Slid, stop her mouth.

MAMMON   Is't best?

FACE She'll never leave else. If the old man hear her,
We are but faeces, ashes.

SUBTLE [*within*]   What's to do there?

FACE O, we are lost. Now she hears him, she is quiet.   40

          Upon Subtle's entry they disperse [*Exit Face and Doll*]

MAMMON Where shall I hide me?

SUBTLE   How? What sight is here?
Close deeds of darkness, and that shun the light!
Bring him again. Who is he? What, my son!
Oh I have lived too long.

MAMMON   Nay, good, dear father,
There was no unchaste purpose.

SUBTLE   Not? And flee me,   45
When I come in?

MAMMON   That was my error.

SUBTLE   Error?
    Guilt, guilt, my son. Give it the right name. No marvel,
    If I found check in our great work within,
    When such affairs as these were managing!
MAMMON Why, have you so?
SUBTLE   It has stood still this half hour,   50
    And all the rest of our less works gone back.
    Where is the instrument of wickedness,
    My lewd false drudge?
MAMMON   Nay, good sir, blame not him.
    Believe me, 'twas against his will, or knowledge.
    I saw her by chance.
SUBTLE   Will you commit more sin,   55
    T' excuse a varlet?
MAMMON   By my hope, 'tis true, sir.
SUBTLE Nay, then I wonder less, if you, for whom
    The blessing was prepared, would so tempt heaven,
    And lose your fortunes.
MAMMON   Why, sir?
SUBTLE   This'll retard
    The work, a month at least.
MAMMON   Why, if it do,   60
    What remedy? But think it not, good father;
    Our purposes were honest.
SUBTLE   As they were,
    So the reward will prove.
        A great crack and noise within
                How now! Aye me.
    God and all saints be good to us.
        [*Enter Face*]
                What's that?
FACE O sir, we are defeated! All the works   65
    Are flown *in fumo*; every glass is burst.°
    Furnace, and all rent down, as if a bolt
    Of thunder had been driven through the house.
    Retorts, receivers, pelicans, bolt-heads,
    All struck in shivers!   70
        Subtle falls down as in a swoon
    [*To Mammon*] Help, good sir! Alas,
    Coldness and death invades him. Nay, Sir Mammon,
    Do the fair offices of a man! You stand
    As you were readier to depart than he.

One knocks
Who's there? [*Looks out*] My lord her brother is come.
MAMMON   Ha, Lungs?   75
FACE His coach is at the door. Avoid his sight,
For he's as furious as his sister is mad.
MAMMON Alas!
FACE   My brain is quite undone with the fume, sir,
I ne'er must hope to be mine own man again.
MAMMON Is all lost, Lungs? Will nothing be preserved,   80
Of all our cost?
FACE   Faith, very little, sir.
A peck of coals, or so, which is cold comfort, sir.
MAMMON O, my voluptuous mind! I am justly punished.
FACE And so am I, sir.
MAMMON   Cast from all my hopes—
FACE Nay, certainties, sir.
MAMMON   By mine own base affections.   85
Subtle seems to come to himself
SUBTLE O, the curs'd fruits of vice and lust!
MAMMON   Good father,
It was my sin. Forgive it.
SUBTLE   Hangs my roof
Over us still, and will not fall? O justice
Upon us, for this wicked man!
FACE   Nay, look, sir,
You grieve him now with staying in his sight.   90
Good sir, the nobleman will come too, and take you,
And that may breed a tragedy.
MAMMON   I'll go.
FACE Aye, and repent at home, sir. It may be
For some good penance you may ha' it yet,
A hundred pound to the box at Bedlam—
MAMMON   Yes.   95
FACE For the restoring such as ha' their wits.
MAMMON   I'll do't.
FACE I'll send one to you to receive it.
MAMMON   Do.
Is no projection left?
FACE   All flown, or stinks, sir.
MAMMON Will nought be saved that's good for medicine, thinkst
thou?   100

FACE I cannot tell, sir. There will be, perhaps,
　　　Something, about the scraping of the shards,
　　　Will cure the itch—[*aside*] though not your itch of mind, sir—
　　　It shall be saved for you, and sent home. Good sir,
　　　This way, for fear the lord should meet you.
　　　　　[*Exit Mammon*]
SUBTLE   Face.   105
FACE Aye.
SUBTLE   Is he gone?
FACE   Yes, and as heavily
　　　As all the gold he hoped for were in his blood.
　　　Let us be light, though.
SUBTLE   Aye, as balls, and bound
　　　And hit our heads against the roof for joy;
　　　There's so much of our care now cast away.   110
FACE Now to our Don.
SUBTLE   Yes, your young widow by this time
　　　Is made a countess, Face; she's been in travail
　　　Of a young heir for you.
FACE   Good, sir.
SUBTLE   Off with your case,°
　　　And greet her kindly, as a bridegroom should,
　　　After these common hazards.
FACE   Very well, sir.   115
　　　Will you go fetch Don Diego off the while?
SUBTLE And fetch him over too, if you'll be pleased, sir;°
　　　Would Doll were in her place, to pick his pockets now.
FACE Why, you can do it as well, if you would set to't.
　　　I pray you prove your virtue.
SUBTLE   For your sake, sir.°   120
　　　　　[*Exeunt*]

4.6

　　　[*Enter*] Surly [*and*] Dame Pliant
SURLY Lady, you see into what hands you are fallen;
　　　'Mongst what a nest of villains! And how near
　　　Your honour was to have catched a certain clap
　　　(Through your credulity) had I but been
　　　So punctually forward, as place, time,   5

And other circumstance would ha' made a man;
For you're a handsome woman: would yo' were wise, too.
I am a gentleman, come here disguised,
Only to find the knaveries of this citadel,
And where I might have wronged your honour, and have not,   10
I claim some interest in your love. You are,
They say, a widow, rich; and I am a bachelor,
Worth nought. Your fortunes may make me a man,
As mine ha' preserved you a woman. Think upon it,
And whether I have deserved you, or no.

PLIANT   I will, sir.   15
SURLY And for these household-rogues, let me alone
    To treat with them.
        [*Enter Subtle*]
SUBTLE   How doth my noble Diego?
    And my dear madam, Countess? Hath the Count
    Been courteous, lady? Liberal? And open?
    Donzel, methinks you look melancholic,   20
    After your *coitum*, and scurvy! Truly,
    I do not like the dullness of your eye;
    It hath a heavy cast, 'tis upsee Dutch,
    And says you are a lumpish whore-master.
    Be lighter, I will make your pockets so.   25
        He falls to picking of them
SURLY Will you, Don bawd and pick-purse? How now? Reel you?
    Stand up, sir; you shall find, since I am so heavy,
    I'll gi' you equal weight.
SUBTLE   Help, murder!
SURLY   No, sir.
    There's no such thing intended. A good cart
    And a clean whip shall ease you of that fear.°   30
    I am the Spanish Don that should be cozened.
    Do you see? Cozened? Where's your Captain Face?
    That parcel-broker, and whole-bawd, all rascal.
        [*Enter Face*]
FACE How, Surly!
SURLY   O, make your approach, good Captain.
    I've found from whence your copper rings and spoons   35
    Come, now, wherewith you cheat abroad in taverns.°
    'Twas here, you learned t' anoint your boot with brimstone,
    Then rub men's gold on't, for a kind of touch,

And say 'twas nought, when you had changed the colour,
That you might ha't for nothing? And this Doctor,   40
Your sooty, smoky-bearded compeer, he
Will close you so much gold in a bolt's-head,
And, on a turn, convey i'the stead another
With sublimed mercury, that shall burst i' the heat,
And fly out all *in fumo*!
    [*Exit Face*]
                       Then weeps Mammon;   45
Then swoons his worship. Or he is the Faustus°
That casteth figures and can conjure, cures
Plague, piles, and pox, by the ephemerides,
And holds intelligence with all the bawds,
And midwives of three shires? While you send in—   50
Captain—what, is he gone?—damsels with child,
Wives that are barren, or the waiting-maid
With the green-sickness? [*Seizing Subtle*] Nay, sir, you must tarry
Though he be 'scaped, and answer by the ears, sir.°

4.7

    [*Enter*] *Face* [*and*] *Kestrel*

FACE [*to Kestrel*] Why, now's the time, if ever you will quarrel
    Well (as they say) and be a true-born child.
    The Doctor and your sister both are abused.
KESTREL Where is he? Which is he? He is a slave
    What e'er he is, and the son of a whore. [*To Surly*] Are you   5
    The man, sir, I would know?
SURLY   I should be loath, sir,
    To confess so much.
KESTREL   Then you lie i'your throat.
SURLY   How?
FACE [*to Kestrel*] A very arrant rogue, sir, and a cheater,
    Employed here, by another conjurer
    That does not love the Doctor, and would cross him   10
    If he knew how—
SURLY   Sir, you are abused.
KESTREL   You lie;
    And 'tis no matter.

FACE   Well said, sir. He is
  The impudent'st rascal—
SURLY   You are indeed. Will you hear me, sir?
FACE By no means. Bid him be gone.
KESTREL   Be gone, sir, quickly.
SURLY This's strange! Lady, do you inform your brother.   15
      [*She tries to speak to Kestrel*]
FACE There is not such a foist in all the town.
  The Doctor had him, presently; and finds, yet,°
  The Spanish count will come here. [*Aside*] Bear up, Subtle.
SUBTLE Yes, sir, he must appear within this hour.
FACE And yet this rogue would come in a disguise,   20
  By the temptation of another spirit,
  To trouble our art, though he could not hurt it.
KESTREL   Aye,
  I know—[*To Dame Pliant*] Away, you talk like a foolish mauther.
      [*Exit Dame Pliant*]
SURLY Sir, all is truth she says.
FACE   Do not believe him, sir;
  He is the lying'st swabber! Come your ways, sir.   25
SURLY You are valiant out of company.
KESTREL   Yes, how then, sir?
      [*Enter Drugger*]
FACE Nay, here's an honest fellow too, that knows him,
  And all his tricks. [*Aside to Drugger*] Make good what I say, Abel,
  This cheater would ha' cozened thee o'the widow.—
  He owes this honest Drugger, here, seven pound,   30
  He has had on him, in two-penny'orths of tobacco.
DRUGGER Yes sir. And he's damned himself three terms to pay me.°
FACE And what does he owe for lotium?
DRUGGER   Thirty shillings, sir:
  And for six syringes.
SURLY   Hydra of villainy!
FACE [*to Kestrel*] Nay, sir, you must quarrel him out o'the house.
KESTREL   I will.   35
  Sir, if you get not out o' doors, you lie,
  And you are a pimp.
SURLY   Why, this is madness, sir,
  Not valour in you; I must laugh at this.
KESTREL It is my humour: you are a pimp and a trig,
  And an Amadis de Gaule, or a Don Quixote.°   40

DRUGGER Or a Knight o'the Curious Coxcomb. Do you see?
      [*Enter Ananias*]
ANANIAS Peace to the household.
KESTREL   I'll keep peace for no man.
ANANIAS Casting of dollars is concluded lawful.
KESTREL Is he the constable?
SUBTLE   Peace, Ananias.
FACE [*to Kestrel*]   No, sir.
KESTREL [*to Surly*] Then you are an otter, and a shad, a whit,   45
   A very tim.
SURLY   You'll hear me, sir?
KESTREL   I will not.°
ANANIAS What is the motive?
SUBTLE   Zeal, in the young gentleman,
   Against his Spanish slops—
ANANIAS   They are profane,
   Lewd, superstitious, and idolatrous breeches.
SURLY New rascals!
KESTREL   Will you be gone, sir?
ANANIAS   Avoid, Satan,   50
   Thou art not of the light. That ruff of pride
   About thy neck betrays thee, and is the same
   With that, which the unclean birds, in seventy-seven,
   Were seen to prank it with on divers coasts.°
   Thou look'st like Antichrist in that lewd hat.°   55
SURLY I must give way.
KESTREL   Be gone, sir.
SURLY   But I'll take
   A course with you—
ANANIAS   Depart, proud Spanish fiend!
SURLY Captain, and Doctor—
ANANIAS   Child of perdition!
KESTREL   Hence, sir.
      [*Exit Surly*]
   Did I not quarrel bravely?
FACE   Yes, indeed, sir.
KESTREL Nay, an' I give my mind to't, I shall do't.   60
FACE O, you must follow, sir, and threaten him tame.
   He'll turn again else.
KESTREL   I'll re-turn him, then.
      [*Exit Kestrel*]

FACE Drugger, this rogue prevented us for thee.
   We had determined that thou shouldst ha' come
   In a Spanish suit, and ha' carried her so; and he,   65
   A brokerly slave, goes, puts it on himself.
   Hast brought the damask?

DRUGGER   Yes, sir.

FACE   Thou must borrow
   A Spanish suit. Hast thou no credit with the players?

DRUGGER Yes, sir; did you never see me play the fool?°

FACE I know not, Nab. [*Aside*] Thou shalt, if I can help it—   70
   Hieronimo's old cloak, ruff, and hat will serve.°
   I'll tell thee more when thou bringst 'em.
      [*Exit Drugger*]

ANANIAS (*Subtle hath whispered with him this while*)
                          Sir, I know
   The Spaniard hates the brethren, and hath spies
   Upon their actions; and that this was one
   I make no scruple. But the holy synod   75
   Have been in prayer and meditation for it.
   And 'tis revealed no less to them than me,
   That casting of money is most lawful.

SUBTLE   True.
   But here I cannot do it; if the house
   Should chance to be suspected, all would out,   80
   And we be locked up in the Tower for ever,
   To make gold there (for the state), never come out;
   And, then, are you defeated.

ANANIAS   I will tell
   This to the elders and the weaker brethren,
   That the whole company of the separation   85
   May join in humble prayer again.

SUBTLE   And fasting.

ANANIAS Yea, for some fitter place. The peace of mind
   Rest with these walls.

SUBTLE   Thanks, courteous Ananias.
     [*Exit Ananias*]

FACE What did he come for?

SUBTLE   About casting dollars,
   Presently, out of hand. And so I told him   90
   A Spanish minister came here to spy
   Against the faithful—

FACE   I conceive. Come, Subtle,
   Thou art so down upon the least disaster!
   How wouldst thou ha' done, if I had not helped thee out?
SUBTLE I thank thee, Face, for the angry boy, i'faith.   95
FACE Who would ha' looked it should ha' been that rascal?
   Surly? He had dyed his beard, and all. Well, sir,
   Here's damask come to make you a suit.
SUBTLE   Where's Drugger?
FACE He is gone to borrow me a Spanish habit;
   I'll be the Count, now.
SUBTLE   But where's the widow?   100
FACE Within, with my lord's sister: Madam Doll
   Is entertaining her.
SUBTLE   By your favour, Face,
   Now she is honest, I will stand again.
FACE You will not offer it?
SUBTLE   Why?
FACE   Stand to your word,
   Or—here comes Doll! She knows—
      [Enter Doll]
SUBTLE   You're tyrannous still.   105
FACE Strict for my right. How now, Doll? Hast told her
   The Spanish Count will come?
DOLL   Yes, but another is come
   You little looked for!
FACE   Who's that?
DOLL   Your master;
   The master of the house.
SUBTLE   How, Doll!
FACE   She lies.
   This is some trick. Come, leave your quiblins, Dorothy.   110
DOLL Look out and see.
SUBTLE   Art thou in earnest?
DOLL   'Slight,
   Forty o'the neighbours are about him, talking.
FACE [at the window] 'Tis he, by this good day.
DOLL   'Twill prove ill day,
   For some on us.
FACE   We are undone, and taken.
DOLL Lost, I'm afraid.
SUBTLE   You said he would not come,   115

While there died one a week within the liberties.°
FACE No, 'twas within the walls.
SUBTLE   Was't so? Cry you mercy;
    I thought the liberties. What shall we do now, Face?
FACE Be silent: not a word if he call or knock.
    I'll into mine old shape again, and meet him,   120
    Of Jeremy the butler. I' the meantime,
    Do you two pack up all the goods and purchase
    That we can carry i' the two trunks. I'll keep him
    Off for today, if I cannot longer; and then
    At night, I'll ship you both away to Ratcliffe,°   125
    Where we'll meet tomorrow, and there we'll share.
    Let Mammon's brass and pewter keep the cellar;
    We'll have another time for that. But, Doll,
    Pray thee, go heat a little water, quickly,
    Subtle must shave me.
        [*Exit Doll*]
                  All my Captain's beard   130
    Must off, to make me appear smooth Jeremy.
    You'll do't?
SUBTLE   Yes, I'll shave you, as well as I can.
FACE And not cut my throat, but trim me?
SUBTLE   You shall see, sir.°
    [*Exeunt*]

5.1

[Enter] Lovewit [and] Neighbours

LOVEWIT Has there been such resort, say you?
1ST NEIGHBOUR   Daily, sir.
2ND NEIGHBOUR And nightly, too.`
3RD NEIGHBOUR   Aye, some as brave as lords.
4TH NEIGHBOUR Ladies and gentlewomen.
5TH NEIGHBOUR   Citizens' wives.
1ST NEIGHBOUR And knights.
6TH NEIGHBOUR   In coaches.
2ND NEIGHBOUR   Yes, and oyster-women.
1ST NEIGHBOUR Beside other gallants.
3RD NEIGHBOUR   Sailors' wives.
4TH NEIGHBOUR   Tobacco-men.   5
5TH NEIGHBOUR Another Pimlico!
LOVEWIT   What should my knave advance,°
To draw this company? He hung out no banners
Of a strange calf, with five legs, to be seen?
Or a huge lobster with six claws?
6TH NEIGHBOUR   No, sir.
3RD NEIGHBOUR We had gone in then, sir.
LOVEWIT   He has no gift   10
Of teaching i' the nose, that e'er I knew of!°
You saw no bills set up, that promised cure
Of agues or the toothache?
2ND NEIGHBOUR   No such thing, sir.
LOVEWIT Nor heard a drum struck, for baboons, or puppets?
5TH NEIGHBOUR Neither, sir.
LOVEWIT   What device should he bring forth now?   15
I love a teeming wit, as I love my nourishment.
Pray God he ha' not kept such open house
That he hath sold my hangings and my bedding,
I left him nothing else. If he have eat 'em,
A plague o'the moth, say I. Sure he has got   20
Some bawdy pictures, to call all this ging;
The friar and the nun; or the new motion
Of the knight's courser covering the parson's mare;
The boy of six year old, with the great thing;

Or 't may be he has the fleas that run at tilt   25
Upon a table, or some dog to dance?
When saw you him?

1ST NEIGHBOUR   Who, sir, Jeremy?

2ND NEIGHBOUR   Jeremy butler?
We saw him not this month.

LOVEWIT   How!

4TH NEIGHBOUR   Not these five weeks, sir.

1ST NEIGHBOUR These six weeks, at the least.

LOVEWIT   Y'amaze me, neighbours!

5TH NEIGHBOUR Sure, if your worship know not where he is,   30
He's slipped away.

6TH NEIGHBOUR   Pray God he be not made away!

LOVEWIT Ha? It's no time to question, then.

> *He knocks*

6TH NEIGHBOUR   About
Some three weeks since, I heard a doleful cry,
As I sat up a-mending my wife's stockings.

LOVEWIT This's strange! That none will answer! Didst thou hear   35
A cry, sayst thou?

6TH NEIGHBOUR   Yes, sir, like unto a man
That had been strangled an hour, and could not speak.

2ND NEIGHBOUR I heard it too, just this day three weeks, at two
o'clock
Next morning.

LOVEWIT   These be miracles, or you make 'em so!   40
A man an hour strangled, and could not speak,
And both you heard him cry?

3RD NEIGHBOUR   Yes, downward, sir.

LOVEWIT Thou art a wise fellow; give me thy hand, I pray thee.
What trade art thou on?

3RD NEIGHBOUR   A smith, an't please your worship.

LOVEWIT A smith? Then lend me thy help to get this door open.   45

3RD NEIGHBOUR That I will presently, sir, but fetch my tools—
> [*Exit 3rd Neighbour*]

1ST NEIGHBOUR Sir, best to knock again afore you break it.

5.2

LOVEWIT I will.
   [*Knocks. Enter Face, dressed as Jeremy*]
FACE   What mean you, sir?
1ST, 2ND, 4TH NEIGHBOURS   O, here's Jeremy!
FACE Good sir, come from the door.
LOVEWIT   Why! What's the matter?
FACE Yet farther, you are too near, yet.
LOVEWIT   I'the name of wonder!
 What means the fellow?
FACE   The house, sir, has been visited.
LOVEWIT What? With the plague? Stand thou then farther.
FACE   No, sir, 5
 I had it not.
LOVEWIT Who had it then? I left
 None else but thee i'the house!
FACE   Yes, sir. My fellow,
 The cat that kept the buttery, had it on her
 A week before I spied it, but I got her
 Conveyed away i'the night. And so I shut 10
 The house up for a month—
LOVEWIT   How!
FACE   Purposing then, sir,
 T' have burnt rose-vinegar, treacle, and tar,
 And ha' made it sweet, that you should ne'er ha' known it,
 Because I knew the news would but afflict you, sir.
LOVEWIT Breathe less, and farther off. Why, this is stranger! 15
 The neighbours tell me all, here, that the doors
 Have still been open—
FACE   How, sir!
LOVEWIT   Gallants, men and women,
 And of all sorts, tag-rag, been seen to flock here
 In threaves, these ten weeks, as to a second Hoxton,
 In days of Pimlico, and Eye-bright!
FACE   Sir,° 20
 Their wisdoms will not say so!
LOVEWIT   Today, they speak
 Of coaches and gallants; one in a French hood
 Went in, they tell me; and another was seen

In a velvet gown at the window? Divers more
Pass in and out!
FACE   They did pass through the doors then,   25
Or walls, I assure their eyesights, and their spectacles;
For here, sir, are the keys, and here have been
In this my pocket, now, above twenty days!
And for before, I kept the fort alone, there.
But that 'tis yet not deep i'the afternoon,   30
I should believe my neighbours had seen double
Through the blackpot, and made these apparitions!
For on my faith to your worship, for these three weeks
And upwards, the door has not been opened.
LOVEWIT   Strange!
1ST NEIGHBOUR Good faith, I think I saw a coach!
2ND NEIGHBOUR   And I too,   35
I'd ha' been sworn!
LOVEWIT   Do you but think it now?
And but one coach?
4TH NEIGHBOUR   We cannot tell, sir; Jeremy
Is a very honest fellow.
FACE   Did you see me at all?
1ST NEIGHBOUR No. That we are sure on.
2ND NEIGHBOUR   I'll be sworn o' that.
LOVEWIT Fine rogues, to have your testimonies built on!   40
        [Enter 3rd Neighbour with tools]
3RD NEIGHBOUR Is Jeremy come?
1ST NEIGHBOUR   O, yes; you may leave your tools;
We were deceived, he says.
2ND NEIGHBOUR   He's had the keys,
And the door has been shut these three weeks.
3RD NEIGHBOUR   Like enough.
LOVEWIT Peace, and get hence, you changelings.
        [Enter Surly and Mammon]
FACE [aside]   Surly come!°
And Mammon made acquainted? They'll tell all.   45
How shall I beat them off? What shall I do?
Nothing's more wretched than a guilty conscience.°

5.3

[Enter] Surly [and Sir Epicure] Mammon

SURLY No, sir, he was a great physician. This,
    It was no bawdy-house, but a mere chancel.
    You knew the lord, and his sister.

MAMMON   Nay, good Surly—

SURLY The happy word, 'be rich'—

MAMMON   Play not the tyrant—

SURLY Should be today pronounced to all your friends.   5
    And where be your andirons now? And your brass pots
    That should ha' been golden flagons, and great wedges?

MAMMON Let me but breathe. What! They ha' shut their doors,
    Methinks!

SURLY   Aye, now 'tis holiday with them.

MAMMON   Rogues,
    Cozeners, impostors, bawds!

    Mammon and Surly knock

FACE   What mean you, sir?   10

MAMMON To enter if we can.

FACE   Another man's house?
    Here is the owner, sir. Turn you to him,
    And speak your business.

MAMMON   Are you, sir, the owner?

LOVEWIT Yes, sir.

MAMMON   And are those knaves, within, your cheaters?

LOVEWIT What knaves? What cheaters?

MAMMON   Subtle, and his Lungs.   15

FACE The gentleman is distracted, sir! No lungs
    Nor lights ha' been seen here these three weeks, sir,
    Within these doors, upon my word!

SURLY   Your word,
    Groom arrogant?

FACE   Yes, sir, I am the housekeeper,
    And know the keys ha' not been out o' my hands.   20

SURLY This's a new Face?

FACE   You do mistake the house, sir!
    What sign was't at?

SURLY   You rascal! This is one
    O' the confederacy. Come, let's get officers,

And force the door.

LOVEWIT   Pray you stay, gentlemen.

SURLY No, sir, we'll come with warrant.

MAMMON   Aye, and then   25
We shall ha' your doors open.
          [Exeunt Mammon and Surly]

LOVEWIT   What means this?

FACE I cannot tell, sir!

1ST NEIGHBOUR   These are two o'the gallants,
That we do think we saw.

FACE   Two o'the fools?
You talk as idly as they. Good faith, sir,
I think the moon has crazed 'em all!
          [Enter Kestrel]
          [Aside]   Oh me,   30
The angry boy come too? He'll make a noise,
And ne'er away till he have betrayed us all.

KESTREL (*knocks*) What rogues, bawds, slaves, you'll open the door
     anon.
Punk, cockatrice, my suster. By this light   35
I'll fetch the marshal to you. You are a whore,
To keep your castle—

FACE   Who would you speak with, sir?

KESTREL The bawdy Doctor, and the cozening Captain,
And Puss, my suster.

LOVEWIT   This is something, sure!

FACE Upon my trust, the doors were never open, sir.   40

KESTREL I have heard all their tricks told me twice over,
By the fat knight and the lean gentleman.

LOVEWIT Here comes another.
          [Enter Ananias, Tribulation]

FACE *[aside]*   Ananias too?
And his pastor?

TRIBULATION   The doors are shut against us.
          They beat too, at the door

ANANIAS Come forth, you seed of sulphur, sons of fire,   45
Your stench, it is broke forth; abomination
Is in the house.

KESTREL   Aye, my suster's there.

ANANIAS   The place,
It is become a cage of unclean birds.

KESTREL Yes, I will fetch the scavenger, and the constable.
TRIBULATION You shall do well.
ANANIAS   We'll join, to weed them out.   50
KESTREL You will not come then? Punk device, my suster!°
ANANIAS Call her not sister. She is a harlot, verily.
KESTREL I'll raise the street.
LOVEWIT   Good gentlemen, a word.
ANANIAS Satan, avoid, and hinder not our zeal.
         [*Exeunt Ananias, Tribulation, Kestrel*]
LOVEWIT The world's turned Bedlam.
FACE   These are all broke loose,   55
    Out of St Katherine's, where they use to keep,°
    The better sort of mad-folks.
1ST NEIGHBOUR   All these persons
    We saw go in, and out, here.
2ND NEIGHBOUR   Yes, indeed, sir.
3RD NEIGHBOUR These were the parties.
FACE   Peace, you drunkards. Sir,
    I wonder at it! Please you, to give me leave   60
    To touch the door; I'll try, an' the lock be changed.
LOVEWIT It 'mazes me!
FACE   Good faith, sir, I believe
    There's no such thing. 'Tis all *deceptio visus*.°
    [*Aside*] Would I could get him away.
DAPPER (*cries out within*) Master Captain, Master Doctor.   65
LOVEWIT Who's that?
FACE [*aside*]   Our clerk within, that I forgot! [*To Lovewit*] I
    know not, sir.
DAPPER [*within*] For God's sake, when will her Grace be at leisure?
FACE   Ha!
    Illusions, some spirit o'the air! [*Aside*] his gag is melted,
    And now he sets out the throat.
DAPPER [*within*]   I am almost stifled—°   70
FACE [*aside*] Would you were altogether.
LOVEWIT   'Tis i'the house.
    Ha! List.
         [*Another cry within*]
FACE   Believe it, sir, i'the air!
LOVEWIT   Peace, you—
DAPPER [*within*] Mine aunt's Grace does not use me well.
SUBTLE [*within*]   You fool,

Peace, you'll mar all.

FACE [*to Subtle within*] Or you will else, you rogue.

LOVEWIT O, is it so? Then you converse with spirits!   75
  Come sir. No more o' your tricks, good Jeremy;
  The truth, the shortest way.

FACE   Dismiss this rabble, sir.
  [*Aside*] What shall I do? I am catched.

LOVEWIT   Good neighbours,
  I thank you all. You may depart.
        [*Exeunt Neighbours*]

                                      Come sir,
  You know that I am an indulgent master,
  And therefore conceal nothing. What's your medicine,   80
  To draw so many several sorts of wildfowl?

FACE Sir, you were wont to affect mirth and wit—
  But here's no place to talk on't i' the street.
  Give me but leave to make the best of my fortune,   85
  And only pardon me th' abuse of your house:
  It's all I beg. I'll help you to a widow,
  In recompense, that you shall gi' me thanks for,
  Will make you seven years younger, and a rich one.
  'Tis but your putting on a Spanish cloak;   90
  I have her within. You need not fear the house,
  It was not visited.

LOVEWIT   But by me, who came°
  Sooner than you expected.

FACE   It is true, sir.
  Pray you forgive me.

LOVEWIT   Well, let's see your widow.
        [*Exeunt*]

5.4

        [*Enter*] Subtle [*and*] Dapper

SUBTLE How! Ha' you eaten your gag?

DAPPER   Yes faith, it crumbled
  Away i' my mouth.

SUBTLE   You ha' spoiled all then.

DAPPER   No,

I hope my aunt of Fairy will forgive me.

SUBTLE Your aunt's a gracious lady, but in troth
    You were to blame.

DAPPER   The fume did overcome me,   5
    And I did do't to stay my stomach. Pray you
    So satisfy her Grace. Here comes the Captain.
       [Enter Face]

FACE How now! Is his mouth down?

SUBTLE   Aye! He has spoken!

FACE *[to Subtle]* A pox, I heard him, and you too. *[Aloud]* He's
    undone, then.   10
       Face and Subtle talk aside
    I have been fain to say the house is haunted
    With spirits, to keep churl back.

SUBTLE   And hast thou done it?

FACE Sure, for this night.

SUBTLE   Why, then triumph and sing
    Of Face so famous, the precious king
    Of present wits.

FACE   Did you not hear the coil   15
    About the door?

SUBTLE   Yes, and I dwindled with it.

FACE Show him his aunt, and let him be dispatched:
    I'll send her to you.
       [Exit Face]

SUBTLE *[Aloud]*   Well sir, your aunt her Grace,
    Will give you audience presently, on my suit,
    And the Captain's word that you did not eat your gag,   20
    In any contempt of her Highness.

DAPPER   Not I, in troth, sir.
       [Enter] Doll like the Queen of Fairy

SUBTLE Here she is come. Down o' your knees, and wriggle;
       [Dapper approaches on his knees]
    She has a stately presence. Good. Yet nearer,
    And bid, 'God save you.'

DAPPER   Madam.

SUBTLE   And your aunt.

DAPPER And my most gracious aunt, God save your Grace.   25

DOLL Nephew, we thought to have been angry with you,
    But that sweet face of yours hath turned the tide,
    And made it flow with joy, that ebbed of love.

Arise, and touch our velvet gown.

SUBTLE   The skirts,
And kiss 'em. So.
        [*Dapper kisses her hem*]

DOLL   Let me now stroke that head.   30
Much, nephew, shalt thou win; much shalt thou spend;
Much shalt thou give away: much shalt thou lend.

SUBTLE [*aside*] Aye, much, indeed. [*Aloud*] Why do you not thank
    her Grace?

DAPPER I cannot speak for joy.

SUBTLE   See, the kind wretch!   35
Your Grace's kinsman right.

DOLL   Give me the bird.°
Here is your fly in a purse, about your neck, cousin;
Wear it, and feed it, about this day sennight,
On your right wrist—

SUBTLE   Open a vein, with a pin,
And let it suck but once a week; till then   40
You must not look on't.

DOLL   No. And, kinsman,
Bear yourself worthy of the blood you come on.

SUBTLE Her Grace would ha' you eat no more Woolsack pies,°
Nor Dagger furmety.

DOLL   Nor break his fast°
In Heaven and Hell.

SUBTLE   She's with you everywhere!°   45
Nor play with costermongers at mumchance, tray-trip,
God-make-you-rich (when as your aunt has done it); but keep
The gallant'st company, and the best games—

DAPPER   Yes, sir.

SUBTLE Gleek and primero; and what you get, be true to us.

DAPPER By this hand, I will.

SUBTLE   You may bring's a thousand pound,   50
Before tomorrow night—if but three thousand,
Be stirring—an you will.

DAPPER   I swear I will then.°

SUBTLE Your fly will learn you all games.

FACE [*within*]   Ha' you done there?

SUBTLE Your Grace will command him no more duties?

DOLL   No;
But come and see me often. I may chance   55

To leave him three or four hundred chests of treasure,
And some twelve thousand acres of Fairyland,
If he game well and comely, with good gamesters.
SUBTLE There's a kind aunt! Kiss her departing part
But you must sell your forty mark a year, now.   60
DAPPER Aye, sir, I mean.
SUBTLE   Or gi't away; pox on't.
DAPPER I'll gi't mine aunt. I'll go and fetch the writings.
SUBTLE 'Tis well; away.
        [*Exit Dapper. Enter Face*]
FACE   Where's Subtle?
SUBTLE   Here. What news?
FACE Drugger is at the door; go take his suit,
And bid him fetch a parson presently;   65
Say he shall marry the widow. Thou shalt spend°
A hundred pound by the service!
        [*Exit Subtle*]
                              Now, queen Doll,
Ha' you packed up all?
DOLL   Yes.
FACE   And how do you like
The Lady Pliant?
DOLL   A good dull innocent.
        [*Enter Subtle*]
SUBTLE Here's your Hieronimo's cloak and hat.
FACE   Give me 'em.   70
SUBTLE And the ruff too?
FACE   Yes, I'll come to you presently.
        [*Exit Face*]
SUBTLE Now he is gone about his project, Doll,
I told you of, for the widow.
DOLL   'Tis direct
Against our articles.
SUBTLE   Well, we'll fit him, wench.
Hast thou gulled her of her jewels or her bracelets?   75
DOLL No, but I will do't.
SUBTLE   Soon at night, my Dolly,
When we are shipped, and all our goods aboard,
Eastward for Ratcliff, we will turn our course
To Brainford, westward, if thou sayst the word,
And take our leaves of this o'erweening rascal,   80

This peremptory Face.

DOLL   Content; I'm weary of him.

SUBTLE Thou'st cause, when the slave will run a-wiving, Doll,
      Against the instrument that was drawn between us.

DOLL I'll pluck his bird as bare as I can.

SUBTLE   Yes, tell her
      She must by any means address some present   85
      To the cunning man; make him amends for wronging
      His art with her suspicion; send a ring,
      Or chain of pearl; she will be tortured else
      Extremely in her sleep, say, and ha' strange things
      Come to her. Wilt thou?

DOLL   Yes.

SUBTLE   My fine flitter-mouse,   90
      My bird o'the night; we'll tickle it at the Pigeons,°
      When we have all, and may unlock the trunks,
      And say, this's mine, and thine, and thine, and mine—
            They kiss. [*Enter Face*]

FACE What now, a-billing?

SUBTLE   Yes, a little exalted
      In the good passage of our stock-affairs.   95

FACE Drugger has brought his parson; take him in, Subtle,
      And send Nab back again, to wash his face.

SUBTLE I will; and shave himself?

FACE   If you can get him.
            [*Exit Subtle*]

DOLL You are hot upon it, Face, whate'er it is!

FACE A trick that Doll shall spend ten pound a month by.   100
            [*Enter Subtle*]
      Is he gone?

SUBTLE   The chaplain waits you i'the hall, sir.

FACE I'll go bestow him.
            [*Exit Face*]

DOLL   He'll now marry her, instantly.

SUBTLE He cannot yet, he is not ready. Dear Doll,
      Cozen her of all thou canst. To deceive him
      Is no deceit, but justice, that would break   105
      Such an inextricable tie as ours was.

DOLL Let me alone to fit him.
            [*Enter Face*]

FACE   Come, my venturers,

You ha' packed up all? Where be the trunks? Bring forth.

SUBTLE Here.

FACE   Let's see 'em. Where's the money?

SUBTLE   Here,
In this.

FACE   Mammon's ten pound; eight score before.   110
The brethren's money, this. Drugger's, and Dapper's.
What paper's that?

DOLL   The jewel of the waiting maid's,
That stole it from her lady, to know certain—

FACE If she should have precedence of her mistress?

DOLL   Yes.

FACE What box is that?

SUBTLE   The fishwife's rings, I think: 115
And th' alewife's single money. Is't not, Doll?°

DOLL Yes, and the whistle that the sailor's wife
Brought you, to know an' her husband were with Ward.°

FACE We'll wet it tomorrow; and our silver beakers,
And tavern cups. Where be the French petticoats,   120
And girdles, and hangers?

SUBTLE   Here, i'the trunk,
And the bolts of lawn.

FACE   Is Drugger's damask there?
And the tobacco?

SUBTLE   Yes.

FACE   Give me the keys.

DOLL Why you the keys?

SUBTLE   No matter, Doll, because
We shall not open 'em before he comes.   125

FACE 'Tis true, you shall not open them, indeed;
Nor have 'em forth. Do you see? Not forth, Doll.

DOLL   No!

FACE No, my smock-rampant. The right is, my master
Knows all, has pardoned me, and he will keep 'em.
Doctor, 'tis true—you look—for all your figures;   130
I sent for him, indeed. Wherefore, good partners,
Both he, and she, be satisfied for, here
Determines the indenture tripartite,
'Twixt Subtle, Doll, and Face. All I can do
Is to help you over the wall, o' the backside;   135
Or lend you a sheet to save your velvet gown, Doll.

Here will be officers presently; bethink you
Of some course suddenly to 'scape the dock:
For thither you'll come else. (*Some knock*) Hark you, thunder.

SUBTLE You are a precious fiend!

OFFICER [*without*]   Open the door!   140

FACE Doll, I am sorry for thee, i' faith. But hear'st thou?
    It shall go hard, but I will place thee somewhere;
    Thou shalt ha' my letter to Mistress Amo.

DOLL   Hang you—

FACE Or Madam Caesarean.

DOLL   Pox upon you, rogue,°
    Would I had but time to beat thee.

FACE   Subtle,   145
    Let's know where you set up next; I'll send you
    A customer, now and then, for old acquaintance.
    What new course ha' you?

SUBTLE Rogue, I'll hang myself,
    That I may walk a greater devil than thou,   150
    And haunt thee i'the flock-bed and the buttery.°

        [*Exeunt*]

5.5

        [*Enter*] Lovewit [*in Spanish dress with the Parson*]

LOVEWIT What do you mean, my masters?

MAMMON [*without*]   Open your door,
    Cheaters, bawds, conjurers.

OFFICER [*without*]   Or we'll break it open.

LOVEWIT What warrant have you?

OFFICER [*without*]   Warrant enough, sir, doubt not,
    If you'll not open it.

LOVEWIT   Is there an officer there?

OFFICER [*without*] Yes, two or three for failing.

LOVEWIT   Have but patience,°   5
    And I will open it straight.

        [*Enter Face*]

FACE   Sir, ha' you done?
    Is it a marriage? Perfect?

LOVEWIT   Yes, my brain.

FACE Off with your ruff and cloak then; be yourself, sir.
    [*Lovewit removes his disguise*]
SURLY [*without*] Down with the door.
KESTREL [*without*]   'Slight, ding it open.
LOVEWIT [*opening door*]   Hold!
   Hold, gentlemen, what means this violence?   10
    [*Enter Mammon, Surly, Kestrel, Tribulation, Ananias, and*
    Officers]
MAMMON Where is this collier?
SURLY   And my Captain Face?
MAMMON These day-owls.
SURLY   That are birding in men's purses.
MAMMON Madam Suppository.
KESTREL   Doxy, my suster.
ANANIAS   Locusts
   Of the foul pit.
TRIBULATION   Profane as *Bel and the Dragon*.°
ANANIAS Worse than the grasshoppers or the lice of Egypt.°   15
LOVEWIT Good gentlemen, hear me. Are you officers,
   And cannot stay this violence?
OFFICER   Keep the peace!
LOVEWIT Gentlemen, what is the matter? Whom do you seek?
MAMMON The chemical cozener.
SURLY   And the Captain Pandar.
KESTREL The nun my suster.
MAMMON   Madam Rabbi.
ANANIAS   Scorpions,   20
   And caterpillars.
LOVEWIT   Fewer at once, I pray you.
OFFICER One after another, gentlemen, I charge you,
   By virtue of my staff—
ANANIAS   They are the vessels
   Of pride, lust, and the cart.
LOVEWIT   Good zeal, lie still,
   A little while.
TRIBULATION Peace, Deacon Ananias.   25
LOVEWIT The house is mine here, and the doors are open:
   If there be any such persons as you seek for,
   Use your authority, search on o' God's name.
   I am but newly come to town, and finding
   This tumult 'bout my door (to tell you true)   30

It somewhat 'mazed me; till my man here (fearing
My more displeasure) told me he had done
Somewhat an insolent part, let out my house
(Belike presuming on my known aversion
From any air o'the town, while there was sickness)   35
To a Doctor and a Captain; who, what they are,
Or where they be, he knows not.

MAMMON   Are they gone?
LOVEWIT You may go in, and search, sir.
          [*Mammon, Ananias and Tribulation*] enter [*the house*]
                                Here, I find
The empty walls, worse than I left 'em, smoked,
A few cracked pots, and glasses, and a furnace,   40
The ceiling filled with poesies of the candle,°
And madam with a dildo writ o' the walls.
Only, one gentlewoman I met here,
That is within, that said she was a widow—
KESTREL Aye, that's my suster. I'll go thump her. Where is she?   45
          [*Goes in*]
LOVEWIT And should ha' married a Spanish count, but he,
When he came to't, neglected her so grossly,
That I, a widower, am gone through with her.
SURLY How! Have I lost her then?
LOVEWIT   Were you the Don, sir?
Good faith, now she does blame y' extremely, and says   50
You swore, and told her you had ta'en the pains,
To dye your beard, and umber o'er your face,
Borrowed a suit and ruff, all for her love;
And then did nothing. What an oversight,
And want of putting forward, sir, was this!   55
Well fare an old harquebusier, yet,
Could prime his powder, and give fire, and hit,
All in a twinkling.
          Mammon comes forth
MAMMON   The whole nest are fled!
LOVEWIT What sort of birds were they?
MAMMON   A kind of choughs,
Or thievish daws, sir, that have picked my purse   60
Of eight-score and ten pounds, within these five weeks,
Beside my first materials; and my goods,
That lie i'the cellar—which I am glad they ha' left,

I may have home yet.

LOVEWIT   Think you so, sir?

MAMMON   Aye.

LOVEWIT By order of law, sir, but not otherwise.   65

MAMMON Not mine own stuff?

LOVEWIT   Sir, I can take no knowledge
That they are yours, but by public means.°
If you can bring certificate that you were gulled of 'em,
Or any formal writ out of a court
That you did cozen yourself, I will not hold them.   70

MAMMON I'll rather lose 'em.

LOVEWIT   That you shall not, sir,
By me, in troth. Upon these terms they're yours.
What should they ha' been, sir—turned into gold all?

MAMMON   No.
I cannot tell. It may be they should. What then?

LOVEWIT What a great loss in hope have you sustained!   75

MAMMON Not I; the commonwealth has.

FACE   Aye, he would ha' built
The city new; and made a ditch about it
Of silver, should have run with cream from Hoxton;
That every Sunday in Moorfields, the younkers,
And tits, and tomboys should have fed on, *gratis*.   80

MAMMON I will go mount a turnip-cart, and preach
The end o'the world within these two months. Surly,
What! In a dream?

SURLY   Must I needs cheat myself,
With that same foolish vice of honesty!
Come, let us go and hearken out the rogues.°   85
That Face I'll mark for mine, if e'er I meet him.

FACE If I can hear of him, sir, I'll bring you word
Unto your lodging; for in troth, they were strangers
To me; I thought 'em honest as myself, sir.

        [*Exeunt Surly, Mammon.*] *Tribulation and Ananias come forth*

TRIBULATION 'Tis well, the saints shall not lose all yet. Go,   90
And get some carts—

LOVEWIT   For what, my zealous friends?

ANANIAS To bear away the portion of the righteous,
Out of this den of thieves.

LOVEWIT   What is that portion?

ANANIAS The goods, sometimes the orphans', that the brethren

Bought with their silver pence.

LOVEWIT   What, those i'the cellar   95
The knight Sir Mammon claims?

ANANIAS   I do defy
The wicked Mammon, so do all the brethren,
Thou profane man. I ask thee with what conscience
Thou canst advance that idol against us
That have the seal? Were not the shillings numbered,°   100
That made the pounds? Were not the pounds told out,
Upon the second day of the fourth week,
In the eight month, upon the table dormant,
The year, of the last patience of the saints,°
Six hundred and ten?

LOVEWIT   Mine earnest vehement botcher,   105
And deacon also, I cannot dispute with you,
But if you get you not away the sooner,
I shall confute you with a cudgel.

ANANIAS   Sir.

TRIBULATION Be patient, Ananias.

ANANIAS   I am strong,
And will stand up, well girt, against an host   110
That threaten Gad in exile.

LOVEWIT   I shall send you°
To Amsterdam, to your cellar.

ANANIAS   I will pray there,
Against thy house: may dogs defile thy walls,
And wasps and hornets breed beneath thy roof,
This seat of falsehood, and this cave of coz'nage.   115
        [*Exeunt Ananias and Tribulation*]

LOVEWIT Another too?
        Enter Drugger

DRUGGER   Not I sir, I am no brother.

LOVEWIT Away you Harry Nicholas! Do you talk?°
        He beats him away

FACE No, this was Abel Drugger. (*To the Parson*) Good sir, go
And satisfy him; tell him all is done:
He stayed too long a-washing of his face.   120
The Doctor, he shall hear of him at Westchester;
And of the Captain, tell him, at Yarmouth, or
Some good port-town else, lying for a wind.
        [*Exit Parson. Enter Kestrel and Dame Pliant*]

If you get off the angry child, now, sir—
KESTREL (*to his sister*) Come on, you ewe, you have matched most
    sweetly, ha' you not?   125
    Did not I say, I would never ha' you tupped
    But by a dubbed boy, to make you a lady-tom?
    'Slight, you are a mammet! O, I could touse you now.
    Death, mun' you marry with a pox?
LOVEWIT   You lie, boy:
    As sound as you: and I am aforehand with you.
    [*Draws his sword and dagger*]
KESTREL   Anon?   130
LOVEWIT Come, will you quarrel? I will feeze you, sirrah.
    Why do you not buckle to your tools?
KESTREL   God's light!°
    This is a fine old boy, as e'er I saw!
LOVEWIT What, do you change your copy now? Proceed,
    Here stands my dove: stoop at her, if you dare.°   135
KESTREL 'Slight I must love him! I cannot choose, i'faith!
    An I should be hanged for't! Suster, I protest,
    I honour thee for this match.
LOVEWIT   O, do you so, sir?
KESTREL Yes, an thou canst take tobacco, and drink, old boy,
    I'll give her five hundred pound more, to her marriage,   140
    Than her own state.
LOVEWIT   Fill a pipe-full, Jeremy.
FACE Yes, but go in and take it, sir.
LOVEWIT   We will.
    I will be ruled by thee in anything, Jeremy.
KESTREL 'Slight, thou art not hidebound! Thou art a jovy boy!
    Come, let's in, I pray thee, and take our whiffs.   145
LOVEWIT Whiff in with your sister, brother boy.
    [*Exeunt Kastril, Dame Pliant*]
    That master
    That had received such happiness by a servant,
    In such a widow, and with so much wealth,
    Were very ungrateful if he would not be   150
    A little indulgent to that servant's wit,
    And help his fortune, though with some small strain
    Of his own candour. Therefore, gentlemen,
    And kind spectators, if I have outstripped
    An old man's gravity, or strict canon, think   155

What a young wife and a good brain may do:
Stretch age's truth sometimes, and crack it too.
Speak for thyself, knave.

FACE   So I will, sir. Gentlemen,
My part a little fell in this last scene,
Yet 'twas decorum. And though I am clean   160
Got off, from Subtle, Surly, Mammon, Doll,
Hot Ananias, Dapper, Drugger, all
With whom I traded; yet I put myself
On you, that are my country; and this pelf°
Which I have got, if you do quit me, rests   165
To feast you often, and invite new guests.
     [*Exeunt*]

This comedy was first
acted in the year
1610
by the King's Majesty's
Servants.
The principal comedians were
Richard Burbage   John Heminges
John Lowin   William Ostler
Henry Condell   John Underwood
Alexander Cook   Nicholas Tooley
Robert Armin   William Egleston
With the allowance of the Master of the Revels.

BARTHOLOMEW FAIR

The Prologue
to The King's Majesty.

Your Majesty is welcome to a fair;
Such place, such men, such language and such ware,
You must expect: with these, the zealous noise
Of your land's faction, scandalized at toys,°
As babies, hobby-horses, puppet plays,   5
And suchlike rage, whereof the petulant ways
Yourself have known, and have been vexed with long.
These for your sport, without particular wrong,°
Or just complaint of any private man,
Who of himself, or shall think well or can,   10
The maker doth present, and hopes tonight
To give you for a fairing, true delight.

THE PERSONS OF THE PLAY

JOHN LITTLEWIT, a proctor
SOLOMON, his man
WIN LITTLEWIT, his wife
DAME PURECRAFT, her mother
and a widow
ZEAL-OF-THE-LAND BUSY, her
suitor, a Banbury° man
WINWIFE, his rival, a gentleman
QUARLOUS, his companion, a
gamester
BARTHOLOMEW COKES, an
esquire of Harrow
HUMPHREY WASP, his man
ADAM OVERDO, a Justice of Peace
DAME OVERDO, his wife
GRACE WELLBORN, his ward
LANTERN LEATHERHEAD, a
hobby-horse seller
JOAN TRASH, a gingerbread
woman
EZEKIEL EDGWORTH, a cutpurse
NIGHTINGALE, a ballad-singer
URSULA, a pig-woman
MOONCALF, her tapster

JORDAN KNOCKEM, a
horse-corser and ranger of
Turnbull°
VAL CUTTING,° a roarer
CAPTAIN WHIT, a bawd
PUNK ALICE, mistress of the
game°
TROUBLE-ALL, a madman
3 WATCHMEN [Haggis, Bristle,
and Poacher, a beadle]
COSTERMONGER
CORNCUTTER
MOUSETRAP MAN, [also called
Tinderbox man]
CLOTHIER [Northern]
WRESTLER [Puppy]
PASSENGERS
PORTERS
DOORKEEPERS [Filcher,
Sharkwell]
PUPPETS
STAGE-KEEPER
BOOK-HOLDER
SCRIVENER

The Induction on the Stage.

[Enter] Stage-keeper

STAGE-KEEPER Gentlemen, have a little patience, they are e'en upon
coming, instantly. He that should begin the play, Master Littlewit,
the proctor, has a stitch new fallen in his black silk stocking; 'twill
be drawn up ere you can tell twenty. He plays one o' the
Arches,° that dwells about the Hospital,° and he has a very pretty   5
part. But for the whole play, will you ha' the truth on't? I am
looking, lest the poet hear me, or his man, Master Brome,° behind
the arras. It is like to be a very conceited scurvy one, in plain
English. When 't comes to the Fair once, you were e'en as good
go to Virginia, for anything there is of Smithfield. He has not hit   10
the humours—he does not know 'em; he has not conversed with
the Bartholomew-birds, as they say; he has ne'er a sword-and-
buckler man in his Fair, nor a Little Davy,° to take toll o' the
bawds there, as in my time, nor a Kindheart,° if anybody's teeth
should chance to ache in his play. Nor a juggler with a well-   15
educated ape to come over the chain for the King of England and
back again for the Prince, and sit still on his arse for the Pope and
the King of Spain! None o' these fine sights! Nor has he the
canvas-cut i' the night for a hobby-horse-man° to creep in to his
she-neighbour and take his leap there! Nothing! No, an some   20
writer (that I know) had had but the penning o' this matter, he
would ha' made you such a jig-a-jog i' the booths, you should ha'
thought an earthquake had been i' the Fair! But these master-
poets, they will ha' their own absurd courses; they will be informed
of nothing! He has, sir-reverence, kicked me three or four times   25
about the tiring-house, I thank him, for but offering to put in, with
my experience. I'll be judged by you, gentlemen, now, but for one
conceit of mine! Would not a fine pump upon the stage ha' done
well for a property now? And a punk set under upon her head,
with her stern upward, and ha' been soused by my witty young   30
masters o' the Inns o' Court?° What think you o' this for a show,
now? He will not hear o' this! I am an ass! I! And yet I kept the
stage in Master Tarlton's° time, I thank my stars. Ho! An that man
had lived to have played in *Bartholomew Fair*, you should ha' seen
him ha' come in, and ha' been cozened i' the cloth-quarter so   35
finely! And Adams,° the rogue, ha' leaped and capered upon him,

and ha' dealt his vermin° about, as though they had cost him
nothing. And then a substantial watch to ha' stolen in upon 'em,
and taken 'em away with mistaking words, as the fashion is, in the
stage-practice.   40

    [*Enter*] *Book-holder* [*and*] *Scrivener* [*carrying documents*]

BOOK-HOLDER How now? What rare discourse are you fallen upon?
Ha? Ha' you found any familiars here, that you are so free? What's
the business?

STAGE-KEEPER Nothing, but the understanding° gentlemen o' the
ground here asked my judgement.   45

BOOK-HOLDER Your judgement, rascal? For what? Sweeping the
stage? Or gathering up the broken apples for the bears° within?
Away, rogue, it's come to a fine degree in these spectacles when
such a youth as you pretend to a judgement.

    [*Exit Stage-keeper*]

And yet he may, i' the most o' this matter i'faith: for the author   50
hath writ it just to his meridian, and the scale of the grounded
judgements here, his play-fellows in wit. Gentlemen, not for want
of a prologue, but by way of a new one, I am sent out to you here
with a scrivener, and certain articles drawn out in haste between
our author and you; which if you please to hear, and as they appear   55
reasonable, to approve of, the play will follow presently. Read,
scribe, gi' me the counterpane.

SCRIVENER Articles of Agreement indented between the spectators
or hearers at the Hope on the Bankside in the county of Surrey on
the one party; and the author of *Bartholomew Fair* in the said place 60
and county on the other party; the one and thirtieth day of October
1614, and in the twelfth year of the reign of our Sovereign Lord,
James, by the grace of God King of England, France,° and Ireland,
Defender of the Faith. And of Scotland the seven and fortieth.°

    Imprimis It is covenanted and agreed, by and between the   65
parties abovesaid, that the said spectators and hearers, as well
the curious and envious as the favouring and judicious, as also the
grounded judgements and understandings, do for themselves
severally covenant and agree, to remain in the places their money
or friends have put them in, with patience, for the space of two   70
hours and an half, and somewhat more. In which time the author
promiseth to present them, by us, with a new sufficient play called
Bartholomew Fair, merry, and as full of noise as sport; made to
delight all, and to offend none, provided they have either the wit
or the honesty to think well of themselves.   75

It is further agreed that every person here have his or their freewill of censure, to like or dislike at their own charge, the author having now departed with his right it shall be lawful for any man to judge his six pen'orth, his twelve pen'orth, so to his eighteen pence, two shillings, half a crown, to the value of his 80 place, provided always his place get not above his wit. And if he pay for half a dozen, he may censure for all them too, so that he will undertake that they shall be silent. He shall put in for censures here as they do for lots at the lottery;° marry, if he drop but sixpence at the door, and will censure a crown's worth, it is 85 thought there is no conscience or justice in that.

It is also agreed that every man here exercise his own judgement, and not censure by contagion, or upon trust, from another's voice, or face, that sits by him, be he never so first in the Commission of Wit.° As also, that he be fixed and settled in his censure, that what 90 he approves or not approves today, he will do the same tomorrow, and if tomorrow, the next day, and so the next week (if need be), and not to be brought about by any that sits on the bench with him, though they indict and arraign plays daily. He that will swear, *Jeronimo*° or *Andronicus*° are the best plays, yet shall pass unex- 95 cepted at, here, as a man whose judgement shows it is constant, and hath stood still these five and twenty or thirty years. Though it be an ignorance, it is a virtuous and staid ignorance; and next to truth, a confirmed error does well; such a one the author knows where to find him. 100

It is further covenanted, concluded and agreed, that how great soever the expectation be, no person here is to expect more than he knows, or better ware than a Fair will afford; neither to look back to the sword-and-buckler age of Smithfield, but content himself with the present. Instead of a Little Davy to take toll o' 105 the bawds, the author doth promise a strutting horse-courser with a leer drunkard, two or three to attend him in as good equipage as you would wish. And then for Kindheart, the tooth-drawer, a fine oily pig-woman with her tapster to bid you welcome, and a consort of roarers for music. A wise Justice of Peace *meditant*, instead of a 110 juggler with an ape. A civil cutpurse *searchant*. A sweet singer of new ballads *allurant*: and as fresh an hypocrite, as ever was broached, *rampant*.° If there be never a servant-monster i'the Fair, who can help it? he says; nor a nest of antics? He is loath to make Nature afraid in his plays, like those that beget Tales, Tempests, 115 and such like drolleries, to mix his head with other men's heels, let the concupiscence of jigs and dances° reign as strong as it will amongst you; yet if the puppets will please anybody, they shall be entreated to come in.

In consideration of which, it is finally agreed by the foresaid hearers and spectators that they neither in themselves conceal, nor suffer by them to be concealed, any state-decipherer, or politic picklock of the scene, so solemnly ridiculous as to search out who was meant by the gingerbread-woman, who by the hobby-horseman, who by the costermonger, nay, who by their wares. Or that will pretend to affirm, on his own inspired ignorance, what Mirror° of Magistrates is meant by the Justice, what great lady by the pig-woman, what concealed statesman by the seller of mousetraps, and so of the rest. But that such person, or persons so found, be left discovered to the mercy of the author, as a forfeiture to the stage and your laughter aforesaid. As also, such as shall so desperately or ambitiously play the fool by his place aforesaid, to challenge the author of scurrility because the language somewhere savours of Smithfield, the booth, and the pig-broth; or of profaneness because a madman cries, 'God quit you' or 'bless you'. In witness whereof, as you have preposterously put to your seals already (which is your money) you will now add the other part of suffrage, your hands. The play shall presently begin. And though the Fair be not kept in the same region that some here, perhaps, would have it, yet think that therein the author hath observed a special decorum, the place being as dirty as Smithfield, and as stinking every whit.

Howsoever, he prays you to believe his ware is still the same, else you will make him justly suspect that he that is so loath to look on a baby or an hobby-horse here, would be glad to take up a commodity° of them, at any laughter, or loss, in another place.

[*Exeunt*]

1.1

[Enter] Littlewit *[reading a licence]*

LITTLEWIT A pretty conceit, and worth the finding! I ha' such luck
to spin out these fine things still, and like a silk-worm, out of
myself. Here's Master Bartholomew Cokes, of Harrow o'the hill,
i'the county of Middlesex, Esquire, takes forth his licence to marry
Mistress Grace Wellborn of the said place and county—and when   5
does he take it forth? Today! The four and twentieth of August!
Bartholomew day! Bartholomew upon Bartholomew! There's the
device! Who would have marked such a leapfrog chance now? A
very less than ambs-ace on two dice!° Well, go thy ways, John
Littlewit, proctor John Littlewit—one o' the pretty wits o' Paul's,°   10
the Little Wit of London (so thou art called) and something
beside. When a quirk or a quiblin does 'scape thee, and thou dost
not watch, and apprehend it, and bring it afore the constable of
conceit (there now, I speak quib too), let 'em carry thee out o' the
Archdeacon's Court° into his kitchen, and make a Jack° of thee   15
instead of a John. (There I am again la!)

[Enter] Win [Littlewit]

Win, good morrow, Win. Aye, marry, Win! Now you look finely
indeed, Win! This cap does convince! You'd not ha' worn it, Win,
nor ha' had it velvet, but a rough country beaver, with a copper
band, like the coney-skin woman of Budge Row!° Sweet Win, let   20
me kiss it! And her fine high shoes, like the Spanish lady!° Good
Win, go a little; I would fain see thee pace, pretty Win! By this
fine cap, I could never leave kissing on't.

WIN Come, indeed la, you are such a fool, still!

LITTLEWIT No, but half a one, Win, you are the t'other half: man   25
and wife make one fool, Win. (Good!) Is there the proctor, or
doctor indeed, i' the diocese, that ever had the fortune to win him
such a Win? (There I am again!) I do feel conceits coming upon
me, more than I am able to turn tongue to. A pox o' these
pretenders to wit, your Three Cranes, Mitre, and Mermaid° men!   30
Not a corn of true salt nor a grain of right mustard amongst them
all. They may stand for places or so, again' the next wit fall,
and pay twopence in a quart more for their canary than other men.
But gi' me the man can start up a justice of wit out of six-shillings beer,° and give the law to all the poets and poet-suckers i'   35

town, because they are the players' gossips? 'Slid, other men
have wives as fine as the players, and as well dressed. Come hither,
Win.

    [*Kisses her*]

1.2

    [*Enter*] *Winwife*

WINWIFE Why, how now, Master Littlewit! Measuring of lips? Or
  moulding of kisses? Which is it?

LITTLEWIT Troth, I am a little taken with my Win's dressing here!
  Does't not fine, Master Winwife? How do you apprehend, sir? She
  would not ha' worn this habit. I challenge all Cheapside° to show   5
  such another—Moorfields,° Pimlico Path,° or the Exchange,° in a
  summer evening—with a lace to boot as this has. Dear Win, let
  Master Winwife kiss you. He comes a-wooing to our mother, Win,
  and may be our father perhaps, Win. There's no harm in him,
  Win.   10

WINWIFE None i' the earth, Master Littlewit.

    [*Kisses her*]

LITTLEWIT I envy no man my delicates, sir.

WINWIFE Alas, you ha' the garden where they grow still! A wife here
  with a strawberry breath, cherry lips, apricot cheeks, and a soft
  velvet head, like a melocoton.   15

LITTLEWIT Good i'faith! Now dullness upon me, that I had not that
  before him, that I should not light on't as well as he! Velvet head!

WINWIFE But my taste, Master Littlewit, tends to fruit of a later
  kind: the sober matron, your wife's mother.

LITTLEWIT Aye! We know you are a suitor, sir. Win and I both wish   20
  you well; by this licence here, would you had her, that your two
  names were as fast in it, as here are a couple. Win would fain have
  a fine young father i'law, with a feather, that her mother might
  hood it and chain° it with Mistress Overdo. But you do not take
  the right course, Master Winwife.   25

WINWIFE No, Master Littlewit? Why?

LITTLEWIT You are not mad enough.

WINWIFE How? Is madness a right course?

LITTLEWIT I say nothing, but I wink upon Win. You have a friend,
  one Master Quarlous, comes here sometimes?   30

WINWIFE Why? He makes no love to her, does he?

LITTLEWIT Not a tokenworth° that ever I saw, I assure you. But—

WINWIFE What?

LITTLEWIT He is the more madcap o' the two. You do not appre-
hend me.   35

WIN You have a hot coal i' your mouth, now, you cannot hold.

LITTLEWIT Let me out with it, dear Win.

WIN I'll tell him myself.

LITTLEWIT Do, and take all the thanks, and much good do thy
pretty heart, Win.   40

WIN Sir, my mother has had her nativity-water cast lately by the
cunning-men in Cow Lane,° and they ha' told her her fortune, and
do ensure her she shall never have happy hour, unless she marry
within this sennight, and when it is, it must be a madman, they
say.   45

LITTLEWIT Aye, but it must be a gentleman madman.

WIN Yes, so the t'other man of Moorfields says.

WINWIFE But does she believe 'em?

LITTLEWIT Yes, and has been at Bedlam° twice since, every day, to
enquire if any gentleman be there, or to come there, mad!   50

WINWIFE Why, this is a confederacy, a mere piece of practice upon
her, by these impostors!

LITTLEWIT I tell her so; or else say I that they mean some young
madcap gentleman (for the devil can equivocate as well as a
shopkeeper) and therefore would I advise you to be a little madder   55
than Master Quarlous, hereafter.

WIN Where is she? Stirring yet?

LITTLEWIT Stirring! Yes, and studying an old elder, come from
Banbury, a suitor that puts in here at meal-tide, to praise the
painful brethren, or pray that the sweet singers may be restored;   60
says a grace as long as his breath lasts him! Sometime the spirit
is so strong with him, it gets quite out of him, and then my
mother, or Win, are fain to fetch it again with malmsey, or *aqua
coelestis*.

WIN Yes indeed, we have such a tedious life with him for his diet,   65
and his clothes too; he breaks his buttons, and cracks seams at
every saying he sobs out.

LITTLEWIT He cannot abide my vocation, he says.

WIN No, he told my mother a proctor was a claw of the Beast, and
that she had little less than committed abomination in marrying   70
me so as she has done.

LITTLEWIT Every line, he says, that a proctor writes, when it comes
to be read in the Bishop's Court, is a long black hair, combed out
of the tail of Antichrist.°

WINWIFE When came this proselyte?   75

LITTLEWIT Some three days since.

1.3

[Enter] Quarlous

QUARLOUS O sir, ha' you ta'en soil,° here? It's well a man may reach
you after three hours' running, yet! What an unmerciful companion art thou, to quit thy lodging at such ungentlemanly hours!
None but a scattered covey of fiddlers, or one of these rag-rakers
in dunghills, or some marrowbone man° at most, would have been   5
up when thou wert gone abroad, by all description. I pray thee
what ailest thou, thou canst not sleep? Hast thou thorns i' thy
eyelids or thistles i' thy bed?

WINWIFE I cannot tell. It seems you had neither i' your feet, that
took this pain to find me.   10

QUARLOUS No, an I had, all the lyam-hounds o' the city should have
drawn after you by the scent rather. Master John Littlewit! God
save you, sir. 'Twas a hot night with some of us, last night, John.
Shall we pluck a hair o' the same wolf today, proctor John?

LITTLEWIT Do you remember, Master Quarlous, what we dis-   15
coursed on last night?

QUARLOUS Not I, John—nothing that I either discourse or do. At
those times I forfeit all to forgetfulness.

LITTLEWIT No? Not concerning Win? Look you, there she is, and
dressed as I told you she should be. Hark you sir, had you forgot?   20

QUARLOUS By this head, I'll beware how I keep you company, John,
when I am drunk, an you have this dangerous memory! That's
certain.

WINWIFE Why sir?

QUARLOUS Why? We were all a little stained last night, sprinkled   25
with a cup or two, and I agreed with Proctor John here to come
and do somewhat with Win (I know not what 'twas) today; and he
puts me in mind on't now; he says he was coming to fetch me:
before truth, if you have that fearful quality, John, to remember,
when you are sober, John, what you promise drunk, John, I shall   30

take heed of you, John. For this once, I am content to wink at you.° Where's your wife?

Come hither, Win.

He kisseth her

WIN Why, John! Do you see this, John? Look you! Help me, John.

LITTLEWIT O Win, fie, what do you mean, Win? Be womanly, Win? Make an outcry to your mother, Win? Master Quarlous is an honest gentleman, and our worshipful good friend, Win; and he is Master Winwife's friend, too. And Master Winwife comes a suitor to your mother, Win, as I told you before, Win, and may perhaps be our father, Win. They'll do you no harm, Win; they are both our worshipful good friends. Master Quarlous! You must know Master Quarlous, Win; you must not quarrel with Master Quarlous, Win.

QUARLOUS No, we'll kiss again and fall in.°

LITTLEWIT Yes, do, good Win.

[Quarlous kisses Win again]

WIN I'faith you are a fool, John.

LITTLEWIT A fool-John she calls me, do you mark that, gentlemen? Pretty littlewit of velvet! A fool-John!

QUARLOUS She may call you an apple-John, if you use this.°

WINWIFE Pray thee forbear, for my respect somewhat.

QUARLOUS Hoy-day! How respective you are become o' the sudden! I fear this family will turn you reformed too; pray you come about again. Because she is in possibility to be your daughter-in-law, and may ask you blessing hereafter, when she courts it to Tottenham° to eat cream—well, I will forbear, sir, but i'faith, would thou wouldst leave thy exercise of widow-hunting once, this drawing after an old reverend smock° by the splay foot! There cannot be an ancient tripe or trillibub° i' the town, but thou art straight nosing it; and 'tis a fine occupation thou'lt confine thyself to, when thou hast got one—scrubbing a piece of buff, as if thou hadst the perpetuity of Pannier Alley° to stink in; or perhaps, worse, currying a carcass that thou hast bound thyself to alive. I'll be sworn, some of them that thou art or hast been a suitor to, are so old as no chaste or married pleasure can ever become 'em. The honest instrument of procreation has, forty years since, left to belong to 'em. Thou must visit 'em as thou wouldst do a tomb, with a torch, or three handfuls of link, flaming hot, and so thou mayst hap to make 'em feel thee, and after, come to inherit according to thy inches.° A sweet course for a man to waste the

brand of life for, to be still raking himself a fortune in an old   70
woman's embers; we shall ha' thee, after thou hast been but a
month married to one of 'em, look like the quartan ague° and the
black jaundice met in a face, and walk as if thou hadst borrowed
legs of a spinner and voice of a cricket. I would endure to hear
fifteen sermons a week 'fore her, and such coarse and loud ones as   75
some of 'em must be; I would e'en desire of Fate, I might dwell
in a drum, and take in my sustenance with an old broken tobacco
pipe and a straw. Dost thou ever think to bring thine ears or
stomach to the patience of a dry grace as long as thy tablecloth,
and droned out by thy son here, that might be thy father, till all   80
the meat o' thy board has forgot it was that day i' the kitchen? Or
to brook the noise made in a question of predestination, by the
good labourers and painful eaters assembled together, put to 'em
by the matron, your spouse, who moderates with a cup of wine,
ever and anon, and a sentence out of Knox° between? Or the   85
perpetual spitting, before and after a sober drawn exhortation of
six hours, whose better part was the 'hum-ha-hum'? Or to hear
prayers groaned out over thy iron chests, as if they were charms
to break 'em? And all this for the hope of two apostle-spoons, to
suffer! And a cup to eat a caudle in! For that will be thy legacy.   90
She'll ha' conveyed her state° safe enough from thee, an she be a
right widow.

WINWIFE Alas, I am quite off that scent now.

QUARLOUS How so?

WINWIFE Put off by a brother of Banbury, one that they say is come   95
·here, and governs all already.

QUARLOUS What do you call him? I knew divers of those Banburians
when I was in Oxford.

WINWIFE Master Littlewit can tell us.

LITTLEWIT Sir! Good Win, go in, and if Master Bartholomew Cokes   100
his man come for the licence—the little old fellow—let him speak
with me. What say you, gentlemen?
      [*Exit Win*]

WINWIFE What call you the reverend elder you told me of, your
Banbury man?

LITTLEWIT Rabbi Busy, sir. He is more than an elder; he is a   105
prophet, sir.

QUARLOUS O, I know him! A baker, is he not?

LITTLEWIT He was a baker, sir, but he does dream now, and see
visions; he has given over his trade.

QUARLOUS I remember that too—out of a scruple he took, that (in   110
spiced conscience) those cakes he made were served to bride-ales,
maypoles, morrises, and such profane feasts and meetings; his
Christian name is Zeal-of-the-Land.

LITTLEWIT Yes, sir, Zeal-of-the-Land Busy.

WINWIFE How, what a name's there!   115

LITTLEWIT O, they have all such names, sir; he was witness for Win
here—they will not be called godfathers—and named her Win-
the-fight. You thought her name had been Winifred, did you
not?

WINWIFE I did indeed.   120

LITTLEWIT He would ha' thought himself a stark reprobate, if it had.

QUARLOUS Aye, for there was a blue-starch woman° o' the name, at
the same time. A notable hypocritical vermin it is; I know him.
One that stands upon his face° more than his faith, at all times;
ever in seditious motion, and reproving for vain-glory; of a most   125
lunatic conscience and spleen, and affects the violence of singu-
larity in all he does. (He has undone a grocer here, in Newgate
market, that broke with him, trusted him with currants, as arrant
a zeal as he, that's by the way.) By his profession, he will ever be
i' the state of innocence, though, and childhood; derides all   130
antiquity; defies any other learning than inspiration; and what
discretion soever years should afford him, it is all prevented in
his original ignorance. Ha' not to do with him, for he is a fellow
of a most arrogant and invincible dullness, I assure you. Who is
this?   135

1.4

[Enter] Wasp [with Win]

WASP By your leave, gentlemen, with all my heart to you, and God
you° good morrow; Master Littlewit, my business is to you. Is this
licence ready?

LITTLEWIT Here, I ha' it for you in my hand, Master Humphrey.

WASP That's well; nay, never open or read it to me, it's labour in   5
vain, you know. I am no clerk; I scorn to be saved by my
book—° i'faith I'll hang first. Fold it up o' your word and gi' it
me; what must you ha' for't?

LITTLEWIT We'll talk of that anon, Master Humphrey.

WASP Now, or not at all, good Master Proctor; I am for no anons, I   10
assure you.

LITTLEWIT Sweet Win, bid Solomon send me the little black box
within, in my study.

WASP Aye, quickly, good mistress, I pray you, for I have both eggs
o' the spit, and iron i' the fire. Say what you must have, good   15
Master Littlewit.

      [*Exit Win*]

LITTLEWIT Why, you know the price, Master Numps.

WASP I know? I know nothing, I. What tell you me of knowing, now
I am in haste? Sir, I do not know, and I will not know, and I scorn
to know, and yet (now I think on't) I will, and do know, as well as   20
another; you must have a mark for your thing here, and eightpence
for the box; I could ha' saved twopence i' that, an I had brought
it myself, but here's fourteen shillings for you. Good Lord! How
long your little wife stays! Pray God, Solomon, your clerk, be not
looking i' the wrong box, Master Proctor.   25

LITTLEWIT Good i'faith! No, I warrant you, Solomon is wiser than
so, sir.

WASP Fie, fie, fie, by your leave, Master Littlewit, this is scurvy, idle,
foolish and abominable; with all my heart, I do not like it.

      [*Walks aside*]

WINWIFE Do you hear? Jack Littlewit, what business does thy pretty   30
head think this fellow may have, that he keeps such a coil with?

QUARLOUS More than buying of gingerbread i' the Cloister° here
(for that we allow him) or a gilt pouch i' the Fair?

LITTLEWIT Master Quarlous, do not mistake him; he is his master's
both-hands, I assure you.   35

QUARLOUS What? To pull on his boots, a-mornings, or his stockings,
does he?

LITTLEWIT Sir, if you have a mind to mock him, mock him softly,
and look t'other way; for if he apprehend you flout him once, he
will fly at you presently. A terrible testy old fellow, and his name   40
is Wasp too.

QUARLOUS Pretty insect! Make much on him.

WASP [*returning*] A plague o'this box, and the pox too, and on him
that made it, and her that went for't, and all that should ha' sought
it, sent it, or brought it! Do you see, sir?   45

LITTLEWIT Nay, good Master Wasp.

WASP Good Master Hornet, turd i' your teeth, hold you your
tongue; do not I know you? Your father was a 'pothecary, and sold

clysters, more than he gave, iwis. And turd i' your little wife's teeth
too   50
     [*Enter Win with the box*]
—here she comes—'twill make her spit, as fine as she is, for all her
velvet-custard on her head, sir.

LITTLEWIT O! Be civil, Master Numps.

WASP Why, say I have a humour not to be civil; how then? Who shall
    compel me? You?   55

LITTLEWIT Here is the box now.

WASP Why a pox o' your box, once again; let your little wife stale in
    it, an she will. Sir, I would have you to understand, and these
    gentlemen too, if they please—

WINWIFE With all our hearts, sir.   60

WASP That I have a charge, gentlemen.

LITTLEWIT They do apprehend, sir.

WASP Pardon me, sir, neither they nor you can apprehend me yet
    (you are an ass). I have a young master; he is now upon his making
    and marring; the whole care of his well-doing is now mine. His   65
    foolish schoolmasters have done nothing but run up and down the
    country with him, to beg puddings and cake-bread of his tenants,
    and almost spoiled him; he has learned nothing but to sing catches,
    and repeat 'Rattle bladder rattle' and 'O Madge'. I dare not let him
    walk alone for fear of learning of vile tunes which he will sing at   70
    supper and in the sermon-times! If he meet but a carman i' the
    street, and I find him not talk to keep him off on him, he will
    whistle him and all his tunes over at night in his sleep! He has a
    head full of bees! I am fain now, for this little time I am absent,
    to leave him in charge with a gentlewoman. 'Tis true, she is a   75
    Justice of Peace his wife, and a gentlewoman o' the hood, and his
    natural sister; but what may happen under a woman's govern-
    ment, there's the doubt. Gentlemen, you do not know him; he is
    another manner of piece than you think for—but nineteen year
    old, and yet he is taller than either of you, by the head, God   80
    bless him.

QUARLOUS [*aside to Winwife*] Well, methinks this is a fine fellow!

WINWIFE [*to Quarlous*] He has made his master a finer by this
    description, I should think.

QUARLOUS [*to Winwife*] 'Faith, much about one; it's cross and pile,   85
    whether for a new farthing.°

WASP I'll tell you, gentlemen—

LITTLEWIT Will't please you drink, Master Wasp?

WASP Why, I ha' not talked so long to be dry, sir; you see no dust
or cobwebs come out o' my mouth, do you? You'd ha' me gone,   90
would you?

LITTLEWIT No, but you were in haste e'en now, Master Numps.

WASP What an I were? So I am still, and yet I will stay too. Meddle
you with your match, your Win, there; she has as little wit as her
husband, it seems. I have others to talk to.   95

LITTLEWIT She's my match indeed, and as little wit as I, good!

WASP We ha' been but a day and a half in town, gentlemen, 'tis true;
and yesterday i' the afternoon, we walked London to show the
city to the gentlewoman he shall marry, Mistress Grace; but
afore I will endure such another half-day with him, I'll be drawn   100
with a good gibcat through the great pond at home, as his
Uncle Hodge was!° Why, we could not meet that heathen thing,°
all day, but stayed him; he would name you all the signs over, as
he went, aloud; and where he spied a parrot or a monkey, there he
was pitched, with all the little long-coats about him, male and   105
female; no getting him away! I thought he would ha' run mad o'the
black boy in Bucklersbury° that takes the scurvy, roguy tobacco
there.

LITTLEWIT You say true, Master Numps; there's such a one indeed.

WASP It's no matter; whether there be or no. What's that to you?   110

QUARLOUS He will not allow of John's reading at any hand.°

1.5

[Enter] Cokes, Mistress Overdo [and] Grace

COKES O Numps! Are you here, Numps? Look where I am, Numps!
And Mistress Grace, too! Nay, do not look angerly, Numps. My
sister is here, and all; I do not come without her.

WASP What the mischief, do you come with her? Or she with you?

COKES We came all to seek you, Numps.   5

WASP To seek me? Why, did you all think I was lost? Or run away
with your fourteen shillings' worth of small ware, here? Or that I
had changed it i' the Fair for hobby-horses? 'Sprecious—to seek
me!

MISTRESS OVERDO Nay, good Master Numps, do you show discre-   10
tion, though he be exorbitant (as Master Overdo says) an't be but
for conservation of the peace.

WASP Mary gip,° Goody She-Justice, Mistress French-hood!° Turd
i' your teeth; and turd i' your French-hood's teeth, too, to do you
service, do you see? Must you quote your Adam to me? You think   15
you are Madam Regent° still, Mistress Overdo, when I am in
place? No such matter, I assure you; your reign is out when I am
in, dame.

MISTRESS OVERDO I am content to be in abeyance, sir, and be
governed by you; so should he too, if he did well; but 'twill be   20
expected you should also govern your passions.

WASP Will't so forsooth? Good Lord! How sharp you are, with being
at Bedlam yesterday! Whetstone° has set an edge upon you, has he?

MISTRESS OVERDO Nay, if you know not what belongs to your
dignity, I do, yet, to mine.   25

WASP Very well, then.

COKES Is this the licence, Numps? For love's sake, let me see't. I
never saw a licence.

WASP Did you not so? Why, you shall not see't then.

COKES An' you love me, good Numps.   30

WASP Sir, I love you, and yet I do not love you, i' these fooleries;
set your heart at rest; there's nothing in't but hard words; and what
would you see't for?

COKES I would see the length and the breadth on't, that's all; and I
will see't now, so I will.   35

WASP You sha' not see it here.

COKES Then I'll see't at home, and I'll look upo' the case here.

WASP Why, do so. [*Shows him the box*] A man must give way to him
a little in trifles, gentlemen. These are errors, diseases of youth,
which he will mend when he comes to judgement and knowledge   40
of matters. I pray you conceive so, and I thank you. And I pray
you pardon him, and I thank you again.

QUARLOUS Well, this dry nurse, I say still, is a delicate man.

WINWIFE And I am for the cosset, his charge! Did you ever see a
fellow's face more accuse him for an ass?   45

QUARLOUS Accuse him? It confesses him one without accusing.
What pity 'tis yonder wench should marry such a cokes?

WINWIFE 'Tis true.

QUARLOUS She seems to be discreet, and as sober as she is handsome.

WINWIFE Aye, and if you mark her, what a restrained scorn she casts   50
upon all his behaviour and speeches!

COKES Well, Numps, I am now for another piece of business more,
the Fair, Numps, and then—

WASP Bless me! Deliver me, help, hold me! The Fair!

COKES Nay, never fidge up and down, Numps, and vex itself. I am   55
   resolute Bartholomew, in this; I'll make no suit on't to you; 'twas
   all the end of my journey, indeed, to show Mistress Grace my Fair.
   I call't my Fair, because of Bartholomew; you know my name is
   Bartholomew, and Bartholomew Fair.

LITTLEWIT That was mine afore, gentlemen—this morning. I had   60
   that i'faith, upon his licence; believe me, there he comes after me.

QUARLOUS Come, John, this ambitious wit of yours, I am afraid, will
   do you no good i' the end.

LITTLEWIT No? Why sir?

QUARLOUS You grow so insolent with it, and overdoing, John, that   65
   if you look not to it, and tie it up, it will bring you to some obscure
   place in time, and there 'twill leave you.

WINWIFE Do not trust it too much, John; be more sparing, and use
   it but now and then. A wit is a dangerous thing in this age; do not
   overbuy it.   70

LITTLEWIT Think you so, gentlemen? I'll take heed on't hereafter.

WIN Yes, do, John.

COKES A pretty little soul, this same Mistress Littlewit! Would I
   might marry her.

GRACE [aside] So would I, or anybody else, so I might 'scape you.   75

COKES Numps, I will see it, Numps, 'tis decreed. Never be melancholy for the matter.

WASP Why, see it, sir, see it, do see it! Who hinders you? Why do
   you not go see it? 'Slid, see it.

COKES The Fair, Numps, the Fair!   80

WASP Would the Fair and all the drums and rattles in't were i' your
   belly for me; they are already i' your brain. He that had the means
   to travel your head, now, should meet finer sights than any are i'
   the Fair, and make a finer voyage on't, to see it all hung with
   cockleshells, pebbles, fine wheat-straws, and here and there a   85
   chicken's feather and a cobweb.

QUARLOUS Good faith, he looks, methinks, an you mark him, like
   one that were made to catch flies, with his Sir Cranion° legs.

WINWIFE And his Numps to flap 'em away.

WASP God be w'you, sir; there's your bee in a box, and much good   90
   do't you.
       [Gives Cokes the box and starts to leave]

COKES Why, your friend and Bartholomew,° an you be so contumacious.

QUARLOUS What mean you, Numps?

WASP I'll not be guilty, I, gentlemen.   95

MISTRESS OVERDO You will not let him go, brother, and lose him?

COKES Who can hold that will away? I had rather lose him than the
Fair, I wusse.

WASP You do not know the inconvenience, gentlemen, you persuade
to, nor what trouble I have with him in these humours. If he go   100
to the Fair, he will buy of everything to a baby there; and
household-stuff for that too. If a leg or an arm on him did not grow
on, he would lose it i' the press. Pray heaven I bring him off with
one stone! And then he is such a ravener after fruit! You will not
believe what a coil I had t'other day to compound a business   105
between a Catherine-pear woman and him about snatching! 'Tis
intolerable, gentlemen.

WINWIFE O, but you must not leave him now to these hazards, Numps.

WASP Nay, he knows too well I will not leave him, and that makes
him presume—well, sir, will you go now? If you have such an itch   110
i' your feet to foot it to the Fair, why do you stop? Am I your
tarriers? Go, will you go, sir? Why do you not go?

COKES O Numps! Have I brought you about? Come, Mistress Grace,
and sister, I am resolute Bat, i'faith, still.

GRACE Truly, I have no such fancy to the Fair, nor ambition to see   115
it; there's none goes thither of any quality or fashion.

COKES O Lord, sir! You shall pardon me, Mistress Grace, we are
enow of ourselves to make it a fashion; and for qualities, let Numps
alone, he'll find qualities.

    [Exeunt Cokes, Wasp, Mistress Overdo, Grace]

QUARLOUS What a rogue in apprehension is this, to understand her   120
language no better!

WINWIFE Aye, and offer to marry to her! Well, I will leave the chase
of my widow for today, and directly to the Fair. These flies cannot,
this hot season, but engender us excellent creeping sport.

QUARLOUS A man that has but a spoonful of brain would think so.   125
Farewell, John.

    [Exeunt Quarlous and Winwife]

LITTLEWIT Win, you see 'tis in fashion to go to the Fair, Win; we
must to the Fair too, you and I, Win. I have an affair i' the Fair,
Win, a puppet-play of mine own making—say nothing—that I writ
for the motion man, which you must see, Win.   130

WIN I would I might, John, but my mother will never consent to
such a—'profane motion', she will call it.

LITTLEWIT Tut, we'll have a device, a dainty one. (Now, Wit, help
at a pinch, good Wit come, come, good Wit, an't be thy will.) I

have it, Win, I have it i'faith, and 'tis a fine one. Win, long to eat   135
of a pig, sweet Win, i' the Fair; do you see? I' the heart o'the Fair,
not at Pie Corner.° Your mother will do anything, Win, to satisfy
your longing, you know; pray thee long, presently, and be sick o'
the sudden, good Win. I'll go in and tell her. Cut thy lace° i' the
meantime and play the hypocrite, sweet Win.   140

WIN No, I'll not make me unready for it. I can be hypocrite enough,
though I were never so straitlaced.

LITTLEWIT You say true; you have been bred i' the family, and
brought up to 't. Our mother is a most elect hypocrite,° and has
maintained us all this seven year with it, like gentlefolks.   145

WIN Aye, let her alone, John; she is not a wise wilful widow for
nothing, nor a sanctified sister for a song. And let me alone too; I
ha' somewhat o' the mother° in me, you shall see. Fetch her, fetch
her, ah, ah.

[*Exit Littlewit*]

1.6

[*Enter Dame*] *Purecraft* [*with Littlewit*]

PURECRAFT Now the blaze of the beauteous discipline° fright away
this evil from our house! How now, Win-the-Fight, child; how do
you? Sweet child, speak to me.

WIN Yes, forsooth.

PURECRAFT Look up, sweet Win-the-Fight, and suffer not the   5
enemy to enter you at this door, remember that your education has
been with the purest. What polluted one was it that named first
the unclean beast, pig, to you, child?

WIN Uh, uh.

LITTLEWIT Not I, o' my sincerity, mother: she longed above three   10
hours, ere she would let me know it. Who was it, Win?

WIN A profane black thing with a beard, John.

PURECRAFT O! Resist it, Win-the-Fight, it is the Tempter, the
wicked Tempter; you may know it by the fleshly motion of pig. Be
strong against it, and its foul temptations in these assaults, whereby   15
it broacheth flesh and blood, as it were, on the weaker side; and pray
against its carnal provocations, good child, sweet child, pray.

LITTLEWIT Good mother, I pray you that she may eat some pig, and
her bellyful, too; and do not you cast away your own child, and

perhaps one of mine, with your tale of the Tempter. How do you,   20
Win? Are you not sick?

WIN Yes, a great deal, John. Uh, uh.

PURECRAFT What shall we do? Call our zealous brother Busy hither,
for his faithful fortification in this charge of the Adversary; child,
my dear child, you shall eat pig, be comforted, my sweet child.   25

  [*Exit Littlewit*]

WIN Aye, but i' the Fair, mother.

PURECRAFT I mean i' the Fair, if it can be any way made or found
lawful.

  [*Enter Littlewit*]

Where is our brother Busy? Will he not come? Look up, child.

LITTLEWIT Presently, mother, as soon as he has cleansed his beard.   30
I found him, fast by the teeth i' the cold turkey pie i' the cupboard,
with a great white loaf on his left hand, and a glass of malmsey on
his right.

PURECRAFT Slander not the brethren, wicked one.

LITTLEWIT Here he is now, purified, mother.   35

  [*Enter Zeal-of-the-Land Busy*]

PURECRAFT O brother Busy! Your help here to edify, and raise us
up in a scruple; my daughter Win-the-Fight is visited with a
natural disease of women, called 'a longing to eat pig'.

LITTLEWIT Aye sir, a Bartholomew pig: and in the Fair.

PURECRAFT And I would be satisfied from you, religiously-wise,   40
whether a widow of the sanctified assembly, or a widow's daughter,
may commit the act without offence to the weaker sisters.

BUSY Verily, for the disease of longing, it is a disease, a carnal
disease, or appetite, incident to women; and as it is carnal, and
incident, it is natural, very natural. Now pig, it is a meat, and a   45
meat that is nourishing, and may be longed for, and so consequent-
ly eaten; it may be eaten; very exceeding well eaten. But in the
Fair, and as a Bartholomew pig, it cannot be eaten, for the very
calling it a Bartholomew pig, and to eat it so, is a spice of idolatry,
and you make the Fair no better than one of the high places.° This   50
I take it, is the state of the question. A high place.

LITTLEWIT Aye, but in state of necessity, place should give place,
Master Busy (I have a conceit left, yet).

PURECRAFT Good Brother Zeal-of-the-Land, think to make it as
lawful as you can.   55

LITTLEWIT Yes, sir, and as soon as you can; for it must be, sir; you
see the danger my little wife is in, sir.

PURECRAFT Truly, I do love my child dearly, and I would not have her miscarry, or hazard her first fruits, if it might be otherwise.

BUSY Surely it may be otherwise, but it is subject to construction, 60 subject, and hath a face of offence with the weak, a great face, a foul face, but that face may have a veil put over it, and be shadowed, as it were; it may be eaten, and in the Fair, I take it, in a booth, the tents of the wicked. The place is not much, not very much, we may be religious in midst of the profane, so it be eaten 65 with a reformed mouth, with sobriety, and humbleness; not gorged in with gluttony or greediness; there's the fear: for, should she go there, as taking pride in the place, or delight in the unclean dressing, to feed the vanity of the eye or the lust of the palate, it were not well, it were not fit, it were abominable, and not good. 70

LITTLEWIT Nay, I knew that afore, and told her on't; but courage, Win, we'll be humble enough; we'll seek out the homeliest booth i' the Fair, that's certain. Rather than fail, we'll eat it o' the ground.

PURECRAFT Aye, and I'll go with you myself, Win-the-Fight, and 75 my brother Zeal-of-the-Land shall go with us too, for our better consolation.

WIN Uh, uh.

LITTLEWIT Aye, and Solomon too, Win—the more the merrier. [*Aside*] Win, we'll leave Rabbi Busy in a booth—Solomon, my 80 cloak.

    [*Enter Solomon with cloak*]

SOLOMON Here, sir.

BUSY In the way of comfort to the weak, I will go and eat. I will eat exceedingly, and prophesy; there may be a good use made of it, too, now I think on't: by the public eating of swine's flesh, to 85 profess our hate and loathing of Judaism, whereof the brethren stand taxed.° I will therefore eat, yea, I will eat exceedingly.

LITTLEWIT Good, i'faith, I will eat heartily too, because I will be no Jew; I could never away with° that stiff-necked generation. And truly, I hope my little one will be like me, that cries for pig so, i' 90 the mother's belly.

BUSY Very likely, exceeding likely, very exceeding likely.

    [*Exeunt*]

2.1

[Enter] Justice Overdo [disguised as a madman]

JUSTICE Well, in justice' name, and the King's; and for the Commonwealth! Defy all the world, Adam Overdo, for a disguise and
all story; for thou hast fitted thyself, I swear. Fain would I meet
the Lynceus° now, that eagle's eye, that piercing Epidaurian°
serpent (as my Quintus Horace calls him) that could discover a   5
justice of peace (and lately of the Quorum°) under this covering.
They may have seen many a fool in the habit of a justice, but never
till now a justice in the habit of a fool. Thus must we do, though,
that wake for the public good; and thus hath the wise magistrate
done in all ages. There is a doing of right out of wrong, if the way   10
be found. Never shall I enough commend a worthy worshipful
man,° sometime a capital member of this city, for his high wisdom
in this point, who would take you, now the habit of a porter, now
of a carman, now of the dog-killer in this month of August;° and
in the winter, of a seller of tinder-boxes. And what would he do   15
in all these shapes? Marry, go you into every alehouse, and down
into every cellar; measure the length of puddings, take the gauge
of black pots and cans, aye, and custards with a stick; and their
circumference with a thread; weigh the loaves of bread on his
middle finger; then would he send for 'em, home; give the   20
puddings to the poor, the bread to the hungry, the custards to his
children; break the pots and burn the cans himself; he would not
trust his corrupt officers; he would do't himself. Would all men in
authority would follow this worthy precedent! For (alas) as we are
public persons, what do we know? Nay, what can we know? We   25
hear with other men's ears; we see with other men's eyes; a foolish
constable or a sleepy watchman is all our information; he slanders
a gentleman by the virtue of his place, as he calls it, and we by the
vice of ours, must believe him. As, a while agone, they made me,
yea me, to mistake an honest zealous pursuivant for a seminary,   30
and a proper young Bachelor of Music for a bawd. This we are
subject to, that live in high place; all our intelligence is idle, and
most of our intelligencers, knaves; and by your leave, ourselves
thought little better, if not arrant fools, for believing 'em. I, Adam
Overdo, am resolved therefore to spare spy-money hereafter, and   35
make mine own discoveries. Many are the yearly enormities of this

Fair, in whose Courts of Piepowders° I have had the honour during the three days sometimes to sit as judge. But this is the special day for detection of those foresaid enormities. Here is my black book for the purpose; this the cloud that hides me; under this covert I shall see and not be seen. On, Junius Brutus!° And as I began, so I'll end: in Justice' name, and the King's; and for the Commonwealth. 40

2.2

[Enter] Leatherhead [and] Trash

LEATHERHEAD The Fair's pestilence dead, methinks; people come not abroad today, whatever the matter is. Do you hear, sister Trash, lady o' the basket? Sit farther with your gingerbread-progeny there, and hinder not the prospect of my shop, or I'll ha' it proclaimed i' the Fair what stuff they are made on. 5

TRASH Why, what stuff are they made on, brother Leatherhead? Nothing but what's wholesome, I assure you.

LEATHERHEAD Yes, stale bread, rotten eggs, musty ginger and dead honey, you know.

JUSTICE *[aside]* Aye! Have I met with enormity so soon? 10

LEATHERHEAD I shall mar your market, old 'Joan.

TRASH Mar my market, thou too-proud pedlar? Do thy worst; I defy thee, aye, and thy stable of hobby-horses. I pay for my ground as well as thou dost, and thou wrong'st me, for all thou art parcel-poet, and an engineer. I'll find a friend shall 15 right me and make a ballad of thee, and thy chattel all over. Are you puffed up with the pride of your wares? Your arse-dine?

LEATHERHEAD Go to, old Joan, I'll talk with you anon; and take you down too, afore Justice Overdo; he is the man must charm you. 20 I'll ha' you i' the Piepowders.

TRASH Charm me? I'll meet thee face to face, afore his worship, when thou dar'st and though I be a little crooked o' my body, I'll be found as upright in my dealing as any woman in Smithfield, I. Charm me? 25

JUSTICE *[aside]* I am glad to hear my name is their terror, yet; this is doing of justice.

[Enter Passengers]

LEATHERHEAD What do you lack? What is't you buy? What do you
lack? Rattles, drums, halberts, horses, babies o' the best? Fiddles
o' the finest?   30
        Enter Costermonger [and Nightingale]
COSTERMONGER Buy any pears, pears, fine, very fine pears!
TRASH Buy any gingerbread, gilt gingerbread!
NIGHTINGALE [*sings*] *Hey, now the Fair's a-filling!*
                O, for a tune to startle
                The birds o' the booths here billing   35
                Yearly with old Saint Bartle!
                The drunkards they are wading,
                The punks and chapmen trading;
                Who'd see the Fair without his lading?
Buy any ballads; new ballads?   40
        [*Enter Ursula*]
URSULA Fie upon't! Who would wear out their youth and prime
thus, in roasting of pigs, that had any cooler vocation? Hell's a kind
of cold cellar to't, a very fine vault, o' my conscience! What,
Mooncalf?
MOONCALF [*within*] Here, mistress.   45
NIGHTINGALE How now Ursula? In a heat, in a heat?
URSULA [*to Mooncalf*] My chair, you false faucet you; and my
morning's draught, quickly, a bottle of ale, to quench me, rascal.
I am all fire and fat, Nightingale; I shall e'en melt away to the
first woman, a rib again, I am afraid. I do water the ground in   50
knots as I go, like a great garden-pot; you may follow me by the
S's I make.
NIGHTINGALE Alas, good Urs; was 'Zekiel here this morning?
URSULA 'Zekiel? What 'Zekiel?
NIGHTINGALE 'Zekiel Edgworth, the civil cutpurse; you know him 55
well enough—he that talks bawdy to you still. I call him my
secretary.
URSULA He promised to be here this morning, I remember.
NIGHTINGALE When he comes, bid him stay; I'll be back again
presently.   60
URSULA Best take your morning's dew in your belly, Nightingale.
(*Mooncalf brings in the chair*) Come, sir, set it here. Did not I bid
you should get this chair let out o' the sides for me, that my hips
might play? You'll never think of anything till your dame be
rump-galled. 'Tis well, changeling; because it can take in your   65
grasshopper's thighs, you care for no more. Now you look as you

had been i' the corner o' the booth, fleaing your breech with a
candle's end, and set fire o' the Fair. Fill, stoat, fill.

JUSTICE [*aside*] This pig-woman do I know, and I will put her in for
my second enormity; she hath been before me, punk, pinnace and
bawd, any time these two and twenty years, upon record i' the
Piepowders.

URSULA Fill again, you unlucky vermin.

MOONCALF Pray you be not angry, mistress; I'll ha' it widened anon.

URSULA No, no, I shall e'en dwindle away to't, ere the Fair be done,
you think, now you ha' heated me! A poor vexed thing I am. I feel
myself dropping already, as fast as I can; two stone o' suet a day
is my proportion. I can but hold life and soul together with this
(here's to you, Nightingale) and a whiff of tobacco, at most.
Where's my pipe now? Not filled? Thou arrant incubee.

NIGHTINGALE Nay, Ursula, thou'lt gall between the tongue and the
teeth with fretting, now.

URSULA How can I hope—that ever he'll discharge his place of trust
tapster, a man of reckoning under me—that remembers nothing I
say to him?
      [*Exit Nightingale*]
But look to't, sirrah, you were best; threepence a pipeful I will ha'
made of all my whole half pound of tobacco, and a quarter of a
pound of coltsfoot mixed with it too, to eke it out. I that have dealt
so long in the fire will not be to seek in smoke now. Then six and
twenty shillings a barrel I will advance o' my beer, and fifty
shillings a hundred o' my bottle-ale; I ha' told you the ways how
to raise it. Froth your cans well i' the filling, at length, rogue, and
jog your bottles o' the buttock, sirrah, then skink out the first glass,
ever, and drink with all companies, though you be sure to be
drunk; you'll misreckon the better, and be less ashamed on't. But
your true trick, rascal, must be to be ever busy, and mis-take away
the bottles and cans in haste before they be half drunk off, and
never hear anybody call (if they should chance to mark you) till
you ha' brought fresh, and be able to forswear 'em. Give me a
drink of ale.

JUSTICE [*aside*] This is the very womb and bed of enormity, gross,
as herself! This must all down for enormity, all, every whit on't.
      One knocks

URSULA Look who's there, sirrah! Five shillings a pig is my price, at
least; if it be a sow-pig, sixpence more; if she be a great-bellied
wife, and long for't, sixpence more for that.

JUSTICE [*aside*] *O tempora! O mores!*° I would not ha' lost my discovery of this one grievance for my place and worship o' the Bench. How is the poor subject abused here! Well, I will fall in with her, and with her Mooncalf, and win out wonders of enormity. [*To Ursula*] By thy leave, goodly woman, and the fatness 110 of the Fair, oily as the King's constable's lamp, and shining as his shoeing-horn! Hath thy ale virtue, or thy beer strength, that the tongue of man may be tickled, and his palate pleased in the morning? Let thy pretty nephew here go search and see.

URSULA What new roarer is this? 115

MOONCALF O Lord! Do you not know him, mistress? 'Tis mad Arthur of Bradley,° that makes the orations. Brave Master, old Arthur of Bradley, how do you? Welcome to the Fair! When shall we hear you again, to handle your matters? With your back again' a booth, ha? I ha' been one o' your little disciples i' my days! 120

JUSTICE Let me drink, boy, with my love, thy aunt here, that I may be eloquent; but of thy best, lest it be bitter in my mouth, and my words fall foul on the Fair.

URSULA Why dost thou not fetch him drink? And offer him to sit?

MOONCALF Is't ale or beer, Master Arthur? 125

JUSTICE Thy best, pretty stripling, thy best; the same thy dove drinketh and thou drawest on holy days.

URSULA Bring him a sixpenny bottle of ale; they say a fool's handsel is lucky.

JUSTICE Bring both, child. Ale for Arthur and beer for Bradley. Ale 130 for thine aunt, boy.

    [*Exit Mooncalf*]

[*Aside*] My disguise takes to the very wish and reach of it. I shall by the benefit of this, discover enough and more, and yet get off with the reputation of what I would be: a certain middling thing between a fool and a madman. 135

2.3

    [*Enter*] *Knockem*

KNOCKEM What! My little lean Ursula! My she-bear! Art thou alive yet, with thy litter of pigs, to grunt out another Bartholomew Fair? Ha!

URSULA Yes, and to amble afoot, when the Fair is done, to hear you groan out of a cart, up the heavy hill. 5

KNOCKEM Of Holborn,° Ursula, mean'st thou so? For what? For
what, pretty Urs?

URSULA For cutting halfpenny purses, or stealing little penny dogs
out o' the Fair.

KNOCKEM O! Good words, good words, Urs.   10

JUSTICE [aside] Another special enormity. A cutpurse of the sword,
the boot, and the feather! Those are his marks.

    [Enter Mooncalf with the ale]

URSULA You are one of those horse-leeches that gave out I was dead
in Turnbull Street of a surfeit of bottle ale and tripes?

KNOCKEM No, 'twas better meat, Urs: cows' udders, cows' udders!   15

URSULA Well, I shall be meet with your mumbling mouth one day.

KNOCKEM What? Thou'lt poison me with a newt in a bottle of ale,
wilt thou? Or a spider in a tobacco pipe, Urs? Come, there's no
malice in these fat folks. I never fear thee, an I can 'scape thy lean
Mooncalf here. Let's drink it out, good Urs, and no vapours!   20

    [Exit Ursula]

JUSTICE Dost thou hear, boy? [Gives him money] There's for thy ale,
and the remnant for thee. Speak in thy faith of a faucet, now; is
this goodly person before us here, this vapours, a knight of the
knife?

MOONCALF What mean you by that, Master Arthur?   25

JUSTICE I mean a child of the horn-thumb, a babe of booty, boy; a
cutpurse.

MOONCALF O Lord, sir! Far from it. This is Master Dan Knockem
—Jordan,° the ranger of Turnbull. He is a horse-corser, sir.

JUSTICE Thy dainty dame, though, called him cutpurse.   30

MOONCALF Like enough, sir; she'll do forty such things in an hour
(an you listen to her) for her recreation, if the toy take her i' the
greasy kerchief;° it makes her fat, you see. She battens with it.

JUSTICE [aside] Here might I ha' been deceived now, and ha' put a
fool's blot upon myself, if I had not played an after-game o'   35
discretion.

    Ursula comes in again, dropping

KNOCKEM Alas poor Urs, this's an ill season for thee.

URSULA Hang yourself, hackney-man.

KNOCKEM How, how, Urs? Vapours? Motion breed vapours?

URSULA Vapours? Never tusk nor twirl your dibble, good Jordan; I   40
know what you'll take to a very drop. Though you be captain o'
the roarers, and fight well at the case of pisspots,° you shall not
fright me with your lion-chap, sir, nor your tusks. You angry? You

are hungry. Come, a pig's head will stop your mouth and stay your
stomach at all times.   45
KNOCKEM Thou art such another mad merry Urs still! Troth, I do
make conscience of vexing thee now i' the dog-days,° this hot
weather, for fear of foundering thee i' the body and melting down
a pillar of the Fair. Pray thee take thy chair again, and keep state;
and let's have a fresh bottle of ale and a pipe of tobacco—and no   50
vapours. I'll ha' this belly o' thine taken up and thy grass scoured,°
wench. Look! Here's Ezekiel Edgworth, a fine boy of his inches as
any is i' the Fair! Has still money in his purse, and will pay all
with a kind heart; and good vapours.

2.4

[*Enter*] *Edgworth, Nightingale, Corncutter, Tinderbox Man*
[*and*] *Passengers*
EDGWORTH That I will, indeed, willingly, Master Knockem. [*To
Mooncalf*] Fetch some ale and tobacco.
[*Exit Mooncalf*]
LEATHERHEAD What do you lack, gentlemen? Maid, see a fine
hobby-horse for your young master; cost you but a token a week
his provender.   5
CORNCUTTER Ha' you any corns i' your feet and toes?
TINDERBOX MAN Buy a mousetrap, a mousetrap, or a tormentor for
a flea!
TRASH Buy some gingerbread!
NIGHTINGALE Ballads, ballads! Fine new ballads: 10
Hear for your love and buy for your money.
A delicate ballad o' 'The Ferret and the Coney.'
'A Preservative again the Punk's Evil.'
Another of 'Goose-green Starch, and the Devil.'
'A Dozen of Divine Points', and 'The Godly Garters.'   15
'The Fairing of Good Counsel', of an ell and three quarters.
What is't you buy?
'The Windmill blown down by the Witch's Fart!'
Or 'Saint George, that O! did break the dragon's heart!'
EDGWORTH Master Nightingale, come hither, leave your mart a   20
little.
NIGHTINGALE O my secretary! What says my secretary?

[Enter Mooncalf with ale and tobacco]

JUSTICE Child o' the bottles, what's he? What's he?

MOONCALF A civil young gentleman, Master Arthur, that keeps
company with the roarers, and disburses all still. He has ever   25
money in his purse. He pays for them, and they roar for him:° one
does good offices for another. They call him the secretary, but he
serves nobody. A great friend of the ballad-man's—they are never
asunder.

JUSTICE What pity 'tis so civil a young man should haunt this   30
debauched company! Here's the bane of the youth of our time
apparent. A proper penman, I see't in his countenance; he has a
good clerk's look with him, and I warrant him a quick hand.

MOONCALF A very quick hand, sir.

[Exit Mooncalf]

EDGWORTH *[to Nightingale]* All the purses and purchase I give you   35
today by conveyance, bring hither to Ursula's presently. Here we
will meet at night in her lodge, and share. Look you choose good
places for your standing i' the Fair when you sing, Nightingale.

This they whisper, that Overdo hears it not

URSULA Aye, near the fullest passages; and shift 'em often.

EDGWORTH And i' your singing, you must use your hawk's eye   40
nimbly, and fly the purse to a mark,° still—where 'tis worn, and
o' which side—that you may gi' me the sign with your beak, or
hang your head that way i' the tune.

URSULA Enough, talk no more on't; your friendship, masters, is not
now to begin. Drink your draught of indenture,° your sup of   45
covenant, and away! The Fair fills apace, company begins to come
in, and I ha' ne'er a pig ready yet.

KNOCKEM Well said! Fill the cups and light the tobacco; let's give
fire i' the works and noble vapours.

EDGWORTH And shall we ha' smocks, Ursula, and good whimsies,   50
ha?

URSULA Come, you are i' your bawdy vein! The best the Fair will
afford, Zekiel, if bawd Whit keep his word.

[Enter Mooncalf]

How do the pigs, Mooncalf?

MOONCALF Very passionate, mistress, one on 'em has wept out an   55
eye.° Master Arthur o' Bradley is melancholy here; nobody talks
to him. Will you any tobacco, Master Arthur?

JUSTICE No, boy, let my meditations alone.

MOONCALF He's studying for an oration now.

JUSTICE [*aside*] If I can, with this day's travail, and all my policy, but 60
  rescue this youth here out of the hands of the lewd man and the
  strange woman,° I will sit down at night, and say with my friend
  Ovid, *Iamque opus exegi, quod nec Jovis ira, nec ignis, &c.*°

KNOCKEM Here Zekiel; here's a health to Ursula, and a kind vapour.
  Thou hast money i' thy purse still, and store! How dost thou come 65
  by it? Pray thee vapour thy friends some in a courteous vapour.
    [*Exit Ursula*]

EDGWORTH Half I have, Master Dan Knockem, is always at your
  service.

JUSTICE [*aside*] Ha, sweet nature! What goshawk would prey upon
  such a lamb? 70

KNOCKEM Let's see what 'tis, Zekiel! Count it, come, fill him to
  pledge me.

2.5

  [*Enter*] *Winwife* [*and*] *Quarlous*

WINWIFE We are here before 'em, methinks.

QUARLOUS All the better; we shall see 'em come in now.

LEATHERHEAD What do you lack, gentlemen, what is't you lack? A
  fine horse? A lion? A bull? A bear? A dog or a cat? An excellent
  fine Bartholomew bird? Or an instrument? What is't you lack? 5

QUARLOUS 'Slid! Here's Orpheus among the beasts, with his fiddle
  and all!

TRASH Will you buy any comfortable bread, gentlemen?

QUARLOUS And Ceres selling her daughter's picture in gingerwork!

WINWIFE That these people should be so ignorant to think us 10
  chapmen for 'em! Do we look as if we would buy gingerbread? Or
  hobby-horses?

QUARLOUS Why, they know no better ware than they have, nor
  better customers than come. And our very being here makes us fit
  to be demanded as well as others. Would Cokes would come! 15
  There were a true customer for 'em.

KNOCKEM [*to Edgworth*] How much is't? Thirty shillings? Who's
  yonder? Ned Winwife? And Tom Quarlous, I think! Yes (gi' me
  it all, gi' me it all. Master Winwife! Master Quarlous! Will
  you take a pipe of tobacco with us? Do not discredit me now, 20
  Zekiel.

WINWIFE Do not see him! He is the roaring horse-courser. Pray thee
let's avoid him; turn down this way.

QUARLOUS 'Slud, I'll see him, and roar with him too, an he roared
as loud as Neptune;° pray thee go with me.   25

WINWIFE You may draw me to as likely an inconvenience, when you
please, as this.°

QUARLOUS Go to then, come along we ha' nothing to do, man, but
to see sights now.

KNOCKEM Welcome Master Quarlous and Master Winwife! Will you   30
take any froth and smoke with us?

QUARLOUS Yes, sir, but you'll pardon us if we knew not of so much
familiarity between us afore.

KNOCKEM As what, sir?

QUARLOUS To be so lightly invited to smoke and froth.   35

KNOCKEM A good vapour! Will you sit down, sir? This is old
Ursula's mansion. How like you her bower? Here you may ha'
your punk and your pig in state, sir, both piping hot.

QUARLOUS I had rather ha' my punk cold,° sir.

JUSTICE [aside] There's for me: punk! And pig!   40

URSULA (she calls [from] within) What, Mooncalf? You rogue.

MOONCALF By and by; the bottle is almost off, mistress; here Master
Arthur.

URSULA [within] I'll part you and your playfellow there, i' the
guarded coat, an you sunder not the sooner.   45

KNOCKEM Master Winwife, you are proud, methinks; you do not
talk nor drink; are you proud?

WINWIFE Not of the company I am in, sir, nor the place, I assure
you.

KNOCKEM You do not except at the company, do you? Are you in   50
vapours, sir?

MOONCALF Nay, good Master Dan Knockem, respect my mistress'
bower, as you call it; for the honour of our booth, none o' your
vapours here.

    Ursula comes out with a firebrand

URSULA Why, you thin lean polecat, you; an they have a mind to be   55
i' their vapours, must you hinder 'em? What did you know,
vermin, if they would ha' lost a cloak, or such a trifle? Must you
be drawing the air of pacification here, while I am tormented,
within, i' the fire, you weasel?

MOONCALF Good mistress, 'twas in the behalf of your booth's credit   60
that I spoke.

URSULA Why? Would my booth ha' broke if they had fallen out in't, sir? Or would their heat ha' fired it? In, you rogue, and wipe the pigs, and mend the fire, that they fall not, or I'll both baste and roast you, till your eyes drop out, like 'em. (Leave the bottle   65
behind you, and be cursed a while.)

[*Exit Mooncalf*]

QUARLOUS Body o' the Fair! What's this? Mother o' the bawds?

KNOCKEM No, she's mother o' the pigs, sir, mother o' the pigs!

WINWIFE Mother o' the Furies, I think, by her firebrand.

QUARLOUS Nay, she is too fat to be a Fury, sure; some walking sow   70
of tallow!

WINWIFE An inspired vessel of kitchen-stuff!

She drinks this while

QUARLOUS She'll make excellent gear for the coach-makers here in Smithfield to anoint wheels and axle-trees with.

URSULA Aye, aye, gamesters, mock a plain plump soft wench o' the   75
suburbs,° do, because she's juicy and wholesome. You must ha' your thin pinched ware, pent up i' the compass of a dog-collar—or 'twill not do—that looks like a long laced conger, set upright; and a green feather, like fennel, i' the jowl on't.

KNOCKEM Well said, Urs, my good Urs; to 'em Urs.   80

QUARLOUS Is she your quagmire, Dan Knockem? Is this your bog?°

NIGHTINGALE We shall have a quarrel presently.

KNOCKEM How? Bog? Quagmire? Foul vapours! Hum'h!

QUARLOUS Yes, he that would venture for't, I assure him, might sink   85
into her and be drowned a week ere any friend he had could find where he were.

WINWIFE And then he would be a fortnight weighing up° again.

QUARLOUS 'Twere like falling into a whole shire of butter: they had need be a team of Dutchmen° should draw him out.   90

KNOCKEM Answer 'em, Urs, where's thy Bartholomew wit now? Urs, thy Bartholomew wit?

URSULA Hang 'em, rotten, roguy cheaters! I hope to see 'em plagued one day (poxed they are already, I am sure) with lean playhouse poultry,° that has the bony rump sticking out like the ace of spades   95
or the point of a partisan, that every rib of 'em is like the tooth of a saw and will so grate 'em with their hips and shoulders, as (take 'em altogether) they were as good lie with a hurdle.

QUARLOUS Out upon her, how she drips! She's able to give a man the sweating sickness° with looking on her.   100

URSULA Marry look off, with a patch° o' your face and a dozen i'
your breech, though they be o' scarlet, sir. I ha' seen as fine
outsides as either o' yours bring lousy linings to the brokers ere
now, twice a week.

QUARLOUS Do you think there may be a fine new cuckingstool i' the   105
Fair to be purchased? One large enough, I mean. I know there is
a pond° of capacity for her.

URSULA For your mother, you rascal! Out, you rogue, you hedge-
bird, you pimp, you pannier-man's bastard, you.

QUARLOUS Ha, ha, ha.   110

URSULA Do you sneer, you dog's-head, you trendle-tail! You look as
you were begotten atop of a cart in harvest-time, when the whelp
was hot and eager. Go, snuff after your brother's bitch, Mistress
Commodity; that's the livery you wear; 'twill be out at the elbows
shortly. It's time you went to't, for the t'other remnant.   115

KNOCKEM Peace, Urs, peace, Urs—They'll kill the poor whale, and
make oil of her—pray thee go in.

URSULA I'll see 'em poxed first, and piled, and double piled.°

WINWIFE Let's away; her language grows greasier than her pigs.

URSULA Does't so, snotty nose? Good Lord! Are you snivelling? You   120
were engendered on a she-beggar in a barn when the bald thrasher,
your sire, was scarce warm.

WINWIFE Pray thee, let's go.

QUARLOUS No, faith; I'll stay the end of her now. I know she cannot
last long; I find by her similes, she wanes apace.   125

URSULA Does she so? I'll set you gone. Gi' me my pigpan hither a
little I'll scald you hence, an you will not go.
[*Exit Ursula*]

KNOCKEM Gentlemen, these are very strange vapours! And very idle
vapours, I assure you.

QUARLOUS You are a very serious ass, we assure you.   130

KNOCKEM Humph! Ass? And serious? Nay, then pardon me my
vapour. I have a foolish vapour, gentlemen; any man that does
vapour me, the ass, Master Quarlous—

QUARLOUS What then, Master Jordan?

KNOCKEM I do vapour him the lie.°   135

QUARLOUS Faith, and to any man that vapours me the lie, I do
vapour that.
[*Strikes Knockem*]

KNOCKEM Nay, then, vapours upon vapours.
Ursula comes in with the scalding-pan

EDGWORTH, NICHTINGALE 'Ware the pan, the pan, the pan; she
　　comes with the pan, gentlemen.   140
　　　　They fight. She falls with it.
　　God bless the woman.
URSULA Oh.
　　　　[*Exeunt Quarlous, Winwife*]
TRASH What's the matter?
JUSTICE Goodly woman!
MOONCALF Mistress!   145
URSULA Curse of hell, that ever I saw these fiends! O! I ha' scalded
　　my leg, my leg, my leg, my leg! I ha' lost a limb in the service!
　　Run for some cream and salad oil, quickly. [*To Mooncalf*] Are you
　　under-peering, you baboon? Rip off my hose, an you be men, men,
　　men.   150
MOONCALF Run you for some cream, good mother Joan. I'll look to
　　your basket.
　　　　[*Exit Joan Trash*]
LEATHERHEAD Best sit up i' your chair, Ursula. Help, gentlemen.
　　　　[*They lift her up*]   ·
KNOCKEM Be of good cheer, Urs; thou hast hindered me the
　　currying of a couple of stallions here, that abused the good   155
　　race-bawd° o' Smithfield; 'twas time for 'em to go.
NIGHTINGALE I' faith, when the pan came; they had made you run
　　else. [*To Edgworth*] This had been a fine time for purchase, if you
　　had ventured.
EDGWORTH Not a whit; these fellows were too fine to carry money.   160
KNOCKEM Nightingale, get some help to carry her leg out o' the
　　air; take off her shoes; body o' me, she has the mallanders,
　　the scratches, the crown scab, and the quitter bone° i' the t'other
　　leg.
URSULA O, the pox, why do you put me in mind o' my leg thus, to   165
　　make it prick and shoot? Would you ha' me i' the Hospital° afore
　　my time?
KNOCKEM Patience, Urs, take a good heart; 'tis but a blister as big
　　as a windgall; I'll take it away with the white of an egg, a little
　　honey, and hog's grease; ha' thy pasterns well rolled, and thou   170
　　shalt pace again by tomorrow. I'll tend thy booth and look to thy
　　affairs the while; thou shalt sit i' thy chair, and give directions, and
　　shine *Ursa major.*°
　　　　[*Exeunt Ursula, Knockem, Mooncalf*]

2.6

[Enter] Cokes, Wasp, Mistress Overdo [and] Grace

JUSTICE These are the fruits of bottle-ale and tobacco! The foam of
the one, and the fumes of the other! Stay, young man, and despise
not the wisdom of these few hairs, that are grown grey in care of
thee.

EDGWORTH Nightingale, stay a little. Indeed, I'll hear some o'   5
this!

COKES Come, Numps, come, where are you? Welcome into the Fair,
Mistress Grace.

EDGWORTH *[to Nightingale]* 'Slight, he will call company, you shall
see, and put us into doings presently.   10

JUSTICE Thirst not after that frothy liquor, ale; for who knows when
he openeth the stopple what may be in the bottle? Hath not a snail,
a spider, yea, a newt been found there? Thirst not after it, youth;
thirst not after it.

COKES This is a brave fellow, Numps; let's hear him.   15

WASP 'Sblood, how brave is he? In a guarded coat? You were best
truck with him; e'en strip, and truck presently, it will become you.
Why will you hear him? Because he is an ass, and may be a kin to
the Cokeses?

COKES O, good Numps!   20

JUSTICE Neither do thou lust after that tawny weed, tobacco.

COKES Brave words!

JUSTICE Whose complexion is like the Indian's that vents° it!

COKES Are they not brave words, sister?

JUSTICE And who can tell, if, before the gathering and making up   25
thereof, the alligator hath not pissed thereon?

WASP 'Heart, let 'em be brave words, as brave as they will! An they
were all the brave words in a country, how then? Will you away
yet? Ha' you enough on him? Mistress Grace, come you away, I
pray you, be not you accessory. If you do lose your licence, or   30
somewhat else, sir, with listening to his fables, say Numps is a
witch, with all my heart, do, say so.

COKES Avoid i' your satin doublet, Numps.

JUSTICE The creeping venom of which subtle serpent, as some late
writers° affirm neither the cutting of the perilous plant, nor the   35
drying of it, nor the lighting or burning, can any way persway or
assuage.

COKES Good, i' faith! Is't not, sister?

JUSTICE Hence it is that the lungs of the tobacconist are rotted, the liver spotted, the brain smoked like the backside of the pig-woman's booth here, and the whole body within, black as her pan you saw e'en now without.

COKES A fine similitude, that, sir! Did you see the pan?

EDGWORTH Yes, sir.

JUSTICE Nay, the hole in the nose° here, of some tobacco-takers, or the third nostril (if I may so call it), which makes that they can vent the tobacco out, like the ace of clubs, or rather the flower-de-lys, is caused from the tobacco, the mere tobacco! When the poor innocent pox, having nothing to do there, is miserably, and most unconscionably slandered.

COKES Who would ha' missed this, sister?

MISTRESS OVERDO Not anybody but Numps.

COKES He does not understand.

EDGWORTH [aside] Nor you feel.

> He picketh his purse

COKES What would you have, sister, of a fellow that knows nothing but a basket-hilt and an old fox in't? The best music i' the Fair will not move a log.

EDGWORTH [giving purse to Nightingale] In to Ursula, Nightingale, and carry her comfort; see it told.° This fellow was sent to us by fortune for our first fairing.

> [Exit Nightingale]

JUSTICE But what speak I of the diseases of the body, children of the Fair?

COKES That's to us, sister. Brave i' faith!

JUSTICE Hark, O you sons and daughters of Smithfield! And hear what malady it doth the mind. It causeth swearing, it causeth swaggering, it causeth snuffling and snarling, and now and then a hurt.

MISTRESS OVERDO He hath something of Master Overdo, methinks, brother.

COKES So methought, sister, very much of my brother Overdo; and 'tis when he speaks.

JUSTICE Look into any angle o' the town—the Straits, or the Bermudas—° where the quarrelling lesson is read, and how do they entertain the time, but with bottle-ale and tobacco? The lecturer is o' one side, and his pupils o' the other; but the seconds are still bottle-ale and tobacco, for which the lecturer reads and the novices pay. Thirty pound a week in bottle-ale! Forty in tobacco! And ten more in ale again. Then for a suit to drink in, so much, and (that being slavered) so much for another suit, and then a third suit, and a fourth suit! And still the bottle-ale slavereth, and the tobacco stinketh! 80

WASP Heart of a madman! Are you rooted here? Will you never away? What can any man find out in this bawling fellow to grow here for? He is a full handful higher sin' he heard him. Will you fix here? And set up a booth, sir? 85

JUSTICE I will conclude briefly—

WASP Hold your peace, you roaring rascal! I'll run my head i' your chaps else. You were best build a booth and entertain him; make your will, an you say the word, and him your heir! Heart, I never knew one taken with a mouth of a peck afore. 90 By this light, I'll carry you away o' my back, an you will not come.

He gets him up on pick-pack

COKES Stay Numps, stay, set me down! I ha' lost my purse, Numps! O, my purse! One o' my fine purses is gone!

MISTRESS OVERDO Is't indeed, brother? 95

COKES Aye, as I am an honest man, would I were an arrant rogue else! A plague of all roguy, damned cutpurses for me.

WASP Bless 'em with all my heart, with all my heart, do you see! Now, as I am no infidel, that I know of, I am glad on't. Aye, I am; here's my witness! Do you see, sir? I did not tell you of his fables, 100 I? No, no, I am a dull malt-horse, I, I know nothing. Are you not justly served i' your conscience now? Speak i' your conscience. Much good do you with all my heart, and his good heart that has it, with all my heart again.

EDGWORTH [*aside*] This fellow is very charitable; would he had a 105 purse too! But I must not be too bold all at a time.

COKES Nay, Numps, it is not my best purse.

WASP Not your best? Death! Why should it be your worst? Why should it be any, indeed, at all? Answer me to that, gi' me a reason from you, why it should be any? 110

COKES Nor my gold, Numps; I ha' that yet; look here else, sister. [*Shows his other purse*]

WASP Why so, there's all the feeling he has!

MISTRESS OVERDO I pray you, have a better care of that, brother.

COKES Nay, so I will, I warrant you; let him catch this, that catch can. I would fain see him get this, look you here. 115

WASP So, so, so, so, so, so, so, so! Very good.

COKES I would ha' him come again, now, and but offer at it. Sister, will you take notice of a good jest? I will put it just where the other was, and if we ha' good luck, you shall see a delicate fine trap to catch the cutpurse nibbling.   120

EDGWORTH [aside] Faith, and he'll try ere you be out o' the Fair.

COKES Come, Mistress Grace, prithee be not melancholy for my mischance; sorrow wi'not keep it, sweetheart.

GRACE I do not think on't, sir.

COKES 'Twas but a little scurvy white money,° hang it: it may hang   125
the cutpurse one day. I ha' gold left to gi' thee a fairing, yet, as hard as the world goes. Nothing angers me but that nobody here looked like a cutpurse, unless 'twere Numps.

WASP How? I? I look like a cutpurse? Death! Your sister's a cutpurse! And your mother and father, and all your kin were cutpurses! And   130
here is a rogue is the bawd o' the cutpurses, whom I will beat to begin with.

They speak all together, and Wasp beats the Justice

JUSTICE Hold thy hand, child of wrath, and heir of anger, make it not Childermass day° in thy fury, or the feast of the French Bartholomew,° parent of the Massacre.   135

COKES Numps, Numps.

MISTRESS OVERDO Good Master Humphrey.

WASP You are the Patrico, are you? The patriarch of the cutpurses? You share, sir, they say; let them share this with you. Are you i' your hot fit of preaching again? I'll cool you.   140

JUSTICE Murder, murder, murder.

[*Exeunt*]

3.1

[Enter] Whit, Haggis, Bristle, Leatherhead [and] Trash

WHIT Nay, 'tish all gone, now! Dish 'tish, phen tou vilt not be phitin
call, Mashter Offisher! Phat ish a man te better to lishen out
noishes for tee, an tou art in an oder 'orld, being very shuffishient
noishes and gallantsh too, one o' their brabblesh would have fed
ush all dish fortnight; but tou art so bushy about beggersh stil, tou   5
hast no leshure to intend shentlemen, an't be.

HAGGIS Why, I told you, Davy Bristle.

BRISTLE Come, come, you told me a pudding, Toby Haggis; a matter
of nothing; I am sure it came to nothing! You said, 'let's go to
Ursula's', indeed; but then you met the man with the monsters,   10
and I could not get you from him. An old fool, not leave seeing
yet?

HAGGIS Why, who would ha' thought anybody would ha' quarrelled
so early? Or that the ale o' the Fair would ha' been up so soon?

WHIT Phy? Phat o'clock toest tou tink it ish, man?   15

HAGGIS I cannot tell.

WHIT Tou art a vishe vatchman, i' te meanteem.

HAGGIS Why, should the watch go by the clock, or the clock by the
watch, I pray?

BRISTLE One should go by another, if they did well.   20

WHIT Tou art right now! Phen didst tou ever know or hear of a
shuffishient vatchman, but he did tell the clock, phat bushiness
soever he had?

BRISTLE Nay, that's most true, a sufficient watchman knows what
o'clock it is.   25

WHIT Shleeping or vaking! Ash well as te clock himshelf, or te jack
dat shtrikes him!

BRISTLE Let's enquire of Master Leatherhead, or Joan Trash here.
Master Leatherhead, do you hear, Master Leatherhead?

WHIT If it be a Ledderhead, tish a very tick Ledderhead, tat sho   30
mush noish vill not peirsh him.

LEATHERHEAD I have a little business now, good friends; do not
trouble me.

WHIT Phat? Because o' ty wrought neet cap, and ty phelvet sherkin,
man? Phy? I have sheen tee in ty ledder sherkin ere now, mashter   35
o' de hobby-horses, as bushy and as stately as tou sheem'st to be.

368

TRASH Why, what an' you have, Captain Whit? He has his choice of
jerkins, you may see by that, and his caps too, I assure you, when
he pleases to be either sick or employed.

LEATHERHEAD God a mercy Joan, answer for me.   40

WHIT Away, be not sheen i' my company, here be shentlemen, and
men of vorship.

    [*Exeunt Haggis, Bristle*]

3.2

    [*Enter*] *Quarlous* [*and*] *Winwife*

QUARLOUS We had wonderful ill luck to miss this prologue o' the
purse, but the best is we shall have five acts of him ere night. He'll
be spectacle enough! I'll answer for't.

WHIT Oh Creesh! Duke Quarlous, how dosht tou? Tou dosht not
know me, I fear? I am te vishesht man, but Justish Overdo, in all   5
Bartholomew Fair, now. Gi' me twelvepence from tee, I vill help
tee to a vife vorth forty marks for't, an't be.

QUARLOUS Away, rogue, pimp, away!

WHIT And she shall show tee as fine cut'ork for't in her shmock too,
as tou cansht vishe i'faith; vilt tou have her, vorshipful Vinvife? I   10
vill help tee to her, here, be an't be, in te pig-quarter, gi' me ty
twelvepence from tee.

WINWIFE Why, there's twelvepence; pray thee wilt thou be gone?

WHIT Tou art a vorthy man, and a vorshipful man still.

QUARLOUS Get you gone, rascal.   15

WHIT I do mean it, man. Prinsh Quarlous, if tou hasht need on me,
tou shalt find me here, at Ursula's I vill see phat ale and punk ish
i' te pigshty for tee, bless ty good vorship.

    [*Exit Whit*]

QUARLOUS Look who comes here! John Littlewit!

WINWIFE And his wife, and my widow, her mother—the whole   20
family.

    [*Enter Busy, Purecraft, Littlewit, Win*]

QUARLOUS 'Slight, you must gi' em all fairings, now!

WINWIFE Not I, I'll not see 'em.

QUARLOUS They are going a-feasting. What schoolmaster's that is
with 'em?   25

WINWIFE That's my rival, I believe, the baker!

BUSY So, walk on in the middle way, fore-right; turn neither to the right hand nor to the left. Let not your eyes be drawn aside with vanity, nor your ear with noises.

QUARLOUS O, I know him by that start!   30

LEATHERHEAD What do you lack? What do you buy, pretty mistress? A fine hobby-horse to make your son a tilter? A drum to make him a soldier? A fiddle to make him a reveller? What is't you lack? Little dogs for your daughters? Or babies, male or female?

BUSY Look not toward them; hearken not! The place is Smithfield,   35 or the field of Smiths, the grove of hobby-horses and trinkets. The wares are the wares of devils, and the whole Fair is the shop of Satan! They are hooks and baits, very baits, that are hung out on every side to catch you, and to hold you as it were, by the gills and by the nostrils, as the fisher doth; therefore you must not look, nor   40 turn toward them. The heathen man could stop his ears with wax, against the harlot o' the sea;° do you the like, with your fingers, against the bells of the Beast.

WINWIFE What flashes comes from him!

QUARLOUS O, he has those of his oven! A notable hot baker 'twas,   45 when he plied the peel. He is leading his flock into the Fair now.

WINWIFE Rather driving 'em to the pens; for he will let 'em look upon nothing.

[Enter Knockem, Whit]

KNOCKEM Gentlewomen, the weather's hot! Whither walk you? Have a care o' your fine velvet caps; the Fair is dusty. Take a sweet   50 delicate booth, with boughs here i' the way, and cool yourselves i' the shade, you and your friends. The best pig and bottle-ale i' the Fair, sir. (*Littlewit is gazing at the sign, which is the Pig's Head with a large writing under it*) Old Ursula is cook, there you may read: the pig's head speaks it. Poor soul, she has had a stringhalt, the   55 maryhinchco,° but she's prettily amended.

WHIT A delicate show-pig, little mistress, with shweet sauce and crackling like de bay-leaf i' de fire, la! Tou shalt ha' de clean side o' de table-clot and di glass vashed with phatersh of Dame Annessh Cleare.°   60

LITTLEWIT This's fine, verily: 'Here be the best pigs, and she does roast 'em as well as ever she did', the pig's head says.

KNOCKEM Excellent, excellent, mistress, with fire o' juniper and rosemary° branches! The oracle of the pig's head, that, sir.

PURECRAFT Son, were you not warned of the vanity of the eye? Have   65 you forgot the wholesome admonition so soon?

LITTLEWIT Good mother, how shall we find a pig if we do not look about for't? Will it run off o' the spit into our mouths, think you? As in Lubberland?° And cry, *wee, wee*?

BUSY No, but your mother, religiously wise, conceiveth it may offer itself by other means to the sense, as by way of steam, which I think it doth here in this place. Huh, huh—yes, it doth. (*Busy scents after it like a hound*) And it were a sin of obstinacy, great obstinacy, high and horrible obstinacy, to decline or resist the good titillation of the famelic sense, which is the smell. Therefore be bold—huh, huh, huh—follow the scent. Enter the tents of the unclean for once, and satisfy your wife's frailty. Let your frail wife be satisfied; your zealous mother, and my suffering self, will also be satisfied.

LITTLEWIT Come, Win, as good winny here as go farther and see nothing.

BUSY We 'scape so much of the other vanities, by our early entering.

PURECRAFT It is an edifying consideration.

WIN This is scurvy, that we must come into the Fair and not look on't.

LITTLEWIT Win, have patience, Win, I'll tell you more anon.
      [*Exeunt into the booth Busy, Purecraft, Littlewit, Win*]

KNOCKEM Mooncalf, entertain within there; the best pig i' the booth, a porklike pig. These are Banbury-bloods, o' the sincere stud,° come a pig-hunting. Whit, wait, Whit, look to your charge.
      [*Exit Whit*]

BUSY [*within*] A pig prepare presently; let a pig be prepared to us.
      [*Enter Mooncalf, Ursula*]

MOONCALF 'Slight, who be these?

URSULA Is this the good service, Jordan, you'd do me?

KNOCKEM Why, Urs? Why, Urs? Thou'lt ha' vapours i' thy leg again presently, pray thee go in, 't may turn to the scratches else.

URSULA Hang your vapours, they are stale, and stink like you. Are these the guests o' the game you promised to fill my pit withal today?

KNOCKEM Aye, what ail they, Urs?

URSULA Ail they? They are all sippers, sippers o' the city. They look as they would not drink off two penn'orth of bottle-ale amongst 'em.

MOONCALF A body may read that i' their small printed ruffs.°

KNOCKEM Away, thou art a fool, Urs, and thy Mooncalf too, i' your ignorant vapours, now! Hence! Good guests, I say, right hypocrites,

good gluttons. In, and set a couple o' pigs o' the board, and half a   105
dozen of the biggest bottles afore 'em, and call Whit. I do not love
to hear innocents abused. Fine ambling hypocrites! And a stone-
puritan° with a sorrel head, and beard: good-mouthed gluttons,
two to a pig. Away!

    [Exit Mooncalf]

URSULA Are you sure they are such?   110

KNOCKEM O' the right breed. Thou shalt try 'em by the teeth, Urs.
Where's this Whit?

    [Enter Whit]

WHIT Behold, man, and see, what a worthy man am ee!
  With the fury of my sword, and the shaking of my beard,
  I will make ten thousand men afeared.   115

KNOCKEM Well said, brave Whit! In, and fear the ale out o' the
bottles into the bellies of the brethren and the sisters; drink to the
cause, and pure vapours.

    [Exeunt Knockem, Whit, Ursula]

QUARLOUS My roarer is turned tapster, methinks. Now were a fine
time for thee, Winwife, to lay aboard° thy widow; thou'lt never be   120
master of a better season or place. She that will venture herself
into the Fair and a pig-box will admit any assault, be assured of
that.

WINWIFE I love not enterprises of that suddenness, though.

QUARLOUS I'll warrant thee, then, no wife out o' the widows'   125
hundred. If I had but as much title to her as to have breathed once
on that strait stomacher of hers, I would now assure myself to carry
her yet, ere she went out of Smithfield. Or she should carry me,
which were the fitter sight, I confess. But you are a modest
undertaker, by circumstances and degrees. Come, 'tis disease in   130
thee, not judgement; I should offer at all together. Look, here's the
poor fool again, that was stung by the wasp erewhile.

3.3

    [Enter Justice] Overdo

JUSTICE I will make no more orations, shall draw on these tragical
conclusions. And I begin now to think that, by a spice of collateral
justice, Adam Overdo deserved this beating; for I, the said
Adam, was one cause (a by-cause) why the purse was lost—and

my wife's brother's purse too, which they know not of yet. But   5
I shall make very good mirth with it at supper (that will be the
sport) and put my little friend Master Humphrey Wasp's choler
quite out of countenance, when, sitting at the upper end o' my
table, as I use, and drinking to my brother Cokes and Mistress
Alice Overdo, as I will, my wife, for their good affection to old   10
Bradley, I deliver to 'em, it was I that was cudgelled, and show
'em the marks. To see what bad events may peep out o' the tail of
good purposes! The care I had of that civil young man I took fancy
to this morning (and have not left it yet) drew me to that
exhortation, which drew the company, indeed, which drew the   15
cutpurse; which drew the money; which drew my brother Cokes
his loss; which drew on Wasp's anger; which drew on my beating:
a pretty gradation! And they shall ha' it i' their dish, i' faith, at
night for fruit; I love to be merry at my table. I had thought once,
at one special blow he ga' me, to have revealed myself; but then (I   20
thank thee, fortitude) I remembered that a wise man (and who is
ever so great a part o' the commonwealth in himself) for no
particular disaster ought to abandon a public good design. The
husbandman ought not, for one unthankful year, to forsake the
plough; the shepherd ought not, for one scabbed sheep, to throw   25
by his tar-box; the pilot ought not, for one leak i' the poop, to quit
the helm; nor the alderman ought not, for one custard more° at
a meal, to give up his cloak; the constable ought not to break his
staff and forswear the watch, for one roaring night; nor the piper
o' the parish (*ut parvis componere magna solebam*)° to put up his   30
pipes, for one rainy Sunday. These are certain knocking conclusions, out of which, I am resolved, come what come can—come
beating, come imprisonment, come infamy, come banishment, nay,
come the rack, come the hurdle (welcome all)—I will not discover
who I am till my due time; and yet still all shall be, as I said ever,   35
in Justice' name, and the King's, and for the Commonwealth.

    [*Exit Justice Overdo*]

WINWIFE What does he talk to himself, and act so seriously? Poor
fool!

QUARLOUS No matter what. Here's fresher argument, intend that.

3.4

[Enter] Cokes, Mistress Overdo, Grace [and] Wasp [carrying goods]

COKES Come, Mistress Grace, come sister, here's more fine sights
yet, i' faith. God's lid, where's Numps?

LEATHERHEAD What do you lack, gentlemen? What is't you buy?
Fine rattles? Drums? Babies? Little dogs? And birds for ladies?
What do you lack?   5

COKES Good honest Numps, keep afore. I am so afraid thou'lt lose
somewhat; my heart was at my mouth when I missed thee.

WASP You were best buy a whip i' your hand to drive me.

COKES Nay, do not mistake, Numps; thou art so apt to mistake. I
would but watch the goods. Look you now, the treble fiddle was   10
e'en almost like to be lost.

WASP Pray you take heed you lose not yourself. Your best way were
e'en get up and ride for more surety. Buy a token's worth of great
pins to fasten yourself to my shoulder.

LEATHERHEAD What do you lack, gentlemen? Fine purses, pouches,   15
pin-cases, pipes? What is't you lack? A pair o' smiths° to wake you
i' the morning? Or a fine whistling bird?

COKES Numps, here be finer things than any we ha' bought, by odds!
And more delicate horses, a great deal! Good Numps, stay, and
come hither.   20

WASP Will you scorse with him? You are in Smithfield; you may fit
yourself with a fine easy-going streetnag for your saddle again'
Michaelmas-term, do. Has he ne'er a little odd cart for you, to
make a caroche on, i' the country, with four pied hobbyhorses?
Why the measles should you stand here with your train, cheaping   25
of dogs, birds, and babies? You ha' no children to bestow 'em on,
ha' you?

COKES No, but again' I ha' children, Numps, that's all one.

WASP Do, do, do, do. How many shall you have, think you? An I
were as you, I'd buy for all my tenants, too. They are a kind o'   30
civil savages that will part with their children for rattles, pipes, and
knives. You were best buy a hatchet or two, and truck with 'em.

COKES Good Numps, hold that little tongue o' thine, and save it a
labour. I am resolute Bat, thou know'st.

WASP A resolute fool you are, I know, and a very sufficient coxcomb, 35
with all my heart; nay, you have it, sir, an you be angry, turd i' your
teeth, twice (if I said it not once afore) and much good do you.

WINWIFE [*to Quarlous*] Was there ever such a self-affliction? And so impertinent?

QUARLOUS [*to Winwife*] Alas! His care will go near to crack him; let's in, and comfort him.   40

WASP Would I had been set i' the ground, all but the head on me, and had my brains bowled at, or threshed out, when first I underwent this plague of a charge!

QUARLOUS How now, Numps! Almost tired i' your protectorship?   45
Overparted? Overparted?

WASP Why, I cannot tell, sir, it may be I am. Does't grieve you?

QUARLOUS No, I swear does't not, Numps, to satisfy you.

WASP Numps? 'Sblood, you are fine and familiar! How long ha' we been acquainted, I pray you?   50

QUARLOUS I think it may be remembered, Numps, that? 'Twas since morning, sure.

WASP Why, I hope I know't well enough, sir; I did not ask to be told.

QUARLOUS No? Why then?

WASP It's no matter why; you see with your eyes, now, what I said   55
to you today? You'll believe me another time?

QUARLOUS Are you removing the Fair, Numps?

WASP A pretty question! And a very civil one! Yes, faith, I ha' my lading, you see, or shall have anon; you may know whose beast I am by my burden. If the pannier-man's jack° were ever better   60
known by his loins of mutton, I'll be flayed, and feed dogs for him, when his time comes.

WINWIFE How melancholy Mistress Grace is yonder! Pray thee let's go enter ourselves in grace with her.

COKES Those six horses, friend, I'll have—   65

WASP How!

COKES And the three Jew's trumps;° and half a dozen o' birds, and that drum (I have one drum already) and your smiths (I like that device o' your smiths very pretty well) and four halberts—and (le'me see) that fine painted great lady, and her three women for   70
state, I'll have.

WASP No, the shop; buy the whole shop, it will be best, the shop, the shop!

LEATHERHEAD If his worship please.

WASP Yes, and keep it during the Fair, bobchin.   75

COKES Peace, Numps. Friend, do not meddle with him, an you be wise, and would show your head above board. He will sting thorough your wrought night-cap, believe me. A set of these

violins I would buy too, for a delicate young noise I have i' the
country, that are every one a size less than another, just like your   80
fiddles. I would fain have a fine young masque at my marriage,
now I think on't; but I do want such a number o' things. And
Numps will not help me now, and I dare not speak to him.

TRASH Will your worship buy any gingerbread, very good bread,
comfortable bread?   85

COKES Gingerbread! Yes, let's see.
    He runs to her shop

WASP There's the t'other springe?

LEATHERHEAD Is this well, goody Joan? To interrupt my market, in
the midst and call away my customers? Can you answer this at the
Piepowders?   90

TRASH Why, if his mastership have a mind to buy, I hope my ware
lies as open as another's; I may show my ware as well as you yours.

COKES Hold your peace; I'll content you both: I'll buy up his shop
and thy basket.

WASP Will you, i' faith?   95

LEATHERHEAD Why should you put him from it, friend?

WASP Cry you mercy! You'd be sold too, would you? What's the
price on you? Jerkin and all, as you stand? Ha' you any qualities?

TRASH Yes, goodman angry-man, you shall find he has qualities, if
you cheapen him.   100

WASP Gods so, you ha' the selling of him! What are they? Will they
be bought for love or money?

TRASH No indeed, sir.

WASP For what then? Victuals?

TRASH He scorns victuals, sir; he has bread and butter at home,   105
thanks be to God! And yet he will do more for a good meal, if the
toy take him i' the belly. Marry, then they must not set him at
lower end;° if they do, he'll go away, though he fast. But put him
atop o' the table, where his place is, and he'll do you forty fine
things. He has not been sent for and sought out for nothing, at   110
your great city suppers, to put down Coryate, and Cokeley,° and
been laughed at for his labour; he'll play you all the puppets i' the
town over, and the players, every company, and his own company
too; he spares nobody!

COKES I'faith?   115

TRASH He was the first, sir, that ever baited the fellow i' the bear's
skin,° an't like your worship. No dog ever came near him since.
And for fine motions!

COKES Is he good at those too? Can he set out a masque, trow?

TRASH O Lord, master! Sought to far and near, for his inventions;   120
and he engrosses all, he makes all the puppets i' the Fair.

COKES Dost thou, in troth, old velvet jerkin? Give me thy hand.

TRASH Nay sir, you shall see him in his velvet jerkin, and a scarf
too, at night, when you hear him interpret Master Littlewit's
motion.   125

COKES Speak no more, but shut up shop presently, friend. I'll buy
both it and thee too, to carry down with me, and her hamper
beside. Thy shop shall furnish out the masque, and hers the
banquet. I cannot go less, to set out anything with credit. What's
the price, at a word, o' thy whole shop, case and all, as it stands?   130

LEATHERHEAD Sir, it stands me in six and twenty shillings seven-
pence halfpenny, besides three shillings for my ground.

COKES Well, thirty shillings will do all, then! And what comes yours
to?

TRASH Four shillings and elevenpence, sir, ground and all, an't like   135
your worship.

COKES Yes, it does like my worship very well, poor woman; that's
five shillings more. What a masque shall I furnish out for forty
shillings (twenty pounds Scotch°)! And a banquet of gingerbread!
There's a stately thing! Numps! Sister! And my wedding gloves   140
too! (That I never thought on afore). All my wedding gloves,
gingerbread! O me! What a device will there be to make 'em eat
their fingers' ends! And delicate brooches for the bride-men and
all! And then I'll ha' this posy put to 'em: *For the best grace*,
meaning Mistress Grace, my wedding posy.   145

GRACE I am beholden to you, sir, and to your Bartholomew-wit.

WASP You do not mean this, do you? Is this your first purchase?

COKES Yes faith, and I do not think, Numps, but thou'lt say, it was
the wisest act that ever I did in my wardship.

WASP Like enough! I shall say anything, I!   150

3.5

[Enter] Justice Overdo, Edgworth [and] Nightingale

JUSTICE *[aside]* I cannot beget a project, with all my political brain,
yet; my project is how to fetch off this proper young man from his
debauched company. I have followed him all the Fair over, and

still I find him with this songster; and I begin shrewdly to suspect
their familiarity; and the young man of a terrible taint, poetry!   5
With which idle disease, if he be infected, there's no hope of him
in a state-course. *Actum est* of him for a commonwealth's-man° if
he go to't in rhyme once.

EDGWORTH [*to Nightingale*] Yonder he is buying o' gingerbread: set
in quickly, before he part with too much on his money.   10

NIGHTINGALE [*sings*]
     My masters and friends, and good people, draw near, &c.

COKES Ballads! Hark, hark! Pray thee, fellow, stay a little! Good
Numps, look to the goods. What ballads hast thou? Let me see, let
me see myself.   15

     He runs to the ballad man

WASP Why so! He's flown to another lime-bush; there he will flutter
as long more, till he ha' ne'er a feather left. Is there a vexation like
this, gentlemen? Will you believe me now? Hereafter shall I have
credit with you?

QUARLOUS Yes faith, shalt thou, Numps, and thou art worthy on't,   20
for thou sweatest for't. [*To Winwife*] I never saw a young pimp
errant and his squire better matched.

WINWIFE Faith, the sister comes after 'em well, too.

GRACE Nay, if you saw the Justice her husband, my guardian, you
were fitted for the mess; he is such a wise one his way—   25

WINWIFE I wonder we see him not here.

GRACE O! He is too serious for this place, and yet better sport than
the other three, I assure you, gentlemen, where'er he is, though 't
be o' the bench.

COKES How dost thou call it? '*A Caveat against cutpurses*'? A good   30
jest, i'faith; I would fain see that demon, your cutpurse you talk
of, that delicate-handed devil. They say he walks hereabout; I
would see him walk now. (*He shows his purse boastingly*) Look you,
sister, here, here, let him come, sister, and welcome. Ballad-man,
does any cutpurses haunt hereabout? Pray thee raise me one or   35
two; begin and show me one.

NIGHTINGALE Sir, this is a spell against 'em, spick and span
new; and 'tis made as 'twere in mine own person, and I sing it
in mine own defence. But 'twill cost a penny alone, if you buy
it.   40

COKES No matter for the price. Thou dost not know me, I see; I am
an odd Bartholomew.

MISTRESS OVERDO Has't a fine picture, brother?

COKES O sister, do you remember the ballads over the nursery-
chimney at home o' my own pasting up? There be brave pictures!   45
Other manner of pictures than these, friend.

WASP Yet these will serve to pick the pictures out o' your pockets,
you shall see.

COKES So I heard 'em say. Pray thee mind him not, fellow, he'll have
an oar in everything.   50

NIGHTINGALE It was intended sir, as if a purse should chance to be
cut in my presence, now, I may be blameless, though; as by the
sequel will more plainly appear.

COKES We shall find that i' the matter. Pray thee begin.

NIGHTINGALE To the tune of 'Paggington's Pound',° sir,   55

COKES [sings] Fa, la la la, la la la, fa la la la. Nay, I'll put thee in
tune, and all! Mine own country dance! Pray thee begin.

NIGHTINGALE It is a gentle admonition, you must know, sir, both to
the purse-cutter and the purse-bearer.

COKES Not a word more, out o' the tune, an thou lov'st me. Fa, la   60
la la, la la la, fa la la la. Come, when?

NIGHTINGALE [sings]
> My masters and friends and good people draw near,
> And look to your purses, for that I do say;

COKES Ha, ha, this chimes! Good counsel at first dash.

NIGHTINGALE And though little money in them you do bear,   65
> It cost more to get, than to lose in a day.

COKES Good!

NIGHTINGALE You oft have been told,
> Both the young and the old,
> And bidden beware of the cutpurse so bold;   70

COKES Well said! He were to blame that would not i'faith.

NIGHTINGALE Then if you take heed not, free me from the curse,
> Who both give you warning for and the cutpurse.°
> Youth, youth, thou hadst better been starved by thy
> nurse,
> Than live to be hangèd for cutting a purse.   75

COKES Good i'faith, how say you, Numps? Is there any harm i' this?

NIGHTINGALE It hath been upbraided to men of my trade,
> That oftentimes we are the cause of this crime.

COKES The more coxcombs they that did it, I wusse.

NIGHTINGALE Alack and for pity, why should it be said?   80
> As if they regarded or places or time.
> Examples have been

> *Of some that were seen,*
> *In Westminster Hall, yea the pleaders between°*
> *Then why should the judges be free from this curse,*   85
> *More than my poor self, for cutting the purse?*

COKES God a mercy for that! Why should they be more free indeed?
He sings the burden with him

NIGHTINGALE AND COKES

> *Youth, youth, thou hadst better been starved by thy*
> *nurse,*
> *Than live to be hangèd for cutting a purse.*

COKES That again, good ballad-man, that again. O rare! I would fain   90
rub mine elbow° now, but I dare not pull out my hand. On, I pray
thee; he that made this ballad shall be poet to my masque.

NIGHTINGALE *At Worcester 'tis known well, and even i' the jail,*
> *A knight of good worship did there show his face,*
> *Against the foul sinners, in zeal for to rail,*   95
> *And lost (ipso facto) his purse in the place.°*

COKES Is it possible?

NIGHTINGALE *Nay, once from the seat*
> *Of judgement so great,*
> *A judge there did lose a fair pouch of velvet.*   100

COKES I' faith?

NIGHTINGALE *O Lord for thy mercy, how wicked or worse,*
> *Are those that so venture their necks for a purse!*
> *Youth, youth, etc.*

COKES [*singing with Nightingale*] *Youth, youth, etc.* Pray thee stay a   105
little, friend, yet. O' thy conscience, Numps, speak, is there any
harm i' this?

WASP To tell you true, 'tis too good for you, 'less you had grace to
follow it.

JUSTICE [*aside*] It doth discover enormity, I'll mark it more; I ha' not 110
liked a paltry piece of poetry so well, a good while.

COKES [*sings*] *Youth, youth, etc*! Where's this youth, now? A man
must call upon him, for his own good, and yet he will not appear.
Look here, here's for him (*he shows his purse*); handy-dandy, which
hand will he have? On, I pray thee, with the rest, I do hear of him,   115
but I cannot see him, this Master Youth, the cutpurse.

NIGHTINGALE *At plays and at sermons, and at the sessions,*
> *'Tis daily their practice such booty to make:*
> *Yea, under the gallows, at executions,*
> *They stick not the stare-abouts' purses to take.*   120

> *Nay one without grace,*
> *At a far better place,*
> *At court, and in Christmas, before the King's face.*°

COKES That was a fine fellow! I would have him now.

NIGHTINGALE *Alack then for pity, must I bear the curse,*   125
> *That only belongs to the cunning cutpurse?*

COKES But where's their cunning now, when they should use it?
They are all chained now, I warrant you. *Youth, youth, thou hadst*
better, etc. The rat-catchers' charms° are all fools and asses to this!
A pox on 'em, that they will not come! That a man should have   130
such a desire to a thing, and want it.

QUARLOUS [*to Winwife*] 'Fore God, I'd give half the Fair, an 'twere
mine, for a cutpurse for him, to save his longing.

COKES Look you sister, here, here, where is't now? Which pocket
isn't in? For a wager?   135

> *He shows his purse again*

WASP I beseech you leave your wagers and let him end his matter,
an't may be.

COKES O, are you edified, Numps?

JUSTICE [*aside*] Indeed he does interrupt him, too much: there
Numps spoke to purpose.   140

COKES Sister, I am an ass, I cannot keep my purse. ([*Shows it*] *again*)
On, on, I pray thee, friend.

NIGHTINGALE *But O, you vile nation of cutpurses all,*
> *Relent and repent, and amend and be sound,*
> *And know that you ought not, by honest men's fall,*   145
> *Advance your own fortunes, to die above ground,*
> *And though you go gay,*
> *In silks as you may,*
> *It is not the highway to heaven, as they say.*

WINWIFE [*aside to Quarlous*] Will you see sport? Look, there's a   150
fellow gathers up to him, mark.

> *Edgworth gets up to him and tickles him in the ear with a straw*
> *twice to draw his hand out of his pocket*

QUARLOUS Good, i'faith! O he has lighted on the wrong pocket.

WINWIFE He has it, 'fore God he is a brave fellow; pity he should
be detected.

NIGHTINGALE *Repent then, repent you, for better, for worse,*   155
> *And kiss not the gallows for cutting a purse.*
> *Youth, youth, thou hadst better been starved by thy*
> *nurse,*

Than live to be hangèd for cutting a purse.

ALL An excellent ballad! An excellent ballad!

EDGWORTH Friend, let me ha' the first, let me ha' the first, I pray   160
you.

COKES Pardon me, sir. First come, first served; and I'll buy the whole
bundle too.

[*Edgworth gives the purse to Nightingale*]

WINWIFE [*aside*] That conveyance was better than all, did you see't?
He has given the purse to the ballad-singer.   165

QUARLOUS Has he?

EDGWORTH Sir, I cry you mercy; I'll not hinder the poor man's
profit; pray you mistake me not.

COKES Sir, I take you for an honest gentleman, if that be mistaking;
I met you today afore. Ha! Humh! O God! My purse is gone, my   170
purse, my purse, &c.

WASP Come, do not make a stir, and cry yourself an ass thorough
the Fair afore your time.

COKES Why, hast thou it, Numps? Good Numps, how came you by
it? I mar'l!   175

WASP I pray you seek some other gamester to play the fool with. You
may lose it time enough, for all your Fair-wit.

COKES By this good hand, glove and all, I ha' lost it already, if thou
hast it not; feel else, and Mistress Grace's handkercher, too, out o'
the t'other pocket.   180

WASP Why, 'tis well; very well, exceeding pretty, and well.

EDGWORTH Are you sure you ha' lost it, sir?

COKES O God! Yes; as I am an honest man, I had it but e'en now,
at 'Youth, youth'.

NIGHTINGALE I hope you suspect not me, sir.   185

EDGWORTH Thee? That were a jest indeed! Dost thou think the
gentleman is foolish? Where hadst thou hands, I pray thee? Away
ass, away.

[*Exit Nightingale*]

JUSTICE [*aside*] I shall be beaten again, if I be spied.

EDGWORTH Sir, I suspect an odd fellow, yonder, is stealing away.   190

MISTRESS OVERDO Brother, it is the preaching fellow! You shall
suspect him. He was at your t'other purse, you know! Nay, stay,
sir, and view the work you ha' done; an you be beneficed at the
gallows and preach there, thank your own handiwork.

COKES Sir, you shall take no pride in your preferment; you shall be   195
silenced quickly.

[*They seize Overdo*]

JUSTICE What do you mean, sweet buds of gentility?

COKES To ha' my pennyworths out on you, bud! No less than two
purses a day serve you? I thought you a simple fellow, when my
man Numps beat you i' the morning, and pitied you—   200

MISTRESS OVERDO So did I, I'll be sworn, brother; but now I see he
is a lewd and pernicious enormity (as Master Overdo calls him).

JUSTICE [*aside*] Mine own words turned upon me like swords.

COKES Cannot a man's purse be at quiet for you i' the master's
pocket, but you must entice it forth and debauch it?   205

WASP Sir, sir, keep your debauch, and your fine Bartholomew-terms
to yourself and make as much on 'em as you please. But gi' me this
from you i' the meantime; I beseech you, see if I can look to this.

[*Wasp tries to take the box with the licence*]

COKES Why, Numps?

WASP Why? Because you are an ass, sir; there's a reason the shortest   210
way, an you will needs ha' it. Now you ha' got the trick of losing,
you'd lose your breech, an't 'twere loose. I know you, sir, come,
deliver. (*Wasp takes the licence from him*) You'll go and crack the
vermin you breed now, will you? 'Tis very fine, will you ha' the
truth on't? They are such retchless flies as you are, that blow   215
cutpurses abroad in every corner; your foolish having of money
makes 'em. An there were no wiser than I, sir, the trade should lie
open for you, sir, it should i'faith, sir. I would teach your wit to
come to your head, sir, as well as your land to come into your
hand, I assure you, sir.   220

WINWIFE Alack, good Numps.

WASP Nay, gentlemen, never pity me; I am not worth it. Lord send
me at home once, to Harrow o' the Hill again; if I travel any more,
call me Coryate, with all my heart.

[*Exeunt Wasp, Cokes, Mistress Overdo; Justice Overdo is
carried off*]

QUARLOUS Stay, sir, I must have a word with you in private. Do you   225
hear?

EDGWORTH With me, sir? What's your pleasure, good sir?

QUARLOUS Do not deny it. You are a cutpurse, sir; this gentleman
here, and I, saw you, nor do we mean to detect you (although we
can sufficiently inform ourselves toward the danger of concealing   230
you), but you must do us a piece of service.

EDGWORTH Good gentlemen, do not undo me; I am a civil young
man, and but a beginner, indeed.

QUARLOUS Sir, your beginning shall bring on your ending, for us. We are no catchpoles nor constables. That you are to undertake, is this: you saw the old fellow with the black box, here? 235

EDGWORTH The little old governor, sir?

QUARLOUS That same. I see you have flown him to a mark° already. I would ha' you get away that box from him, and bring it us.

EDGWORTH Would you ha' the box and all, sir? Or only that that is in't? I'll get you that, and leave him the box to play with still (which will be the harder o' the two), because I would gain your worships' good opinion of me. 240

WINWIFE He says well; 'tis the greater mastery, and 'twill make the more sport when 'tis missed. 245

EDGWORTH Aye, and 'twill be the longer a-missing, to draw on the sport.

QUARLOUS But look you do it now, sirrah, and keep your word, or—

EDGWORTH Sir, if ever I break my word with a gentleman, may I never read word at my need.° Where shall I find you? 250

QUARLOUS Somewhere i' the Fair, hereabouts. Dispatch it quickly.

[*Exit Edgworth*]

I would fain see the careful fool deluded! Of all beasts, I love the serious ass—he that takes pains to be one, and plays the fool, with the greatest diligence that can be. 255

GRACE Then you would not choose, sir, but love my guardian, Justice Overdo, who is answerable to that description in every hair of him.

QUARLOUS So I have heard. But how came you, Mistress Wellborn, to be his ward, or have relation to him, at first?

GRACE Faith, through a common calamity: he bought me, sir; and now he will marry me to his wife's brother, this wise gentleman that you see, or else I must pay value o' my land. 260

QUARLOUS 'Slid, is there no device of disparagement°, or so? Talk with some crafty fellow, some picklock o' the law! Would I had studied a year longer i' the Inns of Court, an't had been but i' your case. 265

WINWIFE [*aside*] Aye, Master Quarlous, are you proffering?

GRACE You'd bring but little aid, sir.

WINWIFE [*aside*] I'll look to you i' faith, gamester.—An unfortunate foolish tribe you are fallen into, lady; I wonder you can endure 'em. 270

GRACE Sir, they that cannot work their fetters off must wear 'em.

WINWIFE You see what care they have on you, to leave you thus.

GRACE Faith, the same they have of themselves, sir. I cannot greatly
complain if this were all the plea I had against 'em.   275

WINWIFE 'Tis true! But will you please to withdraw with us a little,
and make them think they have lost you? I hope our manners ha'
been such hitherto, and our language, as will give you no cause to
doubt yourself in our company.

GRACE Sir, I will give myself no cause; I am so secure of mine own   280
manners as I suspect not yours.

QUARLOUS Look where John Littlewit comes.

WINWIFE Away, I'll not be seen by him.

QUARLOUS No, you were not best; he'd tell his mother, the widow.

WINWIFE Heart, what do you mean?   285

QUARLOUS Cry you mercy, is the wind there? Must not the widow
be named?
      [*Exeunt Quarlous, Winwife, Grace*]

3.6

      [*Enter*] *Littlewit* [*and*] *Win*

LITTLEWIT Do you hear, Win, Win?

WIN What say you, John?

LITTLEWIT While they are paying the reckoning, Win, I'll tell you a
thing, Win: we shall never see any sights i' the Fair, Win, except
you long still, Win, good Win, sweet Win, long to see some   5
hobby-horses and some drums and rattles and dogs and fine
devices, Win. The bull with the five legs, Win, and the great hog.
Now you ha' begun with pig, you may long for anything, Win, and
so for my motion, Win.

WIN But we sha' not eat o' the bull; and the hog, John; how shall I   10
long then?

LITTLEWIT O yes, Win! You may long to see as well as to taste, Win.
How did the 'pothecary's wife, Win, that longed to see the
anatomy, Win? Or the lady, Win, that desired to spit i' the great
lawyer's mouth after an eloquent pleading? I assure you they   15
longed, Win; good Win, go in, and long.
      [*Exeunt Littlewit and Win*]

TRASH I think we are rid of our new customer, brother Leatherhead;
we shall hear no more of him.
      They plot to be gone

LEATHERHEAD All the better; let's pack up all and be gone before he find us.   20

TRASH Stay a little, yonder comes a company; it may be we may take some more money.

[*Enter Knockem, Busy*]

KNOCKEM Sir, I will take your counsel, and cut my hair, and leave vapours. I see that tobacco, and bottle-ale, and pig, and Whit, and very Ursula herself, is all vanity.   25

BUSY Only pig was not comprehended in my admonition; the rest were. For long hair, it is an ensign of pride, a banner, and the world is full of those banners, very full of banners. And bottle-ale is a drink of Satan's, a diet-drink of Satan's, devised to puff us up and make us swell in this latter age° of vanity, as the smoke   30 of tobacco to keep us in mist and error. But the fleshly woman which you call Ursula is above all to be avoided, having the marks upon her of the three enemies of man the world, as being in the Fair; the devil, as being in the fire; and the flesh, as being herself.   35

[*Enter Dame Purecraft*]

PURECRAFT Brother Zeal-of-the-land! What shall we do? My daughter Win-the-fight is fallen into her fit of longing again.

BUSY For more pig? There is no more, is there?

PURECRAFT To see some sights i' the Fair.

BUSY Sister, let her fly the impurity of the place, swiftly, lest she   40 partake of the pitch thereof. Thou art the seat of the Beast,° O Smithfield, and I will leave thee. Idolatry peepeth out on every side of thee.

KNOCKEM [*aside*] An excellent right hypocrite! Now his belly is full, he falls a-railing and kicking, the jade. A very good vapour! I'll in,   45 and joy Ursula with telling how her pig works; two and a half he eat to his share. And he has drunk a pailful. He eats with his eyes as well as his teeth.

[*Exit Knockem*]

LEATHERHEAD What do you lack, gentlemen? What is't you buy? Rattles, drums, babies—   50

BUSY Peace, with thy apocryphal wares, thou profane publican: thy bells, thy dragons, and thy Toby's dogs.° Thy hobby-horse is an idol, a very idol, a fierce and rank idol; and thou the Nebuchad-nezzar,° the proud Nebuchadnezzar of the Fair, that set'st it up for children to fall down to and worship.   55

LEATHERHEAD Cry you mercy, sir, will you buy a fiddle to fill up
    your noise?
        [*Enter Littlewit, Win*]
LITTLEWIT Look Win; do look o' God's name, and save your
    longing. Here be fine sights.
PURECRAFT Aye child, so you hate 'em, as our brother Zeal does,   60
    you may look on 'em.
LEATHERHEAD Or what do you say to a drum, sir?
BUSY It is the broken belly of the Beast, and thy bellows there are
    his lungs, and these pipes are his throat, those feathers are of his
    tail, and thy rattles the gnashing of his teeth.   65
TRASH And what's my gingerbread, I pray you?
BUSY The provender that pricks him up. Hence with thy basket of
    popery, thy nest of images, and whole legend° of gingerwork.
LEATHERHEAD Sir, if you be not quiet the quicklier, I'll ha' you
    clapped fairly by the heels for disturbing the Fair.   70
BUSY The sin of the Fair provokes me; I cannot be silent.
PURECRAFT Good brother Zeal!
LEATHERHEAD Sir, I'll make you silent, believe it.
LITTLEWIT I'd give a shilling you could, i'faith, friend.
LEATHERHEAD Sir, give me your shilling; I'll give you my shop if I   75
    do not, and I'll leave it in pawn with you i' the meantime.
LITTLEWIT A match i' faith, but do it quickly, then.
        [*Exit Leatherhead*]
BUSY Hinder me not, woman. (*He speaks to the widow*) I was moved
    in spirit to be here this day in this Fair, this wicked and foul Fair
    and fitter may it be called a foul than a Fair—to protest against the   80
    abuses of it, the foul abuses of it, in regard of the afflicted saints
    that are troubled, very much troubled, exceedingly troubled, with
    the opening of the merchandise of Babylon again, and the peeping
    of popery upon the stalls, here, here, in the high places.° See you
    not Goldilocks, the purple strumpet, there? In her yellow gown   85
    and green sleeves? The profane pipes, the tinkling timbrels? A
    shop of relics!
LITTLEWIT Pray you forbear, I am put in trust with 'em.
BUSY And this idolatrous grove of images, this flasket of idols, which
    I will pull down—   90
        Overthrows the gingerbread
TRASH O my ware, my ware, God bless it!
BUSY In my zeal, and glory to be thus exercised.

Leatherhead enters with officers

LEATHERHEAD Here he is. Pray you lay hold on his zeal; we cannot sell a whistle, for him, in tune. Stop his noise first!

BUSY Thou canst not; 'tis a sanctified noise. I will make a loud and 95 most strong noise, till I have daunted the profane enemy. And for this cause—

LEATHERHEAD Sir, here's no man afraid of you or your cause. You shall swear it i' the stocks, sir.

BUSY I will thrust myself into the stocks, upon the pikes of the land. 100

LEATHERHEAD Carry him away.

PURECRAFT What do you mean, wicked men?

BUSY Let them alone; I fear them not

[Exit Busy with officers followed by Dame Purecraft]

LITTLEWIT Was not this shilling well ventured, Win, for our liberty? Now we may go play, and see over the Fair, where we list, 105 ourselves. My mother is gone after him, and let her e'en go, and loose us.

WIN Yes John, but I know not what to do.

LITTLEWIT For what, Win?

WIN For a thing I am ashamed to tell you, i'faith, and 'tis too far to 110 go home.

LITTLEWIT I pray thee be not ashamed, Win. Come, i'faith thou shalt not be ashamed. Is it anything about the hobby-horse man? An't be, speak freely.

WIN Hang him, base bobchin, I scorn him. No, I have very great, 115 what sha'call'um, John.

LITTLEWIT O! Is that all, Win? We'll go back to Captain Jordan to the pig-woman's, Win. He'll help us, or she with a dripping pan, or an old kettle, or something. The poor greasy soul loves you, Win, and after we'll visit the Fair all over, Win, and see my puppet 120 play, Win; you know it's a fine matter, Win.

[Exeunt Littlewit and Win]

LEATHERHEAD Let's away; I counselled you to pack up afore, Joan.

TRASH A pox of his Bedlam purity. He has spoiled half my ware; but the best is, we lose nothing if we miss our first merchant.

LEATHERHEAD It shall be hard for him to find or know us when we 125 are translated, Joan.

[Exeunt]

4.1

[Enter] Trouble-all, Bristle, Haggis, Cokes [and] Justice Overdo

TROUBLE-ALL My masters, I do make no doubt but you are officers.

BRISTLE What then, sir?

TROUBLE-ALL And the King's loving and obedient subjects.

BRISTLE Obedient, friend? Take heed what you speak, I advise you;
Oliver° Bristle advises you. His loving subjects, we grant you, but   5
not his obedient, at this time, by your leave. We know ourselves a
little better than so; we are to command, sir, and such as you are
to be obedient. Here's one of his obedient subjects going to the
stocks, and we'll make you such another, if you talk.

TROUBLE-ALL You are all wise enough i' your places, I know.   10

BRISTLE If you know it, sir, why do you bring it in question?

TROUBLE-ALL I question nothing, pardon me. I do only hope you
have warrant for what you do, and so, quit you, and so, multiply
you.°

He goes away again

HAGGIS What's he? Bring him up to the stocks there. Why bring you   15
him not up?

[Trouble-all] comes again

TROUBLE-ALL If you have Justice Overdo's warrant, 'tis well; you
are safe; that is the warrant of warrants. I'll not give this button
for any man's warrant else.

BRISTLE Like enough, sir, but let me tell you, an you play away your   20
buttons thus, you will want 'em ere night, for any store I see about
you. You might keep 'em, and save pins, I wusse.

[Trouble-all] goes away

JUSTICE *[aside]* What should he be, that doth so esteem and advance
my warrant? He seems a sober and discreet person! It is a comfort
to a good conscience to be followed with a good fame in his   25
sufferings. The world will have a pretty taste by this, how I can
bear adversity; and it will beget a kind of reverence toward me
hereafter, even from mine enemies, when they shall see I carry my
calamity nobly, and that it doth neither break me nor bend me.

HAGGIS Come, sir, here's a place for you to preach in. Will you put   30
in your leg?

They put him in the stocks

JUSTICE That I will, cheerfully.

BRISTLE O' my conscience, a seminary! He kisses the stocks.

COKES Well, my masters, I'll leave him with you; now I see him bestowed, I'll go look for my goods and Numps.   35

HAGGIS You may, sir, I warrant you; where's the t'other bawler? Fetch him too; you shall find 'em both fast enough.

    [Exit Cokes]

JUSTICE *[aside]* In the midst of this tumult, I will yet be the author of mine own rest, and not minding their fury, sit in the stocks in that calm as shall be able to trouble a triumph.   40

TROUBLE-ALL *(comes again)* Do you assure me upon your words? May I undertake for you, if I be asked the question, that you have this warrant?

HAGGIS What's this fellow, for God's sake?

TROUBLE-ALL Do but show me Adam Overdo, and I am satisfied.   45

    Goes out

BRISTLE He is a fellow that is distracted, they say, one Trouble-all. He was an officer in the Court of Piepowders here last year, and put out on° his place by Justice Overdo.

JUSTICE *[aside]* Ha!

BRISTLE Upon which he took an idle conceit, and's run mad upon't.   50
So that ever since, he will do nothing but by Justice Overdo's warrant: he will not eat a crust, nor drink a little, nor make him in his apparel: ready. His wife, sir-reverence, cannot get him make his water or shift his shirt without his warrant.

JUSTICE *[aside]* If this be true, this is my greatest disaster! How   55
am I bound to satisfy this poor man, that is of so good a nature to me, out of his wits, where there is no room left for dissembling!

TROUBLE-ALL *(comes in)* If you cannot show me Adam Overdo, I am in doubt of you; I am afraid you cannot answer it.

    Goes again

HAGGIS Before me, neighbour Bristle, and now I think on't better,   60
Justice Overdo is a very parantory person.

BRISTLE O! Are you advised of that? And a severe justicer, by your leave.

JUSTICE *[aside]* Do I hear ill o' that side, too?

BRISTLE He will sit as upright o' the bench, an you mark him, as a   65
candle i' the socket, and give light to the whole court in every business.

HAGGIS But he will burn blue,° and swell like a bile (God bless us) an he be angry.

BRISTLE Aye, and he will be angry too, when he list, that's more; 70
and when he is angry, be it right or wrong, he has the law on's
side ever. I mark that too.

JUSTICE [*aside*] I will be more tender hereafter. I see compassion may
become a Justice, though it be a weakness, I confess, and nearer a
vice than a virtue. 75

HAGGIS Well, take him out o' the stock again. We'll go a sure way
to work; we'll ha' the ace of hearts of our side, if we can.

They take the Justice out. [*Enter Poacher, Busy and Purecraft*]

POACHER Come, bring him away to his fellow, there. Master Busy,
we shall rule your legs, I hope, though we cannot rule your tongue.

BUSY No, minister of darkness, no, thou canst not rule my tongue, 80
my tongue it is mine own, and with it I will both knock and mock
down your Bartholomew abominations, till you be made a hissing
to the neighbour parishes round about.

HAGGIS Let him alone; we have devised better upon't.

PURECRAFT And shall he not into the stocks then? 85

BRISTLE No, mistress, we'll have 'em both to Justice Overdo, and let
him do over 'em as is fitting. Then I and my gossip Haggis and
my beadle Poacher are discharged.

PURECRAFT I thank you, blessed, honest men!

BRISTLE Nay, never thank us, but thank this madman that comes 90
here; he put it in our heads.

[*Trouble-all*] *comes again*

PURECRAFT Is he mad? Now heaven increase his madness, and bless
it, and thank it; sir, your poor handmaid thanks you.

TROUBLE-ALL Have you a warrant? An you have a warrant, show it.

PURECRAFT Yes, I have a warrant out of the Word, to give thanks 95
for removing any scorn intended to the brethren.

TROUBLE-ALL It is Justice Overdo's warrant that I look for. If you have
not that, keep your word, I'll keep mine. Quit ye, and multiply ye.

[*Exeunt all but Trouble-all*]

4.2

[*Enter*] *Edgworth* [*and*] *Nightingale*

EDGWORTH Come away Nightingale, I pray thee.

TROUBLE-ALL Whither go you? Where's your warrant?

EDGWORTH Warrant? For what, sir?

TROUBLE-ALL For what you go about; you know how fit it is. An you
   have no warrant, bless you, I'll pray for you; that's all I can do.   5
      Goes out
EDGWORTH What means he?
NIGHTINGALE A madman that haunts the Fair; do you not know
   him? It's marvel he has not more followers after his ragged heels.
EDGWORTH Beshrew him, he startled me. I thought he had known
   of our plot. Guilt's a terrible thing! Ha' you prepared the   10
   costermonger?
NIGHTINGALE Yes, and agreed for his basket of pears; he is at the
   corner here, ready. And your prize, he comes down, sailing that
   way, all alone, without his protector; he is rid of him, it seems.
EDGWORTH Aye, I know; I should ha' followed his protectorship for   15
   a feat I am to do upon him, but this offered itself so i' the way, I
   could not let it 'scape. Here he comes. Whistle! Be this sport called
   'Dorring the Dotterel'.°
      [*Enter Cokes*]
NIGHTINGALE (*whistles*) Wh, wh, wh, wh, etc.
COKES By this light, I cannot find my gingerbread-wife nor my   20
   hobby-horse man in all the Fair, now, to ha' my money again. And
   I do not know the way out on't, to go home for more. Do you hear,
   friend, you that whistle? What tune is that you whistle?
NIGHTINGALE A new tune I am practising, sir.
COKES Dost thou know where I dwell, I pray thee? Nay, on with thy   25
   tune, I ha' no such haste for an answer. I'll practise with thee.
      [*Enter Costermonger*]
COSTERMONGER Buy any pears, very fine pears, pears fine!
      Nightingale sets his foot afore him, and he falls with his basket
COKES Gods so! A muss, a muss, a muss, a muss.
COSTERMONGER Good gentleman, my ware, my ware! I am a poor
   man. Good sir, my ware.   30
NIGHTINGALE [*to Cokes*] Let me hold your sword, sir, it troubles
   you.
COKES Do, and my cloak, an thou wilt; and my hat too.
      *Cokes falls a-scrambling whilst [Edgworth and Nightingale] run
      away with his things*
EDGWORTH A delicate great boy! Methinks he out-scrambles 'em all.
   I cannot persuade myself, but he goes to grammar-school yet, and   35
   plays the truant today.
NIGHTINGALE Would he had another purse to cut, Zekiel.

EDGWORTH Purse? A man might cut out his kidneys, I think, and he
    never feel 'em, he is so earnest at the sport.

NIGHTINGALE His soul is halfway out on's body at the game.   40

EDGWORTH Away, Nightingale; that way!

    [*Exit Nightingale*]

COKES I think I am furnished for Catherine pears for one undermeal.
    Gi' me my cloak.

COSTERMONGER Good gentleman, give me my ware.

COKES Where's the fellow I ga' my cloak to? My cloak? And my hat?   45
    Ha! God's lid, is he gone? Thieves, thieves! Help me to cry,
    gentlemen.

    He runs out

EDGWORTH Away, costermonger, come to us to Ursula's.

    [*Exit Costermonger*]

    Talk of him to have a soul? 'Heart, if he have any more than a
    thing given him instead of salt, only to keep him from stinking,   50
    I'll be hanged afore my time, presently. Where should it be, trow?
    In his blood? He has not so much toward it in his whole body as
    will maintain a good flea; and if he take this course, he will not ha'
    so much land left as to rear a calf within this twelvemonth. Was
    there ever green plover so pulled?° That his little overseer had   55
    been here now, and been but tall enough to see him steal pears in
    exchange for his beaver-hat and his cloak thus! I must go find him
    out next, for his black box and his patent (it seems) he has of his
    place, which I think the gentleman would have a reversion° of, that
    spoke to me for it so earnestly.   60

    [*Exit Edgworth. Cokes*] *comes again*

COKES Would I might lose my doublet, and hose, too, as I am an
    honest man, and never stir, if I think there be anything but
    thieving and cozening i' this whole Fair. Bartholomew Fair, quoth
    he; an ever any Bartholomew had that luck in't that I have had,
    I'll be martyred for him, and in Smithfield,° too. I ha' paid for my   65
    pears; a rot on 'em, I'll keep 'em no longer. (*Throws away his
    pears*). You were choke-pears to me; I had been better ha' gone to
    mumchance for you, I wusse. Methinks the Fair should not have
    used me thus; an 'twere but for my name's sake, I would not ha'
    used a dog o' the name so. O, Numps will triumph now!   70

    Trouble-all comes again

    Friend, do you know who I am? Or where I lie? I do not myself,
    I'll be sworn. Do but carry° me home, and I'll please thee; I ha'

money enough there. I ha' lost myself, and my cloak and my hat,
and my fine sword, and my sister, and Numps, and Mistress Grace
(a gentlewoman that I should ha' married) and a cutwork handker-   75
cher she ga' me, and two purses today. And my bargain o'
hobby-horses and gingerbread, which grieves me worst of all.

TROUBLE-ALL By whose warrant, sir, have you done all this?

COKES Warrant? Thou art a wise fellow, indeed—as if a man need a
warrant to lose anything with.   80

TROUBLE-ALL Yes, Justice Overdo's warrant a man may get and lose
with; I'll stand to't.

COKES Justice Overdo? Dost thou know him? I lie there, he is my
brother-in-law; he married my sister. Pray thee show me the way.
Dost thou know the house?   85

TROUBLE-ALL Sir, show me your warrant; I know nothing without
a warrant, pardon me.

COKES Why, I warrant thee. Come along, thou shalt see. I have
wrought pillows there, and cambric sheets, and sweet bags° too.
Pray thee guide me to the house.   90

TROUBLE-ALL Sir, I'll tell you; go you thither yourself, first, alone;
tell your worshipful brother your mind; and but bring me three
lines of his hand, or his clerk's, with 'Adam Overdo' underneath.
Here I'll stay you; I'll obey you, and I'll guide you presently.

COKES [aside] 'Slid, this is an ass; I ha' found him. Pox upon me,   95
what do I talking to such a dull fool? Farewell. You are a very
coxcomb, do you hear?

TROUBLE-ALL I think I am. If Justice Overdo sign to it, I am, and
so we are all; he'll quit us all, multiply us all.

[Exeunt]

4.3

[Enter] Grace, [and] Quarlous [and] Winwife with their swords
drawn

GRACE Gentlemen, this is no way that you take: you do but breed
one another trouble and offence, and give me no contentment at
all. I am no she that affects to be quarrelled for, or have my name
or fortune made the question of men's swords.

QUARLOUS 'Sblood, we love you.   5

GRACE If you both love me, as you pretend, your own reason will tell
you but one can enjoy me; and to that point there leads a directer

line, than by my infamy, which must follow if you fight. 'Tis true,
I have professed it to you ingenuously, that rather than to be yoked
with this bridegroom is appointed me, I would take up any   10
husband, almost upon any trust. Though subtlety would say to me,
I know, he is a fool, and has an estate, and I might govern him and
enjoy a friend° beside. But these are not my aims; I must have a
husband I must love, or I cannot live with him. I shall ill make one
of these politic wives!   15

WINWIFE Why, if you can like either of us, lady, say which is he,
    and the other shall swear instantly to desist.

QUARLOUS Content, I accord to that willingly.

GRACE Sure you think me a woman of an extreme levity, gentlemen,
    or a strange fancy, that, meeting you by chance in such a place as   20
    this, both at one instant, and not yet of two hours' acquaintance,
    neither of you deserving afore the other of me, I should so forsake
    my modesty (though I might affect one more particularly) as to
    say, 'This is he' and name him.

QUARLOUS Why, wherefore should you not? What should hinder   25
    you?

GRACE If you would not give it to my modesty, allow it yet to my
    wit; give me so much of woman and cunning as not to betray
    myself impertinently. How can I judge of you so far as to a choice
    without knowing you more? You are both equal and alike to me   30
    yet—and so indifferently affected by me as each of you might be
    the man if the other were away. For you are reasonable creatures:
    you have understanding and discourse. And if fate send me an
    understanding husband, I have no fear at all but mine own
    manners shall make him a good one.   35

QUARLOUS Would I were put forth to making° for you, then.

GRACE It may be you are; you know not what's toward you. Will you
    consent to a motion of mine, gentlemen?

WINWIFE Whatever it be, we'll presume reasonableness, coming
    from you.   40

QUARLOUS And fitness, too.

GRACE I saw one of you buy a pair of tables, e'en now.

WINWIFE Yes, here they be, and maiden ones too, unwritten in.

GRACE The fitter for what they may be employed in. You shall write,
    either of you,° here, a word, or a name—what you like best—but   45
    of two, or three syllables at most; and the next person that comes
    this way (because Destiny has a high hand in business of this
    nature) I'll demand which of the two words he or she doth

approve; and according to that sentence, fix my resolution and
affection without change.   50

QUARLOUS Agreed. My word is conceived already.

WINWIFE And mine shall not be long creating after.

GRACE But you shall promise, gentlemen, not to be curious to know,
which of you, it is, taken; but give me leave to conceal that till you
have brought me either home, or where I may safely tender myself.   55

WINWIFE Why, that's but equal.

QUARLOUS We are pleased.

GRACE Because I will bind both your endeavours to work together,
friendly and jointly, each to the other's fortune, and have myself fitted
with some means to make him that is forsaken a part of amends.   60

QUARLOUS These conditions are very courteous. Well, my word is
out of the *Arcadia*, then: 'Argalus'.°

WINWIFE And mine out of the play: 'Palemon'.°

> *Trouble-all comes again*

TROUBLE-ALL Have you any warrant for this, gentlemen?

QUARLOUS, WINWIFE Ha!   65

TROUBLE-ALL There must be a warrant had, believe it.

WINWIFE For what?

TROUBLE-ALL For whatsoever it is, anything indeed, no matter
what.

QUARLOUS 'Slight, here's a fine ragged prophet, dropped down i' the   70
nick!

TROUBLE-ALL Heaven quit you, gentlemen.

QUARLOUS Nay, stay a little. Good lady, put him to the question.

GRACE You are content, then?

WINWIFE, QUARLOUS Yes, yes.   75

GRACE Sir, here are two names written—

TROUBLE-ALL Is Justice Overdo one?

GRACE How, sir? I pray you read 'em to yourself—it is for a wager
between these gentlemen—and with a stroke or any difference,
mark which you approve best.   80

TROUBLE-ALL They may be both worshipful names for aught, I
know, mistress, but Adam Overdo had been worth three of 'em, I
assure you, in this place; that's in plain English.

GRACE This man amazes me! I pray you, like one of 'em, sir.

TROUBLE-ALL I do like him there, that has the best warrant.   85
Mistress, to save your longing (and multiply him) it may be this.
[*Marks the book*] But I am aye still for Justice Overdo, that's my
conscience. And quit you.

[*Exit Trouble-all*]

WINWIFE Is't done, lady?

GRACE Aye, and strangely as ever I saw! What fellow is this, trow?   90

QUARLOUS No matter what, a fortune-teller we ha' made him. Which is't, which is't?

GRACE Nay, did you not promise, not to enquire?

QUARLOUS 'Slid, I forgot that; pray you pardon me. Look, here's our Mercury come; the licence arrives i' the finest time, too! 'Tis but   95
scraping out Cokes his name, and 'tis done.

[*Enter Edgworth*]

WINWIFE How now lime-twig? Hast thou touched?

EDGWORTH Not yet, sir; except you would go with me and see't, it's not worth speaking on. The act is nothing without a witness. Yonder he is, your man with the box fallen into the finest   100
company, and so transported with vapours; they ha' got in a northern clothier, and one Puppy, a western man, that's come to wrestle before my Lord Mayor,° anon, and Captain Whit, and one Val Cutting, that helps Captain Jordan to roar, a circling boy,° with whom your Numps is so taken, that you may strip him of his   105
clothes, if you will. I'll undertake to geld him for you, if you had but a surgeon ready to sear him. And Mistress Justice there, is the goodest woman! She does so love 'em all over, in terms of justice and the style of authority, with her hood upright—that I beseech you come away, gentlemen, and see't.   110

QUARLOUS 'Slight, I would not lose it for the Fair; what'll you do, Ned?

WINWIFE Why, stay here about for you; Mistress Wellborn must not be seen.

QUARLOUS Do so, and find out a priest i' the meantime; I'll bring the licence. [*To Edgworth*] Lead, which way is't?   115

EDGWORTH Here, sir, you are o' the backside o' the booth already; you may hear the noise.

[*Exeunt*]

4.4

[*Enter*] *Knockem, Northern, Puppy, Cutting, Whit, Wasp* [*and*]
Mistress Overdo

KNOCKEM Whit, bid Val Cutting continue the vapours for a lift,°
Whit, for a lift.

NORTHERN I'll ne mare, I'll ne mare, the eale's too meeghty.

KNOCKEM How now! My Galloway nag, the staggers? Ha! Whit, gi'
him a slit i' the forehead. Cheer up, man; a needle and thread to
stitch his ears. I'd cure him now, an I had it, with a little butter
and garlic, long-pepper, and grains. Where's my horn? I'll gi' him
a mash, presently, shall take away this dizziness.

PUPPY Why, where are you, zurs? Do you vlinch and leave us i' the
zuds,° now?

NORTHERN I'll ne mare, I'is e'en as vull as a piper's bag, by my
troth, I.

PUPPY Do my northern cloth zhrink i' the wetting, ha?

KNOCKEM Why, well said, old flea-bitten, thou'lt never tire,° I see.

They fall to their vapours, again

CUTTING No, sir, but he may tire, if it please him.

WHIT Who told dee sho? That he vuld never teer, man?

CUTTING No matter who told him so, so long as he knows.

KNOCKEM Nay, I know nothing, sir, pardon me there.

[*Enter Edgworth and Quarlous*]

EDGWORTH [*to Quarlous*] They are at it still, sir, this they call
vapours.

WHIT He shall not pardon dee, Captain; dou shalt not be pardoned.
Pre'de shweetheart, do not pardon him.

CUTTING 'Slight, I'll pardon him, an I list, whosoever says nay to't.

QUARLOUS Where's Numps? I miss him.°

Here they continue their game of vapours, which is nonsense;
every man to oppose the last man that spoke, whether it
concerned him or no

WASP Why, I say nay to't.

QUARLOUS O there he is!

KNOCKEM To what do you say nay, sir?

WASP To anything, whatsoever it is, so long as I do not like it.

WHIT Pardon me, little man, dou musht like it a little.

CUTTING No, he must not like it at all, sir; there you are i' the wrong.

WHIT I tink I be; he musht not like it, indeed.

CUTTING Nay, then he both must and will like it, sir, for all you.

KNOCKEM If he have reason, he may like it, sir.

WHIT By no meansh, Captain, upon reason; he may like nothing
upon reason.

WASP I have no reason, nor I will hear of no reason, nor I will look
for no reason, and he is an ass that either knows any or looks for't
from me.

CUTTING Yes, in some sense you may have reason, sir.

WASP Aye, in some sense, I care not if I grant you.   40

WHIT Pardon me, thou ougsht to grant him nothing, in no shensh,
    if dou doe love dyshelf, angry man.

WASP Why then, I do grant him nothing; and I have no sense.

CUTTING 'Tis true, thou hast no sense indeed.

WASP 'Slid, but I have sense, now I think on't better, and I will grant   45
    him anything, do you see?

KNOCKEM He is i' the right, and does utter a sufficient vapour.

CUTTING Nay, it is no sufficient vapour, neither; I deny that.

KNOCKEM Then it is a sweet vapour.

CUTTING It may be a sweet vapour.   50

WASP Nay, it is no sweet vapour, neither, sir; it stinks, and I'll stand
    to't.

WHIT Yes, I tink it dosh shtink, Captain. All vapour dosh shtink.

WASP Nay, then it does not stink, sir, and it shall not stink.

CUTTING By your leave, it may, sir.   55

WASP Aye, by my leave, it may stink; I know that.

WHIT Pardon me, thou knowesht nothing; it cannot by thy leave,
    angry man.

WASP How can it not?

KNOCKEM Nay, never question him, for he is i' the right.   60

WHIT Yesh, I am i' de right, I confesh it; so ish de little man too.

WASP I'll have nothing confessed that concerns me. I am not in the
    right, nor never was i' the right, nor never will be i' the right, while
    I am in my right mind.

CUTTING Mind? Why, here's no man minds you, sir, nor anything   65
    else.

       They drink again

PUPPY Vriend, will you mind this that we do?

QUARLOUS [*to Edgworth*] Call you this vapours? This is such belching
    of quarrel as I never heard. Will you mind your business, sir?

EDGWORTH You shall see, sir.   70

NORTHERN I'll ne maire, my waimb warkes too mickle with this
    auready.

EDGWORTH Will you take that, Master Wasp, that nobody should
    mind you?

WASP Why? What ha' you to do? Is't any matter to you?   75

EDGWORTH No, but methinks you should not be unminded, though.

WASP Nor, I wu'not be, now I think on't; do you hear, new
    acquaintance, does no man mind me, say you?

CUTTING Yes, sir, every man here minds you, but how?

WASP Nay, I care as little how as you do; that was not my question.   80

WHIT No, noting was ty question; tou art a learned man, and I am a valiant man, i'faith la; tou shalt speak for me, and I vill fight for tee.

KNOCKEM Fight for him, Whit? A gross vapour; he can fight for himself.

WASP It may be I can, but it may be I wu'not, how then?   85

CUTTING Why, then you may choose.

WASP Why, and I'll choose whether I'll choose or no.

KNOCKEM I think you may, and 'tis true; and I allow it for a resolute vapour.

WASP Nay, then, I do think you do not think, and it is no resolute   90 vapour.

CUTTING Yes, in some sort he may allow you.

KNOCKEM In no sort, sir, pardon me, I can allow him nothing. You mistake the vapour.

WASP He mistakes nothing, sir, in no sort.   95

WHIT Yes, I pre dee now, let him mistake.

WASP A turd i' your teeth, neuer pre dee mee, for I will have nothing mistaken.

KNOCKEM Turd, ha, turd? A noisome vapour! Strike, Whit.

They fall by the ears. [Exit Edgworth with licence from box]

MISTRESS OVERDO Why, gentlemen, why gentlemen, I charge you   100 upon my authority, conserve the peace. In the King's name, and my husband's, put up your weapons. I shall be driven to commit you myself, else.

QUARLOUS Ha, ha, ha.

WASP Why do you laugh, sir?   105

QUARLOUS Sir, you'll allow me my Christian liberty. I may laugh, I hope.

CUTTING In some sort you may, and in some sort you may not, sir.

KNOCKEM Nay, in some sort, sir, he may neither laugh nor hope in this company.   110

WASP Yes, then he may both laugh and hope in any sort, an't please him.

QUARLOUS Faith, and I will then, for it doth please me exceedingly.

WASP No exceeding neither, sir.

KNOCKEM No, that vapour is too lofty.   115

QUARLOUS Gentlemen, I do not play well at your game of vapours; I am not very good at it, but—

CUTTING Do you hear, sir? I would speak with you in circle!
    He draws a circle on the ground
QUARLOUS In circle, sir? What would you with me in circle?
CUTTING Can you lend me a piece, a jacobus, in circle?   120
QUARLOUS 'Slid, your circle will prove more costly than your
    vapours, then. Sir, no, I lend you none.
CUTTING Your beard's not well turned up, sir.
QUARLOUS How, rascal? Are you playing with° my beard? I'll break
    circle with you.   125
    They draw all, and fight
PUPPY, NORTHERN Gentlemen, gentlemen!
KNOCKEM Gather up, Whit, gather up, Whit, good vapours.
    [*Knockem and Whit take the swords and cloaks. Exit Knockem
    with the stolen goods*]
MISTRESS OVERDO What mean you? Are you rebels? Gentlemen?
    Shall I send out a sergeant-at-arms or a writ o' rebellion against
    you? I'll commit you, upon my womanhood, for a riot, upon my   130
    justicehood, if you persist.
    [*Exeunt Quarlous, Cutting*]
WASP Upon your justice-hood? Marry, shit o' your hood! You'll
    commit? Spoke like a true Justice of Peace's wife, indeed, and a
    fine female lawyer! Turd i' your teeth for a fee, now.
MISTRESS OVERDO Why, Numps, in Master Overdo's name, I   135
    charge you.
WASP Good Mistress Underdo, hold your tongue.
MISTRESS OVERDO Alas! Poor Numps.
WASP Alas! And why alas from you, I beseech you? Or why poor
    Numps, Goody Rich?° Am I come to be pitied by your tuftaffeta   140
    now? Why mistress, I knew Adam, the clerk, your husband, when
    he was Adam scrivener, and writ for twopence a sheet, as high as
    he bears his head now, or you your hood, dame.
    The watch [Bristle and Poacher] comes in
    What are you, sir?
BRISTLE We be men, and no infidels. What is the matter here, and   145
    the noises? Can you tell?
WASP Heart, what ha' you to do? Cannot a man quarrel in quietness,
    but he must be put out on't by you? What are you?
BRISTLE Why, we be His Majesty's Watch, sir.
WASP Watch? 'Sblood, you are a sweet watch, indeed. A body would 150
    think, an you watched well o'nights, you should be contented to

sleep at this time o'day. Get you to your fleas and your flock-beds, you rogues, your kennels, and lie down close.

BRISTLE Down? Yes, we will down, I warrant you! Down with him in His Majesty's name, down, down with him, and carry him away   155
to the pigeon-holes!

    [Bristle and Poacher seize Wasp]

MISTRESS OVERDO I thank you, honest friends, in the behalf o' the Crown and the peace, and in Master Overdo's name, for suppressing enormities.

WHIT Stay, Bristle, here ish anoder brash o' drunkards [*points to*   160
Northern and Puppy], but very quiet, special drunkards, will pay dee five shillings very well. Take 'em to dee, in de graish o' God. One of 'em does change cloth for ale in the Fair here, te t'oder ish a strong man, a mighty man, my Lord Mayor's man, and a wrastler. He has wrashled so long with the bottle, here, that the   165
man with the beard° hash almosht streek up hish heelsh.

BRISTLE 'Slid, the Clerk o' the Market° has been to cry him all the Fair over, here, for my lord's° service.

WHIT Tere he ish, pre de taik him hensh, and make ty best on him.

    [Exeunt Bristle and Poacher with Wasp, Northern, and Puppy]

How now woman o' shilk, vat ailsh ty shweet faish? Art tou   170
melancholy?

MISTRESS OVERDO A little distempered with these enormities. Shall I entreat a courtesy of you, Captain?

WHIT Entreat a hundred, velvet voman, I vill do it; shpeak out.

MISTRESS OVERDO I cannot with modesty speak it out, but—   175

    [Whispers to him]

WHIT I vill do it, and more, and more, for dee. What, Ursula, an't be bitch, an't be bawd, an't be!

    [Enter Ursula]

URSULA How now, rascal? What roar you for, old pimp?

WHIT Here, put up de cloaks, Ursh; de purchase; pre dee now, shweet Ursh, help dis good brave voman to a jordan, an't be.   180

URSULA 'Slid, call your Captain Jordan to her, can you not?

WHIT Nay, pre dee leave dy consheits, and bring the velvet woman to de—

URSULA I bring her? Hang her! Heart, must I find a common pot for every punk i' your purlieus?   185

WHIT O good voordsh, Ursh; it ish a guest o' velvet, i'fait la.

URSULA Let her sell her hood and buy a sponge, with a pox to her. My vessel is employed, sir. I have but one, and 'tis the bottom of

an old bottle. An honest proctor and his wife are at it within; if
she'll stay her time, so.   190

WHIT As soon ash tou cansht, shwet Ursh. Of a valiant man I tink I
am the patientsh man i' the world, or in all Smithfield.

[*Exit Ursula. Enter Knockem*]

KNOCKEM How now Whit? Close vapours, stealing your leaps?
Covering in corners, ha?

WHIT No, fait, Captain, dough tou beesht a vishe man, dy vit is a   195
mile hence, now. I vas procuring a shmall courtesy for a woman
of fashion here.

MISTRESS OVERDO Yes, Captain, though I am Justice of Peace's
wife, I do love men of war and the sons of the sword, when they
come before my husband.   200

KNOCKEM Say'st thou so, filly? Thou shalt have a leap° presently,
I'll horse thee myself, else.

[*Enter Ursula*]

URSULA Come, will you bring her in now? And let her take her turn?

WHIT Gramercy, good Ursh, I tank dee.

MISTRESS OVERDO Master Overdo shall thank her.   205

[*Exit Mistress Overdo*]

4.5

[*Enter*] *Littlewit* [*and*] *Win*

LITTLEWIT Good Gammer Urs, Win and I are exceedingly beholden
to you, and to Captain Jordan and Captain Whit. Win, I'll be bold
to leave you i' this good company, Win; for half an hour or so,
Win, while I go; and see how my matter goes forward, and if the
puppets be perfect; and then I'll come and fetch you, Win.   5

WIN Will you leave me alone with two men, John?

LITTLEWIT Aye, they are honest gentlemen, Win, Captain Jordan
and Captain Whit; they'll use you very civilly, Win. God b'w'you,
Win.

[*Exit Littlewit*]

URSULA [*to Knockem and Whit*] What's her husband gone?   10

KNOCKEM On his false gallop, Urs, away.

URSULA An you be right Bartholomew-birds, now show yourselves
so: we are undone for want of fowl i' the Fair, here. Here will be
Zekiel Edgworth, and three or four gallants with him at night, and

I ha' neither plover nor quail° for 'em. Persuade this between you   15
two to become a bird o' the game, while I work the velvet woman
within (as you call her).

KNOCKEM I conceive thee, Urs! Go thy ways.

   [*Exit Ursula*]

Dost thou hear, Whit? Is't not pity my delicate dark chestnut
here—with the fine lean head, large forehead, round eyes, even   20
mouth, sharp ears, long neck, thin crest, close withers, plain back,
deep sides, short fillets, and full flanks: with a round belly, a plump
buttock, large thighs, knit knees, straight legs, short pasterns,
smooth hoofs, and short heels—should lead a dull honest woman's
life, that might live the life of a lady?   25

WHIT Yes, by my fait and trot, it is, Captain; de honest woman's life
is a scurvy dull life, indeed, la.

WIN How, sir? Is an honest woman's life a scurvy life?

WHIT Yes fait, shweetheart, believe him, de leef of a bondwoman!
But if dou vilt hearken to me, I vill make tee a free-woman and a   30
lady; dou shalt live like a lady, as te Captain saish.

KNOCKEM Aye, and be honest too, sometimes; have her wires and
her tires, her green gowns° and velvet petticoats.

WHIT Aye, and ride to Ware and Romford° i' dy coash, shee de
players, be in love vit 'em; sup vit gallantsh, be drunk, and cost de   35
noting.

KNOCKEM Brave vapours!

WHIT And lie by twenty on 'em, if dou pleash, shweetheart.

WIN What, and be honest still? That were fine sport.

WHIT Tish common, shweetheart; tou mayst do it, by my hand. It   40
shall be justified to ty husband's faish, now; tou shalt be as honest
as the skin between his hornsh, la!

KNOCKEM Yes, and wear a dressing, top and top-gallant,° to compare with e'er a husband on 'em all, for a fore-top. It is the vapour
of spirit in the wife to cuckold, nowadays, as it is the vapour of   45
fashion in the husband not to suspect. Your prying cat-eyed citizen
is an abominable vapour.

WIN Lord, what a fool have I been!

WHIT Mend then, and do everything like a lady hereafter; never
know ty husband from another man.   50

KNOCKEM Nor any one man from another, but i' the dark.

WHIT Aye, and then it ish no dishgrash to know any man.

   [*Enter Ursula*]

URSULA Help, help here!

KNOCKEM How now? What vapour's there?

URSULA O you are a sweet ranger, and look well to your walks!   55
Yonder is your punk of Turnbull, Ramping Alice, has fallen upon;
the poor gentlewoman within, and pulled her hood over her ears,
and her hair through it.

Alice enters, beating the Justice's wife

MISTRESS OVERDO Help, help, i' the King's name.

ALICE A mischief on you! They are such as you are that undo us,   60
and take our trade from us, with your tuftaffeta haunches.

KNOCKEM How now, Alice!

ALICE The poor common whores can ha' no traffic for the privy rich
ones; your caps and hoods of velvet call away our customers, and
lick the fat from us.   65

URSULA Peace you foul ramping jade, you—

ALICE Od's foot, you bawd in grease,° are you talking?

KNOCKEM Why, Alice, I say.

ALICE Thou sow of Smithfield, thou!

URSULA Thou tripe of Turnbull!   70

KNOCKEM Catamountain vapours! Ha!

URSULA You know where you were tawed lately, both lashed and
slashed you were in Bridewell.

ALICE Aye, by the same token, you rid that week, and broke out the
bottom o'the cart,° night-tub.   75

KNOCKEM Why, lion face! Ha! Do you know who I am? Shall I tear
ruff, slit waistcoat, make rags of petticoat? Ha! Go to, vanish, for
fear of vapours. Whit, a kick, Whit, in the parting vapour.

[Exit Alice, kicked by Knockem and Whit]

Come brave woman, take a good heart; thou shalt be a lady, too.

WHIT Yes fait, dey shal all both be ladies, and write Madam. I vill   80
do't myself for dem. *Do* is the vord, and *D* is the middle letter of
Madam DD, put 'em together and make deeds, without which all
words are alike, la.

KNOCKEM 'Tis true. Ursula, take 'em in, open thy wardrobe, and fit
'em to their calling. Green gowns, crimson petticoats, green   85
women! My Lord Mayor's green women! Guests o' the game, true
bred. I'll provide you a coach to take the air in.

WIN But do you think you can get one?

KNOCKEM O, they are as common as wheelbarrows where there are
great dunghills. Every pettifogger's wife has 'em, for first he buys   90
a coach that he may marry, and then he marries that he may be
made cuckold in't—for if their wives ride not to their cuckolding,

they do 'em no credit. Hide and be hidden, ride and be ridden, says the vapour of experience.

[*Exeunt Ursula, Win, Mistress Overdo*]

4.6

[*Enter*] *Trouble-all*

TROUBLE-ALL By what warrant does it say so?

KNOCKEM Ha! Mad child o' the Piepowders, art thou there? Fill us a fresh can, Urs; we may drink together.

TROUBLE-ALL I may not drink without a warrant, Captain.

KNOCKEM 'Sblood, thou'll not stale without a warrant, shortly.   5
Whit, give me pen, ink and paper. I'll draw him a warrant presently.

TROUBLE-ALL It must be Justice Overdo's.

KNOCKEM I know, man. Fetch the drink, Whit.

[*Knockem writes on a paper*]

WHIT I pre dee now, be very brief, Captain; for de new ladies stay   10
for dee.

KNOCKEM Oh, as brief as can be, here 'tis already. 'Adam Overdo.'

[*Gives paper to Trouble-all*]

TROUBLE-ALL Why, now I'll pledge you, Captain.

KNOCKEM Drink it off. I'll come to thee, anon, again.

[*Exeunt Knockem, Whit, Trouble-all. Enter Quarlous, Edgworth*]

QUARLOUS (*to the cutpurse*) Well, sir, you are now discharged; beware   15
of being spied hereafter.

EDGWORTH Sir, will it please you enter in here at Ursula's and take part° of a silken gown, a velvet petticoat, or a wrought smock? I am promised such, and I can spare any gentleman a moiety.

QUARLOUS Keep it for your companions in beastliness; I am none of   20
'em, sir. If I had not already forgiven you a greater trespass, or thought you yet worth my beating, I would instruct your manners, to whom you made your offers. But go your ways, talk not to me, the hangman is only fit to discourse with you; the hand of beadle is too merciful a punishment for your trade of life.   25

[*Exit Edgworth*]

I am sorry I employed this fellow, for he thinks me such: *facinus quos inquinat, aequat*.° But it was for sport. And would I make it serious, the getting of this licence is nothing to me, without other circumstances concur. I do think how impertinently I labour, if the word be not mine that the ragged fellow marked; and what advantage I have given Ned Winwife in this time now, of working her, though it be mine. He'll go near to form to her what a debauched rascal I am, and fright her out of all good conceit of me. I should do so by him, I am sure, if I had the opportunity. But my hope is in her temper, yet; and it must needs be next to despair, that is grounded on any part of a woman's discretion. I would give, by my troth, now, all I could spare, to my clothes and my sword, to meet my tattered soothsayer again, who was my judge i' the question, to know certainly whose word he has damned or saved—for till then I live but under a reprieve. I must seek him. Who be these?

Enter Wasp with the officers

WASP Sir, you are a Welsh cuckold, and a prating runt, and no constable.

BRISTLE You say very well. Come, put in his leg in the middle roundel,° and let him hole there.

WASP You stink of leeks, metheglin, and cheese, you rogue.

BRISTLE Why, what is that to you, if you sit sweetly in the stocks in the meantime? If you have a mind to stink too, your breeches sit close enough to your bum. Sit you merry, sir.

[They put him in the stocks]

QUARLOUS How now, Numps?

WASP It is no matter how; pray you look off.

QUARLOUS Nay, I'll not offend you, Numps. I thought you had sat there to be seen.

WASP And to be sold, did you not? Pray you mind your business, an you have any.

QUARLOUS Cry you mercy, Numps. Does your leg lie high enough?

[Enter Haggis]

BRISTLE How now, neighbour Haggis, what says Justice Overdo's worship to the other offenders?

HAGGIS Why, he says just nothing. What should he say? Or where should he say? He is not to be found, man. He ha' not been seen i' the Fair, here, all this livelong day, never since seven o'clock i' the morning. His clerks know not what to think on't. There is no court of Piepowders yet. Here they be returned.

[Enter officers with Busy and Justice Overdo]

BRISTLE What shall be done with 'em, then, in your discretion?

407

HAGGIS I think we were best put 'em in the stocks, in discretion   65
(there they will be safe in discretion) for the valour of an hour, or
such a thing, till his worship come.

BRISTLE It is but a hole matter, if we do, neighbour Haggis. [*To
Wasp*] Come, sir, here is company for you. Heave up the stocks.

WASP [*aside*] I shall put a trick upon your Welsh diligence, perhaps.   70
*As they open the stocks, Wasp puts his shoe on his hand, and
slips it in for his leg*

BRISTLE [*to Busy*] Put in your leg, sir.
They bring Busy, and put him in

QUARLOUS What, Rabbi Busy! Is he come?

BUSY I do obey thee; the lion may roar, but he cannot bite. I am glad
to be thus separated from the heathen of the land, and put apart   75
in the stocks for the holy cause.

WASP What are you, sir?

BUSY One that rejoiceth in his affliction, and sitteth here to prophesy
the destruction of fairs and May-games, wakes and Whitsun
ales,° and doth sigh and groan for the reformation of these abuses.   80
[*They put the Justice in*]

WASP [*to Overdo*] And do you sigh and groan too, or rejoice in your
affliction?

JUSTICE I do not feel it, I do not think of it; it is a thing without me.
Adam, thou art above these batteries, these contumelies. *In te
manca ruit fortuna*, as thy friend Horace says; thou art one, *quem   85
neque pauperies, neque mors, neque vincula terrent*. And therefore, as
another friend of thine says (I think it be thy friend Persius), *non
te quaesiveris extra*.°

QUARLOUS What's here? A Stoic i' the stocks? The fool is turned
philosopher.   90

BUSY Friend, I will leave to communicate my spirit with you, if I
hear any more of those superstitious relics, those lists of Latin, the
very rags of Rome and patches of Popery.

WASP Nay, an you begin to quarrel, gentlemen, I'll leave you. I ha'
paid for quarrelling too lately. Look you, a device, but shifting in   95
a hand for a foot. God b'w'you.
He gets out

BUSY Wilt thou then leave thy brethren in tribulation?

WASP For this once, sir.
[*Exit Wasp*]

BUSY Thou art a halting neutral—stay him there, stop him—that will
not endure the heat of persecution.   100

BRISTLE How now, what's the matter?

BUSY He is fled, he is fled, and dares not sit it out.

BRISTLE What, has he made an escape? Which way? Follow, neighbour Haggis.

      [Exeunt Bristle and Haggis. Enter Dame Purecraft]   105

PURECRAFT O me! In the stocks! Have the wicked prevailed?

BUSY Peace, religious sister; it is my calling, comfort yourself, an
extraordinary calling, and done for my better standing, my surer
standing hereafter.

    The madman enters

TROUBLE-ALL By whose warrant, by whose warrant, this?

QUARLOUS O, here's my man, dropped in, I looked for.   110

JUSTICE Ha!

PURECRAFT O good sir, they have set the faithful here to be
wondered at, and provided holes for the holy of the land.

TROUBLE-ALL Had they warrant for it? Showed they Justice Overdo's hand? If they had no warrant, they shall answer it.   115

      [Enter Bristle and Haggis]

BRISTLE Sure you did not lock the stocks sufficiently, neighbour Toby!

HAGGIS No? See if you can lock 'em better.

BRISTLE *[checks the lock]* They are very sufficiently locked, and truly,
yet something is in the matter.

TROUBLE-ALL True, your warrant is the matter that is in question;   120
by what warrant?

BRISTLE Madman, hold your peace. I will put you in his room else,
in the very same hole, do you see?

QUARLOUS *[aside]* How? Is he a madman?

TROUBLE-ALL Show me Justice Overdo's warrant, I obey you.   125

HAGGIS You are a mad fool; hold your tongue.

      [Exeunt Bristle and Haggis]

TROUBLE-ALL In Justice Overdo's name, I drink to you, and here's
my warrant.

    Shows his can

JUSTICE *[aside]* Alas, poor wretch! How it earns my heart° for him!

QUARLOUS *[aside]* If he be mad, it is in vain to question him. I'll try   130
though. *[To Trouble-all]* Friend, there was a gentlewoman showed
you two names, some hour since, Argalus and Palemon, to mark
in a book. Which of 'em was it you marked?

TROUBLE-ALL I mark no name but Adam Overdo; that is the name
of names. He only is the sufficient magistrate, and that name I   135
reverence show it me.

QUARLOUS [*aside*] This fellow's mad indeed: I am further off, now, than afore.

JUSTICE [*aside*] I shall not breathe in peace till I have made him some amends.   140

QUARLOUS [*aside*] Well, I will make another use of him, is come in my head; I have a nest of beards in my trunk,° one something like his.

[*Exit Quarlous.*] *The watchmen come back again*

BRISTLE This mad fool has made me that I know not whether I have locked the stocks or no; I think I locked 'em.   145

[*Checks the lock*]

TROUBLE-ALL Take Adam Overdo in your mind, and fear nothing.

BRISTLE 'Slid, madness itself. Hold thy peace, and take that.

[*Strikes him*]

TROUBLE-ALL Strikest thou without a warrant? Take thou that.

The madman fights with 'em, and they leave open the stocks

BUSY We are delivered by miracle; fellow in fetters, let us not refuse the means; this madness was of the spirit. The malice of the enemy 150
hath mocked itself.

[*Exeunt Justice Overdo and Busy*]

PURECRAFT Mad do they call him? The world is mad in error, but he is mad in truth. I love him o' the sudden (the cunning man said all true) and shall love him more and more. How well it becomes a man to be mad in truth! O that I might be his yoke-fellow, and 155
be mad with him! What a many should we draw to madness in truth with us!

[*Exit Trouble-all.*] *The watch, missing them, are affrighted*

BRISTLE How now? All 'scaped? Where's the woman? It is witch-craft! Her velvet hat is a witch, o' my conscience, or my key, t'one!° The madman was a devil and I am an ass; so bless me, my 160
place, and mine office.

[*Exeunt*]

5.1

[Enter] Leatherhead, Filcher [and] Sharkwell. [They begin to erect a puppet theatre]

LEATHERHEAD Well, luck and Saint Bartholomew! Out with the sign of our invention,° in the name of wit, and do you beat the drum the while. All the fowl i' the Fair, I mean all the dirt in Smithfield, (that's one of Master Littlewit's carwhitchets now) will be thrown at our banner today, if the matter does not please the people. O 5 the motions that I, Lantern Leatherhead, have given light to i' my time, since my Master Pod° died! *Jerusalem* was a stately thing, and so was *Nineveh*, and *The City of Norwich*, and *Sodom and Gomorrah*; with the rising o' the prentices; and pulling down the bawdy houses there, upon Shrove Tuesday; but *The Gunpowder* 10 *Plot*,° there was a get-penny! I have presented that to an eighteen- or twenty-pence audience nine times in an afternoon. Your home-born projects prove ever the best; they are so easy and familiar. They put too much learning i' their things nowadays, and that I fear will be the spoil o' this. Littlewit? I say, Mickle- 15 wit! If not too mickle! Look to your gathering there, goodman Filcher.

FILCHER I warrant you, sir.

LEATHERHEAD An there come any gentlefolks, take twopence a piece, Sharkwell. 20

SHARKWELL I warrant you, sir, threepence an we can.

[Exeunt]

5.2

The Justice comes in like a porter

JUSTICE This later disguise I have borrowed of a porter shall carry me out to all my great and good ends, which, however interrupted, were never destroyed in me. Neither is the hour of my severity yet come, to reveal myself, wherein, cloud-like, I will break out in rain and hail, lightning and thunder, upon the head of enormity. Two 5 main works I have to prosecute: first, one is to invent some satisfaction for the poor kind wretch who is out of his wits for my sake—and yonder I see him coming. I will walk aside and project for it.

[Enter Winwife, Grace]

WINWIFE I wonder where Tom Quarlous is, that he returns not; it may be he is struck° in here to seek us.

GRACE See, here's our madman again.

[Enter Quarlous]

QUARLOUS *[aside]* I have made myself as like him as his gown and cap will give me leave.

[Enter Dame Purecraft]

PURECRAFT Sir, I love you, and would be glad to be mad with you in truth.

Quarlous in the habit of the madman is mistaken by Mistress Purecraft

WINWIFE How! My widow in love with a madman?

PURECRAFT Verily, I can be as mad in spirit as you.

QUARLOUS By whose warrant? Leave your canting. *[To Grace]* Gentlewoman, have I found you?—Save ye, quit ye, and multiply ye—Where's your book? 'Twas a sufficient name I marked, let me see't, be not afraid to show't me.

He desires to see the book of Mistress Grace

GRACE What would you with it, sir?

QUARLOUS Mark it again and again, at your service.

GRACE Here it is, sir; this was it you marked.

QUARLOUS 'Palemon'? Fare you well, fare you well.

WINWIFE How, Palemon!

GRACE Yes, faith, he has discovered it to you now, and therefore 'twere vain to disguise it longer; I am yours, sir, by the benefit of your fortune.

WINWIFE And you have him, Mistress, believe it, that shall never give you cause to repent her benefit, but make you rather to think that in this choice she had both her eyes.°

GRACE I desire to put it to no danger of protestation.

[Exeunt Grace and Winwife]

QUARLOUS *[aside]* Palemon the word, and Winwife the man?

PURECRAFT Good sir, vouchsafe a yokefellow in your madness; shun not one of the sanctified sisters, that would draw with you in truth.

QUARLOUS Away, you are a herd of hypocritical proud ignorants, rather wild than mad fitter for woods and the society of beasts than houses and the congregation of men. You are the second part° of the society of canters, outlaws to order and discipline, and the only

privileged church-robbers° of Christendom. Let me alone. [*Aside*]
Palemon the word, and Winwife the man?

PURECRAFT [*aside*] I must uncover myself unto him, or I shall never
enjoy him, for all the cunning men's promises. Good sir, hear me,   45
I am worth six thousand pound; my love to you is become my rack;
I'll tell you all, and the truth, since you hate the hypocrisy of the
parti-coloured° brotherhood. These seven years I have been a
wilful holy widow, only to draw feasts and gifts from my entangled
suitors. I am also by office an assisting sister of the deacons, and a   50
devourer, instead of a distributer, of the alms. I am a special maker
of marriages for our decayed brethren with our rich widows, for a
third part of their wealth, when they are married, for the relief of
the poor elect; as also our poor handsome young virgins with our
wealthy bachelors or widowers to make them steal from their   55
husbands when I have confirmed them in the faith, and got all put
into their custodies. And if I ha' not my bargain, they may sooner
turn a scolding drab into a silent minister° than make me leave
pronouncing reprobation and damnation unto them. Our elder,
Zeal-of-the-Land, would have had me, but I know him to be the   60
capital knave of the land, making himself rich by being made
feoffee in trust° to deceased brethren, and cozening their heirs by
swearing the absolute gift° of their inheritance. And thus having
eased my conscience and uttered my heart with the tongue of my
love, enjoy all my deceits together, I beseech you. I should not   65
have revealed this to you, but that in time I think you are mad,
and I hope you'll think me so too, sir.

QUARLOUS Stand aside, I'll answer you presently. (*He considers with
himself of it*) Why should not I marry this six thousand pound, now
I think on't? And a good trade too, that she has beside, ha? The   70
t'other wench Winwife is sure of; there's no expectation for me
there! Here I may make myself some saver, yet, if she continue
mad—there's the question. It is money that I want; why should I
not marry the money, when 'tis offered me? I have a licence and
all; it is but razing out one name and putting in another. There's   75
no playing with a man's fortune! I am resolved! I were truly mad
an I would not! [*To Dame Purecraft*] Well, come your ways, follow
me; an you will be mad, I'll show you a warrant!
        He takes her along with him
PURECRAFT Most zealously it is that I zealously desire.
        The Justice calls him
JUSTICE Sir, let me speak with you.   80

QUARLOUS By whose warrant?

JUSTICE The warrant that you tender and respect so; Justice Overdo's! I am the man, friend Trouble-all, though thus disguised (as
the careful magistrate ought) for the good of the republic, in the
Fair, and the weeding out of enormity. Do you want a house or   85
meat or drink or clothes? Speak whatsoever it is, it shall be
supplied you. What want you?

QUARLOUS Nothing but your warrant.

JUSTICE My warrant? For what?

QUARLOUS To be gone, sir.   90

JUSTICE Nay, I pray thee stay. I am serious, and have not many
words, nor much time to exchange with thee; think what may do
thee good.

QUARLOUS Your hand and seal will do me a great deal of good;
nothing else in the whole Fair, that I know.   95

JUSTICE If it were to any end, thou should'st have it willingly.

QUARLOUS Why, it will satisfy me; that's end enough to look on; an
you will not gi' it me, let me go.

JUSTICE Alas! Thou shalt ha' it presently: I'll but step into the
scrivener's hereby, and bring it. Do not go away.   100

(*The Justice goes out*)

QUARLOUS [*aside*] Why, this madman's shape will prove a very
fortunate one, I think! Can a ragged robe produce these effects? If
this be the wise Justice, and he bring me his hand, I shall go near
to make some use on't.

And [*the Justice*] *returns*

He is come already!   105

JUSTICE Look thee! Here is my hand and seal, Adam Overdo; if there
be anything to be written above in the paper, that thou want'st
now, or at any time hereafter, think on't; it is my deed, I deliver
it so. Can your friend write?

QUARLOUS Her hand for a witness, and all is well.   110

JUSTICE With all my heart.

He urgeth Mistress Purecraft

QUARLOUS [*aside*] Why should not I ha' the conscience to make this
a bond of a thousand pound, now? Or what I would else?

JUSTICE Look you, there it is; and I deliver it as my deed again.

QUARLOUS Let us now proceed in madness.   115

He takes her in with him

JUSTICE Well, my conscience is much eased; I ha' done my part;
though it doth him no good, yet Adam hath offered satisfaction!

The sting is removed from hence. Poor man, he is much altered
with his affliction; it has brought him low! Now for my other work,
reducing the young man I have followed so long in love from the   120
brink of his bane to the centre of safety. Here, or in some such like
vain place, I shall be sure to find him. I will wait the good time.

5.3

[Enter] Cokes, Sharkwell [and] Filcher

COKES How now? What's here to do? Friend, art thou the master of
the monuments?°

SHARKWELL 'Tis a motion, an't please your worship.

JUSTICE *[aside]* My fantastical brother-in-law, Master Bartholomew
Cokes!   5

COKES A motion, what's that? (*He reads the Bill*) 'The ancient
modern history of Hero and Leander, otherwise called *The Touchstone of true Love*, with as true a trial of friendship between Damon
and Pythias,° two faithful friends o' the Bankside?'° Pretty i' faith;
what's the meaning on't? Is't an interlude? Or what is't?   10

FILCHER Yes, sir, please you come near, we'll take your money
within.

The boys o' the Fair follow him

COKES Back with these children; they do so follow me up and down.

[Enter Littlewit]

LITTLEWIT By your leave, friend.

FILCHER You must pay, sir, an you go in.   15

LITTLEWIT Who, I? I perceive thou know'st not me. Call the master
o' the motion.

SHARKWELL What, do you not know the author, fellow Filcher? You
must take no money of him; he must come in *gratis*. Master
Littlewit is a voluntary; he is the author.   20

LITTLEWIT Peace, speak not too loud; I would not have any notice
taken that I am the author till we see how it passes.

COKES Master Littlewit, how dost thou?

LITTLEWIT Master Cokes! You are exceeding well met. What, in
your doublet and hose, without a cloak or a hat?   25

COKES I would I might never stir, as I am an honest man, and by
that fire;° I have lost all i' the Fair, and all my acquaintance too.
Didst thou meet anybody that I know, Master Littlewit? My man

Numps, or my sister Overdo, or Mistress Grace? Pray thee,
Master Littlewit, lend me some money to see the interlude here.   30
I'll pay thee again, as I am a gentleman. If thou'lt but carry me
home, I have money enough there.

LITTLEWIT O sir, you shall command it. What, will a crown serve
you?

COKES I think it will. What do we pay for coming in, fellows?   35

FILCHER Twopence, sir.

COKES Twopence? There's twelvepence, friend; nay, I am a gallant,
as simple as I look now, if you see me with my man about me, and
my artillery again.

LITTLEWIT Your man was i' the stocks e'en now, sir.   40

COKES Who, Numps?

LITTLEWIT Yes, faith.

COKES For what, i'faith? I am glad o' that; remember to tell me on't
anon; I have enough now! What manner of matter is this, Master
Littlewit? What kind of actors ha' you? Are they good actors?   45

LITTLEWIT Pretty youths, sir, all children, both old and young;
here's the master of 'em—
      [*Enter Leatherhead*]

LEATHERHEAD (*whispers to Littlewit*) Call me not Leatherhead, but
Lantern.°

LITTLEWIT Master Lantern, that gives light to the business.   50

COKES In good time,° sir, I would fain see 'em; I would be glad to
drink with the young company. Which is the tiring-house?

LEATHERHEAD Troth, sir, our tiring-house is somewhat little; we are
but beginners yet, pray pardon us; you cannot go upright in't.

COKES No? Not now my hat is off? What would you have done with   55
me if you had had me feather and all, as I was once today? Ha'you
none of your pretty impudent boys now, to bring stools, fill
tobacco, fetch ale, and beg money, as they have at other houses?
Let me see some o' your actors.

LITTLEWIT Show him 'em, show him 'em. Master Lantern, this is a   60
gentleman that is a favourer of the quality.

JUSTICE [*aside*] Aye, the favouring of this licentious quality is the
consumption of many a young gentleman; a pernicious enormity.

COKES What, do they live in baskets?
      He [*Leatherhead*] *brings them out in a basket*

LEATHERHEAD They do lie in a basket, sir; they are o' the small   65
players.

COKES These be players minors, indeed. Do you call these players?

LEATHERHEAD They are actors, sir, and as good as any, none dispraised, for dumb shows; indeed, I am the mouth of 'em all!

COKES Thy mouth will hold 'em all. I think one Taylor would go near to beat all this company, with a hand bound behind him.

LITTLEWIT Aye, and eat 'em all, too, an' they were in cakebread.

COKES I thank you for that, Master Littlewit, a good jest! Which is your Burbage now?

LEATHERHEAD What mean you by that, sir?

COKES Your best actor. Your Field?°

LITTLEWIT Good i'faith! You are even with me, sir.

LEATHERHEAD This is he that acts young Leander, sir. He is extremely beloved of the womenkind, they do so affect his action, the green gamesters° that come here; and this is lovely Hero; this with the beard, Damon; and this, pretty Pythias; this is the ghost of King Dionysius° in the habit of a scrivener,° as you shall see anon, at large.

COKES Well, they are a civil company, I like 'em for that. They offer not to fleer, nor jeer, nor break jests, as the great players do. And then there goes not so much charge to the feasting of 'em or making 'em drunk as to the other, by reason of their littleness. Do they use to play perfect? Are they never flustered?

LEATHERHEAD No, sir. I thank my industry and policy for it; they are as well governed a company, though I say it—And here is young Leander, is as proper an actor of his inches; and shakes his head like an ostler.

COKES But do you play it according to the printed book?° I have read that.

LEATHERHEAD By no means, sir.

COKES No? How then?

LEATHERHEAD A better way, sir; that is too learned and poetical for our audience. What do they know what Hellespont is? 'Guilty of true love's blood'? Or what Abydos is? Or 'the other Sestos° hight'?

COKES Th'art i' the right; I do not know myself.

LEATHERHEAD No, I have entreated Master Littlewit to take a little pains to reduce it to a more familiar strain for our people.

COKES How, I pray thee, good Master Littlewit?

LITTLEWIT It pleases him to make a matter of it, sir. But there is no such matter, I assure you. I have only made it a little easy and modern for the times, sir, that's all; as, for the Hellespont, I imagine our Thames here; and then Leander, I make a dyer's son,

about Puddle Wharf;° and Hero a wench o' the Bankside, who
going over one morning to old Fish Street,° Leander spies her land   110
at Trig Stairs,° and falls in love with her. Now do I introduce
Cupid, having metamorphosed himself into a drawer, and he
strikes Hero in love with a pint of sherry, and other pretty passages
there are o' the friendship, that will delight you, sir, and please
you of judgement.   115

COKES I'll be sworn they shall; I am in love with the actors already,
and I'll be allied to them presently. (They respect gentlemen, these
fellows.) Hero shall be my fairing; but which of my fairings? Le'me
see—i'faith, my fiddle! And Leander my fiddle-stick; then Damon
my drum, and Pythias my pipe, and the ghost of Dionysius, my   120
hobby-horse. All fitted.

5.4

[Enter] Winwife [and] Grace

WINWIFE Look, yonder's your Cokes gotten in among his playfel-
lows; I thought we could not miss him at such a spectacle.

GRACE Let him alone, he is so busy, he will never spy us.

LEATHERHEAD Nay, good sir.
        Cokes is handling the puppets

COKES I warrant thee, I will not hurt her, fellow; what, dost think   5
me uncivil? I pray thee, be not jealous; I am toward a wife.

LITTLEWIT Well, good Master Lantern, make ready to begin, that I
may fetch my wife; and look you be prefect—you undo me else i'
my reputation.

LEATHERHEAD I warrant you, sir. Do not you breed too great an   10
expectation of it; among your friends that's the only hurter of these
things.

LITTLEWIT No, no, no.
        [Exit Littlewit]

COKES I'll stay here and see; pray thee let me see.

WINWIFE How diligent and troublesome he is!   15

GRACE The place becomes him, methinks.

JUSTICE *[aside]* My ward, Mistress Grace, in the company of a
stranger? I doubt I shall be compelled to discover myself before
my time!

[*Enter Knockem, Whit, Edgworth, Win, Mistress Overdo, the ladies masked*]

The doorkeepers speak

FILCHER Twopence a piece, gentlemen, an excellent motion.   20

KNOCKEM Shall we have fine fireworks, and good vapours?

SHARKWELL Yes, Captain, and waterworks too.

WHIT I pree dee, take a care o' dy shmall lady, there, Edgworth; I will look to dish tall lady myself.

LEATHERHEAD Welcome, gentlemen; welcome gentlemen.   25

WHIT Predee, mashter o' de monshtersh, help a very sick lady, here, to a chair to shit in.

LEATHERHEAD Presently, sir.

They bring Mistress Overdo a chair

WHIT Good fait now, Ursula's ale, and aqua-vitae ish to blame for't; shit down, shweetheart, shit down, and shleep a little.   30

EDGWORTH [*to Win*] Madam, you are very welcome hither.

KNOCKEM Yes, and you shall see very good vapours.

JUSTICE [*aside*] (*by° Edgworth*) Here is my care come! I like to see him in so good company, and yet I wonder that persons of such fashion should resort hither!   35

EDGWORTH This is a very private house,° madam.

The cutpurse courts Mistress Littlewit

LEATHERHEAD Will it please your ladyship sit, madam?

WIN Yes, goodman. They do so all-to-be-madam° me, I think they think me a very lady!

EDGWORTH What else, madam?   40

WIN Must I put off my mask to him?

EDGWORTH O, by no means.

WIN How should my husband know me, then?

KNOCKEM Husband? An idle vapour. He must not know you, nor you him; there's the true vapour.   45

JUSTICE [*aside*] Yea, I will observe more of this. [*To Whit*] Is this a lady, friend?

WHIT Aye, and dat is anoder lady, shweetheart; if dou hasht a mind to 'em, give me twelvepence from tee, and dou shalt have eder-oder on 'em!   50

JUSTICE [*aside*] Aye? This will prove my chiefest enormity. I will follow this.

EDGWORTH Is not this a finer life, lady, than to be clogged with a husband?

WIN Yes, a great deal. When will they begin, trow, in the name o'   55
the motion?

EDGWORTH By and by, madam, they stay but for company.

KNOCKEM Do you hear, puppet master, these are tedious vapours;
when begin you?

LEATHERHEAD We stay but for Master Littlewit, the author, who is   60
gone for his wife; and we begin presently.

WIN That's I, that's I.

EDGWORTH That was you, lady; but now you are no such poor thing.

KNOCKEM Hang the author's wife, a running vapour! Here be ladies
will stay for ne'er a Delia° o' 'em all.   65

WHIT But hear me now, here ish one o' de ladish ashleep; stay till
she but vake, man.

    [Enter Wasp]

WASP How now, friends? What's here to do?

    The doorkeepers [speak] again

FILCHER Twopence apiece, sir, the best motion in the Fair.

WASP I believe you lie; if you do, I'll have my money again and beat   70
you.

WINWIFE Numps is come!

WASP Did you see a master of mine come in here, a tall young squire
of Harrow o' the Hill, Master Bartholomew Cokes?

FILCHER I think there be such a one within.   75

WASP Look he be, you were best; but it is very likely. I wonder I
found him not at all the rest. I ha' been at the eagle, and the black
wolf, and the bull with the five legs and two pizzles (he was a calf
at Uxbridge Fair, two years agone), and at the dogs that dance the
morris, and the hare o' the tabor,° and missed him at all these!   80
Sure this must needs be some fine sight that holds him so, if it
have him.

COKES Come, come, are you ready now?

LEATHERHEAD Presently, sir.

WASP Hoyday, he's at work in his doublet and hose. Do you   85
hear, sir? Are you employed, that you are bareheaded, and so
busy?

COKES Hold your peace, Numps; you ha' been i' the stocks, I hear.

WASP Does he know that? Nay, then the date of my authority is out;
I must think no longer to reign, my government is at an end. He   90
that will correct another must want fault in himself.

WINWIFE Sententious Numps! I never heard so much from him
before.

LEATHERHEAD Sure, Master Littlewit will not come. Please you take
 your place, sir, we'll begin.   95
COKES I pray thee do, mine ears long to be at it, and my eyes too.
 O Numps, i' the stocks, Numps? Where's your sword, Numps?
WASP I pray you intend your game, sir, let me alone.
COKES Well, then, we are quit for all. Come, sit down, Numps; I'll
 interpret to thee. Did you see Mistress Grace? It's no matter,   100
 neither, now I think on't; tell me anon.
WINWIFE A great deal of love and care he expresses.
GRACE Alas! Would you have him to express more than he has?
 That were tyranny.
   [*The curtains of the puppet theatre open*]
COKES Peace, ho; now, now.   105
LEATHERHEAD *Gentles, that no longer your expectations may wander,*
 Behold our chief actor, amorous Leander,
 With a great deal of cloth, lapped about him like a scarf,
 For he yet serves his father, a dyer at Puddle Wharf,
 Which place we'll make bold with, to call it our Abydos,   110
 As the Bankside is our Sestos, and let it not be denied us.
 Now, as he is beating, to make the dye take the fuller,°
 Who chances to come by, but fair Hero *in a sculler?*
 And seeing Leander's naked leg and goodly calf,
 Cast at him, from the boat, a sheep's eye and a half.   115
 Now she is landed, and the sculler come back;
 By and by, you shall see what Leander *doth lack.*
PUPPET LEANDER *Cole, Cole, old Cole.*
LEATHERHEAD *That is the sculler's name without control.*
PUPPET LEANDER *Cole, Cole, I say, Cole.*   120
LEATHERHEAD *We do hear you.*
PUPPET LEANDER *Old Cole.*
LEATHERHEAD *Old Cole? Is the dyer turned collier? How do you sell?*°
PUPPET LEANDER *A pox o' your manners, kiss my hole here, and smell.*
LEATHERHEAD *Kiss your hole and smell? There's manners indeed.*   125
PUPPET LEANDER *Why, Cole, I say, Cole.*
LEATHERHEAD *It's the sculler you need!*
PUPPET LEANDER *Aye, and be hanged.*
LEATHERHEAD *Be hanged? Look you yonder,*
 Old Cole, you must go hang with Master Leander.   130
PUPPET COLE *Where is he?*
PUPPET LEANDER *Here, Cole. What fairest of fairs*
 Was that fare that thou landedst but now at Trig-stairs?

COKES What was that, fellow? Pray thee tell me; I scarce understand
'em.   135

LEATHERHEAD Leander does ask, sir, *what fairest of fairs*
Was the fare that he landed but now at Trig-stairs?

PUPPET COLE *It is lovely Hero.*

PUPPET LEANDER *Nero?*

PUPPET COLE *No, Hero.*   140

LEATHERHEAD *It is Hero.*
Of the Bankside, he saith, to tell you truth without erring,
Is come over into Fish Street to eat some fresh herring.
Leander says no more, but as fast as he can,
Gets on all his best clothes, and will after to the Swan.°   145

COKES Most admirable good, is't not?

LEATHERHEAD *Stay, sculler.*

PUPPET COLE *What say you?*

LEATHERHEAD *You must stay for Leander,*
And carry him to the wench.   150

PUPPET COLE *You rogue, I am no pandar.*

COKES He says he is no pandar. 'Tis a fine language; I understand it
now.

LEATHERHEAD *Are you no pandar, Goodman Cole? Here's no man says*
you are.   155
You'll grow a hot Cole, it seems; pray you stay for your fare.

PUPPET COLE *Will he come away?*

LEATHERHEAD *What do you say?*

PUPPET COLE *I'd ha' him come away.*

LEATHERHEAD *Would you ha' Leander come away? Why pray, sir, stay.*   160
You are angry, Goodman Cole; I believe the fair maid
Came over wi' you a' trust. Tell us sculler, are you paid?

PUPPET COLE *Yes, Goodman Hogrubber o' Pict-hatch.*°

LEATHERHEAD *How, Hogrubber o' Pict-hatch?*

PUPPET COLE *Aye Hogrubber o' Pict-hatch. Take you that.*   165
           The puppet strikes him over the pate

LEATHERHEAD *O, my head!*

PUPPET COLE *Harm watch, harm catch.*°

COKES 'Harm watch, harm catch', he says. Very good i' faith; the
sculler had like to ha' knocked you, sirrah.   170

LEATHERHEAD Yes, but that his fare called him away.

PUPPET LEANDER *Row apace, row apace, row, row, row, row, row.*

LEATHERHEAD *You are knavishly loaden, sculler, take heed where you go.*

PUPPET COLE *Knave i' your face, Goodman Rogue.*

PUPPET LEANDER *Row, row, row, row, row, row.*   175

COKES He said 'knave i' your face', friend.

LEATHERHEAD Aye, sir, I heard him. But there's no talking to these
watermen, they will ha' the last word.

COKES God's my life! I am not allied to the sculler, yet; he shall be
Dauphin my boy.° But my fiddle-stick° does fiddle in and out too   180
much; I pray thee speak to him on't; tell him, I would have him
tarry in my sight more.

LEATHERHEAD I pray you be content; you'll have enough on him, sir.
Now gentles, I take it, here is none of you so stupid,
But that you have heard of a little god of love, called Cupid;   185
Who out of kindness to Leander, hearing he but saw her,
This present day and hour, doth turn himself to a drawer.
And because he would have their first meeting to be merry,
He strikes Hero in love to him, with a pint of sherry.
Which he tells her from amorous Leander is sent her,   190
Who after him into the room of Hero doth venture.

> Puppet Leander goes into Mistress Hero's room
> [Enter Puppet Jonas, the drawer]

PUPPET JONAS *A pint of sack, score a pint of sack i' the Coney°.*

COKES Sack? You said but e'en now it should be sherry.°

PUPPET JONAS *Why so it is; sherry, sherry, sherry.*

COKES 'Sherry, sherry, sherry'. By my troth he makes me merry. I   195
must have a name for Cupid too. Let me see, thou mightst help
me now, an thou wouldest, Numps, at a dead lift,° but thou art
dreaming o' the stocks still! Do not think on't, I have forgot it.
'Tis but a nine days' wonder, man; let it not trouble thee.

WASP I would the stocks were about your neck, sir; condition I° hung   200
by the heels in them till the wonder were off from you, with all
my heart.

COKES Well said, resolute Numps. But hark you, friend, where is the
friendship, all this while, between my drum, Damon, and my pipe,
Pythias?   205

LEATHERHEAD You shall see by and by, sir.

COKES You think my hobby-horse is forgotten° too. No, I'll see 'em
all enact before I go; I shall not know which to love best, else.

KNOCKEM This gallant has interrupting vapours, troublesome
vapours, Whit; puff with him.   210

WHIT No, I pre dee, Captain, let him alone. He is a child i'faith, la.

LEATHERHEAD *Now, gentles, to the friends, who in number are two,*
And lodged in that ale-house, in which fair Hero, does do.

Damon (for some kindness done him the last week)
Is come fair Hero, in Fish Street, this morning to seek: 215
Pythias does smell the knavery of the meeting,
And now you shall see their true friendly greeting.

PUPPET PYTHIAS *You whoremasterly slave, you.*

COKES 'Whoremasterly slave, you'? Very friendly and familiar, that.

PUPPET DAMON *Whore-master i' thy face,*   220
  Thou hast lain with her thyself, I'll prove't i' this place.

COKES Damon says Pythias has lain with her himself; he'll prove't in
  this place.

LEATHERHEAD *They are whoremasters both, sir that's a plain case.*

PUPPET PYTHIAS *You lie like a rogue.*   225

LEATHERHEAD *Do I lie like a rogue?*

PUPPET PYTHIAS *A pimp and a scab.*

LEATHERHEAD *A pimp and a scab?*
  I say between you, you have both but one drab.

PUPPET DAMON *You lie again.*   230

LEATHERHEAD *Do I lie again?*

PUPPET DAMON *Like a rogue again.*

LEATHERHEAD *Like a rogue again?*

PUPPET PYTHIAS *And you are a pimp again.*

COKES 'And you are a pimp again', he says.   235

PUPPET DAMON *And a scab again.*

COKES 'And a scab again', he says.

LEATHERHEAD *And I say again, you are both whore-masters again,*
  And you have both but one drab again.

         [Leatherhead and the puppets] fight

PUPPETS DAMON AND PYTHIAS *Dost thou, dost thou, dost thou?*   240

LEATHERHEAD *What, both at once?*

PUPPET PYTHIAS *Down with him, Damon.*

PUPPET DAMON *Pink his guts, Pythias.*

LEATHERHEAD *What, so malicious?*
  Will ye murder me, masters, both, i' mine own house?   245

COKES Ho! Well acted my drum, well acted my pipe, well acted still.

WASP Well acted, with all my heart.

LEATHERHEAD *Hold, hold your hands.*

COKES Aye, both your hands, for my sake! For you ha' both done
  well.   250

PUPPET DAMON *Gramercy, pure Pythias.*

PUPPET PYTHIAS *Gramercy, dear Damon.*

COKES Gramercy to you both, my pipe and my drum.

PUPPETS DAMON AND PYTHIAS *Come now, we'll together to break-*
 fast to Hero. 255
LEATHERHEAD 'Tis well, you can now go to breakfast to Hero.
 You have given me my breakfast, with a hone and honero.°
COKES How is't friend, ha' they hurt thee?
LEATHERHEAD O, no!
 Between you and I, sir, we do but make show. 260
 Thus, gentles, you perceive, without any denial,
 'Twixt Damon and Pythias here, friendship's true trial.
 Though hourly they quarrel thus, and roar each with other,
 They fight you no more than does brother with brother.
 But friendly together, at the next man they meet, 265
 They let fly their anger, as here you might see't.
COKES Well, we have seen't, and thou hast felt it, whatsoever thou
 sayest. What's next? What's next?
LEATHERHEAD *This while young Leander with fair Hero is drinking,*
 And Hero grown drunk, to any man's thinking! 270
 Yet was it not three pints of sherry could flaw her,
 Till Cupid, distinguished like Jonas the drawer,
 From under his apron, where his lechery lurks,
 Put love in her sack. Now mark how it works.
PUPPET HERO *O Leander, Leander, my dear, my dear Leander,* 275
 I'll for ever be thy goose, so thou'lt be my gander.
COKES Excellently well said, fiddle! She'll ever be his goose, so he'll
 be her gander; was't not so?
LEATHERHEAD Yes, sir, but mark his answer, now.
PUPPET LEANDER *And sweetest of geese, before I go to bed,* 280
 I'll swim o'er the Thames, my goose, thee to tread.
COKES Brave! He will swim o'er the Thames and tread his goose
 tonight, he says.
LEATHERHEAD Aye, peace, sir, they'll be angry if they hear you
 eavesdropping, now they are setting their match.° 285
PUPPET LEANDER *But lest the Thames should be dark, my goose, my*
 dear friend,
 Let thy window be provided of a candle's end.
PUPPET HERO *Fear not, my gander, I protest I should handle*
 My matters very ill, if I had not a whole candle. 290
PUPPET LEANDER *Well then, look to't, and kiss me to boot.*
LEATHERHEAD *Now, here comes the friends again, Pythias and*
 Damon,
   Damon and Pythias enter

And under their cloaks, they have of bacon, a gammon.

PUPPET PYTHIAS *Drawer, fill some wine here.*   295

LEATHERHEAD *How, some wine there?*
   There's company already, sir, pray forbear!

PUPPET DAMON *'Tis Hero.*

LEATHERHEAD *Yes, but she will not be taken,*
   After sack and fresh herring, with your Dunmow bacon.°   300

PUPPET PYTHIAS *You lie, it's Westfabian.*

LEATHERHEAD *'Westphalian'° you should say.*

PUPPET DAMON *If you hold not your peace, you are a coxcomb, I*
   would say.

      Leander and Hero are kissing

PUPPET PYTHIAS *What's here? What's here? Kiss, kiss upon kiss.*   305

LEATHERHEAD *Aye, wherefore should they not? What harm is in this?*
   'Tis Mistress Hero.

PUPPET DAMON *Mistress Hero's a whore.*

LEATHERHEAD *Is she a whore? Keep you quiet, or, sir knave, out of door.*

PUPPET DAMON *Knave out of door?*   310

PUPPET HERO *Yes, knave, out of door.*

      Here the puppets quarrel and fall together by the ears

PUPPET DAMON *Whore out of door.*

PUPPET HERO *I say, knave, out of door.*

PUPPET DAMON *I say, whore, out of door.*

PUPPET PYTHIAS *Yea, so say I too.*   315

PUPPET HERO *Kiss the whore o' the arse.*

LEATHERHEAD *Now you ha' something to do:*
   You must kiss her o' the arse, she says.

PUPPETS DAMON AND PYTHIAS *So we will, so we will.*
      [They kick her]

PUPPET HERO *O my haunches, o my haunches, hold, hold.*   320

LEATHERHEAD *Stand'st thou still?*
   Leander, where art thou? Stand'st thou still like a sot,
   And not offer'st to break both their heads with a pot?
   See who's at thine elbow, there! Puppet Jonas and Cupid.

PUPPET JONAS *Upon 'em Leander, be not so stupid.*   325

PUPPET LEANDER *You goat-bearded slave!*
      They fight

PUPPET DAMON *You whoremaster knave*

PUPPET LEANDER *Thou art a whoremaster.*

PUPPET JONAS *Whoremasters all.*

LEATHERHEAD *See, Cupid with a word has ta'en up the brawl.*   330

KNOCKEM These be fine vapours!

COKES By this good day they fight bravely! Do they not, Numps?

WASP Yes, they lacked but you to be their second, all this while.

LEATHERHEAD *This tragical encounter, falling out thus to busy us,*
   It raises up the ghost of their friend Dionysius,   335
   Not like a monarch, but the master of school,°
   In a scrivener's furred gown, which shows he is no fool,
   For therein he hath wit enough to keep himself warm.
   'O Damon', he cries, 'and Pythias, what harm,
   Hath poor Dionysius done you in his grave,   340
   That after his death, you should fall out thus, and rave,
   All call amorous Leander whoremaster knave?'

PUPPET DIONYSIUS *I cannot, I will not, I promise you, endure it.*

5.5

   [Enter Busy]

BUSY Down with Dagon,° down with Dagon! 'Tis I will no longer endure your profanations.

LEATHERHEAD What mean you, sir?

BUSY I will remove Dagon there, I say, that idol, that heathenish idol, that remains, as I may say, a beam, a very beam, not a beam   5 of the sun, nor a beam of the moon, nor a beam of a balance, neither a house-beam nor a weaver's beam, but a beam in the eye,° in the eye of the brethren; a very great beam, an exceeding great beam; such as are your stage-players, rhymers and morris-dancers, who have walked hand in hand, in contempt of the brethren and   10 the cause, and been borne out by instruments of no mean countenance.°

LEATHERHEAD Sir, I present nothing but what is licensed by authority.

BUSY Thou art all license, even licentiousness itself, Shimei!°   15

LEATHERHEAD I have the Master of the Revels'° hand for't, sir.

BUSY The Master of the Rebels' hand, thou hast—Satan's! Hold thy peace; thy scurrility shut up thy mouth. Thy profession is damnable, and in pleading for it, thou dost plead for Baal.° I have long opened my mouth wide and gaped, I have gaped as the oyster   20 for the tide, after thy destruction, but cannot compass it by suit or dispute; so that I look for a bickering ere long, and then a battle.

KNOCKEM Good Banbury-vapours.

COKES Friend, you'd have an ill match on't if you bicker with him here; though he be no man o' the fist, he has friends that will go to cuffs for him. Numps, will not you take our side? 25

EDGWORTH Sir, it shall not need; in my mind, he offers him a fairer course—to end it by disputation! Hast thou nothing to say for thyself in defence of thy quality?

LEATHERHEAD Faith, sir, I am not well studied in these controversies between the hypocrites and us. But here's one of my motion, Puppet Dionysius, shall undertake him, and I'll venture the cause on't. 30

COKES Who? My hobby-horse? Will he dispute with him?

LEATHERHEAD Yes, sir, and make a hobby-ass of him, I hope. 35

COKES That's excellent! Indeed he looks like the best scholar of 'em all. Come, sir, you must be as good as your word now.

BUSY I will not fear to make my spirit and gifts known! Assist me zeal; fill me, fill me, that is, make me full.

WINWIFE What a desperate, profane wretch is this! Is there any ignorance, or impudence like his? To call his zeal to fill him against a puppet? 40

QUARLOUS I know no fitter match than a puppet to commit with an hypocrite!

BUSY First, I say unto thee, idol, thou hast no calling. 45

PUPPET DIONYSIUS *You lie, I am called Dionysius.*

LEATHERHEAD The motion says you lie; he is called Dionysius i' the matter, and to that calling he answers.

BUSY I mean no vocation, idol, no present lawful calling.

PUPPET DIONYSIUS *Is yours a lawful calling?* 50

LEATHERHEAD The motion asketh if yours be a lawful calling?

BUSY Yes, mine is of the spirit.

PUPPET DIONYSIUS *Then idol is a lawful calling.*

LEATHERHEAD He says, then idol is a lawful calling! For you called him idol, and your calling is of the spirit. 55

COKES Well disputed, hobby-horse!

BUSY Take not part with the wicked, young gallant. He neigheth and hinnyeth; all is but hinnying sophistry. I call him idol again. Yet, I say, his calling, his profession is profane, it is profane, idol.

PUPPET DIONYSIUS *It is not profane!* 60

LEATHERHEAD It is not profane, he says.

BUSY It is profane.

PUPPET DIONYSIUS *It is not profane.*

BUSY It is profane.

PUPPET DIONYSIUS *It is not profane.* 65

LEATHERHEAD Well said, confute him with 'not', still. You cannot bear him down with your base noise, sir.

BUSY Nor he me, with his treble creaking,° though he creak like the chariot wheels of Satan; I am zealous for the cause—

LEATHERHEAD As a dog for a bone. 70

BUSY And I say it is profane, as being the page of Pride, and the waiting woman of Vanity.

PUPPET DIONYSIUS *Yea? What say you to your tire-women, then?*

LEATHERHEAD Good.

PUPPET DIONYSIUS *Or feather-makers i' the Friars, that are o' your* 75 *faction of faith?° Are not they with their perukes and their puffs, their fans and their huffs, as much pages of Pride and waiters upon Vanity? What say you? What say you? What say you?*

BUSY I will not answer for them.

PUPPET DIONYSIUS *Because you cannot, because you cannot. Is a* 80 *bugle-maker a lawful calling? Or the confect-makers? Such you have there. Or your French fashioner? You'd have all the sin within yourselves, would you not? Would you not?*

BUSY No, Dagon.

PUPPET DIONYSIUS *What then, Dagonet?° Is a puppet worse than these?* 85

BUSY Yes, and my main argument against you is that you are an abomination; for the male among you putteth on the apparel of the female, and the female of the male.°

PUPPET DIONYSIUS *You lie, you lie, you lie abominably.*

COKES Good, by my troth, he has given him the lie thrice. 90

PUPPET DIONYSIUS *It is your old stale argument against the players, but it will not hold against the puppets, for we have neither male nor female° amongst us. And that thou may'st see, if thou wilt, like a malicious purblind zeal as thou art!*

    The puppet takes up his garment

EDGWORTH By my faith, there he has answered you, friend, by plain 95 demonstration.

PUPPET DIONYSIUS *Nay, I'll prove, against e'er a rabbin of 'em all, that my standing is as lawful as his; that I speak by inspiration as well as he; that I have as little to do with learning as he; and do scorn her helps as much as he.* 100

BUSY I am confuted, the cause hath failed me.

PUPPET DIONYSIUS *Then be converted, be converted.*

LEATHERHEAD Be converted, I pray you, and let the play go on!

BUSY Let it go on, for I am changed, and will become a beholder
with you!   105

COKES That's brave i' faith. Thou hast carried it away, hobby-horse.
On with the play!

JUSTICE Stay, now do I forbid, I Adam Overdo! Sit still, I charge you.
The Justice discovers himself

COKES What, my brother-i'law!

GRACE My wise guardian!   110

EDGWORTH Justice Overdo!

JUSTICE It is time to take enormity by the forehead, and brand it; for
I have discovered enough.

5.6

*[Enter] Quarlous (like the madman) [and Dame] Purecraft
(a while after)*

QUARLOUS Nay, come, mistress bride. You must do as I do now.
You must be mad with me, in truth. I have here Justice Overdo
for it.

JUSTICE *[to Quarlous]* Peace good Trouble-all; come hither, and you
shall trouble none. (*To the cutpurse and Mistress Littlewit*) I will take   5
the charge of you, and your friend too; you also, young man, shall
be my care, stand there.

EDGWORTH Now, mercy upon me.
The rest are stealing away

KNOCKEM Would we were away, Whit; these are dangerous vapours;
best fall off with our birds, for fear o' the cage.   10

JUSTICE Stay, is not my name your terror?

WHIT Yesh, faith, man, and it ish for tat we would be gone, man.
[Enter Littlewit]

LITTLEWIT O gentlemen, did you not see a wife of mine? I ha' lost
my little wife, as I shall be trusted, my little pretty Win. I left her
at the great woman's house in trust yonder, the pig-woman's, with   15
Captain Jordan and Captain Whit, very good men, and I cannot
hear of her. Poor fool, I fear she's stepped aside. Mother, did you
not see Win?

JUSTICE If this grave matron be your mother, sir, stand by her, *et*
digito compesce labellum,° I may perhaps spring a wife for you anon.   20
Brother Bartholomew, I am sadly sorry to see you so lightly given,
and such a disciple of enormity, with your grave governor
Humphrey; but stand you both there in the middle place; I will
reprehend you in your course. Mistress Grace, let me rescue you
out of the hands of the stranger.   25

WINWIFE Pardon me, sir, I am a kinsman of hers.

JUSTICE Are you so? Of what name, sir?

WINWIFE Winwife, sir.

JUSTICE Master Winwife? I hope you have won no wife of her, sir. If
you have, I will examine the possibility of it at fit leisure. Now to   30
my enormities: look upon me, O London! And see me, O Smithfield; the example of Justice, and Mirror of Magistrates, the true
top of formality° and scourge of enormity. Hearken unto my
labours, and but observe my discoveries, and compare Hercules
with me, if thou dar'st, of old; or Columbus, Magellan, or our   35
countryman Drake° of later times. Stand forth, you weeds of
enormity and spread.° (*To Busy*) First, Rabbi Busy, thou super-
lunatical hypocrite; (*to Leatherhead*) next, thou other extremity,
thou profane professor of puppetry, little better than poetry; (*to the*
horse courser and cutpurse) then thou strong debaucher and seducer   40
of youth—witness this easy and honest young man; (*then Captain*
Whit) now thou esquire of dames, madams, and twelvepenny ladies;
(*and Mistress Littlewit*) now my green madam herself, of the price.
Let me unmask your ladyship.

   [*He removes the mask*]

LITTLEWIT O my wife, my wife, my wife!   45

JUSTICE Is she your wife? *Redde te Harpocratem!*°

   Enter Trouble-all [*hiding his nakedness with a dripping-pan,*
   followed by Ursula and Nightingale]

TROUBLE-ALL By your leave, stand by, my masters; be uncovered.

URSULA O! stay him, stay him. Help to cry, Nightingale; my pan,
my pan!

JUSTICE What's the matter?   50

NIGHTINGALE He has stolen Gammer Ursula's pan.

TROUBLE-ALL Yes, and I fear no man but Justice Overdo.

JUSTICE Ursula? Where is she? O the sow of enormity, this! (*To*
Ursula and Nightingale) Welcome, stand you there; you, songster,
there.   55

URSULA An please your worship, I am in no fault. A gentleman stripped him in my booth, and borrowed his gown and his hat; and he ran away with my goods, here, for it.

JUSTICE (*to Quarlous*) Then this is the true madman, and you are the enormity! 60

QUARLOUS You are i' the right; I am mad but from the gown outward.

JUSTICE Stand you there.

QUARLOUS Where you please, sir.

> *Mistress Overdo [wakes up and] is sick and her husband is silenced*

MISTRESS OVERDO O! lend me a basin, I am sick, I am sick. Where's 65 Master Overdo? Bridget,° call hither my Adam.

JUSTICE How?

WHIT Dy very own wife, i' fait, worshipful Adam.

MISTRESS OVERDO Will not my Adam come at me? Shall I see him no more then? 70

QUARLOUS Sir, why do you not go on with the enormity? Are you oppressed with it? I'll help you. Hark you, sir, i' your ear: your 'innocent young man' you have ta'en such care of all this day, is a cutpurse that hath got all your brother Cokes his things, and helped you to your beating and the stocks; if you have a mind to 75 hang him now, and show him your magistrate's wit, you may— but I should think it were better recovering the goods, and to save your estimation in pardoning him. I thank you, sir, for the gift of your ward,° Mistress Grace. [*Shows him the paper*] Look you, here is your hand and seal, by the way. Master Winwife, give you joy, 80 you are Palemon; you are possessed o' the gentlewoman, but she must pay me value,° here's warrant for it. And honest madman, there's thy gown and cap again; I thank thee for my wife. (*To the widow*) Nay, I can be mad, sweetheart, when I please, still; never fear me. And careful Numps, where's he? I thank him for my 85 licence.

WASP How!

QUARLOUS 'Tis true, Numps.

WASP I'll be hanged then.

QUARLOUS Look i' your box, Numps. (*Wasp misseth the licence*) [*To 90 Justice*] Nay, sir, stand not you fixed here like a stake in Finsbury° to be shot at, or the whipping post i' the Fair, but get your wife out o' the air, it will make her worse else; and remember you are but Adam, flesh and blood! You have your frailty; forget your

other name of Overdo, and invite us all to supper. There you and   95
I will compare our discoveries, and drown the memory of all
enormity in your biggest bowl at home.

COKES How now, Numps, ha' you lost it? I warrant 'twas when thou
wert i' the stocks. Why dost not speak?

WASP I will never speak while I live, again, for aught I know.   100

JUSTICE Nay, Humphrey, if I be patient, you must be so too; this
pleasant conceited gentleman hath wrought upon my judgement,
and prevailed. I pray you take care of your sick friend, Mistress
Alice,° and my good friends all—

QUARLOUS And no enormities.   105

JUSTICE I invite you home with me to my house, to supper: I will
have none fear to go along, for my intents are *ad correctionem, non
ad destructionem; ad aedificandum, non ad diruendum*:° so lead on.

COKES Yes, and bring the actors along, we'll ha' the rest o' the play
at home.   110

   [*Exeunt*]

The Epilogue°

Your Majesty hath seen the play, and you
   Can best allow it from your ear and view.
You know the scope of writers, and what store
   Of leave is given them, if they take not more,
And turn it into licence. You can tell   5
   If we have used that leave you gave us well;
Or whether we to rage or licence break,
   Or be profane, or make profane men speak.
This is your power to judge, great sir, and not
   The envy of a few. Which if we have got,   10
We value less what their dislike can bring.
   If it so happy be, t'have pleased the King.

EXPLANATORY NOTES

Volpone

NOTES TO DEDICATION

TWO . . . UNIVERSITIES: Oxford and Cambridge, at both of which *Volpone* was performed, probably in the summers of 1606 and 1607.
POEM: play.

NOTES TO THE EPISTLE

The polemical tone of the epistle marks it as part of the second phase of the debate known as the War of the Theatres, an acrimonious exchange of insults in which Jonson's principal antagonists were the playwrights John Marston and Thomas Dekker; the warring factions had been reconciled in 1604, but hostilities had broken out again in 1606. Some of the more acerbic passages derive from Jonson's 'Apologetical Dialogue' of 1602.

1 *sisters*: Oxford and Cambridge.

presently excellent: instantaneous in its excellence.

3 *and that*: and that it is true.

6 *benefit . . . friend*: the benefit of an enhanced reputation that derives from the generous patronage of the universities.

8 *your act*: the warm reception which the universities gave to *Volpone*.

9 *mere*: not needing support.

10 *hear so ill*: are so ill spoken of (imitates Latin *tam male audiunt*).

11 *subject*: Jonson, the recipient of the generosity of the universities.

13 *mistress*: the muse of poetry.

14 *But*: were it not.

20–1 *impossibility . . . good man*: a Stoic commonplace, here translated from the Greek of the ancient geographer Strabo (*Geography* 1. ii. 5).

21–7 *He that is said . . . mankind*: a loose translation from the Latin text of a treatise on the art of poetry by Antonio Minturno, the sixteenth-century bishop of Ugento.

27 *him*: it.

35–6 *abortive features*: bad plays.

39–40 *for my particular*: as for myself.

44 *youngest infant*: most recent play—either *Sejanus* or *Eastward Ho!*, both of which were performed in 1605; Jonson was summoned before the Privy Council for alleged papist and treasonable elements in *Sejanus*, and briefly imprisoned for a passage in *Eastward Ho!* that was thought to be anti-Scottish and therefore offensive to King James.

48 *allowed*: licensed by the censor, the Master of the Revels.

48-9 *those . . . mine*: three of Jonson's collaborative plays—*The Isle of Dogs* (now lost), *Sejanus*, and *Eastward Ho!*—had created difficulties with the authorities; Jonson was imprisoned for his part in the first and third, and had to cut his collaborator's contribution to *Sejanus* before it could be published.

51 *mimic*: means both 'burlesque actor' and 'feeble imitator'.

56 *carried*: carried out.

obnoxious to construction: liable to misinterpretation.

57 *Application*: the identification of fictional characters and plot-elements with real people and events.

66 *entrench . . . styles*: engrave with insolent styluses; a stylus could be used as an engraving tool and as an offensive weapon.

69 *providing*: foreseeing.

70 *fools and devils*: stock comic characters in Tudor drama.

74 *sibi . . . odit*: Horace, *Satires* II. i. 23, translated by Jonson in *Poetaster* (3.5.41) as: 'in satires each man, though untouched, complains | As he were hurt; and hates such biting strains.'

75-6 *And men . . . sports*: and men might justly blame the author, should he persist, for creating such vituperation merely for his own selfish amusement.

77 *misc'line interludes*: variety shows (Latin *ludi miscelli*).

85 *name*: the name of poet, though there may be a specific reference to the name 'Horace', which Jonson had used for a character modelled on himself in *Poetaster*; Thomas Dekker had satirized Jonson (calling him 'Horace') in *Satiromastix, or the Untrussing of the Humorous Poet*.

87 *vernaculous*: ill-bred, scurrilous (Jonson's coinage from Latin *vernaculus*, a slave bred at home).

92 *crown*: in antiquity the ivy crown signified accomplishments in poetry and in learning.

97 *comic law*: The conventions of ancient comedy had been transformed by Renaissance literary theorists into a system of rules. Jonson is defending the ending of *Volpone*, in which the severity of the punishments is at odds with the 'laws' of comedy.

99-100 *of industry*: deliberately.

104 *lines of example*: learned Renaissance commentators read the frivolous comedies of Plautus and Terence with leaden seriousness, and detected in them a grave morality that is not apparent to modern readers.

109 *elsewhere*: refers to Jonson's lost commentary on Horace's *Ars Poetica*, the manuscript of which was destroyed in a fire at his home in 1623.

111 *understanding*: men of understanding.

116 *primitive habit*: original clothing.

119 *affected*: aspired to.

120 *worthily*: deservedly.

123 *genus irritabile*: Horace, *Epistles* II. ii. 102: '[poets are] an easily provoked breed.'

124 *Cinnamus*: an ancient Roman hairdresser and surgeon who, according to Martial (VI. lxiv. 24–6), was famed for his skill in removing brands. Jonson's repeated allusions to Cinnamus recall that in 1598 he had been branded on the thumb when he escaped hanging for murder.

NOTES TO THE PERSONS OF THE PLAY

Volpone: (It.) literally means 'fox', figuratively refers to a cunning and fraudulent person.

Magnifico: a Venetian nobleman.

Mosca: (It.) house-fly.

Parasite: In ancient comedy the *parasitus* was a witty buffoon who managed to live at another's expense; the term literally means 'he who eats at another's table', and such characters were therefore associated with flies.

Voltore: an obsolete form of modern Italian *avvoltaio*, 'vulture' (an image traditionally associated with lawyers).

Corbaccio: a pejorative form of Italian *corvo* ('raven').

Corvino: (It.) adjective meaning 'like a raven'.

Avvocati: in Venice the term *avvocato* could be used of a magistrate.

Notaro: an obsolete form of modern Italian *notaio* ('notary').

Register: clerk of the court.

Nano: (It.) dwarf.

Castrone: (It.) literally refers to a castrated animal, figuratively to a blockhead or fool.

Gregge: (It.) literally a flock or herd of animals, here used with reference to a human crowd.

Politic: means both 'a moralizing commentator on public affairs' and (in the abbreviated form 'Pol' which sometimes appears in the play) 'parrot'.

Peregrine: means both 'traveller' and (in the context of the other animal names) 'hunting hawk'.

Bonario: an Italian adjective meaning 'good-natured, kindly'.

Fine: delicate.

Celia: heavenly (Lat. *caelica*).

Commendatori: officers of the court; for their distinctive hats see 5.9.16–17.

Mercatori: (It.) traders.

Androgino: (It.) a person who is both male and female.

Servitore: (It.) a servant.

NOTES TO THE ARGUMENT

This acrostic prologue imitates those that were prefixed (in late antiquity) to the comedies of Plautus. As the acrostic could not be conveyed in performance, 'The Argument' may have been written for a playbill, but was probably composed for the printed version of the text.

2 *state*: estate.

5 *are told*: and are exposed.

7 *sold*: betrayed into slavery.

NOTES TO PROLOGUE

1 *God*: the Quarto reading; in the Folio changed to 'yet' to comply with regulations prohibiting profanity in plays.

5 *bid to credit*: asked to believe.

9 *some*: specifically John Marston, in the prologue to *The Dutch Courtesan*. Lines 9–18 echo Jonson's defence of himself in the 'Apologetical Dialogue' that Jonson appended to *Poetaster.*January 31, 1995

12 *a year about them*: in *Satiromastix* Thomas Dekker had abused Jonson with the words 'you and your itchy poetry break out like Christmas, but once a year' (5.2.217).

13 *his creature*: his play *Volpone*, which did not exist two months previously.

17 *co-adjutor*: a collaborator of equal standing, as opposed to an untrained assistant ('novice'), qualified apprentice ('journeyman') or more important collaborator ('tutor').

21 *quaking custards*: refers both to the custom of a jester jumping into a huge bowl of custard at the annual Lord Mayor's Feast and also to Marston's *Satires* ii: 'Let custards quake, my rage must freely run', a passage that Jonson had previously mocked in *Poetaster* 5.3.525.

23 *gull*: dupe.

ends: tags.

26 *Bedlam*: St Mary of Bethlehem, the London mental asylum.

faction: competitor.

28 *fable*: plot.

29 *quick*: lively.

31 *laws*: Renaissance Italian critics had transformed Aristotle's observations about the conventions of ancient drama into a set of prescriptive rules that limited the action of a play to one day ('time') and one location ('place'), and insisted that comic characters ('persons') be lower- or middle-class.

33 *gall and copperas*: the ingredients of ink; gall is a substance created by insects on oak trees, and copperas is iron sulphate. The gall-bladder was associated with rancour, and copperas with vitriol.

34 *salt*: used in the Latinate sense of 'wit'; the ink-pot was cleaned with salt.

1.1 The scene is set in a room with a bed in Volpone's house. Mosca would have revealed Volpone's treasure by opening a curtain covering one of the doorways at the back of the stage.

3 *world's soul*: an English version of the neoplatonic *anima mundi*, the divine power which gives and sustains life. The pun on *sol* (Lat. 'sun'), which recurs in l. 10, alludes to the solar mysticism of Italian Renaissance philosophers; there is a secondary pun (which recurs in 4.5.96–7) on 'sol', the English term for the Italian coins known as *soldi*.

5 *celestial ram*: the constellation of Aries, which in astrology (though not in astronomy) the sun enters on 21 March, the beginning of spring (hence 'teeming earth')

8 *day*: the day when God created light (Gen. 1: 2–4)

10 *centre*: centre of the earth.

son of Sol: in alchemy gold was said to be the child of the sun.

15 *that age*: the Golden Age, during which, according to Ovid (*Metamorphoses* i. 101–2), the earth yielded its riches without being wounded by the plough (cf. ll. 33 ff.).

19 *they*: the classical poets, who often described Venus, the goddess of love and Cupid's mother, as 'golden'.

22 *Riches*: Mammon, who is dumb because (proverbially) 'silence is golden'.

24 *price of souls*: a blasphemous allusion to the price that Jesus paid (his life) for the souls of men (1 Cor. 6: 20: 'ye are bought with a price').

thee: Riches, trust in whom is said in Mark 10: 24 (where 'Riches' is not personified in the Authorized Version) to inhibit entry into heaven.

25–7 *Thou . . . wise*: the phrasing derives from Horace, *Satire* II. iii. 94–7.

28–9 *Riches . . . nature*: a blasphemous inversion of Prov. 16: 6: 'How much better is it to get wisdom than gold.'

31 *purchase*: used in the slang sense of 'acquisition by dishonest means'.

34 *fat*: fatten.

36 *'em*: refers ambiguously both to the corn that the men grind, and to the grinding down of the men by their labour.

37 *subtle glass*: delicate glass, which was (and is) blown on the Venetian island of Murano.

39 *I . . . bank*: the 'public bank' is the Banco di Rialto, which was then the only public bank in Europe. 'Turn' refers to abuses of '*il giro*', the bank's system of 'turning around' (i.e. transferring) money without the use of cash.

40 *usure private*: operate as a private money-lender charging excessive rates of interest.

41 *Soft*: plays on the senses of 'vulnerable', 'docile', and 'tasty'.

42 *melting*: tender, with a play on melted butter.

glibly refers both to the ease of swallowing and to the glib talk that enables the money-lender to swallow his victim.

Dutch: Dutch fondness for butter was proverbial.

43 *ne'er purge for't*: i.e. digest an heir's fortune so thoroughly that no laxative is necessary; the joke also implies that the money-lenders will not suffer punishment.

53–61 *like the thresher . . . soft beds*: the phrasing derives from Horace, *Satire* II. iii. 111–19.

56 *mallows*: a distasteful wild plant, said in Job 30: 4 to be eaten by famine victims.

58 *Romagna*: (here pronounced Ròman-ya), a sweet wine, Greek in origin, produced in an area south of Venice.

Candian: Candia is the Italian term for Crete.

59 *lees . . . vinegar*: sediment from the inferior wines of Lombardy.

63 *observer*: obsequious disciple.

66 *Hold thee*: plays on the senses of 'stop talking!' and 'keep this [money] for yourself'.

68 *term*: who term.

71 *cocker . . . genius*: indulge my appetites (Lat. *genio indulgere*).

75 *observe*: treat with obsequious respect.

76 *clients*: those dependent on noblemen, and thus of lower rank than Volpone.

82 *engross*: monopolize.

85 *suffer*: permit.

88 *still . . . hand*: always leading them on.

89 *cherry*: in the game of chop-cherry the player tried to bite a cherry hanging on a string.

1.2 [*dramatic entertainment*]: this interlude is an entertainment based on *Gallus* (or *The Cock*), a satirical dialogue between a cobbler and his cock written by Lucian (AD *c.*120–*c.*180), a Syrian author who wrote in Greek and was one of the favourite ancient authors of Renaissance Europe; details of the transmigrations of the soul of Pythagoras are taken from the biography of Pythagoras by Diogenes Laertius, a Greek writer of the third century AD.

1 *room*: i.e. make room, the traditional shout of actors as they entered a room in a large house to perform an entertainment.

2 *university show*: a university play, performed in Latin.

3 *rehearse*: recite.

4 *false pace*: refers to the old-fashioned irregular four-stress metre and forced rhymes of Nano's lines.

6 *Pythagoras*: ancient Greek philosopher and mathematician who believed in metempsychosis, the transmigration of the soul.

7 *juggler*: primarily 'wizard', but also 'trickster' and 'buffoon'.

8 *fast and loose*: the name of a contemporary game, here referring to the soul, which is apparently tied 'fast' to the body but can be made 'loose' by the magician.

Apollo: Greek god of the sun.

9 *Aethalides*: the herald of the Argonauts, the legendary Greek heroes who sought the golden fleece.

Mercurius his son: son of Mercury (herald of the gods), who had bestowed on Aethalides an omniscient memory; Jonson regarded this form of the genitive as pedantic.

12 *Euphorbus*: in Homer's *Iliad*, the defender of Troy who wounded Patroclus and was later killed by Menelaus; his hair was bound with gold threads. In Lucian and Diogenes, Pythagoras claimed to have been Euphorbus in an earlier incarnation.

13 *cuckold*: Menelaus, king of Sparta, whose wife Helen was abducted by Paris.

14 *Hermotimus*: an ancient Greek sage whose soul was said to separate regularly from his body; his wife took advantage of its temporary absence and burnt his body, thus forcing his soul to find a new home.

charta: (1) the script that he is holding; or (2) Lucian's *Gallus*.

16 *Pyrrhus*: identified by Diogenes (viii. 5) only as a fisherman from Delos; the allusion mocks the occasional and selective eating of fish by Pythagoreans.

17 *Sophist*: philosopher, here referring to Pythagoras, whom Lucian calls the Sophist of Greece.

18 *piece*: depreciatory term for 'woman'.

19 *Aspasia*: friend of Socrates and mistress of the Athenian statesman Pericles; she was formerly a prostitute (*meretrix*).

20 *of*: primarily 'from', but also 'like'.

21 *Crates*: ancient Greek philosopher of the Cynic school, members of which renounced all possessions and social institutions.

itself: the soul.

22 *Since*: since then.

24 *cobbler's cock*: in Lucian's dialogue the cobbler's cock claims to have within it the soul of Pythagoras.

26 *By Quatre!*: Pythagoreans swore 'by the holy Four', a reference to the tetrad, an arithmetical notation that represented the number ten as the sum of the first four integers; the tetrad was believed to be the underlying mathematical principle of the cosmos.

27 *musics*: the music of the spheres, a Pythagorean doctrine according to which the various speeds at which the heavenly spheres revolved produced a series of notes which collectively constituted a cosmic octave that was inaudible to human ears, but could be represented in harmonious living and in music.

trigon: the Pythagorean equilateral triangle, which consisted of ten dots (one at the top, two in the second row, three in the third, and four in the base line), was the geometrical representation of the tetrad.

golden thigh: a traditional attribute of Pythagoras.

28 *elements*: in Pythagorean doctrine the four elements were earth, air, fire, and water.

shift: are transmuted into different forms.

29 *translation*: transference from one person to another.

30 *reformation*: the Protestant Reformation.

32 *heresy*: Jonson was almost certainly a furtive Catholic in 1606.

33 *forbid meats*: forbidden food; Pythagoreans did not eat meat or beans, and were forbidden certain kinds of fish.

34 *Carthusian*: the nuns and monks in this austere order were forbidden to buy fish, though they could eat it if it were given to them; the slang meaning of 'fish' ('prostitute') and 'entered' produce a sexual innuendo.

35 *dogmatical silence*: both the Pythagoreans and the Carthusians observed periods of silence.

40 *eating of beans*: forbidden by Pythagoras because flatulence was thought to allow the breath of life to escape from the body; in the seventeenth century beans were used to feed mules.

43 *precise . . . brother*: describes Puritans, who are characterized as fastidious in religious observance (*precise*), ostentatious in morals (*pure*), and presuming to be guided by the light of God (*illuminate*), and who addressed each other as 'brother'.

44 *devour*: who devour.

46 *nativity*: Puritans avoided the Roman Catholic associations of the suffix '-mas' by referring to Christmas as 'Nativity'.

47 *nation*: sect (i.e. the Puritans).

62 *that*: folly.

66 *song*: the song draws on a passage in *Encomium Moriae* ('The Praise of Folly'), a satire published in 1511 by the Dutch humanist Erasmus. The identification of the singers as Nano and Castrone is suggested by l. 61 and supported by their joint exit at l. 82.

69 *selves*: themselves.

72 *sport*: amorous play.

73 *bauble*: literally the court fool's stick, and metaphorically his penis.

81 *he, he, he*: initially a pronoun but then dissolves into a giggle.

85 *furs*: furs were worn by the sick for warmth; Volpone may have worn a fox-fur. The inner nightcap kept the hair in place, and the outer warmed the head.

my . . . changing: my bed is being changed.

88 *clients*: in ancient Rome, plebians under the patronage of a patrician. The duties of a client included a daily salutation and a formal greeting at the levee (*admissio*) of his patron. Clients presented themselves in formal dress at dawn to deliver a greeting and escort the patron to work, and in return for these services received gifts of money or food (*sportula*). The scenes that follow are a parody of the *admissio*.

95–7 *a fox . . . gaping crow*: it was well known that foxes sometimes pretend to be dead in order to capture carrion birds (in this case Voltore, the vulture) who approach what they assume to be a carcass; cf. Horace, *Satire* II. v. 55–7.

106 *foot-cloths*: richly ornamented cloths draped over the mount of a nobleman.

108 *mule*: mules were ridden by legal officials on ceremonial occasions, but were also proverbial for their stupidity.

112 *reverend purple*: the ceremonial hood of a doctor of divinity was purple.

113 *ambitious*: means both 'aspiring' and 'towering'.

124 *harpies*: winged monsters described by Virgil (*Aeneid* iii. 210 ff.) as birds with women's faces.

126–9 *Now . . . hopes*: a parody both of prayer and of the poets' practice of invoking the Muses.

126 *phthisic*: (pronounced 'tizik') dasthma.

130 *uh . . . Oh—*: represents four coughs and a groan.

1.3.4 *notes*: tokens (with reference to the plate).

6 *Patron*: the term encourages Voltore to acknowledge the superior relation of Volpone as wealthy patron to his clients.

10 *of St Mark*: from one of the goldsmiths in Piazza San Marco.

21–2 *Your love . . . unanswered*: this plate gives the taste of your love.

33 *inscribed*: recorded as.

35 *family*: the 'household book' containing the names of servants.

36 *your worship*: respectful term of address, not in this period restricted to magistrates.

50 *know*: acknowledge.

we: a royal plural.

51–66 *He ever liked . . . a sequin!*: adapted from chapter 93 (on advocates) of Cornelius Agrippa's *De incertitudine et vanitate scientiarum et artium* (1531), an attack on the pretentions of learned men, translated in 1569 as *Of the Vanity and Uncertainty of Arts and Sciences*.

51 *course*: professional demeanour.

took: pleased

53 *large*: equivocates between senses that imply compliment ('great', 'numerous') and those that are critical ('improper in speech', 'pompous', 'prolix').

58 *forkèd*: equivocal.

58–9 *take . . . put it up*: accept money from opposing parties, and pocket it.

provoking: glances ironically at the legal sense of 'lodging an appeal'.

73 *but*: only.

76 *Anon*: a servant's response: 'Coming!'

78 *Put . . . face*: look businesslike.

1.4.2 *stand . . . multiply*: Mosca displays the plate (probably on the bedhead); his phrasing is at once blasphemous (in its recollection of 'be fruitful and multiply', Gen. 1: 22) and bawdy ('stand' can mean 'have an erection'; cf. *impotent*, 1.3).

4 *This*: Volpone.

11 *but slumbers*: only dozes.

20–36 *He has no faith . . . any man*: adapted from chapter 83 (on the art of medicine) of Agrippa's *De incertitudine* (see note to 1.3.51–66).

21 *your*: used impersonally, implying contempt (also ll. 23, 25).

35 *him*: the judge.

39–54 *his face . . . he breathes*: Mosca describes the symptoms (drawn from Hippocrates) of 'strong apoplexy'; in production Volpone would have demonstrated each symptom with comic exaggeration.

46 *from his brain*: loss of brain fluid was thought to signal the final stages of fatal apoplexy.

49 *resolvèd*: primarily 'drooping', but also 'watery'.

53 *left*: ceased.

62 *testament*: refers to personal property, whereas a will concerns 'real property' (i.e. land and certain land rights).

67 *By . . . scale*: by the measure of your own behaviour.

70 *weigh down*: outweigh.

72 *to*: compared to.

elixir: a substance used by alchemists to change base metals into gold; taken as a medicine, this 'elixir of life' was said to prolong life indefinitely.

73 *aurum . . . potabile*: Lat. touchable gold (i.e. coins), if not drinkable gold; potable gold, i.e. gold in a solution of oil, was valued as a cordial (a medicine that stimulates the heart).

80 *venture*: i.e. the bag of gold sequins.

96 *colour*: pretence.

97 *taking*: attractive.

but: is it only.

99 *enforce*: emphasize.

100 *watchings*: maintaining a vigil at the bedside of a sick person.

103 *proper issue*: own legitimate child.

124 *rook*: plays on the name of the bird, and on the senses of 'swindler' and 'simpleton'.

raven: the English form of 'Corbaccio'.

128 *brother*: Bonario (Corbaccio's son), but the phrasing recalls Jacob's cheating of his brother Esau out of the blessing of their father (Gen. 27).

133 *let . . . sides*: release my constricting clothes.

134 *this hope*: i.e. of becoming Volpone's legatee.

137 *hold*: constrain myself.

140 *give 'em words*: deceive them (Lat. *dare verba*).

141 *oil*: i.e. flattery.

144–51 *So many . . . life!*: an adaptation of Pliny's *Natural History* VII. xlix. 167–9.

156 *Aeson*: Jason's father, whose youth was restored by the magic of Medea.

159 *all . . . air*: he dismisses old age as a delusion.

1.5.9 *orient*: from the east, and therefore of the finest quality.

14 *carat*: a measure of the weight of precious stones, including pearls; the figure of 24 carats suggests another sense, that of the maximum purity of gold as measured in twenty-fourths.

22–3 *The weeping . . . visor*: translates *haeredis fletus sub persona risus est*, a well-known phrase attributed to Publilius Syrus, a Roman writer of mimes in the first century BC.

visor: mask.

39 *blind harper*: plays on the sense of 'perceive' (l. 38) meaning 'understand', alluding ironically to the tradition of the blind bard who is proverbially credited with compensatory understanding.

46 *common fable*: widely held belief.

48 *true father*: biological father, not merely the *paterfamilias* who was the head of a household.

56 *once*: finally.

75 *take*: take back from Volpone's clenched fist.

90 *purchase*: see note to 1.1.31.

99 *squire*: primarily 'servant', but also 'apple-squire', i.e. pimp.

110 *O' . . . year*: the metaphor reduces Celia to a sacrificial animal, which in the Mosaic law had to be 'of the first year, without blemish'.

114 *blood*: means both 'blushes' and 'sexual passion'.

127 *he*: Corvino, who questions his servants whenever he leaves or returns home.

130 *shape*: theatrical role, i.e. that of a dying man.

2.1.1 *to . . . soil*: a well-worn cliché ('soil', country).

10 *knowing men's . . . Ulysses*: this commonplace originates in *Odyssey* i. 3.

12 *Laid . . . height*: designed for this latitude.

14 *licence*: an early form of passport, which in Jonson's time often forbade travel to Italy and (l. 15) contact with unlicensed travellers.

17 *ambassador*: since 1604 the English ambassador in Venice had been the poet Sir Henry Wotton, to whom all licensed travellers had to be presented.

18 *vents our climate*: a pretentious way of saying 'comes from our country'.

22 *should build*: is reported to have built; the nesting of birds on ships was thought to be a bad omen, and the appearance of a raven to portend evil.

24 *trow?*: in your opinion?

29 *courtesans*: Venetian upper-class prostitutes (*cortigiane*, as opposed to lower-class *meretrici* or *puttane*) were renowned for their beauty, sumptuous clothing, and graceful manners.

30–1 *the spider . . . flower*: proverbial; in this case the flower is the courtesan, the spider (who sucks poison from the flower) is the male customer who contracts syphilis, and the bee (who sucks honey from the flower) is Lady Would-be (with a play on her name).

34 *lion's . . . Tower*: a lioness called Elizabeth had given birth in the Tower of London on 5 August 1604 and again on 26 February 1605.

your: used impersonally, as in ll. 36, 74, and 86.

36 *fires at Berwick*: in 1333 Edward III had defeated the Scots at the Battle of Halidon Hill, near Berwick-upon-Tweed; a luminous atmospheric phenomenon (possibly the aurora borealis) at Berwick on 7 December 1604 gave rise to reports of a ghostly re-staging of the battle.

37 *new star*: the supernova (on which Kepler wrote a treatise, *De Stella Nova*) that had appeared on 30 September 1604 and remained visible for seventeen months.

38 *meteors*: atmospheric phenomena, i.e. the 'fires' and the new star.

40 *bridge*: London Bridge; on 19 January 1606 a porpoise was captured alive at West Ham (which is below London Bridge); Sir Politic turns one porpoise into three, and Peregrine mockingly doubles the figure.

41 *sturgeon*: the joke is that sturgeon were common in the Thames; if they were caught above London Bridge they could be claimed by the Lord Mayor.

46 *a whale*: in January 1606 a whale was sighted proceeding up the Thames; Peregrine locates the sighting in Woolwich because of the naval dockyard there.

49 *Stade fleet*: the ships of the English Merchant Adventurers resident in Stade, an inland port near Hanover.

50 *Archdukes*: the official title of the rulers of the Spanish Netherlands: the Cardinal Archduke Albert of Austria and his wife the Infanta Isabella (half-sister of Philip III of Spain). In 1604 King James had negotiated a peace treaty with Philip and the Archdukes; Jonson is mocking the common English view that the Catholic signatories could not be trusted.

51 *Spinola*: Ambrogio de Spinola commanded the Spanish army in the Netherlands; he was popularly said to have hired a whale to swim up the Thames and blow water through its blowhole, thus drowning the people of London.

53 *Stone*: a London fool whose date of death is unknown; he was still alive in March 1605, when he was released from prison.

62 *That*: i.e. not that.

63 *unknown*: not known for what he was.

69 *Low Countries*: the United Provinces (now the Netherlands) and the Spanish Netherlands (now Belgium).

70 *cabbages*: the Low Countries exported large quantities of red cabbages and brussels sprouts.

72–4 *oranges . . . cockles*: the fruits were all costly and exotic, as were oysters from Colchester (in Essex) and cockles from Selsey (in Sussex).

78 *concealed statesman*: disguised political agent.

80 *toothpick*: see note to 4.1.139.

81–2 *Why . . . cipher*: mocks the high fashion for presenting food cut into unnatural shapes by suggesting that the meat served in a 'public ordinary' was carved to form a message in code (*character*).

85 *In polity*: craftily.

87 *to't*: besides.

88 *baboons*: baboons had been shown in London since about 1603, and had become one of the sights of the city.

90 *Mammalucci*: (It.) Mamelukes, the Egyptian sultans (unrelated to baboons, China, and French plots); the transferred sense of *mammalucco*, meaning 'fool' or 'simpleton', reflects on Sir Politic.

91 *plot*: conspiracy, but (by reference to the collateral form 'plat') also placket, the slit at the top of a skirt.

113 *vulgar grammar*: a grammar book in the vernacular (i.e. Italian–English, not Italian–Latin); there may be a specific reference to John Florio's *Second Fruits* (1591), the sixth dialogue of which contains 'rules for travel'.

118 *ingenuous race*: honourable family.

119 *I . . . it*: i.e. it is not my profession.

121 *kind*: role (of advising travellers).

2.2.2 *mount a bank*: a 'mountebank' was an itinerant quack who sold his medicines from an elevated platform; his sales pitch was an entertainment featuring flights of rhetoric, music, and song. The term derives from It. *monta in banco*, 'mount on a bench'.

12 *cabinet counsellors*: confidential advisers.

13 *only languaged*: most eloquent.

22 *Scoto of Mantua*: leader of a *commedia dell'arte* troupe licensed by the Duke of Mantua; he had performed conjuring tricks before Queen Elizabeth in 1576.

27 *in . . . Piazza*: facing the main square (St Mark's).

s.d. *disguised*: on Volpone's disguise see 2.5.11–15.

28 *zany*: a mountebank's comic assistant (*zanni*) who imitated his master's gestures.

Gregge: literally a flock or herd. The choice of *gregge* rather than *crotto* (crowd) sustains the animal imagery, at least in the printed text, and may imply that the crowd should be dressed to suggest the features of birds or animals.

follo: the text has *follow*, but Jonson has tried to reproduce the Italian word for 'madman' (actually *folle*; cf. *folletto*, elf) for the crowd's mocking of the dwarf Nano, who has just become visible. Sir Politic (and the compositor) thought that the word was English.

36 *portico . . . Procuratia*: the arcade of the *Procuratie Vecchie*, the official residence of the Procurators of St Mark (senior government administrators) on the north side of St Mark's Square.

41 *cold . . . feet*: a genuine proverb (*aver freddo a' piedi*) meaning 'forced to sell cheaply in order to buy necessities'.

44 *Buttone*: a rival mountebank, apparently invented by Volpone.

45 *galleys*: warships, which were crewed by condemned prisoners.

46 *Bembo's*: Pietro Bembo (1470–1547), the son of a Venetian diplomat, was a famous poet, literary theorist, and (from 1539) cardinal; the pause before 'cook' implies a sexual relationship.

48 *ground ciarlatani*: charlatans who performed standing on their cloaks rather than on a mountebank's platform.

49 *feats of activity*: acrobatics.

50–1 *Boccaccio*: Giovanni Boccaccio (1313–75), whose *Decameron* contained 100 tales.

51 *Tabarin*: Giovanni Tabarin, famous late-sixteenth-century Venetian *zanni*.

53 *Christians*: Venetians, who had fought four naval wars with the Ottoman Turks, who were Moslems.

58 *turdy . . . fartical*: such elaborate comic polysynthesis, which can be found in Shakespeare (*Love's Labour's Lost* 5.1) and Rabelais (*Gargantua* 7), derives ultimately from Aristophanes (e.g. the six-line word at the end of *Ecclesiazusae*).

60 *scartoccios*: Anglicized plural of *scartoccio*, a twist of wrapping paper.

63 *salad-eating*: the carnivorous English were contemptuous of the Italian taste for raw vegetables.

87 *humid . . . catarrh*: medicine still used Galenic terminology; the discharge (*flux*) is *phlegm*, one of the four *humours*, each of which corresponded to one of the elements of Empedocles (*earth, air, fire, water*). In this case a flow (techically 'defluxion', hence *flux*) of the watery (*humid*) humour,

phlegm (*catarrh* or rheum) into the arm or shoulder is said to have caused rheumatism.

91 *hath only*: alone has.

92–4 *hot . . . dry*: combinations of hot and cold, moist and dry were deemed to characterize the humours (e.g. phlegm was cold and moist); *windy* is a blunder, corrected by Peregrine to *dry*

101 *retired nerves*: shrunken muscles.

103–4 *torsion . . . guts*: cramps in the small intestine.

104 *melancolia hypochondriaca*: the hypochondria, the organs beneath the ribs, were supposed to be the seat of melancholy.

105 *receipt . . . bill*: prescription.

108–9 *theoric . . . art*: the medical theory and practice of Aesculapius, god of medicine.

110 *Zan Frittata*: the stage name of a famous Venetian zany (literally John Omelet).

112 *most . . . I*: i.e. I'm astonished.

113 *but*: except in.

114 *Broughton's*: Hugh Broughton (1549–1612), Puritan divine and Hebrew scholar; see *Alchemist* 3.2.237–8, 4.5.1–32, and notes.

115 *Hippocrates or Galen*: Hippocrates was a Greek physician (fifth century BC), idealized in the Renaissance; he was credited with a corpus of eighty-seven treatises. *Galen* (AD 129–99), the Greek physician, anatomist, and physiologist, was said to have written nearly 500 books. Famous editions of their works had been printed in Venice in 1525 (Galen) and 1526 (Hippocrates).

122 *Tobacco*: introduced to England in 1586; smoking was controversial, but tobacco tea was prescribed as medicine.

sassafras: the dried bark of the American sassafras tree was used in medicine as a nutritive.

123 *guacum*: a drug derived from the resin of the central American guaiacum tree.

124 *Lully's*: various alchemical works were attributed to Ramon Llull (1235?–1316), the Catalan poet, theologian, and missionary.

125 *Gonswart*: unidentified; possibly Cornelius Hamsfort, physician to Christian III of Denmark, the grandfather of Anne of Denmark (James I's queen).

126 *Paracelsus*: Swiss medical reformer (1493–1541), who resisted the orthodoxy of vegetative drugs and instead prescribed chemical remedies, thus changing alchemy from the science of making gold to a branch of medicine; he was alleged to keep either a medicine or the philosophers' stone in the hollow pommel of his sword.

129 *oglio del Scoto*: (It.) Scoto's oil.

133–4 *Signory . . . Sanità*: the governing body of the Venetian department of public health; it granted licences to physicians and mountebanks.

141 *experimented receipts*: tested remedies.

149 *in fumo*: (It.) up in smoke.

160 *pallone*: Jonson's text has *balloo*, a garbled form of *pallone*, a game in which a ball is struck with a bat tied to the arm.

171 *Montalto*: Felice Peretti, the Franciscan who became Inquisitor for Venice (1557), cardinal (from 1570), and pope (Sixtus V, 1585–90).

Fernese: either Alessandro Farnese, cardinal (from 1493) and later pope (Paul III, 1534–49), or his grandson (also Alessandro), whom he named as a cardinal in 1534 (aged 14).

171–2 *great . . . Tuscany*: in 1569 the title of Grand Duke of Tuscany was conferred by Pius V on Cosimo I de' Medici.

189 *Moist of hand*: indicative of youthful sexual energy.

193 *achès . . . bones*: 'bone-ache' was venereal disease.

194 *nones*: nonce, i.e. purpose.

200 *six—pence*: the dash indicates the point at which Volpone notices Peregrine and Sir Politic, hence the sudden change to English money.

204–5 *toss . . . handkerchiefs*: money was thrown in tied handkerchiefs to the mountebank, who then returned the goods in the handkerchiefs.

208 *double pistolet*: Spanish coin (acceptable in Venice) of high value.

233 *jacks*: upright staves connecting the keys to the quills that pluck the strings of the virginal; they move up and down as the keys are depressed and released.

2.3.1 *Blood*: F has 'Spite'. The Q reading makes Corvino's line a continuation of Volpone's unfinished sentence.

2–9 *Come down! . . . town*: Corvino assumes that he has interrupted a *commedia dell'arte* performance. In such comedies actors and actresses with fixed roles improvised on a three-act plot outline (*scenario*, hence Corvino's *scene*). *Flaminio* was a young lover, *Franciscina* a saucy maidservant; *Pantalone* was a specifically Venetian character, an elderly miser (hence *di Besogniosi*, 'of the paupers') married to a young wife and often cuckolded in the course of the play.

2.4.9 *liver*: the seat of passion.

21 *angel*: alludes both to Beelzebub (Lord of the Flies and therefore Mosca's angelic mentor) and to the name of a coin (cf. *crown*, l. 24).

30 *colour*: red, hence vulpine.

2.5.10 *call . . . whistle*: bird lures.

11 *copper*: cheap substitute for gold in theatrical costumes.

12 *saffron*: used as a glaze on burnished tinfoil to produce imitation gold. *toadstone*: a stone said to have been taken from the head of a toad and to have medicinal properties.

17 *fricace . . . mother*: massage for hysteria.

18–19 *mount*: literally 'become a mountebank', but also 'copulate'.

21 *cittern*: lute-like instrument associated by dramatists with prostitutes. *Lady Vanity*: common name (from the morality play tradition) for a seductress.

24 *save . . . dowry*: courts could award the dowry of a convicted adulteress to her husband.

24–5 *Dutchman . . . Italian*: Germans (called 'Dutchmen') were associated with restraint, Italians with unbridled passion.

55–6 *conjurer . . . laid*: the magic circle protected conjurors from the wrath of devils that they had summoned and subsequently consigned to hell.

58–61 *backwards*: the rear of the house, with a secondary suggestion of buggery.

67 *pain*: on pain.

70 *anatomy*: both 'corpse for dissection' and 'subject for moral analysis'.

2.6.14 *tumbling*: used in both acrobatic and sexual senses.

15 *forcèd*: means both 'contrived' and 'enforced' (by necessity).

20 *fasting spittle*: the spittle of a hungry man, i.e. Scoto.

32–5 *resolved . . . by him*: a biblical remedy (1 Kings 1: 1–4).

44 *opinion*: good opinion.

47 *present him*: i.e. with a young woman.

48 *briefly . . . somewhat*: quickly decide on a course of action.

59 *God's so*: a mild oath in which Italian *cazzo* (penis) has been adapted to form an English oath ('God's soul').

61 *Signor Lupo*: Mr Wolf (It.); the phrase glances at the medical sense of 'wolf' (ulcer) and possibly at the English court physician John Wolfgang Rumler, who was known as 'Mr Wolf'.

65 *spirit*: literally 'semen', but also a demonic spirit.

71 *blood . . . affections*: passions and feelings.

74 *coming*: coming around.

85 *directly . . . possession*: a technical legal phrase (here used ironically) referring to the legal seizing of property without the assistance of an intermediary.

95 *free motion*: unprompted suggestion.

2.7.4 *lightness . . . occasion*: slightness of my motive.

9 *do . . . world*: copulate however well they are guarded.

3.1.11 *liberally*: 'freely', but plays on the sense of 'liberal arts' or 'sciences'.

14 *bare town-art*: skills needed merely to survive in the city.

17 *bait that sense*: feed the sense of hearing.

21 *legs and faces*: bows and flattering smiles.

22 *lick . . . moth*: 'pick vermin off the beard and clothing of his master', but also 'eliminate a rival parasite'.

28 *Present . . . occasion*: ready to pander to any whim or deal with any situation.

29 *visor*: 'mask', hence 'role, expression'.

3.2.17 *St Mark*: here invoked as patron saint of Venice.

23 *fain*: 'compelled', but also 'eager'.

spin . . . raiment: ironic evocation of Matt. 6: 28.

39 *main . . . manners*: serious breach of good conduct.

49 *for . . . respect*: for this reason alone.

65 *common . . . earth*: a Latinism (*terrae filius*), meaning 'of obscure or unknown parentage'.

3.3.5 *known delicates*: acknowledged favourites.

23 *fair return*: 'favourable reply', but also 'substantial profit'. 28–9 *this . . . the other*: Lady Politic and Celia.

3.4. This scene imitates many details of the declamation *De Muliere Loquaci* ('The Talkative Woman') by the Greek rhetorician Libanius of Antioch (AD 314–*c*.393). Lady Would-be's costume should suggest a parrot (a green dress with a red collar), and her nose should be red.

31 *return*: i.e. to England.

38 *entertainment*: pronounced as five syllables.

47 *golden mediocrity*: Horace's *aurea mediocritas* (*Odes* II. x. 5), the 'golden mean' between extremes of attitude and behaviour.

51–65 *The passion . . . poultice?*: Lady Would-be diagnoses *passion of the heart*, a condition that ranges from heartburn to palpitations and melancholy, and prescribes a wide range of medicines for various diseases (see Glossary).

72 *Plato*: music formed part of the education of men (not women) in the *Republic*.

73 *Pythagoras*: see note to 1.2.27.

76 *poet*: Sophocles (*Ajax* 293).

79–81 *poets . . . d'Adria?*: the joke is that Lady Would-be thinks that these medieval and Renaissance poets are contemporaries of Plato; Cieco d'Adria ('the blind man of Adria') is the dramatist Luigi Groto (1541–85).

86 *Pastor Fido*: pastoral play (1589) by Battista Guarini, translated into English as *The Faithful Shepherd* (1602).

90 *Montagnié*: this spelling (from Q) indicates pronunciation as four syllables; the essays of Michel de Montaigne (1533–92) had been translated into English in 1603.

96–7 *Aretine . . . obscene*: Pietro Aretino's 'Sonnets of Lust' (*Sonnetti Lussuriosi*, 1523) were written to illustrate sixteen obscene drawings by Giulio Romano, which were widely circulated in Europe in engravings by Marcantonio Raimondi.

104 *politic bodies*: governments.

107–10 *Settling . . . faeces*: Lady Politic applies alchemical terms to 'humour'; *faeces* means sediment (not 'excrement').

110–12 *assassinates*: was still felt as an Arabism, and its association with Plato would be regarded as grotesquely inappropriate.

118 *lie you*: lie.

120 *quite . . . purpose*: missing the point.

3.5.5 *bells*: passing bells (rung to mark a death) rang frequently in times of plague.

36–8 *primero . . . encounter*: *primero* was a card game in which technical terms include *go less* (i.e. make a smaller bet), *lie* (i.e. place a bet), *draw* (i.e. take a card from the deck), and *encounter* (i.e. to pick a winning card); the sustained sexual innuendo articulates Volpone's fantasy of a sexual encounter with Celia.

3.7.4 *horns*: the symbol of a cuckold.

5 *ply . . . place*: work so eagerly and impetuously to secure an office at court.

9 *except . . . me*: unless you were to tell me.

61 *Aretine*: see note to 3.4.97.

63 *critic in*: connoisseur of.

64 *And*: if.

76 *prostitute*: Corvino naïvely understands the word in its obsolete sense of 'offering with devotion'.

79 *proper*: plays on various senses: 'lovely', 'legal', 'suitable for the occasion', 'respectable'.

80 *only* . . . : the only beauty of the highest value.

96 *eat . . . coals*: Porcia, the faithful wife of Brutus, killed herself by eating burning coals.

98–9 *rip . . . nose*: such mutilations of prostitutes were not a legal punishment in Venice, but were none the less common.

101–2 *I will . . . alive*: the threat made by the rapist Tarquin to the chaste Lucrece.

117 *watched . . . time*: waited for this opportunity.

120 *Crocodile*: the crocodile was said to lure its victims with false tears.

121 *Expecting*: waiting for an opportunity.

154 *Proteus*: sea-god who could change shape at will; his sea-colour was blue. *hornèd flood*: Acheloüs, Greek river whose horned deity could change shape.

162 *Valois*: King Henri III of France, who was entertained in Venice in 1574.

163 *Antinous*: probably the boy who was minion to the emperor Hadrian (if the entertainment reflected Henry's sexual tastes), but possibly the suitor of Penelope in the *Odyssey*.

166 *Song*: an imitation of the fifth song of Catullus.

178 *his*: Corvino's.

192 *queen*: Cleopatra, who famously drank a priceless pearl dissolved in vinegar.

194 *eyes . . . Mark*: unidentified, but possibly a jewel in the treasury of St Mark's cathedral and its fictional 'brother' in Aretino's comedy *Il Marescalco*.

195 *Lollia Paulina*: wife of the emperor Caligula, attended a banquet covered in emeralds and pearls that were the 'spoils of provinces' administered by her corrupt grandfather Marcus Lollius.

202–5 *parrots . . . dish*: the alleged diet of the dissolute emperor Elagabalus; he promised the phoenix to some guests but gave them gold instead; he scented his baths (l. 212) with roses.

215 *unicorns . . . breath*: unicorns were deemed to be rare (not imaginary), and panthers were thought to lure victims with the sweetness of their breath.

217 *preparèd gold*: see note to 1.4.73.

221 *Ovid's tales*: the *Metamorphoses*.

222 *Europa . . . Jove*: Jove disguised himself as a bull to abduct Europa.

230 *Grand Signor*: Sultan of Turkey.

234 *transfuse*: kisses were thought to intermingle the souls of the lovers.

236–9 *That . . . pined*: concludes the song of Catullus.

237 *tell them*: count the number of kisses.

240 *pierced—or eyes . . .* : the dashes (from Q) indicate gasping fear.

242 *sounds . . . you*: proclaims that you are a man.

262 *Nestor*: aged Greek commander at the siege of Troy; he was thought to be impotent, and Juvenal (*Satires* vi. 326) gives him a hernia.

3.8.14 *die . . . Romans*: commit suicide rather than surrender.

15 *Grecians*: ancient Greeks (i.e. dissolute), though the form allows an ironic play on the sense of 'classical scholars' at the university performances.

20 *Make . . . good*: i.e. maintain your defence as an invalid, whatever happens.

3.9.22 *foists*: 'tricks', with a play on 'fustiness'.

32 *disclaiming in*: disowning.

4.1.2–3 *me . . . instructions*: 'that I might give you some rules for travellers'.

20 *be a saver in*: 'neither win or lose by' (a gambling metaphor).

26–7 *Nick . . . this mind*: Niccolò Machiavelli (1469–1527) argued that religion should be subordinated to the needs of the state, and the political philosopher Jean Bodin (1530–96) advocated religious toleration as a means of ensuring civil peace; neither was 'of this mind'.

28 *fork*: not yet common in England.

29 *mettle . . . glass*: i.e. acquire an expert knowledge of the glass made on the Venetian island of Murano; puns on 'metal' (molten glass).

40 *Contarine*: Anglicized (trisyllabic) form of Contarini, referring to Cardinal Gasparo Contarini's book on the Venetian constitution, which had been translated in 1599 as *The Commonwealth and Government of Venice*.

41 *Dealt . . . Jews*: borrowed money from Jews who lived in the Venetian Ghetto.

54 *one . . . States*: someone from the United Provinces (the Netherlands).

56 *chandler*: candlemaker (an inference from the greasiness of the letter).

74–5 *Great Council . . . forty . . . ten*: the ascending hierarchy of the government of Venice.

means: means of access.

91 *Arsenale*: the Venetian naval dockyard, at which there had been a famous explosion in 1569.

106 *Lazaretto*: a plague hospital on an outlying island.

110 *onions*: peeled onions were thought to absorb plague infection.

119 *perpetual motion*: one of the (futile) aims of contemporary science; Sir Politic implies that he has found the secret.

455

130 *Turk*: the traditional enemy of Venice.

136–8 *A rat . . . threshold*: the details associate Sir Politic with the character of the superstitious man as described by the Greek author Theophrastus (*c*.370–*c*.287 BC), in his *Characters*.

139 *toothpicks*: a fashionable accessory for courtiers.

141 *ragion[i] del stato*: 'reasons of state', a catch-phrase used to justify immoral acts for political purposes.

4.2.2 *fast*: 'secure', but also 'firmly attached' to his courtesan.

both: fast and loose; see note to 1.2.8.

6 *it*: her make-up.

20 *But*: 'as recently as'; Lady Would-be has misunderstood 'as soon' (i.e. 'at an early age') as a reference to the time of day.

35 *The Courtier*: refers to Book 3 of Baldassare Castiglione's *Il Cortegiano* (1528).

47 *light land-siren*: promiscuous seductress; the sirens were monsters that lured sailors to their deaths with beautiful songs.

48 *Sporus*: a catamite of Nero, who had him castrated, dressed him in woman's clothes, and 'married' him in a public ceremony.

49 *Poetic . . . storms!*: the sirens appear in classical poetry, and Sporus was historical.

51 *Whitefriars' nation*: prostitutes, who enjoyed immunity from arrest in the 'sanctuary' of Whitefriars, an area of London.

54 *St George*: patron of England, and of virtuous women in distress.

60 *carnival*: the annual Venetian carnival was characterized as riotous and carnal.

61 *liberty of conscience*: a popular phrase among Puritans, here used iron-ically to refer to freedom to act immorally.

65 *'gainst . . . occasion*: in preparation for an occasion of real need.

66 *go to*: a derisive colloquialism ('come off it').

68 *invite me home*: i.e. for a sexual encounter.

4.3.3 *no aristocracy*: alludes to Machiavelli's much-resented view that Vene-tian patricians could not be deemed a true aristocracy because they were in commerce.

17–18 *use . . . conceive*: Lady Would-be means 'use my acquaintance so-cially' and 'understand'; Peregrine understands the terms as 'use sex-ually' and 'make pregnant', and replies with a quibble on *acquainted* ('quaint' is slang for 'pudenda').

23 *salt-head*: both 'seasoned experience' (playing on 'salt' as opposed to 'fresh') and 'lechery' (playing on the sense of 'salacious').

4.4.1 *carriage ... business*: 'how the business is to be managed'. Celia and Bonario are making their statements to the court off-stage, and the others have planned a consistent response.

6 *truth*: i.e. that Corvino attempted to prostitute Celia.

12 *Croaker*: Corbaccio, with reference to his manner of speech.

14 *mummia*: medicine allegedly made from the flesh of ancient Egyptian mummies.

15 *buffalo*: refers to Corvino's cuckold's horns and (in Italian) to his stupidity.

22 *French Hercules*: Lucian had portrayed Hercules (father of the Gauls) as an eloquent old man.

27 *her*: Lady Would-be.

4.5.7 *monstrous*: trisyllabic ('monsterous').

65 *him*: Bonario.

79 *Mischief ... begins*: a witty reversal of a maxim of the Roman historian Valerius Maximus (IX. i. 2), in which Voltore's 'ever' would be translated as 'never'.

85 *stale ... practice*: prostitute used to entice victims into his fraudulent plot.

90 *in ... gentleman*: of Volpone.

102 *creature*: dependent on God (and therefore forbidden to commit suicide) and a dependant of Corvino, whose perjury will compromise her.

107 *Abhors ... in him*: i.e. abhors its knowledge of Bonario; 'I deny that I am his father'.

111–19 *swine ... jennet*: animals associated with filth (swine), lechery (goat and partridge), cruelty (wolf), filial ingratitude (viper), and resistance to discipline (jennet, a Spanish breed of horse).

123 *cedar*: characterized as tall, strong, and gluey.

124 S.D. *indicating* Corvino holds his fingers to his forehead in a V shape to represent the cuckold's horns.

125 *horn*: the cuckold's horns, and also the horn-book, a spelling primer covered with thin transparent horn.

130 *Catholic*: Q has 'Christian'. When Q was published Jonson was Roman Catholic; when F, Anglican.

4.6.2 *chameleon*: reptile that changes colour, hence a symbol of fraud and cunning.

3 *tears ... hyena*: an inept conflation of the tears of the crocodile and the anthropomorphic voice of the hyena, both of which lured victims to their deaths.

7 *been exorbitant*: exceeded the linguistic proprieties of the court.

7–8 *You . . . strong*: in Q and F these lines are individually attributed to the Fourth Avvocato, so one attribution must be a misprint.

20 S.D. *Lady . . . him*: an inference from 5.2.96.

21 *convince*: both 'overpower' the bold tongues and 'convict'.

32 *strappado*: form of torture used to extract confessions; the victim is lifted by a rope binding his arms behind his back, and let down half-way with a jerk.

34 *help*: i.e. help rid.

51 *hot . . . fleshed*: eager and inured.

66 *want living*: lack a livelihood.

71 *other*: i.e. that Corvino had pandered Celia to Volpone.

81 *in*: in the inventory.

92 *take . . . notice*: pretend to take no notice (because Lady Would-be is present).

5.1.3 *this . . . moment*: a moment ago.

8 *A many*: opposite of 'a few'.

16 *make me up*: restore me.

17 *heat . . . blood*: in Renaissance physiology wine was thought to convert quickly into blood, which the heart turned to 'vital heat' that gave the drinker courage.

5.2.2–3 *And wrought . . . before us?*: parodies the biblical image of the path of life.

32 *Did . . . rare*: wasn't the lawyer (Voltore) brilliant?

45 *under favour*: deferentially; the parentheses mock Voltore.

48 *By that*: to judge by that; Volpone entered at 'the latter end' of Voltore's speech.

50 *Draw . . . aggravate*: organize under headings, then bring charges.

51 *vehement figures*: passionate rhetoric.

52 *shift . . . shirt*: change his undershirt (because he was sweating).

69 *gown*: see note to 5.3.105.

70 *take . . . as*: act as if.

81 *cap*: the caps of Venetian (and English) gentlemen were worn indoors, and only doffed to social superiors; Mosca keeps his patrician's hat on and thus insults the visitors.

88 *stark dull*: 'utterly numb', but Volpone's reply plays on the sense of 'blunt'.

90 *round-back*: refers to Corbaccio's stoop.

91 *crump . . . touch*: will curl up for you like a wood-louse when touched.

93 *rope . . . dagger*: emblems of suicidal despair.

98–105 *Why . . . beauty*: parodies Lady Would-be's extravagant speech.

102 *girdle*: the margin of F glosses as *Cestus*, the embroidered belt of Venus which made its wearer irresistible.

103–5 *Acrisius*: king of Argos, imprisoned his daughter Danaë; *Jove* circumvented her guards by hiding in a shower of gold (*shroud*).

106 *The lady, sir?*: Mosca speaks ironically of Lady Would-be; Volpone assumes a reference to Celia, and Mosca seeks clarification.

107 *jealous of*: devoted to (implying devotion to his wealth).

111 *artificer*: plays on the senses 'craftsman' and 'trickster'.

5.3.3 *suits . . . tissue*: sets of bed-hangings interwoven with gold or silver thread.

11 *thread*: Clotho spun the thread of life, which was then measured and cut by the other Fates.

21 *i'their garters*: plays on 'hangings' to suggest suicide.

22 *gasp*: last gasp.

25 *glazen-eyes*: Corbaccio wears reading glasses (cf. *four eyes*, l. 63).

40 *what*: her sexual favours.

53 *on good terms*: expressly.

58–9 *extraordinary . . . title*: supernumerary, and a cuckold in name alone.

68 *three legs*: refers to Corbaccio's cane, and to his age (by allusion to the riddle of the Theban sphinx ('what has four, two, and three feet?'), which associated the walking-stick with old age.

81–101 *O, cry . . . purge, sir*: a parody of Voltore's forensic oratory.

96 *Conceive . . . for*: do understand that I will pay.

102 *lettuce*: used as a laxative.

105 *habit*: Venetian patricians wore a distinctive black gown when outdoors.

119 *cursed*: the fox was proverbially cursed when he escaped.

5.4.4 *Zant*: Zante, an Ionian island in Venetian possession.

Aleppo: Syrian trading city in Ottoman possession.

5 *Book of Voyages*: a travel book such as Richard Hakluyt's *Principal Navigations . . . of the English Nation* (1589).

6 *his . . . story*: the story of his gulling.

9 *Know . . . approaches*: know when it is your cue to enter.

14 *family . . . female*: Sir Politic, like the Venetians, has female servants; Peregrine implies that he is in a brothel (cf. 4.3.20).

16 *him whole*: his undivided attention.

21 *Bolognan sausages*: *mortadella* was available in England.

23 *tidings*: the stateman's word is 'intelligence' (2.1.68).

24 *wills you stay*: means 'wants you to stay', but is interpreted by Peregrine as a command to 'wait till he deigns to receive you', hence the indignant tone of his message in ll. 25–6.

return: reply to.

42 *better*: more incriminating, because plays were scrutinized for sedition.

43 *essays*: elsewhere attacked by Jonson for their second-hand knowledge; Sir Politic's knowledge is by implication third-hand.

55 *Fitted . . . extremities*: 'adapted (Q has *Apted*) for these emergencies', with a play on 'extremities', meaning 'limbs'.

60 *device*: 'contrivance', but understood by the audience as 'emblem', in this case an image of prudent self-reliance and impregnability (in its shell) and of persistence (as illustrated in Aesop's fable of the hare and the tortoise).

62 S.D. *more*: an inference from ll. 61 and 76; in Jacobean theatres smoke was released through the trap-door in the stage floor.

74 *fearful*: 'frightening', but also 'frightened'.

77–8 *Fleet street . . . fair*: lawyers and their clients congregated in the City during the terms of the Inns of Court; puppet-shows were performed in nearby Fleet Street. *Smithfield* was the site of Bartholomew Fair. Jonson's play *Bartholomew Fair* includes a puppet-show in the final act.

5.5.1 *him*: the *commendatore* of 5.3.114.

6–7 *Fox . . . hole*: refers to the children's game, Fox-in-the-Hole.

on: of.

13 *will needs be*: insists on being.

5.6.5 *come upon him*: make my claim on Mosca.

19 *autumn*: autumnal harvest of grapes.

5.7.2 *make legs*: bow and scrape.

8 *tenement . . . reparations*: house in disrepair.

20 *decrease*: a malapropism (hence 'mistaking') for 'increase', characteristic of the dramatic presentation of minor court officials; cf. *Bartholomew Fair*, Induction 330–3.

5.8.11–14 *fine bird . . . emptiness*: refers to Aesop's fable of the fox that tricked the crow into dropping a cheese from its beak by asking to hear its wonderful singing.

12 *emblems*: moralistic symbolic engravings.

15 *privilege . . . place*: immunity conferred within the precincts of the ducal palace, within which was the Scrutineo.

17 *two sequins*: a red cap with two gilt buttons was part of the uniform of the *commendatore*.

23–4 *I . . . stand*: 'I would be a wise man if I could endure'.

5.9.1 *flesh-fly*: blow-fly, which in the summer deposits its eggs in carrion; puns on the literal meaning of 'Mosca'.

9 *mule*: see note to 1.2.107.

10 *Justinian*: the *Corpus Juris Civilis*, a Roman code of law commissioned by the emperor Justinian.

16 *I know*: confirms Voltore's accusation, but after a pause introduces a denial.

5.10.4 *Once win*: for once prevail.

10 *possessed*: i.e. by the devil, the 'false spirit' of l. 49.

15 *Speak forward*: carry on.

30 *The other*: Mosca.

5.11.4 *dull devil*: stupor induced by the wine drunk in 5.1.

21 *upon*: on the raising of.

5.12.1 S.D. *Notaro*: included in the headnote by Q and F, but not given any words; either he is not meant to be on stage, or he is intended to squirm in silence at l. 13.

1 *These things*: Voltore's notes.

2–3 *gentleman . . . gentlewoman*: Bonario and Celia.

9–10 *possession . . . obsession*: demons possessed bodies from within, whereas obsession was an external siege of the body.

19 *stood affected*: reacted.

20 *Do I live*: 'as sure as I am alive'; a conventional expression, but, as the audience knows and Voltore does not, literally true.

24–31 *Stop your wind . . . bat's wings*: the symptoms of possession are characteristic of contemporary accounts of faked exorcisms.

27 *running away*: contorting uncontrollably.

49 *make . . . stool*: make way for him; bring him a seat.

54 *o' the hinge*: running smoothly.

61 *come about*: changed direction.

64–5 *Demand . . . Sir*: 'let us question Voltore'; 'Sir' indicates that Voltore is addressed, even though Volpone answers.

75 *pass*: be allowed to apply (to a man of my new rank).

84 *allied*: related by marriage.

93 *it*: of it.

95 *knot*: the complication of the plot, which is resolved in the denouement (literally, the untying of the knot).

115 *I . . . him*: attributed by Q and F to Voltore.

thy: (also *thou*, l. 116 and *thee*, l. 118) are forms of address to inferiors.

120 *hospital . . . Incurabili*: a private charity on the Dorsoduro, founded in 1522 for the housing and maintenance of beggars, prostitutes, and orphans; it was popularly associated with Francis Xavier and Ignatius Loyola, both of whom had worked there briefly.

125 *mortifying*: plays on various meanings: in a physical sense, 'killing', 'bruising', or 'rendering gangrenous [in irons]'; in a (blasphemous) religious sense of 'mortification of the flesh' through abstinence; in the culinary sense of 'making tender by hanging', ironic because foxes were thought to be inedible; and (possibly) in the Scottish legal sense of 'disposing of property for charitable purposes'.

131 *San Spirito*: the Monastery of the Holy Spirit, on the Dorsoduro beside the Giudecca Canal.

136 *Grand Canal*: Jonson's spelling ('Grand Canale') is a garbled attempt to render the Italian *Canal Grande*, which was known in English as the Great Channel.

152 S.D. *re-enters*: the Jacobean convention for epilogues is not known, so it is possible that the cast stayed on the stage for the epilogue.

157 *fare jovially*: behave cheerfully.

NOTES TO COLOPHON

The colophon appears only in F.

1605: the legal year began on 25 March and ended on 24 March; it is likely that the play was first acted in March 1606, which in the old calendar appears as 1605.

principal comedians: Richard Burbage, Henry Condell, William Sly, John Heminges, John Lowin, and Alexander Cooke were all principal actors in the King's Men, and acted in the plays of Shakespeare and Jonson. The part of Volpone was played by Burbage, who had acted the major tragic roles in Shakespeare's plays; Mosca was probably played by Condell, Corbaccio by Heminges, Sir Politic by Lowin (who later became associated with the part of Falstaff); it is possible that Sly played Voltore and Cooke played Lady Would-be.

allowance: the Master of Revels, then Sir Edmund Tilney, was an officer appointed by the crown to license (or 'allow') plays for performance and (from 1607) printing. In 1606 the Master was Sir Edmund Tilney; in 1616 Sir George Buc.

Epicene

NOTES TO DEDICATION

4 *Sir Francis Stuart*: Francis Stuart (or Stewart), second son of the Earl of Moray, and knighted in 1610, was one of Jonson's literary companions at the Mermaid Tavern.

7 *dumb piece*: both 'silent play' (*Epicene* had been suppressed in 1610) and 'silent woman'.

17 *accusation*: performances of *Epicene* had been banned because Lady Arabella Stuart, the king's first cousin, had complained that the play 'introduced [at 5.1.20–1] an allusion to her person and the part played by the Prince of Moldavia' (translated from the Italian cipher of the report of the Venetian ambassadors, 8/18 February 1610, in *Calendar of State Papers: Venetian*). Stephano Janiculo, who pretended to be Bodgan, Prince of Moldavia, had in 1608 announced in Venice that he was engaged to marry Lady Arabella; he already had a Venetian wife.

NOTES TO THE PERSONS OF THE PLAY

Morose: peevish and sullen; still felt as a Latinism, from *morosus*.

Dauphine Eugenie: a *Dauphine* is the wife of a French *Dauphin*, the heir to the throne; the feminine form suggests sexual ambivalence. *Eugenie* is a (feminine) Greek word (*eugeneia*) meaning 'nobility of birth'; he should have a ribanded love-lock (4.6.36).

Clerimont: probably from the French adverb *clairement* ('clearly, plainly').

Epicene: in Greek and Latin grammar, a noun which can denote either sex without changing its grammatical gender; Jonson's transferred sense (of one who partakes of the characteristics of both sexes) would have been felt as a joke deriving from the grammatical term.

John Daw: the jackdaw, a bird associated with garrulity, theft, and ill fortune (in 1604 parliament had rejected a bill sponsored by a Puritan after a jackdaw flew through the Chamber); Daw's costume should include a grey ruff (3.2.21) and voluminous stuffed breeches (4.5.104).

La Foole: a pseudo-French feminine form of 'the fool'.

Otter: an amphibious animal (1.4.24), hence sexually ambivalent.

Centaure: French form of 'centaur', a mythical semi-human with horse's body and man's head; centaurs were always male (but cf. 4.5.42), and were known for their savagery and lustfulness.

collegiates: members of a college, here a ladies' salon.

Mavis: song-thrush, but also 'ugly face' (5.2.33).

NOTES TO [FIRST] PROLOGUE

3 *bays*: the poet's wreath was made from the leaves of the bay laurel.

5 *particular likings*: narrow tastes, here those of the audiences of the private theatres.

7 *mingle . . . breasts*: share neither thoughts nor feelings.

8 *make*: who make.

12 *And though . . . some*: 'though not every part of the play pleases them, there will be some parts'.

23 *city-wires*: fashionable city wives who use wire to shape the contours of their hair and ruffs.

24 *Whitefriars*: both the theatre in which *Epicene* was performed and the disreputable area of London (see *Volpone*, note to 4.2.51).

27 *broken meat*: left-overs.

NOTES TO 'ANOTHER'

2 *to . . . delight*: maxim from Horace, *Ars Poetica* 343–4.

12 *application*: the interpretation of literature as a commentary on contemporary individuals, in this case the slur perceived by Lady Arabella Stuart (see note to Dedication 17).

1.1 S.D. *making . . . ready*: dressing.

1 *got . . . perfect*: memorized.

19 *rushes*: green rushes were strewn on the floors of apartments.

20 S.D. *Boy sings*: starts to sing the song printed in ll. 82–93.

24 *post-horse*: a horse used to carry mail by stages, here used in the transferred sense of the passing stages of the day.

27 *article . . . time*: moment (Lat. *articulus temporis*).

32–3 *Puppy . . . Whitemane's*: 'horses o' the time' (Jonson's marginal note).

33 *spend aloud*: 'spend conspicuously', playing on the secondary sense of 'bark like a hound' (on seeing the game).

52 *common disease*: discontent caused by lack of patronage.

57 *tedious fellow*: Seneca, whom Truewit has been paraphrasing (*De Brevitate Vitae* III. 5), not Plutarch's *Moralia*; cf. 2.3.40–50.

69 *courtiers . . . madams*: ladies from the court and the country.

70 *from*: apart from.

110 *Aldgate*: the principal eastern gate of the city wall of London was rebuilt in 1609–10; it was flanked by statues of women representing Peace and Charity.

130 *Sick . . . uncle*: adapting 'sick of the mother' (hysteria).

136 *been . . . divers*: been busy making various.

144 *Shrove Tuesday*: the last day before Lent, hence a pretext for the vandalizing of brothels and theatres by gangs of apprentices.

149 *bellman*: night-watchman, who called the hours by ringing a bell.

158–9 *cried his games*: announced the next bear-baiting.

167 *reason . . . ringing*: the virulent plague (*sickness*) of 1609 occasioned a seemingly perpetual tolling of passing bells; cf. *Volpone* 3.5.5–7.

170 *turned . . . man*: dismissed a servant.

1.2.2 *I am here*: as surely as I stand here.

9–10 *acts and monuments*: John Foxe's 'Book of Martyrs' was entitled *Acts and Monuments*; Morose is a martyr to noise.

12 *gives . . . of*: authorizes your.

14–15 *Tower Wharf*: the anniversary of the coronation of King James on 25 July 1603 was marked with the firing of cannons on Tower Wharf, beside the Tower of London.

51 *Let . . . stars*: even though I am fated.

1.3.14 *Decameron*: Boccaccio's collection of tales, largely concerned with amorous 'sport'.

20 *mutines why*: rebels because.

23 *water*: water transport with which to cross or travel along the Thames.

33 *put her out*: distract her so that she loses step.

give plays: finance private performances.

35 *Strand*: main street between London and Westminster, populated by gentry and aristocracy.

37 *Exchange*: the New Exchange, opened on the south side of the Strand in 1609, contained fashionable shops for ladies.

40 *their women*: the reading of the first state of F, which would mean 'the ladies' maidservants'; the corrected second state has *there*, which would make 'women' a slighting reference to ladies who would alight from their carriages at his lodging.

48 *marshal him*: 'show him in'.

49 *truncheon*: plays on 'marshal's baton' and 'cudgel'.

1.4.12 *dispense with*: excuse (affected usage).

16 *terrible boys*: 'roaring boys', gangs of raucous and violent youths.

24 *animal amphibium*: zoological Latin: amphibious animal; by implication an animal with two natures, here a man unnaturally playing the subservient part of a wife.

25 *china-woman*: literally 'proprietress of a shop selling oriental goods', but the ambiguity of 'visited' and 'entertainment' suggests a courtesan.

38 *coat*: coat-of-arms, but by implication the motley coat of the court fool.

53 *or . . . azure . . . gules*: heraldic terms for gold, blue, and red.

55 *knighted in Ireland*: a doubtful honour, because the Earl of Essex had bestowed so many knighthoods in the course of his Irish campaign of 1599 that the honour was said to have been cheapened.

55 *Island voyage*: the Azores expedition of 1597, at which the English gentlemen, who deserted in large numbers, were said to have dressed more like masquers than soldiers.

Caliz: a botched conflation of *Cadiz* and its English exonym, *Cales*, referring to the English capture of Cadiz in 1596.

59 *eye*: London, by analogy with ancient Athens, the 'eye of Greece'.

59–60 *take up*: borrow.

63 *commodity*: in order to circumvent regulations governing the charging of interest, money-lenders made borrowers take part of their loan in the form of a commodity, which would then be bought back at a lower price.

68 *have . . . afore*: take precedence of.

2.1.9 S.D. *At . . . signs*: 'at the breaks in the text, the servant always makes legs (bowing by bending one leg and drawing back the other) or signs'.

33 S.D. *One . . . without*: 'someone blows a post-horn offstage'; a messenger (*post*) who had come by horse would thus announce himself.

2.2 Truewit's speeches are imitations of Juvenal, Satire VI.

2 *Fishes*: fish were proverbially mute.

2–3 *Pythagoreans*: members of the religious society founded by Pythagoras kept a vow of silence.

4 *Harpocrates . . . club*: Egyptian god, depicted iconographically as a child with his finger at his mouth and therefore misconstrued by Greeks as a god of silence; the *club* derives from confusion with Hercules.

7 *O . . . manners*: echoes the Ciceronian tag 'O times, o manners' (*O tempora, o mores*).

19–20 *London . . . fall*: at a low ebb-tide, when one could not drown oneself from the bank, one could jump from London Bridge, the piers of which created rapids.

21 *Bow*: the old church of St Mary-le-Bow, in Cheapside.

22 *Paul's*: the spire of old St Paul's Cathedral was 489 feet high.

27–8 *fly . . . arse*: in fly and spider fights, the fly was nudged towards the spider with a straw.

31 *preachings*: in uncorrected state of F, *parleys*; possibly amended to remove a potential allusion to the Hampton Court Conference of 1604, which was called to discuss Puritan requests for reforms in the Anglican Church.

mad folks: viewing the inmates of Bedlam was a popular amusement.

32–3 *Ethelred's . . . Edward*: Ethelred (II) the Unready (king of England, 978–1016) and his son St Edward the Confessor (king, 1042–66).

40 *Begged . . . 'em*: lodged a petition for right of succession to their property.

58 *roses*: shoe-roses, knotted ribbons worn on the shoes.

69 *silenced brethren*: Puritans who had lost their licences to preach in the wake of the Hampton Court Conference.

70 *family*: probably glances at the Family of Love, a proscribed religious sect.

72 *zealous*: associated with the zeal of Puritans.

73 *holy cause*: Puritanism.

88–9 *she-friend or cousin*: woman friend, intimate friend; but both terms could imply 'prostitute'.

100 *Salisbury*: site of fashionable horse-races.

Bath: fashionable spa.

102 *Daniel . . . Spenser*: the eight-book edition of Samuel Daniel's verse epic on the *Civil Wars* had been published in 1609, thus provoking comparisons with Edmund Spenser's *The Faerie Queene*.

t'other youth: a private joke, possibly referring to Shakespeare, Jonson's friend and middle-aged contemporary.

104 *state . . . question*: in rhetoric, the principal point in contention.

121 *rises*: possibly a misprint for 'rinses'.

135 *physic*: medicine; barbers also practised medicine.

2.3.39 *chimes . . . close*: jingles, and rhymes at the end of each phrase.

40–1 *Seneca . . . Plutarch*: the comic confusion extends the joke of 1.1.56–60 by implying depths of wisdom in verses that are platitudinous and unoriginal.

42 *the dor on*: a scoffing dismissal.

43 *by . . . light*: 'by God's light' (a mild oath).

59 *chines*: in *Iliad* vii. 321 Ajax is given the back (*chine*) of an ox.

59–60 *dunging . . . bees*: in *Georgics* i. 79–81 and iv.

62–4 *Pindarus . . . rest*: Daw's litany of classical poets, all highly esteemed in Jonson's time, includes *Seneca the tragedian*, who was then believed to be

467

a separate person from the Stoic philosopher, and *Politian*, the fifteenth-century Florentine humanist Angelo Poliziano.

72–3 *Syntagma . . . Bible*: *Syntagma juris civilis* has not been identified, but may be a systematically arranged version of the *Corpus juris civilis*, the collective name for Justinian's works on Roman law; the *Corpus juris canonici* is the title of the collection of medieval canon law published in 1582; the *King of Spain's Bible* is the *Complutensian Polyglot* (1517), the revised version (1572) of which had been financed by King Philip II and was known as the *Biblia Regia* or *Filipina*.

81 *Vatablus . . . Symancha*: eminent sixteenth-century scholars. François Vatable was a French Hebraist and authority on Aristotle; Pietro Pomponazzi was an Italian philosopher and theologian; Didacus of Simancas was a Spanish jurist who wrote on canon law.

87–8 *extraordinary . . . ordinary*: *extraordinary* means 'supernumerary', but is also an ironic pun; *in ordinary* refers to a regular official, but also puns on the sense of 'undistinguished'.

105–6 *noble . . . family*: the poetry of Sir Philip Sidney, who had died in 1586, had been published after his death with the encouragement of his family.

123–4 *consentire . . . gravida*: (Lat.) 'she seems to consent, and eventually becomes pregnant'.

2.4.66 *Fortune . . . providence*: 'By accident? Pure foresight on my part.'

89 *I am one*: (of the guests).

95 *quarter-feast*: feast given on the quarter-days (Lady Day, Midsummer, Michaelmas, Christmas) when rents due to La Foole have been paid.

97–8 *will . . . wit*: 'would sacrifice his best friends to his wit'.

105–6 *in jure civili*: (Lat.) 'in civil law' (*in* is in roman type in F, as if it were English, but it must be Latin, because the following words are ablatives).

135 *mole*: proverbially blind.

135–6 *mushroom . . . fresh*: mushrooms spring up overnight, and so are 'fresh' and (in this metaphor) inexperienced.

2.5.16–17 *composition . . . blood*: an extended musical metaphor; *temper* refers to the re-tuning of instruments for purposes of practical harmony, *height* to high pitch. The idea that Epicene is attuned to him is repeated in l. 23, where her voice 'has the just length' of his ears; *height . . . blood* implies sexual incitement.

38 *jump right*: tally.

64 *French intelligences*: news of the latest French fashions.

93 *tenth . . . letter*: supplicatory letters secured by Dauphine from the nobility.

97 *it*: archaic form of 'his' or 'its' used in baby-talk; in this speech used contemptuously.

99 *Coleharbour*: Cold Harborough, a section of Upper Thames Street that had become a debtors' sanctuary.

102 *Cranes*: the Three Cranes, a tavern on Upper Thames Street.

Bear: tavern at the south end of old London Bridge.

105–6 *tenth . . . bond*: a debtor's creditors were paid in a fixed order, so the tenth man received very little.

106 *commodity*: see note to 1.4.63.

108 *brown*: the epithet, which suggests coarseness, is transferred from bread to baker to widow.

110 *How*: a punning reference to Edmund Howes, chronicler of London and allegedly a police informer.

113 *Constantinople . . . Virginia*: bolt-holes for debtors and criminals.

114–15 *Doll . . . Common*: generic names for prostitutes. Doll Tearsheet appears in *2 Henry IV*; cf. Doll Common in *Alchemist*.

115 *may eat*: by pimping for his wife.

2.6.5 *appointed . . . hither*: arranged to meet him here.

11–12 *omnia secunda . . . saltat senex*: a Latin tag: 'everything bodes well, the old man is dancing.'

16 *silenced ministers*: banned Puritan preachers (see note to 2.2.69) whose sermons would have been long and loud.

17 *purely*: 'like a Puritan', but playing on the sense of 'exquisitely'.

18 *Cum privilegio*: Lat. 'with authority', the formula used in licences to publish books.

23 *bonis avibus*: (Lat.) 'the omens being favourable'.

36 *other place*: Otter's house.

54 *Sphinx*: female monster, here invoked as a poser of riddles.

55 *Bear Garden*: see 3.1 headnote.

57 *cups*: drinking-mugs with lids shaped like animals, all of which were baited.

64 *speak him*: reveal his character.

3.1. The metaphor of baiting animals runs through the scene. Bears, bulls, and (on special occasions) horses with apes tied to their backs were chained to a *stake* (42), tormented (hence *worry*, 47) and killed by bulldogs in *Paris Garden* (14), the arena in Southwark; the action was prolonged by officials (under the command of the *Master of the Garden*, 25) who would *stave off* (43) the dogs. Baitings in the presence of the king were conducted in the courtyard of *Banqueting House* (41), in the palace in Whitehall. *Ned Whiting* and *George Stone* (42) were famous bears; the latter was killed in the presence of the king of Denmark in 1606. There was considerable Puritan opposition to the baiting of animals.

1 *pauca verba*: (Lat.) 'few words'.

6 *Shrove Tuesday*: see note to 1.1.144.

7 *Whitsuntide . . . staff*: cap suitable for the holiday that follows Whit Sunday (seven weeks after Easter) and fool's staff of office.

13 *in rerum natura*: (Lat.) 'in the nature of things' (cf. 3.2.5).

21 *Poetarum Pegasus*: (Lat.) 'the Pegasus of poets'; the hoof of Pegasus opened the spring of Hippocrene, the water of which inspired poets.

22 *taurus*: (Lat.) 'bull'; Jupiter assumed the form of a bull in order to abduct Europa.

34–5 *horse . . . suits*: fodder for your horse and a servant's allowance of food and clothing.

3.2. Mistress Otter's phrasing is pretentious throughout the scene.

3 *obnoxious . . . difficil*: botched Latinisms: 'offensive or troublesome.'

5 *in . . . natura*: in existence.

6 *sic . . . superis*: as those above decree.

7 *intimate 'em*: botched courtly coinage, meaning 'become intimate with (i.e. depart to join) your animals'.

8 *toasts . . . butter*: a traditional accompaniment to woodcock, but also means 'wimp'; woodcocks were easily snared, and were therefore associated with gullibility.

14 *Anabaptist*: refers derisively to Baptists, who, like other Puritans, required a licence to preach.

licence: plays on the sense 'lack of restraint'.

21 *my subject*: Otter.

35 *omnia bene*: all is well.

better . . . hinges: running more smoothly.

38 *What . . . vicar*: what sort of vicar is he?

40 *out . . . picked*: with a thin, reedy voice.

42–3 *omnem . . . lapidem*: leave no stone unturned.

46 *ad manum*: [I shall be] at hand.

52 *pageant*: the Lord Mayor's Show, an annual pageant on 9 November marking the inauguration of the Lord Mayor of London.

55 *China stuffs*: Chinese fabrics.

55 *Artemidorus*: Artemidorus Daldinus, second-century Greek author of a treatise on the interpretation of dreams, not translated into English until 1644.

64 *Ware*: see note to 5.1.56.

65 *doublet*: garment normally worn by men.

67 *a leash of*: three (from hunting: three hounds or hawks).

75 *And . . . favour*: with your permission.

81 *no . . . place*: no credit for it, except for providing the place.

3.3.25 *given . . . dor*: ridiculed you.

30 *saver . . . man*: 'saviour of your manhood', with a play on 'main', the score in the dice game of hazard which, when cast, enabled the other players to recoup their stakes (hence *savers*).

52 *his own*: the truth about his own character.

57 *make one*: join in.

61 *bare-headed*: like a servant (gentlemen wore hats indoors).

69 *bare*: the doffing of hats (with sexual innuendo).

88 *by tradition*: what is given to them (Lat. *traditio*).

100 *festinate*: Otter's mistaken form of Lat. *festinanter* or post-classical *festinato* ('quickly').

111 *decora*: 'decorum' was still felt as a Latinism, so Otter pedantically offers the plural form, which here means 'pretty'.

112 *Pasiphaë*: wife of Minos, king of Crete; she mated with a bull, and their offspring was the minotaur (*minos + tauros*, bull).

113 *Callisto*: mother of Arcas by Zeus, was stellified as the Great Bear, *Ursa Major*.

114 *Ursula*: diminuative of *ursa* ('female bear'), hence a laboured reference to *Ursa Minor*, the wrong constellation.

117 *ex . . . Metamorphosi*: 'out of Ovid's *Metamorphoses*'; Pasiphaë, who was not transformed, occurs in Ovid's *Ars Amatoria*, not in *Metamorphoses*.

3.4.6 S.D. *as . . . cold*: Puritan preachers were said to speak with a nasal twang.

11 *catches . . . cloth-workers*: a trade dominated by Puritans and by militantly Protestant Flemish refugees; 'catches' is a gibe at the vulgarity of the music that they sang.

30 *civil coat*: sober profession.

36 *innocent . . . Hospital*: probably 'a child from Christ's Hospital' but possibly 'a lunatic from Bedlam' (Bethlehem Hospital).

37 *hands thus*: crossed limply in front of her.

plaice mouth: the puckered mouth of a flat-fish.

42 *stock . . . competent*: asset always appropriate.

51 *Penthesilia*: queen of the Amazons, a mythical race of female warriors.

52 *Semiramis*: ancient Assyrian who killed her lovers; after the death of her second husband she wore men's clothes at court and on the battlefield.

distaff: the emblem of manhood was a sword, of womanhood a distaff.

3.5.9 *owl*: regarded as an omen of ill fortune.

15 *night-crow*: another omen of ill fortune; ornithologically unidentified, but possibly a nightjar.

17 *left-handed*: sinister; in classical divination the flight of birds to the left was a bad omen.

21 *conduit . . . bake-house*: to the women who meet at the water-pipe or the bakery.

22 *infantry . . . court*: the 'blackguard', i.e. the lowest servants of the royal household; they followed the court on progress, carrying kitchenware.

23–4 *lippis . . . notum*: 'familiar to the bleary-eyed and to barbers' (Horace, *Satires* I. vii. 3).

39–40 *town bull*: bull owned collectively by a village to service the cows of all the farmers.

40 *mountain goat*: is a fanciful contrast (the real animal had not yet been discovered).

49 *make to herself*: anticipate.

55 *cittern*: a flat-backed lute, often kept by barbers for the use of customers and patients.

57 *ten plagues*: visited on Egypt after the Pharaoh refused to allow the Israelites to leave (Exodus 7–9).

60–1 *pox . . . hair*: barbers were no longer surgeons, but they retained the right to let blood and draw teeth, and often practised medicine.

67 *balls*: balls of soap.

76 *carving . . . paper*: barbers sold lanterns cut out of oiled paper.

77 *bawd . . . basin*: pimps and brothel-keepers were carted through the streets to the sound of drummed basins, which were rented from barbers.

79 *lotium*: stale urine, which was used by barbers to flatten hair.

81–2 *earwax . . . string*: barber-surgeons cleaned ears and pulled teeth; drawn teeth were hung on strings.

84 *millstones*: 'grinders', hence molars.

89 *set up*: in business; Morose's reply plays on the sense 'set hair'.

92 *too high set*: with reference to a gambling stake, a metaphor sustained in *go less*.

102–4 *chimney-sweepers . . . collier's*: dirty customers whose presence would discourage trade.

105 *chance-medley*: legal term for killing in self-defence, here used loosely for manslaughter 'without malice aforethought'.

3.6.2 *Another flood*: like the deluge of Genesis 7.

14 *'tis . . . me*: 'fate has decided that I shall be a cuckold' (the jackdaw was proverbially a thief).

18 *steal a marriage*: marry secretly.

27 *bear*: bear the sexual burden.

28 *oppressed*: has a secondary sense of 'ravished'.

29–30 *faculty . . . it*: ability (to bear the weight of a man) if she does not yet know how.

51 *set . . . side*: become partners as in a card game.

61 *Let . . . alone*: leave it to me.

65 *scarfs . . . gloves*: presented to guests at a wedding.

66 *colours*: of the bride and groom, carried or worn by their respective families and friends.

72 *strong meats*: solid food (a Hellenism); the contrast with milk suggests an allusion to Hebrews 5: 12–14.

77 *mere rusticity*: absolute boorishness.

80 *garters*: after the wedding ceremony the bride's garters were given to one of the attendants.

86 *friend*: lover (i.e. Daw).

88 *it*: an illicit rendezvous.

94 *groom*: plays on the senses 'bridegroom' and 'servant'.

95 *grafted*: with cuckold's horns.

101 *begin . . . cup*: 'drink your health in a manner that you will find unpleasant' (by cuckolding you).

3.7.6 *hair . . . guts*: horsehair for the bow, rosin to rub on it, and catgut for the strings of the viol.

13 *ass*: donkey, proverbial for obstinacy and stupidity.

14 *hanging . . . ears*: compares the tails of Morose's nightcaps to the drooping ears of an exhausted donkey.

17 *more reputation*: greater honour.

S.D. *sewing . . . meat*: directing the serving of the food.

33 *in ordinary*: see note to 2.3.87–8.

37 *heralds*: court officials whose duties included settling questions of precedence.

4.1 Truewit's observations on women and courtship (31–114) are imitations of passages in Ovid's *Ars Amatoria*, a witty and ironic treatise on the 'art of love'.

15 *faith . . . article*: playful allusion to the Anglican Thirty-nine Articles of faith.

18 *go . . . jest*: die laughing.

19 *nest . . . nightcaps*: it was common to wear two nightcaps, but the idea of a set (*nest*) of nightcaps fitting inside each other is comic exaggeration.

22 *saddler's horse*: a wooden horse and rider used to display a saddle in front of a saddler's shop.

29–30 *come . . . thee*: come round to your opinion.

37–8 *carve . . . act*: carve the air, gesture.

45–6 *measure . . . voice*: a graceful walk and a lilting voice.

51 *Amadis de Gaule*: French prose version of the Spanish romance *Amadís de Gaula*.

Don Quixote: the first part of Cervantes's *Don Quijote de la Mancha* had been published in 1605.

58 *droning*: sucking as if drawing in air in order to blow the reed of a bagpipe, which was still a common English instrument.

60 *the near*: nearer (comparative form of 'nigh').

65 *doubt to*: doubt that he can.

67 *Penelope*: wife of Odysseus, to whom she remained faithful throughout his twenty-year absence.

68 *Ostend*: Flemish port taken by the Spanish on 20 September 1604 after a three-year siege.

85 *height . . . line*: the high and low wards in fencing.

91–2 *credit . . . back*: as testimony to your sexual prowess.

96 *than . . . safety*: than the safe keeping of your head on your shoulders.

107 *second parts*: supporting roles (Lat. *secundae partes*).

112 *out . . . her*: against your interests to court her.

132 *Medea*: sorceress who helped Jason to secure the Golden Fleece and restored the youth of Aeson (Jason's father).

Forman: Simon Forman (1552–1611), astrologer and quack doctor whose clients included many court ladies.

4.2.7 *course*: plays on the senses 'round of drinks' and 'attack by dogs on baited animal'.

12–13 *set . . . his*: the posture for drinking contests.

16 *Et . . . cantu*: 'and the trumpets sounded with a hoarse sound' (*Aeneid* VIII. 2).

17 *Well said*: well done.

22 *off . . . spurs*: strip him of his knighthood.

39 *Iacta . . . alea*: 'the die is cast' (Caesar's words on crossing the Rubicon).

49 *ass . . . circle*: like a donkey driving a rotary mill (with an obscene pun on 'circle').

53 *tribus verbis*: in three words, i.e. briefly.

61 *Tritons*: sea-gods who blew conch shells.

62 *Nunc . . . libero*: 'now is the time to drink, now with free foot [to dance]': Horace, *Odes* I. xxxviii. 1, introducing his ode on the downfall of Cleopatra, the destroyer of men.

63 S.D. *above*: possibly 'within', but more likely Morose appears briefly on the upper stage.

64 *sons . . . earth*: bastards (Lat. *terrae filii*).

67 *clogdogdo*: meaning unknown; possibly Bear Garden slang or a nonce-word.

68–9 *mala bestia*: evil beast.

81 *viper*: represented treachery towards one's nourisher and protector; *mandrake*: poisonous plant whose divided roots were said to resemble the human male.

83 *mercury . . . bones*: ingredients of cosmetics.

89 *German clock*: said to need constant repair and adjustment.

91 *quarters*: plays on the senses 'quarter-strokes' (of a clock), 'rooms', and 'quarter-blows' (in fencing).

done . . . right: matched me drink for drink.

107 S.D. *descends*: there was no direct access from the upper stage, so Morose must have entered from the side, having walked downstairs offstage.

109 *Mary Ambree*: said, in the ballad tradition, to have dressed as a man and participated in the Siege of Ghent (1584).

110 *stentors*: Stentor, the Greek herald at Troy, was said to have had a voice as loud as the shout of fifty men.

111 *ill . . . Day*: Morose's grumpy phrase recalls 'Evil May Day', the term that commemorated the May Day riots of 1517.

galley-foist: state barge that on 9 November took the new Lord Mayor up the Thames to Westminster for his installation; hundreds of boats filled with revellers joined the annual procession.

126 *that is on*: Otter's head, with its cuckold's horns, could be the model for a replacement cover for the tankard.

128 *Ratcliffe*: rough area on the Thames in Stepney; one of the 'liberties' of London, and therefore not subject to its legal jurisdiction.

129 *bona spes*: good hope.

4.3.5 *made you*: were you doing.

13 *I'll . . . Morose*: the masculine form of address, replacing the earlier 'Master Morose'.

16 *milk . . . honey*: as in the Promised Land (Exodus 3: 8).

34 *new one*: new phrase (used sarcastically of La Foole's cliché).

43 *Cockpit*: private theatre and cockpit in Whitehall.

4.4.11 *supererogatory*: a technical Roman Catholic theological term (repudiated in Anglican Article 14) referring to acts that are not obligatory.

12 *Westminster Hall*: now the vestibule of the Houses of Parliament, but then the great hall of the Palace of Westminster.

13 *fall . . . stag*: signalled by the barking of hounds and the sounding of huntsmen's horns.

Tower Wharf: see note to 1.2.14–15.

14 *London Bridge*: the nineteen bridge-piers created noisy rapids.

Billingsgate: fish market and dock on wharf east of London Bridge.

33 *notes . . . kindness*: tokens of behaviour appropriate to a woman.

48–50 *how . . . has*: (comic) symptoms of madness drawn from Plautus, *Menaechmi* 829–30.

53 *Pliny*: the *Natural History* of the Roman author Pliny the Elder contains sections on the medical applications of plants, animals, and minerals.

Paracelsus: sixteenth-century Swiss-German authority on medicine.

60–2 *insania . . . fanaticus*: madness, insanity, or melancholic ecstasy . . . going out [of one's mind] . . . proceeds from melancholy to madness.

63 *have . . . alive*: be dissected in an anatomy class while still alive.

75–6 *Doni's Philosophy*: Sir Thomas North's *Moral Philosophy of Doni*, a translation of the Italian version of the Fables of Bidpai, a famous collection of ancient Hindu stories. Sir Amorous mistakenly thinks that the European tale of Reynard the Fox appears in this collection.

83 *Seneca . . . Plutarch*: first-century AD authors, the Hispano-Roman Seneca the Younger and the Greek Plutarch; both wrote treatises on moral philosophy.

87 *Ethics*: the *Nichomachean Ethics*, *Eudemian Ethics*, and *Magna Moralia* were all attributed to Aristotle.

94 *exercise*: plays on the senses 'participating in a ceremony', 'training an animal' (hence *tame*), and 'undergoing a martyr's ordeal'.

95–6 *The . . . Salve*: Thomas Brecon's popular sixteenth-century tract offering advice to the sick.

96–7 *Greene's . . . Wit*: the dramatist Robert Greene's popular deathbed confessional and hortatory pamphlet (1592), described as *cheap* because it only cost one groat (fourpence).

118 *disfurnish you*: deprive you (of your small amount of wit).

133–4 *canon lawyer*: lawyer specializing in ecclesiastical law. Divorce could only be granted by a private Act of Parliament, but judicial separation 'from board and bed' (*a mensa et thoro*) was granted by ecclesiastical courts.

148 *set . . . nick*: unclear, but probably 'cheated me out of my money'.

4.5.8 *if . . . keeper*: parodies Genesis 4: 9.

10 *upon posts*: by running errands.

11 *three suits*: like a servant (see note to 3.1.34–5).

15 *to . . . hand*: without effort on your part.

26 *studies*: the Whitefriars theatre had three doors at the rear of the stage; the *studies* were supposed to lie behind the doors on either side, and the *arras* (30) was a curtain covering the middle door.

28 *Guelphs . . . Ghibellines*: feuding political factions supporting popes (*Guelphs*) and emperors (*Ghibellines*) in late medieval northern Italy.

37 *taken up*: resolved.

41–2 *wedding . . . at*: Pirithous, king of the Lapiths, invited the centaurs to his wedding to Hippodamia; a battle ensued when a drunken centaur attempted to abduct the bride.

42 *she-one*: in classical myth centaurs were always male.

51 *put . . . up*: do not sheathe it.

66 *do . . . right*: agree to a duel.

89–90 *fellow . . . possession*: claimants to disputed property often took control of the property with the help of armed assistants.

93 *principal*: original, i.e. La Foole.

false brother: treacherous associate.

100 *justice . . . hall*: characteristically hung with armour and weaponry.

101 *'sessed*: assessed for the provision of armed soldiers for the king.

102 *at . . . foils*: to fence with so many different swords.

103 *St Pulchre's*: St Sepulchre's, populous parish near Newgate.

104 *breeches*: 'slops', fashionable baggy breeches with stuffed legs.

125 *resolved him*: concluded that he was.

137 *tempt . . . breeches*: test the capacity of your breeches to hold urine.

154 *in snuff*: offended.

158 *walks . . . down*: paces around the house like a patrol checking on the vigilance of sentries.

167 *put it on*: adopt it.

179 *Sir A-jax*: the flushing toilet, described by its inventor Sir John Harington in *The Metamorphosis of A-jax* (1596), punning on 'a jakes', i.e. privy.

233–4 *magis . . . feriendo*: more in suffering than in doing, more in submitting than in assaulting.

261 *Seneca*: here invoked as the exponent of Stoicism.

286 *starting off*: shying away like a horse.

290 *at . . . blunt*: to be beaten with a foil, a blunt-edged sword with a capped point.

293–4 *gules . . . nombre*: parodies heraldic terminology: *gules*, red, i.e. bloody; *sans nombre*, innumerable.

305 *all hid*: the cry in the game of hide-and-seek.

310–11 *Damon . . . Pythias*: Pythias (the Renaissance form of Phintias), sentenced to death by Dionysius of Syracuse, returned to save his friend Damon who had offered himself as bail.

4.6.24 *set . . . brake*: assume a fixed expression; a *brake* is a frame to constrain the leg of a horse while it is being shod.

25 *in form*: in place.

27 *French hermaphrodite*: probably Henri III, king of France (1551–89), a flagrant transvestite.

68 *Pylades . . . Orestes*: in Greek myth, husband and brother of Electra, and types of faithful friendship; together they avenged the murder of Agamemnon, the father of Orestes.

93 *had . . . forth*: took it away.

4.7.4 *begged*: been the subject of a legal petition submitted by a courtier in anticipation of the sequestration of Morose's property as that of a criminal.

18 *you . . . resolved*: you want your case to be decided in your favour.

41 *civil . . . welt*: the gown of a civil lawyer, with a border of fur.

42 *canonical . . . sleeves*: the gown of a proctor (canon lawyer) in an ecclesiastical court.

45–7 *without . . . sake*: the disclaimer is Jonson's attempt to fend off the difficulties occasioned by his satire on the legal profession in *Poetaster* 6.

5.1.20 *Nomentack*: Virginia Indian brought to England as a hostage in 1608 and sent back in May 1609.

21 *Prince . . . mistress*: despite the fact that 'his' refers to Daw, Lady Arabella Stuart understood this phrase to imply that she was the mistress of Stephano Janiculo. See note to Dedication 17.

22 *latitude*: both 'breadth' and 'freedom from moral strictures'.

26–7 *carry . . . you*: jibes at the effeminacy of the knights.

37 *come . . . Tripoli*: vault, tumble.

56 *great . . . Ware*: huge painted and carved Elizabethan bed capable of sleeping twelve people; then at the Saracen's Head in Ware, now in the Victoria and Albert Museum in London.

62 *bath*: medicinal bath for the treatment of lice and venereal disease.

5.2.3 *make out*: contrive.

22 *Fidelia*: Latin for 'pot' (so she will 'contain' knowledge) with a play on *fidelis*, her role ('confidante') and her name ('Trusty').

27–8 *make . . . to*: place any trust in.

32 *pargets*: plasters; normally with reference to walls, here used derisively of make-up.

47 *you . . . tell*: disclosure of fairy gifts was deemed to be unlucky.

50 *caution*: Centaure's warning about Haughty.

56 *enter . . . physic*: let it be known that I was taking a purgative (and therefore staying indoors).

61–2 *knights reformados*: officers of 'reformed' (i.e. disbanded) companies who retained their ranks; the semi-Anglicized Hispanic apposite suggests an order of knights.

74 *sooth . . . more*: one or two cries of 'sooth!' ('indeed!').

75 *set . . . hands*: signed the affidavit.

5.3 The comedy centres on the presentation of the impediments to marriage in canon law. Cutbeard plays the part of a canon lawyer expounding the grounds on which a marriage can be declared null and void; Otter assumes the role of a vigilant Puritan divine.

8 *l'envoy*: Anglicized French (with the article assimilated) term for the conclusion of a poem, here applied to a play.

12 *be out*: forget your lines.

37 *positive divinity*: branch of theology that treats matters of fact, custom, or enactment, as opposed to 'natural theology', which deals with principles and universal laws.

55 *perpetual . . . Eltham*: Cornelius Drebbel, the Dutch scientist, displayed a machine that allegedly demonstrated perpetual motion at Eltham Palace, in Kent.

63 *à divertendo*: derived from the Latin word for 'separating'.

78 *impedimentum erroris*: an impediment arising from a mistake.

80 *error personae*: mistaken identity.

82 *error fortunae*: mistake concerning financial circumstances.

84 *error qualitatis*: mistake concerning character.

89 *ante . . . copulam*: before the legal union, but not after it.

90–1 *nec . . . benedictionem*: not after the blessing of the marriage.

91–2 *contract*: betrothal (not marriage).

94–6 *conditio . . . condition*: social status, in this case that of slave or free woman, creates obstacles of ownership and eligibility.

97–8 *sublatae . . . Christians*: abolished in Protestant countries; Spanish slaving was condemned by the English, who did not trade in slaves till 1620.

105 *discipline*: the laws of the Church of England, which had overturned the Roman Catholic law that a person who had taken a 'solemn vow' (of chastity) could not marry.

107 *degrees*: the Calvinist version of the degrees of consanguinity (closeness of blood relationship) had been given canonical authority in England in 1603.

111 *cognatio spiritualis*: a spiritual blood relationship.

113 *absurd . . . superstitious*: Otter's reply reflects growing Puritan opposition to infant baptism and the idea of godparents.

118 *crimen adulterii*: crime of adultery.

123 *You . . . you*: a caustic reference to the power of the consistory courts to examine those suspected of Roman Catholicism; Jonson had been examined in 1606.

130 *if . . . orders*: under Roman Catholic law nuns took solemn vows, whereas 'sisters' took simple vows; solemn vows were irrevocable, so former nuns could never marry.

134–5 *ligamen . . . before*: bond; if you had been married previously.

137–8 *publica . . . affinitas*: public decency . . . an unconsummated (earlier) marriage.

139–40 *affinitas . . . impedimentum*: relationship arising from a betrothal . . . slight impediment.

142 *affinitas . . . fornicatione*: relationship arising from fornication.

143 *vera affinitas*: true relationship.

145 *quae . . . matrimonio*: (than the relationship) which derives from legal marriage.

146–7 *nascitur . . . caro*: it follows from this that through their physical union, two people are made one flesh.

149–50 *Ita . . . generat*: thus he who fathers a child through fornication is equally a true father.

151 *Et . . . generatur*: and he is truly a son who is thus fathered; a contentious view, as in law a bastard son was *filius nullius*, the son of nobody.

154 *si . . . nequibis*: if by chance you are unable to copulate.

155 *impedimentum gravissimum*: a most weighty impediment.

156 *manifestam frigiditatem*: evident impotence.

160 *morbus . . . insanabilis*: a chronic and incurable disease.

168 *reddere debitum*: honour his obligation.

omnipotentes: all-powerful men (Otter's error for *impotentes*, impotent men).

169 *lobster*: insults Otter for his ruddy complexion.

170–1 *minime . . . matrimonium*: least fit to contract a marriage.

172–3 *unmatrimonial*: because Otter's confused case-endings are not grammatically 'married'.

176 *post matrimonium*: after marriage.

frigiditate praeditus: one who suffers from frigidity.

179–80 *uti . . . sorore*: use his wife as a wife may keep her as a sister.

181 *merely apostatical*: utterly heretical.

184–5 *Haec . . . retractant*: these things prohibit uniting in marriage and revoke a marriage already made (a quotation from Thomas Aquinas).

188 *In aeternum*: forever.

190–1 *prorsus . . . torum*: absolutely useless for the marriage-bed.

191 *praestare . . . datam*: fulfil the promise given.

192 *convalere*: recover.

196 *simulare . . . uxoris*: pretend to be frigid out of hatred for his wife.

197 *adulter manifestus*: a manifest adulterer.

199 *prostitutor uxoris*: a pander to his wife.

202 *manifeste frigidus*: manifestly frigid.

207 *frigiditatis causa*: on grounds of frigidity.

210 *libellum divortii*: a bill of divorce.

216 *in . . . conscientiae*: at the bar of conscience (proverbial).

219 *Exercendi potestate*: the power of putting into effect.

5.4.8 *changes*: as in bell-ringing.

12 *one*: Otter (4.2.94).

24 *of . . . inches*: courageous.

44 *uncarnate*: without a body; Centaure's coinage, from 'incarnate'.

45 *offer it*: attempt to do such a thing.

61 *de . . . uxoris*: on behalf of the wife.

68–9 *in . . . qualitatis*: see 5.3.84.

70 *carry it*: act.

75 *dirimere . . . reddere*: cancel the contract and render it null and void; cf. 5.3.69–70, where a distinction is drawn.

108 *to . . . hand*: delivered into my hands.

114 *except . . . knights*: object to them as proven cowards, and therefore inadmissible as witnesses.

125 *virgo . . . nuptias*: a virgin before marriage.

127 *ratum coniugium*: a valid union.

181 *protest before*: declare in advance.

186 *iustum impedimentum*: just impediment.

187 *in . . . gradu*: in the first degree.

201 *garland*: the bay wreath, symbol of victory.

206 *on*: about.

208 *stuck . . . upon*: played a trick on.

209 *this Amazon*: Mistress Otter.

214–15 *make . . . faces*: learn new bows and smirks.

221 *insectae*: possibly a misprint (for the neuter plural *insecta*), but possibly a comic reflection of recent arguments that all insects were gendered and did not arise from putrefaction or spontaneous generation; in this case the feminine plural implies effeminacy.

223 *of years*: an adult.

NOTES TO COLOPHON

Children . . . Revels: a boys' company under the patronage of Queen Anne; it received its patent on 4 January 1610, so '1609' may be 'old style' (calculating the year's end as 24 March) or the name may have been applied retroactively to a performance in December 1609.

principal comedians: on Field, see note to *Bartholomew Fair* 5.3.76. Barkstead, a poet and dramatist, played Morose. The part of La Foole was played by Attwell, who joined an adult company (Lady Elizabeth's Men) in 1613. Blaney, Carey, and Penn also joined adult companies; nothing is known of Allin and Smith.

The Alchemist

NOTES TO DEDICATORY EPISTLE

3 *Mary . . . Wroth*: eldest daughter of Robert Sidney, first Earl of Leicester; married Sir Robert Wroth in 1604, author (in 1621) of *Urania*, a romance

modelled on the *Arcadia* of her uncle Sir Philip Sidney; her married name could also be spelt 'Worth', hence 'most deserving her name'.

5–8 *truth . . . hecatomb*: possibly a sign of Jonson's reconversion to Protestantism, as it seems to repudiate (in language borrowed from Seneca, *De Beneficiis* I. vi. I) the Roman Catholic doctrine that sacraments confer grace *ex opere operato*, through the act performed, regardless of the spiritual state of the priest or the recipient.

NOTES TO EPISTLE TO THE READER

9 *naturals*: natural abilities, with a play on the sense of 'fool'.

13 *excellent vice*: extraordinary viciousness.

31 *numerous*: plays on the sense of 'harmonious'.

NOTES TO THE PERSONS OF THE PLAY

Doll: diminutive of Dorothy (3.3.32), but also generic name for a mistress.

Lovewit: the name is never spoken.

Pertinax: (Lat.): 'stubborn'; also the name of a Roman emperor who ruled for three months in AD 193 and was deposed because of his zeal for reform (which alienated the Senate) and for discipline (which estranged the Praetorians).

Amsterdam: seat of the expatriate British community of Puritans.

Ananias: name of nine biblical characters, meaning 'Yahweh has been gracious'; probably named after the Damascan who baptized Saul of Tarsus (Acts 9: 10–19), but identified by Subtle as 'the varlet that cozened the Apostles' (2.5.72–3).

Kestrel: a species of hawk, but also (by confusion with 'coistrel') 'rascal'.

Mutes: possibly a misprint for 'Mute', as the silent chaplain of 5.5 is the only possible candidate.

NOTES TO THE ARGUMENT

2 *sickness hot*: the play was written in the wake of a particularly virulent epidemic of plague in London in 1609 and 1610.

6 *narrow practice*: mere swindling and prostitution.

12 *selling . . . flies*: 'flies' are 'attendant demons' or 'spies'

stone: the philosophers' stone, for changing base metals to gold.

NOTES TO PROLOGUE

19 *apply*: interpret dramatic characters and action as references to contemporary people and events (and so institute legal proceedings against the author).

1.1.1 *thy worst*: do your worst.

3 *strip you*: i.e. of your servant's livery.

4 *out . . . sleights*: stop you playing your tricks.

7 *strong water*: acid (in the bottle).

16 *livery . . . thrum*: a badly-paid (£3 a year) servant dressed in shabby livery made of waste thread (*thrum*).

17 *Friars*: Blackfriars, the area of London in which the play was acted, and the name of the theatre.

18 *vacations*: law courts alternated between *term* and *vacation*; the law terms corresponded with the London social seasons, and the gentry left London during the vacations.

19 *suburb-captain*: bogus captain (*apocryphal*) living by dishonest means in the suburbs beyond the legal jurisdiction of London.

25 *Pie Corner*: area of cheap food stalls around the Magpie Inn, in Smithfield.

28 *pinched-horn*: like a shoehorn, thin with hunger.

29–30 *Roman . . . worms*: obscure; probably 'sallow and full of blackheads'.

31 *artillery yard*: Artillery Garden, a military practice range.

36 *felt of rug*: hat made of frieze, a coarse woollen cloth.

38 *algebra*: associated with alchemy through false derivation from Geber, the alleged Arab author of a series of medieval treatises on alchemy.

52–3 *chippings . . . men*: scraps of food (*chippings*) and beer were given to the poor over a half-door (*buttery-hatch*), but Face has locked the half-door, kept the scraps, and sold the beer to distillers (*aqua-vitae men*).

55 *post . . . pair*: a card game. *letting . . . counters*: supplying of gambling chips in return for tips.

56 *marks*: an accounting measure (not a coin) worth 13*s.* 4*d.* (67p.); 20 marks = £13. 6*s.* 6*d.* (£13.33).

69 *third region*: the upper (and purest) region of the air.

70 *spirit . . . quintessence*: in alchemical medicine humans were deemed to consist of salt (body), sulphur (soul), and mercury (spirit); all material substances were said to be composed of four elements (earth, water, air, fire); the fifth element (*quintessence*), pure essence, was one of the substances that alchemists sought to distil. On alchemy see Introduction, pp. xvii–xviii.

71 *philosophers' work*: the philosophers' stone, the powdered form of which could transmute base metals into gold.

79 *fly . . . projection*: explode at the final stage of alchemical transmutation.

83 *equi-clibanum*: accusative form (treating *past* as a Latin adjective) of *equi-clibanus*, an oven warmed by the mild heat of fermenting horse dung.

85 *deaf John's*: unidentified tavern.

90–3 *hang . . . Paul's*: begins as a curse ('be hanged') and ends as a threat to hang a picture of Subtle and his trickery in St Paul's Cathedral, where posters were regularly displayed.

94 *cozening . . . coal*: deceiving by placing silver inside a coal which, when burnt, leaves behind a silver nugget that has apparently been produced by alchemy

95 *with . . . shears*: by divination (of the identity of thieves).

96 *Erecting . . . houses*: casting horoscopes in the twelve signs (*houses*) of the zodiac.

97 *taking . . . glass*: calling up spirits with the use of a crystal ball.

98 *Told . . . cut*: a broadside with rubric headings and a woodcut portrait.

99 *Ratsey*: highwayman who wore a grotesque mask; broadsides were sold at his execution on 27 March 1605.

106 *lying . . . basket*: eating more than his share of the food brought to prisoners.

110 *republic*: joint interests, commonwealth, with a play on Doll's surname and her status as a 'public thing' (Lat. *respublica*).

112–13 *tricesimo . . . Eight*: laws were dated by regnal years; the statute of 1541 making sorcery and witchcraft felonies was therefore dated 33 Henry VIII.

114 *laundering . . . it*: bathing coins in acid to dissolve some of the gold, and clipping the edges of coins (which were not milled).

121 *dog-bolt*: obscure, but probably the bolt from a cross-bow, here animated by *snarling*.

128–9 *Puritan . . . feather*: the feather-merchants of Blackfriars were Puritans; cf. *Bartholomew Fair* 5.5.76.

131 *primacy . . . divisions*: prime share of the profits.

133 *powder . . . with*: in alchemy, the 'powder of projection' (taken from the philosophers' stone) was thrown into a crucible of molten base metal; here used metaphorically of the fraudster's art.

137 *Fall . . . couples*: co-operate like a pair of hounds when hunting.

139 *term*: see note to 1.1.18.

150 *'Ods precious*: by God's precious blood.

152 *Sol . . . Luna*: (Lat.) sun and moon; slang for gold and silver.

165 *king came in*: soon after his accession in 1603 King James ruled against Puritan demands for ecclesiastical change at the Hampton Court Conference.

167 *from . . . ride*: breathless to see me carted as a whore.

168–9 *hole . . . ear-rent*: to have your ears cropped in the pillory.

170 *Don Provost*: the provost-marshal, here used loosely of the hangman, who was entitled to the clothes of his victims.

175 *Claridiana*: heroine of *The Mirror of Princely Deeds and Knighthood*, the English version of a romance by Diego Ortuñez de Calahorra.

178–9 *longest . . . Particular*: Face and Subtle will draw straws to establish who will sleep with Doll.

191 *Dagger*: a tavern in Holborn, the borough of two of the Inns of Court.

1.2.10 *broke . . . him*: broached the matter with him.

17 *Read*: Simon Read, a Southwark physician who was accused in 1607 of having raised spirits in order to recover stolen money; he was subsequently pardoned.

26 *chiaus . . . Turk*: *chiaus* (modern Turkish *çavus*), messenger, with reference to the deceptions of the Turk Mustafa, who claimed in 1607 to be the *chiaus* of Sultan Ahmed and so was lavishly entertained.

42 *horse . . . halter*: may you be carted to the gallows.

46 *Clim . . . Claribels*: a late medieval outlaw remembered in *The Ballad of Adam Bell* and a 'lewd knight' in Spenser's *Fairie Queene* IV. ix. 20.

47 *five . . . flush*: the highest possible hand in the card game of primero.

50 *Vicar*: the vicar-general, who represented the bishop or archbishop in ecclesiastical courts, which tried cases of sorcery.

54 *six . . . hands*: court-hand, chancery-hand, English secretary hand, French secretary hand, Roman, and Italic.

56 *Testament*: so Q; F has *Xenophon*, probably to appease the censor, but possibly to suggest passing off a classical text as a New Testament, thus invalidating the oath.

61 *velvet head*: the velvet down on a stag's antlers and the velvet cap of a physician.

69 *assumpsit*: (Lat.) 'he undertook', a legal term clarified in 1602 to refer to an implied promise to pay, without an express agreement.

81–2 *set . . . it*: bet against him, for he will win.

100 *o' . . . score*: on credit (because Dapper will have taken all their cash).

109 *dead . . . Isaac*: John Holland and his son John Isaac Holland, fifteenth-century Dutch alchemists whose works had recently been published in England (hence Jonson's assumption that the son was still alive).

111–12 *put . . . cloak*: reduce to their last garment, possibly with specific reference to the gowns of the six Clerks of Chancery.

128 *born . . . head*: a good omen.

152 *for . . . know*: I can assure you.

1.3.5 *Free . . . Grocers*: a full member of the Grocers' Company, with which the Apothecaries' ('druggers') Society was merged from 1606 to 1617; members of the Company could sell tobacco.

9 *plot on't*: ground-plan of it.

23–7 *tobacco . . . clouts*: sun-cured tobacco deteriorated *en route* to England, and was revivified and adulterated by these means.

29 *conserve . . . beans*: roses preserved with sugar (used as medicine) and the aromatic flowers of French beans.

30–1 *maple . . . juniper*: tobacco is smoked in Drugger's shop, hence the maple block for cutting tobacco, the tongs to hold the coal used to light the pipe, the clay pipes from Winchester, and the slow juniper fire to dry the pipes.

32 *goldsmith*: banking was controlled by goldsmiths, who were therefore despised as usurers.

37 *called . . . scarlet*: appointed sheriff of London.

40 *fine for't*: sheriffs were chosen by the king, and the office was compulsory; one could be excused in return for a cash payment.

56 *house . . . Libra*: in astrology the planet governing the zodiacal sign in the ascendant at the time of one's birth is deemed to be the lord of one's horoscope. Subtle substitutes Mercury for Venus as lord of Libra (represented as scales, hence *balance*) in order to predict a successful mercantile career.

59 *Ormus*: Hormuz, a Portuguese island in the Persian Gulf used for trans-shipping spices from south-east Asia.

65–6 *Mathlai . . . Thiel*: the angels of Wednesday, the day of Mercury; Jonson has taken the information from Pietro d'Albano's *Heptameron, seu Elementa Magica* (1567?).

79 *give a say*: attempt.

1.4.14 *magisterium*: Subtle means 'masterpiece' (Lat. *praeclarum opus*), but instead uses the Latin word for 'director' or 'instruction'.

20 *Reaching . . . dose*: offering his medicine.

Moorfields: area beyond the city walls where lepers (who could not enter the city) could beg.

21 *pomander-bracelets*: made of aromatic paste and worn as a prophylactic against plague.

2.1.2 *In . . . orbe*: in the New World.

4 *Great . . . Ophir*: Solomon was said to have secured the gold for the temple at Jerusalem from Ophir, which was reached in the course of a

voyage of three years (1 Kings 9–10); Ophir had been variously located, but Inca gold had made Peru a candidate.

8 *spectatissimi*: (Lat.) [numbered among the] most respected [citizens].

9 *hollow die*: dice (singular form) loaded for cheating.

10–14 *No more . . . commodity*: unscrupulous Jacobean money-lenders evaded the usury laws by forcing borrowers to accept worthless commodities as part of their loans. Here a prostitute (*livery-punk*) induces a young man to seal an agreement, and he in turn beats the servant who brought the commodity; the prostitute may be the commodity.

17 *Madam Augusta*: a brothel-madam, probably coined from Juvenal's 'whore empress' (*meretrix Augusta*, Satire 118).

18 *sons . . . hazard*: gentleman-soldiers and gamblers.

19 *golden calf*: statue worshipped by idolatrous Israelites (Exodus 32).

21 *go . . . ensign*: carry on drinking and gambling instead of responding to the call to return to their military units.

22 *start . . . viceroys*: beget viceroys (playing on the sense of 'kings of vice').

26 *fire-drake*: fiery dragon, hence by comic implication the alchemist's assistant who pumps the bellows and blows on the fire.

33 *Lothbury*: street of London's coppersmiths.

35 *Devonshire . . . Cornwall*: counties where copper and tin were mined.

39–40 *Mercury . . . Venus . . . Moon . . . Sun*: in alchemy, astrological signs of mercury, copper, silver, and gold.

41 *ad infinitum*: without limit.

47–8 *flower . . . elixir*: synonyms for the philosophers' stone.

55 *renew . . . eagle*: Psalm 103: 5.

56 *fifth age*: years between 50 and 65.

58 *patriarchs*: the longevity of the patriarchs from Adam (930 years) to Noah (950 years) was attributed to their possession of the stone and elixir.

62 *vestals of Pict-hatch*: ironic reference to the prostitutes of Pict-hatch (a district of brothels near the Charterhouse) as vestal virgins, servants of Vesta, Roman goddess of the hearth (hence *fire*, here referring to syphilis).

64 *nature naturized*: scholastic philosophers distinguished between *natura naturata*, created nature, and *natura naturans*, the creative power of nature; the stone is here said to be the former, a created rather than a creating object; alchemy thus avoided the charge of blasphemy.

71 *players . . . praises*: because the theatres were closed during outbreaks of plague.

76 *he . . . waterwork*: Peter Moris, a Dutchman who in 1582 built a water-pump on an arch of London Bridge and supplied private houses with piped water.

81–3 *book . . . Adam*: various medieval alchemical treatises were attributed to Adam, Moses, and Miriam, and the 'Song of Solomon' was sometimes read as an alchemical allegory.

84 *High Dutch*: German, which was claimed to be the language of Adam by Joannes Goropius Becanus in 1569.

88 *Irish wood*: said to be protected from insects by the blessing of St Patrick.

89–104 *Jason's . . . stone*: alchemists interpreted classical myths as allegories (*abstract riddles*, 104) of the alchemical process.

89 *Jason's fleece*: the difficult quest of the Greek hero Jason for the Golden Fleece was interpreted by the alchemists as a quest for an alchemical treatise written on the back of the fleece (*ram-vellum*, 91).

92 *Pythagoras' . . . tub*: the golden thigh attributed to the Greek philosopher Pythagoras and the box from which Pandora released plagues and natural disasters were both interpreted as accounts of alchemical transformations.

94–100 *bulls . . . fixed*: Jason had to harness two fire-breathing bulls to a plough, plough a field, sow the teeth of a dragon killed by Cadmus, and kill the warriors that sprang up from the teeth; he accomplished the task with the assistance of the sorceress Medea. Mammon interprets the story as an alchemical experiment.

96 *mercury sublimate*: chloride of mercury.

98 *helm*: the helm of the Argo and the spouted lid of the alembic.

99 *Mars . . . field*: the field of battle (Mars was the god of war) and iron, for which Mars was the astrological sign.

101 *Hesperian garden*: where the golden apples grew; Hercules killed the guardian dragon and secured the apples.

Cadmus: built Thebes with the men that sprang up from the dragon's teeth.

102 *Jove*: seduced Danaë in a shower of golden rain.

Midas: whose touch turned everything to gold.

Argus: the watchman with 100 eyes, was charmed to sleep by Hermes (Mercury), and his eyes were given to the peacock's tail, which was also an alchemical symbol (2.2.27).

103 *Demogorgon*: the primal god described by Boccaccio in *De Genealogia Deorum*.

2.2.3 *red ferment*: the antepenultimate stage of the process of transmutation.

8 *Give . . . affront*: treat lords as your social equals.

9 *Blushes . . . bolt's-head*: is the flask reddening?

14–16 *covering . . . thatch*: strip the lead off the roofs of churches and let them stand bare-headed, like their congregations, or replace the lead with wooden tiles.

26–8 *pale . . . agni*: the colours of the alchemical sequence are described symbolically: yellow, green (the *green lion* was a 'spirit' with the power to transmute), grey (the crow's beak), multi-coloured (the peacock's tail), pure white (the swan), and the red blood of the lamb (*sanguis agni*).

33 *seraglio*: the security of the harem of the Turkish sultan was the responsibility of a body of black eunuchs headed by a 'master of the maidens'; Face is disguised as the alchemist's 'lungs' (servant in charge of the bellows), so his face may be blackened by smoke.

36 *Equal with Solomon*: Solomon had 700 wives and 300 concubines (1 Kings 11: 3); alchemists attributed his wisdom to possession of the philosophers' stone. The phrase plays on the sense of 'stone' as 'kidney stone'.

39 *Hercules*: who inseminated the fifty daughters of King Thespius in one night.

40 *blood and spirit*: the requisite colour and purity.

42–5 *Tiberius . . . imitated*: the emperor Tiberius was said to have furnished his villa on Capri with erotic pictures illustrating the poetry of the Greek poetess Elephantis; similarly, the Italian poet Pietro Aretino wrote a series of obscene sonnets (*Sonnetti Lussuriosi*, 1523) to accompany sixteen pornographic designs by Giulio Romano. Aretino is deemed *dull* by comparison with Mammon's fantasies.

48 *succubae*: whores, i.e. concubines (classical Latin), as opposed to Renaissance Latin *succubi*, demons in female form; the latter would be blasphemous.

62–3 *Eloquent . . . fart*: in 1607 Sir Henry Ludlow, one of the *eloquent burgesses* (members) of parliament, rejected a message from the House of Lords by breaking wind noisily; this flatulent reply was celebrated in several poems which circulated in manuscript, including Jonson's Epigram 133, ll. 107–10.

67 *for them*: as far as these sexual boasters are concerned.

76 *spirit . . . Sol*: distillate of gold.

77 *Apicius*: proverbial cognomen of several Roman gourmets; Cleopatra was said to have drunk a pearl dissolved in vinegar.

91 *Persian*: Sardanapalus, the last king of Assyria, celebrated for his voluptuousness and luxury.

94 *gums . . . air*: aromatic gums and perfume (*air*) from the Middle East, the site of the Garden of Eden.

97 *homo frugi*: a temperate man.

100 *That . . . so*: 'the man who makes it, sir, is so.'

2.3.30–1 *triple . . . spirit*: the human soul was united with the body by the activity of three spirits (vital, natural, and animal); here the union is mystically attributed to the stone.

32 *Ulenspiegel*: low-German form of Till Eulenspiegel, eponymous trick-ster-hero of a famous German *Volksbuch*; 'Ulen' is printed in F as a separate word (cf. ll. 249 and 260), which is either a mistake or a joke.

40 *gripe's egg*: vessel shaped like the large egg of a vulture.

41 *in balneo*: in a sand-bath, for heating (cf. *sand-heat*, 58).

44 *philosophers' wheel*: the alchemical cycle.

46 *Sulphur o'nature*: pure sulphur, which when mixed with mercury was said to produce gold.

48 *covetise*: covetousness, which would disqualify Mammon.

61 *St Mary's bath*: water-bath (for heating) allegedly invented by Moses' sister Miriam (the Hebrew form of 'Mary').

62 *lac virginis*: the milk of the Virgin Mary, i.e. mercury.

64 *salt of Mercury*: mercuric oxide.

68 *crow's head*: black.

71 *hay . . . a-pitching*: the net is being set [by the hole from which the rabbits are *bolted* (88) by a *ferret* (80)].

73 *nipped . . . digestion*: slowly extracted in a sealed container.

75 *liquor . . . Mars*: molten iron.

79 *signed . . . seal*: hermetically sealed.

82 *Let . . . die*: let that experiment finish.

83 *In embrion*: classical Greek, correcting Renaissance form *embryo*, meaning 'ready to be developed'.

has . . . on: has turned white.

99 *oil of Luna*: viscous silvery mixture.

kemia: classical Greek, correcting Renaissance Greek *kymia*, meaning 'prepared for alchemical analysis'.

100 *philosophers' vinegar*: mercury (used as a solvent).

103 *in . . . vaporoso*: in a vapour bath.

128 *eggs in Egypt*: in Ptolemaic Egypt eggs were incubated in dunghills.

134 *in potentia*: capable of coming into being.

140 *remote matter*: in scholastic philosophy, substance before it is determined and actualized by form.

144 *Materia liquida*: liquid matter, which in Subtle's Aristotelian account of the generation of metals from an exhalation trapped under the surface of the earth, is an oily vapour produced by the sun shining on water.

148 *propria materia*: a specific substance.

157 *all . . . means*: the intermediate stages.

172–3 *bees . . . creatures*: insects were believed to arise spontaneously from putrefaction.

186 *sal . . . mercury*: all substances were deemed to be based on salt, sulphur, and mercury.

187 *oil . . . life*: obscure, but possibly sublimated oil (cf. l. 98) and base metal.

189 *toad . . . panther*: colours in the alchemical process.

190 *firmament*: pronounced 'fir'ment': the canopy of the sky, the astrological equivalent of the precious stone azure.

192 *red . . . woman*: interpenetrating sulphur and mercury.

203 *symbols*: Egyptian hieroglyphics were not yet recognized as word-signs, phonograms, and determinatives, and were instead thought to be mystical symbols.

208 *Sisyphus*: Greek god who betrayed the secrets of the gods (here assumed to be alchemical) and was condemned to roll a stone up a hill forever; close to the summit the stone always rolled down again.

228 *Bradamante*: warrior heroine of Ariosto's *Orlando Furioso*.

233–6 *Paracelsian . . . recipes*: Paracelsus, the sixteenth-century pioneer of pharmaceutical chemistry, overturned the orthodoxy of the pharmacopoeia inherited from the second-century physician Galen of Pergamum.

238 *This*: he, i.e. Surly.

241 *Broughton*: Hugh Broughton, Puritan Old Testament scholar then in self-imposed exile in Holland; here (and throughout the scene) with secondary reference to Bess Broughton, a famous prostitute who had died from the syphilis which she passed to many men.

289 *lapis mineralis*: stone hidden in the earth (Renaissance Latin).

lunary: fern (moonwort), deemed able to unlock secrets.

291 *lutum sapientis*: paste for sealing vessels.

292 *menstruum simplex*: plain solvent.

293–4 *quick-silver . . . sulphur*: used in alchemy and in the treatment of syphilis.

295 *Temple Church*: chapel shared by the Inner and Middle Temples, used (by implication, improperly) for the transaction of legal business.

303 *by attorney*: not in my own person.

309 *quainter*: puns on sexual sense of 'quaint' meaning female pudendum.

316–17 *philosopher . . . weep*: in late antiquity Democritus and Heraclitus became known as the laughing and weeping philosophers respectively, a characterization that passed into Renaissance iconography.

326 *Bantam*: trading centre in Java; since 1602 site of pepper factory run by the East India Company.

331–2 *jack . . . weights*: the mechanism (jack) for turning spits was powered by falling weights (as in a long-case clock).

332 *I . . . ear*: expression of endearment.

335 *Set . . . bench*: as a judge.

chain: of office.

336 *vermin*: puns on 'ermine', with which the state robes of judges and peers were trimmed.

337 *Count Palatine*: earl of Chester, duke of York, or palsgrave of the Rhine.

2.4.5 *firks mad*: goes wild.

18 *more gudgeons*: more fish swimming into the net.

20 *Anabaptist*: 're-baptizers', a radical sect that advocated believers' baptism. In 1534 a group of radical Anabaptists proclaimed a Kingdom of the Saints in Münster; the city fell after a long siege, and the sect was thereafter tainted with a reputation for fanaticism. Anabaptists in England consisted mainly of refugees from the Low Countries.

29–30 *holy . . . saints*: English Puritan exiles in the Netherlands.

2.5.5 *Terra damnata*: sediment (*ground*).

8 *Lullianist . . . artis?*: 'a follower of Ramon Llull (the medieval Catalan mystic and alchemist)? Of George Ripley (the fifteenth-century English alchemist)? A son of the art?'

10 *sapor . . . styptic*: in the alchemical continuum of nine tastes (*sapors*), 'less sour' and 'yet less sour'.

13 *Knipperdollink*: Bernhard Knipperdollink, one of the Anabaptists of Münster who presided over the reign of terror in 1534–5; when the city fell he was executed.

13–15 *ars . . . knowledge*: synonyms for 'alchemy' from Latin ('the sacred art'), Greek ('gold-making'), a Greek coinage by Paracelsus ('separating and uniting'), and two Greek coinages apparently by Jonson ('all-nature' and 'all-ruling').

17 *All . . . Hebrew*: Hebrew was thought by some Puritans to be the language which was spoken by God at the creation, and by unfallen Adam and Eve.

27 *aqua regis*: mixture of nitric and hydrochloric acid.

28 *trine . . . spheres*: garbled Paracelsian alchemy, conflating the favourable aspect of planets separated by 120° with an obscure instruction to allow a solution to pass three times through the sphere of the seven planets.

29 *proper ... Malleation*: the distinctive attribute of metals (as opposed to minerals) is malleability under the hammer.

30 *ultimum ... Antimonium*: the 'utmost punishment of gold' is antimony, the trisulphide that punishes gold by making it unmalleable.

32 *very fugitive*: because of its volatility.

41 *spirit ... body*: in Paracelsian alchemy, mercury, sulphur, and salt.

71 *paper ... pin-dust*: twist of metal filings (a by-product of pin manufacturing).

72–3 *varlet ... Apostles*: Ananias cheats the Apostles in Acts 5: 1–11.

80 *Piger Henricus*: 'lazy Henry', a multi-chambered furnace.

81 *sericon ... bufo*: two of the ingredients used in the alchemical process. 'Sericon' is red tincture; 'bufo' is black (literally 'toad').

82–3 *hope ... perish*: Presbyterians favoured abolishing episcopacy in favour of church government by elders.

84–6 *aquiety ... annulled*: the alchemical process will be stopped, and all the ingredients will be reduced to their basic elements of mercury (*aqueity*), salt (*terreity*), and sulphur.

2.6.2 *Bayards*: Bayard, the horse of Renaud de Montauban in the Charlemagne legend, was thrown into a river with a millstone round his neck, but managed to escape; he represents dogged and foolhardy persistence.

20 *Dee*: John Dee, Elizabethan astrologer and alchemist.

24 *hieroglyphic*: see note to 2.3.202–3.

33 *hood*: Dame Pliant imitates the fashion for hats by wearing her French hood on the top of her head (*a cop*) rather than on the back.

42 *blown abroad*: whispered in public.

55 *glass ... water*: love-philtre.

64 *by line*: according to set rules.

87 *in tail*: plays on the sexual sense and on the legal sense of 'entail', a mechanism by which estates were passed down undivided through a family.

89 *grains*: of weight, to balance her lack of moral weight.

3.1.6 *language ... Canaan*: a mistake by Jonson (or Ananias), as the 'language of Canaan' is Hebrew (Isaiah 19: 18).

8 *mark ... Beast*: a sign of damnation (Revelation 19: 20).

23 *bell-founders*: Puritans associated bells with the Catholic mass (cf. 3.2.61).

27–8 *give ... motives*: make allowance for the forces that motivate.

33 *menstruous ... Rome*: in 1604 the vestiarian controversy was revived by a requirement that ministers wear the surplice (here *cloth and rag*);

Puritans favoured the black Geneva gown, and identified the Scarlet Woman (hence *menstruous*) of Revelation 17 with the Church of Rome.

36 *Heidelberg*: headquarters of the Calvinists.

38 *silenced saints*: see note to *Epicene* 2.69.

40 *one of Scotland*: an appeal to the authority of the home of Presbyterianism.

41 *aurum potabile*: drinkable gold (here, a bribe).

3.2.3 *Furnus . . . circulatorius*: 'furnace of sloth' (2.5.80), 'circulation tower' (for continuous refining).

23–4 *Hollanders . . . fleet*: the vast fleet of the Dutch East India Company was (rightly) seen as a military threat to the activities of the English East India Company, so *your friends* is an edged remark.

31 *incombustible stuff*: sulphurs refined to resist fire.

33 *feat of body*: sexual intercourse.

43 *Christ-tide*: a Puritan substitute which avoided the Popish 'mass' in Christmas; Subtle re-institutes the mass in 'massy' (45).

48–9 *The king . . . Indies*: a cruel joke, as Henri IV had been assassinated on 14 May 1610 and had been succeeded by his 8-year-old son Louis XIII, and Philip III had gone bankrupt in 1607 because of the collapse of silver shipments from the Indies.

50 *lords . . . temporal*: bishops and peers in the House of Lords.

52 *temporal lords*: Puritans opposed episcopacy, and so could not be spiritual lords.

54 *Long-winded exercises*: Puritans opposed set prayers, and their 'conceived' prayers were notoriously lengthy.

55 *'ha' . . . 'hum'*: Puritan mannerisms.

63 *it . . . down*: the alchemical process will be terminated.

72 *Nor . . . day*: nor seize the security on a loan that is only one day overdue.

78 *scrupulous bones*: in moral theology, a scruple is an unfounded fear of sin; Puritans relentlessly argued (like a dog chewing *bones*) the sinfulness of practices such as those in ll. 79–82.

81 *doublets*: worn exclusively by men; cross-dressing was forbidden (Deut. 22: 5).

86–7 *libel . . . ears*: be punished for your opposition to episcopacy by having your ears clipped.

106 *traditions*: in 1546 the Council of Trent gave Scripture and tradition equal authority; Protestants insisted on the sole sufficiency of the Bible.

113 *by revelation*: the 'continuous revelation' claimed by Anabaptists by being 'filled with the Spirit'.

125 *gi' . . . in*: exchange it.

131–2 *second . . . month*: Ananias avoids the pagan names of the days and months.

138–9 *ignis . . . cineris*: the grades of heat, from the lowest, produced with horse dung (*fimus equinus*), through heating in a sand oven (*balneus*) and in ash (*cinis*), to burning heat (*ignis ardens*).

150 *We . . . magistrate*: some Puritans refused to recognize the right of civil courts to judge matters of conscience.

151 *This's . . . coin*: Ananias is ignorant (perhaps wilfully) of the illegality (since 1554) of forging foreign coins.

156 *case . . . conscience*: scholastic procedure (*casus conscientiae*) adopted by Protestants whereby principles of faith are applied to a particular case.

3.3.2 *the round*: the circular aisle of the Temple Church.

8 *black boy*: Subtle's job blackens his face and hands.

12 *for . . . conscience*: because he is a Protestant.

14 *hoys*: small boats rigged as sloops (thus a pun on *slops*).
   round trunks: stuffed knee-breeches.

15 *pieces of eight*: Spanish dollars (worth eight *reales*).

16–17 *bath . . . colour*: 'bath' is a pretext (*colour*) because a bath-house was a euphemism for a brothel.

17 *make his battery*: attack; as a foreign invader he will land at *Dover*, which is a *Cinque Port*, one of the (originally) five fortified ports on the south-east coast of England.

24 *John Leidens*: Anabaptist followers of Johann Buckholdt of Leiden, leader of the rising in Münster in 1534–5, and afterwards executed with his father-in-law Knipperdollink (2.5.13).

33 *Yes . . . camp*: line cited from Kyd's *Spanish Tragedy* 1.2.1.

38 *small parties*: raiding parties.

41 *Dousabel*: 'sweet and lovely'; possibly a romance name.

46 *great frost*: of 1607–8, when the Thames froze.

47 *bees . . . basin*: according to Virgil (*Georgics* iv. 64) swarming bees can be settled by banging pots together.

49 *God's gift*: the literal meaning (in Greek) of 'Dorothy'.

56 *in bank*: safely stored.

70 *tickle . . . mother-tongue*: amuse him by speaking English and licking and kissing him.

71 *Verdugoship*: mock title based on Spanish *verdugo*, 'hangman'.

82 *angry boy*: 'roaring boy', an upper-class hooligan like Cutting in *Bartholomew Fair*.

3.4.13 *Good time*: all in good time.

39 *in diameter*: a direct lie.

40 *ordinarily*: puns on 'ordinary' (eating-house).

60–1 *set . . . Christmas*: give him the best seat at the gambling tables at court throughout the Christmas season.

72 *buttered shrimps*: an allegedly aphrodisiac dish.

79 *by . . . posts*: as fast as a post-horse.

81 *naked boy*: catamite.

84 *As . . . long*: because earth was the basest of the four elements.

85–6 *In . . . term*: the 'seasons' when the wealthy were in London coincided with the law terms, so in the vacations there was less money about.

90 *commodity*: see note to 2.1.10–14.

105 *suster*: 'sister' pronounced in a provincial dialect.

108 *pass it*: let that pass.

119 *Seacoal Lane*: poor area outside London's walls.

120 *pellitory . . . wall*: a shrub used medicinally.

124 *waterwork*: see note to 2.1.76.

142–7 *six score . . . Marys*: coins of the reigns of Henry VIII (*old Harry*), Edward VI, Mary, Philip and Mary, Elizabeth, and James. 'Marys' were rare because she ruled for only six months before marrying the future Philip II of Spain. Philip and Marys are *best of all* to Face's treacherous mind because they commemorate the instigator of the Spanish Armada and the bloody persecutor of Protestants.

3.5.33 *spur-rial*: gold coin struck by Edward IV in 1465; the blazing sun stamped on the reverse was said to resemble the rowel of a spur.

57 *lay . . . back*: from the fire.

4.1.39 *Guinea-bird*: prostitute.

57 *Austriac*: the Habsburg dynasty that ruled the Holy Roman Empire (including the Duchy of Austria) was noted for large lower lips.

59 *Valois*: the ruling house of France, referred to in the past tense because they had been succeeded by the Bourbons in 1589.

60–1 *Medici . . . Florence*: family of the grand dukes of Tuscany.

91 *Kelly*: the alchemist Edward Kelly, who twice visited the court of Rudolf II (emperor 1576–1611) in Prague, failed to produce the philosophers' stone, and in consequence died in 1595 in an imperial prison (hence the play on *chains*).

93–4 *Aesculapius . . . Thunderer*: 'Thunderer' is an epithet (*tonans*) of Jove, who killed Aesculapius because he had learnt to bring the dead back to life.

102 *mere solecism*: utter impropriety.

146 *Nero's Poppaea*: in order to marry his mistress Poppaea, the emperor Nero murdered his mother and divorced his wife, whom he subsequently murdered; he later killed Poppaea with a kick when she was pregnant.

157 *free state*: republic such as Venice or (since 1609) the United Provinces.

4.2.6–7 *for . . . fall*: 'that my captain's disguise (*suit*) could conceal me.'

9 *hit . . . nostrils*: obscure: perhaps 'lead you by a ring through the nose'.

13 *terrae fili*: Latin idiom (vocative), 'bastard'; Subtle's 'boy of land' is a literal translation that comically snatches back the insult.

21 *grammar*: the correct 'grammar' of quarrelling stipulated an indirect approach, not instant confrontation ('you lie'); Kestrel broke the rules in order to ensure that he could make the first accusation ('I am aforehand').

22 *render causes*: or lose the choice of weapons.

23–8 *Your first . . . perfect*: quarrelling is described in terms of fashionable neo-Aristotelian logic.

40 *subtlety*: plays on the senses of 'exquisiteness' and 'sweetness' as well as on his name.

42 *myrobalan*: plum-like fruit said to be sweet before it is ripe.

43 *in . . . frontis*: Renaissance Latin: on a vein on the forehead.

45 *linea fortunae*: line of fortune, the vertical line from the middle of the wrist to the base of the middle finger.

46 *stella*: star, one of the complex system of marks on the hand. *in monte Veneris*: on the mountain of Venus, i.e. the ball of the thumb.

47 *junctura anularis*: Renaissance Latin: on the first joint of the ring-finger.

59 *dark glass*: crystal ball.

4.3.10 *serve*: plays on the sexual sense of 'service' (an animal).

21 *Don John*: stock name for a Spaniard, like *Diego* (37).

22 *Señores . . . mercedes*: 'Gentlemen, I kiss your honours' hands.'

27–8 *collar . . . knife*: pig's neck cut beneath the ear and slashed to resemble a ruff.

31 *D'Alva*: Fernando Alvarez, duke of Alba, the brutal governor of the Spanish Netherlands; in 1568 his Council of Blood unjustly condemned and executed Count Egmont, a leader of the Dutch Revolt.

33–4 *fortification . . . sets*: the pleats (*sets*) of Surly's ruff are compared to a castle's crenellations, which house rockets (*squibs*).

35 *Por . . . casa*: 'By God, gentlemen, a most exquisite house.'

37 *but's action*: than his gestures.

47 *See . . . monsters*: see the sights, including the lions in the Tower of London.

48 *Con . . . señora*: 'With your permission, may one see this lady?'

62–4 *Entiendo . . . vida*: 'I understand that the lady is so beautiful that I desire to see her as the great fortune of my life.'

69 *Which . . . chance*: whichever of us happens.

76–7 *E'en . . . me*: a version of Subtle's judgement (*doom*) in ll. 13–16.

77 *work her*: work on her to entertain the Spaniard.

80 *Señores . . . tanto*: 'Gentlemen, why so much delay?'

82 *Puede . . . amor*: 'perhaps you are mocking my love.'

93 *Por . . . barbas*: 'By this honoured beard.'

94–5 *Tengo . . . traición*: 'I fear, gentlemen, that you are somehow deceiving me.'

96–8 *presto . . . bathada*: Subtle is attempting to speak Spanish.

4.4.10 *Stoup . . . garb*: method of bowing is the most elegant.

29 *eighty-eight*: 1588, the year of the Armada.

32 *rush*: either a rush from the floor of the stage or a rush burning in a lamp.

33–4 *cry . . . mackerel*: become a fruit-seller or a fish-seller.

43–4 *idolaters . . . Barer*: courtiers wore hats indoors, but removed them as a gesture of respect.

47–8 *Exchange . . . china-houses*: see note to *Epicene* 1.3.37.

Bedlam: Bethlehem Hospital (then in Bishopsgate), where the mentally ill were incarcerated; viewing the inmates was a popular amusement in court circles.

50 *goose-turd bands*: yellowish-green collars.

53–4 *Qué . . . mata*: 'Why, gentlemen, does she not come? This delay is killing me.'

56 *En . . . Gallantissima*: pseudo-Spanish: 'A fine lady, Don! Most fine!'

57–8 *Por . . . vida*: 'By all the gods, the most perfect beauty that I have seen in my life.'

61–2 *law French*: the Anglo-Norman French of the English legal system, rare after 1600. It is far from courtly, e.g. the prisoner 'ject un brickbat a le dit justice que narrowly mist'.

63–4 *El . . . Diós*: 'The sun has lost its light with the radiance of this lady. God bless me!'

69 *Por . . . acude*: 'Why does she not come?'

71 *Por . . . tarda*: 'For the love of God, what is it that is making her hesitate?'

76–7 *Señora . . . hermosura*: 'My lady, my person is most unworthy to approach such beauty.'

80 *Señora . . . entremos*: 'Lady, if it be convenient, let us go in.'

83 *the word*: her cue to throw a fit.

92 *erection . . . figure*: from casting her horoscope.

4.5. Doll's ravings are drawn from *A Concent of Scripture* (1590), an attempt to reconcile biblical chronology with secular sources, written by Hugh Broughton (see note to 2.3.238).

1–3 *For . . . Ptolemy*: the generals of Alexander the Great—Perdiccas, Antigonus, Seleucus (Nicator), and Ptolemy (Soter)—acrimoniously divided his empire between them after his death.

5 *Gog*: ruler of the northern hordes that threatened Israel.

10 *fourth chain*: the last of Broughton's four periods of history.

14 *Salem*: commonly identified as Jerusalem.

16 *tongue . . . Javan*: Hebrew and Greek.

19–20 *communion . . . consonants*: impinges on the contemporary debate about the relationship between consonantal Hebrew (i.e. the text written without vowels) and early medieval Massoretic vocalization.

25 *Talmud*: the Mishnah (Jewish oral law, written in Hebrew) and the Gemara (rabbinical commentary on the Mishnah, written in Aramaic).

27 *Heber's house*: the kingdom of God (mistranscribed in all texts as 'Helen's').

Ismaelite: the unbelieving descendants of Ishmael.

28 *Togarma*: biblical country east of Assyria.

30 *King . . . Cittim*: *Abaddon* is Hell, *Cittim* (Shittim) is Moab; Broughton identifies both rulers with the pope.

31 *Kimchi*: Jewish exegete and grammarian (*c.*1160–1235). *Onkelos*: ancient Aramaic paraphrase (Targum) of the Pentateuch.

32 *Aben-Ezra*: Jewish philologist and exegete (*c.*1093–1167); Browning's Rabbi Ben Ezra.

34–6 *fifth . . . straight*: the first four monarchies of Assyria, Persia, Greece, and Rome (the Catholic Church) were to be superseded by the fifth monarchy of Christ.

66 *in fumo*: in smoke.

113 *case*: disguise as Lungs.

116–17 *fetch . . . over*: get the better of him.

120 *prove ... virtue*: test your skill.

4.6.29–30 *cart ... whip*: Face will be tied to a cart and whipped through the streets.

36 *cheat*: by selling blanched copper as silver.

46 *Faustus*: Dr Faustus, the eponymous hero of Marlowe's play, was an early sixteenth-century German necromancer who was said to have turned from theology to sorcery, lived extravagantly for the twenty-four-year term of a pact with the devil, and at the end of the term to have been dragged off to hell.

54 *by ... ears*: in the pillory.

4.7.17 *had ... presently*: found him out immediately.

32 *damned ... me*: broke his promises to pay me over three law terms.

40 *Amadis ... Quixote*: see note to *Epicene* 4.1.51.

45–6 *whit ... tim*: obscure; possibly 'a trifle, a mere nothing'.

53–4 *unclean ... coasts*: Puritans searched for portents such as the 'unclean ... bird' of Revelation 18: 2; strange birds with ruffs had been seen on the Lincolnshire coast in 1586, and Ananias is probably alluding to a later visitation.

55 *lewd hat*: Surly's hat resembles the triple-crowned papal tiara, which was said to identify the pope with the Antichrist.

69 *play the fool*: a theatrical joke, as Robert Armin, who probably played Drugger, had in other plays (e.g. *King Lear*) played the part of the fool.

71 *Hieronimo*: hero of Kyd's *Spanish Tragedy*, a part that Jonson had acted.

116 *liberties*: areas outside the walls of London, and not subject to its legal jurisdiction.

125 *Ratcliff*: dock-side area in Stepney.

132–3 *shave ... trim*: both have secondary sense of 'cheat'.

5.1.6 *Pimlico*: not modern Pimlico, but a tavern in *Hoxton* (5.2.19).

11 *nose*: through which Puritan preachers were said to speak.

5.2.20 *Eye-bright*: another tavern in Hoxton.

44 *changelings*: plays on the senses 'inconsistent' and 'idiots'.

47 *Nothing's ... conscience*: translation of Plautus, *Mostellaria* 544–5.

5.3.51 *Punk device*: arrant whore.

55 *St Katherine's*: hospital then near the Tower of London.

62 *deceptio visus*: optical illusion.

67 *sets ... throat*: raises his voice.

92 *visited*: by the plague.

5.4 The trunks that have been packed (66, 106) were presumably brought on stage at the beginning of the scene.

36 *bird*: the *fly* (35), or familiar spirit.

43 *Woolsack*: tavern in Farringdon.

44 *Dagger*: see note to 1.1.191.

45 *Heaven . . . Hell*: taverns in Westminster.

51–2 *if . . . stirring*: even if there is only £3,000 to be gambled for.

66 *spend*: i.e. have available for spending.

91 *Pigeons*: the Three Pigeons, at Brentford (*Brainford*, l. 77); John Lowin (see *Volpone*, 'Notes to Colophon') later became its landlord.

116 *single money*: small change.

118 *Ward*: Captain John Ward, an English pirate then based in Tunis, the subject of ballads and of two pamphlets published in 1609.

143–4 *Amo . . . Caesarean*: generic names for brothel madams.

151 *flock-bed . . . buttery*: where the butler sleeps and eats.

5.5.5 *for failing*: to ensure success.

14 *Bel . . . Dragon*: Old Testament apocryphal book, declared canonical by the Council of Trent, printed in the Authorized Version, and rejected as profane by Puritans.

15 *grasshoppers . . . lice*: two of the plagues of Egypt (Exodus 8: 10).

41 *poesies of the candle*: written with (or on) candle smoke.

67 *public means*: due process of law.

85 *hearken out*: ask the whereabouts of.

100 *seal*: the mark (on the forehead) of the elect (Revelation 9: 4).

104 *last . . . saints*: millenarian sects eagerly awaited the rule of the saints that would precede the second coming of Christ.

111 *Gad . . . exile*: the exiled brethren, who identified themselves with the tribe of Gad, son of Jacob (Geneis 49: 19).

117 *Nicholas*: Anglicized name of Hendrick Niclaes (*c*.1502–*c*.1580), founder of the Family of Love, an Anabaptist sect suppressed in England but still active.

132 *buckle . . . tools*: draw your sword and dagger.

135 *stoop*: swoop like a kestrel on its prey.

163–4 *put . . . country*: legal phrase, 'submit to trial by jury'.

Bartholomew Fair

NOTES TO PROLOGUE

The prologue was recited at the performance before King James at Whitehall on Tuesday, 1 November 1614.

4 *faction*: the Puritans, who were opposed to many royal policies and practices.

8 *particular wrong*: satire directed at individuals.

NOTES TO THE PERSONS OF THE PLAY

Banbury: Oxfordshire market-town dominated by zealous Puritans, who in 1610 had destroyed the ancient Cross celebrated in the nursery rhyme.

horse-courser . . . Turnbull: literally, dealer in horses that have been broken in and park-keeper, here applied to the brothels of Turnbull (now Turnmill) Street.

Cutting: highwayman's nickname.

mistress . . . game: prostitute.

NOTES TO INDUCTION

The Induction was played at the public performance at the Hope on Monday, 31 October 1614, not at the court performance the following evening.

5 *Arches*: a lawyer in the Court of Arches, the popular name (derived from St Mary-le-Bow, where it met) for the provincial court of the Archbishop of Canterbury.

Hospital: St Bartholomew's, in Smithfield.

7 *Brome*: Richard Brome, servant and dramatic apprentice to Jonson.

13 *Little Davy*: a well-known thug.

14 *Kindheart*: itinerant dentist who had become a literary 'character'.

19 *hobby-horse man*: frequenter of prostitutes.

31 *masters . . . Court*: students of law.

33 *Tarlton*: Richard Tarlton (d. 1588), actor and clown; in one of *Tarlton's Jests* (1613) he loses his clothes in the *cloth-quarter*.

36 *Adams*: John Adams, clown who acted with Tarlton in the Queen's Men.

37 *dealt . . . vermin*: scattered his fleas.

44 *understanding*: a pun, alluding to the groundlings who stood below the stage.

47 *bears*: the Hope playhouse, on the South Bank, was used once a fortnight for bear-baiting.

63 *France*: the English claim to the French throne was not formally renounced until the Treaty of Amiens (1802).

64 *seven . . . fortieth*: an error for 'forty-eight'; James's forty-seventh Scottish regnal year had ended on 23 July 1614.

84 *lottery*: the Virginia Company lottery of 1612.

89–90 *Commission . . . Wit*: an imagined group of critics on a judicial *bench* (93).

95 *Jeronimo*: Kyd's *Spanish Tragedy* (*c*.1590) and its protagonist Hieronimo.

   Andronicus: Shakespeare's *Titus Andonicus* (1592).

110–13 *meditant . . . rampant*: a parody of Law French, which inflected English words (*searchant*), adapted Latin words (*meditant*), and hardened ordinary French words (*allurant* and the heraldic *rampant*) into technical terms.

113–17 *servant-monster . . . dances*: an attack on Shakespeare's late plays. Caliban is the 'servant-monster' in *The Tempest*, and *dances* and *drolleries* are included in *The Winter's Tale*.

126 *Mirror*: 'paragon', but the phrase recalls both the Tudor *Mirror for Magistrates* (1559) and George Whetstone's *Mirror for Magistrates of Cities* (1584).

146 *commodity*: see note to *Alchemist* 2.1.10–14.

1.1.9 *very . . . dice*: truly less likely than a double ace (Lat. *ambas as*), i.e. two ones on a throw of the dice.

10 *pretty . . . Paul's*: fashionable wits who frequented St Paul's Cathedral.

15 *Archdeacon's Court*: the lowest ecclesiastical court (abolished in 1963), above which were the Consistory (or Bishop's) Court (note to 1.2.58–74) and the Court of Arches (note to Induction 5), which was the highest court.

   Jack: plays on the sense of a mechanism for turning a spit.

20 *Budge Row*: street of furriers.

21 *Spanish lady*: unidentified English widow who had visited Spain and thereafter dressed in a Spanish fashion.

30 *Three . . . Mermaid*: taverns frequented by theatrical and literary society.

35 *six-shillings beer*: 'small [i.e. weak] beer', sold cheaply for 6*s*. a barrel.

1.2.5 *Cheapside*: neighbourhood of the cloth trade.

6 *Moorfields*: had been drained and (in 1606) laid out as a public park.

   Pimlico Path: near the Pimlico tavern in Hoxton (cf. *The Alchemist* 5.1.6. and note).

   Exchange: New Exchange, fashionable shopping arcade in the Strand, opened in 1609.

24 *hood ... chain*: assert her social superiority by virtue of her husband's insignia of civic office.

32 *tokenworth*: when small change was scarce, tradesmen issued privately minted tokens instead of coins; a 'tokenworth' is the smallest amount.

42 *has ... Lane*: astrologers (*cunning men*) in Cow Lane (now King Street) have appropriated the medical technique of using urine samples to diagnose disease in order to cast a horoscope (*nativity*).

49 *Bedlam*: Hospital of St Mary of Bethlehem, the lunatic asylum.

58–74 *elder ... Antichrist*: Busy is described as a puritanical *elder* in a clandestine Presbyterian congregation in the Puritan town of *Banbury*; *meal-tide* parodies the Puritan substitution of 'Christ-tide' for 'Christmas' in order to avoid the papal 'mass' (cf. *The Alchemist* 3.2.43 and note); *sweet singers* derives from the (Puritan) Geneva Bible (2 Samuel 23: 1) and was applied to Puritans, who wanted to be *restored* to the pulpits from which they had been excluded in 1604; the gibe about *grace* before meals refers to the Puritan rejection of set prayers in favour of (long) extempore prayers. Puritan objections to drunkenness and gluttony are mocked in Busy's drinking habits (*aqua coelestis* was an expensive distilled cordial) and expanding girth. Littlewit's *vocation* as an ecclesiastical lawyer makes him an instrument of the bishops, hence (in Puritan eyes) of the *Beast* of the Book of Revelation; the Consistory (*Bishop's*) *Court* is denounced as an instrument of the Pope, who was identified with the *Antichrist*.

1.3.1 *ta'en soil*: hunting term used of a stag which has taken refuge in water.

5 *marrowbone man*: obscure play on 'rag-and-bone man'; possibly (following 'fiddlers') musician playing on bones, possibly bare-knuckle fighter.

31–2 *wink ... you*: overlook your fault.

44 *fall in*: 'be reconciled', with a suggestion of 'copulate'.

49 *apple ... this*: 'shrivelled apple if you behave like a pander.'

54–5 *courts ... Tottenham*: sets off like a lady of the court to visit Tottenham Court, an inn famous for cakes and cream.

56–7 *drawing ... smock*: tracking an old woman.

58 *tripe ... trillibub*: bag of entrails.

61 *perpetuity ... Alley*: perpetual lease on the alley of the leather-sellers.

68–9 *come ... inches*: imitates Juvenal on the gigolo (*Satires* i. 40–1).

72 *quartan ague*: paroxysmal fever recurring every four days.

85 *Knox*: John Knox, the Scottish reformer, whose *Treatise on Predestination* (1560) was popular with Puritans.

91 *conveyed ... state*: transferred her estate.

122 *blue-starch woman*: seller of starch (for ruffs), of which Puritans disapproved.

124 *stands . . . face*: depends on his appearance.

1.4.2 *God you*: God grant you.

6-7 *be . . . book*: plead benefit of clergy. A convicted felon could escape hanging by reading Psalm 51: 1, the 'neck verse'; Jonson had done so in 1598.

32 *Cloister*: the Fair extended into the parish of Christ Church, the cloister of which was used as a market.

85-6 *much . . . farthing*: 'virtually identical; it's the nap or pile of a cloth, the head or tail of a coin, a toss-up.'

100-2 *drawn . . . was*: practical joke said to be played on gullible peasants (*Hodge* is the rustic form of 'Roger'), who bet that they cannot be pulled through a pond by a tom-cat (*gibcat*), and are then dragged across the pond by those who are 'guiding' the cat.

102 *that heathen thing*: outlandish sights.

107 *Bucklersbury*: street of the apothecaries, whose products included tobacco.

111 *reading . . . hand*: interpretation on any account.

1.5.13 *Mary gip*: St Mary of Egypt, a mythical fifth-century hermit; the oath is conflated with *gip* ('get out!').

French-hood: Mistress Overdo should be wearing the fashionable small wired bonnet worn in the portraits of Mary I of England and Mary Queen of Scots.

16 *Madam Regent*: ruler in the absence of her husband.

23 *Whetstone*: unidentified, but possibly a Bedlam official or inmate, with a play on the stone used for sharpening tools.

88 *Sir Cranion*: crane-fly (daddy-long-legs), with a play on Greek *cranion*, skull, i.e. bony.

92 *your . . . Bartholomew*: 'goodbye', phrased like the subscription of a letter, with reference to the disciple of Jesus (hence 'your friend and disciple').

137 *Pie Corner*: see note to *Alchemist* 1.1.25.

139 *Cut . . . lace*: cut the laces of your bodice.

144 *hypocrite*: actor; a jibe at Puritan usage, because actors were condemned by Puritans as hypocrites because they pretended to be someone else.

148 *mother*: plays on the sense of 'hysteria'.

1.6.1 *beauteous discipline*: godly practice.

50 *high places*: after the construction of Solomon's temple, worship in 'high places' (*bamoth*) became associated with idolatry, and the sites were destroyed by Josiah (2 Kings 23).

87 *stand taxed*: are accused (because of their emphasis on the Old Testament).

89 *away with*: abide.

2.1 The Whitehall accounts record payment for 'canvas for the booths . . . for a play called Bartholomew Fair', which suggests that booths were erected on the stages at Whitehall and the Hope. They were probably erected in the course of Act 2 and remained on stage for the remainder of the play.

4 *Lynceus*: Argonaut whose sight was preternaturally keen.

Epidaurian: sharp-eyed serpents were sacred to Aesculapius, whose shrine was at Epidaurus; Horace uses the phrase in *Satires* I. iii. 26–7.

6 *Quorum*: a group of named justices specified for a commission of the peace.

12 *man*: the description parallels in many details the activities of Thomas Middleton, the reforming Lord Mayor of London in 1613–14.

14 *August*: the month in which plague was most virulent and dogs suspected of infection were killed (see note to 2.3.47).

36 *Courts . . . Piepowders*: the royal franchise for a fair brought with it the right to convene a court; by the seventeenth century these courts had been reduced in jurisdiction to matters arising within the limits of the fair while the fair was being held; the name refers to the dusty feet (*pedes pulverosi*, *pieds poudrés*) of the itinerant pedlars at the fairs.

41 *Junius Brutus*: traditional founder of the Roman Republic; his nickname (*brutus*, stupid) was later explained as a ruse to escape from the Tarquins; he was a brutal judge, and sentenced his own sons to death.

2.2.105 *O . . . mores*: 'O the times, the habits!', Cicero's cry in his oration accusing Catiline of conspiracy.

116 *Arthur . . . Bradley*: eponymous hero of a Robin Hood ballad.

2.3.6 *Holborn*: Holborn Hill, leading from Newgate to the gallows at Tyburn.

29 *Jordan*: Knockem's nickname, meaning 'chamber-pot'.

32–3 *i' . . . kerchief*: in the head.

42 *case of pisspots*: plays on 'case of pistols'.

47 *dog-days*: hot period dating from the heliacal rising of Sirius, the Dog-star, which on the Greenwich latitude takes place at the beginning of August; dogs were popularly believed to run mad during this period (see note to 2.1.14).

48–51 *foundering . . . scoured*: farrier's terminology includes *foundering thee i' the body* (causing equine rheumatism by overfeeding or watering in hot weather), *taken up* (reduced), and *scoured* (purged).

2.4.26 *roar for him*: distract the victim in order to assist the cutpurse.

41 *fly . . . mark*: indicate its location (a term from falconry).

45 *Drink . . . indenture*: drink to your agreement.

55–6 *wept . . . eye*: indicating that a roasting pig is almost cooked.

62 *strange woman*: prostitute (imitating biblical usage).

63 *Iamque . . . &c*: from the closing words of Ovid's *Metamorphoses*: 'my work is finished, a work which neither the wrath of Jove nor fire [nor sword nor the gnawing tooth of time will ever destroy].'

2.5.6–25 *Orpheus . . . Ceres . . . Neptune*: condescending classical allusions: Orpheus was traditionally depicted singing and playing his lyre to wild beasts; Ceres, the goddess of the Roman plebians, was the mother of Proserpina, who was usually depicted as goddess of the underworld; Neptune's roar was heard in storms at sea and volcanoes.

26–7 *You . . . this*: 'I am always game to be involved in a spectacle as delightfully absurd as this one.'

39 *cold*: plays on the sense 'not inflamed with syphilis'.

75–6 *wench . . . suburbs*: prostitute operating beyond the legal jurisdiction of London.

81–2 *quagmire . . . bog*: horse-dealers were said to disguise the poor legs of horses by standing them in deep wet clay.

88 *weighing up*: being raised up (like a sunken ship).

90 *Dutchmen*: said to be lovers of butter.

94–5 *playhouse poultry*: prostitutes who solicited in the theatres.

100 *sweating sickness*: febrile disease of which there were epidemics in England.

101 *patch*: used to hide syphilitic scabs.

105–7 *cuckingstool . . . pond*: scolds were tied to a stool and ducked in Smithfield pond, which was then stagnant.

118 *double piled*: plays on the senses 'threadbare', 'afflicted with haemorrhoids', and 'rendered bald [pilled] by syphilis'.

135 *lie*: plays on 'lye', as in urine.

156 *race-bawd*: mother of the bawds, by analogy to 'race-mare', a breeding mare.

162–3 *mallanders . . . bone*: equine diseases of leg and hoof.

166 *Hospital*: St Bartholomew's, in Smithfield.

173 *Ursa major*: the constellation of the Great Bear.

2.6.23 *vents*: plays on the senses 'sells' and 'exhales'.

34–5 *some . . . writers*: including James I, whose *Counterblast to Tobacco* had appeared in 1604.

45 *hole . . . nose*: an effect of syphilis.

59 *see it told*: have it counted.

72–3 *Straits . . . Bermudas*: disreputable alleys near King's Cross.

125 *white money*: silver coins.

134 *Childermass day*: Holy Innocents' Day, 28 December, commemorates Herod's massacre of the children of Bethlehem.

134–5 *French Bartholomew*: the massacre of Protestants in France started on St Bartholomew's Day (24 August) 1572.

3.1 Whit speaks Jacobean stage-Irish; Haggis, stage-Scots; Bristle, stage-Welsh.

3.2.41–2 *heathen . . . sea*: a garbled classical reference: in Homer there were two sirens, not one (*the harlot*), and it was the crew, not Ulysses (*the heathen man*), who plugged their ears with wax to shut out the singing of the sirens.

55–6 *stringhalt . . . maryhinchco*: synomyns for a twitching disorder in a horse's legs.

59–60 *Dame . . . Cleare*: a well in Hoxton named after a thirteenth-century Londoner (Annis Clare) who drowned herself in it.

63–4 *juniper and rosemary*: burnt to purify the air with their fragrance.

69 *Lubberland*: legendary country of idleness and plenitude where roasted pigs run about asking to be eaten.

88–9 *sincere stud*: pure breed.

102 *small . . . ruffs*: small, meticulously folded (*printed*) ruffs were worn by Puritans.

107–8 *stone-puritan*: 'randy Puritan', coined by analogy to 'stone-horse' (stallion).

120 *lay aboard*: attack one ship from another alongside.

3.3.27 *one . . . more*: one extra guest.

30 *ut . . . solebam*: 'as I compared great things with small' (Virgil, *Eclogues* i. 23).

3.4.16 *pair o'smiths*: clocks that struck quarter-hours had two hammers.

60 *pannier-man's jack*: hawker's ass, which when it died would be sold for dog-food.

66 *Jew's trumps*: Jew's harps (simple musical instruments).

108 *lower end*: end of the table for low-ranking guests.

111 *Coryate . . . Cokeley*: the traveller Thomas Coryate, to whose *Crudities* (1611) Jonson added commendatory verses, had been a fool in the household of Prince Henry. Cokeley was another well-known fool.

116–17 *baited . . . skin*: refers to an entertainment staged at the Fortune in 1612 in which actors dressed as dogs almost killed an actor in a bear's skin.

139 *pounds Scotch*: an independent currency till 1709; in 1614 one Scots pound was worth slightly less than two English shillings.

3.5.7 *Actum . . . man*: 'he is finished as a reputable citizen', an adaptation of *actum est de republica* ('it is all over with the commonwealth').

55 *Pagginton's Pound*: popular dance-tune (no. 178 in the Fitzwilliam Virginal Book).

73 *both . . . and*: warns both you and also.

84 *Westminster Hall*: hall in the Palace of Westminster, seat of the English common law courts until 1884.

91 *rub . . . elbow*: in glee.

96 *ipso facto*: an obvious inference from the facts.

123 *court . . . face*: on Christmas Day 1611 John Selman was caught stealing a purse in the King's Chapel at Whitehall; he was subsequently executed.

129 *rat-catchers' charm*: music, as in the story of the Pied Piper.

238 *flown . . . mark*: noticed him.

251 *read . . . need*: read neck-verse (see note to 1.4.6–7).

260–3 *bought . . . disparagement*: the highly unpopular Court of Wards and Liveries (established 1540, abolished 1660) gave the king the right to sell the guardianship of royal wards, including minors who were heirs to the king's tenants. The guardianship of Grace has been sold by the crown to Overdo. Should she marry without Overdo's permission, she would have to pay compensation unless she could prove *disparagement*, i.e. that he had tried to marry her to one of inferior degree.

3.6.30 *latter age*: last age; in Puritan eschatology, the end of the world.

41 *Beast*: in the Book of Revelation, the Antichrist.

52 *bells . . . dogs*: Bel and the Dragon and the Book of Tobit (here *Toby*, with reference to the dog in Punch and Judy shows) are books in the Apocrypha (hence *apocryphal*), the inter-testamental books rejected by Puritans as uncanonical.

53–4 *Nebuchadnezzar*: Babylonian king who forced his people (and the captured Israelites) to worship a golden idol (Daniel 3).

68 *nest . . . legend*: Puritans were iconoclastic and disapproved of saints, so the gingerbread images of St Bartholomew are denounced by Busy as a collection of saints' lives (*legend*).

84 *high places*: see note to 1.6.50.

4.1.5 *Oliver*: called Davy at 3.1.7.

13–14 *quit . . . you*: may God forgive you and give you children.

48 *put out on*: dislodged from.

68 *burn blue*: blue flame in a candle was a bad omen.

4.2.18 *Dorring the Dotterel*: hoaxing the simpleton; the dotterel (a species of plover) is often very tame, and so was easy to trap.

55 *green . . . pulled*: a lapwing (with a play on green as 'inexperienced') so easily plucked.

58–9 *patent . . . reversion*: Edgworth assumes that Quarlous aspires to secure Wasp's entitlement (*patent*) to his governorship and transfer the right of succession (*reversion*) to himself.

65 *martyred . . . Smithfield*: many Protestant martyrs under the Marian persecution (e.g. John Rogers) had been executed at Smithfield.

72 *but carry*: only lead (to his rooms, where he 'lies').

89 *sweet bags*: of scented herbs, to perfume the linen.

4.3.13 *enjoy . . . friend*: have a lover.

36 *put . . . making*: apprenticed for instruction.

44–5 *shall . . . you*: shall each write.

62 *Argalus*: noble lover of Parthenia in Sidney's *Arcadia* (1581).

63 *Palemon*: knight in Boccaccio and Chaucer ('The Knight's Tale'), rival to Arcite for the hand of Emilia; the *play* in which the story is dramatized is *Two Noble Kinsmen* (*c*.1613), by Shakespeare and John Fletcher.

103 *wrestle . . . Mayor*: at the opening of the Fair a wrestling match was staged in the presence of the Lord Mayor of London.

104 *circling boy*: obscure, but possibly explained by 4.4.118–25.

4.4.1 *for . . . lift*: in preparation for a theft.

9–10 *i' . . . zuds*: in difficulty.

14 *flea-bitten . . . tire*: proverbially, a flea-bitten horse never tires.

24 *I miss him*: I don't see him in the company.

124 *playing with*: mocking.

140 *Goody Rich*: 'Goody' was used like 'Mrs' of lower-class married women; 'Rich' may refer to the Rich family, which received tolls and dues from the cloth fair.

166 *man . . . beard*: beer-jug decorated with a bearded face.

167 *Clerk . . . Market*: official responsible for administration of the Fair and collection of tolls.

168 *my lord's*: the Lord Mayor.

201 *have a leap*: be mounted in copulation (like a female horse).

4.5.13–15 *fowl . . . plover . . . quail*: prostitutes.

32–3 *wires . . . green gowns*: wires were used to stiffen ruffs and hair; 'green' suggested seduction on the grass, and was associated with prostitutes.

34 *Ware and Romford*: places outside the city used for assignations.

43 *top . . . top-gallant*: in full sail.

67 *in grease*: fattened for slaughter.

75 *rid . . . cart*: prostitutes were carted through the streets.

4.6.17–18 *take part*: partake.

26–7 *such . . . aequat*: 'such [as he is]: guilt levels those whom it contaminates' (Lucan, *Pharsalia* v. 290).

44–5 *middle roundel*: the stocks have three holes, one for each of Wasp, Busy, and Overdo, so only one leg of each victim is stocked.

79–80 *May-games . . . ales*: festivals condemned as heathen by Puritans.

83–8 *I . . . extra*: as Quarlous notes, Overdo strikes a *Stoic* pose. His opening sentence sets out distinctions from the Greek of Epictetus. The first two Latin quotations are taken from Horace's *Satires* ii. 7, which articulates the Stoic view that only the wise man is free: 'in her assaults upon you Fortune only harms herself'; 'undaunted by poverty, death and chains'; the phrase from Persius (*Satires* i. 7) means 'consult no-one outside of yourself'.

129 *earns my heart*: grieves me.

142 *beards . . . trunk*: trunk hose was often stuffed with wool.

160 *t' one*: the one or the other.

5.1 A puppet theatre should be brought on stage.

2 *sign . . . invention*: banner announcing the puppet-plays.

7 *Pod*: 'Pod was a master of motions before him' (folio marginal note).

7–11 *Jerusalem . . . Plot*: puppet shows on biblical themes (the entry of Jesus into *Jerusalem*, Jonah's journey in the whale's belly to *Ninevah*, and the destruction of *Sodom and Gomorrah*), national myths (*The City of Norwich*, which was said to have been built in an hour), and recent events (*The Gunpowder Plot* of 1605). The annual *Shrove Tuesday* rioting of the London apprentices (which included attacks on *bawdy houses*) may have been the subject of a separate puppet-show, but is here conflated with *Sodom and Gomorrah*.

5.2.11 *is struck*: has gone.

33 *she . . . eyes*: the Renaissance conflation of Love and Fortune (*Fortuna Amoris*) is sometimes represented as blind or blindfolded.

40 *second part*: the first part is the society of thieves, who have their own jargon.

42 *privileged church-robbers*: thefts from churchs were often blamed on Puritans who thought the furnishings idolatrous.

48 *parti-coloured*: 'multicoloured', with a play on the sense of 'factional'.

58 *silent minister*: Puritans who lost their licences to preach in the wake of the Hampton Court Conference of 1604.

62 *feoffee in trust*: trustee to whom legal (as opposed to beneficial) ownership of a freehold has been granted.

63 *absolute gift*: unconditional transfer of legal and beneficial ownership.

5.3.2 *master . . . monuments*: an analogy to the official at Westminster Abbey responsible for the collection of fees from visitors to the monuments.

7–9 *Hero . . . Pythias*: the puppet-show is a conflation of Marlowe's *Hero and Leander* (1598) and Richard Edwards's rhymed play *Damon and Pythias* (*c*.1564).

Bankside: district on the south bank of the Thames.

27 *that fire*: obscure; either the fire in Ursula's booth or 'by hellfire'.

48–9 *Call . . . Lantern*: to prevent being recognized by Cokes.

51 *In . . . time*: 'as soon as possible, please.'

70–6 *Taylor . . . Burbage . . . Field*: Joseph Taylor and Nathan Field were members of the company that acted the play; Richard Burbage and William Ostler (d. December 1614)—his name is punned on, l. 92—were actors in the King's Men.

79–80 *affect . . . gamesters*: admire his acting, the promiscuous women.

82 *Dionysius*: Dionysius II, tyrant of Syracuse, who in Edwards's version of the story (which reverses the characters) sentences Damon to death.

habit . . . scrivener: fur-trimmed gown.

93 *printed book*: Marlowe's *Hero and Leander*, which Leatherhead quotes in ll. 98–100.

98–9 *Hellspont . . . Sestos*: Abydos and Sestos were ancient Greek towns separated by the Hellespont (now Dardanelles), the strait that divides European and Asiatic Turkey.

109 *Puddle Wharf*: on the north bank of the Thames near St Paul's.

110 *Fish Street*: centre of the wet-fish trade, near St Paul's.

111 *Trig Stairs*: steps descending to the Thames, close to Puddle Wharf.

5.4.33 s.d. *by*: referring to.

36 *private house*: exclusive theatre.

38 *all-to-be-madam*: constantly call me 'madam'.

65 *Delia*: eponymous lady of Samuel Daniel's sonnet sequence (1592).

80 *hare . . . tabor*: hare that plays a tabor (a kind of drum).

112 *the fuller*: more thoroughly.

123 *How . . . sell?*: What is your price?

145 *Swan*: the tavern (not the theatre).

163 *Pict-hatch*: district associated with prostitution.

168 *Harm . . . catch*: 'if you seek trouble, you will find it.'

180 *Dauphin . . . boy*: a phrase from a (lost) ballad.

    my fiddle-stick: Leander.

192 *Coney*: name of a room in the tavern.

193 *Sack . . . sherry*: Cokes does not realize that sherry is a kind of sack.

197 *dead lift*: pinch.

200 *condition I*: 'on the condition that I'.

207 *my . . . forgotten*: refrain from a (lost) ballad.

257 *a . . . honero*: 'alas and alack', refrain from an Irish ballad.

285 *setting their match*: agreeing a time to meet.

300 *Dunmow bacon*: at Little Dunmow (in Essex), a jury of six bachelors and six unmarried women awarded a side of bacon to any couple who could prove conjugal harmony for a year and a day.

302 *Westphalian*: ham from the German duchy of Westphalia.

336 *master . . . school*: Dionysius II was believed to have started a school after he was overthrown and banished to Corinth.

5.5.1 *Dagon*: principal god of the Philistines.

  7 *beam . . . eye*: a great fault (with reference to Matthew 7: 3).

11–12 *instruments . . . countenance*: courtly patrons of the theatre.

15 *Shimei*: man who cursed King David (2 Samuel 16: 5–14).

16 *Master of the Revels*: official who licensed plays.

19 *Baal*: god of the Canaanites.

68 *treble creaking*: the high-pitched voice used by Leatherhead for the puppets, playing on *base* as 'bass'.

75–6 *feather-makers . . . faith*: the trade in fashionable feathered clothing was dominated by the Puritans of Blackfrairs; the puppet argues that it is hypocritical for Puritans to condemn the wearing of fashions that they have manufactured.

85 *Dagonet*: King Arthur's fool.

87–8 *abomination . . . male*: quoting Deuteronomy 22: 5.

92–3 *neither . . . female*: quoting St Paul: 'there is neither male nor female, for ye are all one in Christ Jesus' (Galatians 3: 28).

5.6.19–20 *et . . . labellum*: and put a finger to your lips (Juvenal, *Satires* i. 160).

33 *top . . . formality*: apogee of legal propriety.

34–6 *Hercules . . . Columbus . . . Magellan . . . Drake*: each explorer discovered more than his predecessor. The labours of Hercules took him to the mythical island of Erythea at the western extremity of the known world; Columbus reached America; Ferdinand Magellan led the expedition which first circumnavigated the world, but was killed in the Philippines; Francis Drake led the first English circumnavigation.

37 *enormity . . . spread*: widespread enormity.

46 *Redde te Harpocratem*: 'make yourself like Harpocrates', the Egyptian god who was portrayed as a child with a finger to his lips.

66 *Bridget*: a slip, either Jonson's or Mrs Overdo's, for 'Grace'.

78–9 *gift . . . ward*: Quarlous has filled in the paper that Overdo signed with a warrant authorizing the transfer of the guardianship of Grace from Overdo to himself.

81–2 *she . . . value*: Quarlous demands the compensation that Overdo would have demanded (see note to 3.5.260–3).

91 *Finsbury*: public area north of the city, used by archers.

103–4 *Mistress Alice*: Mrs Overdo (see 3.3.10), not Punk Alice.

108 *ad . . . diruendum*: 'for improvement, not destruction; for building up, not tearing down' (adapted from Horace, *Epistles* i. i. 100), possibly intended as a compliment to the king, who had quoted the same words in a speech to parliament in 1609.

NOTES TO EPILOGUE

The epilogue was written for the court performance on 1 November 1614.

GLOSSARY

ablution washing away of impurities
above board openly
abroad out of the house
absolute perfect
abuse deceive
accident unforeseen event
accidents preconditions for success
(*Vol.* Epistle)
accoutred equipped
a-days often
Adelantado (Sp.) provincial
governor
admire wonder
adulterate counterfeit
adultery adulteration
advantage opportunity
advertised advised
advertisement information
advises dispatches
affect (verb) aim for; love
affections sentiments
after-game second game (to reverse
the result of the first)
again' in anticipation of
a'known acknowledged
alembics vessels used for distilling
alkali caustic soda
allow license (a play)
altogether without interruption
aludel earthenware pot used as a
condenser
amalgama mercury compound
ambitious swelling
amused puzzled, bemused
an if
anatomy skeleton with intact skin
andirons metal bars supporting fuel in
a fire
anenst opposite
angel gold coin worth 10 shillings
anon in a moment
answer (verb) repay; justify
antic grotesque dance
antique antiquated, grotesque

apocryphal uncanonical, lacking in
authority
apostle-spoon christening spoon with
figure of an apostle on the handle
appellation (legal) appeal
apprehend feel
aquafortis nitric acid used in etching
aqua-vitae distilled spirits
argaile coarse cream of tartar
argent-vive mercury
argument subject
arras tapestry hanging
arsedine imitation gold leaf
artillery equipment
ascension (alchemy) sublimation
assiduity frequency
athanor alchemist's slow-burning
furnace
atone reconcile
attached seized
attachment writ of arrest or seizure
of property
aunt (slang) prostitute
avoid (imperative) go away!
azoth (alchemy) mercury

baby doll
bagattino Venetian coin of very little
value
bait snack
balance pair of scales
band collar
bane wolf's bane, an aconite
compound used to poison wolves
banquet snack; dessert
barbary barb (large North African
horse)
barbel fish with four barbels (Lat.
barba) hanging from its mouth
barley-meal used in poultice of red
cloth to treat heartburn
barricado barricade
basilisk legendary reptile able to kill
with its glance

basket-hilt protective handle for a sword

Bat diminutive of Bartholomew

bate abate

bate subtract (*Vol.* 2.2.202)

battens fattens

bawdry obscene language and incident

bearward keeper of bears for baiting

beaver hat made of beaver's fur

bedfere bedfellow

beech-coal high-quality charcoal made from beech

beldame hag

benefit act of kindness

benevolences charitable gifts

berlina Italian: pillory

biggin baby-bonnet or lawyer's cap

bile mispronunciation of boil

bird (verb) hunt birds

bird-eyed startled

birdlime sticky substance put on twigs to trap birds (applied metaphorically in *Ep.* 2.2.121)

black-moors negroes

blackpot beer jug

blanket (verb) toss in a blanket

blanks space left for names in an otherwise complete document

bloods gallants

bobchin simpleton with a jerky chin

bolt (verb) shoot

bona-roba prostitute (It. *buona-roba*)

bone-ache syphilis

bonnibel bonny lass

book (verb) make a note of

book-holder prompter

(to) boot into the bargain

bore penetrate

borne managed

botch (noun) boil

botcher tailor who repairs clothes

both-hands guardian

bound on the way

brabblesh (i.e. brabbles) brawls

brach bitch

brave splendid, (of people) well-born

bravery fashionably-dressed gentleman; fine clothes

bravo hired thug

bray crush with a pestle

brazier worker in brass

breathe exercise (a horse)

brickbat piece of brick used for throwing

bride-ale archaic term for 'bridal', a wedding feast

Bridewell London prison

briefly shortly

broad indecent

brock badger

brokerly interfering

brook (verb) endure

broom-man seller of brooms

brunt crisis

buckler small round shield

buff-doublet leather jacket

bugle-maker manufacturer of glass beads

bugloss herb used as a heart stimulant

burden refrain of a song

business proper conduct

busy meddling

butter-teeth front teeth

buzz exclamation of contempt

by-cause secondary cause, because

cage (slang) prison

calcine to powder by roasting

caliver light musket

callet prostitute

calver slice (fish) while still alive

calx residue

canaglia (It.) mob

canary sweet wine

candle-rents rents from decaying houses

candour reputation

canon rule

cant thieves' slang

canting pious jargon; thieves' argot

cape-man merchant

car cart

carbuncle ruby

careful hard won (*Vol.* 3.2.21)

carnaliter (Lat.) carnally

caroche carriage

carman carter

carpet tapestry table covering

carriage bearing; management

carve gesture affectedly

carwitchet quibble

casa house

cast (noun) in falconry, two birds
released simultaneously;
(participle) cashiered;
(verb) forecast, calculate

casuist moral theologian specializing
in cases of conscience

catamountain leopard or panther

cataplasm poultice

catastrophe denouement (of a play)

catch round; part-song

catchpole sheriff's officer

cates delicacies

Catherine pear small early pear

caudle warm drink for invalids

cause purpose

cautions precautions

cave (Lat.) beware

censure (noun) sentence; (verb) judge

cantuple hundred-fold

ceration mollification to produce a
waxen consistency

certain few (Vol. 5.10.33)

change exchange

chap jaw

chapman dealer

character character sketch

charges cost

charming enchantment

chattel wares

cheapen bargain for

chief, in chiefly

chimera mythical tripartite beast with
lion's head, goat's body, and dragon's
tail

china-house shop selling oriental goods

chiromancy palmistry

choke-pear a coarse variety of pear;
(figuratively) an impediment or gag

chough bird in crow family

chrysosperm (alchemy) seed of gold

churl countryman

cibation (alchemy) infusion with
liquids

cinoper cinnabar, red mercuric sulphide

ciphering alchemy

circumstance ceremony (Vol.
2.2.180); detail; (plural)
circumstantialities

citron-rind lemon-peel, used to aid
digestion

cittern wire stringed instrument
resembling a lute

clap harm; venereal disease

clarissimo Venetian patrician

clerk scholar

close (noun) secret; (verb) hide

clot-poll blockhead

clout cloth

clyster enema

coact compel

coaetanei (Lat.) contemporaries

coat party, i.e. their own side (Vol.
2.1.95)

cockatrice basilisk

cockpit arena in which cocks (roosters)
fought

cocted boiled

codling an immature apple

cognatio (Lat.) consanguinity

cohobation repeated distillation

coil disturbance

cokes simpleton

Cole slang name for a pander

collateral indirect

collect recollect

collections conclusions

collier charcoal merchant

colours knight's heraldic colours

coltsfoot herb used to adulterate
tobacco

comfortable refreshing

coming (adj.) forthcoming

comment lie (Lat. commentum)

commit engage in battle

commodity self-interest, gain

Commonwealth country

communicable affable; communicative

companion fellow (used
contemptuously or familiarly)

compeer equal, companion

compendious expeditious

composition legal settlement of a debt

conceit idea, opinion

conceive understand

concent harmony

concumbere (Lat.) have sexual
intercourse

conditions financial settlement

coney rabbit
confect-maker manufacturer of sweets
confederacy conspiracy
conference consultation
confirm reassure
confound astound
conjurer astrologer
conscience inward knowledge
consideration recompense
considerative thoughtful
consistory governing body of church
constancy composure
contemn treat with contempt
continent (adj.) chaste
contrary (verb) contradict, oppose
control (noun) restraint, check
contumacious insubordinate
conundrum whim, caprice
conveyance legal document for transferring property; sleight of hand
cope-man dealer, merchant
cope-stitch stitch used to embroider edges
copy copiousness
coral red coral, hung from the neck to fend off melancholy
corpus (Lat.) collection of writings
correspondence communication
corsive corrosive
cosset spoilt child
costermonger fruit-seller
costive reluctant; constipated
couch bed
counterpane copy of an indenture
court-hand script used in legal documents
courtless uncourtly
courtling courtier
cover copulate (used of horses)
coverlid bedcover, quilt
coxcomb fool's cap
coz cousin
cozen cheat
crack craze
crackers firecrackers
crass dense
creature dependant
credit reputation
crewel thin worsted yarn
crinkle shrink

crocodile person whose tears are disingenuous
cross impediment; affliction
crosslet melting-pot
crotchet perverse whim
crown English silver coin or Italian scudo
crude suffering from indigestion (Vol. 2.2.95)
cucurbite gourd-shaped retort
culverin cannon
cumber encumbrance
cunning (adj.) skilful; (noun) ingenuity; worldly knowledge
cunning man/woman fortune-teller
curious fastidious
currant-butt cask for currants or currant wine
curried scraped like leather
currier horse-groom
curry (verb) groom (a horse)
custard open meat or fruit pie
customed well-patronized
cut slash in gown revealing silk lining
cut'ork cutwork, lace embroidery

dabchick small waterfowl
dainty awkward, difficult; delicate, delightful
damask patterned silk
dear esteemed
decoction boiling down
decorum propriety
defalk reduce prices
degrees sizes
delate report (a crime)
delicate (adj.) delightful, fine; (pl. noun) delicacies
demerit merit blame
derive pass down
destine allot
detect inform on
device scheme
devotion disposal
diaper patterned linen
dibble beard shaped like a trowel
diet-drink medicine
dimensions rules
discourse rationality
discover disclose

discretion judgement
disfavour disfigure
dishonest unchaste
disple (verb) chastise, whip
distaff cleft stick on to which thread is wound for weaving
distemper upset
distempered troubled
distinctly properly (Lat. *distincte*)
distinguished dressed
distracted perplexed, confused
divers various [*sc*. people]
doctor barrister
doctrine teaching
dog-leech quack doctor
Doll diminutive of 'Dorothy'
dollar Dutch coin: *daler* (now *daalder*)
domine Lat. vocative: master; term of respectful address to member of learned profession
Don Spanish title (in English often used mockingly)
Donzel pseudo-Spanish: little Don
dotes (noun) natural endowments
doubt fear, suspect
doubtfulness ambiguity
down open
drab (noun) filthy woman, slut
draught drain, privy
drawer barman in a tavern
dropping dripping with sweat
dubbed knighted
ducat a silver coin (It. *ducato*)
duello (It.) duel
dulcify wash the salts out of a substance
dumb dumbness
dysenteria (Lat.) dysentery

eachwhere everywhere
easy co-operative
e'er ever
elder Presbyterian church officer
elecampane plant used for stomach complaints
elect (Puritan usage) one predestined to salvation
election judgement
elephantiasis (Lat.) a kind of leprosy
ell 45 inches

emp'ric empiric, alchemist
emulation contention
engage involve
engagements obligations
engine contrivance
engineer designer
enow plural form of 'enough'
ensign token
ensure assure
entiendo (Sp.) I understand
entrails lining
entreaty entertainment
entrench engrave
ephemerides astronomical almanacs
epididymis tube carrying sperm from testes
epithalamium wedding song or poem
equal just
equipage array of servants
erection nobility of mind and bearing
Erycine Venus, so called after her temple at Eryx in Sicily
esquire order of gentry below rank of knight
event outcome
exact (verb) command close attention
exalt (alchemy) concentrate
example precedent
except unless
except at take exception to
exception objection, fault-finding
execution seizure by writ of a debtor's goods
exercise religious observance
exhibition allowance
exploded clapped and hooted off the stage (a Latinism)
extempore (Lat.) improvised
extensive capable of extension

fable subject of gossip
fabulist story-teller
facinorous criminal
fact crime
faction quarrel
faculty talent
faeces sediment, dead matter
fain obliged
fair available (*Vol.* 2.1.97)
fairing present bought at a fair

fairly completely
faithful ready to believe
fall flat collar
false treacherous
fame reputation
famelic stimulating hunger
familiar attendant evil spirit
family household
fant'sied fancifully described
far-fet imported
fashioner tailor, dressmaker
fatal fateful
fatness richness
faucet tap for a barrel
favour loveliness
feat (adj.) dainty
featherman dealer in feathers
feeze flog
ferment (alchemy) purify through
  infusion
fidge fidget
figs haemorrhoids, piles
figure horoscope; role
firk stir; leap about
fix (alchemy) stabilize
flasket long shallow basket
flaw make drunk
flawed flayed
fleer smile obsequiously; mock
Fleming inhabitant of Flanders
flexible pliable
flitter-mouse bat
flock-bed stuffed mattress
flux flow, discharge
fly familiar spirit
foil setting for jewels
foist rogue, pickpocket
follow a hunting cry
footing dance step
'fore me an emphatic asseveration
forehead assurance (*Vol.* Epistle);
  capacity to blush (*Vol.* 4.2.53)
fore-right straight ahead
fore-top fore-top sail, the sail above
  the fore-sail
form formulate
formal elaborate
forsooth a pseudo-genteel oath
fox sword (*BF* 2.6.56)
frail rush basket for figs and raisins

frame devise
freight topic
frequent copious
Friars Blackfriars
fricace massage
fricatrice prostitute
front forehead
frontless shameless
froward perverse
fubbed cheated
fucus cosmetic rouge
fume smoke, vapour
furmety boiled wheat
fury Greek avenging goddess
fustian pretentious, worthless

gall blister
gallant (adj.) beautiful, finely dressed
Galloway small, strong breed of horse
gamester gambler or player of a game
gammer title for countrywoman;
  feminine form of 'gaffer'
garb bearing
gat got
gazet Venetian coin of little value (It.
  gazzetta)
gazzette (It.) news-sheets
genius attendant spirit
gentle noble
gentleman-usher gentleman in the
  service of a nobleman
gentleness elegance
get beget
ging crowd
gird taunt
glass mirror
glass-men glass-blowers
glebe soil
gleek a card-game
go walk
god-make-you-rich backgammon
God's precious by God's precious
  blood (oath)
gods so form of 'cadso' (It. *cazzo*,
  penis), spelt to resemble an oath
godwit species of sandpiper
going ability to walk (*Vol.* 1.4.148)
goings-out endings
gold-end man itinerant jeweller
goods benefits

gor-crow carrion crow

Gorgon female monster whose gaze turned those who saw her to stone

gossip (noun) close friend; godfather

govern determine

gracias (Sp.) thank you

grains malt residue, used as fodder

gramercy thanks

grandee Spanish nobleman

gravity dignity

green-sickness chlorosis, anaemia

groatsworth four-pence worth

groom servant

groom-porter official who regulated gambling at royal court

guard of clothes: trimmed with lace

gull dupe

gun-stones cannonballs

habergeon soldier wearing mail jacket

habit clothing, costume

halbert weapon combining spear and battle-axe

half partner (*Ep.* 1.4.63)

halter noose

halting wavering

hammerman metal-worker

hand handwriting

handsel first takings of the day

handy-dandy children's game of guessing which hand hides an object

hanger belt loop for holding a sword

hanging tapestry

hapless unfortunate

haply perhaps

ha'p'orth half-penny worth

happiness skill

harlot rascal, villain (used of men)

harquebusier musketeer

hautboy oboe

have possess sexually (*Vol.* 3.7.225)

hearken enquire

hearse-cloth funeral pall

'heart 'by God's heart' (a mild oath)

heautarit (Arabic) mercury

hecatomb great public sacrifice (literally 100 oxen)

hedge-bird vagrant

heifer cow that has not yet calved, hence 'bride'

height latitude

hernia ventosa (Lat.) a hernia causing flatulence

heterogene of several kinds

high-country mountain

hight named (archaic)

hinny whinny (of a horse)

his a neuter possessive (i.e. its)

hog-louse wood-louse

hogrubber swineherd

homogene of one kind

honest (verb) honour

honesty decorum

hoodwink blindfold

hopyard field for cultivation of hops

horn (verb) cuckold

horn-mad fearful of being cuckolded

horn-thumb thimble protecting cutpurse's thumb from the knife

horse-corser dealer in horses

horse-leech farrier

hoy a small boat

huffs shoulder pads

humanity secular learning (opposite of 'divinity')

humour temperament, state of mind

hundred subdivision of a county; a division of land

hurdle sledge used to carry traitors to execution

hyacinth blue precious stone

hydra mythical water serpent with seven heads

Hymen Greek personification of marriage

idle unreliable

i'fac in faith (a mild oath)

iliaco passio colic

imbibition steeping in liquid

impertinent irrelevant; trivial

impertinently unsuitably, pointlessly

impotent decrepit

imprimis (Renaissance Lat.) in the first place

impudence shamelessness

impulsion prompting

inceration mollification to produce a waxen consistency

incline agree

incontinence sexual promiscuity

incubee child fathered by a demon

indeed a mild asseveration regarded as falsely genteel

indifferent impartial

infirmity weakness

inform form

ingle catamite

innocent simpleton

instrument legal document

intelligence information

intend attend; attend to

intergatory interrogatory; written question in a civil action

interlude short comedy

interpret give voice to

invent discover

itch scabies

iwis certainly

jack mechanical figure that strikes a clock-bell

jacobus gold sovereign issued at accession of King James as king of England

jennet small Spanish horse

jig comic interlude

jolt-head blockhead

jovial, jovy influenced by Jupiter (hence 'cheerful')

judicial judicious

July-flowers gillyflowers

just exactly

kibes chilblains

kibrit (alchemy) sulphur

kitling kitten

knack snapping sound

knave servant

knocking decisive

knot nexus; criss-crossed lines; (ornithological) species of sandpiper

know copulate with (*Vol.* 4.6.37)

knowing (adj.) learned

lading freight

laid carefully plotted

Lambeth disreputable area in south London

lamprey species of eel-like fish

larum alarum

lato latten (a metal resembling brass)

lawn a linen (like cambric)

learn teach

learnedly expertly

leave leave off, stop

leer (adj.) leering

lent slow

lewd ignorant, base, obscene

lies stays

lift (thieves' slang) theft

light window; (pl.) lungs of beasts used to feed domestic animals

lightly commonly

lily-pot ornamental vase

lime-bush bush smeared with lime to trap birds

linen underwear

linener draper

link tow and pitch, for making torches

liquid (adj.) transparent

list (noun) strip

list (verb) choose

livre French coin

loaden heavy-laden

lock chastity belt (*Vol.* 2.5.57); curled love-lock

lodestone magnetic oxide of iron

long-coats children (wearing petticoats)

long-pepper powdered condiment made from fruit-spikes of peppers

longings belongings, wealth

loo shout to incite a dog

loose (adj.) dissolute; (alchemy: noun) solution; (verb) dissolve

lotium stale urine used by barbers

lover friend

lurch (verb) cheat

lust delight

lute enclose in clay

lyam-hound bloodhound (held by a leash, 'lyam')

macerate soften by soaking

madrigal lyrical love poem

magazine storehouse

magisterium masterpiece (i.e. the alchemical process)

magnesia salty water

maintenance means of subsistence

maker author; poet

mal caduco (It.) falling sickness (i.e. epilepsy)

malapert impudently

malmsey strong sweet wine

malt-horse dray-horse

mammet puppet

manage (noun) management

mania madness

manikin small man, puppet

mankind (adj.) unnaturally masculine, like a virago

manners moral conduct

mansion apartment

manumit set (slave) free

marcasite iron pyrites

mark Scottish coin

marks plague-marks

mar'l marvel

marry a mild oath (with vestigial reference to the Virgin Mary)

Mars god of war

marshall court official responsible for prisoners

mart market, selling

'marvel I marvel

Mas' Master

massy weighty

mastery masterpiece

mate person (used contemptuously) (*Vol.* 3.3.6)

mauther (English dialect) large awkward girl

meat food

Medusa a Gorgon (*q.v.*)

meet even

melancholy madness

melocoton peach grafted on a quince

menstrue solvent

mercer dealer in fabrics, especially silk and velvet

merchant customer

Mercury god of eloquence and duplicity

merds excrement

mere absolute

mess dining party (usually four people)

metheglin Welsh mead (*meddyglyn*)

metoposcopy science of reading character from facial features

mickle great

mill-jade horse powering a mill by walking in circles

mining (verb) undermining

minister agent

mocenigo Venetian coin

modern commonplace, ordinary

modesty deference; moderation

moiety portion; share

mooncalf misshapen product of a blighted birth

more greater

morris morris-dance

mortification destruction of active quality of a chemical

moscatelli muscatel wines

motion (verb) propose

motion emotion

motion puppet, puppet-show

movables furniture

move propose (*Vol.* 3.7.21)

much 'not bloody likely' (*Vol.* 4.4.20)

mulct punish with a fine

mumchance dice game

musk secretion of musk-deer used medicinally

muss scramble

myrobalane oriental fruit used to alleviate fever

mystery craft, occupation

nag small riding-horse

ne nor

near (adv.) closely

neeze sneeze

nick turning-point

night-tub chamberpot

noble gold coin worth 6*s.* 8*d.* (34p)

noddle (slang) head (jocular)

noise band of musicians

nomenclator announcer of guests' names

Numps diminutive of Humphrey

nun (slang) whore

obnoxious liable

obsequy obsequiousness

observance obsequiously dutiful service

obstancy legal objection

obstreperous noisy

odour fragrance
offices affairs, responsibilities
ohimè (It.) alas!
old familiar (*Vol.* 4.1.9)
oleosity oiliness
oppilations obstructions
oppone oppose
oppress overwhelm
or either (as in 'or . . . or', meaning
    'either . . . or')
ordinary public eating-house
    (pronounced 'ord-nry')
organ instrument
original originator
osteria (It.) inn
other other or others
out abroad (*Vol.* 2.1.8,101)
over-leavened puffed up
overparted given a part too difficult to
    play
over-reached outwitted
owe acknowledge

painful painstaking
painter cosmetician
pallet straw mattress
pannier-man hawker
paralysis (Lat.) palsy
parantory mispronunciation of
    peremptory
parcel (adj.) part-time; (pl. noun) lots
parcel-broker part-time middleman
parcel-gilt partly gilded silverware
parley peace conference
parlous shrewd
particular intimate (*Alc.* 4.1.77);
    personal
partisan long-handled spear with
    axe-head
parts talents (*Vol.* 3.1.2)
party-bawd fellow pimp
pass-time watch
passant passing (across the stage)
passenger passer-by
passionate sad
patents monopolies
patrico (thieves' slang) parson
pavan a stately dance
peck dry measure equivalent to two
    gallons

peculiar particular
peel long-handled baker's shovel
pelf wealth
pelican vessel for circular distillation
pensioner retainer
peremptory stubborn
perfect complete
perplexed intricate
personate impersonate
perspective optical device for
    producing special effects
persway diminish
pertinacy pertinacity
peruke wig
pescheria (It.) fish-market
pestilence plaguily
pestling crushing, as with a pestle
petard bomb for breaching walls
petronel large cavalry pistol
pettifogger minor lawyer
petulant insolent
philtre love potion
phlegma watery substance obtained by
    distillation
phrase idiom
phreneticus (Lat.) delirious
phthisic tuberculosis
physic medical science; medicine
piazza (It.) square
pick-pack carried on the shoulders
    like a pack
pick-tooth toothpick (a fashionable
    accessory)
picture (slang) coin (stamped with
    portrait of the king)
pieced patched
pierce mend (with a needle)
piety filial devotion
pigeon-holes stocks
pined tormented
pink stab
pinnace intermediary
pipkin small earthenware pot
pistolet Spanish gold coin
pizzle penis
plain flat
play-books printed plays
plight condition
poetasters untalented poets
poet-sucker young poet

point appoint (*Vol.* 2.5.43)
points laces
politic (adj.) scheming; (noun) moralizing commentator on public affairs
political shrewd
polity diplomatic cunning
pome-citrons citrons and lemons
portague Portuguese gold coin worth up to £4. 10s (£4.50)
possess inspire (*Vol.* 2.6.96); have the attention of (*Vol.* 5.4.17)
posture role
posy motto
potate liquid
poulter poulterer
powder-corns grains of gunpowder
pox syphilis
practice/practise plot
praesto (Lat.) at your service
precise puritanical
premises beginnings; previous events; anticipations
preposterous inverted in position or order; back to front; foolish; monstrous
presage warn
present (verb) give a present
presently at once
president presiding
pretender claimant
prevaricate go astray (the Latin sense)
prevent come before; forestall
price worth
primero card game played for money
privy (adj.) exclusive
prize role (*Vol.* 5.2.15); contest
proctor lawyer in ecclesiastical courts
prodigious monstrous
prodigy monster
profecto (Lat.) truly
profess practise
profession declaration of faith
professor one who professes (Christianity); practitioner
proficient (noun) pupil
progress monarch's journey to the provinces
project scheme; (alchemy) to cast on to a hot metal in order to transmute into gold

prolepses anachronisms
proper handsome
properties stage props
property instrument
proportion guess
protest assert, avow
prove endure; experience; test
publish make known
puck-fist puff-ball fungus (hence 'boaster')
pudding sausage
puff fabric gathered in a bunch
puffin seabird with brightly coloured bill
punk prostitute
punkettee child prostitute
purblind blinkered
purchase winnings
purlieu suburb
purse-net rabbit-snare with draw-strings
pursuivant warrant-officer
putrefaction decomposition
put up place inside

quacksalvers fake doctors who sell ointments (salves)
qualify (alchemy) dilute
quality acting profession; rank
quarlous contentious
quarter quarter of the year, as divided by quarter-days
quean prostitute
queen-apple the queening, a red apple
quest enquiry, petition
quiblin quibble; pun; trick
quick alive
quintessence purest form
quirk legalistic evasion; quip
quit (adj.) quits, even; acquitted
quit (verb) acquit, repay
quote make notes

rabbin early medieval Jewish exegete
race family
rack metal bracket supporting a spit; torture
radii (Lat.) rays
railing abusive
raked covered

rankness exuberance
rapt carried
rare(ly) excellent(ly)
receipt recipe, formula
recipient receptacle for condensing distilled matter
recitation performance
rectify distil
reduce restore (*Vol.* Epistle); lead back
reference (legal) submission of a dispute for consideration
reform revise
register damper (on a furnace)
relations reports (*Vol.* 2.1.96)
remnant quotation
reprobate (Puritan usage) one predestined to damnation
resty lazy (of a horse)
retchless heedless
reverberate warm with reflected heat
reversion right of succession
rheum watery discharge
Rialto commercial centre of Venice
rifle (verb) gamble
ring circular door-knocker
ritely ritually
roarer rowdy
rochet red gurnard
rook crow; also simpleton
roundly plainly
rouse (noun) draught of liquor
rub annoy
rude unpolished

sack-lees wine-dregs
sad grave
sadness seriousness
Saffi (It.) police
saint (Puritan usage): one of the godly elect
sal salt
sal-tartar carbonate of potash
salad (alchemy) oil (gold, salt, sulphur) and vinegar (mercury)
salt (adj.) salacious; (noun) salt-cellar
sanguine humour of cheerful and amorous person
satyr lustful mythological creature, half man, half animal
'save God save you (a mild oath)

saver compensation
scab rascal
scald scabbed
scandal offence
scarab dung-beetle
scavenger official responsible for street-cleaning
scene stage (Lat. *scena*)
science recognized branch of knowledge
scorse barter
scotomy dizziness
scrivener professional scribe
Scrutineo Venetian lawcourt
sear (up) cauterize
search (noun) extent; (verb) examine
second (verb) support; confirm; follow
secretary confidant
seed-pearl tiny pearl used as heart stimulant
seminary recusant priest trained in continental seminary
sempster tailor
sennight week
sentences maxims, opinions (Lat. *sententia*)
separation Puritan usage: God's chosen people
sequin a gold coin (It. *zecchino*) or button
seraglio harem
sèrene poisonous dew
sergeant minor court official
servant lover dedicated to the service of his lady
sever distinguish
several separate
severally one by one
sewer servant responsible for dining room
sforzato (It.) galley-slave, prisoner
shad herring
shambles meat-market, slaughterhouse
shamefaced shy
shark cheat
shift (verb) change clothes
shreds scraps of knowledge (*Vol.* 2.2.15)
sickness plague
signor (It.) Mr (pron. 'seen-your')

simples medicinal plants

sincere pure

sirrah form of address to a social inferior

sir-reverence saving your reverence

skink pour

slaughter punishment

'slid by God's eyelid (a mild oath)

'slight by God's light (a mild oath)

slip (verb) omit

slops fashionable puffed breeches

'slud by God's blood (a mild oath)

smock-rampant arrant whore

sod(den) boiled (archaic past participle of 'seethe')

soft (imperative) wait

Sol sun-god; in alchemy, gold

sol French coin of little value

solemn formal

solution alchemy: liquefication

some-deal somewhat

sophisticate (verb) adulterate

sophisticated adulterated

sorrel chestnut-coloured (of horses)

Sophy Shah of Persia

Soria (It.) Syria

spark fashionable young man

speaks bespeaks, defines (Vol. 2.1.25)

spice species

spinner spider

spittle hospital for the poor

spoon-meat food for babies and invalids

'sprecious by God's precious blood

spring raise from cover (of birds)

springe snare

spruce dapper

squire (noun, slang) pimp; (verb) escort

stage-keeper servant employed by a theatre to set and sweep the stage

staggers dizziness in horses

stained tipsy

stale urine, urinate (used of animals)

standing profession

start outburst

start up beget

state (noun) estate; dignity of manner; ceremoniousness; (verb) instate (Vol. 3.9.36)

state-course career in public service

state-face grave facial expression

statelijh (Dutch) stately

stateswoman female politician (a satirical coinage)

staunch cautious

stay (noun) gag

stay (verb) wait, wait for

stepdame stepmother

still always

stomacher ornamental covering worn under a bodice

stone testicle

store (noun) supply; plenty

straight straight-away (Vol. 1.4.124)

stranger foreigner

strangury impeded urination

strip expose to ridicule

style representation

sublimate (noun) arsenic, a rat-poison

sublime (verb) (alchemy) vaporize

subtle cunning

success result

sudden quick

suffering submissive (Vol. 1.2.62)

suffrage consent

suits law-suits

superlative exaggerated

suppository prostitute

suscitability excitability

suspicion doubt

swabber sailor; lout

syntagma a systematically arranged treatise

table writing-tablet

taffeta-sarsnet glossy silk originally made by Saracens

talc mica

tan-boy young man or woman

tapster tavern-keeper

tar-box container for tar-salve for treating skin disorders in sheep

target shield

tarrier obstructor

tart keen of taste

taw flog

tawed tanned

tax censure

tender (verb) cherish

term season during which courts were in session; (pl.) jargon (*Vol.* 2.2.15); menses

Terra Firma Venetian mainland possessions (*Lat.* 'solid earth')

thorough through

threave crowd

throughly thoroughly, throughout

tie obligation (*Vol.* 2.1.106)

tilter jouster

tilt-feather plume from the helmet of a jousting knight

tilting (noun) joust

timeless untimely

tincture (alchemy) golden tinge of a metal

tire (noun) headdress; (pl.) clothes, especially hats

tire-woman dressmaker

tiring-house dressing-room at theatre

tit young man or woman

titillation perfume

titvilitium (*Lat.*) trifle (coined by Plautus, *Casina* 347)

tobacconist smoker

token tavern-token issued by shopkeeper in lieu of small change

tonight last night

tormentor trap

touch (noun) test of the quality of gold (which is rubbed against a touchstone)

touch (verb) accuse

touse beat

toward ahead of; in prospect of

toy object of little value; whim

traded experienced

train (noun) fuse; (verb) trap

translate transfer; transform

travail work (also 'travel')

traverse portable curtain used as a screen

tray-trip dice game

tread copulate with (of birds)

tremor cordis heart palpitations

trencher wooden dinner-plate

trencher-rascal scoundrel only interested in eating

trendle-tail mongrel dog with curled tail

trig fop

trivial ungenerous

trouble mar

trow [I] wonder

truck deal; trade

trunk speaking-tube connecting rooms in a house

trust give credit

try test

tuftaffeta tufted silk

tupped mated (used of sheep)

tusk bluster

tutty crude zinc oxide

unbrace expose

uncase disrobe

under-meal afternoon meal

undertake guarantee

undertaker guarantor; adventurer

unequal unjust

unguento (It.) ointment

unintelligent unaware

unscrew placate

upsee dull (Dutch: *op zijn*)

utter sell (*Vol.* 2.2.17)

vail tip, gratuity

valour quantity

vapour mood, humour

varlet court sergeant; rascal

vegetal like a plant, characterized by physical life and growth

vegetous lively

velvet-custard velvet hat shaped like a custard pie

venery sexual pleasure

venting selling

venture speculative commercial enterprise

vertiginè (It.) dizziness

very true

vesture garment

vice device; mechanism for controlling a puppet

virginal small keyboard instrument

virtual powerful

virtue efficacy

visitor official inspector

visor mask

vitiate defile sexually

vitriol sulphuric acid

vivification recovery of a substance from a solution
voluntary unpaid volunteer
votum (Lat.) vow

wade stagger
wag mischievous child
waimb (womb) belly
wait street musician
wanton playful
warrant (verb) assure
waterman (Thames) boatman
waterworks machinery powered by water; pageant performed on water
welt border
Westchester Chester
whether which (*Vol.* 3.3.4)
whiff tobacco smoke
whimsy promiscuous woman; capriciousness
whindle whine
wight man (archaic)
will (noun) sexual desire (*Vol.* 2.7.8)

wind-fucker kestrel (a kind of hawk); (not obscene)
windgall tumour on a horse's leg
winny stay
wire-drawn protracted
wit intelligence and imagination
witch wizard
withal as well
without unless (*Ep.* 4.5.276); outside
wittol complaisant cuckold
woman maidservant
wood crowd (*Ep.* 2.2.70); collection
Word (Puritan usage) Bible
wot know
write reckon (*Ep.* 2.2.30)
wrought embroidered
wusse certainly

younker youngster

zarnich trisulphide of arsenic
Zephyrus personification of the west wind

The Oxford World's Classics Website

www.worldsclassics.co.uk

- Information about new titles
- Explore the full range of Oxford World's Classics
- Links to other literary sites and the main OUP webpage
- Imaginative competitions, with bookish prizes
- Peruse the Oxford World's Classics Magazine
- Articles by editors
- Extracts from Introductions
- A forum for discussion and feedback on the series
- Special information for teachers and lecturers

www.worldsclassics.co.uk

American Literature

British and Irish Literature

Children's Literature

Classics and Ancient Literature

Colonial Literature

Eastern Literature

European Literature

History

Medieval Literature

Oxford English Drama

Poetry

Philosophy

Politics

Religion

The Oxford Shakespeare

A complete list of Oxford Paperbacks, including Oxford World's Classics, Oxford Shakespeare, Oxford Drama, and Oxford Paperback Reference, is available in the UK from the Academic Division Publicity Department, Oxford University Press, Great Clarendon Street, Oxford OX2 6DP.

In the USA, complete lists are available from the Paperbacks Marketing Manager, Oxford University Press, 198 Madison Avenue, New York, NY 10016.

Oxford Paperbacks are available from all good bookshops. In case of difficulty, customers in the UK can order direct from Oxford University Press Bookshop, Freepost, 116 High Street, Oxford OX1 4BR, enclosing full payment. Please add 10 per cent of published price for postage and packing.